Practical Argument
A Text and Anthology

Laurie G. Kirszner
University of the Sciences, Emeritus

Stephen R. Mandell
Drexel University

Bedford/St. Martin's
Boston ■ New York

For Bedford/St. Martin's

Executive Editor: John E. Sullivan III
Senior Production Editor: Peter Jacoby
Senior Production Supervisor: Jennifer Peterson
Executive Marketing Manager: Molly Parke
Editorial Assistant: Laura Horton
Indexer: Melanie Belkin
Photo Researcher: Sheri Blaney
Permissions Manager: Kalina K. Ingham
Art Director: Lucy Krikorian
Text Design: Jerilyn Bockorick
Cover Design: Billy Boardman
Cover Photos: Mortarboard: Photographed by Derek E. Rothchild.
   Credit cards: Photographed by Walker and Walker; © Getty Images.
Composition: Cenveo® Publisher Services
Printing and Binding: RR Donnelley and Sons

President, Bedford/St. Martin's: Denise B. Wydra
Presidents, Macmillan Higher Education: Joan E. Feinberg and Tom Scotty
Editor in Chief: Karen S. Henry
Director of Development: Erica T. Appel
Director of Marketing: Karen R. Soeltz
Production Director: Susan W. Brown
Associate Production Director: Elise S. Kaiser
Managing Editor: Shuli Traub

Manufactured in the United States of America.

8 7 6 5 4 3
f e d c b a

For information, write: Bedford/St. Martin's, 75 Arlington Street, Boston, MA 02116   (617-399-4000)

ISBN 978-1-4576-2237-3

Acknowledgments
Acknowledgments and copyrights are continued at the back of the book on pages 851–857, which constitute an extension of the copyright page. It is a violation of the law to reproduce these selections by any means whatsoever without the written permission of the copyright holder.

In recent years, more and more college composition programs have integrated argumentation into their first-year writing sequence, and there are good reasons for this. Argumentation is central to academic and public discourse, so students who are skilled at argumentation are able to participate in the dynamic, ongoing discussions that take place both in their classrooms and in their communities. Clearly, argumentation teaches valuable critical-thinking skills that are necessary for academic success and for survival in today's media-driven society.

What has surprised and troubled us as teachers, however, is that many college argument texts are simply too difficult. Frequently, a divide exists between the pedagogy of these texts and students' ability to understand it. In many cases, technical terminology and excessively abstract discussions lead to confusion instead of clarity. The result is that students' worst fears are realized: instead of feeling that they are part of a discourse community, they see themselves marginalized as outsiders who will never be able to understand, let alone master, the principles of argumentation.

Recognition that students struggle to master important principles of argumentative thinking and writing, we drew on our years of classroom experience to create an innovative book: *Practical Argument: A Text and Anthology*. In this second edition, *Practical Argument* remains a straightforward, accessible, and visually stimulating introduction to argumentative writing that explains concepts in understandable, everyday language and illustrates them with examples that actually mean something to students. *Practical Argument* is an alternative for instructors who see currently available argument texts as too big, too complicated, and too intimidating for their students. Its goal is to demystify the study of argument. Thus, *Practical Argument* focuses on the things that students need to know, omitting the confusing, overly technical concepts they often struggle with. For example, *Practical Argument* emphasizes the basic principles of classical argument and downplays the more complex Toulmin logic, treating it as simply an alternative way of envisioning argument. *Practical Argument* works because its approach is "practical"; it helps students to make connections between what they learn in the classroom and what they experience in their lives outside of it. As they do so, they become comfortable with the rhetorical skills that are central to effective argumentation. We believe there's no other book like it.

Organization

Practical Argument, both a text and a reader, includes in one book everything students and instructors need for an argument course.

- **Part 1, Understanding Argument,** discusses the role of argument in everyday life and the value of studying argument, offers definitions of what argument is and is not, explains the means of persuasion (appeals to logic, emotion, and authority), and defines and illustrates the basic elements of argument (thesis, evidence, refutation, and concluding statement).

- **Part 2, Reading and Responding to Arguments,** explains and illustrates critical thinking and reading; visual argument; writing a rhetorical analysis; logic and fallacies; and Rogerian, Toulmin, and oral arguments.

- **Part 3, Writing an Argumentative Essay,** traces and illustrates the process of planning, drafting, and revising an argumentative essay.

- **Part 4, Using Sources to Support Your Argument,** covers locating and evaluating print and Internet sources; summarizing, paraphrasing, quoting, and synthesizing sources; documenting sources in MLA style; and avoiding plagiarism.

- **Part 5, Strategies for Argument,** explains and illustrates some of the most common kinds of arguments—definition arguments, causal arguments, evaluation arguments, proposal arguments, arguments by analogy, and ethical arguments.

- **Part 6, Debates, Casebooks, and Classic Arguments,** includes both contemporary and classic arguments. The contemporary arguments are arranged in four pro-con debates and five in-depth casebooks on issues such as whether study drugs should be banned and whether the "glass ceiling" is a myth. The eleven classic arguments include well-known pieces by writers such as Jonathan Swift, George Orwell, Martin Luther King Jr., and Rachel Carson.

- **Appendixes.** Appendix A provides instruction on writing literary arguments, and Appendix B covers APA documentation style.

Key Features

Concise in a Thoughtful Way

Practical Argument covers everything students need to know about argument but doesn't overwhelm them. It limits technical vocabulary to what students and instructors actually require to understand and discuss important concepts in argument and argumentative writing. In short, *Practical Argument* is argument made accessible.

Argument Step by Step, Supported by Helpful Apparatus

Practical Argument takes students through a step-by-step process of reading and responding to others' arguments and writing, revising, and editing their own arguments. The book uses a classroom-tested, exercise-driven approach that encourages students to participate actively in their own learning process. Chapters progress in a clear, easy-to-understand sequence: students are asked to read arguments, identify their key elements, and develop a response to an issue in the form of a complete, documented argumentative essay based on in-book focused research.

Exercises and writing assignments for each selection provide guidance for students as they work toward creating a finished piece of writing. Throughout the text, checklists, grammar-in-context and summary boxes, and source and gloss notes provide support In addition, more than a dozen unique templates for paragraph-length arguments—located in the end-of-chapter exercises—provide structures that students can use for guidance as they write definition arguments, causal arguments, evaluation arguments, proposal arguments, arguments by analogy, ethical arguments, and so on. (In addition, many sentence templates appear in the questions that follow the readings.)

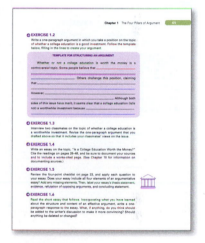

A Thematically Focused Approach with Compelling Chapter Topics

Students learn best when they care about and are engaged in an issue. For this reason *Practical Argument* uses readings and assignments to help students learn argumentation in the context of one high-interest contemporary issue per chapter. Chapter topics include college costs, the drinking age, and internships—issues that have real meaning in students' lives.

Readings on Relevant and Interesting Issues

Ninety-four accessible professional readings—on issues that students will want to read about and debate—are included in the text, with numerous selections from college newspapers and blogs introducing authentic student voices into the text. Topics include privacy in the age of Facebook, online versus classroom education, and the question of whether we should eat meat. Many visual selections appear throughout in conjunction with textual readings. Seventeen sample student essays (more than in any other argument book), including

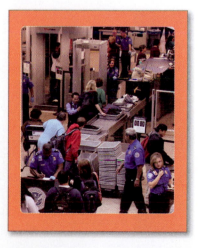

complete MLA and APA research papers, provide realistic models for student writers as well as additional student voices. (Many of these student essays include helpful annotations.) An additional twenty-eight selections are organized as debates and casebooks on questions such as whether the United States needs a federal DREAM Act and whether everyone should have the right to attend college. A collection of eleven classic arguments offers more challenging approaches to enduring issues.

To help students better understand the context of the sources included in *Practical Argument*, each is marked with an icon that shows how it was originally presented.

Book   Magazine or journal   National newspaper   Speech

Poem   Student essay   Student newspaper   Web site

An Open and Inviting Full-Color Design

The fresh, contemporary look of *Practical Argument* will engage students. This open, colorful design eliminates the sea of dense type that is typical of many other argument books. Over a hundred photographs and other visuals—such as graphic novel excerpts, cartoons, advertisements, realia, templates, charts and graphs, Web pages, and fine art—provide appealing, real-world examples. The use of open space and numerous images reinforces the currency of the book's themes and also creates an inviting and visually stimulating format.

New to This Edition

Essays, Topics, and Images

The second edition includes eighty-eight engaging new professional essays on such timely topics as controversial sports mascots and student loan debt. These essays have been carefully selected for their high-interest subject matter as well as for their effectiveness as sources and as teaching models for student writing. There are also three new student essays and twenty-two new images that provide even better examples for students.

Debates, Casebooks, and Classic Arguments

New debate and casebook topics include publicizing the addresses of sex offenders, America's safety after 9/11, and more. The classic argument section now features more recent selections, including essays by James Baldwin and Betty Friedan.

More Help with the Writing Process and Academic Writing

In response to instructor requests, we have added more coverage of the writing process—more on developing the body of an essay, more on editing and proofreading, more on the rhetorical situation, and more grammar help. We have also provided more help with academic writing, including additional material on finding sources. Finally, we have included additional templates—for example, templates for thesis statements, paraphrase, and summary.

 Online Quizzes in e-Pages

Practical Argument now features e-Pages with more than 200 online quizzes. These multiple-choice quizzes cover both the argument instruction and the readings, so you can easily assess how well your students understand the material you assign. Students have free access to e-Pages quizzes with the purchase of a new book. (See the inside back cover for details, or go to **bedfordstmartins.com/practicalargument**.)

You Get More Digital Choices for Practical Argument

Practical Argument doesn't stop with a book. Online, you'll find both free and affordable premium resources to help students get even more out of the book and your course. You'll also find convenient instructor resources, such as downloadable sample syllabi, classroom activities, and even a nationwide community of teachers. To learn more about or order any of the products below, contact your Bedford/St. Martin's sales representative, e-mail sales support (**sales_support@bfwpub.com**), or visit the Web site at **bedfordstmartins.com**.

Student Site for Practical Argument

bedfordstmartins.com/practicalargument Send students to free and open resources, choose flexible premium resources to supplement your print text, or upgrade to an expanding collection of innovative digital content.

> **Free and open resources.** *Practical Argument* provides students with free, easy-to-access reference materials, visual tutorials, and support for working with sources.

- Three free tutorials from *ix visual exercises* by Cheryl Ball and Kristin Arola
- *TopLinks* with reliable online sources
- *The Bedford Bibliographer*, a tool for collecting source information and making a bibliography in MLA, APA, and *Chicago* styles

An interactive e-book. *Practical Argument* is available in an e-book format. With all the content of the print book, the ***Practical Argument e-Book*** lets students easily search, highlight, and bookmark. Instructors can customize and rearrange chapters, add and share notes, and link to quizzes and activities. Loaded with quizzes on both the argument instruction and the readings, the e-book gives students flexible options for thinking and writing about argument. The ***Practical Argument e-Book*** can be purchased alone or packaged at a discount with the print book. To order the e-book packaged with the print book, use ISBN 978-1-4576-6391-8.

Bonus online readings. Even if you don't order the e-book, you can package the additional online readings free with the print textbook. For more information about the extra selections, visit the catalog page at **bedfordstmartins.com/practicalargument/catalog**.

Multiple formats. Students can purchase *Practical Argument* as a print book or in popular e-book formats for computers, tablets, and e-readers. For more details, visit **bedfordstmartins.com/ebooks**.

VideoCentral. This growing collection of videos for the writing class captures real-world, academic, and student writers talking about how and why they write. **VideoCentral** can be packaged for free with *Practical Argument*. An activation code is required. To order Video-Central packaged with the print book, use ISBN 978-1-4576-6375-8.

Re:Writing Plus. All of Bedford/St. Martin's premium digital content for composition is gathered into one online collection called ***Re:Writing Plus***. It includes hundreds of model documents, the first-ever peer-review game, and VideoCentral. ***Re:Writing Plus*** can be purchased separately or packaged with the print book at a significant discount. An activation code is required. To order ***Re:Writing Plus*** packaged with *Practical Argument*, use ISBN 978-1-4576-6366-6.

i-series Add more value to your text by choosing one of the following tutorial series, which are free when packaged with *Practical Argument*. This popular series presents multimedia tutorials in a flexible format—because there are things you can't do in a book. To learn more about package options or any of the products below, contact your Bedford/St. Martin's sales representative or visit **bedfordstmartins.com**.

- *ix visualizing composition 2.0* (available online) helps students put into practice key rhetorical and visual concepts. To order *ix visualizing composition 2.0* packaged with the print book, use ISBN 978-1-4576-6363-5.

- *i-claim: visualizing argument 2.0* (available online) uses six tutorials, an illustrated glossary, and over seventy multimedia arguments to show students how to analyze and compose arguments in words, images, and sounds. To order *i-claim: visualizing argument 2.0* packaged with the print book, use ISBN 978-1-4576-6358-1.

- *i-cite: visualizing sources* (available online as part of *Re:Writing Plus*) brings research to life through an animated introduction, four tutorials, and hands-on source practice. To order *i-cite: visualizing sources* packaged with the print book, use ISBN 978-1-4576-6359-8.

Instructor Resources

You have a lot to do in your course. Bedford/St. Martin's wants to make it easy for you to find the support you need—and to find it quickly.

- *Resources for Teaching Practical Argument* is available in print (ISBN 978-1-4576-4896-0) and in PDF that can be downloaded from **bedfordstmartins.com/practicalargument**. In addition to chapter overviews and teaching tips, it includes sample syllabi and suggestions for classroom activities.

- *Teaching Central* (**bedfordstmartins.com/teachingcentral**) offers the entire list of Bedford/St. Martin's print and online professional resources in one place. You'll find landmark reference works, sourcebooks on pedagogical issues, award-winning collections, and practical advice for the classroom—all free for instructors.

- *Bits* (**bedfordbits.com**) collects creative ideas for teaching a range of composition topics in an easily searchable blog. A community of teachers—leading scholars, authors, and editors—discusses research, grammar and style, revision, technology, peer review, and much more. Take, use, adapt, and pass the ideas around. Then come back to the site to comment or share your own suggestions.

- **Bedford Coursepacks** allow you to easily integrate our most popular content into your own course management system. For details, visit **bedfordstmartins.com/coursepacks**.

Acknowledgments

For the first edition of *Practical Argument*, the following reviewers examined the manuscript and gave us valuable feedback: Heidi E. Ajrami, Victoria College; Sonja Andrus, Collin College; Joseph E. Argent, Gaston College; Jerry Ball, Arkansas State University; Christine Berni, Austin Community College; Mary Cantrell, Tulsa Community College; Irene Clark, California State University–Northridge; Cathy A. D'Agostino, New Trier Township High School; Sidney Dobrin, University of Florida; MacGregor Frank, Guilford Technical Community College; David Gruber, North Carolina State University; Joseph Haske, South Texas College; Ann Jagoe, North Central Texas College; Loretta McBride, Southwest Tennessee Community College; Susan Miller-Cochran, North Carolina State University; Susan O'Neal, Tulsa Community College; Brian Reed, Langston University; Sylvia Ross, Tidewater Community College; John Schaffer, Blinn College; Ann Spurlock, Mississippi State University; Mary Stahoviak-Hall, Victoria College; John Williamson, Highlands High School; and our anonymous reviewer from American River College. We are grateful for their help.

We are grateful to those reviewers who provided feedback for the second edition: Kirk Adams, Tarrant County College; Craig Albin, Missouri State University at West Plains; James Allen, College of DuPage; Diana Badur, Black Hawk College; Josh Beach, University of Texas at San Antonio; Jacqueline Blackwell, Thomas Nelson Community College; Shannon Blair, Central Piedmont Community College; Clinton Burhans, Central Michigan University; Rhonda Dean-Kyncl, University of Oklahoma; James Decker, Illinois Central College; Darren DeFrain, Wichita State University; Tammy DiBenedetto, Riverside City College; Sara Dustin, Edison State College; Tracy Ferrell, University of Colorado at Boulder; MacGregor Frank, Guilford Technical Community College; Linda Franklin, North Central Texas College; Rod Freeman, Estrella Mountain Community College; Christopher Garland, University of Florida; Julie Gibson, Greenville Technical College; Randy Gonzales, University of Southern Mississippi; Rochelle Gregory, North Central Texas College; William Hays, Delta State University; Victoria Hollis, Auburn University at Montgomery; Anneliese Homan, State Fair Community College; Leslie Janac, Blinn College; Joanna Johnson, University of Texas at Arlington; Joseph Jones, University of Memphis; Ben Kiely, North Hennepin Community College; Erin Lehman, Ivy Tech Community College–Columbus/Franklin; David Lipton, Long Beach City College; Michelle Long, Lakeland Community College; Wendy Lym, Austin Community College; John Mammen, Brookhaven College; Kara Manning, University of Southern Mississippi; Tiffany Messerschmidt, Polk State College; Joanne Messman, Greenville Technical College; Lonetta Oliver, St. Louis Community College at Florissant Valley; Rachel Pierce, Miles College; Christine Rai, Montgomery College; Rufel Ramos, Eastfield College; Beth Richards, University of Hartford; Kevin Roberts, Monmouth

College; Harvey Rubinstein, Hudson County Community College; Kathie Russell, Santa Fe College; Brandy Schillace, Winona State University; Zahir Small, Santa Fe College; Andrea Spofford, University of Southern Mississippi; Pat Tyrer, West Texas A&M University; Everett Wade, University of Memphis; Andrea Wood, Winona State University; and Penny Zang, Greenville Technical College.

We thank John Bostwick, Jessica Carroll, and Jeff Ousborne for their assistance.

At Bedford/St. Martin's, Joan Feinberg, Denise Wydra, Karen Henry, Steve Scipione, Leasa Burton, and John Sullivan were involved and supportive from the start of the project. John, in particular, helped us shape this book and was with us every step of the way with encouragement and valuable advice. It's been a genuine pleasure working with him. Alyssa Demirjian and Laura Horton were an important part of our team, helping with many details. Peter Jacoby, senior production editor, patiently and efficiently shepherded the book through the production process, along with Shuli Traub. Others who made valuable contributions were Jerilyn Bockorick, Anna Palchik, and Lucy Krikorian, who developed the design; Karita dos Santos, Molly Parke, and Emily Rowin, who were instrumental in marketing the book; Sheri Blaney, who found art and obtained permission for it; and Keely Leonard, who handled text permissions. We are grateful for their help.

Finally, we would like to thank each other for lunches past—and for many, many lunches to come.

Laurie G. Kirszner
Stephen R. Mandell

BRIEF CONTENTS

CONTENTS

Comprehension quizzes on argument instruction and readings at
bedfordstmartins.com/practicalargument.

Comprehension quizzes at
bedfordstmartins.com/practicalargument.

Comprehension quizzes at
bedfordstmartins.com/practicalargument.

Comprehension quizzes at
bedfordstmartins.com/practicalargument.

Comprehension quizzes at
bedfordstmartins.com/practicalargument.

e Comprehension quizzes at
bedfordstmartins.com/practicalargument.

6 Rogerian Argument, Toulmin Logic, and Oral Arguments 185

e Comprehension quizzes at
bedfordstmartins.com/practicalargument.

PART

3   Writing an Argumentative Essay   239

7   Planning, Drafting, and Revising an Argumentative Essay   241

Comprehension quizzes at
bedfordstmartins.com/practicalargument.

In the final version of the paper developed throughout this chapter, a student argues that colleges should create green campuses.

Comprehension quizzes at bedfordstmartins.com/practicalargument.

PART 4 Using Sources to Support Your Argument 273

Comprehension quizzes at
bedfordstmartins.com/practicalargument.

Comprehension quizzes at
bedfordstmartins.com/practicalargument.

11 Avoiding Plagiarism   351

PART

5   **Strategies for Argument**   393

12   **Definition Arguments**   397

Comprehension quizzes at
bedfordstmartins.com/practicalargument.

Comprehension quizzes at
bedfordstmartins.com/practicalargument.

Comprehension quizzes at
bedfordstmartins.com/practicalargument.

Comprehension quizzes at bedfordstmartins.com/practicalargument.

Comprehension quizzes at
bedfordstmartins.com/practicalargument.

17   Ethical Arguments   589

Comprehension quizzes at
bedfordstmartins.com/practicalargument.

PART
6 Debates, Casebooks, and Classic Arguments 635

Comprehension quizzes at
bedfordstmartins.com/practicalargument.

Comprehension quizzes at
bedfordstmartins.com/practicalargument.

25   Is the Glass Ceiling a Myth or a Reality?   715

26   Does the United States Need a Federal DREAM Act?   739

e Comprehension quizzes at
bedfordstmartins.com/practicalargument.

CLASSIC ARGUMENTS

27

Comprehension quizzes at
bedfordstmartins.com/practicalargument.

1

Understanding Argument

An Introduction to Argument

Recognizing Arguments

Arguments are everywhere. Whenever you turn on the television, read a newspaper or magazine, talk to friends and family, enter an online discussion, or engage in a debate in one of your classes, you encounter arguments. In fact, it is fair to say that much of the interaction that takes place in society involves argument. Consider, for example, a lawyer who tries to persuade a jury that a defendant is innocent, a doctor who wants to convince a patient to undergo a specific form of treatment, a lawmaker who wants to propose a piece of legislation, an executive who wants to institute a particular policy, an activist who wants to pursue a particular social agenda, a parent who wants to convince a child to study harder, a worker who wants to propose a more efficient way of performing a task, an employee who thinks that he or she deserves a raise, or a spokesperson in an infomercial whose goal is to sell something: all these people are engaging in argument.

In college, you encounter arguments on a daily basis; in fact, both class discussions and academic writing often take the form of argument. Consider, for example, the following questions that might be debated (and written about) in a first-year writing class:

- Do the benefits of bottled water outweigh the costs?
- Should college campuses go green?
- Should every American go to college?
- Should we eat meat?
- Is the glass ceiling a myth or a reality?
- Is *Wikipedia* a legitimate research source?

What these questions have in common is that they all call for argumentation. To answer these questions, students would be expected to state their opinions and support them.

For comprehension quizzes, see bedfordstmartins.com/practicalargument.

WHY INSTRUCTORS ASSIGN ARGUMENT

Instructors assign argumentative essays for a number of reasons. Here are just a few:

- To encourage students to develop and defend a position
- To help students learn to look closely at their own and other people's ideas
- To give students the tools they need to convince others of the validity of their ideas
- To help students learn to resolve conflicting points of view

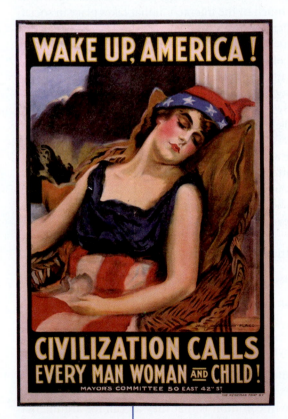

World War I propaganda poster (1917)

Defining Argument

Now for the obvious question: exactly what is an argument? Perhaps the best way to begin is by explaining what argument is *not*. An argument (at least an academic argument) is not a **quarrel** or an angry exchange. The object of argument is not to attack someone who disagrees with you or to beat an opponent into submission. For this reason, the shouting matches that you routinely see on television or hear on talk radio are not really arguments. Argument is also not **spin**—the positive or biased slant that politicians routinely put on facts—or **propaganda**—information (or misinformation) that is spread to support a particular viewpoint. Finally, argument is not just a contradiction or denial of someone else's position. Even if you establish that an opponent's position is wrong, you still have to establish that your own position has merit by presenting evidence to support it.

There is a basic difference between **formal arguments**—those that you develop in academic discussion and writing—and **informal arguments**—those that occur in daily life, where people often get into arguments about politics, sports, social issues, and personal relationships. These everyday disputes are often just verbal fights in which one person tries to outshout another. Although they sometimes include facts, they tend to rely primarily on emotion and unsupported opinions. Moreover, such everyday arguments do not have the formal structure of academic arguments: they do not establish a logical link between a particular viewpoint and reliable supporting evidence. There is also no real effort to address opposing arguments. In general, these arguments tend to be disorganized, emotional disputes that have more to do with criticizing an opponent than with advancing and supporting a position on an issue. Although such informal arguments can serve as starting points for helping you think about issues, they do not have the structure or the intellectual rigor of formal arguments.

So exactly what is an argument—or, more precisely, what is an academic argument? An **academic argument** takes a stand, presents evidence, and uses logic to convince an audience to accept (or at least consider) the writer's position. Of course, academic arguments can get heated, but at their core they are civil exchanges. Writers of academic arguments strive to be fair and to show respect for others—especially for those who present opposing arguments.

Keep in mind that arguments take positions with which reasonable people may disagree. For this reason, an argument never actually proves anything. (If it did, there would be no argument.) The best that an argument can do is to convince other people to accept (or at least acknowledge) the validity of its position.

An angry exchange is not an academic argument.

WHAT KINDS OF STATEMENTS ARE NOT DEBATABLE?

To be suitable for argument, a statement must be **debatable**: in other words, there must be conflicting opinions or conflicting facts that call the validity of the statement into question. For this reason, the following types of statements are generally *not* suitable for argument:

- **Statements of fact:** A statement of fact can be verified, so it is not debatable. For example, there is no point in arguing that your school makes instructors' lectures available as podcasts. This is a question of fact that can easily be checked. You can, however, argue that making instructors' lectures available as podcasts would (or would not) enhance education at your school. This is a debatable statement that can be supported by facts and examples.

- **Statements of personal preference or taste:** Expressions of personal preference or taste are not suitable for argument. For example, if you say that you don't like the taste of diet soft drinks, no one can legitimately argue that you are wrong. This statement is beyond dispute because it is a matter of personal taste. You could, however, argue that diet soft drinks should not be sold in school cafeterias because they contribute to obesity. To support this position, you would supply evidence—facts, statistics, and expert opinion.

NOTE

Although personal expressions of religious belief are difficult to debate, the interpretation of religious doctrine is a suitable subject for argument—and so are the political, social, philosophical, and theological effects of religion on society.

It is a mistake to think that all arguments have just two sides—one right side and one wrong side. In fact, most arguments that you encounter in college focus on issues that are quite complex. For example, if you were considering the question of whether the United States should ban torture, you could certainly answer this question with a yes or a no, but this would be an oversimplification. To examine the issue thoroughly, you would have to consider it from a number of angles:

- Should torture be banned in all situations?

- Should torture be used as a last resort to elicit information that could prevent an imminent attack?

- What actually constitutes torture? For example, is sleep deprivation torture? What about a slap on the face? Loud music? A cold cell? Are "enhanced interrogation techniques"—such as waterboarding—torture?

- Who should have the legal right to approve interrogation techniques?

If you were going to write an argument about this issue, you would have to take a position that adequately conveyed its complex nature—for example, "Although torture may be cruel and even inhuman, it is sometimes necessary." To do otherwise might be to commit the **either/or fallacy** (see p. 140)—to offer only two choices when there are actually many others.

Arguments in Real Life

In blogs, work-related proposals, letters to the editor, emails to businesses, letters of complaint, and other types of communication, you formulate arguments that are calculated to influence readers. Many everyday situations call for argument:

- A proposal to the manager of the UPS store where you work to suggest a more efficient way of sorting packages

- A letter to your local newspaper in which you argue that creating a walking trail would be good use of your community's tax dollars

- An email to your child's principal asking her to extend after-school hours

- A letter to a credit card company in which you request an adjustment to your bill

- A blog post in which you argue that the federal government could do more to relieve the student loan burden

Because argument is so prevalent, the better your arguing skills, the better able you will be to function—not just in school but also in the wider world. When you have a clear thesis, convincing support, and effective refutation of opposing arguments, you establish your credibility and go a long way toward convincing readers that you are someone worth listening to.

Presenting a good argument does not guarantee that readers will accept your ideas. It does, however, help you to define an issue and to express your position clearly and logically. If you present yourself as a well-informed, reasonable person who is attuned to the needs of your readers—even those who disagree with you—you increase your chances of convincing your audience that your position is worth considering.

Arguments are also central to our democratic form of government. Whether the issue is taxation, health care, border control, the environment, abortion, gun ownership, energy prices, gay marriage, terrorism, or cyber-bullying, political candidates, media pundits, teachers, friends, and family members all try to influence the way we think. So in a real sense, argument is the way that all of us participate in the national (or even global) conversation about ideas that matter. The better you understand the methods of argumentation, the better able you will be to recognize, analyze, and respond to the arguments that you hear. By mastering the techniques of argument, you will become a clearer thinker, a more informed citizen, and a person who is better able to influence those around you.

Occupy Wall Street
protest

Winning and Losing Arguments

People often talk of "winning" and "losing" arguments, and of course, the aim of many arguments is to defeat an opponent. In televised political debates, candidates try to convince viewers that they should be elected. In a courtroom, a defense attorney tries to establish a client's innocence. In a job interview, a potential employee tries to convince an employer that he or she is the best-qualified applicant. However, the goal of an argument is not always to determine a winner and a loser. Sometimes the goal of an argument is to identify a problem and suggest solutions that could satisfy those who hold a number of different positions on an issue.

If, for example, you would like your college bookstore to lower the price of items (such as sweatshirts, coffee mugs and backpacks) with a school logo, you could simply state your position and then support it with evidence. A more effective way of approaching this problem, however, might be to consider all points of view and find some middle ground. For example, how would lowering these prices affect the bookstore? A short conversation with the manager of the bookstore might reveal that the revenue generated by these products enables the bookstore to discount other items—such as art supplies and computers—as well as to hire student help. Therefore, decreasing the price of products with college logos would negatively affect some students. Even so, the high prices also make it difficult for some students to buy these items.

To address this problem, you could offer a compromise solution: the price of items with college logos could be lowered, but the price of other items—such as magazines and snacks—could be raised to make up the difference.

Logos, Pathos, and Ethos

To be effective, an argument has to be persuasive. **Persuasion** is a general term that refers to how a speaker or writer influences an audience to adopt a particular belief or to follow a specific course of action.

In the fifth century BCE, the philosopher Aristotle considered the issue of persuasion. Ancient Greece was primarily an oral culture (as opposed to written or print culture), so persuasive techniques were most often used in speeches. Public officials had to speak before a citizens' assembly, and people had to make their cases in front of various judicial bodies. The more persuasive the presentation, the better the speaker's chance of success. In *The Art of Rhetoric*, Aristotle examines the three different means of persuasion that a speaker can use to persuade listeners (or writers):

- The appeal to reason (*logos*)
- The appeal to the emotions (*pathos*)
- The appeal to authority (*ethos*)

Aristotle

The Appeal to Reason (Logos)

According to Aristotle, argument is the appeal to reason or logic (***logos***). He assumed that at their core, human beings are logical and therefore would respond to a well-constructed argument. For Aristotle, appeals to reason focus primarily on the way that an argument is organized, and this organization is determined by formal logic, which uses deductive and inductive reasoning to reach valid conclusions. Aristotle believed that appeals to reason convince an audience that a conclusion is both valid and true (see Chapter 5 for a discussion of deductive and inductive reasoning and logic). Although Aristotle believed that ideally, all arguments should appeal to reason, he knew that given the realities of human nature, reason alone was not always enough. Therefore, when he discusses persuasion, he also discusses the appeals to *ethos* and *pathos*.

Logos *in Action*

Notice how the ad below for the Toyota Prius, a popular hybrid automobile, appeals primarily to reason. It uses facts as well as a logical explanation of how the car works to appeal to reason (as well as to the consumer's desire to help the environment).

You can assess the effectiveness of *logos* (the appeal to reason) in an argument by asking the following questions:

- Does the argument have a clear thesis? In other words, can you identify the main point the writer is trying to make?

- Does the argument include the facts, examples, and expert opinion needed to support the thesis?

- Is the argument well organized? Are the points the argument makes presented in logical order?

- Can you detect any errors in logic (**fallacies**) that undermine the argument's reasoning?

The Appeal to the Emotions (Pathos)

Aristotle knew that an appeal to the emotions (*pathos*) could be very persuasive because it adds a human dimension to an argument. By appealing to an audience's sympathies and by helping them to identify with the subject being discussed, emotional appeals can turn abstract concepts into concrete examples that can compel people to take action. After December 7, 1941, for example, explicit photographs of the Japanese attack on Pearl Harbor helped convince Americans that retaliation was both justified and desirable. Many Americans responded the same way when they saw pictures of planes crashing into the twin towers of the World Trade Center on September 11, 2001.

Although an appeal to the emotions can add to an already strong argument, it does not in itself constitute proof. Moreover, certain kinds of emotional appeals—appeals to fear, hatred, and prejudice, for example—are considered unfair and are not acceptable in college writing. In this sense, the pictures of the attacks on Pearl Harbor and the World Trade Center would be unfair arguments if they were not accompanied by evidence that established that retaliation was indeed necessary.

Pathos *in Action*

The following ad makes good use of the appeal to the emotions. Using a picture of polar bears defaced by graffiti, the ad includes a caption encouraging people to respect the environment. Although the ad contains no supporting evidence, it is effective nonetheless.

What will it take before we respect the planet?

You can assess the effectiveness of *pathos* (the appeal to the emotions) in an argument by asking the following questions:

- Does the argument include words or images designed to move readers?
- Does the argument use emotionally loaded language?
- Does the argument include vivid descriptions or striking examples calculated to appeal to readers' emotions?

- Are the values and beliefs of the writer apparent in the argument?
- Does the tone seem emotional?

The Appeal to Authority (Ethos)

Finally, Aristotle knew that the character and authority of a speaker or writer (*ethos*) could contribute to the persuasiveness of an argument. If the person making the argument is known to be honorable, truthful, knowledgeable, and trustworthy, audiences will likely accept what he or she is saying. If, on the other hand, the person is known to be deceitful, ignorant, dishonest, uninformed, or dishonorable, audiences will probably dismiss his or her argument—no matter how persuasive it might seem. Whenever you analyze an argument, you should try to determine whether the writer is worth listening to—in other words, whether the writer has **credibility**. (For a discussion of how to establish credibility and demonstrate fairness in your own writing, see Chapter 7.)

Ethos *in Action*

The following ad uses an appeal to authority. It uses an endorsement by the popular tennis star Venus Williams to convince consumers to buy Reebok sneakers. (Recent studies suggest that consumers react positively to ads that feature products endorsed by famous athletes.)

Venus Williams in an ad endorsing Reebok

You can assess the effectiveness of *ethos* (the appeal to authority) in an argument by asking the following questions:

- Does the person making the argument demonstrate knowledge of the subject?

- What steps does the person making the argument take to present its position as reasonable?

- Does the argument seem fair?

- If the argument includes sources, do they seem both reliable and credible? Does the argument include proper documentation?

- Does the person making the argument demonstrate respect for opposing viewpoints?

The Rhetorical Triangle

The relationship among the three kinds of appeals in an argument is traditionally represented by a triangle.

LOGOS (reason)
Focuses on the text

ETHOS (authority)
Focuses on the writer

PATHOS (emotions)
Focuses on the audience

In the diagram above—called the **rhetorical triangle**—all sides of the triangle are equal, implying that the three appeals occur in an argument in equal measure. In reality, however, this is seldom true. Depending on the audience, purpose, and situation, an argument may include all three appeals or just one or two. Moreover, one argument might emphasize reason, another might stress the writer's authority (or credibility), and still another might appeal mainly to the emotions. (In each of these cases, one side of the rhetorical triangle would be longer than the others.) In academic writing, for example, the appeal to reason is used most often, and the appeal to the emotions is less common. As Aristotle recognized, however, the three appeals often work together (to varying degrees) to create an effective argument.

Each of the following paragraphs makes an argument against smoking, illustrating how the appeals are used in an argument. Although each paragraph includes all three of the appeals, one appeal in each paragraph outweighs the others. (Keep in mind that each paragraph is aimed at a different audience.)

APPEAL TO REASON (*LOGOS*)

Among young people, the dangers of smoking are clear. According to the World Health Organization, smoking can cause a variety of problems in young people—for example, lung problems and shortness of breath. Smoking also contributes to heart attacks, strokes, and coronary artery disease (72). In addition, teenage smokers have an increased risk of developing lung cancer as they get older (CDC). According to one study, teenage smokers see doctors or other health professionals at higher rates than those who do not smoke (Ardly 112). Finally, teenagers who smoke tend to abuse alcohol and marijuana as well as engage in other risky behaviors (CDC). Clearly, tobacco is a dangerous drug that has serious health risks for teenage smokers. In fact, some studies suggest that smoking takes thirteen to fourteen years off a person's life (American Cancer Society).

APPEAL TO THE EMOTIONS (*PATHOS*)

Every day, almost four thousand young people begin smoking cigarettes, and this number is growing (Family First Aid). Sadly, most of you have no idea what you are getting into. For one thing, smoking yellows your teeth, stains your fingers, and gives you bad breath. The smoke also gets into your hair and clothes and makes you smell. Also, smoking is addictive; once you start, it's hard to stop. After you've been smoking for a few years, you are hooked, and as television commercials for the nicotine patch show, you can have a hard time breaking the habit. Finally, smoking is dangerous. In the United States, one out of every five deaths can be attributed to smoking (Teen Health). If you have ever seen anyone dying of lung cancer, you understand how bad long-term smoking can be. Just look at the pictures on the Internet of diseased, blackened lungs, and it becomes clear that smoking does not make you look cool or sophisticated, no matter what cigarette advertising suggests.

APPEAL TO AUTHORITY (*ETHOS*)

My advice to those who are starting to smoke is to reconsider—before it's too late. I began using tobacco over ten years ago when I was in high school. At first, I started using snuff because I was on the baseball team and wanted to imitate the players in the major leagues. It wasn't long before I had graduated to cigarettes—first a few and then at least a pack a day. I heard the warnings from teachers and the counselors from the D.A.R.E. program, but they didn't do any good. I spent almost all my extra money on cigarettes. Occasionally, I would stop—sometimes for a few days, sometimes for a few weeks—but I always started again. Later, after I graduated, the health plan at my job covered smoking cessation treatment, so I tried everything—the patch, Chantix, therapy, and even hypnosis. Again, nothing worked. At last, after I had been married for four years, my wife sat me down and begged me to quit. Later that night, I threw away my cigarettes and haven't smoked since. Although I've gained some weight, I now breathe easier, and I am able to concentrate better than I could before. Had I known how difficult quitting was going to be, I never would have started in the first place.

Defining Your Audience

When you write argumentative essays, you don't write in a vacuum; you write for real people who may or may not agree with you. As you are writing, it is easy to forget this fact and address a general group of readers. However, doing this would be a mistake. Defining your audience and keeping this audience in mind as you write is important because it helps you decide what material to include and how to present it.

One way to define an audience is by its **traits**—the age, gender, interests, values, preconceptions, and level of education of audience members. Each of these traits influences how audience members will react to your ideas, and understanding them helps you determine how to construct your argument. For instance, suppose you were going to write an essay with the following thesis:

> Although college is expensive, its high cost is justified.

How you approach this subject would depend on the audience you were addressing. For example, college students, parents, and college administrators would have different ideas about the subject, different perspectives, different preconceptions, and different levels of knowledge. Therefore, the argument you write for each of these audiences would be different from the others in terms of content, organization, and type of appeal.

- **College students** have a local and personal perspective. They know the school and have definite ideas about the value of the education they are getting. Most likely, they come from different backgrounds and have varying financial needs. Depending on their majors, they have different expectations about employment (and salary) when they graduate. Even with these differences, however, these students share certain concerns. Many probably have jobs to help cover their expenses. Many also have student loans that they will need to start paying after graduation.

An argumentative essay addressing this audience could focus on statistics and expert opinion that establish the worth of a college degree in terms of future employment, job satisfaction, and lifetime earnings.

■ **Parents** probably have limited knowledge of the school and the specific classes their children are taking. They have expectations—both realistic and unrealistic—about the value of a college degree. Some parents may be able to help their children financially, and others may be unable to do so. Their own life experiences and backgrounds probably color their ideas about the value of a college education. For example, parents who have gone to college may have different ideas about the value of a degree from those who haven't.

An argumentative essay addressing this audience could focus on the experience of other parents of college students. It could also include statistics that address students' future economic independence and economic security.

■ **College administrators** have detailed knowledge about college and the economic value of a degree. They are responsible for attracting students, scheduling classes, maintaining educational standards, and providing support services. They are familiar with budget requirements, and they understand the financial pressures involved in running a school. They also know how tuition dollars are spent and how much state and federal aid the school needs to stay afloat. Although they are sympathetic to the plight of both students and parents, they have to work with limited resources.

An argumentative essay addressing this audience could focus on the need to make tuition more affordable by cutting costs and providing more student aid.

Another way to define an audience is to determine whether it is *friendly*, *hostile*, or *neutral*.

■ A **friendly audience** is sympathetic to your argument. This audience might already agree with you or have an emotional or intellectual attachment to you or to your position. In this situation, you should emphasize points of agreement and reinforce the emotional bond that exists between you and the audience. Don't assume, however, that because this audience is receptive to your ideas, you do not have to address their concerns or provide support for your points. If readers suspect that you are avoiding important issues or that your evidence is weak, they will be less likely to take your argument seriously—even though they agree with you.

■ A **hostile audience** disagrees with your position and does not accept the underlying assumptions of your argument. For this reason, you have to work hard to overcome their preconceived opinions, presenting your points clearly and logically and including a wide range of evidence. To show that you are a reasonable person, you should treat these readers with respect even though they happen to disagree with you. In addition, you should show that you have taken the time to consider their arguments and that you value their concerns. Even with all these efforts, however, the best you may be able to do is get them to admit that you have made some good points in support of your position.

■ A **neutral audience** has no preconceived opinions about the issue you are going to discuss. (When you are writing an argument for a college class, you should assume that you are writing for a neutral audience.) For this reason, you need to provide background information about the issue and about the controversy surrounding it. You should also summarize opposing points of view, present them logically, and refute them effectively. This type of audience may not know much about an issue, but it is not necessarily composed of unsophisticated or unintelligent people. Moreover, even though such readers are neutral, you should assume that they are **skeptical**—that is, that they will question your assumptions and require supporting evidence before they accept your conclusions.

> **NOTE**
>
> Some audiences are so diverse that they are difficult to categorize. In this case, it is best to define the audience yourself—for example, *concerned parents*, *prudent consumers*, or *serious students*—and then address them accordingly.

Keep in mind that identifying a specific audience is not something that you do at the last minute. Because your audience determines the kind of argument you present, you should take the time to make this determination before you begin to write.

CHAPTER

1

The Four Pillars of Argument

Is a College Education Worth the Money?

In recent years, more and more high school graduates have been heading to college, convinced that higher education will enhance their future earning power. At the same time, the cost of a college education has been rising, and so has the amount of student-loan debt carried by college graduates. (In recent years, tuition at private colleges has gone up some 4.5% per year, with tuition at public schools rising close to 8% per year. As of 2012, average student-loan debt was almost $27,000.) This situation has led some observers to wonder if the high cost of college actually pays off—not only in dollars but also in future job satisfaction. Will a college degree protect workers who are threatened by high unemployment, the rise of technology, the declining power of labor unions, and the trend toward outsourcing? Given the high financial cost of college, do the rewards of a college education—emotional, and intellectual as well as financial—balance the sacrifices that students make in time and money? These and other questions have no easy answers.

Later in this chapter, you will be introduced to readings that highlight the pros and cons of investing in a college education, and you will be asked to write an argumentative essay in which you take a position on this controversial topic.

In a sense, you already know a lot more than you think you do about how to construct an argumentative essay. After all, an argumentative essay is a variation of the thesis-and-support essays that you have been writing in your college classes: you state a position on a topic, and then you support this position. However, argumentative essays also involve some special concerns in terms of structure, style, and purpose. Throughout this book, we introduce you to the unique features of argument. In this chapter, we focus on structure.

 For comprehension quizzes, see **bedfordstmartins.com/practicalargument**.

The Elements of Argument

An argumentative essay includes the same three sections—*introduction*, *body*, and *conclusion*—as any other essay. In an argumentative essay, however, the introduction includes an argumentative **thesis statement**, the body includes both the supporting **evidence** and the **refutation** of opposing arguments, and the conclusion includes a strong, convincing **concluding statement** that reinforces the position stated in the thesis.

The following diagram illustrates one way to organize an argumentative essay.

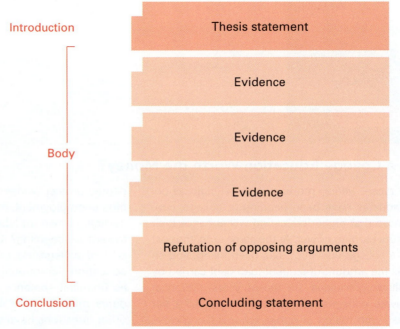

Introduction — Thesis statement

Body — Evidence / Evidence / Evidence / Refutation of opposing arguments

Conclusion — Concluding statement

The elements of an argumentative essay are like the pillars of an ancient Greek temple. Together, the four elements—thesis statement, evidence, refutation of opposing arguments, and concluding statement—help you build a strong argument.

Ancient Greek temple

Thesis Statement

A **thesis statement** is a single sentence that states your position on an issue. An argumentative essay must have an **argumentative thesis**—one that takes a firm stand. For example, on the issue of whether colleges should require all students to study a language other than English, your thesis statement could be any of the following (and other positions are also possible):

- Colleges should require all students to study a foreign language.

- Colleges should require all liberal arts majors to study a foreign language.

- Colleges should require all students to take Spanish, Chinese, or Farsi.

- Colleges should not require any students to study a foreign language.

An argumentative thesis must be **debatable**—that is, it must have at least two sides, stating a position with which some reasonable people might disagree. To confirm that your thesis is debatable, you should see if you can formulate an **antithesis**, or opposing argument. For example, the statement, "Our school has a foreign-language requirement" has no antithesis because it is simply a statement of fact; you could not take the opposite position because the facts would not support it. However, the following thesis statement takes a position that *is* debatable (and therefore suitable for an argumentative thesis):

THESIS	Our school should institute a foreign-language requirement.
ANTITHESIS	Our school should not institute a foreign-language requirement.

(For more on thesis statements, see Chapter 7.)

Evidence

Evidence is the material—facts, observations, expert opinion, examples, statistics, and so on—that supports your thesis statement. For example, you could support your position that foreign-language study should be required for all college students by arguing that this requirement will make them more employable, and you could cite employment statistics to support this point. Alternatively, you could use the opinion of an expert on the topic—for example, an experienced college language instructor—to support the opposite position, arguing that students without an interest in language study are wasting their time in such courses.

You will use both *facts* and *opinions* to support the points you make in your arguments. A **fact** is a statement that can be verified (proven to be true). An **opinion** is always open to debate because it is simply a personal judgment. Of course, the more knowledgeable the writer is, the more credible his or her opinion is. Thus, the opinion of a respected expert on language study will carry more weight than the opinion of a student with no particular expertise on the issue. However, if the student's opinion is supported by facts, it will be much more convincing than an unsupported opinion.

FACTS

- Some community colleges have no foreign-language requirements.

- Some selective liberal arts colleges require all students to take two years or more of foreign-language study.

- At some universities, undergraduates must take as many as fourteen foreign-language credits.

- Some schools grant credit for high school language classes, allowing these courses to fulfill the college foreign-language requirement.

UNSUPPORTED OPINIONS

- Foreign-language courses are not as important as math and science courses.

- Foreign-language study should be a top priority on university campuses.

- Engineering majors should not have to take a foreign-language course.

- It is not fair to force all students to study a foreign language.

SUPPORTED OPINIONS

- The university requires all students to take a full year of foreign-language study, but it is not doing enough to support those who need help. For example, it does not provide enough student tutors, and the language labs have no evening hours.

- According to Ruth Fuentes, chair of the Spanish department, nursing and criminal justice majors who take at least two years of Spanish have an easier time finding employment after graduation than students in those majors who do not study Spanish.

Refutation

Because every argument has more than one side, you should not assume that your readers will agree with you. On the contrary, readers usually need to be convinced that your position on an issue has merit. This means that you need to do more than just provide sufficient evidence in support of your position; you also need to **refute** (disprove or call into question) arguments that challenge your position, possibly acknowledging the strengths of those opposing arguments and then pointing out their shortcomings. For example, if you take a position in favor of requiring foreign-language study for all college students, some readers might argue that college students already have to take too many required courses. After acknowledging the validity of this argument, you could refute it by pointing out that a required foreign-language course could replace another, less important required course. (For more on refutation, see Chapter 7.)

Concluding Statement

After you have provided convincing support for your position and refuted opposing arguments, you should end your essay with a strong **concluding statement** that reinforces your position. (The position that you want readers to remember is the one stated in your thesis, not the opposing arguments that you have refuted.) For example, you might conclude an essay in support of a foreign-language requirement by making a specific recommendation or by predicting the possible negative outcome of *not* implementing this requirement.

⊙ The following student essay includes all four of the elements that are needed to build a convincing argument.

WHY FOREIGN-LANGUAGE STUDY SHOULD BE REQUIRED

NIA TUCKSON

Introduction

"What do you call someone who speaks three languages? Trilingual. 1
What do you call someone who speaks two languages? Bilingual. What do
you call someone who speaks only one language? American." As this old
joke illustrates, many Americans are unable to communicate in a language
other than English. Given our global economy and American companies'
need to conduct business with other countries, this problem needs to be
addressed. A good first step is to require all college students to study a
foreign language.

Thesis statement

First body paragraph:
Evidence

After graduation, many students will work in fields in which speaking 2
(or reading) another language will be useful or even necessary. For example,
health-care professionals will often be called on to communicate with
patients who do not speak English; in fact, a patient's life may depend on
their ability to do so. Those who work in business and finance may need
to speak Mandarin or Japanese; those who have positions in the military
or in the foreign service may need to speak Persian or Arabic. A working
knowledge of one of these languages can help students succeed in their
future careers, and it can also make them more employable.

Second body
paragraph: Evidence

In addition to strengthening a résumé, foreign-language study can also 3
give students an understanding of another culture's history, art, and literature.
Although such knowledge may never be "useful" in a student's career, it can
certainly enrich the student's life. Too narrow a focus on career can turn
college into a place that trains students rather than educates them. In
contrast, expanding students' horizons to include subjects beyond those
needed for their careers can better equip them to be lifelong learners.

Third body paragraph:
Evidence

When they travel abroad, Americans who can speak a language 4
other than English will find that they are better able to understand
people from other countries. As informal ambassadors for the United
States, tourists have a responsibility to try to understand other
languages and cultures. Too many Americans assume that their own

country's language and culture are superior to all others. This shortsighted attitude is not likely to strengthen relationships between the United States and other nations. Understanding a country's language can help students to build bridges between themselves and others.

5   Some students say that learning a language is not easy and that it takes a great deal of time. College students are already overloaded with coursework, jobs, and family responsibilities, and a new academic requirement is certain to create problems. In fact, students may find that adding just six credits of language study will limit their opportunities to take advanced courses in their majors or to enroll in electives that interest them. However, this burden can be eased if other, less important course requirements—such as physical education—are eliminated to make room for the new requirement.

Fourth body paragraph: Refutation of opposing argument

6   Some students may also argue that they, not their school, should be able to decide what courses are most important to them. After all, a student who struggled in high school French and plans to major in computer science might understandably resist a foreign-language requirement. However, challenging college language courses might actually be more rewarding than high school courses were, and the student who struggled in high school French might actually enjoy a college-level French course (or take another language). Finally, a student who plans to major in computer science may actually wind up majoring in something completely different—or taking a job in a country in which English is not spoken.

Fifth body paragraph: Refutation of opposing argument

7   Entering college students sometimes find it hard to envision their personal or professional futures or to imagine where their lives may take them. Still, a well-rounded education, including foreign-language study, can prepare them for many of the challenges that they will face. Colleges can help students keep their options open by requiring at least a year (and preferably two years) of foreign-language study. Instead of focusing narrowly on what interests them today, American college students should take the extra step to become bilingual—or even trilingual—in the future.

Conclusion

Concluding statement

⊛ EXERCISE 1.1

The following essay, "An Immigrant Writes" by Arnold Schwarzenegger—champion body builder, movie star, and former governor of California—includes all four of the basic elements of argument discussed so far. Read the essay, and then answer the questions that follow it, consulting the diagram on page 20 if necessary.

This essay appeared in the *Wall Street Journal* on April 10, 2006.

AN IMMIGRANT WRITES
ARNOLD SCHWARZENEGGER

President Reagan memorably described his "shining city on a hill" as a place   1
that "hummed with commerce and creativity, and if there had to be city walls, the walls had doors, and the doors were open to anyone with the will and the heart to get here." Perhaps because he'd been a border state governor, Reagan understood the challenges and the opportunities presented by immigration. He believed, as I do, that we can have an immigration policy that both strengthens our borders and welcomes immigrants.

Immigration is not just a theory debated on talk shows and on Capitol   2
Hill; in California, it's a reality that we live with every day in our schools, hospitals, and workplaces. When Congress returns from its Easter recess, it must immediately address immigration reform again. I urge Congress to remember that immigrants are good people; but our current immigration system is bad policy. We need a new law.

Already we hear so much talk about so many false choices. We are told   3
that in a free society it's not possible to have border security. We are advised that in order to secure the borders, we must deport 12 million people. Never mind that we don't know who they are or where they are and that it could cost up to $230 billion to do it.

I reject these false choices, and Congress should too. I salute the mem-   4
bers of both parties in Congress who are conducting a civil, serious discussion on this issue. I urge them to agree on legislation based on a simple philosophy: control of the border . . . and compassion for the immigrant. These are the twin pillars around which we must construct a new immigration policy. They are both essential elements in our overall immigration strategy. Without both, our strategy is destined to collapse.

> "I reject these false choices."

To pursue a policy of stronger borders, Congress must get serious about   5
our security. Before 9/11, we gambled that everyone entering our country had good intentions. After 9/11, we cannot afford to take that chance again. A stronger border means more border patrol agents, better equipment, and greater resources. We cannot ask state and local officials to bear the cost and

responsibility of enforcing federal immigration laws. They are not trained or equipped to do it. The presence of the citizens' groups along our border is a reminder of the federal government's failure to do its job. Government officials, not private citizens, are responsible for our borders. They need to do it right—and to do it right now.

6   A stronger border also requires real solutions, not soundbites or symbolic gestures. Building a wall sounds good and a fence may do some good in certain places. But every wall can be scaled with a ladder. Brick walls and chain link fences will not stop the desires and dreams of a father who is desperate to feed his family. And making it a felony to cross the border crosses the line into pure politics. Instead, we need to bring the 12 million undocumented workers out of the shadows and into the light. I support a temporary worker program to allow American businesses to hire foreign workers when no one else will do the job. How ironic it is to hear some of the same voices who complain about the outsourcing of jobs also complain about the use of immigrant workers here in America.

7   Still, we can do more to address the root of immigration. That's why President Clinton was right to help stabilize Mexico's economy in the '90s, and why President Bush is right today to propose a free trade zone° throughout the Americas. By fostering economic growth in other countries, we foster greater security in our own.

An area of international trade that is designed to keep taxes and other costs low

8   To pursue a policy of compassion, Congress must attack the problem, not people. A compassionate immigration policy will fight this battle at the borders, not in our schools and not in our hospitals. Teachers, doctors, and charity workers should not have to choose between helping those in need and enforcing the law. A compassionate immigration policy will acknowledge that immigrants are just like us: They're moms and dads looking for work, wanting to provide for their kids. Any measure that punishes charities and individuals who comfort and help immigrants is not only unnecessary but un-American.

9   Yes, immigration reform is a difficult issue. But it must be guided by a simple goal: compassion for the immigrant, control of the borders. Congress should not rest until it achieves both.

Identifying the Elements of Argument

1. What is this essay's thesis? Restate it in your own words.

2. List the three arguments Schwarzenegger presents as evidence to support his thesis.

3. Summarize the opposing arguments the essay identifies. Then, summarize the refutations of these arguments.

4. Restate the essay's concluding statement in your own words.

Is a College Education Worth the Money?

Reread the At Issue box on page 19, which summarizes questions raised on both sides of this issue. As the following sources illustrate, reasonable people may disagree about this controversial topic.

As you review the sources, you will be asked to answer some questions and to complete some simple activities. This work will help you understand both the content and the structure of the sources. When you have finished, you will be ready to write an essay in which you take a position on the topic, "Is a College Education Worth the Money?"

SOURCES

For comprehension quizzes, see **bedfordstmartins.com/practicalargument**.

This essay appeared in *USA Today* on December 6, 2011.

YES, A COLLEGE EDUCATION IS WORTH THE COSTS

RODNEY K. SMITH

I can imagine a frustrated graduate in an Occupy Wall Street protest carrying   1
a placard reading, "Worthless degree. Will not repay my student loan debt."

A recent Pew Research Center survey revealed that 57% of Americans rate   2
the job that our higher education system is doing in providing value for money
spent by students and their families as only fair (42%) or poor (15%); only 53%
of families report that they are saving to help pay for their children's education.
More than half of those ages 18 to 34 who do not have a bachelor's degree say
they would rather work and make money than pursue higher education.

Concerns regarding student indebtedness and educational quality are legiti-   3
mate, but we are losing our appreciation for education as an investment and
stewardship. Many are more inclined to spend money on a fancy car or on a less-
than-modest home than to invest in education. Many in the rising generation
fail to see education as a stewardship worthy of investment on their part.

We face major unemployment in the United States today. We talk of jobs   4
bills but fail to see the value of education in this calculation. Who populates the
ranks of the unemployed? According to Bureau of Labor Statistics (BLS) for 2010:

- 14.9% of those without a high school diploma

- 10.3% of those with a high school education

- 7% of those with an associate degree

- 5.4% of those with a bachelor's degree

- 2.4% of those with a professional degree

- 1.9% of those with a doctoral degree

See a trend here?

We talk about stimulating the economy by increasing the tax base. Once   5
again, educational attainment correlates with income, according to BLS.
Here's the average weekly income for those who have jobs:

- $444 for those with less than a high school degree

- $626 for those with a high school degree

- $767 for those with an associate degree

- $1,038 for those with a bachelor's degree

- $1,550 for those with a doctoral degree

To worldly wealth, education adds richness. As president of a small liberal 6 arts college with a strong core curriculum, I remember when one of our football players stopped by my office to complain about having to take music history. I urged him to give it his best effort. He was required to attend four concerts. I observed him at each one. At the first, he was disengaged. At the second, he was mildly attentive. At the third, he was enjoying the music. At the fourth, he approached me during intermission and said, "Wasn't the dissonance in the third movement of that last piece wonderful?" Today, as an investment banker, his education provides him with a job and the love of music fills his home.

Graduates enjoy increased opportunities for employment at higher rates 7 of pay, providing them with the wherewithal to pay off debt, if they are wise stewards of that debt. It also brings joy into lives in a world that is increasingly stressful.

Our family views education as an investment and stewardship. My father 8 grew up in Oklahoma during the early years of the Great Depression. He was the only living child of a hardworking farmer and a devoted mother. When Dad completed eighth grade, my grandfather believed his only son would work on the farm. My grandmother, however, understood the door that an education could open even in tough economic times. She persuaded Grandfather to permit Dad to finish high school.

> "Graduates enjoy increased opportunities for employment at higher rates of pay."

Dad worked hard and completed high school at the age of 16. At last, 9 Grandpa was to have his wish. Dad would work on the farm, easing the economic and physical burdens Grandpa carried.

But Grandmother intervened again. She begged Grandpa to permit my 10 father to go to college.

After reflection, Grandpa made the most difficult walk of his lifetime. He 11 walked to the chicken coop, where he did his banking. Taking a shovel in his work-worn hands, Grandpa dug up a mason jar that held all the family's savings. He offered the jar and its precious contents to Dad, saying, "Here boy, go make something of yourself."

Realizing that his family was sacrificing all their savings by investing in his 12 education, Dad became a steward of those funds. He received his bachelor's degree and then went on to the University of Oklahoma, where he graduated second in his law school class in 1936. Dad flipped hamburgers to ensure that the family savings would suffice for him to obtain his education. Jobs were hard to come by when Dad graduated, so he opened his own practice and lived in a home with a dirt floor. He worked long hours, but I remember him sharing the great books he discovered in the course of his education with me.

Our family was changed by the long walk Grandpa took to the chicken coop. 13 Education is more than an investment in our family. It is a treasure. I followed my father to college and law school, and my children have sought higher education. We have been transformed by a sacrifice made two generations ago by a loving, if not fully convinced, grandfather and a persistent grandmother.

○ AT ISSUE: THE FOUR PILLARS OF ARGUMENT

1. Smith states his position in his title, and he develops this position in paragraph 3 when he says, "we are losing our appreciation for education as an investment and stewardship." What does he mean? Paraphrase his thesis by filling in the following template.

    Because a college education is so important, we must _____

    _____

    _____

2. In paragraphs 4 and 5, Smith presents evidence to support his thesis that a college education is a worthwhile investment. What evidence does he give?

3. What appeal is Smith using when he identifies himself as "president of a small liberal arts college with a strong core curriculum" (6)? Does this information strengthen his argument? Why or why not?

4. For the most part, Smith relies on appeals to *logos* and *pathos*: in paragraphs 4–5, he uses *logos* (facts); in paragraphs 8–13, he appeals to *pathos* (emotion). Which of these two appeals do you find more convincing? Why?

5. In paragraph 3, when Smith says, "Concerns regarding student indebtedness and educational quality are legitimate," he is acknowledging an opposing argument. Why do you think he does not refute this argument? Do you think he should have done so?

6. Evaluate Smith's conclusion. Is the appeal he makes here an effective way to end his argument? Can you suggest a stronger concluding statement?

This undated essay is from MartyNemko.com.

WE SEND TOO MANY STUDENTS TO COLLEGE

MARTY NEMKO

Among my saddest moments as a career counselor is when I hear a story like 1 this: "I wasn't a good student in high school, but I wanted to prove to myself that I can get a college diploma—I'd be the first one in my family to do it. But it's been six years and I still have 45 units to go."

I have a hard time telling such people the killer statistic: According to the 2 U.S. Department of Education, if you graduated in the bottom 40% of your high school class and went to college, 76 of 100 won't earn a diploma, even if given 8½ years. Yet colleges admit and take the money from hundreds of thousands of such students each year!

Even worse, most of those college dropouts leave college having learned 3 little of practical value (see below) and with devastated self-esteem and a mountain of debt. Perhaps worst of all, those people rarely leave with a career path likely to lead to more than McWages. So it's not surprising that when you hop into a cab or walk into a restaurant, you're likely to meet workers who spent years and their family's life savings on college, only to end up with a job they could have done as a high school dropout.

Perhaps yet more surprising, even the high school students who are fully 4 qualified to attend college are increasingly unlikely to derive enough benefit to justify the often six-figure cost and four to eight years it takes to graduate—and only 40% of freshmen graduate in four years; 45% never graduate at all. Colleges love to trumpet the statistic that, over their lifetimes, college graduates earn more than nongraduates. But that's terribly misleading because you could lock the college-bound in a closet for four years and they'd earn more than the pool of non-college-bound—they're brighter, more motivated, and have better family connections. Too, the past advantage of college graduates in the job market is eroding: ever more students are going to college at the same time as ever more employers are offshoring ever more professional jobs. So college graduates are forced to take some very nonprofessional jobs. For example, Jill Plesnarski holds a bachelor's degree in biology from the private ($160,000 published total cost for four years) Moravian College. She had hoped to land a job as a medical research lab tech, but those positions paid so little that she opted for a job at a New Jersey sewage treatment plant. Today, although she's since been promoted, she must still occasionally wash down the tower that holds raw sewage.

Or take Brian Morris. After completing his bachelor's degree in liberal arts 5 from the University of California, Berkeley, he was unable to find a decent-paying job, so he went yet deeper into debt to get a master's degree from the private Mills College. Despite those degrees, the best job he could land was teaching a three-month-long course for $3,000. At that point, Brian was married and had a baby, so to support them, he reluctantly took a job as a truck driver. Now Brian says, "I just *have* to get out of trucking."

Colleges are quick to argue that a college education is more about enlight- 6
enment than employment. That may be the biggest deception of all. There is a Grand Canyon of difference between what the colleges tout in their brochures and websites and the reality.

> "Colleges are businesses, and students are a cost item."

Colleges are businesses, and students are a cost item while research is a 7
profit center. So colleges tend to educate students in the cheapest way possible: large lecture classes, with small classes staffed by rock-bottom-cost graduate students and, in some cases, even by undergraduate students. Professors who bring in big research dollars are almost always rewarded, while even a fine teacher who doesn't bring in the research bucks is often fired or relegated to the lowest rung: lecturer.

So, no surprise, in the definitive *Your First College Year* nationwide survey 8
conducted by UCLA researchers (data collected in 2005, reported in 2007), only 16.4% percent of students were very satisfied with the overall quality of instruction they received and 28.2% were neutral, dissatisfied, or very dissatisfied. A follow-up survey of seniors found that 37% reported being "frequently bored in class," up from 27.5% as freshmen.

College students may be dissatisfied with instruction, but despite that, do 9
they learn? A 2006 study funded by the Pew Charitable Trusts found that 50% of college *seniors* failed a test that required them to do such basic tasks as interpret a table about exercise and blood pressure, understand the arguments of newspaper editorials, or compare credit card offers. Almost 20% of seniors had only basic quantitative skills. For example, the students could not estimate if their car had enough gas to get to the gas station.

What to do? Colleges, which receive billions of tax dollars with minimum 10
oversight, should be held at least as accountable as companies are. For example, when some Firestone tires were defective, the government nearly forced it out of business. Yet year after year, colleges turn out millions of defective products: students who drop out or graduate with far too little benefit for the time and money spent. Yet not only do the colleges escape punishment; they're rewarded with ever greater taxpayer-funded student grants and loans, which allow colleges to raise their tuitions yet higher.

What should parents and guardians do? 11

1. If your student's high school grades and SAT or ACT are in the bottom 12
   half of his high school class, resist colleges' attempts to woo him. Their marketing to your child does *not* indicate that the colleges believe he will succeed there. Colleges make money whether or not a student learns, whether or not she graduates, and whether or not he finds good employment. If a physician recommended a treatment that cost a fortune and required years of effort without disclosing the poor chances of it working,

33

she'd be sued and lose in any court in the land. But colleges—one of America's most sacred cows—somehow seem immune.

So let the buyer beware. Consider nondegree options: 13

- Apprenticeship programs (a great portal to apprenticeship websites: www.khake.com/page58.html)

- Short career-preparation programs at community colleges

- The military

- On-the-job training, especially at the elbow of a successful small business owner

2. Let's say your student *is* in the top half of his high school class and is moti-   14
vated to attend college by more than the parties, being able to say she went to college, and the piece of paper. Then have her apply to perhaps a dozen colleges. Colleges vary less than you might think, yet financial aid awards can vary wildly. It's often wise to choose the college that requires you to pay the least cash and take on the smallest loan. College is among the few products where you don't get what you pay for—price does not indicate quality.

3. If your child is one of the rare breed who, on graduating high school,   15
knows what he wants to do and isn't unduly attracted to college academics or the *Animal House* environment that college dorms often are, then take solace in the fact that in deciding to forgo college, he is preceded by scores of others who have successfully taken that noncollege road less traveled. Examples: the three most successful entrepreneurs in the computer industry, Bill Gates, Michael Dell, and Apple cofounder Steve Wozniak, all do not have a college degree. Here are some others: Malcolm X, Rush Limbaugh, Barbra Streisand, PBS *NewsHour*'s Nina Totenberg, Tom Hanks, Maya Angelou, Ted Turner, Ellen DeGeneres, former governor Jesse Ventura, IBM founder Thomas Watson, architect Frank Lloyd Wright, former Israeli president David Ben-Gurion, Woody Allen, Warren Beatty, Domino's pizza chain founder Tom Monaghan, folksinger Joan Baez, director Quentin Tarantino, ABC-TV's Peter Jennings, Wendy's founder Dave Thomas, Thomas Edison, Blockbuster Video founder and owner of the Miami Dolphins Wayne Huizenga, William Faulkner, Jane Austen, McDonald's founder Ray Kroc, Oracle founder Larry Ellison, Henry Ford, cosmetics magnate Helena Rubinstein, Benjamin Franklin, Alexander Graham Bell, Coco Chanel, Walter Cronkite, Walt Disney, Bob Dylan, Leonardo DiCaprio, cookie maker Debbi Fields, Sally Field, Jane Fonda, Buckminster Fuller, DreamWorks cofounder David Geffen, *Roots* author Alex Haley, Ernest Hemingway, Dustin Hoffman, famed anthropologist Richard Leakey, airplane inventors Wilbur and Orville Wright, Madonna, satirist H. L. Mencken, Martina Navratilova, Rosie O'Donnell, Nathan Pritikin (Pritikin diet), chef Wolfgang Puck, Robert Redford, oil billionaire

John D. Rockefeller, Eleanor Roosevelt, NBC mogul David Sarnoff, and seven U.S. presidents from Washington to Truman.

4. College is like a chain saw. Only in certain situations is it the right tool. 16 Encourage your child to choose the right tool for her post–high school experience.

⊘ AT ISSUE: THE FOUR PILLARS OF ARGUMENT

1. Which of the following statements best summarizes Nemko's position? Why?

   - "We Send Too Many Students to College" (title)

   - "There is a Grand Canyon of difference between what the colleges tout in their brochures and websites and the reality" (para. 6).

   - "Colleges, which receive billions of tax dollars with minimum oversight, should be held at least as accountable as companies are" (10).

   - "College is like a chain saw. Only in certain situations is it the right tool" (16).

2. Where does Nemko support his thesis with appeals to logic? Where does he use appeals to the emotions? Where does he use an appeal to authority? Which of these three appeals do you find the most convincing? Why?

3. List the arguments Nemko uses to support his thesis in paragraphs 2–4.

4. In paragraph 4, Nemko says, "Colleges love to trumpet the statistic that, over their lifetimes, college graduates earn more than nongraduates." In paragraph 6, he says, "Colleges are quick to argue that a college education is more about enlightenment than employment." How does he refute these two opposing arguments? Are his refutations effective?

5. Nemko draws an analogy between colleges and businesses, identifying students as a "cost item" (7). Does this analogy—including his characterization of weak students as "defective products" (10)—work for you? Why or why not?

6. What specific solutions does Nemko propose for the problem he identifies? To whom does he address these suggestions—and, in fact, his entire argument?

7. Reread paragraph 15. Do you consider the list of successful people who do not hold college degrees to be effective support for Nemko's position? What kind of appeal does this paragraph make? How might you refute it?

This personal essay is from talk.onevietnam.org, where it appeared on May 9, 2011.

WHAT DOES IT MEAN TO BE A COLLEGE GRAD?

JENNIE LE

After May 14th, I will be a college graduate. By fall, there will be no more a cap- 1 pella rehearsals, no more papers or exams, no more sleepless nights, no more weekday drinking, no more 1 AM milk tea runs, no more San Francisco Bay Area exploring. I won't be with the people I now see daily. I won't have the same job with the same awesome boss. I won't be singing under Sproul every Monday. I won't be booked with weekly gigs that take me all over California. I won't be lighting another VSA Culture Show.

I will also have new commitments: weekly dinner dates with my mom, 2 brother/sister time with my other two brothers, job hunting and career build- ing, car purchasing and maintenance. In essence, my life will be—or at least feel—completely different. From what college alumni have told me, I will soon miss my college days after they are gone.

But in the bigger picture, outside of the daily tasks, what does it mean to hold 3 a college degree? My fellow graduating coworker and I discussed the importance (or lack thereof) of our college degrees: while I considered hanging up my two diplomas, she believed that having a bachelor's was so standard and insubstantial, only a professional degree is worth hanging up and showing off. Now- adays, holding a college degree (or two) seems like the norm; it's not a very outstanding feat.

> "Nowadays, holding a college degree (or two) seems like the norm."

However, I'd like to defend 4 the power of earning a college degree. Although holding a degree isn't as pow- erful as it was in previous decades, stats still show that those who earn bachelor's degrees are likely to earn twice as much as those who don't. Also, only 27% of Americans can say they have a bachelor's degree or higher. Realistically, having a college degree will likely mean a comfortable living and the opportunity to move up at work and in life.

Personally, my degrees validate my mother's choice to leave Vietnam. She 5 moved here for opportunity. She wasn't able to attend college here or in Vietnam or choose her occupation. But her hard work has allowed her children to become the first generation of Americans in the family to earn college degrees: she gave us the ability to make choices she wasn't privileged to make. Being the fourth and final kid to earn my degree in my family, my mom can now boast about having educated children who are making a name for themselves (a son who is a computer-superstar, a second son and future dentist studying at UCSF, another son who is earning his MBA and manages at Mattel, and a daughter who is thankful to have three brothers to mooch off of).

For me, this degree symbolizes my family being able to make and take the opportunities that we've been given in America, despite growing up with gang members down my street and a drug dealer across from my house. This degree will also mean that my children will have more opportunities because of my education, insight, knowledge, and support.   6

Even though a college degree isn't worth as much as it was in the past, it still shows that I—along with my fellow graduates and the 27% of Americans with a bachelor's or higher—will have opportunities unheard of a generation before us, showing everyone how important education is for our lives and our futures.   7

⊖ AT ISSUE: THE FOUR PILLARS OF ARGUMENT

1. What purpose do the first two paragraphs of this essay serve? Do you think they are necessary? Do you think they are interesting? How else could Le have opened her essay?

2. Where does Le state her thesis? Do you think she should have stated it more forcefully? Can you suggest a more effectively worded thesis statement for this essay?

3. In paragraph 3, Le summarizes an opposing argument. Paraphrase this argument. How does she refute it? Can you think of other arguments against her position that she should have addressed?

4. In paragraphs 5–6, Le includes an appeal to the emotions. Does she offer any other kind of supporting evidence? If so, where? What other kinds of evidence do you think she should include? Why?

5. Le begins her conclusion with the statement, "Even though a college degree isn't worth as much as it was in the past, . . ." Does this concluding statement undercut her argument? Do you think she should have addressed this point in her essay instead of simply mentioning it in her conclusion?

This essay appeared on CNN.com on June 3, 2011.

COLLEGE IS A WASTE OF TIME

DALE STEPHENS

I have been awarded a golden ticket to the heart of Silicon Valley: the Thiel Fellowship. The catch? For two years, I cannot be enrolled as a full-time student at an academic institution. For me, that's not an issue; I believe higher education is broken.

I left college two months ago because it rewards conformity rather than independence, competition rather than collaboration, regurgitation rather than learning, and theory rather than application. Our creativity, innovation, and curiosity are schooled out of us.

Failure is punished instead of seen as a learning opportunity. We think of college as a stepping-stone to success rather than a means to gain knowledge. College fails to empower us with the skills necessary to become productive members of today's global entrepreneurial economy.

College is expensive. The College Board Policy Center found that the cost of public university tuition is about 3.6 times higher today than it was 30 years ago, adjusted for inflation. In the book *Academically Adrift*, sociology professors Richard Arum and Josipa Roksa say that 36% of college graduates showed no improvement in critical thinking, complex reasoning, or writing after four years of college. Student loan debt in the United States, unforgivable in the case of bankruptcy, outpaced credit card debt in 2010 and will top $1 trillion in 2011.

Fortunately, there are productive alternatives to college. Becoming the next Mark Zuckerberg or mastering the phrase "Would you like fries with that?" are not the only options.

> "Fortunately, there are productive alternatives to college."

The success of people who never completed or attended college makes us question whether what we need to learn is taught in school. Learning by doing—in life, not classrooms—is the best way to turn constant iteration into true innovation. We can be productive members of society without submitting to academic or corporate institutions. We are the disruptive generation creating the "free agent economy" built by entrepreneurs, creatives, consultants, and small businesses envisioned by Daniel Pink in his book, *A Whole New Mind: Why Right Brainers Will Rule the Future*.

We must encourage young people to consider paths outside college. That's why I'm leading UnCollege: a social movement empowering individuals to take their education beyond the classroom. Imagine if millions of my peers copying their professors' words verbatim started problem-solving in the real world. Imagine if we started our own companies, our own projects, and our own organizations. Imagine if we went back to learning as practiced in French salons, gathering to discuss, challenge, and support each other in improving the human condition.

A major function of college is to signal to potential employers that one is qualified to work. The Internet is replacing this signaling function. Employers are recruiting on LinkedIn, Facebook, StackOverflow, and Behance. People are hiring on Twitter, selling their skills on Google, and creating personal portfolios to showcase their talent. Because we can document our accomplishments and have them socially validated with tools such as LinkedIn Recommendations, we can turn experiences into opportunity. As more and more people graduate from college, employers are unable to discriminate among job seekers based on a college degree and can instead hire employees based on their talents.

Of course, some people want a formal education. I do not think everyone should leave college, but I challenge my peers to consider the opportunity cost of going to class. If you want to be a doctor, going to medical school is a wise choice. I do not recommend keeping cadavers in your garage. On the other hand, what else could you do during your next 50-minute class? How many e-mails could you answer? How many lines of code could you write?

Some might argue that college dropouts will sit in their parents' basements playing *Halo 2*, doing Jell-O shots, and smoking pot. These are valid but irrelevant concerns, for the people who indulge in drugs and alcohol do so before, during, and after college. It's not a question of authorities; it's a question of priorities. We who take our education outside and beyond the classroom understand how actions build a better world. We will change the world regardless of the letters after our names.

◉ AT ISSUE: THE FOUR PILLARS OF ARGUMENT

1. In paragraph 1, Stephens says, "I believe higher education is broken." Is this statement his essay's thesis? Explain.

2. List Stephens's criticisms of college education.

3. Why does Stephens begin by introducing himself as a winner of a Thiel Fellowship? Is this introductory strategy an appeal to *logos*, *ethos*, or *pathos*? Explain.

4. List the evidence that Stephens uses to support his position. Do you think this essay needs more supporting evidence? If so, what kind?

5. In paragraphs 9 and 10, Stephens considers possible arguments against his thesis. What are these opposing arguments? Does he refute them effectively?

6. Throughout this essay, Stephens uses the pronoun *we* (as well as the pronoun *I*). Do these first-person pronouns refer to college students in general? To certain kinds of students? To Thiel fellows? Explain.

The *Washington* Post published this essay on June 3, 2011.

WHAT IS A COLLEGE EDUCATION REALLY WORTH?

NAOMI SCHAEFER RILEY

Did Peter Thiel pop the bubble? That was the question on the minds of parents, taxpayers, and higher education leaders late last month when the cofounder of PayPal announced that he was offering $100,000 to young people who would stay out of college for two years and work instead on scientific and technological innovations. Thiel, who has called college "the default activity," told *USA Today* that "the pernicious side effect of the education bubble is assuming education [guarantees] absolute good, even with steep student fees."

He has lured 24 of the smartest kids in America and Canada to his Silicon Valley lair with promises of money and mentorship for their projects. Some of these young people have been working in university labs since before adolescence. Others have consulted for Microsoft, Coca-Cola, and other top companies. A couple didn't even have to face the choice of putting off college—one enrolled in college at age 12 and, at 19, had left his PhD studies at Stanford to start his own company.

Of course, Thiel's offer isn't going to change the way most universities do business anytime soon. These 24 kids represent the narrowest swath of the country's college-bound youth. (Though it's important to note: When we talk about America having the greatest system of higher education in the world, these are the kind of people we're bragging about.)

There's not much reason to worry that this program is going to produce a nation of dropouts, contrary to the fears of some wags such as James Temple, a columnist for the *San Francisco Chronicle*. Temple called the premise of the fellowships "scary" and worried about the broader message they send. However, as a country, we are still creeping along toward President Obama's dream of universal higher education. Obama sees this not only as a way for all individuals to have the opportunity to reach their full potential but also as a key to the nation's ability to compete in the global marketplace.

But Thiel put a dollar figure on something that certain young people may already have suspected was true. A friend of mine whose son, a budding Internet entrepreneur, just graduated from Yale told me about a conversation that her son reported having with another somewhat successful start-up founder. The latter had dropped out of Harvard Law School to launch his business, and he advised my friend's son to drop out of Yale—venture capitalists would know that he was serious if he was willing to give up that Ivy League diploma. My friend was a little horrified, having already dropped somewhere around $200,000 on her son's education, but it does raise the question: For a smart kid from an upper-middle-class family who went to one of the top high schools in the country and who already has a business going, what does a college diploma mean?

Colleges have long been engaged in an odd deal with students and their 6 parents. Paying for a college education—or taking on a huge amount of debt to finance an education — is a transaction in which most of the buyers and most of the sellers have fundamentally different understandings of the product.

Think about it this way: Suppose I start a print newspaper tomorrow. I 7 might think I'm selling excellent journalism, while my "readers" are actually using my product to line their birdcages. It might work out fine for a while. But the imbalance in this transaction would make it difficult to talk in general terms about improving the product or whether the product is worth what I'm charging. I might think I should improve my grammar and hire more reporters. My customers might want me to make the paper thicker.

In the college transaction, most parents think they're buying their kids a 8 credential, a better job, and a ticket, economically speaking at least, to the American dream. Most college professors and administrators (the good ones, anyway) see their role as producing liberally educated, well-rounded individuals with an appreciation for certain kinds of knowledge. If they get a job after graduation—well, that's nice, too.

The students, for the most part, are not quite sure where they fit into this 9 bargain. Some will get caught up in what they learn and decide to go on to further education. But most will see college as an opportunity to have fun and then come out the other end of the pipeline with the stamp of approval they need to make a decent salary after graduation.

> "Most will see college as an opportunity to have fun."

So does Thiel's offer suggest that a university diploma might be most use- 10 ful lining a birdcage? Yes and no. He has certainly undermined the worth of a credential. But it is universities themselves that have undermined the worth of the education. It is to their detriment that they have done so, certainly, but it is to the detriment of students as well.

In the recent movie *The Social Network*, Mark Zuckerberg is shown devot- 11 ing endless hours in his room to computer programming. He goes to a few parties, but mostly he is engaged in his new business venture, "the Facebook." How is this possible, one might wonder? Was he flunking out of his classes? No. Thanks to the wonders of grade inflation and the lack of a serious core curriculum, it is possible to get through Harvard and a number of other high-price universities acing your computer science classes and devoting very little effort to anything else.

Colleges and universities have allowed their value to slip by letting stu- 12 dents call this an undergraduate education. There is no compelling understanding among students of why they are there. Studying is not how they spend even the bulk of their waking hours, and their classes seem random at best. They may spend Monday in "19th Century Women's Literature," Tuesday in "Animal Behavior," and Wednesday in "Eastern Philosophy," but these courses may bear little relation to any they took the previous semester or any they will take the next.

A 2010 report called "What Will They Learn?," published by the American   13
Council of Trustees and Alumni, an organization that emphasizes traditional education, surveyed the curricula of more than 700 colleges. About 4 percent require students to take a basic economics class. A little more than a quarter of the public institutions and only 5 percent of the private colleges and universities require a single broad survey course in American history or government. And only 61 percent of colleges and universities require students to take a college-level mathematics class.

General education requirements are no longer general at all. They are   14
absurdly specific. At Cornell, you can fill your literature and arts requirement with "Global Martial Arts Film and Literature." And at Northwestern, the math requirement can be fulfilled with "Slavonic Linguistics." It's little wonder that smart students think their time is better spent coding.

So yes, Zuckerberg was wasting his parents' money and his own time. Why   15
pay to be at Harvard if that's what you're going to do? Why not take a class on Dostoyevsky or the history of Christianity or astronomy or ancient history? You are surrounded by some of the most learned people in the world, and you are holed up in your dorm room typing code. (One could place some blame on the students, but it's hard to fault people for not knowing what they don't know.) Surely Thiel has the right idea when it comes to the Zuckerbergs of the world. And colleges have only themselves to blame if they lose some of these very smart young people to his fellowships.

Beyond the top tier, there are also gaping holes in higher education. Exec-   16
utives at U.S. companies routinely complain about the lack of reading, writing, and math skills in the recent graduates they hire. Maybe they too will get tired of using higher education as a credentialing system. Maybe it will be easier to recruit if they don't have to be concerned about the overwhelming student debt of their new employees.

Employers may decide that there are better ways to get high school stu-   17
dents ready for careers. What if they returned to the idea of apprenticeship, not just for shoemakers and plumbers but for white-collar jobs? College as a sorting process for talent or a way to babysit 18-year-olds is not very efficient for anyone involved. Would students rather show their SAT scores to companies and then apply for training positions where they can learn the skills they need to be successful? Maybe the companies could throw in some liberal arts courses along the way. At least they would pick the most important ones and require that students put in some serious effort. Even a 40-hour workweek would be a step up from what many students are asked to do now.

If tuition continues to rise faster than inflation and colleges cannot pro-   18
vide a compelling mission for undergraduate education, we may move further away from Obama's vision of education and closer to Peter Thiel's.

⇒ AT ISSUE: THE FOUR PILLARS OF ARGUMENT

1. Why do you think Riley opens her essay by discussing Peter Thiel's program? Given what she is trying to accomplish in this essay, do you think this is an effective opening strategy? Why or why not?

2. What is the college "transaction" (paras. 6–9)? What is Riley's opinion of this transaction?

3. What is Riley's thesis? Does she present any arguments that challenge her position? If so, where?

4. What criticisms does Riley have of colleges and universities? Of the typical college curriculum?

5. Whom (or what) does Riley blame for the declining value of a college education? Why?

6. Does Riley ever answer the question that her title asks? If so, what answer does she give? How would you answer this question?

7. Reread Riley's conclusion. Whose "vision of education" does she seem to be in favor of—President Obama's or Peter Thiel's? What steps do you think she might propose to turn the vision she favors into a reality?

This media release appeared on Census.gov on September 8, 2011.

EDUCATION IMPACTS WORK-LIFE EARNINGS FIVE TIMES MORE THAN OTHER DEMOGRAPHIC FACTORS, CENSUS BUREAU REPORTS

CENSUS.GOV

According to a new U.S. Census Bureau study, education levels had more effect on earnings over a 40-year span in the workforce than any other demographic factor, such as gender, race, and Hispanic origin. For example, a worker with a professional degree is expected to make more than a worker with an eighth grade education or lower. 1

Some groups, such as non-Hispanic white males, Asian males, and Asian females, benefit more from higher levels of education than other groups over a 40-year career for those with a professional degree. White males with a professional degree make more than double (about $2.4 million more) than that of Hispanic females with the same level of education. 2

(Note: Hispanics may be any race. All references in this news release to race groups such as black or white exclude Hispanic members of the race group in question; that is, all are "non-Hispanic.") 3

Many factors, such as race and Hispanic origin, gender, citizenship, English-speaking ability, and geographic location, do influence work-life earnings, but none had as much impact as education. The estimated impact on annual earnings between a professional degree and an eighth grade education was about $72,000 a year, roughly five times the impact of gender, which was $13,000. 4

These findings come from the report *Education and Synthetic Work-Life Earnings*, which looks at the economic value of educational attainment by estimating the amount of money that people might earn over the course of a 40-year work-life given their level of education. The report also looks at the effect of other factors, such as race and gender groups and other characteristics with regard to this relationship. 5

"This analysis shows that there is a clear and well-defined relationship between education and earnings," said Tiffany Julian, an analyst in the Census Bureau's Housing and Household Economic Statistics Division. "The overall economic value of educational attainment in this report supports the belief that higher levels of education are well-established paths to better jobs and higher earnings." 6

> "There is a clear and well-defined relationship between education and earnings."

Other highlights: 7

- Overall, white males had higher earnings than any other group at every education level, with the exception of those with a master's degree, which was topped by Asian males, and those with a professional degree, where Asian males were not significantly different from white males,

- In general, women in the most economically advantaged race groups usually earn less than men in the most disadvantaged race groups. For example, a white female with a master's degree is expected to earn $2.4 million over a 40-year work-life. In comparison, a Hispanic male with a master's degree is expected to earn $2.8 million.

- For Asian, black, and Hispanic groups whose highest education completed is high school, the difference between each group's work-life earnings was not large compared with the differences between these groups when they had higher levels of education.

- Asian men and women with a bachelor's degree or higher had greater returns on higher education than blacks or Hispanics of either gender. For example, an Asian female with a professional degree made $3.7 million in work-life earnings compared with $2.3 million for a Hispanic female with a professional degree.

- Naturalized citizens saw a small yearly increase in earnings over the native-born population ($1,210), but those who were not citizens made $2,446 less a year than the native-born.

- Language spoken at home had an effect on earnings: those who spoke a language at home other than English saw a decrease in annual earnings after considering all other factors. Even those who speak English "very well" saw a decrease of $989 in annual earnings compared with English-only speakers.

- Geography impacted earnings, showing higher earnings in the Pacific states and in New England and lowest earnings in East South Central states.

Data for this research comes from the 2006–2008 3-year American Community Survey. All estimates are presented in 2008 dollars and represent the amount of estimated money that one can expect to earn from ages 25 to 64.   8

⊘AT ISSUE: THE FOUR PILLARS OF ARGUMENT

1. This media release presents information, but it is not explicitly structured as an argument for or against the question of whether a college education is worth the money. What position (or positions) could the

information in this document support? Suggest some possible thesis statements that could be supported by the evidence presented here.

2. This media release does not include a conclusion. Write a paragraph—including a strong concluding statement—that summarizes the information it presents.

3. For the most part, this media release appeals to *logos* by presenting factual information. Does it also include appeals to *pathos* or *ethos*? Explain.

4. The information summarized in this document supports the idea that "there is a clear and well-defined relationship between education and earnings" (6). Does it also support the idea that a college education is worth the money for every group—males and females; black, white, Asian, and Hispanic groups; and so on?

This graph appeared in the *Wall Street Journal* on November 19, 2011.

IS A COLLEGE DEGREE WORTH THE MONEY?

THE WALL STREET JOURNAL

Report Card

College graduates are more likely to be employed, and earn more, than Americans without an undergraduate degree. Economists disagree on how much credit colleges should get for the difference.

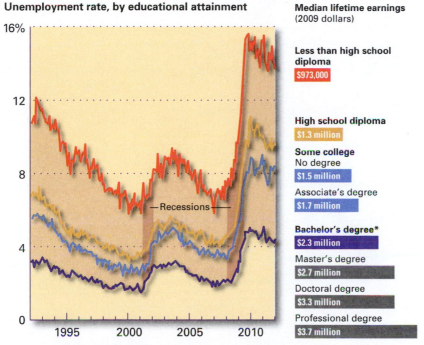

Unemployment rate, by educational attainment

Median lifetime earnings (2009 dollars)

Less than high school diploma
$973,000

High school diploma
$1.3 million

Some college
No degree
$1.5 million

Associate's degree
$1.7 million

Bachelor's degree*
$2.3 million

Master's degree
$2.7 million

Doctoral degree
$3.3 million

Professional degree
$3.7 million

*Unemployment rate is for all people with a bachelor's degree, including those with a more advanced degree.

Sources: Labor Department; Georgetown University Center on Education and the Workforce; National Bureau of Economic Research

⊙ AT ISSUE: THE FOUR PILLARS OF ARGUMENT

1. The graph above presents an argument on the issue of whether a college education is worth the money. In your own words, summarize this argument.

2. Note that the graph does not include information about college costs. Do you think this missing information weakens the graph's argument? Why or why not?

3. Do you think this graph presents a more compelling argument than a paragraph summarizing the same information would convey? Why or why not?

⊘ EXERCISE 1.2

Write a one-paragraph argument in which you take a position on the topic of whether a college education is a good investment. Follow the template below, filling in the lines to create your argument.

> ### TEMPLATE FOR STRUCTURING AN ARGUMENT
>
> Whether or not a college education is worth the money is a controversial topic. Some people believe that _____
> _____
> _____. Others challenge this position, claiming
> that _____
> _____.
> However, _____.
> _____. Although both
> sides of this issue have merit, it seems clear that a college education (is/is
> not) a worthwhile investment because _____
> _____.

⊘ EXERCISE 1.3

Interview two classmates on the topic of whether a college education is a worthwhile investment. Revise the one-paragraph argument that you drafted above so that it includes your classmates' views on the issue.

⊘ EXERCISE 1.4

Write an essay on the topic, "Is a College Education Worth the Money?" Cite the readings on pages 28–48, and be sure to document your sources and to include a works-cited page. (See Chapter 10 for information on documenting sources.)

⊘ EXERCISE 1.5

Review the four-point checklist on page 23, and apply each question to your essay. Does your essay include all four elements of an argumentative essay? Add any missing elements. Then, label your essay's thesis statement, evidence, refutation of opposing arguments, and concluding statement.

⊘ EXERCISE 1.6

Read the short essay that follows. Incorporating what you have learned about the structure and content of an effective argument, write a one-paragraph response to the essay. What, if anything, do you think should be added to the writer's discussion to make it more convincing? Should anything be deleted or changed?

This essay appeared on Businessweek.com in March 2011.

PRACTICAL EXPERIENCE TRUMPS FANCY DEGREES

TONY BRUMMEL

So you got great grades and earned your bachelor's degree? Congratulations. 1
You may have been better off failing college and then starting a venture and
figuring out why you didn't pass your classroom tests.

Being successful in business is absolutely not contingent on having a bach- 2
elor's degree—or any other type of degree, for that matter. A do-or-die work
ethic, passion, unwavering persistence, and vision mean more than anything
that can be taught in a classroom. How many college professors who teach business have actually started a business?

I am the sole owner of the top independent rock record label (according to 3
Nielsen-published market share). Historically, the music industry is thought of
as residing in New York City, Los
Angeles, and Nashville. But I have
blazed my own trail, segregating
my business in its own petri dish here in Chicago. I started the business as a
part-time venture in 1989 with $800 in seed capital. In 2009, Victory Records
grossed $20 million. We've released more than 500 albums, including platinum-
selling records for the groups Taking Back Sunday and Hawthorne Heights.

> "I have blazed my own trail."

Because I never went to college and didn't automatically have industry 4
contacts, I had to learn all of the business fundamentals through trial and error
when I started my own company. The skills I learned on my own have carried
me through 20 years of business. Making mistakes forces one to learn.

If you have a brand that people care about and loyal, hard-working employ- 5
ees coupled with a robust network of smart financial advisers, fellow entrepreneurs, and good legal backup, you will excel. There are plenty of people with
degrees and MBAs who could read the books and earn their diplomas but cannot apply what they learned to building a successful enterprise.

➲ EXERCISE 1.7

Study the image on the cover of this book. What argument could it
suggest about the issue of whether a college education is worth the
money?

2

Reading and Responding to Arguments

2

Thinking and Reading Critically

Do Violent Media Images Trigger Violent Behavior?

In recent years, the popular media seem to have become increasingly violent. This is particularly true of visuals in video games and on some Internet sites, but graphically violent images also appear regularly in films, on TV, in comic books, and even in newspapers. Some research has suggested that these violent images can have a negative effect on those who view them, particularly on adolescents and young children. In fact, some media critics believe that these violent images have helped to create an increasingly violent culture, which in turn has inspired young people to commit violent crimes (including school shootings) such as the massacres at Virginia Tech in 2007 and Newtown, Connecticut, in 2012. Others, however, argue that violent media images are not to blame for such events—and that, in fact, they provide a safe outlet for aggression.

In this chapter and in the chapter that follows, you will be asked to read essays and study images that shed light on the relationship between media violence and violent behavior. In the process, you will learn critical-thinking and active reading strategies that will help you learn to examine and interpret texts and images.

Now that you understand the structure of an argumentative essay, you can turn your attention to reading arguments more closely. These arguments may be the subject of class discussion, or they may be source material for the essays you write. In any case, you will need to know how to get the most out of reading them.

For comprehension quizzes,
see bedfordstmartins.com/practicalargument.

Thinking Critically

When you **think critically**, you do not simply accept ideas at face value. Instead, you question these ideas, analyzing them in order to understand them better. You also challenge their underlying assumptions and form your own judgments about them. Throughout this book, discussions and readings encourage you to think critically. The box below shows you where in this text to find material that will help you develop your critical-thinking skills.

USING CRITICAL-THINKING SKILLS

Reading (see Chapter 2): When you read a text, you use critical-thinking skills to help you understand what the text says and what it suggests. You ask questions and look for answers, challenging the ideas you read and probing for information. *Previewing*, *highlighting*, and *annotating* are active reading strategies that require you to use critical-thinking skills.

Analyzing Visual Texts (see Chapter 3): When you examine an image, you use critical-thinking skills to help you understand what you are seeing, using previewing, highlighting, and annotating to help you analyze the image and interpret its persuasive message.

Writing a Rhetorical Analysis (see Chapter 4): When you write a rhetorical analysis of a text, you use critical-thinking skills to analyze its elements and understand how the writer uses various appeals and rhetorical strategies to influence readers. You also use critical-thinking skills to help you understand the argument's context. Finally, you use critical-thinking skills to evaluate the overall effectiveness of the argument.

Analyzing an Argument's Logic (see Chapter 5): When you analyze an argument's logic, you use critical-thinking skills to help you understand the relationships among ideas, to evaluate the form the argument takes, and to determine whether its conclusions are both valid and true. You also use critical-thinking skills to identify any **logical fallacies** that may undermine the argument.

Writing an Essay (see Chapter 7): When you plan an essay, you use critical-thinking skills to probe a topic, to see what you already know and what you need to find out, to identify your essay's main idea, and to decide how to support it—that is, which ideas to include and how to arrange them. As you draft and revise, you use critical-thinking skills to evaluate your supporting evidence, to make sure your arguments are reasonable and fair, and to decide whether ideas are arranged effectively within paragraphs and in the essay as a whole. *Freewriting*, *brainstorming*, *clustering*, and *outlining* are some activities that require you to use critical-thinking skills.

Refuting Opposing Arguments (see Chapter 7): When you refute opposing arguments, you use critical-thinking skills to identify and evaluate arguments against your position—and to challenge or possibly argue against them.

Evaluating Sources (see Chapter 8): When you evaluate sources, you use critical-thinking skills to assess your sources in terms of their *accuracy*, *credibility*, *objectivity*, and *comprehensiveness* and to determine whether a source is trustworthy and appropriate for your purpose and audience.

Summarizing (see Chapter 9): When you summarize a passage, you use critical-thinking skills to identify the writer's main idea.

Paraphrasing (see Chapter 9): When you paraphrase a passage, you use critical-thinking skills to identify the writer's main idea, the most important supporting details and examples, and the ways in which key ideas are related.

Synthesizing (see Chapter 9): When you synthesize, you use critical-thinking skills to analyze sources and integrate them with your own ideas.

Reading Critically

When you read an argument, you should approach it with a critical eye. Contrary to popular opinion, **reading critically** does not mean arguing with every idea you encounter. What it does mean is commenting, questioning, and judging.

As a critical reader, you do not simply accept that what you are reading is true. Instead, you assess the accuracy of the facts in your sources, and you consider whether opinions are convincingly supported by evidence. You try to judge the appropriateness and reliability of a writer's sources, and you evaluate the scope and depth of the evidence and the relevance of that evidence to the topic. You also consider opposing arguments carefully, measuring them against the arguments developed in your sources. Finally, you watch out for possible **bias** in your sources—and you work hard to keep your own biases in check.

GUIDELINES FOR READING CRITICALLY

As a critical reader, you need to read carefully, keeping the following guidelines in mind:

- Check the accuracy of a source's facts.
- Be sure opinions are supported convincingly.
- Evaluate the sources.
- Evaluate the evidence.
- Consider opposing arguments.
- Be on the lookout for bias—in your sources and in yourself.

Becoming an Active Reader

Reading critically means being an *active* rather than a *passive* reader. Being an **active reader** means participating in the reading process by taking the time to preview a source and then to read it carefully, highlighting and annotating. This process will prepare you to discuss the source with others or to respond in writing to what you have read.

Previewing

When you approach an argument for the first time, you **preview** it to form a general impression of the writer's position on the issue, the argument's key supporting points, and the context for the writer's remarks.

You should begin by looking at the title, the first paragraph (which often contains a thesis statement or overview), and the last paragraph (which often includes a concluding statement or a summary of the writer's key points). You should also look at the topic sentences of the essay's body paragraphs. In addition, you should note any headings, words set in boldface or italic type, and bulleted or numbered lists in the body of the argument. If the argument includes visuals—charts, tables, graphs, photos, and so on—you should look at them as well. Finally, if an argument includes a headnote or background on the author or on the text, be sure to read this material. It can help you to understand the context in which the author is writing.

When you have finished previewing the argument, you should have a good general sense of what the writer wants to communicate.

Careful Reading

Now, you are ready to read through the argument more carefully. As you read, look for words and phrases that help to shape the structure of the argument and signal the arrangement of the writer's ideas. These words and phrases will help you understand the flow of ideas as well as the content and emphasis of the argument.

COMPREHENSION CLUES

- Phrases that signal emphasis (the *primary* reason, the *most important* problem)

- Repeated words and phrases

- Words and phrases that signal addition (*also, in addition, furthermore*)

- Words and phrases that signal time sequence (*first, after that, next, then, finally*)

- Words and phrases that identify causes and effects (*because, as a result, for this reason*)

- Words and phrases that introduce examples (*for example, for instance*)

- Words and phrases that signal comparison (*likewise, similarly, in the same way*)

- Words and phrases that signal contrast (*although, in contrast, on the other hand*)

- Words and phrases that signal contradiction (*however, on the contrary*)

- Words and phrases that signal a move from general to specific (*in fact, specifically, in other words*)

- Words and phrases that introduce summaries or conclusions (*to sum up, in conclusion*)

⊘ EXERCISE 2.1

"Violent Media Is Good for Kids" is an essay by Gerard Jones, a comic book writer and author of several books about popular media. In this essay, which begins on the following page, Jones argues that violent comic books and video games serve a useful function for young people.

In preparation for class discussion and other activities that will be assigned later in this chapter, preview the essay. Then, read it carefully, and answer the questions that follow it.

This article appeared in *Mother Jones* on June 28, 2000.

VIOLENT MEDIA IS GOOD FOR KIDS

GERARD JONES

At 13 I was alone and afraid. Taught by my well-meaning, progressive, English-teacher parents that violence was wrong, that rage was something to be overcome and cooperation was always better than conflict, I suffocated my deepest fears and desires under a nice-boy persona. Placed in a small, experimental school that was wrong for me, afraid to join my peers in their bumptious rush into adolescent boy-hood, I withdrew into passivity and loneliness. My parents, not trusting the violent world of the late 1960s, built a wall between me and the crudest elements of American pop culture.

A scene from Gerard Jones and Will Jacobs's comic book *Monsters from Outer Space*

Then the Incredible Hulk smashed through it.

One of my mother's students convinced her that Marvel Comics, despite their apparent juvenility and violence, were in fact devoted to lofty messages of pacifism and tolerance. My mother borrowed some, thinking they'd be good for me. And so they were. But not because they preached lofty messages of benevolence. They were good for me because they were juvenile. And violent.

The character who caught me, and freed me, was the Hulk: overgendered and undersocialized, half-naked and half-witted, raging against a frightened world that misunderstood and persecuted him. Suddenly I had a fantasy self to carry my stifled rage and buried desire for power. I had a fantasy self who was a self: unafraid of his desires and the world's disapproval, unhesitating and effective in action. "Puny boy follow Hulk!" roared my fantasy self, and I followed.

I followed him to new friends—other sensitive geeks chasing their own inner brutes—and I followed him to the arrogant, self-exposing, self-assertive, superheroic decision to become a writer. Eventually, I left him behind, followed more sophisticated heroes, and finally my own lead along a twisting path to a career and an identity. In my 30s, I found myself writing action movies and comic books. I wrote some Hulk stories, and met the geek-geniuses who created him. I saw my own creations turned into action figures, cartoons, and computer games. I talked to the kids who read my stories. Across generations, genders, and ethnicities I kept seeing the same story: people pulling themselves out of emotional traps by immersing themselves in violent stories. People integrating the scariest, most fervently denied fragments of their psyches° into fuller senses of selfhood through fantasies of superhuman combat and destruction.

Minds or selves

6   I have watched my son living the same story—transforming himself into a bloodthirsty dinosaur to embolden himself for the plunge into preschool, a Power Ranger to muscle through a social competition in kindergarten. In the first grade, his friends started climbing a tree at school. But he was afraid: of falling, of the centipedes crawling on the trunk, of sharp branches, of his friends' derision. I took my cue from his own fantasies and read him old Tarzan comics, rich in combat and bright with flashing knives. For two weeks he lived in them. Then he put them aside. And he climbed the tree.

7

A scene from Gerard Jones and Gene Ha's comic book *Oktane*

8

9

But all the while, especially in the wake of the recent burst of school shootings, I heard pop psychologists insisting that violent stories are harmful to kids, heard teachers begging parents to keep their kids away from "junk culture," heard a guilt-stricken friend with a son who loved Pokémon lament, "I've turned into the bad mom who lets her kid eat sugary cereal and watch cartoons!"

That's when I started the research.

"Fear, greed, power-hunger, rage: these are aspects of our selves that we try not to experience in our lives but often want, even need, to experience vicariously through stories of others," writes Melanie Moore, Ph.D., a psychologist who works with urban teens. "Children need violent entertainment in order to explore the inescapable feelings that they've been taught to deny, and to reintegrate those feelings into a more whole, more complex, more resilient selfhood."

10   Moore consults to public schools and local governments, and is also raising a daughter. For the past three years she and I have been studying the ways in which children use violent stories to meet their emotional and developmental needs—and the ways in which adults can help them use those stories healthily. With her help I developed *Power Play*, a program for helping young people improve their self-knowledge and sense of potency through heroic, combative storytelling.

11   We've found that every aspect of even the trashiest pop-culture story can have its own developmental function. Pretending to have superhuman powers helps children conquer the feelings of powerlessness that inevitably come with being so young and small. The dual-identity concept at the heart of many

superhero stories helps kids negotiate the conflicts between the inner self and the public self as they work through the early stages of socialization. Identification with a rebellious, even destructive, hero helps children learn to push back against a modern culture that cultivates fear and teaches dependency.

At its most fundamental level, what we call "creative violence"—head- 12 bonking cartoons, bloody video games, playground karate, toy guns—gives children a tool to master their rage. Children will feel rage. Even the sweetest and most civilized of them, even those whose parents read the better class of literary magazines, will feel rage. The world is uncontrollable and incomprehensible;

> "Rage can be an energizing emotion."

mastering it is a terrifying, enraging task. Rage can be an energizing emotion, a shot of courage to push us to resist greater threats, take more control, than we ever thought we could. But rage is also the emotion our culture distrusts the most. Most of us are taught early on to fear our own. Through immersion in imaginary combat and identification with a violent protagonist, children engage the rage they've stifled, come to fear it less, and become more capable of utilizing it against life's challenges.

I knew one little girl who went around exploding with fantasies so violent 13 that other moms would draw her mother aside to whisper, "I think you should know something about Emily. . . ." Her parents were separating, and she was small, an only child, a tomboy at an age when her classmates were dividing sharply along gender lines. On the playground she acted out *Sailor Moon*° fights, and in the classroom she wrote stories about people being stabbed with knives. The more adults tried to control her stories, the more she acted out the roles of her angry heroes: breaking rules, testing limits, roaring threats.

A Japanese cartoon series about magical girls

Then her mother and I started helping her tell her stories. She wrote them, 14 performed them, drew them like comics: sometimes bloody, sometimes tender, always blending the images of pop culture with her own most private fantasies. She came out of it just as fiery and strong, but more self-controlled and socially competent: a leader among her peers, the one student in her class who could truly pull boys and girls together.

I worked with an older girl, a middle-class "nice girl," who held herself 15 together through a chaotic family situation and a tumultuous adolescence with gangsta rap. In the mythologized street violence of Ice T, the rage and strutting of his music and lyrics, she found a theater of the mind in which she could be powerful, ruthless, invulnerable. She avoided the heavy drug use that sank many of her peers, and flowered in college as a writer and political activist.

The title character of *Oktane* gets nasty.

16   I'm not going to argue that violent entertainment is harmless. I think it has helped inspire some people to real-life violence. I am going to argue that it's helped hundreds of people for every one it's hurt, and that it can help far more if we learn to use it well. I am going to argue that our fear of "youth violence" isn't well-founded on reality, and that the fear can do more harm than the reality. We act as though our highest priority is to prevent our children from growing up into murderous thugs—but modern kids are far more likely to grow up too passive, too distrustful of themselves, too easily manipulated.

17   We send the message to our children in a hundred ways that their craving for imaginary gun battles and symbolic killings is wrong, or at least dangerous. Even when we don't call for censorship or forbid *Mortal Kombat*, we moan to other parents within our kids' earshot about the "awful violence" in the entertainment they love. We tell our kids that it isn't nice to play-fight, or we steer them from some monstrous action figure to a pro-social doll. Even in the most progressive households, where we make such a point of letting children feel what they feel, we rush to substitute an enlightened discussion for the raw material of rageful fantasy. In the process, we risk confusing them about their natural aggression in the same way the Victorians° confused their children about their sexuality. When we try to protect our children from their own feelings and fantasies, we shelter them not against violence but against power and selfhood.

The people who lived during the reign of Victoria (1819–1901), queen of Great Britain and Ireland, who are often associated with prudish behavior.

Identifying the Elements of Argument

1. What is Jones's thesis? Restate it in your own words.

2. What arguments does Jones present as evidence in support of his thesis?

3. What arguments against his position does Jones identify? How does he refute them?

4. Paraphrase Jones's concluding statement.

Argument

Thesis   Evidence   Refutation   Concluding Statement

Highlighting

After you read an argument, read through it again, this time highlighting as you read. When you **highlight**, you use underlining and symbols to identify the essay's most important points. This active reading strategy will help you to understand the writer's ideas and to see connections among those ideas when you reread.

How do you know what to highlight? As a general rule, you look for the same signals that you looked for when you read the essay the first time—for example, the essay's thesis and topic sentences and the words and phrases that identify the writer's intent and emphasis. This time, however, you physically mark these elements and use various symbols to indicate your reactions to them.

SUGGESTIONS FOR HIGHLIGHTING

- Underline key ideas—for example, ideas stated in topic sentences.

- Box or circle words or phrases you want to remember.

- Place a check mark or a star next to an important idea.

- Place a double check mark or double star next to an especially significant idea.

- Draw lines or arrows to connect related ideas.

- Put a question mark near an unfamiliar reference or a word you need to look up.

- Number the writer's key supporting points or examples.

Here is how a student, Katherine Choi, highlighted the essay "When Life Imitates Video" by John Leo. Choi was preparing to write an essay about the effects of media violence on children and adolescents. She began her highlighting by underlining and starring the thesis statement (para. 2). She then circled references to Leo's two key examples, "Colorado massacre" (1) and "Paducah, Ky." (7) and placed question marks beside them to remind herself to find out more about them. In addition, she underlined and starred some particularly important points (2, 8, 9) as well as what she identified as the essay's concluding statement (11).

This essay first appeared in *U.S. News & World Report* on May 3, 1999.

WHEN LIFE IMITATES VIDEO

JOHN LEO

? Marching through a large building using various bombs and guns to pick off   1
victims is a conventional video-game scenario. In the Colorado massacre, Dylan Klebold and Eric Harris used pistol-grip shotguns, as in some video-arcade games. The pools of blood, screams of agony, and pleas for mercy must have been familiar—they are featured in some of the newer and more realistic kill-for-kicks games. "With each kill," the *Los Angeles Times* reported, "the teens cackled and shouted as though playing one of the morbid video games they loved." And they ended their spree by shooting themselves in the head, the final act in the game *Postal*, and, in fact, the only way to end it.

2   Did the sensibilities created by the modern, video kill games play a role in the Littleton massacre? Apparently so. Note the cool and casual cruelty, the outlandish arsenal of weapons, the cheering and laughing while hunting down victims one by one. All of this seems to reflect the style and feel of the video killing games they played so often.

3   No, there isn't any direct connection between most murderous games and most murders. And yes, the primary responsibility for protecting children from dangerous games lies with their parents, many of whom like to blame the entertainment industry for their own failings.

4   But there is a cultural problem here: We are now a society in which the chief form of play for millions of youngsters is making large numbers of people die. Hurting and maiming others is the central fun activity in video games played so addictively by the young. A widely cited survey of 900 fourth-through eighth-grade students found that almost half of the children said their favorite electronic games involve violence. Can it be that all this constant training in make-believe killing has no social effects?

5   **Dress rehearsal.** The conventional argument is that this is a harmless activity among children who know the difference between fantasy and reality. But the games are often played by unstable youngsters unsure about the difference. Many of these have been maltreated or rejected and left alone most of the time (a precondition for playing the games obsessively). Adolescent feelings of resentment, powerlessness, and revenge pour into the killing games. In these children, the games can become a dress rehearsal for the real thing.

6   Psychologist David Grossman of Arkansas State University, a retired Army officer, thinks "point and shoot" video games have the same effect as military strategies used to break down a soldier's aversion to killing. During World War II, only 15 to 20 percent of all American soldiers fired their weapon in battle. Shooting games in which the target is a man-shaped outline, the Army found, made recruits more willing to "make killing a reflex action."

7   Video games are much more powerful versions of the military's primitive discovery about overcoming the reluctance to shoot. Grossman says Michael Carneal, the schoolboy shooter in Paducah, Ky. showed the effects of video-game lessons in killing. Carneal coolly shot nine times, hitting eight people, five of them in the head or neck. Head shots pay a bonus in many video games. Now the Marine Corps is adapting a version of *Doom*, the hyperviolent game played by one of the Littleton killers, for its own training purposes.

8   More realistic touches in video games help blur the boundary between fantasy and reality—guns carefully modeled on real ones, accurate-looking wounds, screams, and other sound effects, even the recoil of a heavy rifle. Some newer games seem intent on erasing children's empathy and concern for others. Once the intended victims of video slaughter were mostly gangsters or aliens. Now some games invite players to blow away ordinary people who have done nothing wrong—pedestrians, marching bands, an elderly woman with a walker. In these games, the shooter is not a hero, just a violent sociopath. One

ad for a Sony game says: "Get in touch with your gun-toting, testosterone-pumping, cold-blooded murdering side."

These killings are supposed to be taken as harmless over-the-top jokes. But the bottom line is that the young are being invited to enjoy the killing of vulnerable people picked at random. This looks like the final lesson in a course to eliminate any lingering resistance to killing.   9

SWAT teams and cops now turn up as the intended victims of some video-game killings. This has the effect of exploiting resentments toward law enforcement and making real-life shooting of cops more likely. This sensibility turns up in the hit movie *Matrix*: world-saving hero Keanu Reeves, in a mandatory Goth-style, long black coat packed with countless heavy-duty guns, is forced to blow away huge numbers of uniformed law-enforcement people.   10

"We have to start worrying about what we are putting into the minds of our young," says Grossman. "Pilots train on flight simulators, drivers on driving simulators, and now we have our children on murder simulators." If we want to avoid more Littleton-style massacres, we will begin taking the social effects of the killing games more seriously.   11

⊖ EXERCISE 2.2

Look carefully at Katherine Choi's highlighting of John Leo's essay on pages 62–64. How would your own highlighting of this essay be similar to or different from hers?

⊖ EXERCISE 2.3

Reread "Violent Media Is Good for Kids" (pp. 58–61). As you read, highlight the essay by underlining and starring important points, boxing or circling key words, writing question marks beside references that need further explanation, or drawing lines and arrows to connect related ideas. If you do not understand a word or a reference, circle it and put a question mark above it.

Annotating

As you highlight, you should also annotate what you are reading. **Annotating** means making notes—of your questions, reactions, and ideas for discussion or writing—in the margins of the essay or between the lines. Keeping this kind of informal record of ideas as they occur to you will prepare you for class discussion and provide a useful source of material when you write.

As you read an argument and think critically about what you are reading, use the questions in the following checklist to help you make useful annotations.

CHECKLIST

Questions for Annotating

☐ What issue is the writer focusing on?

☐ Does the writer take a clear stand on this issue?

☐ What is the writer's thesis?

☐ What is the writer's purpose (his or her reason for writing)?

☐ What kind of audience is the writer addressing?

☐ Does the argument appear in a popular periodical or a scholarly journal?

☐ Does the writer seem to assume readers will agree with the essay's position?

☐ What evidence does the writer use to support the essay's thesis? Does the writer include enough evidence?

☐ Does the writer consider (and refute) opposing arguments?

☐ Do you understand the writer's vocabulary?

☐ Do you understand the writer's references?

☐ Do you agree with the points the writer makes?

☐ Do the views the writer expresses agree or disagree with the views presented in other essays you have read?

The following pages, which reproduce Katherine Choi's highlighting of John Leo's essay on pages 62–64, also include her marginal annotations. In these annotations, Choi put Leo's thesis and some of his key points into her own words and recorded a few questions that she intended to explore further. She also added notes to clarify his references to the two school shootings. Finally, she identified arguments against Leo's position and his refutation of these arguments.

This essay first appeared in *U.S. News & World Report* on May 3, 1999.

WHEN LIFE IMITATES VIDEO

JOHN LEO

1   Marching through a large building using various bombs and guns to pick off victims is a conventional video-game scenario. In the Colorado massacre, Dylan Klebold and Eric Harris used pistol-grip shotguns, as in some video-arcade games. The pools of blood, screams of agony, and pleas for mercy must have been familiar—they are featured in some of the newer and more realistic kill-for-kicks games. "With each kill," the *Los Angeles Times* reported, "the teens cackled and shouted as though playing one of the morbid video games they loved." And they ended their spree by shooting themselves in the head, the final act in the game *Postal*, and, in fact, the only way to end it.

Columbine H.S., 1999

Thesis
His position: "video kill games" can lead to violent behavior

Did the sensibilities created by the modern, video kill games play a role ₂ in the Littleton massacre? Apparently so. Note the cool and casual cruelty, the outlandish arsenal of weapons, the cheering and laughing while hunting down victims one by one. All of this seems to reflect the style and feel of the video killing games they played so often.

Opposing arguments

No, there isn't any direct connection between most murderous games and ₃ most murders. And yes, the primary responsibility for protecting children from dangerous games lies with their parents, many of whom like to blame the entertainment industry for their own failings.

Refutation

But there is a cultural problem here: We are now a society in which the ₄ chief form of play for millions of youngsters is making large numbers of people die. Hurting and maiming others is the central fun activity in video games played so addictively by the young. A widely cited survey of 900 fourth-through eighth-grade students found that almost half of the children said their favorite electronic games involve violence. Can it be that all this constant training in make-believe killing has no social effects?

True?

Date of survey?

(He means "training" *does* have negative effects, right?)

Dress rehearsal. The conventional argument is that this is a harmless ₅ activity among children who know the difference between fantasy and reality. But the games are often played by unstable youngsters unsure about the difference. Many of these have been maltreated or rejected and left alone most of the time (a precondition for playing the games obsessively). Adolescent feelings of resentment, powerlessness, and revenge pour into the killing games. In these children, the games can become a dress rehearsal for the real thing.

Opposing argument

Refutation

Quotes psychologist (= authority)

Psychologist David Grossman of Arkansas State University, a retired Army ₆ officer, thinks "point and shoot" video games have the same effect as military strategies used to break down a soldier's aversion to killing. During World War II, only 15 to 20 percent of all American soldiers fired their weapon in battle. Shooting games in which the target is a man-shaped outline, the Army found, made recruits more willing to "make killing a reflex action."

1997

Video games are much more powerful versions of the military's primitive ₇ discovery about overcoming the reluctance to shoot. Grossman says Michael Carneal, the schoolboy shooter in Paducah, Ky. showed the effects of video-game lessons in killing. Carneal coolly shot nine times, hitting eight people, five of them in the head or neck. Head shots pay a bonus in many video games. Now the Marine Corps is adapting a version of *Doom*, the hyperviolent game played by one of the Littleton killers, for its own training purposes.

More realistic touches in video games help blur the boundary between ₈ fantasy and reality—guns carefully modeled on real ones, accurate-looking wounds, screams, and other sound effects, even the recoil of a heavy rifle. Some newer games seem intent on erasing children's empathy and concern for others. Once the intended victims of video slaughter were mostly gangsters or aliens. Now some games invite players to blow away ordinary people who have done nothing wrong—pedestrians, marching bands, an elderly woman with a walker. In these games, the shooter is not a hero, just a violent sociopath. One ad for a Sony game says: "Get in touch with your gun-toting, testosterone-pumping, cold-blooded murdering side."

9   These killings are supposed to be taken as harmless over-the-top jokes. But the bottom line is that the young are being invited to enjoy the killing of vulnerable people picked at random. This looks like the final lesson in a course to eliminate any lingering resistance to killing.

10   SWAT teams and cops now turn up as the intended victims of some video-game killings. This has the effect of exploiting resentments toward law enforcement and making real-life shooting of cops more likely. This sensibility turns up in the hit movie *Matrix*: world-saving hero Keanu Reeves, in a mandatory Goth-style, long black coat packed with countless heavy-duty guns, is forced to blow away huge numbers of uniformed law-enforcement people.

11   "We have to start worrying about what we are putting into the minds of our young," says Grossman. "Pilots train on flight simulators, drivers on driving simulators, and now we have our children on murder simulators." If we want to avoid more Littleton-style massacres, we will begin taking the social effects of the killing games more seriously.

Recommendation for action

➔ EXERCISE 2.4

Reread Gerard Jones's "Violent Media Is Good for Kids" (pp. 58–61). As you read, refer to the "Questions for Annotating" checklist (p. 65), and use them as a guide as you write your own reactions and questions in the margins of Jones's essay. In your annotations, note where you agree or disagree with Jones, and briefly explain why. Quickly summarize any points that you think are particularly important. Look up any unfamiliar words or references you have identified, and write down brief definitions or explanations. Think about these annotations as you prepare to discuss the Jones essay in class (and, eventually, to write about it).

➔ EXERCISE 2.5

Exchange essays with another student, and read his or her highlighting and annotating. How are your written responses similar to the other student's? How are they different? Do your classmate's responses help you to see anything new about Jones's essay?

➔ EXERCISE 2.6

The following two brief commentaries from readers of *USA Today* were published on April 17, 2007, following the massacre at Virginia Tech University. Read the readers' comments, and highlight and annotate them. As you read, identify points that support or contradict Gerard Jones's argument. Then, write one or two additional annotations in the margins of Jones's essay to acknowledge these points.

MEDIA VIOLENCE MAY BE REAL CULPRIT BEHIND VIRGINIA TECH TRAGEDY

TIM MILEY, KALAMAZOO, MICHIGAN

Guns are not creating the problem in our society. Rather, it is our mentality 1 ("33 dead after gunfire at dorm, in classrooms," News, Tuesday).

Gratuitous violence is accepted as normal. Our television programs and 2 movies are awash in mindless death and destruction, and that sickness spreads into the city streets. Every day, more U.S. soldiers, sailors, Marines, and helpless Iraqi and Afghani citizens die in the Middle East. Our culture implicitly believes that violence solves problems.

Politicians cannot solve this problem. They created it, with our consent. 3 No law will be able to fix our broken world view.

To put an end to the violence, we must rethink our very relationship with 4 the world. Would our society start to get better if every time we saw a violent TV program we changed the channel or, better yet, turned off the television? Would our collective sickness start to fade if every time a violent scene started in a movie, we walked out of the theater?

TAKE AIM AT GUNS

PATRICK MACKIN, THE VILLAGES, FLORIDA

A careful observer would have noted that there hardly has been any commen- 1 tary on the cause of the horrible Virginia Tech shootings: guns. Why? It probably is because many fear bringing on the wrath of the National Rifle Association and gun owners throughout the world. The NRA will toss out its old cry about our Constitution, a well-regulated militia and the right to bear arms.

The Bureau of Alcohol, Tobacco, Firearms, and Explosives estimates that 2 there are more than 215 million guns in the hands of private citizens. That's a gun for almost every man, woman, and child in our country. The USA leads the world in gun ownership.

Why should we be surprised about what happened at Virginia Tech? We 3 will continue to have horrible, tragic days like those at Columbine High School and Virginia Tech until we wake up and rid ourselves of guns. One disturbed young man buys two guns and then kills 32 students and himself in his expression of his "right to bear arms." When will we ever learn?

● EXERCISE 2.7

The following letter to the editor of a college newspaper takes a position on the issue of how violent media—in this case, video games—influence young people. Read the letter, highlighting and annotating it.

Now, consider how this letter is similar to and different from Gerard Jones's essay (pp. 58–61). First, identify the writer's thesis, and restate it in your own words. Then, consider the benefits of the violent video games the writer identifies. Are these benefits the same as those Jones identifies?

In paragraph 4, the writer summarizes arguments against her position. Does Jones address any of these same arguments? If so, does he refute them in the same way this writer does? Finally, read the letter's last paragraph. How is this writer's purpose for writing different from Jones's?

> This letter to the editor was published on October 22, 2003, in *Ka Leo o Hawai'i*, the student newspaper of the University of Hawaii at Manoa.

DON'T WITHHOLD VIOLENT GAMES

JESSICA ROBBINS

Entertainment and technology have changed. Video games today are more graphic 1 and violent than they were a few years ago. There is a concern about children being influenced by the content of some of these video games. Some states have already passed laws which ban minors from the viewing or purchasing of these video games without an accompanying adult. I believe this law should not exist.

Today's technology has truly enriched our entertainment experience. 2 Today's computer and game consoles are able to simulate shooting, killing, mutilation, and blood through video games. It was such a problem that in 1993 Congress passed a law prohibiting the sale or rental of adult video games to minors. A rating system on games, similar to that placed on movies, was put into place, which I support. This helps to identify the level of violence that a game might have. However, I do not believe that this rating should restrict people of any age from purchasing a game.

Currently there is no significant evidence that supports the argument that 3 violent video games are a major contributing factor in criminal and violent behavior. Recognized universities such as MIT and UCLA described the law as misguided, citing that "most studies and experiments on video games containing violent content have not found adverse effects." In addition, there actually are benefits from playing video games. They provide a safe outlet for aggression and frustration, increased attention performance, along with spatial and coordination skills.

> "There actually are benefits from playing video games."

Some argue that there is research that shows real-life video game play is related 4 to antisocial behavior and delinquency, and that there is need for a law to prevent children from acting out these violent behaviors. This may be true, but researchers have failed to indicate that this antisocial and aggressive behavior is mostly short-term. We should give children the benefit of the doubt. Today's average child is competent and intelligent enough to recognize the difference between the digital representation of a gun and a real 28-inch military bazooka rocket launcher. They are also aware of the consequences of using such weapons on real civilians.

Major software companies who create video games should write Congress 5 and protest this law on the basis of a nonexistent correlation between violence and video games. If the law is modified to not restrict these games to a particular age group, then these products will not be unfairly singled out.

Writing a Critical Response

Sometimes you will be asked to write a **critical response**—a paragraph or more in which you analyze ideas presented in an argument and express your reactions to them.

Before you can respond in writing to an argument, you need to be sure that you understand what the writer means to get across and that you have a sense of how ideas are arranged—and why. You also need to consider how convincingly the writer conveys his or her position.

If you have read the argument carefully, highlighting and annotating it according to the guidelines outlined in this chapter, you should have a good idea what the writer wants to communicate to readers as well as how successfully the argument makes its point.

Before you begin to write a critical response to an argument, you should consider the questions in the checklist on the facing page.

When you write your critical response, begin by identifying your source and its author; then, write a clear, concise summary of the writer's position. Next, analyze the argument's supporting points one by one, considering the strength of the evidence that is presented. Also consider whether the writer addresses all significant opposing arguments and whether those arguments are refuted convincingly. Quote, summarize, and paraphrase the writer's key points as you go along, being careful to quote accurately and not to misrepresent the writer's ideas or distort them by quoting out of context. (For information on summarizing, paraphrasing, quoting, and synthesizing sources, see Chapter 9.) As you write, identify

CHECKLIST

Questions for Critical Reading

☐ What is the writer's general subject?

☐ What purpose does the writer have for presenting this argument?

☐ What is the writer's position?

☐ Does the writer support ideas mainly with facts or with opinion?

☐ What evidence does the writer present to support this position?

☐ Is the evidence convincing? Is there enough evidence?

☐ Does the writer present opposing ideas and refute them effectively?

☐ What kind of audience does the writer seem to be addressing?

☐ Does the writer see the audience as hostile, friendly, or neutral?

☐ Does the writer establish himself or herself as well-informed? As a fair and reasonable person?

☐ Does the writer seem to exhibit bias? If so, how does this bias affect the argument?

arguments you find unconvincing, poorly supported, or irrelevant. At the end of your critical response, sum up your assessment of the argument in a strong concluding statement.

⬇ Katherine Choi, the student who highlighted and annotated "When Life Imitates Video" by John Leo (pp. 62–64), used her highlighting and annotations to help her develop the following critical response to Leo's article.

RESPONSE TO "WHEN LIFE IMITATES VIDEO"

KATHERINE CHOI

1   In "When Life Imitates Video," John Leo takes the position that "video kill games" (para. 2) can actually lead to violent behavior. In fact, he suggests a cause-and-effect connection between such games and the notorious 1999 murder spree at Colorado's Columbine High School, which occurred shortly before Leo wrote his essay.

2   Although Leo acknowledges in paragraph 3 that there is no "direct connection" between video games and this crime and agrees that

Article's source and author identified

Summary of writer's position

Analysis of supporting evidence

parents bear the "primary responsibility" for keeping violent games out of the hands of their children, he insists that our culture is also responsible. He is very critical of our society's dependence on violent video games, which he considers "training in make-believe killing" (para 4). This argument is convincing, up to a point. The problem is that Leo's primary support for this argument is a reference to an unnamed "widely cited survey" (para. 4), for which he provides no date. In addition, his use of a weak rhetorical question at the end of paragraph 4 instead of a strong statement of his position does little to help to support his argument.

Analysis of Leo's discussion of an opposing argument

Leo cites an opposing argument at the beginning of paragraph 5— the "conventional argument" that video games are harmless because children can tell the difference between fantasy and reality. He refutes this argument with unsupported generalizations rather than with specifics, pointing out the possibility that the games will often be played by "unstable youngsters" who channel their "adolescent feelings of resentment, powerlessness, and revenge" into the games.

3

Analysis of supporting evidence

The key piece of supporting evidence for Leo's claim that video games are dangerous comes in paragraph 6 with the expert opinion of a psychology professor who is also a retired army officer. The professor, David Grossman, draws an analogy between adolescents' video games and military training games designed to encourage soldiers to shoot their enemies. Although this analogy is interesting, it is not necessarily valid. For one thing, the army training Grossman refers to took place during World War II; for another, the soldiers were aware that the games were preparing them for actual combat.

4

Analysis of supporting evidence

In paragraph 7, Leo goes on to cite Grossman's comments about the young shooter in a 1997 attack in Paducah, Kentucky, and the Marines' use of *Doom* to train soldiers. Again, both discussions are interesting, and both are relevant to the connection between video games and violence. The problem is that neither discussion establishes a cause-and-effect relationship between violent video games and violent acts.

5

It may be true, as Leo observes, that video games are becoming more and more violent and that the victims in these games are increasingly likely to be police officers. Still, Leo fails to make his point because he never establishes that real-life violence is also increasing; therefore, he is not able to demonstrate a causal connection. His concluding statement— "If we want to avoid more Littleton-style massacres, we will begin taking

6

the social effects of the killing games more seriously"—combines a frightening prediction and a strong recommendation for action. Unfortunately, although Leo's essay will frighten many readers, it does not convincingly establish the need for the action he recommends.

Concluding statement

Work Cited

Leo, John. "When Life Imitates Video." *Practical Argument*. 2nd ed.
Laurie G. Kirszner and Stephen R. Mandell. Boston: Bedford, 2014.
62–64. Print.

⊖ EXERCISE 2.8

Write a one-paragraph critical response to Gerard Jones's essay on pages 58–61. Use the following template to shape your paragraph.

> **TEMPLATE FOR WRITING A CRITICAL RESPONSE**
>
> According to Gerard Jones, violent media can actually have positive effects on young people because _____
> _____
> _____
> _____. Jones also believes that violent media are a positive influence on children because _____
> _____ .
> Jones makes some good points. For example, he says that _____
> _____
> _____
> _____. However, _____
> _____
> _____. All in
> all, _____
> _____ .

⊖ EXERCISE 2.9

Consulting the one-paragraph critical response that you wrote above, write a more fully developed critical response to Gerard Jones's essay on pages 58–61. Refer to the highlighting and annotations that you did for Exercises 2.3 and 2.4. (If you like, you can expand your response with references to recent news events involving violent acts.)

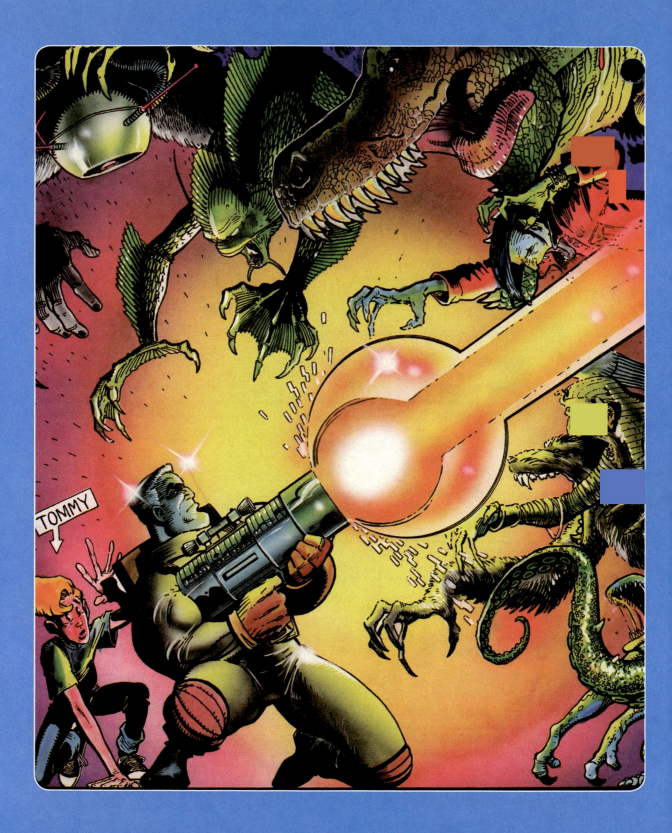

Decoding Visual Arguments

AT ISSUE

Do Violent Media Images Trigger Violent Behavior? (continued)

In Chapter 2, you read two essays focusing on whether violence on TV and in other popular media can be blamed (at least in part) for the violence in our society. Now, you will be introduced to a variety of visual texts that offer additional insights into this issue. At the same time, you will learn how to use the critical-reading strategies that you practiced in Chapter 2 to help you to **decode**, or interpret, visual texts and to use visuals as springboards for discussion and writing or as sources in your essays.

A **visual argument** can be an advertisement, a chart or graph or table, a diagram, a Web page, a photograph, or a painting. Like an argumentative essay, a visual argument can take a position. Unlike an argumentative essay, however, a visual argument communicates its position (and offers evidence to support that position) largely through images rather than words.

Thinking Critically about Visual Arguments

When you approach a visual argument—particularly one that will be the subject of class discussion or writing—you should do so with a critical eye. Your primary goal is to understand the point that the creator of the visual is trying to make, but you also need to understand how the message is conveyed. In addition, you need to evaluate whether the methods used to persuade the audience are both logical and fair.

For comprehension quizzes,
see **bedfordstmartins.com/practicalargument**.

VISUAL TEXTS VERSUS VISUAL ARGUMENTS

Not every visual is an argument; many simply present information. For example, a diagram of a hunting rifle, with its principal parts labeled, tells viewers what the weapon looks like and how it works. However, a photo of two toddlers playing with a hunting rifle could make a powerful argument about the need for gun safety. Conversely, a photo of a family hunting trip featuring a teenager proudly holding up a rifle while his parents look on approvingly might make a positive argument for access to guns.

Using Active Reading Strategies with Visual Arguments

As you learned in Chapter 2, being a critical reader involves responding actively to the text of an argument. The active reading strategies that you practiced in Chapter 2—*previewing, careful reading, highlighting,* and *annotating*—can also be applied to visual arguments.

When you approach a visual argument, you should look for clues to its main idea, or message. Some visuals, particularly advertising images, include words (sometimes called body copy) as well, and this written text often conveys the main ideas of the argument. Apart from words, however, the images themselves can help you understand the visual's purpose, its intended audience, and the argument that it is making.

COMPREHENSION CLUES

- The individual images that appear

- The relative distance (close together or far apart) between images

- The relative size of the images

- The relationship between images and background

- The use of empty space

- The use of color and shading (for example, contrast between light and dark)

- If people are pictured, their activities, gestures, facial expressions, positions, body language, dress, and so on

APPEALS: *LOGOS, PATHOS,* AND *ETHOS*

As you study a visual argument, you should consider the appeal (or appeals) that the visual uses to convince its audience.

- An ad produced by Mothers Against Drunk Drivers (MADD) that includes statistics about alcohol-related auto fatalities might appeal to logic (***logos***).

- Another MADD ad could appeal to the emotions (***pathos***) by showing photographs of an accident scene.

- Still another ad could appeal to authority (***ethos***) by featuring a well-known sports figure warning of the dangers of drunk driving.

(For more on these appeals, see the introduction to this book.)

When you have studied the visual carefully, you should have a good general sense of what it was designed to communicate.

Look at the following image.

This illustration by Todd Davidson first appeared in the *Age* newspaper, Melbourne, Australia, on March 22, 1998.

The visual on the preceding page uses the image of a young child holding a mutilated teddy bear to make an emotional appeal to those concerned about children's exposure to television violence.

The visual includes three dominant images: the child, the teddy bear, and a giant TV screen projecting an image of a hand holding a knife. The placement of the child in the center of the visual, with the teddy bear on one side and the knife on the other, suggests that the child (and, by extension, all children) is caught between the innocence of childhood and the violence depicted in the media. The hand holding the knife on the television screen is an extension of the child's actual arm, suggesting that the innocent world of the child is being taken over by the violent world of the media.

To emphasize this conflict between innocence and violence, the teddy bear is set against a dark background, while the TV, with its disturbing image, is paradoxically set against a light background. (The image of the child is split, with half against each background, suggesting the split between the two worlds the child is exposed to.) The child's gaze is directed at his mutilated teddy bear, apparently the victim of his own violent act. The expression on the child's face makes it clear that he does not understand the violence he is caught up in.

Because it treats subject matter that is familiar to most people—TV violence and children's vulnerability to it—this visual is easy to understand. Its powerful images are not difficult to interpret, and its message is straightforward: TV violence is, at least in part, responsible for real-world violence. The visual's accessibility suggests that it is aimed at a wide general audience (rather than, for example, child psychologists or media analysts).

The visual's purpose is somewhat more complex. It could be to criticize the media, to warn parents and others about the threat posed by media violence, or to encourage the audience to take action.

Now, turn your attention to the graph on the facing page. This graph appeals to logic by using statistics as evidence to support its position. In so doing, it makes a powerful visual argument about the relationship between violent video games and crime. The visual uses accessible graphics and has an open, inviting design; its format is designed to make its information clear to most people who will look at it. The main idea that it conveys might be summarized as follows: "Although video games have become more and more violent, the number of crime victims has actually declined."

This idea is likely to come as a surprise to most people, who might assume a causal relationship between violent video games and violent crime. But as the graph shows, in 1972—when video games did not exist—the crime rate was considerably higher than it was in 2004. Because the information in the graph is intended to contradict its audience's probable assumptions, it seems to have been created to convince people to change the way they look at video games. In other words, it is an argument (and, in fact, it is structured as a **refutation**).

United States Department of Justice, Crime Victims per 1,000 Citizens

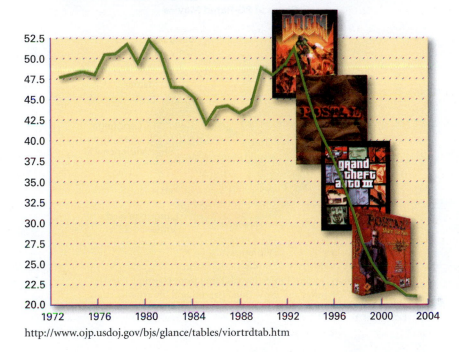

http://www.ojp.usdoj.gov/bjs/glance/tables/viortrdtab.htm

EXERCISE 3.1

Look at the visuals on the pages that follow, and then answer the questions on page 82.

Bill Watterson, *Calvin and Hobbes*, "Graphic Violence in the Media"

©1995 Watterson/Dist. by Universal Press Syndicate

Parenthood Library, Distribution of Language, Sex, and Violence Codes in PG-Rated Movies

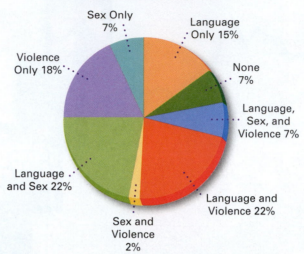

This chart is from "Protecting Children from Harmful Television: TV Ratings and the V-chip," parenthood.library.wisc.edu/Nathanson/Nathanson.html.

Netwellness.org, Homicides per 100,000 Population

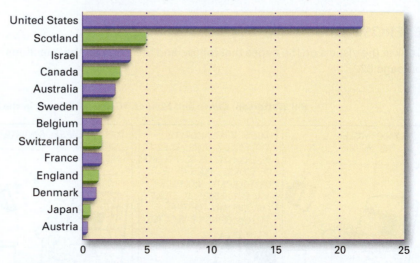

This graph appears in "Violence in the United States," published at netwellness.org/healthtopics/domestictv/violenceUS.cfm.

Boy Shooting Plastic Gun

Robert Mankoff, Killing It: Murders in *New Yorker* Cartoons (by decade)

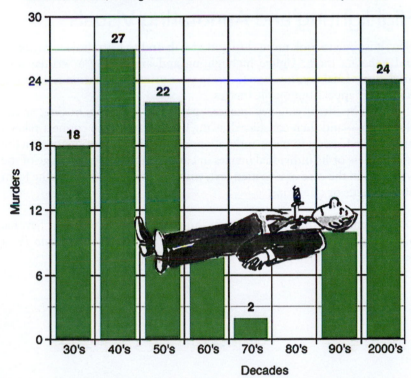

Identifying the Elements of a Visual Argument

1. Are all of the visuals on pages 79–81 arguments, or do you think some were designed solely to present information? Explain.

2. What main idea does each visual communicate? State the main idea of each visual in a single sentence.

3. What elements in each visual support this main idea?

4. If the visual includes words as well as images, are the words necessary?

5. What purpose does each visual seem designed to achieve?

6. What kind of audience do you think each visual is aimed at?

7. Does the visual appeal primarily to *logos*, *pathos*, or *ethos*?

8. Do you think the visual is effective? That is, is it likely to have the desired effect on its intended audience?

Highlighting and Annotating Visuals

Now, it is time to look more closely at visuals and to learn how to *highlight* and *annotate* them. Unlike highlighting and annotating a written text, marking a visual text involves focusing your primary attention not on any words that appear but on the images.

Begin by identifying key images—perhaps by starring, boxing, or circling them—and then consider drawing lines or arrows to connect related images. Next, go on to make annotations on the visual, commenting on the effectiveness of its individual images in communicating the message of the whole. As in the case of a written text, your annotations can be in the form of comments or questions.

⬇ The image on the following page shows how a student, Jason Savona, highlighted and annotated an advertisement for *Grand Theft Auto IV*, a popular violent video game.

Rockstar North, Advertisement for *Grand Theft Auto IV*

Top of gun = taller than tallest building

Huge lone figure looking down on city

"Liberty City" skyline (looks like NY)

Hazy yellow sky

Dark image stands out against lighter background

Name of game centered; large type in contrasting black and white for emphasis

➔ EXERCISE 3.2

Look at the visual or the following page, and then highlight and annotate it to identify its most important images and their relationship to one another. When you have finished, think about how the images work together to communicate a central message to the audience. What argument does this visual make?

Mediaviolence.org, *The Top Games of 2011 Include*

According to CNBC, the Top Games of 2011 Include:
Rage
Bulletstorm
Max Payne
Twisted Metal
Deus Ex 3: Human Revolution

➔ EXERCISE 3.3

Interview a classmate about his or her experiences with video games—
or with actual violence. Does your classmate see any links between the
kinds of videos that are watched by friends and family members and the
violence (or lack of violence) that occurs in his or her community? Write
a paragraph summarizing your interview.

➔ EXERCISE 3.4

Study the three visuals on the following page, all of which appear in
Gerard Jones's essay, "Violent Media Is Good for Kids" (pp. 58–61).
Look at each visual with a critical eye, and then consider how
effectively each one supports the central argument that Jones makes
in his essay.

A scene from Gerard Jones and Will Jacobs's comic book *Monsters from Outer Space*

A scene from Gerard Jones and Gene Ha's comic book *Oktane*

The title character of *Oktane* gets nasty.

Responding Critically to Visual Arguments

As you learned in Chapter 2, a **critical response** analyzes the ideas in a text and expresses your reactions to them. When you respond in writing to a visual argument, you should rely on your highlighting and annotations to help you understand the writer's ideas and see how the words and images work together to make a particular point.

As you prepare to write a critical response to a visual argument, you should keep in mind questions like those in the following checklist.

CHECKLIST

Questions for Responding to Visual Arguments

☐ In what source did the visual appear? What is the target audience for this source?

☐ For what kind of audience was the visual created? Hostile? Friendly? Neutral?

☐ For what purpose was the visual created?

☐ Who (or what organization) created the visual? What do you know about the background and goals of this person or group?

☐ What issue is the visual addressing?

☐ What position does the visual take on this issue? How can you tell? Do you agree with this position?

(*continued*)

☐ Does the visual include words? If so, are they necessary? What points do they make? Does the visual need more—or different—written text?

☐ Does the visual seem to be a *refutation*—that is, an argument against a particular position?

☐ Is the visual effective? Attractive? Interesting? Clear? Convincing?

When you write a critical response, begin by identifying the source and purpose of the visual. Then, state your reaction to the visual, and examine its elements one at a time, considering how effective each is and how well the various elements work together to create a convincing visual argument. End with a strong concluding statement that summarizes your reaction.

⬇ The critical response that follows was written by the student who highlighted and annotated the advertisement for *Grand Theft Auto IV* on page 83.

RESPONSE TO *GRAND THEFT AUTO IV*

JASON SAVONA

Identification of visual's source

Reaction to visual

The advertisement for *Grand Theft Auto IV* presents a disturbing preview of the game. Rather than highlighting the game's features and challenges, this ad promotes the game's violence. As a result, it appeals more to those who are looking for video games that depict murder and other crimes than to those who choose a video game on the basis of the skill it requires.   1

Analysis of visual's elements

The "hero" of this game is Niko Bellic, a war veteran from Eastern Europe who has left his country to build a new life in the fictional Liberty City. Instead of finding peace, he has found a new kind of war. Now, trapped in the corrupt world of organized crime, Bellic is willing to do whatever it takes to fight his way out. His idea of justice is vigilante justice: he makes his own rules. The ad conveys this sense of Bellic as a loner and an outsider by showing him as a larger-than-life figure standing tall and alone against a background of the Liberty City skyline.   2

In the ad, Niko Bellic holds a powerful weapon in his huge hands, and the weapon extends higher than the tallest building behind it,   3 dominating the picture. Clearly, Bellic means business. As viewers look at the picture, the dark image of the gun and the man who holds it comes to the foreground, and everything else—the light brown buildings, the city lights, the yellow sky—fades into the background. In the center, the name of the game is set in large black-and-white type that contrasts with the ad's hazy background, showing the importance of the product's name.

4   This image, clearly aimed at young players of violent video games, would certainly be appealing to those who want to have a feeling of power. What it says is, "A weapon makes a person powerful." This is a very dangerous message.

Concluding statement

⬗ EXERCISE 3.5

Write a one-paragraph critical response to the visual you highlighted and annotated in Exercise 3.2 on pages 83–84. Use the following template to shape your paragraph.

TEMPLATE FOR RESPONDING TO VISUAL ARGUMENTS

A visual posted on the site mediaviolence. org shows _____
_____.

This visual makes a powerful statement about _____
The central image shows _____
_____.

The background enhances the central image because _____
_____
_____.

The visual includes words as well as images. These words suggest _____
_____.
_____.

The goal of the organization that posted the visual seems to be to _____
_____.

The visual (is/is not) effective because _____
_____.

⬗ EXERCISE 3.6

Consulting the one-paragraph critical response that you wrote for Exercise 3.5, write a more fully developed critical response to the visual on page 84. Refer to the highlighting and annotating that you did for Exercise 3.2.

Writing a Rhetorical Analysis

Is It Ethical to Buy Counterfeit Designer Merchandise?

The demand for counterfeit designer merchandise—handbags, shoes, and jewelry—has always been great. Wishing to avoid the high prices of genuine designer goods, consumers spend hundreds of millions of dollars per year buying cheap imitations that are made primarily in factories in China (and in other countries as well). According to United States Customs and Border Protection statistics, the amount of counterfeit goods seized in 2012 had a retail value of $1.5 billion. Naturally, much more counterfeit merchandise gets into the United States than is seized. However hard they try, law enforcement officials cannot stem the tide of counterfeit merchandise that is sold in stores, in flea markets, and by street vendors as well as through the Internet. As long as people want these illegal goods, there will be a market for them.

However, purchasing counterfeit designer goods is not a victimless crime. Buyers are stealing the intellectual property of legitimate businesses that, unlike the manufacturers of fakes, pay their employees fair wages and provide good working conditions. The result is that the sale of counterfeit products eventually drives up prices for legitimate consumers. In addition, because counterfeit goods are of low quality, they do not last as long as the genuine articles. This is not a serious problem when people are buying fake watches and handbags, but it can be life threatening when the counterfeit products include pharmaceuticals, tools, baby food, or automobile parts.

Later in this chapter, you will read a rhetorical analysis of an essay that takes a position on this issue, and you will be asked to write a rhetorical analysis of your own about another essay on this topic.

 For comprehension quizzes, see bedfordstmartins.com/practicalargument.

What Is a Rhetorical Analysis?

In everyday use, the term **rhetoric** has distinctly negative connotations. When a speech is described as being nothing but *rhetoric*, the meaning is clear: the speech consists of empty words and phrases that are calculated to confuse and manipulate listeners. When writing instructors use the term *rhetoric*, however, it means something entirely different. Applied to argument, *rhetoric* refers to how various elements work together to form a convincing and persuasive argument.

When you write a **rhetorical analysis,** you systematically examine the strategies a writer employs to achieve his or her purpose. In the process, you explain how these strategies work together to create an effective (or ineffective) argument. To carry out this task, you consider the argument's **rhetorical situation**, the writer's **means of persuasion**, and the **rhetorical strategies** that the writer uses.

OVERVIEW: "LETTER FROM BIRMINGHAM JAIL" BY MARTIN LUTHER KING JR.

Here and throughout the rest of this chapter, we will be analyzing "Letter from Birmingham Jail" by Martin Luther King Jr., which can be found on page 799 of this book.

In 1963, civil rights leader Martin Luther King Jr. organized a series of nonviolent demonstrations to protest the climate of segregation that existed in Birmingham, Alabama. He and his followers met opposition not only from white moderates but also from some African-American clergymen who thought that King was a troublemaker. During the demonstrations, King was arrested and jailed for eight days. He wrote his "Letter from Birmingham Jail" on April 16, 1963, from the city jail in response to a public statement by eight white Alabama clergymen entitled "A Call for Unity." This statement asked for an end to the demonstrations, which the clergymen called "untimely," "unwise," and "extreme." (Their letter was addressed to the "white and Negro" population of Birmingham, not to King, whom they considered an "outsider.")

King knew that the world was watching and that his response to the white clergymen would have both national and international significance. As a result, he used a variety of rhetorical strategies to convince readers that his demands were both valid and understandable and that contrary to the opinions of some, his actions were well within the mainstream of American social and political thought. Today, King's "Letter from Birmingham Jail" stands as a model of clear and highly effective argumentation.

Martin Luther King Jr. in Birmingham Jail (April 1963)

Considering the Rhetorical Situation

Arguments do not take place in isolation. They are written by real people in response to a particular set of circumstances called the **rhetorical situation**. The rhetorical situation consists of the following five elements:

- The writer
- The writer's purpose
- The writer's audience
- The topic
- The context

By analyzing the rhetorical situation, you are able to determine why the writer made the choices he or she did and how these choices affect the argument.

ANALYZING THE RHETORICAL SITUATION

To help you analyze the rhetorical situation of an argument, look for information about the essay and its author.

1. **Look at the essay's headnote.** If the essay you are reading has a headnote, it can contain useful information about the writer, the issue being discussed, and the structure of the essay. For this reason, it is a good idea to read headnotes carefully.

2. **Look for clues within the essay.** The writer's use of particular words and phrases can sometimes provide information about his or her preconceptions as well as about the cultural context of the argument. Historical or cultural references can indicate what ideas or information the writer expects readers to have.

3. **Search the Web.** Often, just a few minutes online can give you a lot of useful information—such as the background of a particular debate or the biography of the writer. By looking at titles of the other books or essays the writer has written, you may also be able to get an idea of his or her biases or point of view.

The Writer

Begin by trying to determine whether anything in the writer's background (for example, the writer's education, experience, race, gender, political beliefs, religion, age, and experiences) has influenced the content of the argument. Also consider whether the writer seems to have any preconceptions about the subject.

QUESTIONS FOR ANALYZING THE WRITER

- What is the writer's background?
- How does the writer's background affect the content of the argument?
- What preconceptions about the subject does the writer seem to have?

If you were analyzing "Letter from Birmingham Jail," it would help to know that Martin Luther King Jr. was pastor of the Dexter Avenue Baptist Church in Montgomery, Alabama. In 1956, he organized a bus boycott that led to a United States Supreme Court decision that outlawed segregation on Alabama's buses. In addition, King was a leader of the Southern Christian Leadership Conference and strongly believed in nonviolent protest. His books include *Stride towards Freedom* (1958) and *Why We Can't Wait* (1964). His "I Have a Dream" speech, which he delivered on the steps of the Lincoln Memorial on August 28, 1963, is considered by scholars to be one of the most influential speeches of the twentieth century. In 1964, King won the Nobel Prize for peace.

In his letter, King addresses the injustices that he sees in America—especially in the South—and makes a strong case for civil rights for all races. Throughout his argument, King includes numerous references to the New Testament, to philosophers, and to political and religious thinkers. By

"I Have a Dream" speech, Washington, D.C. (August 1963)

doing so, he makes it clear to readers that he is aware of the social, cultural, religious, and political implications of his actions. Because he is a clergyman, King suggests that by battling injustice, he is doing God's work. This point is made clear in the following passage (para. 3):

> But more basically, I am in Birmingham because injustice is here. Just as the prophets of the eighth century B.C. left their villages and carried their "thus saith the Lord" far beyond the boundaries of their home towns, and just as the Apostle Paul left his village of Tarsus and carried the gospel of Jesus Christ to the far corners of the Greco-Roman world, so am I compelled to carry the gospel of freedom beyond my own home town. Like Paul, I must constantly respond to the Macedonian call for aid.

The Writer's Purpose

Next, consider what the writer hopes to achieve with his or her argument. In other words, ask yourself why the author wrote the argument.

QUESTIONS FOR ANALYZING THE WRITER'S PURPOSE

- Does the writer state his or her purpose directly, or is the purpose implied?
- Is the writer's purpose simply to convince or to encourage action?
- Does the writer rely primarily on logic or on emotion?
- Does the writer have a hidden agenda?

It is clear that Martin Luther King Jr. wrote "Letter from Birmingham Jail" to convince readers that even though he had been arrested, his actions were both honorable and just. To get readers to understand that, like Henry David Thoreau, he is protesting laws that he considers wrong, he draws a distinction between just and unjust laws. For him, a law is just if it "squares with the moral law or the law of God" (16). A law is unjust if it "is out of harmony with the moral law" (16). As a clergyman and a civil rights leader, King believed that he had an obligation both to point out the immorality of unjust laws and to protest them—even if it meant going to jail.

The Writer's Audience

To analyze the writer's audience, begin by considering whether the writer seems to see readers as friendly, hostile, or neutral. (For a discussion of types of audiences, see p. 15.) Also, determine how much knowledge the writer assumes that readers have. Then, consider how the writer takes into account factors like the audience's race, religion, gender, education, age, and ethnicity.

Next, decide what preconceptions the writer thinks readers have about the subject. Finally, see if the writer shares any common ground with readers.

QUESTIONS FOR ANALYZING THE WRITER'S AUDIENCE

- Who is the writer's intended audience?

- Does the writer see the audience as informed or uninformed?

- Does the writer see the audience as hostile, friendly, or neutral?

- What values does the writer think the audience holds?

- What does the writer seem to assume about the audience's background?

- On what points do the writer and the audience agree? On what points do they disagree?

In "Letter from Birmingham Jail," King aims his letter at more than one audience. First, he speaks directly to eight clergymen from Birmingham, who are at worst a hostile audience and at best a skeptical one. They consider King to be an outsider whose actions are "unwise and untimely" (1). Before addressing their concerns, King tries to establish common ground, referring to his readers as "fellow clergymen" and "my Christian and Jewish brothers." He then goes on to say that he wishes that the clergymen had supported his actions instead of criticizing them. King ends his letter on a conciliatory note by asking his readers to forgive him if he has overstated his case or been unduly harsh.

In addition to addressing clergymen, King also speaks to white moderates, who he assumes are sympathetic to his cause but concerned about his methods. He knows that he has to influence this segment of his audience if he is to gain wide support for his cause. For this reason, King uses a restrained tone and emphasizes the universality of his message, ending his letter with a plea that is calculated to console and inspire those people who need reassurance (50):

> Let us all hope that the dark clouds of racial prejudice will soon pass away and the deep fog of misunderstanding will be lifted from our fear-drenched communities, and in some not too distant tomorrow the radiant stars of love and brotherhood will shine over our great nation with all their scintillating beauty.

The Topic

Try to learn why the writer has decided to write about a particular topic. Also consider how narrow or broad the topic is, and decide if an argument is sufficiently well developed for the topic.

> ### QUESTIONS FOR ANALYZING THE TOPIC
>
> - What is the topic of the argument?
>
> - Why did the writer decide to write about this particular topic?
>
> - Has the writer developed the topic fully enough?

King addresses complex and emotional issues in "Letter from Birmingham Jail." His topic is apparently racial segregation in Alabama, but he also addresses the problem of indifference among white moderates. In addition, he feels he needs to explain his actions (for example, engaging in nonviolent protests) and to answer those who are urging him to call off the demonstrations. Because of the complexity of his topic, his argument is long and somewhat difficult.

The Context

The **context** is the situation that creates the need for the argument. As you analyze an argument, try to determine the social, historical, economic, political, and cultural events that set the stage for the argument and the part that these events play in the argument itself.

> ### QUESTIONS FOR ANALYZING THE CONTEXT
>
> - What situation (or situations) set the stage for the argument?
>
> - What social, economic, political, and cultural events triggered the argument?
>
> - What historical references situate this argument in a particular place or time?

The immediate context of "Letter to Birmingham Jail" is well known: Martin Luther King Jr. wrote an open letter to eight white clergymen in which he defended his protests against racial segregation. However, the wider social and political context of the letter is less well known.

In 1896, the U.S. Supreme Court ruled in *Plessy v. Ferguson* that "separate but equal" accommodations on railroad cars gave African Americans the equal protection guaranteed by the Fourteenth Amendment of the U.S. Constitution. Well into the twentieth century, this decision was used to justify separate public facilities—including restrooms, water fountains, and even schools and hospitals—for blacks and whites.

In the mid-1950s, state support for segregation of the races and discrimination against African Americans had begun to be challenged. For example, Supreme Court decisions in 1954 and 1955 found that segregation

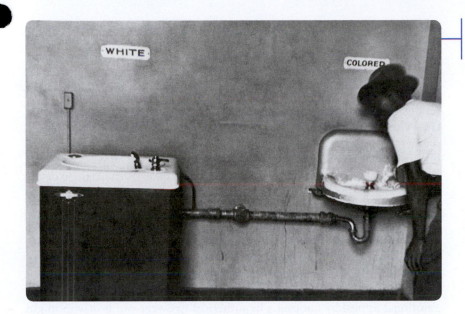

Segregated water fountains in North Carolina (1950)

in the public schools and other publicly financed locations was unconstitutional. At the same time, whites and blacks alike were calling for an end to racial discrimination. Their actions took the form of marches, boycotts, and sit-ins (organized nonviolent protests whose participants refused to move from a public area). Many whites, however, particularly in the South, strongly resisted any sudden changes in race relations.

King's demonstrations in Birmingham, Alabama, took place within this larger social and political context. His campaign was a continuation of the push for equal rights that had been gaining momentum in the United States for decades. King, along with the Southern Christian Leadership Conference, had dispatched hundreds of people to Birmingham to engage in nonviolent demonstrations against those who were determined to keep African Americans from gaining their full rights as citizens.

Considering the Means of Persuasion: *Logos, Pathos, Ethos*

In the introduction to this book, you learned how writers of argument use three means of persuasion—*logos*, *pathos*, and *ethos*—to appeal to readers. You also saw how the **rhetorical triangle** represents the way these three appeals come into play within an argument. (See p. 13 for more information about the rhetorical triangle.) Of course, the degree to which a writer uses each of these appeals depends on the rhetorical situation. Moreover, a single argument can use more than one appeal—for example, an important research source would enhance both the logic of the argument (*logos*) and the credibility of the writer (*ethos*). In "Letter from Birmingham Jail," King uses all three appeals.

The Appeal to Reason (Logos)

In "Letter from Birmingham Jail," King attempts to demonstrate the logic of his position. In paragraph 15, for example, he says that there are two types of laws—just and unjust. He then points out that he has both a legal and a moral responsibility to "disobey unjust laws." In paragraph 16, King supports his position with references to various philosophers and theologians—for example, St. Thomas Aquinas, Martin Buber, and Paul Tillich. He also develops the logical argument that even though all Americans should obey the law, they are responsible to a higher moral authority—God.

The Appeal to the Emotions (Pathos)

Throughout "Letter from Birmingham Jail," King attempts to create sympathy for his cause. In paragraph 14, for example, he catalogues the injustices of life in the United States for African Americans. He makes a particularly emotional appeal by quoting a hypothetical five-year-old boy who might ask, "Daddy, why do white people treat colored people so mean?" In addition, he includes vivid images of racial injustice to provoke anger against those who deny African Americans equal rights. In this way, King creates sympathy (and possibly empathy) in readers.

The Appeal to Authority (Ethos)

To be persuasive, King has to establish his credibility or authority to speak on behalf of the African-American community. In paragraph 2, for example, he reminds readers that he is the president of the Southern Christian Leadership Conference, "an organization operating in every southern state." In paragraph 3, he compares himself to the apostle Paul, who carried the gospel "to the far corners of the Greco-Roman world." In addition, King attempts to show readers that what he is doing is well within the mainstream of American political and social thought. By referring to Thomas Jefferson, Henry David Thoreau, and the 1954 U.S. Supreme Court decision that outlawed segregation in public schools, he tries to demonstrate that he is not the wild-eyed radical that some believe him to be. Thus, King establishes himself in both secular and religious terms as a leader who has both the stature and the authority to present his case.

Considering the Writer's Rhetorical Strategies

Writers use various **rhetorical strategies** to present their ideas and opinions. Here are a few of the elements that you should examine when analyzing and evaluating an argument.

Thesis

The **thesis**—the position that the argument supports—is of primary importance in every argument. When you analyze an argument, you should always ask, "What is the essay's thesis, and why does the writer state it as he or she does?" You should also consider at what point in the argument the thesis is stated and what the effect of this placement is.

In "Letter from Birmingham Jail," Martin Luther King Jr. begins by telling readers that he is "confined here in the Birmingham city jail" and that he is writing his letter to answer clergymen who have called his demonstrations "unwise and untimely." King clearly (and unapologetically) states his thesis ("But more basically, I am in Birmingham because injustice is here") at the beginning of the third paragraph, right after he explains his purpose, so that readers will have no doubt what his position is as they read the rest of his argument.

Organization

The **organization** of an argument—how a writer arranges ideas—is also important. For example, after stating his thesis, King tells readers why he is in Birmingham and what he hopes to accomplish: he wants unjust laws to be abolished and the 1954 Supreme Court ruling to be enforced. King then **refutes**—disproves or calls into question—the specific charges that were leveled at him by the white clergymen who want him to stop his protests.

The structure of "Letter from Birmingham Jail" enables King to make his points clearly, logically, and effectively:

- King begins his argument by addressing the charge that his actions are untimely. If anything, says King, his actions are not timely enough: after all, African Americans have waited more than 340 years for their "constitutional and God-given rights" (14).

- He then addresses the issue of his willingness to break laws and makes the distinction between just and unjust laws.

- After chiding white moderates for not supporting his cause, he addresses their claim that he is extreme. According to King, this charge is false: if he had not embraced a philosophy of nonviolent protest, the streets of the South would "be flowing with blood" (29).

- King then makes the point that the contemporary church must recapture the "sacrificial spirit of the early church" (42). He does this by linking his struggle for freedom with the "sacred heritage of our nation and the eternal will of God" (44).

- King ends his argument by asserting both his humility and his unity with the white clergy.

Evidence

To convince an audience, a writer must support the thesis with **evidence**— facts, observations, expert opinion, and so on. King presents a great deal of evidence to support his arguments. For instance, he uses numerous examples (both historical and personal) as well as many references to philosophers, political thinkers, and theologians (such as Jesus, St. Paul, St. Augustine, Amos, Martin Luther, William Gladstone, and Abraham Lincoln). According to King, these figures, who were once considered "extremists," were not afraid of "making waves" when the need arose. Now, however, they are well within the mainstream of social, political, and religious thought. King also presents reasons, facts, and quotations to support his points.

Stylistic Techniques

Writers also use stylistic techniques to make their arguments more memorable and more convincing. For example, in "Letter from Birmingham Jail," King uses *similes*, *metaphors*, and *allusions* to enhance his argument.

Simile A **simile** is a figure of speech that compares two unlike things using the word *like* or *as*.

> Like a boil that can never be cured so long as it is covered up but must be opened with all its ugliness to the natural medicines of air and light, injustice must be exposed, . . . before it can be cured. (24)

> Isn't this like condemning a robbed man because his possession of money precipitated the evil act of robbery? (25)

Metaphor A **metaphor** is a comparison in which two dissimilar things are compared without the word *like* or *as*. A metaphor suggests that two things that are very different share a quality.

> Frankly, I have yet to engage in a direct-action campaign that was "well-timed" in the view of those who have not suffered unduly from the disease of segregation. (13)

> [W]hen you see the vast majority of your twenty million Negro brothers smothering in an airtight cage of poverty . . . (14)

Allusion An **allusion** is a reference within a work to a person, literary or biblical text, or historical event in order to enlarge the context of the situation being written about. The writer expects readers to recognize the allusion and to make the connection to the text they are reading.

> I would agree with St. Augustine that "an unjust law is no law at all." (15)

> Of course, there is nothing new about this kind of civil disobedience. It was evidenced sublimely in the refusal of Shadrach, Meshach, and Abednego to obey the laws of Nebuchadnezzar, on the ground that a

higher moral law was at stake. (21) [King expects his audience of cler-gymen to recognize this reference to the Book of Daniel in the Old Testament.]

In addition to those stylistic techniques, King also uses *parallelism*, *repetition*, and *rhetorical questions* to further his argument.

Parallelism **Parallelism,** the use of similar grammatical structures to emphasize related ideas, makes a passage easier to follow.

> In any nonviolent campaign there are four basic steps: collection of the facts to determine whether injustices exist; negotiation; self-purification; and direct action. (6)

> Shallow understanding from people of good will is more frustrating than absolute misunderstanding from people of ill will. Lukewarm acceptance is much more bewildering than outright rejection. (23)

> I wish you had commended the Negro sit-inners and demonstrators of Birmingham for their sublime courage, their willingness to suffer, and their amazing discipline in the midst of great provocation. (47)

Repetition Intentional **repetition** involves repeating a word or phrase for emphasis, clarity, or emotional impact.

> "Are you able to accept blows without retaliating?" "Are you able to endure the ordeal of jail?" (8)

> If I have said anything in this letter that overstates the truth and indi-cates an unreasonable impatience, I beg you to forgive me. If I have said anything that understates the truth and indicates my having patience that allows me to settle for anything less than brotherhood, I beg God to forgive me. (49)

Rhetorical questions A **rhetorical question** is a question that is asked to encourage readers to reflect on an issue, not to elicit a reply.

> One may well ask: "How can you advocate breaking some laws and obeying others?" (15)

> Will we be extremists for hate or for love? (31)

Assessing the Argument

No rhetorical analysis of an argument would be complete without an assessment of its effectiveness—whether the rhetorical strategies the writer uses create a clear and persuasive argument or whether they fall short. When you write a rhetorical analysis, you can begin with an assessment of the argument as a whole and go on to support it, or you can begin with a discussion of the various rhetorical strategies that the writer uses and then end with your assessment of the argument.

After analyzing "Letter from Birmingham Jail," you could reasonably conclude that King has written an effective argument that is likely to convince his readers that his presence in Birmingham is both justified and necessary. Using *logos*, *pathos*, and *ethos*, he constructs a multifaceted argument that is calculated to appeal to the various segments of his audience— Southern clergymen, white moderates, and African Americans. In addition, King uses similes, metaphors, and allusions to enrich his argument and to make it more memorable, and he uses parallelism, repetition, and rhetorical questions to emphasize ideas and to reinforce his points. Because it is so clear and powerful, King's argument—in particular, the distinction between just and unjust laws—addresses not only the injustices that were present in 1963 when it was written but also the injustices and inequalities that exist today. In this sense, King has written an argument that has broad significance beyond the audiences for which it was originally intended.

CHECKLIST

Preparing to Write a Rhetorical Analysis

As you read, ask the following questions:

- ☐ Who is the writer? Is there anything in the writer's background that might influence what is (or is not) included in the argument?
- ☐ What is the writer's purpose? What does the writer hope to achieve?
- ☐ What topic has the writer decided to write about? How broad is the topic?
- ☐ What situation created the need for the argument?
- ☐ At what points in the argument does the writer appeal to logic? To the emotions? How does the writer try to establish his or her credibility?

- ☐ What is the argument's thesis? Where is it stated? Why?
- ☐ How does the writer organize the argument? How effective is this arrangement of ideas?
- ☐ What evidence does the writer use to support the argument? Does the writer use enough evidence?
- ☐ Does the writer use similes, metaphors, and allusions?
- ☐ Does the writer use parallelism, repetition, and rhetorical questions?
- ☐ Given your analysis, what is your overall assessment of the argument?

Sample Rhetorical Analysis

In preparation for a research paper, Deniz Bilgutay, a student in a writing class, read the following essay, "Terror's Purse Strings" by Dana Thomas, which makes an argument against buying counterfeit designer goods.

Deniz then wrote the rhetorical analysis that appears on pages 104–106. (Deniz Bilgutay's research paper, "The High Cost of Cheap Counterfeit Goods," uses "Terror's Purse Strings" as a source. See Appendix B.)

This essay appeared in the *New York Times* on August 30, 2007.

TERROR'S PURSE STRINGS

DANA THOMAS

1   Luxury fashion designers are busily putting final touches on the handbags they will present during the spring-summer 2008 women's wear shows, which begin next week in New York City's Bryant Park. To understand the importance of the handbag in fashion today consider this: According to consumer surveys conducted by Coach, the average American woman was buying two new handbags a year in 2000; by 2004, it was more than four. And the average luxury bag retails for 10 to 12 times its production cost.

2   "There is a kind of an obsession with bags," the designer Miuccia Prada told me. "It's so easy to make money."

3   Counterfeiters agree. As soon as a handbag hits big, counterfeiters around the globe churn out fake versions by the thousands. And they have no trouble selling them. Shoppers descend on Canal Street in New York, Santee Alley in Los Angeles, and flea markets and purse parties around the country to pick up knockoffs for one-tenth the legitimate bag's retail cost, then pass them off as real.

4   "Judges, prosecutors, defense attorneys shop here," a private investigator told me as we toured the counterfeit section of Santee Alley. "Affluent people from Newport Beach." According to a study by the British law firm Davenport Lyons, two-thirds of British consumers are "proud to tell their family and friends" that they bought fake luxury fashion items.

5   At least 11 percent of the world's clothing is fake, according to 2000 figures from the Global Anti-Counterfeiting Group in Paris. Fashion is easy to copy: counterfeiters buy the real items, take them apart, scan the pieces to make patterns, and produce almost-perfect fakes.

> "At least 11 percent of the world's clothing is fake."

6   Most people think that buying an imitation handbag or wallet is harmless, a victimless crime. But the counterfeiting rackets are run by crime syndicates that also deal in narcotics, weapons, child prostitution, human trafficking, and terrorism. Ronald K. Noble, the secretary general of Interpol,° told the House of Representatives Committee on International Relations that profits from the sale of counterfeit goods have gone to groups

An international criminal police organization

associated with Hezbollah, the Shiite terrorist group, paramilitary organizations in Northern Ireland, and FARC, the Revolutionary Armed Forces of Colombia.

Sales of counterfeit T-shirts may have helped finance the 1993 World Trade 7 Center bombing, according to the International AntiCounterfeiting Coalition. "Profits from counterfeiting are one of the three main sources of income supporting international terrorism," said Magnus Ranstorp, a terrorism expert at the University of St. Andrews, in Scotland.

Most fakes today are produced in China, a good many of them by children. 8 Children are sometimes sold or sent off by their families to work in clandestine factories that produce counterfeit luxury goods. Many in the West consider this an urban myth. But I have seen it myself.

On a warm winter afternoon in Guangzhou, I accompanied Chinese police 9 officers on a factory raid in a decrepit tenement. Inside, we found two dozen children, ages 8 to 13, gluing and sewing together fake luxury-brand handbags. The police confiscated everything, arrested the owner, and sent the children out. Some punched their timecards, hoping to still get paid. (The average Chinese factory worker earns about $120 a month; the counterfeit factory worker earns half that or less.) As we made our way back to the police vans, the children threw bottles and cans at us. They were now jobless and, because the factory owner housed them, homeless. It was *Oliver Twist* in the 21st century.

What can we do to stop this? Much like the war on drugs, the effort to 10 protect luxury brands must go after the source: the counterfeit manufacturers. The company that took me on the Chinese raid is one of the only luxury-goods makers that works directly with Chinese authorities to shut down factories, and it has one of the lowest rates of counterfeiting.

Luxury brands also need to teach consumers that the traffic in fake goods has many victims. But most companies refuse to speak publicly about counterfeiting—some won't even authenticate questionable items for concerned customers—believing, like Victorians,° that acknowledging despicable actions tarnishes their sterling reputations.

The people who lived during the reign of Victoria (1819–1901), queen of Great Britain and Ireland, who are often associated with prudish behavior

So it comes down to us. If we stop knowingly buying fakes, the supply 12 chain will dry up and counterfeiters will go out of business. The crime syndicates will have far less money to finance their illicit activities and their terrorist plots. And the children? They can go home.

A POWERFUL CALL TO ACTION

DENIZ BILGUTAY

Context

In her *New York Times* essay, "Terror's Purse Strings," writer Dana 1 Thomas uses the opening of New York's fashion shows as an opportunity to expose a darker side of fashion—the impact of imitation designer goods. Thomas explains to her readers why buying counterfeit luxury items, like fake handbags, is a serious problem. Her first goal is to raise awareness of the dangerous ties between counterfeiters who sell fake luxury merchandise and international criminal organizations that support terrorism and child labor. Her second goal is to explain how people can be a part of the solution by refusing to buy the counterfeit goods that finance these criminal activities. By establishing her credibility, building her case slowly, and appealing to both logic and emotions, Thomas succeeds in writing an interesting and informative argument.

2   For Thomas's argument to work, she has to earn her readers' trust. She does so first by anticipating a sympathetic, well-intentioned, educated audience and then by establishing her own credibility. To avoid sounding accusatory, Thomas assumes that her readers are unaware of the problem posed by counterfeit goods. She demonstrates this by presenting basic factual information and by acknowledging what "most people think" or what "many in the West consider": that buying counterfeit goods is harmless. She also acknowledges her readers' high level of education by drawing comparisons with history and literature—specifically, the Victorians and *Oliver Twist*. To further earn the audience's trust, she uses her knowledge and position to gain credibility. As the Paris correspondent for *Newsweek* and as the author of a book on luxury goods, Thomas has credibility. Showing her familiarity with the world of fashion by referring to a conversation with renowned designer Miuccia Prada, she further establishes this credibility. Later in the article, she shares her experience of witnessing the abuse that accompanies the production of fake designer handbags. This anecdote allows her to say, "I've seen it myself," confirming her knowledge not just of the fashion world but also of the world of counterfeiting. Despite her authority, she does not distance herself from readers. In fact, she goes out of her way to identify with them, using informal style and first person, noting "it comes down to us" and asking what "we" can do.

3   In Thomas's argument, both the organization and the use of evidence are effective. She begins her article with statements that are easy to accept, and as she proceeds, she addresses more serious issues. In the first paragraph, she simply asks readers to "understand the

Topic

Analysis of writer's purpose

Thesis statement: Assessment of essay

Analysis of writer's audience

Writer's use of similes, metaphors, allusions

Writer's use of ethos

Analysis of the writer

Analysis of essay's organization

Writer's use of logos

importance of the handbag in fashion today." She demonstrates the wide-ranging influence and appeal of counterfeit designer goods, pointing out that "at least 11 percent of the world's clothing is fake." Thomas then makes the point that the act of purchasing these seemingly frivolous goods can actually have serious consequences. For example, crime syndicates and possibly even terrorist organizations actually run

Writer's use of evidence

"the counterfeiting rackets" that produce these popular items. To support this point, she relies on two kinds of evidence—quotations from terrorism experts (specifically, the leader of a respected international police organization as well as a scholar in the field) and her own personal experience at a Chinese factory. Both kinds of evidence appeal to our

Writer's use of pathos

emotions. Discussions of terrorism, especially those that recall the terrorist attacks on the United States, create fear. Descriptions of child labor in China encourage readers to feel sympathy.

Thomas waits until the end of her argument to present her thesis 4 because she assumes that her readers know little about the problem she is discussing. The one flaw in her argument is her failure to provide the evidence needed to establish connections between some causes and their effects. For example in paragraph 7, Thomas says that the sale of counterfeit T-shirts "may have helped finance the 1993 Word Trade Center bombing." By using the word *may*, she qualifies her claim and weakens her argument. The same is true when Thomas says that profits from the sale of counterfeit goods "have gone to groups associated with Hezbollah, the Shiite terrorist group." Readers are left to wonder what specific groups are "associated with Hezbollah" and whether these groups are in fact terrorist organizations. Without this information, her assertion remains unsupported. In spite of these shortcomings, Thomas's argument is clear and well organized. More definite links between causes and effects, however, would have made it more convincing than it is.

⊙ EXERCISE 4.1

Read the essay "Sweatshop Oppression," by Rajeev Ravisankar, on pages 107–109. Then, write a one-paragraph rhetorical analysis of the essay. Follow the template on pages 108–109, filling in the blanks to create your analysis.

This opinion essay was published in the *Lantern*, the student newspaper of the Ohio State University, on April 19, 2006.

SWEATSHOP OPPRESSION

RAJEEV RAVISANKAR

1   Being the "poor" college students that we all are, many of us undoubtedly place an emphasis on finding the lowest prices. Some take this to the extreme and camp out in front of a massive retail store in the wee hours of the morning on Black Friday,° waiting for the opportunity to buy as much as we can for as little as possible.

The Friday after Thanksgiving, traditionally the biggest shopping day of the year

2   What often gets lost in this rampant, low-cost driven consumerism is the high human cost it takes to achieve lower and lower prices. Specifically, this means the extensive use of sweatshop labor.

3   Many of us are familiar with the term sweatshop,° but have difficulty really understanding how abhorrent the hours, wages, and conditions are. Many of these workers are forced to work 70–80 hours per week making pennies per hour. Workers are discouraged or intimidated from forming unions.

A work environment with long hours, low wages, and difficult or dangerous conditions

4   They must fulfill certain quotas for the day and stay extra hours (with no pay) if these are not fulfilled. Some are forced to sit in front of a machine for hours as they are not permitted to take breaks unless the manager allows them to do so. Unsanitary bathrooms, poor ventilation, and extreme heat, upward of 90 degrees, are also prevalent. Child labor is utilized in some factories as well.

5   Facing mounting pressure from labor rights activists, trade unions, student protests, and human-rights groups, companies claimed that they would make improvements. Many of the aforementioned conditions, however, persist. In many cases, even a few pennies more could make a substantial difference in the lives of these workers. Of course, multi-

> "Corporations . . . are interested in doing anything to increase profits."

national corporations are not interested in giving charity; they are interested in doing anything to increase profits. Also, many consumers in the West refuse to pay a little bit more even if it would improve the lives of sweatshop workers.

6   Free-market economic fundamentalists have argued that claims made by those who oppose sweatshops actually have a negative impact on the plight of the poor in the developing world. They suggest that by criticizing labor and human-rights conditions, anti-sweatshop activists have forced companies to pull out of some locations, resulting in workers losing their jobs. To shift the blame in this manner is to neglect a simple fact: Companies, not the anti-sweatshop protestors, make the decision to shift to locations where they can find cheaper labor and weaker labor restrictions.

Simply put, the onus should always be on companies such as Nike, Reebok, Adidas, Champion, Gap, Wal-Mart, etc. They are to blame for perpetuating a system of exploitation which seeks to get as much out of each worker for the least possible price.

By continuing to strive for lower wages and lower input costs, they are taking part in a phenomenon which has been described as "the race to the bottom." The continual decline of wages and working conditions will be accompanied by a lower standard of living. This hardly seems like the best way to bring the developing world out of the pits of poverty.

So what can we do about it? Currently, the total disregard for human well-being through sweatshop oppression is being addressed by a number of organizations, including University Students against Sweatshops. USAS seeks to make universities source their apparel in factories that respect workers' rights, especially the right to freely form unions.

According to an article in *The Nation*, universities purchase nearly "$3 billion in T-shirts, sweatshirts, caps, sneakers and sports uniforms adorned with their institutions' names and logos." Because brands do not want to risk losing this money, it puts pressure on them to provide living wages and reasonable conditions for workers. Campaigns such as this are necessary if we are to stop the long race to the bottom.

TEMPLATE FOR WRITING A RHETORICAL ANALYSIS

Ravisankar begins his essay by _____ _____ _____. The problem he identifies is _____ _____ _____. Ravisankar assumes his readers are _____ _____ _____. His purpose in this essay is to _____ _____.

In order to accomplish this purpose, he appeals mainly to _____ _____ _____. He also appeals to _____ _____.

In his essay, Ravisankar addresses the main argument against his thesis, the idea that _____ _____ _____.

He refutes this argument by saying _____

_____

_____.

Finally, he concludes by making the point that _____

_____.

Overall, the argument Ravisankar makes is effective [or ineffective] because

_____

_____

_____.

❯ EXERCISE 4.2

Read the following essay, "Where Sweatshops Are a Dream" by Nicholas D. Kristof. Then, write a rhetorical analysis of Kristof's essay. Be sure to consider the rhetorical situation, the means of persuasion, and the writer's rhetorical strategies. End your rhetorical analysis with an assessment of the strengths and weaknesses of Kristof's argument.

This opinion column was published in the *New York Times* on January 15, 2009.

WHERE SWEATSHOPS ARE A DREAM

NICHOLAS D. KRISTOF

Before Barack Obama and his team act on their talk about "labor standards," 1 I'd like to offer them a tour of the vast garbage dump here in Phnom Penh.

This is a Dante-like vision of hell. It's a mountain of festering refuse, a 2 half-hour hike across, emitting clouds of smoke from subterranean fires.

The miasma of toxic stink leaves you gasping, breezes batter you with 3 filth, and even the rats look forlorn. Then the smoke parts and you come across a child ambling barefoot, searching for old plastic cups that recyclers will buy for five cents a pound. Many families actually live in shacks on this smoking garbage.

Mr. Obama and the Democrats who favor labor standards in trade agree- 4 ments mean well, for they intend to fight back at oppressive sweatshops abroad. But while it shocks Americans to hear it, the central challenge in the poorest countries is not that sweatshops exploit too many people, but that they don't exploit enough.

Talk to these families in the dump, and a job in a sweatshop is a cherished 5
dream, an escalator out of poverty, the kind of gauzy if probably unrealistic
ambition that parents everywhere often have for their children.

"I'd love to get a job in a factory," said Pim Srey Rath, a 19-year-old 6
woman scavenging for plastic. "At least that work is in the shade. Here is
where it's hot."

Another woman, Vath Sam Oeun, hopes her 10-year-old boy, scavenging 7
beside her, grows up to get a factory job, partly because she has seen other children run over by garbage trucks. Her boy has never been to a doctor or a dentist and last bathed when he was 2, so a sweatshop job by comparison would be
far more pleasant and less dangerous.

I'm glad that many Americans are repulsed by the idea of importing 8
products made by barely paid, barely legal workers in dangerous factories. Yet
sweatshops are only a symptom of poverty, not a cause, and banning them
closes off one route out of poverty.
At a time of tremendous economic
distress and protectionist pressures,
there's a special danger that tighter
labor standards will be used as an
excuse to curb trade.

> "Sweatshops are only a symptom of poverty, not a cause."

When I defend sweatshops, people always ask me: But would you want 9
to work in a sweatshop? No, of course not. But I would want even less to pull
a rickshaw. In the hierarchy of jobs in poor countries, sweltering at a sewing
machine isn't the bottom.

My views on sweatshops are shaped by years living in East Asia, watching 10
as living standards soared — including those in my wife's ancestral village in
southern China — because of sweatshop jobs.

Manufacturing is one sector that can provide millions of jobs. Yet sweat- 11
shops usually go not to the poorest nations but to better-off countries with
more reliable electricity and ports.

I often hear the argument: Labor standards can improve wages and work- 12
ing conditions, without greatly affecting the eventual retail cost of goods.
That's true. But labor standards and "living wages" have a larger impact on
production costs that companies are always trying to pare. The result is to
push companies to operate more capital-intensive factories in better-off
nations like Malaysia, rather than labor-intensive factories in poorer countries
like Ghana or Cambodia.

Cambodia has, in fact, pursued an interesting experiment by working 13
with factories to establish decent labor standards and wages. It's a worthwhile
idea, but one result of paying above-market wages is that those in charge of
hiring often demand bribes — sometimes a month's salary — in exchange for
a job. In addition, these standards add to production costs, so some factories
have closed because of the global economic crisis and the difficulty of competing internationally.

The best way to help people in the poorest countries isn't to campaign 14 against sweatshops but to promote manufacturing there. One of the best things America could do for Africa would be to strengthen our program to encourage African imports, called AGOA, and nudge Europe to match it.

Among people who work in development, many strongly believe (but 15 few dare say very loudly) that one of the best hopes for the poorest countries would be to build their manufacturing industries. But global campaigns against sweatshops make that less likely.

Look, I know that Americans have a hard time accepting that sweatshops 16 can help people. But take it from 13-year-old Neuo Chanthou, who earns a bit less than $1 a day scavenging in the dump. She's wearing a "Playboy" shirt and hat that she found amid the filth, and she worries about her sister, who lost part of her hand when a garbage truck ran over her.

"It's dirty, hot, and smelly here," she said wistfully. "A factory is better." 17

You have taken my

PARKING

space!

Would you like my disability also?

Understanding Logic and Recognizing Logical Fallacies

AT ISSUE

Have Colleges Gone Too Far to Accommodate Students with Disabilities?

In 1975, the United States Congress passed the Education for All Handicapped Children Act (EHA), later renamed the Individuals with Disabilities Education Act (IDEA), to mandate special accommodations for students with disabilities. Currently, IDEA as well as other federal laws (the Americans with Disabilities Act and the Rehabilitation Act of 1973, for example) require that disabled students between three and twenty-one years of age— regardless of the nature of their disability— be provided with the services they need in all publicly funded schools. Although colleges and universities are not held to the same strict standards as elementary and secondary schools, they are required to make appropriate academic adjustments—for example, to offer accessible housing and classroom buildings, extra time on exams, and access to tutors and note takers—for students who qualify.

In recent years, the number of college students claiming to have disabilities—especially learning disabilities and attention deficit disorders—has increased dramatically. This situation has caused some observers to claim that colleges too readily grant disability status and that some students manipulate the system to gain an advantage over other students. Advocates for the disabled disagree, pointing out that colleges are required by law to help all students with special needs. In addition, they contend that if the number of students with disabilities has increased, it is not because these individuals are dishonest but because they are more aware of their rights than they once were.

Later in this chapter, you will be asked to think more about this issue. You will be given several sources to consider and asked to write a logical argument that takes a position on whether colleges have gone too far to accommodate students with disabilities.

For comprehension quizzes,
see bedfordstmartins.com/practicalargument.

Charlie Sheen arguing with Jimmy Fallon.

The word *logic* comes from the Greek word *logos*, roughly translated as "word," "thought," "principle," or "reason." **Logic** is concerned with the principles of correct reasoning. By studying logic, you learn the rules that determine the validity of arguments. In other words, logic enables you to tell whether a conclusion correctly follows from a set of statements or assumptions.

Why should you study logic? One answer is that knowledge of logic enables you to make valid points and draw sound conclusions, which in turn helps you to present your ideas clearly and effectively. An understanding of logic also enables you to evaluate the arguments of others. When you understand the basic principles of logic, you know how to tell the difference between a strong argument and a weak argument—between one that is well reasoned and one that is not. This ability can help you cut through the tangle of jumbled thought that characterizes many of the arguments you encounter daily—on television, radio, and the Internet; in the press; and from friends. Finally, knowledge of logic enables you to communicate clearly and forcefully. Understanding the characteristics of good arguments helps you to present your own ideas in a coherent and even compelling way.

Specific rules determine the criteria you use to develop (and to evaluate) arguments logically. For this reason, you should become familiar with the basic principles of *deductive* and *inductive reasoning*—two important ways information is organized in argumentative essays. (Keep in mind that a single argumentative essay might contain both deductive reasoning and inductive reasoning. For the sake of clarity, however, we will discuss them separately.)

What Is Deductive Reasoning?

Most of us use deductive reasoning every day—at home, in school, on the job, and in our communities—usually without even realizing it. **Deductive reasoning** begins with **premises**—statements or assumptions on which an argument is based or from which conclusions are drawn. Deductive reasoning moves from general statements, or premises, to specific conclusions. The process of deduction has traditionally been illustrated with a **syllogism**, which consists of a *major premise*, a *minor premise*, and a *conclusion*:

Thomas Jefferson

> **MAJOR PREMISE**   All disabled students should get the special help they need.
>
> **MINOR PREMISE**   Sarah is a disabled student.
>
> **CONCLUSION**   Therefore, Sarah should get the special help she needs.

A syllogism begins with a **major premise**—a general statement that relates two terms. It then moves to a **minor premise**—an example of the statement that was made in the major premise. If these two premises are linked correctly, a **conclusion** that is supported by the two premises logically follows. (Notice that the conclusion in the syllogism above contains no terms that do not appear in the major and minor premises.) The strength of deductive reasoning is that if readers accept the major and minor premises, the conclusion must necessarily follow.

Thomas Jefferson used deductive reasoning in the Declaration of Independence (see p. 770). When, in 1776, the Continental Congress asked him to draft this document, Jefferson knew that he had to write a powerful argument that would convince the world that the American colonies were justified in breaking away from England. He knew how compelling a deductive argument could be, and so he organized the Declaration of Independence to reflect the traditional structure of deductive logic. It contains a major premise, a minor premise (supported by evidence), and a conclusion. Expressed as a syllogism, here is the argument that Jefferson used:

> **MAJOR PREMISE**   When a government oppresses people, the people have a right to rebel against that government.
>
> **MINOR PREMISE**   The government of England oppresses the American people.
>
> **CONCLUSION**   Therefore, the American people have the right to rebel against the government of England.

In practice, deductive arguments are more complicated than the simple three-part syllogism suggests. Still, it is important to understand the basic structure of a syllogism because a syllogism enables you to map out your argument, to test it, and to see if it makes sense.

Constructing Sound Syllogisms

A syllogism is **valid** when its conclusion follows logically from its premises. A syllogism is **true** when the premises are consistent with the facts. To be **sound**, a syllogism must be *both* valid and true.

Consider the following valid syllogism:

MAJOR PREMISE	All state universities must accommodate disabled students.
MINOR PREMISE	UCLA is a state university.
CONCLUSION	Therefore, UCLA must accommodate disabled students.

In the valid syllogism above, both the major premise and the minor premise are factual statements. If both these premises are true, then the conclusion must also be true. Because the syllogism is both valid and true, it is also sound.

However, a syllogism can be valid without being true. For example, look at the following syllogism:

MAJOR PREMISE	All recipients of support services are wealthy.
MINOR PREMISE	Dillon is a recipient of support services.
CONCLUSION	Therefore, Dillon is wealthy.

As illogical as it may seem, this syllogism is valid: its conclusion follows logically from its premises. The major premise states that *recipients of support services*—all such *recipients*—are wealthy. However, this premise is clearly false: some recipients of support services may be wealthy, but more are probably not. For this reason, even though the syllogism is valid, it is not true.

Keep in mind that validity is a test of an argument's structure, not of its soundness. Even if a syllogism's major and minor premises are true, its conclusion may not necessarily be valid.

Consider the following examples of invalid syllogisms.

Syllogism with an Illogical Middle Term

A syllogism with an illogical middle term cannot be valid. The **middle term** of a syllogism is the term that occurs in both the major and minor premises but not in the conclusion. (It links the major term and the minor term together in the syllogism.) A middle term of a valid syllogism must refer to *all* members of the designated class or group—for example, all dogs, all people, all men, or all women.

Consider the following invalid syllogism:

MAJOR PREMISE	All dogs are mammals.
MINOR PREMISE	Some mammals are porpoises.
CONCLUSION	Therefore, some porpoises are dogs.

Even though the statements in the major and minor premises are true, the syllogism is not valid. *Mammals* is the middle term because it appears in both the major and minor premises. However, because the middle term *mammal* does not refer to *all mammals*, it cannot logically lead to a valid conclusion.

In the syllogism that follows, the middle term *does* refer to all members of the designated group, so the syllogism is valid:

MAJOR PREMISE	All dogs are mammals.
MINOR PREMISE	Ralph is a dog.
CONCLUSION	Therefore, Ralph is a mammal.

Syllogism with a Key Term Whose Meaning Shifts

A syllogism that contains a key term whose meaning shifts cannot be valid. For this reason, the meaning of a key term must remain consistent throughout the syllogism.

Consider the following invalid syllogism:

MAJOR PREMISE	Only man is capable of analytical reasoning.
MINOR PREMISE	Anna is not a man.
CONCLUSION	Therefore, Anna is not capable of analytical reasoning.

In the major premise, *man* refers to mankind—that is, to all human beings. In the minor premise, however, *man* refers to males. In the following valid syllogism, the key terms remain consistent:

MAJOR PREMISE	All educated human beings are capable of analytical reasoning.
MINOR PREMISE	Anna is an educated human being.
CONCLUSION	Therefore, Anna is capable of analytical reasoning.

Syllogism with Negative Premise

If *either* premise in a syllogism is negative, then the conclusion must also be negative.

The following syllogism is not valid:

MAJOR PREMISE	Only senators can vote on legislation.
MINOR PREMISE	No students are senators.
CONCLUSION	Therefore, students can vote on legislation.

Because one of the premises of the syllogism above is negative ("No students are senators"), the only possible valid conclusion must also be negative ("Therefore, no students can vote on legislation").

If *both* premises are negative, however, the syllogism cannot have a valid conclusion:

MAJOR PREMISE	Disabled students may not be denied special help.
MINOR PREMISE	Jen is not a disabled student.
CONCLUSION	Therefore, Jen may not be denied special help.

In the syllogism above, both premises are negative. For this reason, the syllogism cannot have a valid conclusion. (How can Jen deserve special help if she is not a disabled student?) To have a valid conclusion, this syllogism must have only one negative premise:

MAJOR PREMISE	Disabled students may not be denied special help.
MINOR PREMISE	Jen is a disabled student.
CONCLUSION	Therefore, Jen may not be denied special help.

Recognizing Enthymemes

An **enthymeme** is a syllogism with one or two parts of its argument—usually, the major premise—missing. In everyday life, we often leave out parts of arguments—most of the time because we think they are so obvious (or clearly implied) that they don't need to be stated. We assume that the people hearing or reading the arguments will easily be able to fill in the missing parts.

Many enthymemes are presented as a conclusion plus a reason. Consider the following enthymeme:

Robert has lied, so he cannot be trusted.

In the statement above, the minor premise and the conclusion are stated, but the major premise is only implied. Once the missing term has been supplied, the logical structure of the enthymeme becomes clear:

> **MAJOR PREMISE**   People who lie cannot be trusted.
>
> **MINOR PREMISE**   Robert has lied.
>
> **CONCLUSION**   Therefore, Robert cannot be trusted.

It is important to identify enthymemes in arguments you read because some writers, knowing that readers often accept enthymemes uncritically, use them intentionally to unfairly influence readers.

Consider this enthymeme:

> Because Liz receives a tuition grant, she should work.

Although some readers might challenge this statement, others will accept it uncritically. When you supply the missing premise, however, the underlying assumptions of the enthymeme become clear—and open to question:

> **MAJOR PREMISE**   All students who receive tuition grants should work.
>
> **MINOR PREMISE**   Liz receives a tuition grant.
>
> **CONCLUSION**   Therefore, Liz should work.

Perhaps some people who receive tuition grants should work, but should everyone? What about those who are ill or who have disabilities? What about those who participate in varsity sports or have unpaid internships? The enthymeme oversimplifies the issue and should not be accepted at face value.

At first glance, the following enthymeme might seem to make sense:

> North Korea is ruled by a dictator, so it should be invaded.

However, consider the same enthymeme with the missing term supplied:

> **MAJOR PREMISE**   All countries governed by dictators should be invaded.
>
> **MINOR PREMISE**   North Korea is a country governed by a dictator.
>
> **CONCLUSION**   Therefore, North Korea should be invaded.

Once the missing major premise has been supplied, the flaws in the argument become clear. Should *all* nations governed by dictators be invaded? Who should do the invading? Who would make this decision? What would be the consequences of such a policy? As this enthymeme illustrates, if the major premise of a deductive argument is questionable, then the rest of the argument will also be flawed.

BUMPER-STICKER THINKING

Bumper stickers often take the form of enthymemes:

- Self-control beats birth control.

- Peace is patriotic.

- A woman's place is in the House . . . and in the Senate.

- Ban cruel traps.

- Evolution is a theory—kind of like gravity.

- I work and pay taxes so wealthy people don't have to.

- The Bible says it, I believe it, that settles it.

- No one needs a mink coat except a mink.

- Celebrate diversity.

Most often, bumper stickers state just the conclusion of an argument and omit both the major and minor premises. Careful readers, however, will supply the missing premises and thus determine whether the argument is sound.

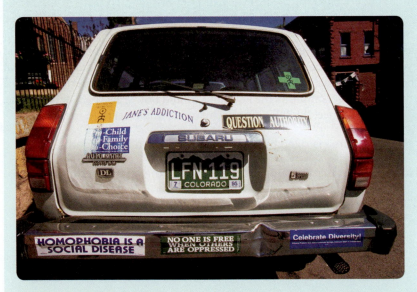

Bumper stickers on a car

⊙ EXERCISE 5.1

Read the following paragraph. Then, restate its main argument as a syllogism.

Drunk Driving Should Be Legalized

In ordering states to enforce tougher drunk driving standards by making it a crime to drive with a blood-alcohol concentration of .08% or higher, government has been permitted to criminalize the content of drivers' blood instead of their actions. The assumption that a driver who has been drinking automatically presents a danger to society even when no harm has been caused is a blatant violation of civil liberties. Government should not be concerned with the probability and propensity of a drinking driver to cause an accident; rather, laws should deal only with actions that damage person or property. Until they actually commit a crime, drunk drivers should be liberated from the force of the law. (From "Legalize Drunk Driving," by Llewellyn H. Rockwell Jr., WorldNetDaily.com)

⊙ EXERCISE 5.2

Read the following paragraphs. Then, answer the questions that follow.

Animals Are Equal to Humans

According to the United Nations, a person may not be killed, exploited, cruelly treated, intimidated, or imprisoned for no good reason. Put another way, people should be able to live in peace, according to their own needs and preferences.

Who should have these rights? Do they apply to people of all races? Children? People who are brain damaged or senile? The declaration makes it clear that basic rights apply to everyone. To make a slave of someone who is intellectually handicapped or of a different race is no more justifiable than to make a slave of anyone else.

The reason why these rights apply to everyone is simple: regardless of our differences, we all experience a life with its mosaic of thoughts and feelings. This applies equally to the princess and the hobo, the brain surgeon and the dunce. Our value as individuals arises from this capacity to experience life, not because of any intelligence or usefulness to others. Every person has an inherent value, and deserves to be treated with respect in order to make the most of their unique life experience. (Excerpted from "Human and Animal Rights," by Animal Liberation.org)

1. What unstated assumptions about the subject does the writer make? Does the writer expect readers to accept these assumptions? How can you tell?

2. What kind of supporting evidence does the writer provide?

3. What is the major premise of this argument?

4. Express the argument that is presented in these paragraphs as a syllogism.

5. Evaluate the syllogism you constructed. Is it true? Is it valid? Is it sound?

⊖ EXERCISE 5.3

Read the following five arguments, and determine whether each is sound. (To help you evaluate the arguments, you may want to try arranging them as syllogisms.)

1. All humans are mortal. Max is human. Therefore, Max is mortal.

2. Alison should order eggs or oatmeal for breakfast. She won't order eggs, so she should order oatmeal.

3. The cafeteria does not serve steak on Friday. Today is not Friday. Therefore, the cafeteria will not serve steak.

4. All reptiles are cold-blooded. Geckos are reptiles. Therefore, geckos are cold-blooded.

5. All triangles have three equal sides. The figure on the board is a triangle. Therefore, it must have three equal sides.

⊖ EXERCISE 5.4

Read the following ten enthymemes, which come from bumper stickers. Supply the missing premises, and then evaluate the logic of each argument.

1. If you love your pet, don't eat meat.

2. War is terrorism.

3. Real men don't ask for directions.

4. Immigration is the sincerest form of flattery.

5. I eat local because I can.

6. Don't blame me; I voted for the other guy.

7. I read banned books.

8. Love is the only solution.

9. It's a child, not a choice.

10. Think. It's patriotic.

Writing Deductive Arguments

Deductive arguments begin with a general principle and reach a specific conclusion. They develop that principle with logical arguments that are supported by evidence—facts, observations, the opinions of experts, and so on. Keep in mind that no single structure is suitable for all deductive (or inductive) arguments. Different issues and different audiences will determine how you arrange your ideas.

In general, deductive essays can be structured in the following way:

INTRODUCTION	Presents an overview of the issue
	States the thesis
BODY	Presents evidence: point 1 in support of the thesis
	Presents evidence: point 2 in support of the thesis
	Presents evidence: point 3 in support of the thesis
	Refutes the arguments against the thesis
CONCLUSION	Brings argument to a close
	Concluding statement reinforces the thesis

⊘ EXERCISE 5.5

The following student essay, "College Should Be for Everyone," includes all the elements of a deductive argument. The student who wrote this essay was responding to the question, "Should everyone be encouraged to go to college?" After you read the essay, answer the questions on page 126, consulting the outline above if necessary.

COLLEGE SHOULD BE FOR EVERYONE

CRYSTAL SANCHEZ

1   Until the middle of the twentieth century, college was largely for the rich. The G.I. Bill, which paid for the education of veterans returning from World War II, helped change this situation. By 1956, nearly half of those who had served in World War II, almost 7.8 million people, had taken advantage of this benefit (U.S. Department of Veterans Affairs). Even today, however, college graduates are still a minority of the population. According to the U.S. Census Bureau, only 27.5% of Americans age twenty-five or older have a bachelor's degree. In many ways, this

Overview of issue

situation is not good for the country. Why should college be just for the privileged few? Because a college education provides important benefits, such as increased wages for our citizens and a stronger democracy for our nation, every U.S. citizen should have the opportunity to earn a college degree.

Thesis statement

Evidence: Point 1

One reason everyone should have the opportunity to go to college   2 is that a college education gives people an opportunity to discover what they are good at. It is hard for people to know if they are interested in statistics or public policy or marketing unless they have the chance to learn about these subjects. College—and only college—can give them this opportunity. Where else can a person be exposed to a large number of courses taught by experts in a variety of disciplines? Such exposure can open new areas of interest and lead to a much wider set of career options—and thus to a better life (Stout). Without college, most people have limited options and never realize their true potential. Although life and work experiences can teach a person a lot of things, the best education is the broad kind that a college education offers.

Evidence: Point 2

Another reason everyone should have the opportunity to go to   3 college is that more and more jobs are being phased out or shipped overseas. Americans should go to college to develop the skills that they will need to get the best jobs that will remain in the United States. Over the last few decades, midlevel jobs have been steadily disappearing. If this trend continues, the American workforce will be divided in two. One part will consist of low-wage, low-skill service jobs, such as those in food preparation and retail sales, and the other part will be high-skill, high-wage jobs, such as those in management and professional fields like business and engineering. According to a recent report, to compete in the future job market, Americans will need the skills that colleges teach. Future workers will need to be problem solvers who can think both critically and creatively and who can adapt to unpredictable situations. They will also need a global awareness, knowledge of many cultures and disciplines, and the ability to communicate in different forms of media. To master these skills, Americans have to be educated ("Ten Skills for the Future Workforce"). If they do not go to college, then they will not be prepared for the high-growth, high-skill jobs of the future.

4   Perhaps the best reason everyone should have the opportunity to go to college is that education is an essential part of a democratic society. Those without the ability to understand and analyze news reports are not capable of contributing to the social, political, and economic growth of the country. Democracy requires informed citizens who will be able to analyze complicated issues in areas such as finance, education, and public health; weigh competing claims of those running for public office; and assess the job performance of elected officials. By providing students with the opportunity to study subjects such as history, philosophy, English, and political science, colleges and universities help them to acquire the critical-thinking skills that they will need to participate fully in American democracy.

Evidence: Point 3

5   Some people oppose the idea that everyone should have the opportunity to attend college. One objection is that educational resources are limited. Some say that if students enter colleges in great numbers they will overwhelm the higher-education system (Stout). This argument exaggerates the problem. As with any other product, if demand rises, supply will rise to meet that demand. In addition, with today's extensive distance-learning options and the availability of open educational resources—free, high-quality, digital materials—it will be possible to educate large numbers of students at a reasonable cost ("Open Educational Resources"). Another objection to encouraging everyone to attend college is that underprepared students will require so much help that they will take time and attention away from better students. This argument is actually a red herring.° Most schools already provide resources, such as tutoring and writing centers, for students who need them. With some additional funding, these schools could expand the services they already provide. This course of action will be expensive, but it is a lot less expensive than leaving millions of young people unprepared for jobs of the future.

Refutation of opposing arguments

An irrelevant side issue used as a diversion

6   A college education gave the returning veterans of World War II many opportunities and increased their value to the nation. Today, a college education could do the same for all our citizens. This country has an obligation to offer all students access to an affordable and useful education. Not only will the students benefit personally, but the nation will also. If we do not adequately prepare students for the future, then we will all suffer the consequences.

Concluding statement

Works Cited

"Open Educational Resources." *Center for American Progress*. Center for American Progress, 7 Feb. 2012. Web. 6 Apr. 2012.

Stout, Chris. "Top Five Reasons Why You Should Choose to Go to College." *Ezine Articles*. EzineArticles.com, 2008. Web. 4 Apr. 2012.

"Ten Skills for the Future Workforce." *The Atlantic.com*. The Atlantic Monthly Group, 22 June 2011. Web. 5 Apr. 2012.

United States. Census Bureau. "Bachelor's Degree Attainment Tops 30 Percent for the First Time, Census Bureau Reports." *US Census Bureau Newsroom*. US Census Bureau, 23 Feb. 2012. Web. 5 Apr. 2012.

---. ---. Dept. of Veterans Affairs. "Born of Controversy: The GI Bill of Rights." *GI Bill History*. United States Department of Veterans Affairs, 20 Oct. 2008. Web. 4 Apr. 2012.

Identifying the Elements of a Deductive Argument

1. Paraphrase this essay's thesis.

2. What arguments does the writer present as evidence to support her thesis? Which do you think is the strongest argument? Which is the weakest?

3. What opposing arguments does the writer address? What other opposing arguments could she have addressed?

4. What points does the conclusion emphasize? Do you think that any other points should be emphasized?

5. Construct a syllogism that expresses the essay's argument. Then, check your syllogism to make sure it is sound.

What Is Inductive Reasoning?

Inductive reasoning begins with specific observations (or evidence) and moves to a general conclusion. You can see how induction works by looking at the following list of observations:

- Nearly 80% of ocean pollution comes from runoff.

- Runoff pollution can make ocean water unsafe for fish and people.

- In some areas, runoff pollution has forced beaches to be closed.

Sign warning of
contaminated water

- Drinking water can be contaminated by runoff.

- More than one third of shellfish growing in waters in the United States
  are contaminated by runoff.

- Each year, millions of dollars are spent to restore polluted areas.

- There is a causal relationship between agricultural runoff and water-
  borne organisms that damage fish.

After studying these observations, you can use inductive reasoning to reach the
conclusion that runoff pollution (rainwater that becomes polluted after it
comes in contact with earth-bound pollutants such as fertilizer, pet waste, sewage, and pesticides) is a problem that must be addressed as soon as possible.

Children learn about the world by using inductive reasoning. For
example, very young children see that if they push a light switch up, the
lights in a room go on. If they repeat this action over and over, they reach
the conclusion that every time they push a switch, the lights will go on. Of
course, this conclusion does not always follow. For example, the light bulb
may be burned out or the switch may be damaged. Even so, their conclusion usually holds true. Children also use induction to generalize about
what is safe and what is dangerous. If every time they meet a dog, the
encounter is pleasant, they begin to think that all dogs are friendly. If at
some point, however, a dog snaps at them, they question the strength of
their conclusion and modify their behavior accordingly.

Scientists also use induction. In 1620, Sir Francis Bacon first proposed
the **scientific method**—a way of using induction to find answers to

questions. When using the scientific method, a researcher proposes a hypothesis and then makes a series of observations to test this hypothesis. Based on these observations, the researcher arrives at a conclusion that confirms, modifies, or disproves the hypothesis.

REACHING INDUCTIVE CONCLUSIONS

Here are some of the ways you can use inductive reasoning to reach conclusions:

- **Particular to general:** This form of induction occurs when you reach a general conclusion based on particular pieces of evidence. For example, suppose you walk into a bathroom and see that the mirrors are fogged. You also notice that the bathtub has drops of water on its sides and that the bathroom floor is wet. In addition, you see a damp towel draped over the sink. Putting all these observations together, you conclude that someone has recently taken a bath. (Detectives use induction when gathering clues to solve a crime.)

- **General to general:** This form of induction occurs when you draw a conclusion based on the consistency of your observations. For example, if you determine that Apple Corporation has made good products for a long time, you conclude it will continue to make good products.

- **General to particular:** This form of induction occurs when you draw a conclusion based on what you generally know to be true. For example, if you have owned several cars made by the Ford Motor Company and they have been reliable cars, then you conclude that a Ford Focus will also be a reliable car.

- **Particular to particular:** This form of induction occurs when you assume that because something works in one situation, it will also work in another similar situation. For example, if Krazy Glue fixed the broken handle of one cup, then you conclude it will probably fix the broken handle of another cup.

Making Inferences

Unlike deduction, which reaches a conclusion based on information provided by the major and minor premises, induction uses what you know to make a statement about something that you don't know. While deductive arguments can be judged in absolute terms (they are either **valid** or **invalid**), inductive arguments are judged in relative terms (they are either **strong** or **weak**).

You reach an inductive conclusion by making an **inference**—a statement about what is unknown based on what is known. (In other words, you look at the evidence and try to figure out what is going on.) For this reason, there is always a gap between your observations and your conclusion. To bridge this gap, you have to make an **inductive leap**—a stretch of the imagination that enables you to draw an acceptable conclusion. Therefore, inductive conclusions are never certain (as deductive conclusions are) but only probable. The more evidence you provide, the stronger and more probable your conclusions (and your argument) are.

Public-opinion polls illustrate how inferences are used to reach inductive conclusions. Politicians and news organizations routinely use public-opinion polls to assess support (or lack of support) for a particular policy, proposal, or political candidate. After surveying a sample population— registered voters, for example—pollsters reach conclusions based on their responses. In other words, by asking questions and studying the responses of a sample group of people, pollsters make inferences about the larger group—for example, which political candidate is ahead and by how much. How solid these inferences are depends to a great extent on the sample populations they survey. In an election, for example, a poll of randomly chosen individuals will be less accurate than a poll of registered voters or likely voters. In addition, other factors (such as the size of the sample and the way questions are worded) can determine the relative strength of the inductive conclusion.

As with all inferences, a gap exists between a poll's data—the responses to the questions—and the conclusion. The larger and more representative the sample, the smaller the inductive leap necessary to reach a conclusion and the more accurate the poll. If the gap between the data and the conclusion is too big, however, the pollsters will be accused of making a **hasty generalization** (see p. 140). Remember, no matter how much support you present, an inductive conclusion is only probable, never certain. The best you can do is present a convincing case and hope that your audience will accept it.

Constructing Strong Inductive Arguments

When you use inductive reasoning, your conclusion is only as strong as the **evidence**—the facts, details, or examples—that you use to support it. For this reason, you should be on the lookout for the following problems that can occur when you try to reach an inductive conclusion.

Generalization Too Broad

The conclusion you state cannot go beyond the scope of your evidence. Your evidence must support your generalization. For instance, you cannot survey just three disabled students in your school and conclude that the school does not go far enough to accommodate students with disabilities. To reach such a conclusion, you would have to consider a large number of disabled students.

Insufficient Evidence

The evidence on which you base an inductive conclusion must be representative, not atypical or biased. For example, you cannot conclude that students are satisfied with the Office of Disability Services at your school by sampling just first-year students. To be valid, your conclusion should be based on responses from a cross-section of disabled students from all years.

Irrelevant Evidence

Your evidence has to support your conclusion. If it does not, it is **irrelevant**. For example, if you assert that many students with disabilities make substantial contributions to your school, your supporting examples must be students with conditions that substantially limit their activities, not those with minor or temporary limitations.

Exceptions to the Rule

There is always a chance that you will overlook an exception that may affect the strength of your conclusion. For example, not everyone who has a disability needs special accommodations, and not everyone who requires special accommodations needs the same services. For this reason, you should avoid using words like *every*, *all*, and *always* and instead use words like *most*, *many*, and *usually*.

➲ EXERCISE 5.6

Read the following arguments, and decide whether each is a deductive argument or an inductive argument.

1. Freedom of speech is a central principle of our form of government. For this reason, students should be allowed to wear T-shirts that call for the legalization of marijuana. _____

2. The Chevy Cruze Eco gets twenty-eight miles a gallon in the city and forty-two miles a gallon on the highway. The Honda Accord gets twenty-three miles a gallon in the city and thirty-three miles a gallon on the highway. Therefore, it makes more sense for me to buy the Chevy Cruze Eco. _____

3. In Edgar Allan Poe's short story "The Cask of Amontillado," Montresor flatters Fortunato. He lures him to his vaults where he stores wine. Montresor then gets Fortunato drunk and chains him to the wall of a crypt. Finally, Montresor uncovers a pile of building material

and walls up the entrance to the crypt. Clearly, Montresor has carefully planned to murder Fortunato for a very long time. _____

4. All people should have the right to die with dignity. Garrett is a terminally ill patient, so he should have access to doctor-assisted suicide. _____

5. Last week, we found unacceptably high levels of pollution in the ocean. On Monday, we also found high levels of pollution. Today, we found even higher levels of pollution. We should close the ocean beaches to swimmers until we can find the source of this problem. _____

⬆ EXERCISE 5.7

Read the following arguments. Then, decide whether they are deductive or inductive. If they are inductive arguments, evaluate their strength. If they are deductive arguments, evaluate their soundness.

1. *The Farmer's Almanac* says that this winter will be very cold. The national weather service also predicts that this winter will be very cold. So, this should be a cold winter.

2. Many walled towns in Europe do not let people drive cars into their centers. San Gimignano is a walled town in Europe. It is likely that we will not be able to drive our car into its center.

3. The window at the back of the house is broken. There is a baseball on the floor. A few minutes ago, I saw two boys playing catch in a neighbor's yard. They must have thrown the ball through the window.

4. Every time I go to the beach I get sunburned. I guess I should stop going to the beach.

5. All my instructors have advanced degrees. George Martin is one of my instructors. Therefore, George Martin has an advanced degree.

6. My last two boyfriends cheated on me. All men are terrible.

7. I read a study published by a pharmaceutical company that said that Vioxx was safe. Maybe the government was too quick to pull this drug off the market.

8. Chase is not very good looking, and he dresses badly. I don't know how he can be a good architect.

9. No fictional character has ever had a fan club. Harry Potter does, but he is the exception.

10. Two weeks ago, my instructor refused to accept a late paper. She did the same thing last week. Yesterday, she also told someone that because his paper was late, she wouldn't accept it. I'd better get my paper in on time.

⊚ **EXERCISE 5.8**

Read the inductive paragraph below, written by student Pooja Vaidya, and answer the questions that follow it.

Years ago, when my friend took me to a game between the Philadelphia Eagles and the Dallas Cowboys in Philadelphia, I learned a little bit about football and a lot about the behavior of football fans. Many of the Philadelphia fans were dressed in green and white football jerseys, each with a player's name and number on the back. One fan had his face painted green and wore a green cape with a large white *E* on it. He ran up and down the aisles in his section and led cheers. When the team was ahead, everyone joined in. When the team fell behind, this fan literally fell on his knees, cried, and begged the people in the stands to support the Eagles. (After the game, several people asked him for his autograph.) A group of six fans sat without shirts. They wore green wigs, and each had one letter of the team's name painted on his bare chest. Even though the temperature was below freezing, none of these fans ever put on his shirt. Before the game, many fans had been drinking at tailgate parties in the parking lot, and as the game progressed, they continued to drink beer in the stadium. By the beginning of the second half, fights were breaking out all over the stadium. Guards grabbed the people who were fighting and escorted them to a holding area under the stadium where a judge held "Eagles Court." At one point, a fan wearing a Dallas jersey tried to sit down in the row behind me. Some of the Eagles fans were so threatening that the police had to escort the Dallas fan out of the stands for his own protection. When the game ended in an Eagles victory, the fans sang the team's fight song as they left the stadium. I concluded that for many Eagles fans, a day at the stadium is an opportunity to engage in behavior that in any other context would be unacceptable and even abnormal.

1. Which of the following statements could you *not* conclude from this paragraph?

   a. All Eagles fans act in outrageous ways at games.

   b. At football games, the fans in the stands can be as violent as the players on the field.

Philadelphia Eagles
fans

   c. The atmosphere at the stadium causes otherwise normal people to act abnormally.

   d. Spectator sports encourage fans to act in abnormal ways.

   e. Some people get so caught up in the excitement of a game that they act in uncharacteristic ways.

2. Paraphrase the writer's conclusion. What evidence is provided to support this conclusion?

3. What additional evidence could the writer have provided? Is this additional evidence necessary, or does the conclusion stand without it?

4. The writer makes an inductive leap to reach the paragraph's conclusion. Do you think this leap is too great?

5. Does this paragraph make a strong inductive argument? Why or why not?

Writing Inductive Arguments

Inductive arguments begin with evidence (specific facts, observations, expert opinion, and so on), draw inferences from the evidence, and reach a conclusion by making an inductive leap. Keep in mind that inductive arguments are only as strong as the link between the evidence and the conclusion, so the stronger this link is, the stronger the argument will be.

Inductive essays frequently have the following structure:

INTRODUCTION   Presents the issue
                   States the thesis

BODY   Presents evidence: facts, observations, expert opinion,
                   and so on
                   Draws inferences from the evidence
                   Refutes the arguments against the thesis

CONCLUSION   Brings argument to a close
                   Concluding statement reinforces the thesis

⊘ EXERCISE 5.9

The following essay includes all the elements of an inductive argument. After you read the essay, answer the questions on page 136, consulting the outline above if necessary.

This essay appeared in *Slate* on September 2, 2006.

PLEASE DO NOT FEED THE HUMANS

WILLIAM SALETAN

Dug

In 1894, Congress established Labor Day to honor those who "from rude nature have delved° and carved all the grandeur we behold." In the century since, the grandeur of human achievement has multiplied. Over the past four decades, global population has doubled, but food output, driven by increases in productivity, has outpaced it. Poverty, infant mortality, and hunger are receding. For the first time in our planet's history, a species no longer lives at the mercy of scarcity. We have learned to feed ourselves.

We've learned so well, in fact, that we're getting fat. Not just the United States or Europe, but the whole world. Egyptian, Mexican, and South African women are now as fat as Americans. Far more Filipino adults are now overweight than underweight. In China, one in five adults is too heavy, and the rate of overweight children is 28 times higher than it was two decades ago. In Thailand, Kuwait, and Tunisia, obesity, diabetes, and heart disease are soaring.

Hunger is far from conquered. But since 1990, the global rate of malnutrition has declined an average of 1.7 percent a year. Based on data from the World Health Organization and the U.N. Food and Agriculture Organization, for every two people who are malnourished, three are now overweight or obese. Among women, even in most African countries, overweight has surpassed underweight. The balance of peril is shifting.

Fat is no longer a rich man's disease. For middle- and high-income Americans, the obesity rate is 29 percent. For low-income Americans, it's

35 percent. Among middle- and high-income kids aged 15 to 17, the rate of overweight is 14 percent. Among low-income kids in the same age bracket, it's 23 percent. Globally, weight has tended to rise with income. But a study in Vancouver, Canada, published three months ago, found that preschoolers in "food-insecure" households were twice as likely as other kids to be overweight or obese. In Brazilian cities, the poor have become fatter than the rich.

Technologically, this is a triumph. In the early days of our species, even 5 the rich starved. Barry Popkin, a nutritional epidemiologist at the University of North Carolina, divides history into several epochs. In the hunter-gatherer era, if we didn't find food, we died. In the agricultural era, if our crops perished, we died. In the industrial era, famine receded, but infectious diseases killed us. Now we've achieved such control over nature that we're dying not of starvation or infection, but of abundance. Nature isn't killing us. We're killing ourselves.

You don't have to go hungry anymore; we can fill you with fats and carbs 6 more cheaply than ever. You don't have to chase your food; we can bring it to you. You don't have to cook it; we can deliver it ready-to-eat. You don't have to eat it before it spoils; we can pump it full of preservatives so it lasts forever. You don't even have to stop when you're full. We've got so much food to sell, we want you to keep eating.

What happened in America is happening everywhere, only faster. Fewer 7 farmers' markets, more processed food. Fewer whole grains, more refined ones. More sweeteners, salt, and trans fats. Cheaper meat, more animal fat. Less cooking, more eating out. Bigger portions, more snacks.

Kentucky Fried Chicken and Pizza Hut are spreading across the planet. 8 Coca-Cola is in more than 200 countries. Half of McDonald's business is overseas. In China, animal-fat intake has tripled in 20 years. By 2020, meat consumption in developing countries will grow by 106 million metric tons, outstripping growth in developed countries by a factor of more than five. Forty years ago, to afford a high-fat diet, your country needed a gross national product per capita of nearly $1,500. Now the price is half that. You no longer have to be rich to die a rich man's death.

Soon, it'll be a poor man's death. The rich have Whole Foods, gyms, and 9 personal trainers. The poor have 7-Eleven, Popeye's, and streets unsafe for walking. When money's tight, you feed your kids at Wendy's and stock up on macaroni and cheese. At a lunch buffet, you do what your ancestors did: store all the fat you can.

That's the punch line: Technology has changed everything but us. We 10 evolved to survive scarcity. We crave fat. We're quick to gain weight and slow to lose it. Double what you serve us, and we'll double what we eat. Thanks to technology, the deprivation that made these traits useful is gone. So is the link between flavors and nutrients. The modern food industry can sell you sweetness

> "We evolved to survive scarcity."

without fruit, salt without protein, creaminess without milk. We can fatten you and starve you at the same time.

And that's just the diet side of the equation. Before technology, adult men 11 had to expend about 3,000 calories a day. Now they expend about 2,000. Look at the new Segway scooter. The original model relieved you of the need to walk, pedal, or balance. With the new one, you don't even have to turn the handlebars or start it manually. In theory, Segway is replacing the car. In practice, it's replacing the body.

In country after country, service jobs are replacing hard labor. The folks 12 who field your customer service calls in Bangalore are sitting at desks. Nearly everyone in China has a television set. Remember when Chinese rode bikes? In the past six years, the number of cars there has grown from six million to 20 million. More than one in seven Chinese has a motorized vehicle, and households with such vehicles have an obesity rate 80 percent higher than their peers.

The answer to these trends is simple. We have to exercise more and change 13 the food we eat, donate, and subsidize. Next year, for example, the U.S. Women, Infants, and Children program, which subsidizes groceries for impoverished youngsters, will begin to pay for fruits and vegetables. For 32 years, the program has fed toddlers eggs and cheese but not one vegetable. And we wonder why poor kids are fat.

The hard part is changing our mentality. We have a distorted body image. 14 We're so used to not having enough, as a species, that we can't believe the problem is too much. From China to Africa to Latin America, people are trying to fatten their kids. I just got back from a vacation with my Jewish mother and Jewish mother-in-law. They told me I need to eat more.

The other thing blinding us is liberal guilt. We're so caught up in the idea 15 of giving that we can't see the importance of changing behavior rather than filling bellies. We know better than to feed buttered popcorn to zoo animals, yet we send it to a food bank and call ourselves humanitarians. Maybe we should ask what our fellow humans actually need.

Identifying the Elements of an Inductive Argument

1. What is this essay's thesis? Restate it in your own words.

2. Why do you think Saletan places the thesis where he does?

3. What evidence does Saletan use to support his conclusion?

4. What inductive leap does Saletan make to reach his conclusion? Do you think he should have included more evidence?

5. Overall, do you think Saletan's inductive argument is relatively strong or weak? Explain.

Recognizing Logical Fallacies

When you write arguments in college, you are obligated to follow certain rules that ensure fairness. Not everyone who writes arguments is this fair or thorough, however. Sometimes you will encounter arguments in which writers attack the opposition's intelligence or patriotism and base their arguments on questionable (or even false) assumptions. As convincing as these arguments can sometimes seem, they are actually not valid because they contain **fallacies**—errors in reasoning that undermine the logic of an argument. Familiarizing yourself with the most common logical fallacies can help you to evaluate the arguments of others and to construct better, more effective arguments of your own.

The following pages define and illustrate some logical fallacies that you should learn to recognize and avoid.

Begging the Question

The fallacy of **begging the question** assumes that a statement is self-evident (or true) when it actually requires proof. A conclusion based on such assumptions cannot be valid. For example, someone who is very religious could structure an argument the following way:

> **MAJOR PREMISE**   Everything in the Bible is true.
>
> **MINOR PREMISE**   The Bible says that Noah built an ark.
>
> **CONCLUSION**   Therefore, Noah's Ark really existed.

A person can accept the conclusion of this syllogism only if he or she also accepts the major premise, which has not been proven true. Some people might find this line of reasoning convincing, but others would not—even if they were religious.

Begging the question occurs any time someone presents a debatable statement as if it were true. For example, look at the following statement:

> You have unfairly limited my right of free speech by refusing to print my editorial in the college newspaper.

This statement begs the question because it assumes what it should be proving—that refusing to print an editorial violates a person's right to free speech.

Circular Reasoning

Closely related to begging the question, **circular reasoning** occurs when someone supports a statement by restating it in different terms. Consider the following statement:

> Stealing is wrong because it is illegal.

The conclusion of the statement on the previous page is essentially the same as its beginning: stealing (which is illegal) is against the law. In other words, the argument goes in a circle.

Here are some other examples of circular reasoning:

- Lincoln was a great president because he is the best president we ever had.

- I am for equal rights for women because I am a feminist.

- Illegal immigrants should be deported because they are breaking the law.

All of the statements above have one thing in common: they attempt to support a statement by simply repeating the statement in different words.

Weak Analogy

An **analogy** is a comparison between two items (or concepts)—one familiar and one unfamiliar. When you make an analogy, you explain the unfamiliar item by comparing it to the familiar item. (For a discussion of argument by analogy, see Chapter 16.)

Although analogies can be effective in arguments, they have limitations. For example, a senator who opposed a government bailout of the financial industry in 2008 made the following argument:

> This bailout is doomed from the start. It's like pouring milk into a leaking bucket. As long as you keep pouring milk, the bucket stays full. But when you stop, the milk runs out the hole in the bottom of the bucket. What we're doing is throwing money into a big bucket and not fixing the hole. We have to find the underlying problems that have caused this part of our economy to get in trouble and pass legislation to solve them.

The problem with using analogies such as this one is that analogies are never perfect. There is always a difference between the two things being compared. The larger this difference, the weaker the analogy—and the weaker the argument that it supports. For example, someone could point out to the senator that the financial industry—and by extension, the whole economy—is much more complex and multifaceted than a leaking bucket. To analyze the economy, the senator would have to expand his discussion beyond this single analogy (which cannot carry the weight of the entire argument) as well as supply the evidence to support his contention that the bailout was a mistake from the start.

Waterfall, by M. C. Escher. The artwork creates the illusion of water flowing uphill and in a circle. Circular reasoning occurs when the conclusion of an argument is the same as one of the premises.

Ad Hominem Fallacy (Personal Attack)

The **ad hominem fallacy** occurs when someone attacks the character or the motives of a person instead of focusing on the issues. This line of reasoning is illogical because it focuses attention on the person making the argument, sidestepping the argument itself.

Consider the following statement:

> Dr. Thomson, I'm not sure why we should believe anything you have to say about this community health center. Last year, you left your husband for another man.

The above attack on Dr. Thomson's character is irrelevant; it has nothing to do with her ideas about the community health center. Sometimes, however, a person's character may have a direct relation to the issue. For example, if Dr. Thomson had invested in a company that supplied medical equipment to the health center, this fact would have been relevant to the issue at hand.

The ad hominem fallacy also occurs when you attempt to undermine an argument by associating it with individuals who are easily attacked. For example, consider this statement:

> I think your plan to provide universal heath care is interesting. I'm sure Marx and Lenin would agree with you.

Instead of focusing on the specific provisions of the health-care plan, the opposition unfairly associates it with the ideas of Karl Marx and Vladimir Lenin, two well-known Communists.

Creating a Straw Man

This fallacy most likely got its name from the use of straw dummies in military and boxing training. When writers create a **straw man**, they present a weak argument that can easily be refuted. Instead of attacking the real issue, they focus on a weaker issue and give the impression that they have effectively refuted an opponent's argument. Frequently, the straw man is an extreme or oversimplified version of the opponent's actual position. For example, during a debate about raising the minimum wage, a senator made the following comment:

> Those who oppose raising the minimum wage are heartless. They obviously don't care if children starve.

Ad hominem attack against Charles Darwin, originator of the theory of evolution by natural selection

Instead of focusing on the minimum wage, the senator misrepresents the opposing position so that it appears cruel. As this example shows, the straw man fallacy is dishonest because it intentionally distorts an opponent's position to mislead readers.

Hasty or Sweeping Generalization (Jumping to a Conclusion)

A **hasty or sweeping generalization** (also called **jumping to a conclusion**) occurs when someone reaches a conclusion that is based on too little evidence. Many people commit this fallacy without realizing it. For example, when Richard Nixon was elected president in 1972, film critic Pauline Kael is supposed to have remarked, "How can that be? No one I know voted for Nixon!" The general idea behind this statement is that if Kael's acquaintances didn't vote for Nixon, then neither did most other people. This assumption is flawed because it is based on a small sample.

Sometimes people make hasty generalizations because they strongly favor one point of view over another. At other times, a hasty generalization is simply the result of sloppy thinking. For example, it is easier for a student to simply say that an instructor is an unusually hard grader than to survey the instructor's classes to see if this conclusion is warranted (or to consider other reasons for his or her poor performance in a course).

Either/Or Fallacy (False Dilemma)

The **either/or fallacy** (also called a **false dilemma**) occurs when a person says that there are just two choices when there are actually more. In many cases, the person committing this fallacy tries to force a conclusion by presenting just two choices, one of which is clearly more desirable than the other. (Parents do this with young children all the time: "Eat your carrots, or go to bed.")

Politicians frequently engage in this fallacy. For example, according to some politicians, you are either pro-life or pro-choice, pro–gun control or anti–gun control, pro-stem-cell research or anti-stem-cell research. Many people, however, are actually somewhere in the middle, taking a much more nuanced approach to complicated issues.

Consider the following statement:

> I can't believe you voted against the bill to build a wall along the southern border of the United States. Either you're for protecting our border, or you're against it.

This statement is an example of the either/or fallacy. The person who voted against the bill might be against the wall but not against all immigration restrictions. The person might favor loose restrictions for some people (for example, migrant workers) and strong restrictions for others (for example, drug smugglers). By limiting the options to just two, the speaker oversimplifies the situation and attempts to force the listener to accept a fallacious argument.

Politicians frequently engage in the either/or fallacy.

Equivocation

The fallacy of **equivocation** occurs when a key term has one meaning in one part of an argument and another meaning in another part. (When a term is used **unequivocally**, it has the same meaning throughout the argument.) Consider the following old joke:

> The sign said, "Fine for parking here," so because it was fine, I parked there.

Obviously, the word *fine* has two different meanings in this sentence. The first time it is used, it means "money paid as a penalty." The second time, it means "good" or "satisfactory."

Most words have more than one meaning, so it is important not to confuse the various meanings. For an argument to work, a key term has to have the same meaning every time it appears in the argument. If the meaning shifts during the course of the argument, then the argument cannot be sound.

Consider the following statement:

> This is supposed to be a free country, but nothing worth having is ever free.

In this statement, the meaning of a key term shifts. The first time the word *free* is used, it means "not under the control of another." The second time, it means "without charge."

Red Herring

This fallacy gets its name from the practice of dragging a smoked fish across the trail of a fox to mask its scent during a fox hunt. As a result, the hounds lose the scent and are thrown off the track. The **red herring** fallacy occurs when a person raises an irrelevant side issue to divert attention from the real issue. Used skillfully, this fallacy can distract an audience and change the focus of an argument.

Political campaigns are good sources of examples of the red herring fallacy. Consider this example from the 2012 presidential race:

> I know Mitt Romney says he is for the middle class, but he and his wife own three homes. How can we believe his tax proposals will help the middle class?

The focus of this argument should have been on Romney's tax proposals—not on the fact that he and his wife own three houses.

Here is red herring fallacy from the 2012 political campaign:

> Barack Obama wants us to vote for him, but his father was a Muslim. How can we possibly trust him with national security?

Again, the focus of these remarks should have been Obama's qualifications, not the fact that his father was a Muslim.

Slippery Slope

The **slippery-slope** fallacy occurs when a person argues that one thing will inevitably result from another. (Other names for the slippery-slope fallacy are the **foot-in-the-door fallacy** and the **floodgates fallacy**.) Both these names suggest that once you permit certain acts, you inevitably permit additional acts that eventually lead to disastrous consequences. Typically, the slippery-slope fallacy presents a series of increasingly unacceptable events that lead to an inevitable, unpleasant conclusion. (Usually, there is no evidence that such a sequence will actually occur.)

We encounter examples of the slippery-slope fallacy almost daily. During a debate on same-sex marriage, for example, an opponent advanced this line of reasoning:

> If we allow gay marriage, then there is nothing to stop polygamy. And once we allow this, where will it stop? Will we have to legalize incest—or even bestiality?

Whether or not you support same-sex marriage, you should recognize the fallacy of this slippery-slope reasoning. By the last sentence of the passage above, the assertions have become so outrageous that they approach parody. People can certainly debate this issue, but not in such a dishonest and highly emotional way.

You Also (Tu Quoque)

The **you also** fallacy asserts that a statement is false because it is inconsistent with what the speaker has said or done. In other words, a person is attacked for doing what he or she is arguing against. Parents often encounter this fallacy when they argue with their teenage children. By introducing an irrelevant point—"You did it too"—the children attempt to distract parents and put them on the defensive:

- How can you tell me not to smoke when you used to smoke?

- Don't yell at me for drinking. I bet you had a few beers before you were twenty-one.

- Why do I have to be home by midnight? Didn't you stay out late when you were my age?

Beware the slippery-slope fallacy

Arguments such as these are irrelevant. People fail to follow their own advice, but that does not mean that their points have no merit. (Of course, not following their own advice does undermine their credibility.)

Appeal to Doubtful Authority

Writers of research papers frequently use the ideas of recognized authorities to strengthen their arguments. However, the sources offered as evidence need to be both respected and credible. The **appeal to doubtful authority** occurs when people use the ideas of nonexperts to support their arguments.

Not everyone who speaks as an expert is actually an authority on a particular issue. For example, when movie stars or recording artists give their opinions about politics, climate change, or foreign affairs—things they may know little about—they are not speaking as experts; therefore, they have no authority. (They *are* experts, however, when they discuss the film or music industries.) A similar situation occurs with the pundits who appear on television news shows. Some of these individuals have solid credentials in the fields they discuss, but others offer opinions even

Actor and director George Clooney speaking about atrocities in Darfur, Sudan, at a rally in Washington, D.C.

though they know little about the subjects. Unfortunately, many viewers accept the pronouncements of these "experts" uncritically and think it is acceptable to cite them to support their own arguments.

How do you determine whether a person you read about or hear is really an authority? First, make sure that the person actually has expertise in the field he or she is discussing. You can do this by checking his or her credentials on the Internet. Second, make sure that the person is not biased. No one is entirely free from bias, but the bias should not be so extreme that it undermines the person's authority. Finally, make sure that you can confirm what the so-called expert says or writes. Check one or two pieces of information in other sources, such as a basic reference text or encyclopedia. Determine if others—especially recognized experts in the field—confirm this information. If there are major points of discrepancy, dig further to make sure you are dealing with a legitimate authority.

Misuse of Statistics

The **misuse of statistics** occurs when data are misrepresented. Statistics can be used persuasively in an argument, but sometimes they are distorted—intentionally or unintentionally—to make a point. For example, a classic ad for toothpaste claims that four out of five dentists recommend Crest toothpaste. What the ad neglects to mention is the number of dentists who were questioned. If the company surveyed several thousand dentists, then this statistic would be meaningful. If the company surveyed only ten, however, it would not be.

Misleading statistics can be much subtler (and much more complicated) than the example above. For example, in 2000, there were 16,653 alcohol-related deaths in the United States. According to the National Highway Traffic Safety Administration (NHTSA), 12,892 of these 16,653 alcohol-related deaths involved at least one driver or passenger who was legally drunk. Of the 12,892 deaths, 7,326 were the drivers themselves, and 1,594 were legally drunk pedestrians. The remaining 3,972 fatalities were nonintoxicated drivers, passengers, or nonoccupants. These 3,972 fatalities call the total number into question because the NHTSA does not indicate which drivers were at fault. In other words, if a sober driver ran a red light and killed a legally drunk driver, the NHTSA classified this death as alcohol-related. For this reason, the original number of alcohol-related deaths—16,653—is somewhat misleading. (The statistic becomes even more questionable when you consider that a person is automatically classified as intoxicated if he or she refuses to take a sobriety test.)

Post Hoc, Ergo Propter Hoc (After This, Therefore Because of This)

The **post hoc** fallacy asserts that because two events occur closely in time, one event must cause the other. Professional athletes commit the post hoc fallacy all the time. For example, one major league pitcher wears the same shirt every time he has an important game. Because he has won several big games while wearing this shirt, he believes it brings him luck.

Many events seem to follow a sequential pattern even though they actually do not. For example, some people refuse to get a flu shot because they say that the last time they got one, they came down with the flu. Even though there is no scientific basis for this link, many people insist that it is true. (The more probable explanation for this situation is that the flu vaccination takes at least two weeks to take effect, so it is possible for someone to be infected by the flu virus before the vaccine starts working.)

Another health-related issue also illustrates the post hoc fallacy. Recently, the U.S. Food and Drug Administration (FDA) studied several products that claim to cure the common cold. Because the study showed that these medications were not effective, the FDA ordered the manufacturers to stop making false claims about their products. Despite this fact, however, many people still buy these products. When questioned, they say the medications actually work. Again, the explanation for this phenomenon is simple. Most colds last just a few days. As the FDA pointed out in its report, people who took the medications would have begun feeling better with or without them.

Non Sequitur (It Does Not Follow)

The **non sequitur** fallacy occurs when a conclusion does not follow from the premises. Frequently, the conclusion is supported by weak or irrelevant evidence—or by no evidence at all. Consider the following statement:

> Megan drives an expensive car, so she must be earning a lot of money.

Megan might drive an expensive car, but this is not evidence that she has a high salary. She could, for example, be leasing the car or paying it off over a five-year period, or it could have been a gift.

Non sequiturs are common in political arguments. Consider this statement:

> Gangs, drugs, and extreme violence plague today's prisons. The only way to address this issue is to release all nonviolent offenders as soon as possible.

This assessment of the prison system may be accurate, but it doesn't follow that because of this situation, all nonviolent offenders should be released immediately.

Scientific arguments also contain non sequiturs. Consider the following statement that was made during a debate on global warming:

> Recently, the polar ice caps have thickened, and the temperature of the oceans has stabilized. Obviously, the earth is healing itself. We don't need to do more to address climate change.

A non sequitur fallacy

Even if you accept the facts of this argument, you need to see more evidence before you can conclude that no action against climate change is necessary. For example, the cooling trend could be temporary, or other areas of the earth could still be growing warmer.

Bandwagon Fallacy

The **bandwagon fallacy** occurs when you try to convince people that something is true because it is widely held to be true. It is easy to see the problem with this line of reasoning. Hundreds of years ago, most people believed that the sun revolved around the earth and that the earth was flat. As we know, the fact that many people held these beliefs did not make them true.

The underlying assumption of the bandwagon fallacy is that the more people who believe something, the more likely it is to be true. Without supporting evidence, however, this form of argument cannot be valid. For example, consider the following statement made by a driver who was stopped by the police for speeding:

> Officer, I didn't do anything wrong. Everyone around me was going the same speed.

The bandwagon fallacy

Mike Baldwin/www.CartoonStock.com

As the police officer was quick to point out, the driver's argument missed the point: he was doing fifty-five miles an hour in a thirty-five-mile-an-hour zone, and the fact that other drivers were also speeding was irrelevant. If the driver had been able to demonstrate that the police officer was mistaken—that he was driving more slowly or that the speed limit was actually sixty miles an hour—then his argument would have had merit. In this case, the fact that other drivers were going the same speed would be relevant because it would support his contention.

Since most people want to go along with the crowd, the bandwagon fallacy can be very effective. For this reason, advertisers use it all the time. For example, a book publisher will say that a book has been on the *New York Times* bestseller list for ten weeks, and a pharmaceutical company will say that its brand of aspirin outsells other brands four to one. These appeals are irrelevant, however, because they don't address the central questions: Is the book actually worth reading? Is one brand of aspirin really better than other brands?

⊖ EXERCISE 5.10

Determine which of the following statements are logical arguments and which are fallacies. If the statement is not logical, identify the fallacy that best applies.

1. Almost all the students I talked to said that they didn't like the senator. I'm sure he'll lose the election on Tuesday.

2. This car has a noisy engine; therefore, it must create a lot of pollution.

3. I don't know how Professor Resnick can be such a hard grader. He's always late for class.

4. A vote for the bill to limit gun sales in the city is a vote against the Second Amendment.

5. It's only fair to pay your fair share of taxes.

6. I had an internship at a government agency last summer, and no one there worked very hard. Government workers are lazy.

7. It's a clear principle of law that people are not allowed to yell "Fire!" in a crowded theater. By permitting protestors to hold a rally downtown, Judge Cohen is allowing them to do just that.

8. Of course this person is guilty. He wouldn't be in jail if he weren't a criminal.

9. Schools are like families; therefore, teachers (like parents) should be allowed to discipline their kids.

10. Everybody knows that staying out in the rain can make you sick.

11. When we had a draft in the 1960s, the crime rate was low. We should bring back the draft.

12. I'm not a doctor, but I play one on TV. I recommend Vicks Formula 44 cough syrup.

13. Some people are complaining about public schools, so there must be a problem.

14. If you aren't part of the solution, you're part of the problem.

15. All people are mortal. James is a person. Therefore, James is mortal.

16. I don't know why you gave me an F for handing in someone else's essay. Didn't you ever copy something from someone else?

17. First, the government stops us from buying assault rifles. Then, it limits the number of handguns we can buy. What will come next? Soon, they'll try to take away all our guns.

18. Shakespeare was the world's greatest playwright; therefore, *Macbeth* must be a great play.

19. Last month, I bought a new computer. Yesterday, I installed some new software. This morning, my computer wouldn't start up. The new software must be causing the problem.

20. Ellen DeGeneres is against testing pharmaceutical and cosmetics products on animals, and that's good enough for me.

❯ EXERCISE 5.11

Read the following essay, and identify as many logical fallacies in it as you can. Make sure you identify each fallacy by name and are able to explain the flaws in the writer's arguments.

This essay is from Buchanan.org, where it appeared on October 31, 1994.

IMMIGRATION TIME-OUT

PATRICK J. BUCHANAN

Proposition 187 "is an outrage. It is unconstitutional. It is nativist. It is   1
racist."—Al Hunt, *Capital Gang*, CNN

That outburst by my columnist colleague, about California's Prop. 187—   2
which would cut off social welfare benefits to illegal aliens—suggests that this
savage quarrel is about more than just money. Indeed, the roots of this dispute

over Prop. 187 are grounded in the warring ideas that we Americans hold about the deepest, most divisive issues of our time: ethnicity, nation, culture.

What do we want the America of the years 2000, 2020, and 2050 to be like? 3 Do we have the right to shape the character of the country our grandchildren will live in? Or is that to be decided by whoever, outside America, decides to come here?

By 2050, we are instructed by the chancellor of the University of Califor- 4 nia at Berkeley, Chang Lin-Tin, "the majority of Americans will trace their roots to Latin America, Africa, Asia, the Middle East, and Pacific Islands."

Now, any man or woman, of any nation or ancestry can come here—and 5 become a good American.

We know that from our history. But by my arithmetic, the chancellor is 6 saying Hispanics, Asians, and Africans will increase their present number of 65 million by at least 100 million in 60 years, a population growth larger than all of Mexico today.

What will that mean for America? Well, South Texas and Southern 7 California will be almost exclusively Hispanic. Each will have tens of millions of people whose linguistic, historic, and cultural roots are in Mexico. Like Eastern Ukraine, where 10 million Russian-speaking "Ukrainians" now look impatiently to Moscow, not Kiev, as their cultural capital, America could see, in a decade, demands for Quebeclike status for Southern California. Already there is a rumbling among militants for outright secession. A sea of Mexican flags was prominent in that L.A. rally against Prop. 187, and Mexican officials are openly urging their kinsmen in California to vote it down.

If no cutoff is imposed on social benefits for those who breach our bor- 8 ders, and break our laws, the message will go out to a desperate world: America is wide open. All you need do is get there, and get in.

Consequences will ensue. Crowding together immigrant and minority 9 populations in our major cities must bring greater conflict. We saw that in the 1992 L.A. riot. Blacks and Hispanics have lately collided in D.C.'s Adams-Morgan neighborhood, supposedly the most tolerant and progressive section of Washington. The issue: bilingual education. Unlike 20 years ago, ethnic conflict is today on almost every front page.

Before Mr. Chang's vision is realized, the United States will have at least 10 two official languages. Today's steady outmigration of "Anglos" or "Euro-Americans," as whites are now called, from Southern Florida and Southern California, will continue. The 50 states will need constant redrawing of political lines to ensure proportional representation. Already we have created the first "apartheid districts" in America's South.

Ethnic militancy and solidarity are on the rise in the United States; 11 the old institutions of assimilation are not doing their work as they once did; the Melting Pot is in need of repair. On campuses we hear demands for separate dorms, eating rooms, clubs, etc., by black, white, Hispanic, and

> "Ethnic militancy and solidarity are on the rise."

Asian students. If this is where the campus is headed, where are our cities going?

If America is to survive as "one nation, one people," we need to call a   12
"time-out" on immigration, to assimilate the tens of millions who have lately arrived. We need to get to know one another, to live together, to learn together America's language, history, culture, and traditions of tolerance, to become a new national family, before we add a hundred million more. And we need soon to bring down the curtain on this idea of hyphenated-Americanism.

If we lack the courage to make the decisions—as to what our country will   13
look like in 2050—others will make those decisions for us, not all of whom share our love of the America that seems to be fading away.

⊜ EXERCISE 5.12

Choose three of the fallacies that you identified in "Immigration Time-Out" for Exercise 5.11. Rewrite each statement in the form of a logical argument.

Have Colleges Gone Too Far to Accommodate Students with Disabilities?

You have taken
my

PARKING
space!

Would you like my
disability also?

Go back to page 113, and reread the At Issue box that gives background on whether colleges have gone too far in accommodating students with disabilities. As the following sources illustrate, this question has a number of possible answers.

As you read this source material, you will be asked to answer questions and to complete some simple activities. This work will help you understand both the content and the structure of the sources. When you are finished, you will be ready to write an argument—either inductive or deductive—that takes a position on whether colleges have gone too far in accommodating students with disabilities.

SOURCES

 California Polytechnic State University, "College Students with Learning Disabilities," p. 153; University of Minnesota, "Do I Have a Disability?," p. 157

 Tamar Lewin, "Fictitious Learning-Disabled Student at the Center of a Lawsuit against College," p. 161

 Arne Duncan, "Keeping the Promise to All America's Children," p. 165

 Charlotte Allen, "College for the Intellectually Disabled," p. 172

 Melissa Felder, "How Yale Supports Students with Disabilities," p. 176

 Rachel Adams, "Bringing Down the Barriers—Seen and Unseen," p. 178

For comprehension quizzes,
see **bedfordstmartins.com/practicalargument**.

This information was posted on the Web site of the Disability Resource Center at California Polytechnic State University.

COLLEGE STUDENTS WITH LEARNING DISABILITIES

CALIFORNIA POLYTECHNIC STATE UNIVERSITY

A Learning Disability (LD) Is:

- A disorder which affects the manner in which individuals with normal or above average intelligence take in, retain, and express information. It is commonly recognized as a significant deficit in one or more of the following areas: oral expression, listening comprehension, written expression, basic reading skills, reading comprehension, mathematical calculation, or problem solving. Individuals with learning disabilities also may have difficulty with sustained attention, time management, or social skills.

- Presumably due to central nervous system dysfunction.

- Cross-cultural. It occurs regardless of racial or ethnic origin.

- Often inconsistent. A learning disability may persist throughout life but the problems manifested may change depending upon the learning demands and the setting. It may cause problems throughout grade school, seem to disappear in high school, and then resurface again in college. It may manifest itself in only one specific academic area, such as math or foreign language, or may impact an individual's performance across a variety of subject areas and disciplines.

- Frustrating! Because a learning disability is not visible, teachers, parents, and peers often do not understand the challenges faced by individuals with learning disabilities. Consequently, many adults with learning disabilities often have to "prove" to others that their invisible impairments are disabling.

A Learning Disability Is Not:

- A form of mental retardation or an emotional disorder.

- Primarily due to other impairments, environmental, or cultural influences. It may occur concomitantly with other disabilities but is not the result of these conditions.

Characteristics of College Students with Learning Disabilities

Many college students with learning disabilities are intelligent, talented, and capable. Typically, they have developed a variety of strategies for compensating for their learning disabilities. However, the degree of severity of the disability varies from individual to individual. Individuals who

"Many college students with learning disabilities are intelligent, talented, and capable."

come from divergent cultural and language backgrounds may exhibit many of the oral and written language behaviors cited below but are not necessarily learning disabled by virtue of this difference alone.

Reading Skills

- Slow reading rate and/or difficulty in modifying reading rate in accordance with material's level of difficulty.

- Uneven comprehension and retention of material read. Difficulty identifying important points and themes.

- Incomplete mastery of phonics, confusion of similar words, difficulty integrating new vocabulary.

- Skips words or lines of printed material.

- Difficulty reading for long periods of time.

Written Language Skills

- Difficulty planning a topic and organizing thoughts on paper.

- Difficulty with sentence structure (e.g., incomplete sentences, run-ons, poor use of grammar, missing inflectional endings).

- Frequent spelling errors (e.g., omissions, substitutions, transpositions), especially in specialized and foreign vocabulary.

- Difficulty effectively proofreading written work and making revisions.

- Compositions are often limited in length.

- Slow written production.

- Poor penmanship (e.g., poorly formed letters, incorrect use of capitalization, trouble with spacing, overly large handwriting).

- Inability to copy correctly from a book or the blackboard. Slow written production.

Oral Language Skills

- Inability to concentrate on and to comprehend spoken language when presented rapidly.

- Difficulty in orally expressing ideas that they seem to understand.

- Difficulty following or having a conversation about an unfamiliar idea.
- Difficulty speaking grammatically correct English.
- Trouble telling a story in the proper sequence.
- Difficulty following oral or written directions.

Mathematical Skills

- Incomplete mastery of basic facts (e.g., mathematical tables).
- Reverses numbers (e.g., 123 to 321 or 231).
- Confuses operational symbols, especially $+$ and $\times$.
- Copies problems incorrectly from one line to another.
- Difficulty recalling the sequence of operational concepts.
- Difficulty understanding key concepts and applications to aid problem solving.
- Difficulty comprehending word problems.

Organizational and Study Skills

- Difficulty with organizational skills.
- Time management difficulties.
- Slow to start and to complete tasks.
- Repeated inability, on a day-to-day basis, to recall what has been taught.
- Difficulty interpreting charts and graphs.
- Lack of overall organization in written notes and compositions.
- Difficulty preparing for and taking tests.
- Inefficient use of library and reference materials.

Attention and Concentration

- Trouble focusing and sustaining attention on academic tasks.
- Fluctuating attention span during lectures.
- Easily distracted by outside stimuli.
- Difficulty juggling multiple task demands and overloads quickly.
- Hyperactivity and excessive movements may accompany the inability to focus attention.

Social Skills

- Some adults with learning disabilities have social skills problems due to their inconsistent perceptual abilities. These individuals may be unable to detect the difference between sincere and sarcastic comments or may be unable to recognize other subtle changes in tone of voice for the same reason that a person with visual perceptual problems may have trouble distinguishing between the letters *b* and *d*. Difficulties in interpreting nonverbal messages may result in lowered self-esteem and may cause some adults with learning disabilities to have trouble meeting people or working cooperatively with others.

This information comes from the Student Services section of the Web site for the University of Minnesota.

DO I HAVE A DISABILITY?

UNIVERSITY OF MINNESOTA

Is what I have a disability? How do I know what a disability is?

> "How do I know what a disability is?"

1

Information about Disabilities

A disability is a physical or mental impairment that substantially limits one or more major life activities such as seeing, hearing, walking, learning, or self-care. While some disabilities are apparent, or visible, the majority of people have invisible disabilities. While an invisible disability may not be apparent, the impact of the condition is real. Some individuals may be reluctant to disclose a disability because of the stigma associated with having a disability. The following is a list of some of the disability conditions served by Disability Services. It is important to note that individuals may experience multiple conditions.

2

Psychiatric Disabilities

A psychiatric disability or mental illness is a health condition that impacts an individual's thinking, feelings, or behavior (or all three) and causes the individual distress and difficulty in functioning. The course of a mental illness is unique for each person and may limit one or more major life activities such as learning or working. Examples of a psychiatric disability include major depression, bipolar disorder, schizophrenia, anxiety disorder, or post-traumatic stress disorder.

3

Attention Deficit Hyperactivity Disorder (ADD/ADHD)

Attention Deficit Hyperactivity Disorder (ADHD) is a neurological condition that affects learning and behavior. ADHD is the result of a chronic disturbance in the areas of the brain that regulate attention, impulse control, and executive functioning. Hyperactivity is not always a symptom. People with a formal diagnosis of ADHD may have difficulties with information processing and concentration. Individuals generally experience symptoms of ADHD in childhood and continue to experience symptoms as adults, but adult diagnoses are not uncommon for college-aged students.

4

Learning Disabilities

A Learning Disability (LD) affects the manner in which individuals acquire, store, organize, retrieve, manipulate, and express information. People who

5

have been diagnosed with a learning disability typically have average to above-average intelligence but exhibit a discrepancy between ability and achievement. Areas affected by LD may include reading, written expression, and math. People with learning disabilities may also experience difficulty with organizational skills, time management, or social/interpersonal skills.

Mobility Impairments

Mobility impairments include a broad range of disabilities that affect a person's independent movement and cause limited mobility. Some mobility impairments are acquired at birth while accidents, illnesses, or the natural process of aging may cause others. Examples of mobility impairments may include paraplegia, multiple sclerosis, quadriplegia, amputation, cerebral palsy, and arthritis. Depending on the severity of the disability, individuals may have limitations related to stamina, manual dexterity, speech, and ability to stand or sit. 6

Systemic Disabilities

Systemic disabilities are medical conditions that affect one or more major body systems. These conditions constitute a disability if they significantly impact one or more major life activities, such as learning. The effects and symptoms of these conditions vary greatly; systemic conditions may include cancer, asthma, HIV/AIDS, epilepsy, chronic fatigue syndrome, or diabetes. 7

Blind and Low Vision

Few individuals are totally blind; many individuals have some useful vision that can be utilized through the use of adaptive devices. Individuals are considered to be legally blind when they meet specific criteria for their vision loss. Someone has low vision when they have decreased visual acuity or visual field that cannot be corrected with ordinary eyeglasses, contact lenses, or medical or surgical procedures. 8

Visual impairments may occur because of birth defects, inherited diseases, injuries, diabetes, glaucoma, cataracts, macular degeneration, and other conditions. Some individuals may use Braille, large print, various assistive technologies, or a combination of these for communication purposes. 9

Deaf and Hard of Hearing

The term *deaf* refers to those individuals who are unable to hear well enough to rely on their hearing and use it as a means of processing information. The term *hard of hearing* refers to those who have some hearing, are able to 10 use it for communication purposes, and who feel reasonably comfortable doing so. Hearing loss is categorized by its severity as mild, moderate, severe, or profound and may affect the hearing in one or both ears. Modes of communication (American Sign Language, captioning, lip reading, assistive listening devices) vary depending on the degree of hearing loss and age of onset. Two people with the same severity of hearing loss may experience it quite differently.

Deaf/Blind

This refers to a dual sensory loss that interferes with the ability of individuals   11
to function effectively in the hearing-sighted world. This term does not necessarily mean total loss of hearing and vision; the range of hearing loss and vision loss varies with individuals. Please see additional descriptions on Deaf/Hard of Hearing and/or Blind/Low-Vision.

Head Injuries

Some head injuries result in cognitive and behavioral impairments. A head   12
injury may affect one or more of the following areas: information processing, memory, communication, motor skills, and other sensory, physical, and psychosocial abilities. There is great variation among individuals in the impact of a head injury.

Brain Injuries

A brain injury is damage caused by an internal or external trauma to the brain.   13
Inflammation or swelling, bleeding, a blow to the head, or excessive force such as shaking or whiplash may cause a brain injury; these traumas may result in cognitive, physical, behavioral, and emotional changes. A brain injury can affect different areas of the brain depending on the type and severity of the accident; as a result, the effects vary widely from person to person. Major causes of brain injury include falls, motor vehicle accidents, violence, concussions, bicycle crashes, lack of oxygen from cardiac arrest, brain inflammation, aneurysms, strokes, and tumors.

Autism Spectrum Disorder

Autism Spectrum Disorder (ASD) is a developmental disability that is charac-   14
terized by social interaction deficits, impaired communication skills, restricted interests, and stereotyped patterns of behavior. People with this disability may have difficulty with understanding social cues, breaks in routines, fine motor skills, stress management, and sensitivity to environmental stimuli. ASD may include high-functioning autism, Asperger's syndrome, or Pervasive Developmental Disorder.

⊙ AT ISSUE: SOURCES FOR DEVELOPING A LOGICAL ARGUMENT

1. The two learning disabilities Web sites on the preceding pages give information to college students. How much knowledge does each site assume readers have? What preconceptions (if any) does each site assume readers have?

2. Which of these sites do you think is more helpful? Why?

3. The California Polytechnic State University site explains what conditions do *not* qualify as learning disabilities. Do you think this material is necessary? Why do you think the University of Minnesota site does not include this information? Should it be added?

4. Do the two sites provide enough information? Too much information? Are the definitions of the various disabilities listed on each site too broad, too narrow, or just right? Explain.

5. Is the purpose of each site just to give information, or do you think one (or both) has a different purpose? Explain.

This article is from the April 8, 1997, edition of the *New York Times*.

FICTITIOUS LEARNING-DISABLED STUDENT AT THE CENTER OF A LAWSUIT AGAINST COLLEGE

TAMAR LEWIN

Boston University had long been one of the nation's leaders in helping learning-disabled students through the rigors of higher education. So two years ago, when Jon Westling, the provost, described "Somnolent Samantha" in a speech complaining of the extremes to which universities are being pushed to accommodate such students, there was every reason to believe that she was real. 1

Mr. Westling, now the president of Boston University, related how Samantha had told him after class that she had a learning disability "in the area of auditory processing" and would need copies of lecture notes, a seat in front, extra time on exams, and a separate room to take them in. And, he said, he was told that Samantha might fall asleep in class, so he should fill her in on material she missed while she dozed. 2

Mr. Westling spoke of Samantha on other occasions, too, affirming that the case was real in an interview with the *New York Times* last year and citing it, again as if it were real, in a letter to the mother of a child with a disability. But now, in documents related to a highly visible lawsuit, Mr. Westling has acknowledged that there was no such student as Somnolent Samantha, that the sleeping young woman was someone he had invented to make a point. 3

Even though Samantha is fictional, she and her inventor are at the heart of an academic debate over how much help, and what academic adjustments, learning-disabled college students are entitled to. 4

Lawyers for Mr. Westling say he is guilty only of daring to voice the politically incorrect view that the field of learning disabilities is still scientifically murky and that universities have the right to set their own academic requirements, even if some disabled students will have trouble fulfilling them. 5

But advocates for the learning-disabled say his dismissive words and his actions—he has tightened the university's policy on handling requests for accommodations—amount to illegal discrimination against those with learning disabilities. 6

In a lawsuit, a class action that goes to trial today in Boston, learning-disabled students at Boston University are charging that the university and Mr. Westling have violated Federal laws requiring that educational institutions provide "reasonable accommodations" to those with learning disabilities. 7

In the last decade, the number of college students identified as having learning disabilities has grown rapidly. In the annual survey by the American Council on Education last fall, 3.1 percent of full-time college freshmen called themselves learning-disabled, compared with 2.2 percent in 1991, the first year 8 the question was asked. Colleges across the nation are grappling with the question of what they must do to accommodate these students.

Learning disabilities are defined as the unexpected failure to learn, despite 9 adequate intelligence, motivation, and instruction. Reading disorders, or dyslexia, are the most common. But both clinically and legally, the field of learning disabilities is evolving. New learning disabilities are still being identified, and there are no clear legal standards on what constitutes reasonable accommodation.

For many years, the Office of Learning Disabilities Support Services at 10 Boston University had a national reputation for its summer program for learning-disabled students, the tutoring it offered, and its policy of helping such students get special assistance, like the aid of a note-taker, extended time on tests, or permission to substitute a course to meet a foreign language or math requirement.

But in 1995, Mr. Westling, then the provost, became suspicious of the 11 diagnoses some students were declaring, the credentials of some of the experts making the diagnoses, and the accommodations the university was being asked to make. After reviewing the files, he said, he was troubled to find poor documentation, vague diagnoses, and evaluations that offered no evidence of any need for the accommodations that had been granted. Some files had no documentation or had documentation for the wrong students.

So Mr. Westling, a humanities professor with no expertise in learning dis- 12 abilities, changed the policy in this area at the end of 1995, taking unto himself the authority that had rested in the Office of Learning Disabilities Support Services. He made himself the final arbiter of applications for accommodations, set up a blanket prohibition against course substitutions for foreign language or math requirements, and required every learning-disabled student receiving any accommodation to re-apply for such aid by submitting a diagnostic evaluation not more than three years old from a doctor or licensed clinical psychologist.

The change created turmoil at the learning-disabilities office, where top 13 officials resigned in protest, and led to confusion at other schools that had looked to Boston University as their model. Many of the university's learning-disabled students—480 of the university's 29,000 students registered with the learning-disabilities office last year—said they felt betrayed since they had come to the college because of the support it offered.

"I was drawn to B.U. because I thought there would be an attitude of 14 understanding about learning disabilities," said Elizabeth Guckenberger, a third-year law student who was discovered to have auditory and visual dyslexia as a freshman at Carleton College in Northfield, Minn.

"I have always had to work very hard," Ms. Guckenberger said. "Things 15 take me much longer than they take my twin sister, who is not dyslexic. I'm doing well in law school, but I need my accommodations. I get a reduced caseload, which means I'm not going to finish in the usual three years, and I get extended time on tests and a quiet room to take them in."

Lawyers for Ms. Guckenberger and the other plaintiffs say the Samantha 16
story shows that Mr. Westling should not be making decisions on which
accommodations to grant.

"That kind of language is evidence of an intent to discriminate," said Wil- 17
liam Hunt, one of the students' lawyers.

The university, however, says advocates for learning-disabled students are 18
on a witch hunt, seeking to vilify Mr. Westling for daring to say what many
other academics around the country think but do not dare express.

"The field of learning disabilities is still a very fluid field," said Larry Els- 19
wit, the university lawyer handling the case, "and throughout the academic
world, there is a great deal of questioning going on. Jon Westling's cardinal sin
was to talk about it."

In the students' original complaint, they charged that Mr. Westling and 20
Boston University were maintaining a "hostile learning environment," a legal
concept borrowed from cases dealing with workplace discrimination and used
recently in cases alleging sexual harassment at schools. Several leading advocacy groups for learning-disabled students joined the students as plaintiffs in
the original complaint.

Judge Patti B. Saris of Federal District Court in Boston, in an order she 21
issued in January to allow the case to proceed as a class action, refused to
allow the advocacy groups to be parties in the case and dismissed the hostile-
environment charge. Judge Saris warned that making an academic liable for
expressing his general views would raise First Amendment concerns. Still, she
said that if a "vociferous administrator with a concern about a perceived
abuse of learning-disability protections" was involved in the daily administration of the policy being challenged, that might "be of some consequence in
this court's determination of the fairness of Boston University's evaluation
procedures."

Since the lawsuit was filed, Boston University's handling of learning disabili- 22
ties has loosened somewhat: some waivers of the requirement for diagnoses
every three years have been granted, and the range of acceptable credentials for
evaluators has been slightly broadened. And the university has accepted a temporary standstill agreement that allows students to keep any accommodations
that had been promised before Mr. Westling changed the policy. With the standstill agreement, Mr. Elswit said, the number of accommodations rose to 178 last
fall, from 118 in 1995 and 117 the previous year. In January, the university hired
a learning-disabilities expert to review applications for accommodations.

But other issues in the lawsuit remain, including the question of whether 23
courses can be substituted for math and foreign language requirements, the
students' demand for an appeals process, and a claim of breach of contract.

"This case is not about Somnolent 24
Samantha," Mr. Elswit said. "It is about a
university's right to set academic standards.
The university's position is that the
Americans with Disabilities Act does not prohibit us from having an academic

> "This case is not about
> Somnolent Samantha."

administrator involved in decisions about academic adjustments. If a student seeks an adjustment to his or her academic program, that is fundamentally an academic issue."

He continued: "Everyone acknowledges, and we do at Boston University, that learning disabilities can make certain elements of learning difficult. As a result, we have in place a broad array of support, adjustments, and alternatives. Within our academic standards, we will do whatever we can to help students with learning disabilities over the bar. Time and a half on tests and note-takers can be fine efforts to help students over the bar. What we won't do is lower the bar." 25

At trial, both sides will present expert witnesses on learning disabilities. They are expected to address the question of who needs accommodations, how widely such help is used or abused, how well it works, and whether periodic retesting should be required for students reporting learning disabilities. 26

Ms. Guckenberger, for her part, remains convinced that Boston University's policy is an expression of hostility to students with learning disabilities. The fact that they used a fictional story to illustrate the problems they were having, she said, means that they did not have any genuine complaints. 27

⊙ AT ISSUE: SOURCES FOR DEVELOPING A LOGICAL ARGUMENT

1. Why did Jon Westling, the provost of Boston University, invent "Somnolent Samantha"? What did he hope to prove? Do you think his tactics were justified? Were they fair?

2. Why are students with learning disabilities at Boston University suing Westling? Do you think their suit has merit? Why or why not?

3. Why did Westling become suspicious of the disabilities that some students were claiming? What did he think these students were hoping to gain?

4. In paragraph 12, Lewin says that Westling is "a humanities professor with no expertise in learning disabilities." How significant is this information? Do you think it suggests that Lewin favors one side of the dispute over the other? Explain.

5. In paragraph 24, Larry Elswit, one of the university's lawyers, says that the case is not about Somnolent Samantha. According to him, "It is about a university's right to set academic standards." Do you agree?

6. The essay ends with the following comment by one of the plaintiffs in the case: "The fact that [the university] used a fictional story to illustrate the problems they were having . . . means that they did not have any genuine complaints." Does this statement seem logical, or is it an example of a logical fallacy? Explain.

The following speech was delivered by the U. S. Secretary of Education on April 21, 2010.

KEEPING THE PROMISE TO ALL AMERICA'S CHILDREN

ARNE DUNCAN

President Obama and I believe that every child deserves a world-class educa- 1 tion. When the president says every child, it is not just rhetoric—he means every child, regardless of his or her skin color, nationality, ethnicity, or ability. The truth is, however, that virtually everyone professes to believe that all children deserve a world-class education.

Yet today, a significant gap between our aspirations and reality persists. 2 And here is the harder, unspoken truth. Subtle, unexpressed prejudices and lingering roadblocks still prevent children with disabilities from receiving the world-class education they deserve. No belief is more pernicious in education than the conviction that disabilities and demography are destiny—that the burdens of poverty, disability, and race mean the children cannot really succeed and should be treated with low expectations.

We should never forget the past. Even in my lifetime, public schools virtu- 3 ally ignored children with disabilities. Many children were denied access to public schools, and those who attended didn't get the individualized instruction and appropriate services they needed and deserved.

Over the past 35 years, we've made great strides in delivering on the prom- 4 ise of a free, appropriate public education for children with disabilities. Thanks to the advocacy and hard work of people and organizations like the Council for Exceptional Children, six million students with disabilities are in school—and millions of them are thriving.

Yet unfortunately, many children with disabilities are not getting a world- 5 class education. The President and I are committed to doing everything in our power to make that bedrock American promise of equal educational opportunity a reality. With the reauthorization of the Elementary and Secondary Education Act, we have a historic opportunity to move closer to fulfilling that promise for all students.

The President has set a goal that, by the end of the decade, America once 6 again will have the highest proportion of college graduates in the world. That ambitious goal will require our educational institutions to produce eight million new graduates with two-year and four-year degrees. We simply cannot achieve that goal without Americans of all ages and abilities going to college and getting degrees in far greater numbers than they are today.

And we know, more than ever before, that in a global economy, a country's economic security depends on the skills and knowledge of its workers. The country 7

"America does not have expendable students."

165

that out-educates us today will out-compete us tomorrow. America does not have expendable students.

But education for all is more than an economic issue. It's a moral issue. I 8 have often said that education is the civil rights issue of our time. In March, I had the opportunity to speak at the Edmund Pettus Bridge in Selma, Alabama, on the 45th anniversary of one of the most important events of the Civil Rights movement. On that bridge, police savagely beat several hundred peaceful protesters with clubs, lashed them with bullwhips, and stung their eyes and throats with tear gas—all because the protesters wanted to secure the right to vote. Our nation wept with shame that day. Within months, Congress passed the landmark Voting Rights Act of 1965.

The civil rights protesters on the Edmund Pettus Bridge weren't in wheel- 9 chairs and they weren't marching on behalf of students with dyslexia, learning disabilities, ADD, or other disabilities. But their spirit and commitment emboldened the disability rights movement. In education, no victory for disability advocates was bigger than the 1975 law that guaranteed students with disabilities the right to a free, appropriate public education. On the 35th anniversary of that law's passage, it's important to remember many students with disabilities were turned away from school altogether. Others were put in separate classrooms—sometimes a place as unwelcoming as a converted broom closet. Very few ever interacted with peers without disabilities. Today, six million students are guaranteed a free, appropriate public education.

Great advocates continue to work tirelessly on behalf of persons with 10 disabilities. In Congress, we are fortunate the education committees are led by two great champions for students with disabilities—Senator Tom Harkin and Representative George Miller. As you know, Senator Harkin has dedicated much of his career to protecting the rights of people with disabilities. He was an author of the Americans with Disabilities Act. Representative Miller is a passionate advocate for people with disabilities. He takes a back seat to no one in his commitment to accountability for educating students with disabilities.

I look forward to working with both of them to reauthorize ESEA. We'll 11 be working closely with Republicans as well, including Senator Enzi, Senator Alexander, and Representative Kline.

Senator Harkin, Chairman Miller, and House Appropriations Committee 12 Chairman David Obey also have introduced legislation to save education jobs. In this tough economy, hundreds of thousands of education professionals could be facing layoffs. Maybe you are one of them—maybe one of your colleagues or friends is. I look forward to working with them to pass an education jobs bill. Education reform and saving education jobs go hand in hand.

Because of the leadership of Senator Harkin, Chairman Miller, and many 13 others, the lives of children with disabilities are so much richer today than a generation ago. The nation has made significant progress for students with disabilities—but we have more work to do.

Today, 57 percent of students with disabilities spend at least 80 percent of   14
their day within the regular school environment. Overall, 95 percent of students with disabilities attend a neighborhood school. We're working to put an end to the days of students with disabilities being bused across town or put into a separate school solely because they have a disability. Students with disabilities are learning alongside their peers. They're eating lunch with them. They're making art with them. They're becoming friends with them. And once they graduate they will be working side-by-side.

I know that you'll be hearing from Tim Shriver on Friday. As the chairman   15
and CEO of the Special Olympics, Tim is a strong advocate for including students with disabilities across community groups. He recounts story after story to illustrate how people with disabilities enrich the lives of all children.

One story he shared with me came in an essay by a girl named Kaitlyn   16
Smith from Conifer High School in Colorado. She wrote about her best friend, Kathleen. Kaitlyn and Kathleen met while they were paired off as partners in P.E. class. They quickly became best friends and they do all of the things best friends do. They eat lunch together every day. When neither of them had a date for the Homecoming dance, they went together as friends.

Kaitlyn wrote that Kathleen taught her what truly matters. It's not dress-   17
ing well, doing your hair right, or making sure everyone likes you. In fact, when high school bullies made fun of Kathleen, her response was to look them in the eye, smile, and ignore them. Kaitlyn wrote about their friendship: "Right from the moment I met her, I knew my best friend was a blessing. I needed someone in my life that was going to change my perspective and give me a different outlook."

Kathleen happens to have Down syndrome. But the story about Kaitlyn's   18
and Kathleen's friendship shows how the inclusion of students with disabilities benefits more than just the student with the disability. Inclusion benefits the whole community. Sometimes, parents, students, and teachers fail to recognize the great leadership that students with disabilities can provide our school communities.

But I'm sure you can tell me hundreds of stories of how inclusion enriched   19
the lives of everyone in a school. These are stories we need to tell, over and over again. So many students with disabilities have gone on to become insightful and effective leaders for children who followed in their wake.

Judy Heumann was the assistant secretary for special education and   20
rehabilitative services under Secretary Riley. She contracted polio when she was 18 months old and grew up using a wheelchair. The New York City Public Schools refused to enroll her—not because she wasn't smart enough, not because she couldn't learn—simply because she used a wheelchair. When she was old enough for 4th grade, she was allowed to enroll in school. She went on to graduate high school and then college. She applied for a job as a teacher in the system and was turned away again. Once again, she didn't give up. She eventually got a job as a teacher—but only after suing the school board.

Judy knows that a disability shouldn't stop any child from attending 21 school, pursuing a career, and making a difference in the lives of others. In addition to eight years of public service at the Department of Education, she has been a strong advocate for persons with disabilities. She has worked with the World Bank to ensure that it addresses disability issues in its work with countries throughout the world. Today, she is the director of the Department of Disability Services in the District of Columbia.

Her work and dedication are reminders of the power of determination 22 and the time-honored truth that disabilities alone do not define us or our work and worth as human beings. Students like Kaitlyn and Kathleen—and adults like Judy—show us that disabilities are not destiny.

The work you do as special education leaders and teachers is vitally 23 important for the students you work with—and our society as well. Children no longer have to fight to be enrolled in school. People who use wheelchairs no longer need to sue simply to have their job application considered by public school districts or other employers. And students like Kathleen can be important parts of a school community—learning with her peers and teaching her peers important lessons about respect, self-confidence, and friendship.

Those are civil rights victories truly worth celebrating. But we haven't ful- 24 filled the promise of education for students with disabilities. The struggle for equal opportunity in our nation's schools and universities did not end with the passage of IDEA or at the foot of the Edmund Pettus Bridge. We will work with schools and enforce laws to ensure that all children, no matter what their race, gender, disability, or national origin, have a fair chance at a good future. We will make sure ESEA doesn't lose track of these students, who in many cases are making significant progress.

The data show us that we're making progress. In 2007, nearly 60 percent 25 of students with disabilities graduated high school with a regular diploma, compared to 32 percent twenty years earlier. And a third of students with disabilities were enrolled in postsecondary education—up from just one in seven two decades ago. More adults with disabilities are employed than ever before. By just about every measure, students with disabilities are better educated today than they were a generation ago.

But while America can justly celebrate those successes, we have a long way 26 to go before we rest on our laurels. The graduation rate, postsecondary enrollment rate, and employment rate are all increasing, but they're still far too low. Too many students with disabilities are leaving school, without the knowledge and skills they truly need to succeed.

From Washington, we're working hard to ensure that we have the right 27 policies and incentives in place to help states and districts accelerate achievement for all students, including those with disabilities. This year, I'm working closely with Democrats and Republicans in Congress to fix the No Child Left Behind Act through the reauthorization of the Elementary and Secondary Education Act. We want the law to be fair, flexible, and focused on the right goals. We want a law that ensures all students are prepared for success in college and careers. Our proposal will set a goal that all students graduate high school ready to succeed in college and careers. We want to make sure that students with disabilities are included in all aspects of ESEA, and to continue to measure achievement gaps and work to close them. We want to align ESEA with the Individuals with Disabilities Education Act so that we create one seamless system that addresses the needs of each child.

Under our proposal, students with disabilities will continue to be full participants in accountability systems. One thing NCLB did right was hold schools accountable for all students and highlighted the achievement gaps between subgroups of students. We absolutely want to continue that. But NCLB doesn't measure student growth. If students start the year two grade levels behind, and, through excellent teaching and strong supports, progress so much that they end the year just below grade level, their school is still labeled a failure instead of a success. 28

Our accountability system will be based mostly on student growth. Schools where students show large gains in learning over the course of the school year will be rewarded. And the emphasis on student growth will ensure that schools have an incentive to improve the academic performance of our highest-achieving students as well. While we will reward and recognize the best schools, the vast majority of schools will have more flexibility to implement locally designed plans to reach the benchmarks they set for themselves. But schools with chronically low performance and persistent achievement gaps will be required to take far-reaching steps to help students. 29

We'll maintain that focus on achievement gaps from NCLB. Our proposal would continue to hold schools accountable for teaching students with disabilities but will also reward them for increasing student learning. Our proposal will also include meaningful district accountability. That means even where achievement gaps aren't apparent in schools with small numbers of students with disabilities, we will see these gaps at the district level and ask districts to focus on closing them. 30

While we're confident that our accountability system will be fair and flexible, we recognize it won't be flawless. To build a first-rate accountability system, states have to significantly improve existing assessments used to measure our students' growth and move beyond fill-in-the-bubble tests. Our ESEA Blueprint and Race to the Top Assessment Competition will invest in that next generation of tests to measure student growth and achievement. And it will enhance states' use of technology and advances in the field of testing to evaluate a range of skills, including those that have traditionally been difficult to measure. 31

The Department plans to support consortia of states, who will design better assessments for the purposes of both measuring student growth and providing feedback to inform teaching and learning in the classroom. All students will benefit from these tests, but the tests are especially important for students with disabilities. 32

169

Today, we have a complicated set of rules around assessing students with [33] disabilities. The majority of students with disabilities take the regular state tests based on the state's standards for all students, with appropriate accommodations to ensure that their results are valid. Students with the most significant cognitive disabilities can take alternate tests based on alternate standards, and other students with disabilities may take an alternate test based on modified standards.

Developing these alternate assessments requires specialized expertise. The [34] Department intends to run an alternate assessments competition that will be managed by the Office of Special Education and Rehabilitative Services, with a notice inviting applications later this year.

We need to move toward assessments that allow practically all students to [35] take tests that report results tracking their progress toward college- or career-readiness. Our Blueprint also recognizes the uniquely transformative power of teachers on students. We will invest almost $4 billion in programs that recruit, prepare, develop, retain, and reward effective teachers. That's an unprecedented amount. Our proposal goes further by bolstering traditional and alternative pathways to teaching—especially for those teaching in high-need areas—such as special education—and those teaching in high-need schools.

This reauthorized ESEA will provide the building block for the reauthori- [36] zation of the IDEA that will follow. Alexa Posny will be leading our work in IDEA reauthorization, and she will be a strong advocate for students with disabilities in ESEA reauthorization as well. You'll be hearing from her tomorrow morning. Alexa and I look forward to hearing your voices and working with you as Congress shapes this very important law.

Before I close, I want to issue a challenge to each of you individually and [37] to the whole field of special education. Everything we do at the U.S. Department of Education is aimed toward meeting the President's goal that by 2020 America once again will lead the world in college completion. We cannot get there unless students are earning postsecondary degrees at record levels. I know you've made tremendous progress over the decades, but there's still significant work to be done. I want to challenge each of you to be personally responsible for the success of your students once they graduate. This will mean helping students not just in school but assisting them to plan their transition from high school to college or careers.

I know you already work hard on this, but I'm asking you to redouble [38] your efforts. The success of your students, the well-being of our communities, and the economic prosperity of our nation depend on creating a cradle-to-career educational pipeline, not an education system that continues to function in its separate silos.

Working together, and with your courage and commitment to challenging [39] the status quo, we can create an education system that delivers a world-class education to every learner. This is a promise we must keep to our nation's students with disabilities, and to all of America's children.

⊘ AT ISSUE: SOURCES FOR DEVELOPING A LOGICAL ARGUMENT

1. At what point in his speech does Duncan appeal to *ethos*? How effective is this appeal?

2. Duncan develops his argument with both deductive and inductive reasoning. Where does he use each strategy?

3. What does Duncan mean when he says that "education for all is more than an economic issue. It's a moral issue" (para. 8)? Do you agree?

4. In paragraphs 8 and 9, Duncan draws an analogy between civil rights protestors in the 1960s and those who are involved in the disability rights movement. How valid is this analogy? At what points (if any) does this comparison break down?

5. What evidence does Duncan present to support his thesis? Should he have included more evidence? If so, what kind?

6. Where does Duncan address arguments against his position? Does he refute these arguments? Are there any other arguments he should have refuted?

This essay was posted on MindingtheCampus.com on September 23, 2010.

COLLEGE FOR THE INTELLECTUALLY DISABLED

CHARLOTTE ALLEN

Here is a new trend: college for people who can't read or write. And no, that doesn't mean the one out of three freshmen whose

> "Here is a new trend: college for people who can't read or write." 1

literacy and numeracy skills are so poor that they have to take remedial courses before they are deemed ready to do college-level work. It means students who literally can't read or write because they are severely cognitively impaired by Down syndrome or some other mental disability. Yet an increasing number of campus administrators have decided that even the "intellectually disabled" (as this group is now called) deserve a college education.

Well, not exactly a college education, since even the most egalitarian 2 administrators concede that people with severe cognitive disabilities can't handle even the most rudimentary of course offerings. Instead, what a host of new programs for the intellectually disabled offer is what the people who run them call "a college experience."

Some 250 campuses around the country offer such courses. Students 3 enrolled in the programs sit in on a class or two per semester that regular students are taking for credit, but they don't receive grades, and their assignments are drastically tailored to fit their limited abilities. Batteries of counselors and tutors (the latter are typically volunteers from the regular student population) help them through, and they fill up the rest of their time with "life skills" seminars and workshops designed to help them use a debit card, take the bus, or get through a job interview, with internships at participating nonprofits, and, presumably, with making friends and soaking up the ivy-covered atmosphere. They don't receive actual college degrees—indeed, according to the U.S. Department of Education, no student enrolled in any college program for the intellectually disabled has to date received even a two-year associate degree—but if they complete their programs in a process that can take years, they typically receive certificates of completion that they can show to prospective employers.

The "college experience" programs represent the latest step in the concept 4 of "mainstreaming" the disabled, including the cognitively disabled, in a process that began in 1973. That's when Congress passed the Education for All Handicapped Children Act (now known as the Individuals with Disabilities Education Act, or IDEA), which established the right to a public-school education for disabled children. A companion law, the Rehabilitation Act of 1973, along with the Americans with Disabilities Act of 1990, outlawed discrimination against the handicapped. Many school districts accordingly dismantled their special-education classes for cognitively impaired youngsters and began seating those children in regular classrooms alongside children of normal abilities, all the way from kindergarten through high school. When those classmates went on to college, their cognitively impaired peers wanted to go, too. As Elise McMillan, codirector of the Center for Excellence in Developmental Disabilities at Vanderbilt University, which began what It calls a "Next Step" program for intellectually disabled young people this year, told the *Chronicle of Higher Education*, "[T]hey have the same dreams and aspirations as their brothers and sisters and other students."

Such sentimental linguistic trafficking in "dreams and aspirations" and 5 "a college experience" in contrast to actual college can be viewed as a harmless if expensive exercise in philanthropy by university administrators— although it does help dilute the value and meaning of a college education, already threatened by grade inflation and the collapse of core curricula. It would be more honest to describe the programs as charity rather than college. The programs may also do some psychological good for the ultra-select group of people they serve (the Vanderbilt program, for example, enrolls only five students at a time). They also likely teach the volunteer tutors and classmates of the cognitively impaired important lessons in compassion for their less fortunate fellow human beings. But it is hard to assess their practical value. Although advocates cite studies showing that intellectually disabled students who complete some sort of postsecondary education earn 1.7 times more per week than their peers who receive no postsecondary education, no students or administrators interviewed by the *Chronicle* or other newspapers pinpointed any specific better-paying jobs offered to enrollees in the programs. One cannot help but wonder whether the programs simply help cognitively impaired students coast along at their parents' (or university) expense in a respectable academic setting instead of going to work at the low-prestige jobs for which their limited abilities qualify them.

More alarmingly, although the programs in the past have been funded 6 largely by state grants and private donations (as well as the tuition paid by their enrollees), the federal government is poised to dump large amounts of taxpayer money into them. In 2008 Congress extended federally guaranteed loans and Pell grants for low-income students to intellectually disabled students enrolled in transition, learning-skills, and other "college experience" programs. Another 2008 law provides for federal grants to institutions of higher learning that set up such programs.

Worst of all, the programs have generated a litigious entitlement men- 7 tality on the part of beneficiaries and their parents. Take the case of Micah Fialka-Feldman, who enrolled in 2003 in the "OPTIONS" program for the intellectually disabled set up by Oakland University in Rochester, Mich. By all accounts Fialka-Feldman, although an extroverted young man who participated in many high school activities as he was mainstreamed along, could neither read nor write. The *Wall Street Journal* described him as having "a cognitive impairment" that interfered with his ability to acquire literacy.

After four years of participating in OPTIONS and taking tutor-assisted classes without acquiring any sort of certificate, Fialka-Feldman decided in 2007 that he wanted to live in a dormitory on the Oakland campus instead of commuting the twenty miles from his home by bus (he said he was inspired by his younger sister's move into a dormitory at Mt. Holyoke College). "I just wanted to be able to live with my friends and have the total college experience," he later told a newspaper reporter.

When the university balked at this demand, saying that its dorms were reserved for full-time students enrolled in four-year degree programs rather than part-timers like Fialka-Feldman who typically lived in off-campus apartments, the young man sued the university under the 1973 Rehabilitation Act. He availed himself of free legal services provided by Michigan Protection and Advocacy Inc., a public-interest law firm. In December 2009 a federal judge ruled that Oakland had violated his rights under the 1973 law and ordered the university to allow him to move into a dorm room in January 2010. The judge also ordered Oakland to pay $102,000 in legal fees to Michigan Protection and Advocacy. By then Fialka-Feldman was 25 years old, well past the graduation age of most on-campus students. He completed the OPTIONS program in June after a single semester of dorm life and some seven years after enrolling at Oakland. The university is appealing the ruling. 8

The Fialka-Feldman lawsuit suggests that what began as a well-intentioned service for cognitively impaired young people who felt disappointed that they could not get into college has hardened into unrealistic expectations that can spell legal trouble for colleges who set up the programs. A recent article on the *US News* website about such programs was followed by angry comments from parents of intellectually disabled students taking issue with critics who questioned the programs' usefulness or propriety. 9

"Should [my daughter] work at Walmart and live below the poverty level for the rest of her life?" wrote one mother. Wrote another: "Why should [my daughter] have to wait on me at McDonald's?" Those comments said a lot— about upper-middle-class disdain for honest but entry-level service work and about the kind of employment for which those with severe cognitive disabilities can realistically qualify even with the best of "life-skills" coaching on a college campus. Such are the perils of deciding to offer a "college experience," or indeed college itself, to people who lack the intellectual qualifications to benefit from higher education. 10

⬣ AT ISSUE: SOURCES FOR DEVELOPING A LOGICAL ARGUMENT

1. Do you understand the context of the problem that Allen discusses? Should she have provided more background information?

2. According to Allen, what is the difference between a college education and a "college experience" (para. 5)? Do you see college experience

programs as harmless—or even beneficial—or do you agree with Allen that they "help dilute the value and meaning of a college education" (5)? Explain.

3. Throughout her essay, Allen uses words and phrases that convey her feelings to readers. (For example, in paragraph 5, she refers to "sentimental linguistic trafficking," and in paragraph 6, she uses the phrase "more alarmingly.") List some other words and phrases like these. Would Allen's essay have been more effective had she used more neutral language? Why or why not?

4. Does Allen ever establish that the programs she opposes are widespread enough to be a problem? Could she be accused of setting up a straw man?

5. In the first five paragraphs of her essay, Allen presents the arguments of those who support "college experience" programs. The rest of her essay is a refutation of these arguments. For example, in paragraph 5, she says that college experience programs do little actual good. In paragraph 6, she says that the federal government "is poised to dump large amounts of taxpayer money into them." Finally, in paragraph 7, she says that the programs have encouraged "a litigious entitlement mentality." Restate these arguments in your own words by filling in the following template.

   Some people defend college experience programs, saying _____

   _____

   _____, but others point out that _____

   _____.

6. What does Allen want to accomplish with her essay? Is her purpose to convince readers of something? To move them to action? What is your reaction to her essay?

This personal essay is from Yale University's *Yale Herald* summer 2000 edition.

HOW YALE SUPPORTS STUDENTS WITH DISABILITIES

MELISSA FELDER

As the only current undergraduate with a hearing impairment and one of a 1
scarce number of students with physical or learning disabilities, I identify
myself first as a Yale student and second as a student with a disability. However, that is not to say that having a hearing loss has not affected my college
experience. It has undeniably shaped my college experiences—just in very
subtle ways.

Although I have become part of the hearing world of Yale, I have had to 2
accept some limitations. Lectures are difficult when the professor is talking on
the stage or meandering around the classroom and not facing me, since I read
lips more proficiently than I hear. When students in the class ask questions or
make comments, it is difficult for me to find them in the crowd and understand what they are saying. Seminars with fast-paced discussions can also be
frustrating, and plays, lectures, and concerts can be bewildering, because
sometimes I cannot understand the performers. However, these frustrations
are but a small part of my experiences and have not stopped me from taking
advantage of all Yale has to offer.

After I presented documentation of my hearing loss, the Resource Office 3
on Disabilities (ROD) has provided me with all the accommodations I have
needed, such as real-time captioning: a court reporter sits next to me in class
and types the lecture, almost verbatim. The lecture appears instantaneously on
a laptop in front of me. While at first it was embarrassing to have to go to class
with a stenographer sitting next to me, I eventually realized that it has its perks:
all the professors know who I am, and so do most students in my classes.
(Unfortunately, since the professors know who I am, I can't cut class!)

After two semesters, I cannot recall a professor who was unwilling to allow 4
the captioning or who would not meet with me during office hours to review
the lectures if I had an especially difficult time understanding. The professors,
along with ROD, have made the transition from the smaller, more intimate setting of high school to the larger setting of college fluid and easy. The University
as a whole is supportive of dis-
abled students and ensures that
their lives are as unaffected by
their disabilities as possible.

> "The University as a whole is
> supportive of disabled students."

However, there are still flaws in the University's treatment of students with 5
disabilities. Although ROD has worked tirelessly to make the University handicapped accessible, many buildings are old and cannot accommodate wheelchair ramps or elevators. Mobility-impaired students cannot visit every dorm

or college, and they cannot gain access to the facilities in all of the colleges. Even some of the newer buildings are not completely accessible.

It will take time before handicapped access is extended to more buildings   6
around campus. Students—disabled and nondisabled alike—should not accept that a "ramp is unfeasible here," or that "this book is too hard to change into Braille." Such excuses are unacceptable. Students with disabilities need to challenge other Yale students, staff, and faculty to create greater access for the disabled. It is not that the University does not care, but when disabled students comprise such a small minority, their voices are not always heard.

⊙ AT ISSUE: SOURCES FOR DEVELOPING A LOGICAL ARGUMENT

1. Where does Felder appeal to *ethos*? Is this appeal effective? How could she make it more effective?

2. Felder suggests that she is managing well in college and that for the most part, Yale has provided her with the special services that she needs. Does her success at Yale undermine her argument in any way? Explain.

3. In paragraph 5, Felder suggests changes that she thinks Yale needs to make. Do you think her demands are reasonable? Is her statement that "excuses are unacceptable" (6) unduly harsh?

4. Does Felder use inductive or deductive reasoning to make her case? Why do you think she chose this strategy?

5. Felder's argument rests on at least two unstated assumptions. First, she believes that disabled students are entitled to a very high degree of service from the university. She also believes that Yale has an obligation to make every facility on campus handicapped accessible. Do you think that these assumptions are self-evident, or could Felder be accused of begging the question?

6. Felder ends her essay by acknowledging that disabled students make up "a small minority" at Yale (6). Is this an effective conclusion, or does it undercut her argument? How else could she have ended her essay?

This article was published in the *Chronicle of Higher Education* on November 6, 2011.

BRINGING DOWN THE BARRIERS—SEEN AND UNSEEN

RACHEL ADAMS

A colleague in a wheelchair goes into an underground passage connecting two campus buildings. Once the entrance locks behind him, he discovers that the door at the other end refuses to open with his swipe card. Although he is a vigorous man of middle age, the maintenance worker who comes to his rescue calls him Pops. 1

A student with a sensory-processing disorder needs to sit in the front row of class and take notes on a laptop computer, but the professor insists that laptops may be used only in the back of the room. After the student explains her situation, he announces to the entire class that he is making a "special exception" for her. 2

I heard these and other stories about broken elevators, stairs without handrails, and inaccessible bathrooms at a recent panel on disability and the university that I organized on campus for students, faculty, and staff from our Office of Disability Services. 3

The news wasn't all so grim. One student with muscular dystrophy was welcomed into the marching band, and another described her professors as generous and accommodating. A professor who had been around since the 1980s insisted that conditions at our university are much better today than they were in the recent past. And the panelists and audience agreed that there was a general climate of acceptance and good will toward accommodating people with disabilities on campus. 4

They also agreed that good will is hardly enough. But neither are the requirements for accommodation mandated by the Americans with Disabilities Act, which fall far short of making college campuses genuinely inclusive environments for people with disabilities. Recent news stories indicate that my university is hardly alone in confronting these problems. At County College of Morris, in New Jersey, a student was told not to participate in class discussions because the instructor found his severe stutter to be disruptive. And a student with epilepsy at Colorado Mountain College was asked to drop a class after she had a seizure that was deemed distracting to other students. 5

> "Good will is hardly enough."

Of course, there's another side to the accessibility story, one that's rarely in the news. Wayne State University, Florida State University, Humboldt State University, and Binghamton University all receive glowing reviews of their services for people with disabilities from *New Mobility*, a magazine for wheelchair users. The University of Illinois at Urbana-Champaign has a 6 program to support study abroad for students with disabilities and what it says is the first collegiate wheelchair basketball teams for both men and women. The University of California at Berkeley, where the Independent Living movement got its start, continues to offer one of the most accessible campuses in the country. But these tend to be the exceptions rather than the rule.

The controversies that have been in the news lately point toward the emergence of newer and more difficult terrain in the struggle for disabled people's rights. On campuses, considerable effort goes into material accommodations, such as building ramps and accessible bathrooms, providing note takers and sign-language interpreters, or securing extra time on exams. But, as important as these provisions are, they do little to meet the needs of students with invisible disabilities like bipolar disorder, chronic fatigue syndrome, epilepsy, or stuttering. And they do not mitigate the more subtle ways that people with disabilities are told that they are unwelcome: locating a ramp behind a Dumpster on a dark loading dock, holding parties and other extracurricular events at inaccessible locations, or offering accommodations only for talks specifically related to the topic of disability.

At Columbia, matters of accommodation are handled by our Office of Disability Services on an individual basis, with virtually no effort to inform faculty and staff about what it means to create a truly inclusive classroom. For example, every semester since the 2007 massacre at Virginia Tech, my colleagues and I have received an e-mail with a list of alarming behaviors that might indicate psychiatric disturbances in our students. We can all agree on the importance of campus safety, but in the absence of any broader effort to educate faculty, the memo creates the disturbing implication that students with psychiatric disabilities are liable to be violent or dangerous.

One problem noted by Lennard J. Davis in a recent article in the *Chronicle* is that universities don't value disability as a form of diversity, as they do race and gender. While on most campuses there is a consensus about the value of including people of different racial and ethnic backgrounds, genders, and sexual orientations, there is no such commitment to the inclusion of people with disabilities. Materials related to disabilities rarely appear on course syllabi; students and faculty with disabilities are almost never featured in promotional brochures and videos. As Davis suggests, there is something wrong with a discourse of diversity that doesn't include people with disabilities, who make up around 10 percent of the world's population.

But there's another important point to be made here. Colleges stand to learn from the lessons of the universal-design movement, which showed that changes in the built environment intended to accommodate people with disabilities ended up benefiting everyone.

A genuine effort to include—not simply to accommodate—people with disabilities could have a radical effect on our teaching and our professional practices. What if the instructor who silenced the stutterer had instead taken his disability as an opportunity to examine the goals and purpose of class

179

participation? What if a professor who was asked to give a disabled student extra time on an exam paused to think about whether 50 minutes was the ideal time for any student to complete the exam?

When our campuses tolerate, but do not welcome, people with disabilities, 12 they undermine the values of democracy, justice, and intellectual freedom that are the core values of higher education. And when we regard students and colleagues with disabilities as nuisances or disruptions, we lose the opportunities they provide to think critically, with fresh eyes, about the assumptions on which our pedagogy and our intellectual projects are based.

⊘ AT ISSUE: SOURCES FOR DEVELOPING A LOGICAL ARGUMENT

1. This article begins with a series of examples. Based on these examples, what inductive conclusion does Adams reach? How strong (or weak) is this conclusion?

2. What kinds of evidence—for example, personal experience or statistics—does Adams present to support the various points she makes? Does she present enough evidence?

3. What is Adams's purpose in writing her essay? For example, does she want to present information, change people's ideas, or move readers to action? Is she appealing mainly to *logos*, *ethos*, or *pathos*?

4. According to Adams, what is the difference between making "a genuine effort to include" people with disabilities (para. 11) and simply accommodating them? Do you think that this distinction is valid, or is Adams splitting hairs?

5. In her conclusion, Adams says, "When our campuses tolerate, but do not welcome, people with disabilities, they undermine the values of democracy, justice, and intellectual freedom that are the core values of higher education." Do you think she is overstating her case? Why or why not?

6. According to the Americans with Disabilities Act, an employer or school must make "reasonable accommodation" for those who qualify. Do you think Adams's requests are reasonable or unreasonable? Explain.

⊖ EXERCISE 5.13

Write a one-paragraph **deductive** argument in which you argue *in favor of* your school doing more to accommodate students with disabilities. Follow the template below, filling in the blanks to create your argument.

> ### TEMPLATE FOR WRITING A DEDUCTIVE ARGUMENT
>
> Each year, more and more students with disabilities are coming to college. All colleges should _____
> _____
> _____. Everyone benefits when _____
> _____.
> For example, _____
> _____. By providing disabled students with all the help they need,
> _____
> _____
> _____. Therefore, _____
> _____.
> Not everyone agrees with this view, however. Some people argue that
> _____
> _____
> _____. This argument misses the point. When colleges welcome and support students with disabilities, _____
> _____
> _____.
> For this reason, colleges should _____
> _____
> _____.

⊖ EXERCISE 5.14

Write a one-paragraph **inductive** argument in which you argue *against* your school doing more to accommodate students with disabilities. Follow the template on the next page, filling in the blanks to create your argument.

TEMPLATE FOR WRITING AN INDUCTIVE ARGUMENT

The number of college students claiming to have learning disabilities is increasing. Some students claim that _____ _____ _____. These students request _____ _____.

Studies have shown that a number of these students do not really need the special services that they are requesting. For example, some students _____ _____ _____. As a result, _____ _____.

The best way for colleges to deal with this problem is to _____ _____ _____. Advocates for the disabled, however, argue that _____ _____ _____. Although this may be true, _____ _____.

For this reason, it is clear that _____ _____.

⮞ EXERCISE 5.15

Interview several of your classmates as well as one or two of your instructors about whether they think your school has gone too far to accommodate students with disabilities. Then, edit the deductive and inductive arguments you wrote for Exercises 5.13 and 5.14 so that they include some of these comments.

⮞ EXERCISE 5.16

Write an essay in which you take a position on the topic, "Have Colleges Gone Too Far to Accommodate Students with Disabilities?" Make sure that your essay is organized primarily as either a deductive argument or an inductive argument. Use the readings on pages 152–180 as source material, and be sure to document all information that you get from these sources. (See Chapter 10 for information on documenting sources.)

⊘ EXERCISE 5.17

Review the logical fallacies discussed on pages 137–148. Then, reread the essay you wrote for Exercise 5.16, and check to see if it contains any fallacies. Underline any fallacies you find, and identify them by name. Then, rewrite each statement so it expresses a logical argument. Finally, revise your draft to eliminate any fallacies you found.

⊘ EXERCISE 5.18

Review the four pillars of argument discussed in Chapter 1. Does your essay include all four elements of an effective argument? Add anything that is missing. Then, label the key elements of your essay.

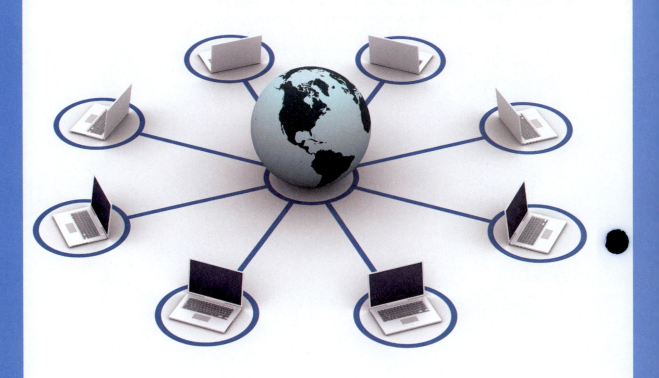

6

Rogerian Argument, Toulmin Logic, and Oral Arguments

AT ISSUE

Is Online Education as Good as Classroom Education?

Online education is a type of instruction designed to take place over a computer network. Beginning in the 1990s, increasing college costs and advances in technology made distance learning a practical and cost-effective option for educators. This method of instruction eventually evolved into the broader concept of online education.

Currently, many colleges and universities offer online courses, both undergraduate and graduate, that often lead to degrees. The National Center for Education Statistics found that from 2000 to 2008, the number of undergraduate students taking at least one online course expanded from 8% to 20%. The percentage of students participating in online education was highest among those enrolled in public two-year colleges, with older students participating in online education to a greater extent than younger students.

The advantages of online education are clear. For colleges and universities, online education programs are very profitable, allowing schools to reach new student populations both nationally and internationally. In addition,

schools can provide instruction without the expense of classrooms, offices, libraries, and bookstores. For students, online education offers the freedom of flexible scheduling, creating extra time for work or family. Finally, students save the cost of commuting to and from school.

Despite the advantages of online education, however, questions remain about its effectiveness. Some educators wonder whether online courses can duplicate the dynamic educational atmosphere that face-to-face instruction provides. Others question whether students learn as well from education delivered by technology as they do from classroom instruction. Finally, because online education classes require more self-discipline than on-campus classes, students find it easy to procrastinate and fall behind in their work.

Later in this chapter, you will be asked to think more about this issue. You will be given several sources to consider and asked to write an argument—using one of the three approaches discussed in this chapter—that takes a position on whether online education is as good as classroom instruction.

A confrontational argument

Understanding Rogerian Argument

The traditional model of argument is **confrontational**—characterized by conflict and opposition. This has been the tradition since Aristotle wrote about argument in ancient Greece. The end result of this model of argument is that someone is guilty and someone is innocent, someone is a winner and someone is a loser, or someone is right and someone is wrong.

Arguments do not always have to be confrontational, however. In fact, the twentieth-century psychologist Carl Rogers contended that in many situations, this method of arguing can actually be counterproductive, making it impossible for two people to reach agreement. According to Rogers, attacking opponents and telling them that they are wrong or misguided puts them on the defensive. The result of this tactic is frequently ill will, anger, hostility—and conflict. If you are trying to negotiate an agreement or convince someone to do something, these are exactly the responses that you do not want. To solve this problem, Rogers developed a new approach to argument—one that emphasizes cooperation over confrontation.

Rogerian argument begins with the assumption that people of good will can find solutions to problems that they have in common. Rogers recommends that you consider those with whom you disagree as colleagues, not opponents. Instead of entering into the adversarial relationship that is assumed in classical argument, Rogerian argument encourages you to enter into a cooperative relationship in which both you and your readers search for **common ground**—points of agreement about a problem. By taking this approach, you are more likely to find a solution that will satisfy everyone.

Structuring Rogerian Arguments

Consider the following situation. Assume that you bought a camera that broke one week after the warranty expired. Also assume that the manager of the store where you purchased the camera has refused to exchange it for another camera. His point is that because the warranty has expired, the store has no obligation to take the camera back. As a last resort, you write a letter to the camera's manufacturer. If you were writing a traditional argument, you would state your thesis—"It is clear that I should receive a new camera"—and then present arguments to support your position. You would also refute opposing arguments, and you would end your letter with a strong concluding statement.

Because Rogerian arguments begin with different assumptions, however, they are structured differently from classical arguments. In a Rogerian argument, you would begin by establishing common ground—by pointing out the concerns you and the camera's manufacturer share. For example, you could say that as a consumer, you want to buy merchandise that will work as advertised. If the company satisfies your needs, you will continue to buy its products. This goal is shared by the manufacturer. Therefore, instead of beginning with a thesis statement that demands a yes or no response, you would point out that you and the manufacturer share an interest in solving your problem.

Establishing common ground

A malfunctioning camera might provide an opportunity to use Rogerian argument.

Next, you would describe *in neutral terms*—using impartial, unbiased language—the manufacturer's view of the problem, defining the manufacturer's concerns and attempting to move toward a compromise position. For example, you would explain that you understand that the company wants to make a high-quality camera that will satisfy customers. You would also say that you understand that despite the company's best efforts, mistakes sometimes happen.

In the next section of your letter, you would present your own view of the problem fairly and objectively. This section plays a major role in convincing the manufacturer that your position has merit. Here, you should also try to concede the strengths of the manufacturer's viewpoint. For example, you can say that although you understand that warranties have time limits, your case has some unique circumstances that justify your claim.

Then you would explain how the manufacturer would benefit from granting your request. Perhaps you could point out that you have been satisfied with other products made by this manufacturer and expect to purchase more in the future. You could also say that instead of requesting a new camera, you would be glad to send the camera back to the factory to be repaired. This suggestion shows that you are fair and willing to compromise.

Finally, your Rogerian argument would reinforce your position and end with a concluding statement that emphasizes the idea that you are certain that the manufacturer wants to settle this matter fairly.

⊃ EXERCISE 6.1

Read through the At Issue topics listed in this book's table of contents. Choose one topic, and then do the following:

1. Summarize your own position on the issue.

2. In a few sentences, summarize the main concerns of someone who holds the opposite position.

3. Identify some common ground that you and someone who holds the opposite position might have.

4. Write a sentence that explains how your position on the issue might benefit individuals (including those who hold opposing views) or society in general.

Writing Rogerian Arguments

Rogerian arguments are typically used to address controversial or emotionally charged issues. By attempting to understand the audience's concerns and by avoiding confrontational language, you demonstrate empathy and respect for the audience. In this way, you define the common ground between your position and that of the audience. By making concessions to the opposition, Rogerian argument tries to avoid an "I win/you lose" situation and reach consensus. Thus, the strength of a Rogerian argument rests on your ability to identify areas of agreement between you and your readers. The more successful you are in doing so, the more persuasive and successful your argument will be.

> **NOTE**
>
> Although the Rogerian approach to argument can be used to develop a whole essay, it can also be part of a more traditional argument. In this case, it frequently appears in the refutation section, where opposing arguments are addressed.

In general, a Rogerian argument can be structured in the following way:

INTRODUCTION	Introduces the problem, pointing out how both the writer and reader are affected (establishes common ground)
BODY	Presents the reader's view of the problem
	Presents the writer's view of the problem (includes evidence to support the writer's viewpoint)
	Shows how the reader would benefit from moving toward the writer's position (includes evidence to support the writer's viewpoint)
	Lays out possible compromises that would benefit both reader and writer (includes evidence to support the writer's viewpoint)
CONCLUSION	Strong concluding statement reinforces the thesis and emphasizes compromise

⊖ EXERCISE 6.2

The following student essay includes all the elements of a Rogerian argument. This essay was written in response to the question, "Is it fair for instructors to require students to turn off their cell phones in class?" After you read the essay, answer the questions on pages 192–193, consulting the outline above if necessary.

WHY CELL PHONES DO NOT BELONG IN THE CLASSROOM

ZOYA KAHN

Thesis statement

Reader's view of the situation

Some college students think it is unfair for instructors to require them to turn off their cell phones during class. Because they are accustomed to constant cell phone access, they don't understand how such a rule is justified. Granted, a strict, no-exceptions policy requiring that cell phones be turned off all over campus is not fair, but neither is a policy that prevents instructors from imposing restrictions ("Official Notices"). Both students and instructors know that cell phone use— including texting—during class can be disruptive. In addition, most would agree that the primary goal of a university is to create a respectful learning environment and that cell phone use during class undercuts this goal. For this reason, it is in everyone's interest for instructors to institute policies that require students to turn off cell phones during class.

Many students believe that requiring them to turn off their cell phones is unfair because it makes them feel less safe. Students are understandably concerned that, with their phones turned off, they will be unreachable during an emergency. For example, text message alerts are part of the emergency response system for most universities. Similarly, cell phones are a way for friends and family to contact students if there is an emergency. For these reasons, many students think that they should be free to make their own decisions concerning cell use. They believe that by turning their phones to vibrate or silent mode, they are showing respect for their classmates. As one student points out, "Only a small percentage of students will misuse their phones. Then, why should every student have to sacrifice for someone's mistakes?" (SchoolBook). After all, most students are honest and courteous. However, those few students who are determined to misuse their phones will do so, regardless of the school's phone policy.

1

2

3   To protect the integrity of the school's learning environment, instructors are justified in requiring students to turn off their phones. Recent studies have shown how distracting cell phones can be during a class. For example, a ringing cell phone significantly impairs students' performance, and a vibrating phone can be just as distracting (End et al. 56–57). In addition, texting in class decreases students' ability to focus, lowers test performance, and lessens students' retention of class material (Tindell and Bohlander 2). According to a recent study, most students believe that texting causes problems, "including a negative impact on classroom learning for the person who is texting, and distraction for those sitting nearby" (Tindell and Bohlander 4). Even more disturbing, cell phones enable some students to cheat. Students can use cell phones to text test questions and answers, to search the Web, and to photograph exams. Although asking students to turn off their phones will not prevent all these problems, it will reduce the abuses, and this will benefit the majority of students.

Writer's view of the situation

4   Students have good reasons for wanting to keep their phones on, but there are even better reasons for accepting some reasonable restrictions. First, when students use cell phones during class, they distract themselves (as well as their classmates) and undermine everyone's ability to learn. Second, having their cell phones on gives students a false sense of security. A leading cell phone company has found that cell phones can actually "detract from school safety and crisis preparedness" in numerous ways. For example, the use of cell phones during a crisis can overload the cell phone system and make it useless. In addition, cell phones make it easy for students to spread rumors and, in some cases, cell phone use has created more panic than the incidents that actually caused the rumors ("Cell Phones").

Benefits of writer's position

5   One possible compromise is for instructors to join with students to create cell phone policies that take into consideration various situations and settings. For example, instructors could require students to turn off their phones only during exams. Instructors could also try to find ways to engage students by using cell phone technology in the classroom. For example, in some schools teachers take advantage of the various functions available on most cell phones—calculators,

Possible compromise

cameras, dictionaries, and Internet browsers ("Cell Phones"). In addition, schools should consider implementing alternative emergency alert systems. Such compromises would ensure safety, limit possible disruptions, reduce the potential for academic dishonesty, and enhance learning.

It is understandable that students want instructors to permit the use of cell phones during class, but it is also fair for instructors to ask students to turn them off. Although instructors should be able to restrict cell phone use, they should also make sure that students understand the need for this policy. It is in everyone's best interest to protect the integrity of the classroom and to make sure that learning is not compromised by cell phone use. To ensure the success of their education, students should be willing to turn off their phones.

Concluding statement

6

Works Cited

"Cell Phones and Text Messaging in Schools." *National School Safety and Security Services.* National School Safety and Security Services, 2012. Web. 29 Jan. 2012.

End, Christian M., Shaye Worthman, Mary Bridget Mathews, and Katharina Wetterau. "Costly Cell Phones: The Impact of Cell Phone Rings on Academic Performance." *Teaching of Psychology* 37.1 (2010): 55–57. *Academic Search Complete.* Web. 30 Jan. 2012.

"Official Notices." *UCLA Registrar's Office, Department of Student Affairs.* UCLA, 24 Oct. 2011. Web. 29 Jan. 2012.

SchoolBook. "Time to Repeal the Cell Phone Ban, Students Say." *New York Times,* 2 Nov. 2011. Web. 29 Jan. 2012.

Tindell, Deborah R., and Robert W. Bohlander. "The Use and Abuse of Cell Phones and Text Messaging in the Classroom: A Survey of College Students." *College Teaching* 60.1 (2012): 1–9. *Academic Search Complete.* Web. 29 Jan. 2012.

Identifying the Elements of a Rogerian Argument

1. Where in the essay does the writer attempt to establish common ground? Do you think she is successful?

2. Where does the writer state her position? What evidence does she supply to support this position?

3. What points does the conclusion emphasize? Other than reinforcing the writer's position, what else is the conclusion trying to accomplish?

4. Does the concluding statement reinforce agreement and compromise?

5. How would this essay be different if it were written as a traditional (as opposed to a Rogerian) argument?

Understanding Toulmin Logic

Another way of describing the structure of argument was introduced by the philosopher Stephen Toulmin in his book *The Uses of Argument* (1958). Toulmin observed that although formal logic is effective for analyzing highly specialized arguments, it is inadequate for describing the arguments that occur in everyday life. Although Toulmin was primarily concerned with the structures of arguments at the level of sentences or paragraphs, his model is also useful when dealing with longer arguments.

In its simplest terms, a **Toulmin argument** has three parts—the *claim*, the *grounds*, and the *warrant*. The **claim** is the main point of the essay— usually stated as the thesis. The **grounds** are the evidence that a writer uses to support the claim. The **warrant** is the inference—either stated or implied—that connects the claim to the grounds.

A basic argument using Toulmin logic would have the following structure.

CLAIM	Online education should be a part of all students' education.
GROUNDS	Students who take advantage of online education get better grades and report less stress than students who do not.
WARRANT	Online education is a valuable educational option.

Notice that the three-part structure above resembles the **syllogism** that is the backbone of classical argument. (See p. 115 for a discussion of syllogisms.)

> **NOTE**
>
> When you use Toulmin logic to construct an argument, you still use deductive and inductive reasoning. You arrive at your claim inductively from facts, observations, and examples, and you connect the grounds and the warrant to your claim deductively.

Constructing Toulmin Arguments

Real arguments—those you encounter in print or online every day—are not as simple as the three-part model on the preceding page implies. To be convincing, arguments often contain additional elements. To account for the demands of everyday debates, Toulmin expanded his model.

CLAIM

The **claim** is the main point of your essay. It is a debatable statement that the rest of the essay will support.

Online education should be a part of all students' education.

REASON

The **reason** is a statement that supports the claim. Often the reason appears in the same sentence, with the claim connected to it by the word *because*. (In an argumentative essay, this sentence is the thesis statement.)

*Online education should be a part of all students' education **because** it enables them to have a more successful and less stressful college experience.*

WARRANT

The **warrant** is the inference that connects the claim and the grounds. The warrant is often an unstated assumption. Ideally, the warrant should be an idea with which your readers will agree. (If they do not agree with it, you will need to supply **backing**.)

Online education is a valuable educational option.

BACKING

The **backing** consists of statements that support the warrant.

My own experience with online education was positive. Not only did it enable me to schedule classes around my job, but it also enabled me to work at my own pace in my courses.

GROUNDS

The **grounds** are the concrete evidence that a writer uses to support the claim. These are the facts and observations that support the thesis. They can also be the opinions of experts that you locate when you do research.

Studies show that students who take advantage of online education often get better grades than students who do not.

Research indicates that students who take advantage of online education are under less stress than those who are not.

QUALIFIERS

The **qualifiers** are statements that limit the claim. For example, they can be the real-world conditions under which the claim is true. These qualifiers can include words such as *most, few, some, sometimes, occasionally, often,* and *usually.*

Online education should be a required part of most students' education.

REBUTTALS

The **rebuttals** are exceptions to the claim. They are counterarguments that identify the situations where the claim does not hold true.

Some people argue that online education deprives students of an interactive classroom experience, but a course chat room can give students a similar opportunity to interact with their classmates.

❯ EXERCISE 6.3

Look through this book's table of contents, and select an At Issue topic that interests you (ideally, one that you know something about). Write a sentence that states your position on this issue. (In terms of Toulmin argument, this statement is the *claim.*)

Then, supply as many of the expanded Toulmin model elements as you can, consulting the description of these elements above.

Reason: _____

_____

Warrant: _____

_____

_____

Backing: _____

_____

_____

Grounds: _____

_____

Qualifiers: _____

_____

_____

Rebuttals: _____

_____

Writing Toulmin Arguments

One of the strengths of the Toulmin model of argument is that it emphasizes that presenting effective arguments involves more than stating ideas in absolute terms. Unlike the classical model of argument, the Toulmin model encourages writers to make realistic and convincing points by including claims and qualifiers and by addressing opposing arguments in down-to-earth and constructive ways. In a sense, this method of constructing an argument reminds writers that arguments do not exist in a vacuum. They are aimed at real readers who may or may not agree with them.

In general, a Toulmin argument can be organized in the following way:

INTRODUCTION   Introduces the problem

States the claim and the reason (and possibly the qualifier)

BODY   Possibly states the warrant

Presents the backing that supports the warrant

Presents the grounds that support the claim

Presents the conditions of rebuttal

States the qualifiers

CONCLUSION   Brings the argument to a close

Strong concluding statement reinforces the claim

➲ EXERCISE 6.4

The following student essay, which includes all the elements of a Toulmin argument, was written in response to the question, "Are cheerleaders athletes?" After you read the essay, answer the questions on page 199, consulting the outline above if necessary.

COMPETITIVE CHEERLEADERS ARE ATHLETES

JEN DAVIS

Recently, the call to make competitive cheerleading an official   1
college sport and to recognize cheerleaders as athletes has gotten
stronger. Critics of this proposal maintain that cheerleading is simply

entertainment that occurs on the sidelines of real sporting events. According to them, although cheerleading may show strength and skill, it is not a competitive activity. This view of cheerleading, however, misses the point. Because competitive cheerleading pits teams against each other in physically and technically demanding athletic contests, it should be recognized as a sport. For this reason, those who participate in the sport of competitive cheerleading should be considered athletes.

Reason

Claim and qualifier

2   Acknowledging cheerleaders as athletes gives them the respect and support they deserve. Many people associate cheerleading with pom-poms and short skirts and ignore the strength and skill competitive cheerleading requires. Like athletes in other female-dominated sports, cheerleaders unfortunately have had to fight to be taken seriously. For example, Title IX, the law that mandates gender equity in college sports, does not recognize competitive cheerleading as a sport. This situation demonstrates a very narrow definition of sports, one that needs to be updated. As one women's sports advocate explains, "What we consider sports are things that men have traditionally played" (qtd. in Thomas). For this reason, women's versions of long-accepted men's sports—such as basketball, soccer, and track—are easy for people to respect and to support. Competitive cheerleading, however, departs from this model and is not seen as a sport even though those who compete in it are skilled, accomplished athletes. As one coach points out, the athleticism of cheerleading is undeniable: "We don't throw balls, we throw people. And we catch them" (qtd. in Thomas).

Warrant

Backing

Grounds

3   Recent proposals to rename competitive cheerleading "stunt" or "team acrobatics and tumbling" are an effort to reshape people's ideas about what cheerleaders actually do. Although some cheerleading squads have kept to their original purpose—to lead fans in cheering on their teams—competitive teams practice rigorously, maintain impressive levels of physical fitness, and risk serious injuries. Like other sports, competitive cheerleading involves extraordinary feats of strength and skill. Cheerleaders perform elaborate floor routines and ambitious stunts, including flips from multilevel human pyramids. Competitive cheerleaders also do what all athletes must do: they compete. Even a critic concedes that cheerleading could be "considered a sport when cheerleading groups compete against one another" (Sandler). Competitive

Backing

Grounds

cheerleading teams do just that; they enter competitive contests, are judged, and emerge as winners or losers.

Rebuttal

Those in authority, however, are slow to realize that cheerleading is a sport. In 2010, a federal judge declared that competitive cheerleading was "too underdeveloped and disorganized" to qualify as a legitimate varsity sport under Title IX (Tigay). This ruling was shortsighted. Before competitive cheerleading can develop as a sport, it needs to be *acknowledged* as a sport. Without their schools' financial support, cheerleading teams cannot recruit, offer scholarships, or host competitions. To address this situation, several national groups are asking the National Collegiate Athletic Association (NCAA) to designate competitive cheerleading as an "emerging sport." By doing this, the NCAA would show its support and help competitive cheerleading to develop and eventually to flourish. This does not mean, however, that all cheerleaders are athletes or that all cheerleading is a sport. In addition, the NCAA does have reason to be cautious when it comes to redefining competitive cheerleading. Some schools have taken sideline cheerleading teams and recategorized them just so they could comply with Title IX. These efforts to sidestep the purpose of the law are, as one expert puts it, "obviously transparent and unethical" (Tigay). Even so, fear of possible abuse should not keep the NCAA from doing what is right and giving legitimate athletes the respect and support they deserve.

Qualifiers

Competitive cheerleaders are athletes in every sense of the word. They are aggressive, highly skilled, physically fit competitors. For this reason, they deserve to be acknowledged as athletes under Title IX and supported by their schools and by the NCAA. Biased and outdated ideas about what is (and what is not) a sport should not keep competitive cheerleading from being recognized as the sport it is. As one proponent puts it, "Adding flexibility to the definition of college athletes is a common sense move that everyone can cheer for" ("Bona Fide"). It is time to give competitive cheerleaders the support and recognition they deserve.

Concluding statement

4

5

Works Cited

"Bona Fide Athletes." Editorial. *USA Today.* Gannett, 16 Oct. 2009. Web. 8 Feb. 2012.

Sandler, Bernice R. "Certain Types of Competition Define Sports." *USA Today* 22 Oct. 2009. *Academic Search Complete.* Web. 7 Feb. 2012.

Thomas, Katie. "Born on the Sideline, Cheering Clamors to Be a Sport."
New York Times. New York Times, 22 May 2011. Web. 5 Feb. 2012.

Tigay, Chanan. "Is Cheerleading a Sport Protected by Title IX?" *CQ*
Researcher 25 Mar. 2011: 276. *Gale Power Search*. Web. 9 Feb. 2012.

Identifying the Elements of a Toulmin Argument

1. Summarize the position this essay takes as a three-part argument that includes the claim, the grounds, and the warrant.

2. Do you think the writer includes enough backing for her claim? What other supporting evidence could she have included?

3. Find the qualifier in the essay. How does it limit the argument? How else could the writer have qualified the argument?

4. Do you think the writer addresses enough objections to her claim? What other arguments could she have addressed?

5. Based on your reading of this essay, what advantages do you think Toulmin logic offers to writers? What disadvantages does it present?

Understanding Oral Arguments

Many everyday arguments—in school, on the job, or in your community— are presented orally. In many ways, an oral argument is similar to a written one: it has an introduction, a body, and a conclusion, and it addresses and refutes opposing points of view. In other, more subtle ways, however, an oral argument is different from a written one. Before you plan and deliver an oral argument, you should be aware of these differences.

The major difference between an oral argument and a written one is that an audience cannot reread an oral argument to clarify information. Listeners have to understand an oral argument the first time they hear it. To help your listeners, you need to design your presentation with this limitation in mind, considering the following guidelines:

- **An oral argument should contain verbal signals that help guide listeners.** Transitional phrases such as "My first point," "My second point," and "Let me sum up" are useful in oral arguments, where listeners do not have a written text in front of them. They alert listeners to information to come and signal shifts from one point to another.

- **An oral argument should use simple, direct language and avoid long sentences.** Complicated sentences that contain elevated language and numerous technical terms are difficult for listeners to follow. For this reason, your sentences should be straightforward and easy to understand.

- **An oral argument should repeat key information.** A traditional rule of thumb for oral arguments is, "Tell listeners what you're going to tell them; then tell it to them; finally, tell them what you've told them." In other words, in the introduction of an oral argument, tell your listeners what they are going to hear; in the body, discuss your points, one at a time; and finally, in your conclusion, restate your points. This intentional repetition ensures that your listeners follow (and remember) your points.

- **An oral argument should include visuals.** Visual aids can make your argument easier to follow. You can use visuals to identify your points as you discuss them. You can also use visuals—for example, charts, graphs, or tables—to clarify or reinforce key points as well as to add interest. Carefully selected visuals help increase the chances that what you are saying will be remembered.

Planning an Oral Argument

The work you do to plan your presentation is as important as the presentation itself. Here is some advice to consider as you plan your oral argument:

1. **Choose your topic wisely.** Try to select a topic that is somewhat controversial so listeners will want to hear your views. You can create interest in a topic, but it is easier to appeal to listeners if they are already interested in what you have to say. In addition, try to choose a topic that you know something about. Even though you will probably do some research, the process will be much easier if you are already familiar with the basic issues.

2. **Know your audience.** Try to determine what your audience already knows about your topic. Also, assess their attitudes toward your topic. Are they friendly? Neutral? Hostile? The answers to these questions will help you decide what information to include and which arguments will most likely be effective (and which will not).

3. **Know your time limit.** Most oral presentations have a time limit. If you run over your allotted time, you risk boring or annoying your listeners. If you finish too soon, it will seem as if you don't know much about your subject. As you prepare your argument, include all the information that you can cover within your time limit. Keep in mind that you will not be able to go into as much detail in a short speech as you will in a long speech, so plan accordingly.

Visual aids can help listeners follow an oral presentation.

4. **Identify your thesis statement.** Like a written argument, an oral argument should have a debatable thesis statement. Keep this statement simple, and make sure that it clearly conveys your position. Remember that in an oral argument, your listeners have to understand your thesis the first time they hear it. (See Chapter 7 for more on developing a thesis statement.)

5. **Gather support for your thesis.** You need to support your thesis convincingly if you expect listeners to accept it. Supporting evidence can be in the form of facts, observations, expert opinion, or statistics. Some of your support can come from your own experiences, but most will come from your research.

6. **Acknowledge your sources.** Remember that all of the information you get from your research needs to be acknowledged. As you deliver your presentation, let listeners know where the information you are using comes from—for example, "According to a 2012 editorial in the *New York Times . . .*" or "As Kenneth Davis says in his book *America's Hidden History. . . .*" This strategy enhances your credibility by showing that you are well informed about your topic. (Including source information also helps you protect yourself from unintentional **plagiarism**. See Chapter 11.)

7. **Prepare your speaking notes.** Effective speakers do not read their speeches. Instead, they prepare **speaking notes**—usually on index cards—that list the points they want to make. (Some speakers write out the full text of their speech or make a detailed outline of their speech

and then prepare the notes from this material.) These notes guide you as you speak, so you should make sure that there are not too many of them and that they contain just key information. (It is a good idea to number your note cards so you can be sure that they remain in the correct order.)

8. **Prepare visual aids.** Visual aids help you to communicate your thesis and your supporting points more effectively. Visuals increase interest in your presentation, and they also strengthen your argument by reinforcing your points and making them easier for listeners to follow and to understand. In addition, visuals can help establish your credibility and thus improve the persuasiveness of your argument.

    You can use the following types of visual aids in your presentations:

    - Diagrams
    - Photographs
    - Slides
    - Flip charts
    - Overhead transparencies
    - Document cameras
    - Handouts
    - Objects

    In addition to these kinds of visual aids, you can also use **presentation software**, such as Microsoft's PowerPoint or the Web-based application *Prezi* (Prezi.com). With presentation software, you can easily create visually appealing and persuasive slides. You can insert scanned photographs or drawings into slides, or you can cut and paste charts, graphs, and tables into them. You can even include YouTube videos and MP3 files. Keep in mind, however, that the images, videos, or sound files that you use must support your thesis; if they are irrelevant, they will distract or confuse your listeners. (See pp. 210–212 for examples of PowerPoint slides.)

9. **Practice your presentation.** As a general rule, you should spend as much time rehearsing your speech as you do preparing it. In other words, practice, practice, practice. Be sure you know the order in which you will present your points and when you will move from one visual to another. Rehearse your speech aloud with just your speaking notes and your visuals until you are confident that you can get through your presentation effectively. Try to anticipate any problems that may arise with your visuals, and solve them at this stage of the process. If possible, practice your speech in the room in which you will actually deliver it. Bring along a friend, and ask for feedback. Finally, cut or add material as needed until you are certain that you can stay within your time limit.

CHECKLIST

Designing and Displaying Visuals

☐ Use images that are large enough for your audience to see and that will reproduce clearly.

☐ Make lettering large enough for your audience to see. Use 40- to 50-point type for titles, 25- to 30-point type for major points, and 20- to 25-point type for less important points.

☐ Use bulleted lists, not full sentences or paragraphs.

☐ Put no more than three or four points on a single visual.

☐ Make sure there is a clear contrast between your lettering and the background.

☐ Don't show your listeners the visual before you begin to speak about it. Display the visual only when you discuss it.

☐ Face your listeners when you discuss a visual. Even if you point to the screen, always look at your listeners. Never turn your back on your audience.

☐ Introduce and discuss each visual. Don't simply show or read the visual to your audience. Always tell listeners more than they can read or see for themselves.

☐ Don't use elaborate visuals or special effects that will distract your audience.

➲ EXERCISE 6.5

Look through the table of contents of this book, and select three At Issue topics that interest you. Imagine that you are planning to deliver an oral argument to a group of college students on each of these topics. For each topic, list three visual aids you could use to enhance your presentation.

Delivering Oral Arguments

Delivery is the most important part of a speech. The way you speak, your interaction with the audience, your posture, and your eye contact all affect your overall presentation. In short, a confident, controlled speaker will have a positive impact on an audience, while a speaker who fumbles with note cards, speaks in a shaky voice, or seems disorganized will lose credibility. To make sure that your listeners see you as a credible, reliable source of information, follow these guidelines:

1. **Accept nervousness.** For most people, nervousness is part of the speech process. The trick is to convert this nervousness into energy that you

can channel into your speech. The first step in dealing with nervousness is to make sure that you have rehearsed enough. If you have prepared adequately, you will probably be able to handle any problem you may encounter. If you make a mistake, you can correct it. If you forget something, you can fit it in later.

DEALING WITH NERVOUSNESS

If nervousness is a problem, the following strategies can help you to relax:

- **Breathe deeply.** Take a few deep breaths before you begin speaking. Research has shown that increased oxygen has a calming effect on the brain.

- **Use visualization.** Imagine yourself delivering a successful speech, and fix this image in your mind. It can help dispel anxiety.

- **Empty your mind.** Consciously try to eliminate all negative thoughts. Think of your mind as a room full of furniture. Imagine yourself removing each piece of furniture until the room is empty.

- **Drink water.** Before you begin to speak, take a few sips of water. Doing so will eliminate the dry mouth that is a result of nervousness.

- **Keep things in perspective.** Remember, your speech is a minor event in your life. Nothing that you do or say will affect you significantly.

---

2. **Look at your audience.** When you speak, look directly at the members of your audience. At the beginning of the speech, make eye contact with a few audience members who seem to be responding positively. As your speech progresses, look directly at as many audience members as you can. Try to sweep the entire room. Don't focus excessively on a single person or on a single section of your audience.

3. **Speak naturally.** Your presentation should sound like a conversation, not like a performance. This is not to suggest that your presentation should include slang, ungrammatical constructions, or colloquialisms; it should conform to the rules of standard English. The trick is to maintain the appearance of a conversation while following the conventions of public speaking. Achieving this balance takes practice, but it is a goal worth pursuing.

4. **Speak slowly.** When you give an oral presentation, you should speak more slowly than you do in normal conversation. This strategy gives listeners time to process what they hear—and gives you time to think about what you are saying.

5. **Speak clearly and correctly.** As you deliver your presentation, speak clearly. Do not drop endings, and be careful to pronounce words correctly. Look up the pronunciation of unfamiliar words in a dictionary, or ask your instructor for help. If you go though an entire speech pronouncing a key term or a name incorrectly, your listeners will question your competence.

6. **Move purposefully.** As you deliver your speech, don't pace, move your hands erratically, or play with your note cards. Try to stand in one spot, with both feet flat on the floor. Move only when necessary—for example, to point to a visual or to display an object. If you intend to distribute printed material to your listeners, do so only when you are going to discuss it. (Try to arrange in advance for someone else to give out your handouts.) If you are not going to refer to the material in your presentation, wait until you have finished your speech before you distribute it. Depending on the level of formality of your presentation and the size of your audience, you may want to stand directly in front of your audience or behind a podium.

7. **Be prepared for the unexpected.** Don't get flustered if things don't go exactly as you planned. If you forget material, work it in later. If you make a mistake, correct it without apologizing. Most of the time, listeners will not realize that something has gone wrong unless you call attention to it. If someone in the audience looks bored, don't worry. You might consider changing your pace or your volume, but keep in mind that the person's reaction might have nothing to do with your presentation. He or she might be tired, preoccupied, or just a poor listener.

Michelle Obama projects confidence and control as she speaks.

8. **Leave time for questions.** End your presentation by asking if your listeners have any questions. As you answer questions, keep in mind the following advice:

   - *Be prepared.* Make sure you have anticipated the obvious counterarguments to your position, and be prepared to address them. In addition, prepare a list of Web sites or other resources that you can refer your audience to for more information.

   - *Repeat a question before you answer it.* This technique enables everyone in the audience to hear the question, and it also gives you time to think of an answer.

   - *Keep control of interchanges.* If a questioner repeatedly challenges your answer or monopolizes the conversation, say that you will be glad to discuss the matter with him or her after your presentation is finished.

   - *Be honest.* Answer questions honestly and forthrightly. If you don't know the answer to a question, say so. Tell the questioner you will locate the information that he or she wants and send it by email. Above all, do not volunteer information that you are not sure is correct.

   - *Use the last question to summarize.* When you get to the last question, end your answer by restating the main point of your argument.

Composing an Oral Argument

The written text of an oral argument is organized just as any other argument is: it has an introduction that gives the background of the issue and states the thesis, it has a body that presents evidence that supports the thesis, it identifies and refutes arguments against the thesis, and it ends with a concluding statement.

In general, an oral argument can be structured in the following way:

INTRODUCTION	Presents the background of the issue
	States the thesis
BODY	Presents evidence: Point 1 in support of the thesis
	Presents evidence: Point 2 in support of the thesis
	Presents evidence: Point 3 in support of the thesis
	Refutes opposing arguments
CONCLUSION	Brings the argument to a close
	Concluding statement restates thesis
	Speaker asks for questions

➔ EXERCISE 6.6

The following oral argument was presented by a student in a speech course in response to the assignment, "Argue for or against the advantages of a 'gap year' between high school and college." (Her PowerPoint slides appear at the end of the speech.) After you read this argument, answer the questions on page 212, consulting the outline above if necessary.

AN ARGUMENT IN SUPPORT OF THE "GAP YEAR"

CHANTEE STEELE

1   *College:* even the word sounded wonderful when I was in high school. Everyone told me it would be the best time of my life. They told me that I would take courses in exciting new subjects and that I'd make lifelong friends. [Show slide 1.] What they didn't tell me was that I would be anxious, confused, and uncertain about my major and about my future. Although this is only my second year in college, I've already changed my major once, and to be honest, I'm still not sure I've made the right decision. But during the process of changing majors, my adviser gave me some reading material that included information about a "gap year." A gap year is a year off between high school and college when students focus on work or community service and learn about themselves—something that would have benefited me. Although gaining popularity in the United States, the gap year still suggests images of spoiled rich kids who want to play for a year before going to college. According to educator Christina Wood, however, in the United Kingdom a gap year is common; it is seen as a time for personal growth that helps students mature (36). [Show slide 2.] In fact, 230,000 British students take a gap year before going to college. As the rest of my speech will show, a well-planned gap year gives students time to mature, to explore potential careers, and to volunteer or travel.   **Thesis statement**

2   [Show slide 3.] Apparently I'm not alone in my uncertainty about my major or about my future. As Holly Bull, a professional gap-year counselor, explains, "The National Research Center for College and University Admissions estimates that over 50% of students switch majors   **Evidence: Point 1 in support of thesis**

at least once" (8). As they go from high school to college, most students have little time to think about what to do with their lives. A gap year before college would give them time to learn more about themselves. According to Wood, "Gap years provide valuable life experiences and maturity so students are more ready to focus on their studies when they return" (37). A year off would give some students the perspective they need to mature and to feel more confident about their decisions. Bull agrees, noting that the gap year helps students choose or confirm the area of study they want to pursue, that it makes them "instantly more mature," and that it "boosts their excitement about learning" (7–8).

Evidence: Point 2 in support of thesis

The gap year gives students many options to explore before going to   3
college. [Show slide 4.] This slide shows just some of the resources students can use as they prepare for their gap year. As you can see, they can explore opportunities for employment, education, and volunteer work. There are even resources for students who are undecided. As David Lesesne, the dean of admissions at Sewanee, says, "Some students do very interesting and enriching things: hike the Appalachian Trail, herd sheep in Crete, play in a rock band, [or even] attend school in Guatemala" (qtd. in Wood 37). Many other students, especially in these economic hard times, use the gap year to earn money to offset the high cost of their education (Wood 35).

Evidence: Point 3 in support of thesis

Taking a gap year can also help students to get into better colleges. According to an article by the dean of admissions at Harvard, "Occasionally students are admitted to Harvard or other colleges in part because they accomplished something unusual during a year off" (Fitzsimmons, McGrath, and Ducey). Depending on the scope of their service or work, a gap year could enable students to earn scholarships that they were not eligible for before. In fact, some colleges actually recommend that students take time off after high school. Harvard is one of several U.S. colleges that "encourages admitted students to defer enrollment for one year to travel, pursue a special project or activity, work, or spend time in another meaningful way" (Fitzsimmons, McGrath, and Ducey). Furthermore, evidence shows that a gap year can help students to be more successful after they begin in college. One Middlebury College admissions officer has calculated that "a single gap semester was the strongest predictor of academic success at his school" (Bull 7). Given this support for the gap year and given the resources that are now available to help students plan it, the negative attitudes about it in the United States are beginning to change.

5   In spite of these benefits, parental concerns about "slackerdom" and money are common. Supporters of the gap year acknowledge that students have to be motivated to make the most of their experiences. Clearly, the gap year is not for everyone. For example, students who are not self-motivated may not benefit from a gap year. In addition, parents worry about how much money the gap year will cost them. This is a real concern when you add the year off to the expense of four years of college (Wood 37). However, if finances are a serious concern, students can spend their gap year working in their own communities or taking advantage of a paid experience like AmeriCorps—which, as the AmeriCorps Web site shows, covers students' room and board *and* offers an educational stipend after students complete the program. [Show slide 5.] Additionally, parents and students should consider the time and money that is wasted when a student who is not ready for college starts school and then drops out.

Refutation of opposing arguments

6   After considering the benefits of a gap year, I have concluded that more students should postpone college for a year. Many students (like me) are uncertain about their goals. We welcome new opportunities and are eager to learn from new experiences and may find a year of service both emotionally and intellectually rewarding. Given another year to mature, many of us would return to school with a greater sense of purpose, focus, and clarity. In some cases, the gap year could actually help us get into better schools and possibly get more financial aid. If we intend to take the college experience seriously, spending a gap year learning about our interests and abilities would help us to become better, more confident, and ultimately more focused students. [Show slide 6.]

Concluding statement

7   Are there any questions?

Works Cited

Bull, Holly. "Navigating a Gap Year." *TeenLife* Feb. 2011: 6–9. Print.

Fitzsimmons, William, Marlyn E. McGrath, and Charles Ducey. "Time Out or Burn Out for the Next Generation." *Harvard College Office of Admissions*. Harvard U, 2011. Web. 7 Apr. 2012.

Wood, Christina. "Should You Take a 'Gap Year'?" *Careers and Colleges* Fall 2007: 36–37. Print.

Slide 1

Slide 2

230,000 students between 18 and 25 take a Gap
Year in the U.K.

—Tom Griffiths, founder and director
of GapYear.com

(qtd. in Christina Wood, "Should You Take a 'Gap Year'?,"
Careers and Colleges Fall 2007)

Slide 3

50% of students change their major at least once.

—National Research Center for College
and University Admissions

Slide 4

A Few Links for the Potential "Gapster"

(links from Holly Bull, "The Possibilities of the Gap Year," *Chronicle of Higher Education* 52.44 [2006])

Employment

Cool Works: CoolWorks.com (domestic jobs)

Working Abroad: WorkingAbroad.org (jobs overseas)

Education

Global Routes: GlobalRoutes.org (semester-long courses)

Sea-mester: Seamester.com (sea voyage programs)

Volunteer Work

AmeriCorps: AmeriCorps.gov

City Year: CityYear.org

Thoughtful Texts for Fence Sitters

Karl Haigler and Rae Nelson, *The Gap-Year Advantage* (Macmillan, 2005)

Colin Hall, *Taking Time Off* (Princeton Review, 2003)

Charlotte Hindle and Joe Bindloss, *The Gap Year Book* (Lonely Planet, 2005)

Slide 5

Slide 6

Identifying the Elements of an Oral Argument

1. Where does this oral argument include verbal signals to help guide readers?

2. Does this oral argument use simple, direct language? What sections of the speech, if any, could be made simpler?

3. Where does this oral argument repeat key information for emphasis? Is there any other information that you think should have been repeated?

4. What opposing arguments does the speaker identify? Does she refute them convincingly?

5. How effective are the visuals that accompany the text of this oral argument? Are there enough visuals? Are they placed correctly? What other information do you think could have been displayed in a visual?

6. What questions would you ask this speaker at the end of her speech?

Is Online Education as Good as Classroom Education?

Go back to page 185, and reread the At Issue box, which gives background about whether online education is as good as classroom instruction. As the following sources illustrate, this question has a number of possible answers.

After you review the sources listed below, you will be asked to answer some questions and to complete some simple activities. This work will help you to understand both the content and the structure of the sources. When you are finished, you will be ready to develop an argument—using one of the three alternative approaches to argument discussed in this chapter—that takes a position on whether online education is as effective as classroom learning.

SOURCES

 Bill Maxwell, "No Short Cuts in Long-Distance Learning," p. 214

 Chris Bustamante, "The Risks and Rewards of Online Learning," p. 217

 David Smith, "Reliance on Online Materials Hinders Learning Potential for Students," p. 221

 Elena Kadvany, "Online Education Needs Connection," p. 224

 John Crisp, "Short Distance Learning," p. 226

 Rachel Farhi, "Online Education Innovators Should Be Wary," p. 229

 Campus Explorer, "Online School Degree Programs," p. 231

 Seattle Central Community College, "Distance Education and *e*-Learning," p. 235

 "Two Views of Online Education," p. 236

 For comprehension quizzes, see bedfordstmartins.com/practicalargument.

This opinion column appeared in the *Tampa Bay Times* on July 24, 2011.

NO SHORT CUTS IN LONG-DISTANCE LEARNING

BILL MAXWELL

Distance learning is one of the national rallying cries of Republican politicians 1 and state education officials seeking cheap ways to graduate more students attending public colleges. Community colleges, the old doormats of post-secondary learning that were founded on the sensible notion that anybody who wants an education should be able to get one, are major players in this Web-based instruction movement.

Economists and social scientists know that if the United States intends to 2 remain an economic leader internationally, a much larger portion of the work force must be educated, including citizens who traditionally have been shunned by colleges: low-income students, working adults, select minorities, and those who need remediation before they can tackle college-level work.

Here is where community colleges come in. They enroll more students 3 than their four-year counterparts. As such, many politicians, with the support of community college presidents and state officials, see these schools as ideal, cost-effective places to boost online learning.

Besides saving the colleges money, online courses reduce scheduling con- 4 flicts for students with families and jobs and other commitments. But according to a recent study released by the Community College Research Center at the Teachers College at Columbia University, Web-based instruction is not the magic bullet for educating more community college students. The research found, in fact, that community college students in online courses fail and drop out more often than students in classroom-based courses.

> "Web-based instruction is not the magic bullet."

Researchers followed the academic history of 51,000 students in the state 5 of Washington between 2004 and 2009 and found an 8 percent gap in comple-tion rates between students in distance courses and those in face-to-face courses. Two other troubling findings of the study were that students with online credits did not graduate or transfer to four-year schools as often as those enrolled in traditional coursework, and those in online remedial courses fared far worse than remedial students in face-to-face courses.

A second study, conducted for the Virginia community college system, 6 found similar gaps between students in distance courses and those in tradi-tional courses.

Postsecondary online courses are here to stay and will play an increasingly 7 critical role in educating a competitive U.S. work force of people who will demand a lot of flexibility. But community colleges should not succumb to the lure of increased funding only to implement slipshod efforts that ill serve their students. While they are increasing their online offerings, community colleges must make student success in these courses a priority.

The very idea of the community college, open enrollment to residents 8 with a high school diploma or its equivalent, sets many students up for failure. Add to that the enticement of distance learning—never having to leave home to take courses—and we get immature students who are in over their heads from the beginning.

What should community colleges do to improve online learning? The 9 Virginia study suggests, among other strategies:

- Students should be tested for their preparedness for online instruction.

- Online students should be given a dose of reality about time management. They need to be taught from the outset that while working at home with the family around can be advantageous, it can become a trap.

- Students need to be trained to navigate the online course-related computer systems necessary to complete their coursework.

- Faculty members should be trained for online instruction so that they can competently guide their students.

- Colleges should improve support services, offering, for example, 24/7 online tutoring.

As the studies show, distance learning is not a panacea for graduating 10 more community college students. But if it is done effectively, it will become an essential part of sustaining the nation's economic viability in the world.

⊙ AT ISSUE: SOURCES FOR USING ALTERNATIVE APPROACHES TO ARGUMENT

1. What assumptions does Maxwell make in paragraph 2? Are these assumptions self-evident, or should he have included evidence to support them?

2. According to Maxwell, what special niche do community colleges occupy?

3. What does Maxwell mean in paragraph 4 when he says, "Web-based instruction is not the magic bullet for educating more community college students"? Why not? According to Maxwell, what problems does research identify in online education for community college students?

4. According to the Virginia study Maxwell cites, what can community colleges do to address the problems that some students have with online education? How realistic are these suggestions?

5. Use Toulmin logic to analyze Maxwell's argument, identifying the argument's claim, its grounds, and its warrant. Does he include qualifiers and rebuttals? If not, should he have? Does Maxwell appeal only to *logos* in his argument, or does he appeal to *pathos* and *ethos* as well? Explain.

6. This newspaper column is an inductive argument, and Maxwell does not state his thesis until his last paragraph. Paraphrase this thesis statement by filling in the following template.

Although online education _____

_____, it can become _____

_____.

This essay is from the online newspaper *Community College Times*. It appeared on November 16, 2011.

THE RISKS AND REWARDS OF ONLINE LEARNING

CHRIS BUSTAMANTE

In 2008, investors wanted to buy Rio Salado College, the nation's largest online 1
public community college headquartered in Tempe, Ariz. The offer was more
than $400 million with plans to convert it into a national, for-profit, online
school.

Rio Salado wasn't for sale, but the offer proved how much demand exists 2
for serving students who find traditional education systems inconvenient and
need the flexibility of online formats.

Online learning may not be the first thing that comes to mind when com- 3
munity colleges consider providing support for student success. But that
mindset is changing. It has to. The 2011 Sloan Survey of Online Learning
reported that more than six million college students in the fall of 2010 took at
least one online course, comprising nearly one-third of all college and university students. The growth rate in online course enrollment far exceeds the
growth rate of the overall higher education student population.

Still, there is healthy skepticism about the proliferation of online learning 4
and views still differ about its value. According to surveys by the Pew Research
Center and the *Chronicle of Higher Education*, less than 30 percent of the public believes that online and classroom courses provide the same educational
value. Half of college presidents share that belief.

Any way you look at it, online learning is an increasingly vital part of pro- 5
ducing the number of qualified graduates needed to meet future workforce
demands—when it is done correctly.

A Calculated Risk

In 1996, Rio Salado, one of 10 Maricopa Community Colleges, took a calculated 6
risk and began offering courses online—16 to start—just when the Internet
was taking off. Critics at the time challenged the quality of online education
and claimed that students wouldn't adjust well to such a radical change in their
learning environment. But Maricopa and Rio Salado pushed ahead, determined
to create an innovative, nontraditional, and nimble approach that is responsive
to and supportive of changing student needs.

The risks have proven to be worth it. While no one could have predicted 7
the economic environment that students and higher education face today,
making the decision to move online proved to be provident for the college and
students. Rio Salado extended educational access to students who found traditional college to be out of reach in Arizona, nationwide, and around the world.

The college currently serves nearly 70,000 students each year, with more than 41,000 enrolled in 600-plus online courses.

Keeping Costs Down

To keep costs down, Rio Salado supports more than 60 certificate and degree 8 programs with just 22 residential faculty and more than 1,400 adjunct faculty. Our "one-course, many sections" model uses a master course approved by the resident faculty and taught by adjunct faculty in more than 6,000 course sections. The college's cost to educate students is as much as 48 percent less than peer institutions nationwide.

Without the expense of a traditional campus, Rio Salado has been able to 9 focus on building and improving its RioLearn platform, a customized learning management system that provides access to course-related resources, instructors, fellow students, and other support services.

Focused on Student Support

Meeting students' needs means providing access to robust, comprehensive 10 support services that are customized for their complex lifestyles, whether they are a working adult, an active military student accessing their coursework online, or someone taking in-person classes in adult basic education, incarcerated reentry, early college, or workforce training programs. Today's students need the resources of round-the-clock instructional and technology helpdesks, tutoring, and virtual library services. Additionally, we never cancel an online class and offer the flexibility of 48 start dates a year.

Students also need real-time support to keep them on track. Predictive analytic technology allows the college to monitor online student engagement and predict by the eighth day of class the level of success students will have in a course. When needed, instructors facilitate interventions to minimize risks and support successful course completion.

Building a culture of unified support focused on completion won't happen overnight. It took 30 years for Rio Salado to get to this point. Our upside-down faculty model has made it possible for the college to adapt a corporate "systems approach," and all Rio Salado staff and faculty participate in a training program to instill a unified commitment to helping students complete their degree programs.

Technical Challenges

Staying ahead of the online curve comes with its share of challenges. Rio Salado 13 had to build its own learning management system because there wasn't one available that would support all of the features that our faculty and students wanted. In partnership with Microsoft and Dell, RioLearn was designed to be scalable to more than 100,000 students.

However, a few years ago, it didn't fully support Mac users. Although students could access their coursework, they had to switch Internet browsers to do so. A new version of RioLearn was launched in 2010 to help students access their courses, regardless of the platform they are using.

We've also learned that many of our students are co-enrolled in traditional colleges and universities. They come to Rio Salado for flexibility, affordability, and convenience to accelerate their degree on their terms. They bank credits and ultimately transfer those credits to complete their degrees at another institution.

A recent report examines Rio Salado's efforts and the experience and perspectives of more than 30 institutions throughout the U.S. addressing similar challenges to ensure student success—especially for low-income, minority, and adult students—and pursuing promising approaches to increase college completion rates.

Reimagining the System

Our country can't continue to allow millions of people who are college material to fall through the cracks. We must find new, convenient, and high-quality educational options for students who might otherwise have missed out on a college education. That means serving more students in more places—especially where college enrollments have been capped—through efforts such as online early college initiatives, by creating cohorts at the high-school level and developing open-source courses.

> "We must find new, convenient, and high-quality educational options for students."

With tuition rising faster than the rate of inflation, and the best-paying jobs requiring some form of postsecondary degree, specialized certification, or licensure, we have to find solutions that lower costs for students. We need to innovate. We need new models of education to leverage public resources through private and public partnerships and increase the capacity to serve nontraditional students through productive and cost-efficient means.

It's encouraging to see the rapid growth in affordable online learning. It has broken down the barriers of time, distance, and affordability without sacrificing high-quality academics. But shoring up its credibility and value for students means heeding some of the lessons learned over the past 15 years. The stakes for getting it right are certainly high and getting higher.

◐ AT ISSUE: SOURCES FOR USING ALTERNATIVE APPROACHES TO ARGUMENT

1. According to Bustamante, "there is healthy skepticism about the proliferation of online learning" (para. 4). What does he mean? What reservations, if any, do you have about the rise of online education?

2. In this essay, where does the claim appear? How is this claim qualified? How does the qualifier set up the rest of the essay?

3. Bustamante's article focuses on the development of one school's online education program. Do you think the risks and rewards he discusses also apply to other schools' online offerings? What factors might account for any differences in other schools' experiences with online learning?

4. What is Bustamante's purpose? What does he want readers to take away from his essay?

5. Does Bustamante ever address opposing arguments? If he does, where? If he does not, should he have addressed them? Explain.

6. What does Bustamante mean when he says that we must reimagine the system of higher education? What problems does he see with the current educational system? How will online education help solve these problems?

This essay was published in the *Daily Nebraskan*, the student newspaper of the University of Nebraska, on November 29, 2011.

RELIANCE ON ONLINE MATERIALS HINDERS LEARNING POTENTIAL FOR STUDENTS

DAVID SMITH

Students of today should be thankful for the . . . plethora of ways available for them to learn. Compared to our grandparents, parents, and even older siblings, we have access to modes of communication and education that would not have been possible even 10 years ago. 1

Students today, not just in college but in high school, middle school, and elementary school, take in and process astounding amounts of information on a daily basis. We have access to TV and the Internet, social media outlets such as Twitter and Facebook, and a nearly inexhaustible supply of ways to keep in contact with and learn about one another. 2

This variety has begun to work its way into academia, as well; more and more, it seems, organized instruction is moving beyond the classroom and into cyberspace. Pencils and paper, once the sole staples of the educational experience, are slowly being ousted by keyboards, webcams, and online dropboxes. 3

Here at the University of Nebraska–Lincoln, this growing prevalence is easy to see. Just look at Blackboard and how some courses are completely dependent upon it. Blackboard has everything from grade tracking and homework assignments to the administration of quizzes and exams. 4

Look at MyRED, which now handles everything from class enrollment and scheduling to residence hall contracts and meal plans. 5

Look at things such as the Love Library's EBSCO search engine, which gives students access to a greater wealth of information than even the most practiced scholar would know what to do with, and online courses such as the Keller Plan, which allow students to complete coursework and earn credit without having to leave their dorm rooms. 6

It's clear to even the most casual observer that taking in and processing information is far easier for the students of today than it was for the students of 100, 50, or even 10 years ago.

> "While the Internet has certainly made learning easier, has it made it better?" 7

But it begs the question: While the Internet has certainly made learning easier, has it made it better? Not necessarily. 8

Think for a moment about the fundamental differences between a traditional course, taught in a classroom, and one conducted entirely via Blackboard's online services. 9

In the former, students are bound by structure and organization. They 10 must attend class on a regular basis or suffer the consequences, typically (though not always) complete regular homework assignments for points, and are constantly reminded of the work that needs to be done by the ever-present figure (or specter) of the professor.

Such is not the case with classes taken outside the classroom. The instruc- 11 tions for such courses are, at least in my experience, pared down to the following: "Read this by this date, this by this date, and this by this date. There are quizzes on Day X, Day Y, and Day Z, and the final exam can be taken at any time during finals week in the testing center. Have a nice semester."

Now, I know that college is supposed to be a place of greater expectations, 12 of increased responsibilities and better time management skills. I get that, I really do. But the sad truth is that all too often, giving a student that kind of freedom doesn't end well.

By removing the sense of structure from a course, you remove the stu- 13 dent's notion that he or she is under any sort of pressure, any sort of time constraint. By removing a constantly present instructor, you remove what is, in many cases, the sole source of motivation students have to do well in a class. You take away the sense of urgency, the sense of immediate requirement, and by extension the student's drive.

Readings are put off or forgotten, material review sessions (if there are 14 any) are blown off or missed, and quizzes and exams are ultimately bombed. More often than not, the student will get caught up with work from the other, more traditional courses on their schedule—the ones they remember they have homework in because it was assigned in class this afternoon or the ones they have to study for because the professor reminded them about the upcoming exam the other day. Unfortunately, another marked difference between traditional and online courses is that the latters are typically far less forgiving when it comes to things such as deadlines and extensions, making it next to impossible for students to get out of the holes they dig themselves into.

The Internet is a powerful tool. It allows us to share, distribute, and 15 absorb more information in a single year than our ancestors absorbed in a lifetime, and its capacity to do those things is constantly growing. What people, educators in particular, need to realize is that no matter how powerful a tool it becomes, the Internet should never become anything more than that: a tool.

There will never be an adequate online substitute for the watchful eye 16 and the stern voice of a professor, or the pressure of an exam time limit that is about to expire, or the dismay and subsequent motivation to improve that can come from a handed-back assignment with a failing grade scrawled on it.

Now . . . off to class. 17

AT ISSUE: SOURCES FOR USING ALTERNATIVE APPROACHES TO ARGUMENT

1. Paragraph 8 expresses Smith's thesis in the form of a question and answer. Paraphrase this thesis statement in one sentence.

2. Why does Smith spend his first seven paragraphs discussing the amount of information currently available to students?

3. In paragraph 8, Smith says that his previous statement "begs the question." What does he mean? Is this statement actually an example of **begging the question**? Explain.

4. How, according to Smith, is online education different from classroom learning? What problems does Smith identify with online learning?

5. In paragraph 13, Smith says that online courses remove "the sense of structure from a course." What evidence does he present to support this statement?

6. What does Smith mean in paragraph 15 when he says that what we "need to realize is that no matter how powerful a tool it becomes, the Internet should never become anything more than that: a tool"? What is he warning against here?

7. Where does Smith use the techniques of Rogerian argument? Does he use these techniques often enough? Does he use them effectively? Explain.

8. In paragraph 16, Smith says, "There will never be an adequate online substitute for the watchful eye and the stern voice of a professor." Do you agree? Do you think this highlights a disadvantage of online education (as Smith intends) or an advantage?

This essay is from the October 9, 2011, edition of the *Daily Trojan*, the student newspaper of the University of Southern California.

ONLINE EDUCATION NEEDS CONNECTION

ELENA KADVANY

From the most trivial of issues (who went to what party this weekend?) to the most traditional of society's establishments (newspapers, music and book industries, Postal Service), the Internet has transformed our lives. But one area remains to be revolutionized digitally: education. 1

Online education is on the rise, pitting those who support the idea of a virtual university for its ability to increase access and revenue against those who believe there is no substitute for real-time, traditional educational experiences. 2

There's one thing wrong with the entire conversation, however: Viewing online education as a new higher-education business model that must supplant the current system is a close-minded view. Why not look at it as a means by which we can strengthen and innovate education by blending digital and traditional elements? 3

Online education began mostly as distance-learning programs for graduate degrees that lend themselves to the medium like engineering or business. 4

USC's Viterbi School of Engineering has a well-established Distance Education Network that offers more than 30 master's degree programs. 5

Now, in times of financial crisis, schools across the country, especially in California, are searching for ways to reinvent themselves. This has led to an expansion of digital courses into the undergraduate sphere. 6

But there is a distinct danger in allowing finance-driven ideas to dominate the dialogue about schools' futures and education in general, especially for undergraduates whose educational experiences and life tracks are so defined by their first four years on a campus. 7

> "There is a distinct danger in allowing finance-driven ideas to dominate."

This is not to say that universities should completely reject online learning. It's great to be able to listen to lectures at home or gain access to classes you can't physically attend or afford. 8

Higher learning, however, is about a level of personal interaction and commitment that can't be re-created online. 9

Before transferring to USC, I spent a semester at the University of San Francisco, where I took a hybrid service-learning Spanish class. It combined conventional in-class instruction twice a week with a once-a-week class online with Blackboard, in addition to a requirement of outside community service hours. 10

This kind of blending shows the innovative potential universities should 11 recognize and seize. The idea of a virtual university should not replace the traditional, but instead should merge with it.

For undergraduates, hybrid classes could be incredibly valuable and much 12 more engaging for a generation that spends so much time online.

Some of the University of California schools have submitted courses in 13 response to an online education pilot project proposed by the University's Office of the President.

Sebastian Thrun, a professor at Stanford University renowned for leading 14 the team that built Google's self-driving car, now offers a free online course, "Introduction to Artificial Intelligence." Enrollment in this class has jumped from 58,000 to 130,000 across the world in the past month, according to the *New York Times*. USC is lucky enough to have generous alumni that keep it more than afloat financially. But as many universities choose to go digital, USC might want to follow suit.

The potential of all things online is vast. And there's no match for the 15 value of real-time, person-to-person educational experiences.

There's no reason universities can't take advantage of both. 16

⊙ AT ISSUE: SOURCES FOR USING ALTERNATIVE APPROACHES TO ARGUMENT

1. In paragraph 2, Kadvany says that online education pits those who support virtual education against those who support traditional classroom education. Do the essays in this At Issue section confirm or challenge Kadvany's point? Explain.

2. In paragraph 3, Kadvany says that it is wrong to view online education as a "higher-education business model" that will displace classroom education. Why does she use the term "business model"? Does she expect this term to have positive or negative connotations for her readers? How can you tell?

3. How has the financial crisis helped to promote the idea of online education? According to Kadvany, what is the danger of letting "finance-driven ideas" (7) dominate the conversation about education?

4. In paragraph 9, Kadvany says that the personal interaction and commitment that characterize higher learning "can't be re-created online." What evidence does she present to support this statement? How convincing is this evidence? What additional evidence could she have used?

5. Does Kadvany ever use the techniques of Rogerian argument? If so, where? If not, should she have used them?

This essay is from the December 14, 2011, edition of the *MetroWest Daily News*.

SHORT DISTANCE LEARNING

JOHN CRISP

The end of the semester at my college always inclines me toward reflection, 1 relief, and mild melancholy. I suspect my students feel the same way, with more inclination, perhaps, toward relief. Five classes have met with me about 30 times each over the course of 15 weeks, five communities of individuals that materialize, coalesce, and disperse in a few months.

Whatever its merits, I've never developed much enthusiasm for online learning. Its proponents contend that a community of learners can develop among students scattered by geography but connected by the Internet, and I'm not in a position to say they're wrong. 2

> "I've never developed much enthusiasm for online learning."

In fact, my purpose isn't to disparage online education. Along with the 3 trend toward a part-time professoriate, the proliferation of online education is probably the most prominent tendency in higher education during the last decade.

Still, I prefer the face-to-face classroom, which seems to me to preserve a 4 fine touch of humanity that warrants reflection during this week of final exams.

Who was in my classes this semester? Many are traditional students, fresh 5 from high school and on their way to a four-year college or university, after a sojourn at my community college. Many are bright, capable, and articulate. Others are shy and reserved. A few are sullen or downright surly. But they're not always my most interesting students.

Consider the young woman who, a decade after high school, finds herself 6 slogging through a developmental writing course before she can even attempt freshman composition. Pardon the cliché, but sometimes you do see a light go on in a student. She begins to listen to her instructor's and classmates' every word, to take notes and to think, to become absorbed in her writing, which over the course of the semester really does get better.

It doesn't always work like that, by any means. Other students are tak- 7 ing my developmental writing class for the second or third time. I like them, but they miss too much class. Some of them have tattoos that betray their gangbanger history; some have been thieves and some have been in prison. And how well can you learn to write amid the violence and futility in the barrio?

Many of them say that's all in the past now, and I believe them. Will they 8 pass this semester? I'm not sure. If they don't, what will become of them?

Momentous life passages occurred as the classes proceeded: At least two 9
women in my five classes this semester were pregnant and one gave birth. Two
students died. One young man, a veteran who had survived tours in Iraq and
Afghanistan, was killed in the second week of the semester, hit by a car while
out for his morning jog.

In mid-semester, a young woman in the same class lost control of her car 10
on the way home from school and died in a one-vehicle rollover. When I told
the class the next week that she wouldn't be coming back, there were some
tears. So we learned about more than just writing this semester.

A middle-aged woman expressed conservative religious beliefs then admitted 11
that she spent two years in prison for marijuana possession. Several veterans can't
sleep at night and some of them drink too much. A young man came to class
so depressed that I took him to one of the college's counselors, and he never
came back.

Another young man and a young woman sat on opposite sides of the class 12
and never spoke up or spoke to anyone else. Then they began to sit together
and talk to each other. A lot. Now I occasionally see them around the campus
together. Does that happen in online classes?

In short, it's all there, a rich mixture of human experiences in one ephem- 13
eral microcosm: birth, mating, sickness, death, frustration, laughter, storytelling, aspiration, failure, and learning.

Good luck, students; the pleasure was mine. 14

AT ISSUE: SOURCES FOR USING ALTERNATIVE APPROACHES TO ARGUMENT

1. Where does Crisp attempt to establish his credibility? How effective is this appeal to *ethos*?

2. To whom is Crisp addressing his argument? Teachers? Students? Parents? Administrators? Others? How do you know?

3. In paragraph 3, Crisp says that his purpose "isn't to disparage online education." What is his purpose?

4. In paragraph 4, Crisp says that he prefers traditional classroom instruction because it preserves "a fine touch of humanity." What does he mean? What evidence does he present in paragraphs 5–12 to support this point? How convincing is this evidence?

5. Draw a **rhetorical triangle** (p. 13) that represents the relative importance of the various appeals in this essay. Which appeal does the longest side of the triangle represent? Which does the shortest side represent? Do you think this is a good balance?

6. In paragraph 2, Crisp briefly addresses an opposing argument. Does he accurately characterize the case for online learning? Should he have spent more time addressing opposing arguments?

7. Crisp ends his essay with a single sentence. Is this sentence an effective concluding statement? Why or why not?

8. Suppose Crisp wanted to present his ideas in a speech. What parts of his essay would you suggest he expand? What parts would you advise him to condense or delete? What visuals would you suggest he include?

This essay appeared on October 5, 2011, in the *Daily Cougar*, the student newspaper of the University of Houston.

ONLINE EDUCATION INNOVATORS SHOULD BE WARY

RACHEL FARHI

Some professors at elite universities are trying to devise a more economical university model, and they are using the Internet to do it.

Sebastian Thrun, a Stanford professor, is an advocate of the online university and has ambitious goals: producing lectures and live, online discussions to thousands of students at a fraction of the cost, rewarding students for honed skills instead of "grades," and eliminating the inefficiency of large campuses.

Thrun is now offering free, online courses on artificial intelligence to over 100,000 students around the world. These courses teach the same material for which Stanford students pay $50,000 per year. Thrun offers dynamic, live lectures that end in a "Statement of Accomplishment" but not Stanford credit. However, the opportunity to learn from the man who led the team that built Google's self-driving car is probably incentive enough to take his course.

The high cost of a college education unfortunately perpetuates immobility between social classes; students from higher socioeconomic classes have almost automatic access, while students from disadvantaged neighborhoods have a much harder time.

Supplementing a student's education with online classes reduces the amount of money he or she has to spend. If students attend class only two days a week and have online courses the other three days, they save on gas, food, university fees, and other costs.

However, what Thrun and other advocates of online universities do not consider are the non-academic skills and values that universities instill in students. Taking courses on a computer at home deprives students of a practical, social education that is necessary in most professions and not taught in high school.

> "Taking courses on a computer at home deprives students of a practical, social education."

How does somebody develop a personal relationship with a professor, or necessary networking skills, when he or she is only one in a class of five thousand, and the only method of communication with peers and professors is through online chat or a discussion board? Professionals, especially service providers, need social skills almost as much as they need qualifications.

Another problem with online courses is cheating from lack of supervision. Thrun portrays students with an idealism that is inspirational but seems to be ignoring reality. Anyone can sit behind a computer screen and take a course, including a friend of a person enrolled in that course. So how do we know who

229

is sitting behind that screen? Without a professor and teaching assistants, to whom is the student accountable?

Reducing the amount of money spent on a college education and increas- 9 ing accessibility does not fix the problem of individual drive, appreciating the significance of one's education, and whether or not students entering these classes can handle the material. Unequal opportunity and training in public schools also makes the "universal accessibility" dream unrealistic. To reap the benefits of these classes, students must have the proper training before they graduate. Otherwise, even a completely free education does no good.

Online courses are a great idea, they are already being used by some degree 10 at most universities, but implementing the online change slowly may make room for constructive criticism and ensure that the system works as well as it could.

⊙ AT ISSUE: SOURCES FOR USING ALTERNATIVE APPROACHES TO ARGUMENT

1. Why does Farhi begin her essay by discussing Sebastian Thrun? How does this discussion prepare readers for the rest of the essay? Elena Kadvany also mentions Sebastian Thrun, in paragraph 14 of her essay "Online Education Needs Connection" (p. 224). Is the point Kadvany makes about Thrun similar to or different from the one Farhi makes?

2. Throughout her essay, Farhi makes statements that she assumes are self-evident. For example, in paragraph 1, she says that some professors are using the Internet to "devise a more economical university model," and in paragraph 5, she says that taking online classes saves students money. Identify other statements that Farhi presents as self-evident. Are they really self-evident, or do they require support?

3. What does Farhi mean when she says that a college education "perpetuates immobility between social classes" (4)? According to her, how does online education address this problem?

4. Where does Farhi discuss opposing arguments? How effectively does she refute them?

5. In the first five paragraphs of her essay, Farhi presents arguments in favor of online education. The rest of her essay discusses the problems with online education, which, according to her, its advocates do not consider. Do these qualifications of her initial position make you more or less likely to accept her thesis, which appears in paragraph 10?

ONLINE SCHOOL DEGREE PROGRAMS

CAMPUS EXPLORER

Find online degrees at online schools and learn more about the benefits of a distance learning program.

What Is an Online School and Distance Learning?

Online schools are academic institutions in which all or the majority of the coursework is completed through a distance learning program. Online schools offer a range of online degrees like online certificate programs, online career training, online bachelor's degrees, and even online master's degrees. An online school may refer to the online branch of a college or university that has a physical campus. It can also refer to schools that strictly offer online degree programs and online courses without a college campus or campuses.

| Online Certificate Programs | Online Associate's Degree—Career Training | Online Bachelor's Degree Programs | Online Master's Degree Programs |

Online Certificate Programs

Administrative Assistant & Secretarial Science

Business Administration & Management

Computer Systems Technology

Corrections

Design & Visual Communications

Early Childhood Education

Educational & Instructional Media Design

Elementary Education and Teaching

General Education

Health and Medical Administrative Services

Health Care Administration/Management

Legal Assistant/Paralegal

Medical Insurance/Biller

Medical Insurance Coding Specialist/Coder

Medical Office Assistant/Specialist

Multimedia Management and Webmaster

Nursing—Registered Nurse Training (RN, ASN, BSN, MSN)

Pharmacy Technician/Assistant

System Administration/Administrator

See All Online Certificate Programs at Online Schools

Online Schools Offering Certificate Programs

Ashworth College Online School

ATI Career Training Online School

Charter College Online School

DeVry University Online School

Fischler School of Education and Human Services Online School

Globe University/Minnesota School of Business Online School

Kaplan University Online School

Keiser University Online School

National American University Online School

Northcentral University Online School

Post University Online School

Rasmussen College Online School

Remington College Online School

Strayer University Online School

Sullivan University Online School

The Art Institute of Pittsburgh Online School

Ultimate Medical Academy Online School

University of Phoenix Online School

Villanova University Online School

See All Online Schools Offering Certificate Programs

Time Requirements for Online Schools

Course requirements and time commitments for online schools and distance learning programs vary depending in part on the type of online degree you're getting, whether you choose to go full-time or part-time, and if you include summer classes in your schedule.

If you want to complete your online degree program as quickly as possible, you may find more flexibility at an online school than at a campus school. Because distance learning programs like online colleges cater to students with busy or inflexible schedules, some online colleges will allow students to accelerate their studies to complete their degree in less time than it would typically take at a campus school.

"You may find more flexibility at an online school than at a campus school."

Is an Online Degree Program Right for You?

Students are increasingly turning to online schools and distance learning over campus schools for many reasons; chief among them are flexibility and affordability. Here are some of the main reasons students seek out online programs for their degrees:

- **Increased flexibility in scheduling classes.** Many online schools offer more online courses in the evening and on weekends than campus schools do because these schools tend to cater to working students and students with other obligations outside the classroom.

- **Saving tuition money.** Enrolling at an online school means you don't have to pay travel, relocation, or room and board cost at a college campus. Also, tuition at online schools may be less than campus schools, partly because schools with a campus need more money to fund items such as classrooms, which aren't necessary with online courses.

- **Independent study.** Distance learning programs allow you to work on your own without the distractions you can find in school settings. You will still be able to interact with professors and other students, but most of this communication will take place online rather than in person.

- **Studying from home.** Online degrees can be completed mostly or completely via home computer, which is especially helpful for students without transportation or who are caring for kids or other family members.

- **To study on the go.** Enrolling in an online college requires access to a working computer with Internet access. If you have a laptop computer, you will be able to stay connected to your online classes and teachers anywhere you can connect to the Web.

What Types of Students Pursue Online Degrees?

Because you can pursue an online degree in everything from certificate programs to master's degrees, a broad variety of students enroll in online programs. Some are recent high school graduates looking for career training or for a more convenient, affordable alternative to a campus college. Others are professionals above the traditional college age who want to expand their skills or develop knowledge in a new area, and some are parents or caregivers who are seeking a degree for future employment or personal enrichment.

Online degrees and online colleges are becoming more prevalent and popular with students' increased access to the Internet. A growing number of students enroll in at least some online courses while studying for their degree.

How Do You Narrow Down Your Search of Online Schools?

When choosing an online college, make sure it offers the type of certificate or degree you're seeking, as well as the areas of study you're interested in. You'll then want to review each school's accreditation and reputation, as well as the accreditation and reputation of the certificate or degree you're pursuing.

While location tends to be less of a factor when selecting an online college than a campus school, find out if the programs you're considering require any in-person training or tests as part of their degree requirements. Certain programs require hands-on training as part of the degree program, so if that is required by the schools you're considering, be sure you have the time and financial means to travel to the required campus to complete the coursework.

➲ AT ISSUE: SOURCES FOR USING ALTERNATIVE APPROACHES TO ARGUMENT

1. This Web page is from Campus Explorer, a site that promotes online learning. Do you think the site's treatment of the pros and cons of online learning is balanced? Why or why not?

2. Can you think of any positive or negative aspects of online education that this Web page neglects to mention?

3. Assume you are writing an argument in favor of online learning. From the Campus Explorer Web page, identify the three strongest arguments *against* online education. How would you refute each of these opposing arguments?

4. Assume you are writing an argument against online learning. From the Campus Explorer Web page, identify the three strongest arguments *in favor of* online education. How would you refute each of these arguments?

This Web page, accessed January 15, 2013, explains the SCCC distance-learning program.

DISTANCE EDUCATION AND *e*-LEARNING
SEATTLE CENTRAL COMMUNITY COLLEGE

AT ISSUE: SOURCES FOR USING ALTERNATIVE APPROACHES TO ARGUMENT

1. What is the purpose of this Web page?

2. What kind of audience does this Web page seem to be addressing? How can you tell?

3. Is the Web page's treatment of distance learning balanced? Explain.

4. What additional information—if any—do you think should have been provided?

5. How do you think John Crisp (p. 226) would respond to this Web page?

The photo at left is by Andy Nelson. The photo at right is by Tanya Constantine.

TWO VIEWS OF ONLINE EDUCATION

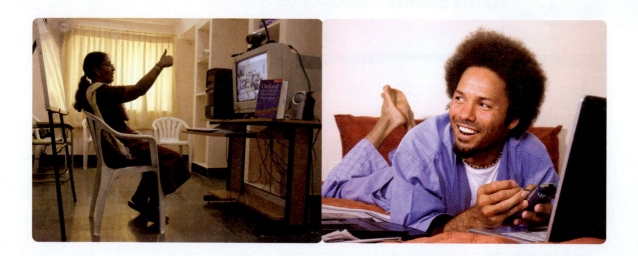

❯ AT ISSUE: SOURCES FOR USING ALTERNATIVE APPROACHES TO ARGUMENT

1. The photo at left above shows an instructor teaching in an online education program. What is your reaction to this picture? Does it present online education in a favorable or an unfavorable light? Explain.

2. The other photo—a student taking an online class—is from a university's Web site that promotes its online education program. What advantages of online education does this picture try to show?

3. Do you think you would do well in an online education environment? Why or why not?

EXERCISE 6.7

Write a one-paragraph **Rogerian** argument in which you argue that the drawbacks of online education have to be addressed before it can be successful. Follow the template below, filling in the blanks to create your argument.

TEMPLATE FOR WRITING A ROGERIAN ARGUMENT

With more and more students taking online courses, both the students and the colleges benefit. For example, _____ _____ _____. In addition, _____ _____.

However, online education does have some drawbacks. For instance, ____ _____ _____.

These problems could be easily solved. First, _____ _____. Second, _____ _____.

If these problems are addressed, both students and colleges would benefit because _____ _____.

EXERCISE 6.8

Write a one-paragraph **Toulmin** argument in which you argue in favor of online education. Follow the template below, filling in the blanks to create your argument.

TEMPLATE FOR WRITING A TOULMIN ARGUMENT

Many colleges and universities have instituted online education programs. These programs are the best way _____ _____.

If colleges are going to meet the rising demand for education, they _____ _____ _____.

The online course I took _____ _____ _____.

Recent studies show that _____

_____. In addition, _____

_____

_____. However, some people argue that _____

_____

_____. They also say that _____

_____.

These arguments _____

_____.

For this reason, online education is _____

_____

_____.

➲ EXERCISE 6.9

Discuss your ideas about online learning with one or two of your classmates. Consider both the strengths and the limitations of this method of teaching. What types of classes do you think it is best suited for? Which classes do you think it would not work for? Then, edit the Rogerian and Toulmin arguments that you wrote for Exercises 6.7 and 6.8 so that they include some of these comments.

➲ EXERCISE 6.10

Write an argumentative essay on the topic, "Is Online Education as Good as Classroom Education?" Use the principles of either Rogerian argument or Toulmin logic to structure your essay. Cite sources in the Reading and Writing about the Issue section on pages 213–236, and be sure to document the sources you use and to include a works-cited page. (See Chapter 10 for information on documenting sources.)

➲ EXERCISE 6.11

 Review the four pillars of argument that are discussed in Chapter 1. Does your essay include all four elements of an effective argument? Add anything that is missing. Then, label the elements of your argument.

➲ EXERCISE 6.12

Assume that you have been asked to present the information in the essay you wrote for Exercise 6.10 as an oral argument. What information would you include? What information would you eliminate? Find two or three visuals that you would use when you deliver your speech. Then, make an outline of your speech and indicate at what points you would display these visuals.

Writing an Argumentative Essay

CHAPTER
7

Planning, Drafting, and Revising an Argumentative Essay

Should College Campuses Go Green?

In recent years, more and more American colleges and universities have been moving toward becoming green, emphasizing **sustainability**—the use of systems and materials that will not deplete the earth's natural resources. Various schools have taken steps such as the following to become green:

- Placing an emphasis on recycling and reducing nonbiodegradable waste
- Creating green buildings and using eco-friendly materials in construction projects
- Instituting new curricula in environmental science
- Monitoring their greenhouse gas emissions and evaluating their carbon footprint
- Growing crops on campus to feed students
- Hiring full-time "sustainability directors"
- Encouraging students to use bikes instead of cars
- Purchasing wind-generated electricity to supply the campus's energy

- Eliminating trays in college cafeterias

Although many schools have launched ambitious programs and projects to reduce their energy dependence, some have been more cautious, citing the high cost of such programs and the need to allocate resources elsewhere. Moreover, some critics of the green movement object to the notion that colleges should help to make students "sustainability literate." Such critics consider the green movement to be an expression of political correctness that at best gives lip service to the problem and at worst threatens academic freedom by furthering a political agenda.

The question remains whether the green movement that is spreading rapidly across college campuses is here to stay or just a fad—or something between these two extremes. This chapter takes you through the process of writing an argumentative essay on the topic of whether college campuses should go green. (Exercises guide you through the process of writing your own argumentative essay.)

Before you can write a convincing argumentative essay, you need to understand the **writing process**. You are probably already familiar with the basic outline of this process, which includes *planning, drafting,* and *revising.* This chapter reviews this familiar process and explains how it applies to the specific demands of writing an argument.

Choosing a Topic

The first step in planning an argumentative essay is to choose a topic you can write about. Your goal is to select a topic that you have some emotional stake in—not simply one that interests you. If you are going to spend hours planning, writing, and revising an essay, then you should care about your topic. At the same time, you should have an open mind about your topic and be willing to consider various viewpoints. Your topic also should be narrow enough to fit the boundaries of your assignment—the time you have to work on the paper and its length and scope.

Typically, your instructor will give you a general assignment, such as the following.

> **Assignment**
> Write a three- to five-page argumentative essay on a topic related to college services, programs, facilities, or curricula.

The first thing you need to do is narrow this general assignment to a topic, focusing on one particular campus service, program, facility, or curriculum. You could choose to write about any number of topics—financial aid, the writing center, athletics, the general education curriculum—taking a position, for example, on who should receive financial aid, whether to expand the writing center, whether college athletes should receive a salary, or why general education requirements are important for business majors.

If you are interested in the environment, however, you might decide to write about the green movement that is spreading across college campuses, perhaps using your observations of your own campus's programs and policies to support your position.

> **Topic**
> The green movement on college campuses

TOPICS TO AVOID

Certain kinds of topics are not appropriate for argumentative essays. For one thing, some topics are just not arguable. For example, you could not write an argumentative essay on a statement of fact, such as the fact that many colleges saw their endowments decline after the financial crisis of 2008. (A fact is not debatable, so there can be no argument.)

Some familiar topics also present problems. These issues—the death penalty, abortion rights, and so on—are important (after all, that's why they are written about) so often, but finding an original argument on either side of the debate can be a challenge. For example, you might have a hard time finding something new to say that would convince some readers that the death penalty is immoral or that abortion is a woman's right. In many people's minds, these issues are "settled." When you write on topics such as these, some readers' strong religious or cultural beliefs are likely to prevent them from considering your arguments, however well supported they might be.

Finally, topics that are very narrow or depend on subjective value judgments—or that take a stand on issues readers simply will not care much about, such as whether one particular video game or TV reality show is more entertaining than another—are unlikely to engage your audience (even if these topics are compelling to you and your friends).

 **EXERCISE 7.1**

In response to the boxed assignment on the previous page, list ten topics that you could write about. Then, cross out any that do not meet the following criteria:

- The topic interests you.
- You know something about the topic.
- You care about the topic.
- You have an open mind about the topic.
- The topic fits the boundaries of your assignment.

Finally, choose one topic to write an essay about.

Thinking about Your Topic

Before you can start to do research, develop a thesis statement, or plan the structure of your argument, you need to think a bit about the topic you have chosen. You can use *invention strategies*, such as **freewriting** (writing without stopping for a predetermined time), **brainstorming** (making quick notes on your topic), or **clustering** (creating a diagram to map out your thoughts) to help you discover ideas you might write about. You can also explore ideas in a writing journal or in conversations with friends, classmates, family members, or instructors.

Freewriting

People say green is good, but I'm not sure why. Why do we need all these containers for different kinds of bottles and cans, white and colored paper, etc., etc.? In middle school, we learned about the "three Rs" to save the environment—one was Recycle, but I forget the other two. Renew? Reuse? Remember? Whatever. OK, I know not to throw trash on the ground, and I know we're supposed to separate bottles from cans, etc. I get that. But does all this time and effort really do any good?

Brainstorming

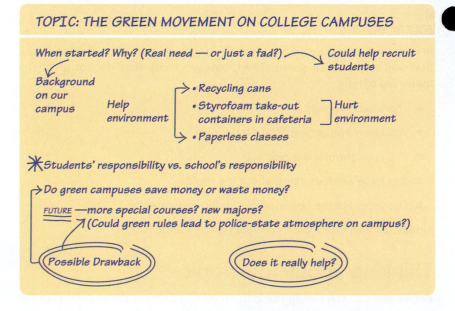

TOPIC: THE GREEN MOVEMENT ON COLLEGE CAMPUSES

When started? Why? (Real need — or just a fad?) → Could help recruit students

Background on our campus

Help environment {
• Recycling cans
• Styrofoam take-out containers in cafeteria
• Paperless classes
} Hurt environment

✳Students' responsibility vs. school's responsibility

→Do green campuses save money or waste money?

FUTURE —more special courses? new majors?
(Could green rules lead to police-state atmosphere on campus?)

(Possible Drawback)   (Does it really help?)

Clustering

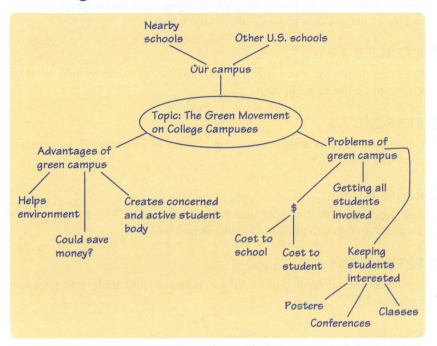

When you finish your preliminary exploration of ideas, you should be able to construct a quick **informal outline** that lists the ideas you plan to discuss.

Informal Outline

Topic: The Green Movement on College Campuses
  History/background
    National
    Our campus
  Positive aspects
    Helps environment
    Attracts new students
  Negative aspects
    Cost
    Enforcement
  Future

By grouping your ideas and arranging them in a logical order, an informal outline like the one above can help lead you to a thesis statement that expresses the position you will take on the issue.

⊜ EXERCISE 7.2

Focusing on the topic you chose in Exercise 7.1, freewrite to think of ideas you might write about in your essay.

⊜ EXERCISE 7.3

Continuing to work with the topic you chose in Exercise 7.1, brainstorm for ideas to write about.

⊜ EXERCISE 7.4

Still working with the topic you chose in Exercise 7.1, draw a cluster diagram to help you think of ideas to write about.

⊜ EXERCISE 7.5

Construct an informal outline for an essay on the topic you chose in Exercise 7.1.

Drafting a Thesis Statement

After you have decided on a topic and thought about how you want to approach it, your next step is to take a stand on the issue you are going to discuss. You do this by expressing your position as a **thesis statement**.

A thesis statement is the central element of any argumentative essay. It tells readers what your position is and also perhaps indicates why you are taking this position and how you plan to support it. As you draft your thesis statement, keep the following guidelines in mind:

- An argumentative thesis statement is not simply a statement of your topic; rather, it expresses the point you will make about your topic.

  TOPIC   The green movement on college campuses

  THESIS STATEMENT   College campuses should go green.

- An argumentative thesis statement should be specific, clearly indicating to readers exactly what position you will take in your essay.

  TOO GENERAL   Colleges need to do more to get students involved in environmental issues.

  REVISED   Colleges should institute programs and classes to show students the importance of using sustainable resources.

■ An argumentative thesis statement should get right to the point, avoiding wordy, repetitive language.

WORDY	Because issues that revolve around the environment are so crucial and important, colleges should do more to increase student involvement in campus projects that are concerned with sustainability.
REVISED	Because environmental issues are so important, colleges should take steps to involve students in campus sustainability projects.

■ Many argumentative thesis statements include words such as *should* and *should not*.

- College campuses should _____.
- Because _____, colleges should _____.
- Even though _____, colleges should not _____.

NOTE

At this point, any thesis that you come up with is tentative. As you think about your topic and as you read about it, you will very likely modify your thesis statement, perhaps expanding or narrowing its scope, rewording it to make it more precise, or even changing your position. Still, the thesis statement that you decide on at this point can help you focus your exploration of your topic.

TENTATIVE THESIS STATEMENT

College campuses should go green.

⊘ EXERCISE 7.6

List five possible thesis statements for the topic you chose in Exercise 7.1. Which thesis statement seems most promising for an essay? Why?

Understanding Your Audience

When you write an argument, your goal is to convince your audience to accept your position as sensible (or even compelling). Sometimes you will be able to change your readers' minds and get them to accept your position—or even take some action in support of it. To make the best possible case to your audience, you need to understand who your audience is—what knowledge, values, beliefs, and opinions your readers might have.

You will also need to have some idea whether your audience is likely to be receptive, hostile, or neutral to the ideas you propose.

In most cases, it makes sense to assume that your readers are **skeptical**—that they have open minds but still need to be convinced. However, if you are writing about a topic that is very controversial, you will need to assume that at least some of your readers will not support your position and may, in fact, be hostile to it. If this is the case, they will be scrutinizing your arguments very carefully, looking for opportunities to argue against them. Your goal in this case is not necessarily to win them over but to make them more receptive to your position—or at least to get them to admit that you have made a good case even though they may disagree with you. At the same time, however, you also have to work to convince those who probably agree with you or are neutral (perhaps because the issue you are discussing is something they haven't thought much about).

An audience of first-year college students who are used to the idea that sound environmental practices make sense might find the idea of a green campus appealing—and, in fact, natural and obvious. An audience of faculty or older students might be more skeptical, realizing that the benefits of green practices might be offset by the time and expense they could involve. College administrators might find the long-term goal of a green campus attractive (and see it as a strong recruitment tool), but they might also be somewhat hostile to your position, anticipating the considerable expense that would be involved. If you wrote an argument on the topic of green campuses, you would need to consider many of these positions—and, if possible, address them.

⊘ EXERCISE 7.7

Consider how different audiences might respond to the thesis statement you found the most promising in Exercise 7.6. Identify five possible groups of readers on your college campus—for example, athletes, history majors, or part-time faculty. Would you expect each group to be neutral, positive, or hostile to your thesis? Why?

Gathering Evidence

After you have a sense of who your audience will be and how they might react to your thesis, you can begin to collect **evidence** to support your thesis. As you look for evidence, you need to evaluate the usefulness and relevance of each of your sources, and you need to be alert for possible bias.

Evaluating the Evidence in Your Sources

As you read each potential source, consider the quality of the supporting evidence that the writer marshals to support his or her position. The more compelling the evidence, the more willing you should be to accept the writer's ideas—and, perhaps, to integrate these ideas into your own essay.

(Don't forget that if you use any of your sources' ideas, you must document them. See Chapter 10 for information on MLA documentation format and Appendix B for information on APA documentation format.)

To be convincing, the evidence that is presented in the sources you review should be *accurate, relevant, representative,* and *sufficient:*

- **Accurate** evidence comes from reliable sources that you have quoted carefully—and not misrepresented by quoting out of context.

- **Relevant** evidence applies specifically (not just tangentially) to the topic under discussion.

- **Representative** evidence is drawn from a fair range of sources, not just those that support your position.

- **Sufficient** evidence is enough facts, statistics, expert opinion, and so on to support the essay's thesis.

(For more detailed information on evaluating sources, see Chapter 8.)

> **NOTE**
>
> Remember, the evidence you use to support your own arguments should also satisfy the four criteria listed above.

Detecting Bias in Your Sources

As you select sources, you should be alert for **bias**—a writer's use of preconceived ideas (rather than factual evidence) as support for his or her arguments. A writer who demonstrates bias may not be trustworthy, and you should approach such a writer's arguments with skepticism. To determine whether a writer is biased, follow these guidelines:

- *Consider what a writer explicitly tells you* about his or her beliefs or opinions. For example, if a writer mentions that he or she is a lifelong member of the Sierra Club, a vegan, and the owner of a house heated by solar energy, then you should consider the possibility that he or she might downplay (or even disregard) valid arguments against a green campus rather than presenting a balanced view.

- *Look for slanted language.* For example, a writer who mocks supporters of environmental issues as *politically correct* or uses pejorative terms such as *hippies* for environmentalists should not earn your trust.

- *Consider the supporting evidence* the writer chooses. Does the writer present only examples that support his or her position and ignore valid opposing arguments? Does the writer quote only those experts who agree with his or her position—for example, only pro- (or only anti-) environmental writers? A writer who does this is presenting an unbalanced (and therefore biased) case.

- *Consider the writer's tone.* A writer whose tone is angry, bitter, or sarcastic should be suspect.

- *Consider any overtly offensive statements or characterizations* that a writer makes. A writer who makes negative assumptions about college students (for example, characterizing them as selfish and self-involved and therefore dismissing their commitment to campus environmental projects) should be viewed with skepticism.

> **NOTE**
>
> Be aware of any biases you hold that might affect the strength or logic of your own arguments. See "Being Fair," page 256.

⊙ EXERCISE 7.8

What evidence might you use to support the thesis statement you decided on in Exercise 7.6?

⊙ EXERCISE 7.9

In writing an essay that supports the thesis statement you have been working with in this chapter, you might not be objective. What biases do you have that you might have to watch for as you research and write about your topic?

⊙ EXERCISE 7.10

Gather evidence to support your thesis statement, evaluating each source carefully (consulting Chapter 8 as necessary). Be on the lookout for bias in your sources.

Refuting Opposing Arguments

As you plan your essay and read sources that will supply your supporting evidence, you will encounter evidence that contradicts your position. You may be tempted to ignore this evidence, but if you do, your argument will be less convincing. Instead, as you do your research, identify the most convincing arguments against your position and prepare yourself to **refute** them (that is, disprove them or call them into question), showing them to be illogical, unfair, or untrue. Indicating to readers that you are willing to address these arguments—and that you can respond effectively to them—will help convince them to accept your position.

Of course, simply saying that your opponent's position is "wrong" or "stupid" is not convincing. You need to summarize opposing arguments accurately and clearly identify their weaknesses. In the case of a strong opposing argument, be sure to acknowledge its strengths before you refute it; if you do not, readers may see you as uninformed or unfair. Also be careful not to create a **straw man**—distorting an opposing argument by oversimplifying it so it can be easily refuted (for example, claiming that environmentalists believe that sustainability should always be a college's first priority in its decisions about allocating resources). This unfair tactic will discourage readers from trusting you and thus will undermine your credibility.

> **NOTE**
>
> Sometimes an opposing argument is so strong that you will not be able to refute it. If you cannot demonstrate that an opposing argument is weak or false, it makes sense to concede the point—perhaps noting that it is not central to your discussion or that it is beside the point—and then move on.

Although refutation is a key element of an argumentative essay, it can also provide the structure for an entire essay. For example, if you are writing an essay for an audience of students who believe they have no time to pay attention to campus environmental issues, you might structure your essay as a refutation. Your essay would discuss and refute each of your audience's objections and then present your own position. A thesis statement such as the following one would indicate that your essay was structured as a refutation:

> **Although protecting the environment may be time-consuming, a green campus should be a priority for every U.S. college student.**

Revising Your Thesis Statement

Before you can draft your argumentative essay and even before you can begin to arrange your ideas, you need to revise your tentative thesis statement so it says exactly what you want it to say.

After you have gathered and evaluated evidence to support your position and considered the merits of opposing ideas, you are ready to refocus your thesis and state it in more definite terms. Although a tentative thesis statement such as "College campuses should go green" is a good start, the thesis that guides your essay's structure should be more specific. In fact, it will be most useful as a guide if it actually acknowledges opposing arguments in its phrasing.

> ### REVISED THESIS STATEMENT
>
> *Despite the expense, colleges should make every effort to create green campuses because doing so improves their own educational environment, ensures their own institution's survival, and helps solve the global climate crisis.*

⊖ EXERCISE 7.11

Consulting the sources you gathered in Exercise 7.10, list all the arguments against the position that you took in your thesis statement. Then, list possible refutations of these arguments. When you have finished, revise your thesis statement so that it is more specific, acknowledging and refuting the most important argument against your position.

After you have revised your thesis statement, you will have a concise blueprint for the essay you are going to write. Now, you are ready to plan your essay's structure and write a first draft.

Structuring Your Essay

As you learned in Chapter 1, an argumentative essay, like other essays, includes an introduction, a body, and a conclusion. In the introduction of an argumentative essay, you state your thesis; in the body paragraphs, you present evidence to support your thesis, and you refute opposing arguments; and in your conclusion, you bring your argument to a close and reinforce your thesis with a strong concluding statement. As you have seen, these four elements—thesis, evidence, refutation, and concluding statement—are like the four pillars of the ancient Greek temple, supporting your argument so that it will stand up to scrutiny.

> ### SUPPLYING BACKGROUND INFORMATION
>
> Depending on what you think your readers know—and what you think they need to know—you might decide to include a background paragraph that supplies information about the issue you are discussing. For example, in an essay about green campuses, you might briefly sum up the history of the U.S. environmental movement and trace its rise on college campuses. If you decide to include a background paragraph, it should be placed right after your introduction, where it can prepare readers for the discussion to follow.

Understanding basic essay structure can help you as you shape your essay. *Using induction and deduction, identifying a strategy for your argument*, and *constructing a formal outline* can also help you develop the body of your essay.

Using Induction and Deduction

Many argumentative essays are structured either **inductively** or **deductively**. (See Chapter 5 for explanations of induction and deduction.) For example, the body of an essay with the thesis statement that is shown on page 252 could have either of the following general structures:

INDUCTIVE STRUCTURE

- Colleges are taking a number of steps to follow green practices.
- Through these efforts, campuses have become more environmentally responsible, and their programs and practices have made a positive difference.
- Because these efforts are helping to save the planet, they should be expanded.

DEDUCTIVE STRUCTURE

- Saving the planet is vital.
- Green campuses can help to save the planet.
- Therefore, colleges should create green campuses.

These strategies offer two options for arranging material in your essay. Many argumentative essays, however, combine induction and deduction or use other strategies to shape their ideas.

Identifying a Strategy for Your Argument

As Part 5 of this book makes clear, there are a variety of different ways to structure an argument, and the strategy you use depends on what you want your argument to accomplish. In this text, we discuss six options for presenting material: *definition arguments, causal arguments, evaluation arguments, proposal arguments, argument by analogy*, and *ethical arguments*.

Any of the six options listed above could guide you as you developed an essay on green campuses:

- You could structure your essay as a **definition argument**, explaining the concept of a green campus and giving examples to show how it operates. (See Chapter 12 for more on definition arguments.)

■ You could structure your essay as a **causal argument**, showing how establishing a green campus could have positive results for students and for the campus. (See Chapter 13 for more on causal arguments.)

■ You could structure your essay as an **evaluation argument**, assessing the strengths and weaknesses of various programs and policies designed to create and sustain a green campus. (See Chapter 14 for more on evaluation arguments.)

■ You could structure your essay as a **proposal argument**, recommending a particular program, service, or course of action and showing how it can support a green campus. (See Chapter 15 for more on proposal arguments.)

■ You could structure your essay as an **argument by analogy**, showing how a college campus is a city in miniature and should therefore be green for the same reasons cities should have responsible environmental policies—to protect its citizens, buildings, natural resources, and institutions. (See Chapter 16 for more on argument by analogy.)

■ You could structure your essay as an **ethical argument**, explaining why creating a green campus is the right thing to do from a moral or ethical standpoint. (See Chapter 17 for more on ethical arguments.)

> **NOTE**
>
> Keep in mind that you might also decide to structure your essay as a **refutation**. (See pp. 22–23 for more on refutation.)

Constructing a Formal Outline

If you like, you can construct a **formal outline** before you begin your draft. (Later on, you can also construct an outline of your finished paper to check the logic of its structure.) A formal outline, which is more detailed and more logically organized than the informal outline shown on page 245, presents your main points and supporting details in the order in which you will discuss them.

A formal outline of the first body paragraph of the student essay on page 267 would look like this:

I. Background of the term *green*
   A. 1960s environmental movement
      1. Political agenda
      2. Environmental agenda
   B. Today's movements
      1. Eco-friendly practices
      2. Green values

Following a formal outline makes the drafting process flow smoothly, but many writers find it hard to predict exactly what details they will use for support or how they will develop their arguments. In fact, your first draft is likely to move away from your outline as you develop your ideas. Still, if you are the kind of writer who prefers to know where you are going before you start on your way, you will probably consider the time you devote to outlining to be time well spent.

⊖ EXERCISE 7.12

Look back at the thesis you decided on earlier in this chapter, and review the evidence you collected to support it. Then, construct a formal outline for your argumentative essay.

Establishing Credibility

Before you begin writing your draft, you need to think about how to approach your topic and your audience. The essay you write will use a combination of *logical*, *emotional*, and *ethical* appeals, and you will have to be careful to use these appeals reasonably. (See the introduction to this book for information on these appeals.) As you write, you will concentrate on establishing yourself as well informed, reasonable, and fair.

Being Well Informed

If you expect your readers to accept your ideas, you will need to establish yourself as someone they should believe and trust. This involves showing your audience that you have a good command of your material—that is, that you know what you are talking about.

If you want readers to listen to what you are saying, you need to earn their respect by showing them that you have done your research, that you have collected evidence that supports your argument, and that you understand the most compelling arguments against your position. For example, discussing your own experiences as a member of a campus or community environmental group, your observations at a Greenpeace convention, and essays and editorials that you have read on both sides of the issue will encourage your audience to accept your ideas on the subject of green campuses.

Being Reasonable

Even if your evidence is strong, your argument will not be convincing if it does not seem reasonable. One way to present yourself as a reasonable person is to **establish common ground** with your readers, stressing possible points of agreement instead of attacking those who might disagree with your position. For example, saying, "We all want our planet to survive" is a more effective strategy than saying, "Those who do not support the concept of a green campus are going to destroy our planet." (For more on establishing common ground, see the discussion of Rogerian argument in Chapter 6.)

Another way to present yourself as a reasonable person is to **maintain a reasonable tone**. Try to avoid absolutes (words like *always* and *never*); instead, use more conciliatory language (*in many cases, much of the time,* and so on). Try not to use words and phrases like *obviously* or *as anyone can see* to introduce points whose strength may be obvious only to you. Do not brand opponents of your position as misguided, uninformed, or deluded; remember, some of your readers may hold opposing positions and will not appreciate your unfavorable portrayal of them.

Finally, be very careful to treat your readers with respect, addressing them as your intellectual equals. Avoid statements that might insult them or their beliefs ("Although some ignorant or misguided people may still think . . ."). And never assume that your readers know less about your topic than you do; they may actually know a good deal more.

Being Fair

If you want readers to respect your point of view, you need to demonstrate respect for them by being fair. It is not enough to support your ideas convincingly and maintain a reasonable tone. You also need to avoid unfair tactics in your argument and take care to avoid **bias**.

In particular, you should be careful not to *distort evidence, quote out of context, slant evidence, make unfair appeals,* or *use logical fallacies.* These unfair tactics may influence some readers in the short term, but in the long run such tactics will alienate your audience.

- **Do not distort evidence. Distorting** (or misrepresenting) **evidence** is an unfair tactic. It is not ethical or fair, for example, to present your opponent's views inaccurately or to exaggerate his or her position and then argue against it. If you want to argue that green programs on college campuses are a good idea, then it is not fair to attack someone who expresses reservations about their cost by writing, "Mr. McNamara's concerns about cost reveal that he has basic doubts about saving the planet." (His concerns reveal no such thing.) It is, however, fair to acknowledge your opponent's reasonable concerns about cost and then go on to argue that the long-term benefits of such programs justify their expense.

- **Do not quote out of context.** It is perfectly fair to challenge someone's stated position. It is not fair, however, to misrepresent that position by **quoting out of context**—that is, by taking the words out of the original setting in which they appeared. For example, if a college dean says, "For schools with limited resources, it may be more important to allocate resources to academic programs than to environmental projects," you are quoting the dean's remarks out of context if you say, "According to Dean Levering, it is 'more important to allocate resources to academic programs than to environmental projects.'"

- **Do not slant evidence.** An argument based on slanted evidence is not fair. **Slanting** involves choosing only evidence that supports your position and ignoring evidence that challenges it. This tactic makes your position seem stronger than it actually is. Another kind of slanting involves using biased language to unfairly characterize your opponents or their positions—for example, using a dismissive term such as *tree-hugger* to describe a concerned environmentalist.

- **Do not make unfair appeals.** If you want your readers to accept your ideas, you need to avoid **unfair appeals** to the emotions, such as appeals to your audience's fears or prejudices. For example, if you try to convince readers of the importance of using green building materials by saying, "Construction projects that do not use green materials doom future generations to a planet that cannot sustain itself," you are likely to push neutral (or even receptive) readers to skepticism or to outright hostility.

- **Do not use logical fallacies.** Using **logical fallacies** (flawed arguments) in your writing will alienate your readers. (See Chapter 5 for information about logical fallacies.)

MAINTAINING YOUR CREDIBILITY

An argument is no place for modesty. Be careful to avoid phrases that undercut your credibility ("Although this is not a subject I know much about") and to avoid apologies ("This is just my opinion"). Be as clear, direct, and forceful as you can, showing readers you are confident as well as knowledgeable. And, of course, be sure to proofread carefully: grammatical and mechanical errors and typos will weaken your credibility.

Drafting Your Essay

Once you understand how to approach your topic and your audience, you will be ready to draft your essay. At this point, you will have selected the sources you will use to support your position as well as identified the strongest arguments against your position (and decided how to refute them). You may also have prepared a formal outline (or perhaps just a list of points to follow).

Now, you need to focus on some guidelines for drafting your essay. As you write, keep the following points in mind:

- **Follow the general structure of an argumentative essay.** State your thesis in your first paragraph, and discuss each major point in a separate paragraph, moving from least to most important point to emphasize your strongest argument. Introduce each body paragraph with a clearly worded topic sentence. Discuss each opposing argument in a separate paragraph, and be sure your refutation appears directly after you summarize each opposing argument. Finally, don't forget to include a strong concluding statement in your essay's last paragraph.

- **Decide how to arrange your material.** As you draft your essay, you may notice that it is turning out to be an ethical argument, an argument by analogy, or another kind of argument that you recognize. If this is the case, you can follow the guidelines outlined in the appropriate chapter in Part 5 of this book.

- **Use evidence effectively.** As you make your points, select the evidence that supports your argument most convincingly. As you write, summarize or paraphrase relevant information from your sources, and respond to this information in your own voice, supplementing material that you find in your sources with your own original ideas and conclusions. (For information on finding and evaluating sources, see Chapter 8; for information on integrating source material into your argumentative essay, see Chapter 9.)

- **Use coordination and subordination to make your meaning clear.** Readers shouldn't have to guess how two points are connected; you should use coordination and subordination to show them the relationship between ideas.

  Choose **coordinating conjunctions**—*and, but, or, nor, for, so,* and *yet*—carefully, making sure you are using the right word for your purpose. (Use *and* to show addition; *but, for,* or *yet* to show contradiction; *or* to present alternatives; and *so* to indicate a causal relationship.)

  Choose **subordinating conjunctions**—*although, because,* and so on—carefully, and place them so that your emphasis will be clear.

  Consider the following two sentences.

  > Achieving a green campus is vitally important. Creating a green campus is expensive.

  If you want to stress the idea that green measures are called for, you would write the following:

> Although creating a green campus is expensive, achieving a green campus is vitally important.

If, on the other hand, you want to place emphasis on the high cost, you would write the following:

> Although achieving a green campus is vitally important, creating a green campus is expensive.

■ **Include transitional words and phrases.** Be sure you have enough transitions to guide your readers through your discussion. You need to supply signals that move readers from sentence to sentence and paragraph to paragraph, and the signals you choose need to make sense in the context of your discussion.

SOME TRANSITIONS FOR ARGUMENT

■ To show causal relationships: *because, as a result, for this reason*

■ To indicate sequence: *first, second, third; then; next; finally*

■ To introduce additional points: *also, another, in addition, furthermore, moreover*

■ To move from general to specific: *for example, for instance, in short, in other words*

■ To identify an opposing argument: *however, although, even though, despite*

■ To grant the validity of an opposing argument: *certainly, admittedly, granted, of course*

■ To introduce a refutation: *however, nevertheless, nonetheless, still*

■ **Define your terms.** If the key terms of your argument have multiple meanings—as *green* does—be sure to indicate what the term means in the context of your argument. Terms like *environmentally friendly, global warming, climate change, environmentally responsible, sustainable,* and *sustainability literacy* may mean very different things to different readers.

■ **Use clear language.** An argument is no place for vague language or wordy phrasing. If you want readers to understand your points, your writing should be clear and direct. Avoid vague words like *good, bad, right,* and *wrong,* which are really just unsupported judgments that do nothing to help you make your case. Also avoid wordy phrases such as *revolves around* and *is concerned with*, particularly in thesis statements and topic sentences.

- **Finally, show your confidence and your mastery of your material.** Avoid qualifying your statements with phrases like *I think, I believe, it seems to me,* and *in my opinion.* These qualifiers weaken your argument by suggesting that you are unsure of your material or that the statements to follow may not be true.

GRAMMAR IN CONTEXT

Using Parallelism

As you draft your argumentative essay, you should express corresponding words, phrases, and clauses in **parallel** terms. The use of matching parts of speech to express corresponding ideas strengthens your argument's impact because it enables readers to follow your line of thought.

In particular, use parallelism in sentences that highlight *paired items* or *items in a series.*

- **Paired Items**

  UNCLEAR   Creating a green campus is important because <u>it sets</u> an example for students and the <u>environment will be protected</u>.

  PARALLEL   Creating a green campus is important because it <u>sets</u> an example for students and <u>protects</u> the environment.

- **Items in a Series**

  UNCLEAR   Students can do their part to support a green campus in four ways—by <u>avoiding</u> bottled water, use of electricity <u>should be limited</u>, and they <u>can recycle</u> packaging and also <u>educating</u> themselves about environmental issues is a good strategy.

  PARALLEL   Students can do their part to support a green campus in four ways—by <u>avoiding</u> bottled water, by <u>limiting</u> use of electricity, by <u>recycling</u> packaging, and by <u>educating</u> themselves about environmental issues.

⊙ EXERCISE 7.13

Keeping the above guidelines in mind, write a draft of an argumentative essay that develops the thesis statement you have been working with.

Revising Your Essay

After you have written a draft of your essay, you will need to revise it. **Revision** is "re-seeing"—looking carefully and critically at the draft you have written. Revision is different from editing and proofreading (discussed on pp. 265–266), which focus on grammar, punctuation, mechanics, and the like. In fact, revision can involve substantial reworking of your essay's structure and content. The strategies discussed on the pages that follow can help you revise your arguments.

Asking Questions

Asking some basic questions, such as those in the two checklists that follow, can help you start the revision process.

> **CHECKLIST**
>
> **Questions about Your Essay's Structure and Style**
>
> ☐ Do you have a clearly stated thesis?
>
> ☐ Are your topic sentences clear and concise?
>
> ☐ Do you provide all necessary background and definitions?
>
> ☐ Do you refute opposing arguments effectively?
>
> ☐ Do you include enough transitional words and phrases to guide readers smoothly through your discussion?
>
> ☐ Have you avoided vague language and wordy phrasing?
>
> ☐ Do you have a strong concluding statement?

> **CHECKLIST**
>
> **Questions about Your Essay's Supporting Evidence**
>
> ☐ Do you support your opinions with *evidence*—facts, observations, examples, statistics, expert opinion, and so on?
>
> ☐ Do you have enough evidence to support your thesis?
>
> ☐ Do the sources you rely on present information accurately and without bias?
>
> ☐ Are your sources' discussions directly relevant to your topic?
>
> ☐ Have you consulted sources that represent a wide range of viewpoints, including sources that challenge your position?

The answers to the questions on the preceding page may lead you to revise your essay's content, structure, and style. For example, you may want to look for additional sources that can provide the kind of supporting evidence you need. Or, you may notice you need to revise the structure of your essay, perhaps rearranging your points so that the most important point is placed last, for emphasis. You may also want to revise your essay's introduction and conclusion, sharpening your thesis statement or adding a stronger concluding statement. Finally, you may decide to add more background material to help your readers understand the issue you are writing about.

Using Outlines and Templates

To check the logic of your essay's structure, you can prepare a revision outline or consult a template.

- To make sure your essay's key points are arranged logically and supported convincingly, you can construct a formal outline of your draft. (See p. 254 for information on formal outlines.) This outline will indicate whether you need to discuss an additional point, add supporting evidence, or refute an opposing argument more fully. It will also show you if paragraphs are arranged in a logical order.

- To make sure your argument flows smoothly from thesis statement to evidence to refutation of opposing arguments to concluding statement, you can refer to one of the paragraph **templates** that appear throughout this book. These templates can help you to construct a one-paragraph summary of your essay.

Getting Feedback

After you have done as much as you can on your own, it is time to get feedback from your instructor and (with your instructor's permission) from your school's writing center or from other students in your class.

Instructor Feedback   You can get feedback from your instructor in a variety of different ways. For example, your instructor may ask you to email a draft of your paper to him or her with some specific questions ("Do I need paragraph 3, or do I have enough evidence without it?" "Does my thesis statement need to be more specific?"). The instructor will then reply with corrections and recommendations. If your instructor prefers a traditional face-to-face conference, you may still want to email your draft ahead of time so that he or she will have had time to read it.

Writing Center Feedback You can also get feedback from a writing center tutor, who can be either a student or a professional. The tutor can give you another point of view about your paper's content and organization and also help you focus on specific questions of style, grammar, punctuation, and mechanics. (Keep in mind, however, that a tutor will not edit or proofread your paper for you; that is your job.)

Peer Review Finally, you can get feedback from your classmates. **Peer review** can be an informal process in which you ask a classmate for advice, or it can be a more structured process, involving small groups working with copies of students' work. Peer review can also be conducted electronically. For example, students can exchange drafts by email or respond to one another's drafts that are posted on the course Web site. They can also use Word's comment tool, as illustrated in the following example.

DRAFT

Colleges and universities have no excuse for ignoring the threat of global warming. Campus leaders need to push beyond efforts to recycle or compost and instead become models of sustainability. Already, many universities are hard at work demonstrating that reducing their institution's environmental impact is not only possible but worthwhile. They are overhauling their entire infrastructure, their buildings, systems, and even curriculum. While many students, faculty, staff, and administrators are excited by these new challenges, some still question this need to go green. Is it worth the money? Is it promoting "a moral and behavioral agenda rather than an educational one"? (Butcher). In fact, greening will ultimately save institutions money while providing their students with a good education. Colleges should make every effort to create green campuses because by doing so they will help solve the global climate crisis.

Comment [LB]: Your first two sentences are a little abrupt. Maybe you could ease into your argument more slowly?

Comment [KS]: I like these two questions. They really got me thinking.

Comment [PL]: Could you be more specific? I'm not sure what you mean.

Comment [PL]: You definitely talk about this in your paper, but you also talk about other reasons to go green. You might consider revising this thesis statement so it matches your argument.

FINAL VERSION

Over the last few years, the pressure to go green has led colleges and universities to make big changes. The threats posed by global warming are inspiring campus leaders to push beyond efforts to recycle to become models of sustainability. Today, in the interest of reducing their environmental impact, many campuses are seeking to overhaul their entire infrastructure—their buildings, their systems, and even their curriculum. While many students, faculty, staff, and administrators are excited by these new challenges, some question this need to go green. Is it worth the money? Is it promoting "a moral and behavioral agenda rather than an educational one"? (Butcher). In fact, greening will ultimately save institutions money while providing their students with the educational opportunities necessary to help them solve the crisis of their generation. Despite the expense, colleges should make every effort to create green campuses because by doing so they will improve their own educational environment, ensure their own institution's survival, and help solve the global climate crisis.

> **NOTE**
>
> Remember that the peer-review process involves *giving* feedback as well as receiving it. When you respond to a classmate's work, be tactful and supportive when pointing out shortcomings or errors, give praise and encouragement whenever possible, and be generous with your suggestions for improvement.

➲ EXERCISE 7.14

Following the guidelines for revision discussed earlier, get some feedback from others, and then revise your argumentative essay.

Adding Visuals

After you have gotten feedback about the ideas in your paper, you might want to consider adding a **visual**—a chart, graph, table, photo, or diagram—to help you make a point more forcefully. For example, in a paper on the green campus movement, you could include anything from photos of students recycling to a chart comparing energy use at different schools. Sometimes a visual can be so specific, so attractive, or so dramatic that its impact will be greater than words would be. At other times, a visual can expand and support a verbal argument.

You can create a visual yourself, or you can download one from the Internet, beginning your search with Google Images. If you download a visual and paste it into your paper, be sure to include a reference to the visual in your discussion to show readers how it supports your argument.

> **NOTE**
>
> Don't forget to label your visual with a figure number, to use proper documentation, and to include a caption explaining what the visual shows, as the student paper that begins on page 267 does. (For information on how to document visuals, see Chapter 10.)

Polishing Your Essay

The final step in the writing process is putting the finishing touches on your essay. At this point, your goal is to make sure that your essay is well organized, convincing, and clearly written, with no distracting grammatical or mechanical errors.

Editing

When you **edit** your revised draft, you review your essay's overall structure, style, and sentence construction, but you focus on grammar, punctuation, and mechanics. Editing is an important step in the writing process because an interesting, logically organized argument will not be convincing if readers are distracted by run-ons and fragments, confusingly placed modifiers, or incorrect verb forms. (Remember, your grammar checker will spot some grammatical errors, but it will miss many others.)

GRAMMAR IN CONTEXT

Pronoun-Antecedent Agreement

A pronoun must always agree in number with its **antecedent**, the word to which it refers. Every pronoun must clearly refer to a particular antecedent.

CONFUSING	College administrators, faculty members, and staff members must work hard to show every student that a green campus will benefit <u>them</u>.
REVISED	College administrators, faculty members, and staff members must work hard to show every student that a green campus will benefit <u>him or her</u>.

Proofreading

When you **proofread** your revised and edited draft, you carefully read every word, trying to spot any remaining punctuation or mechanical errors, as well as any typographical errors (typos) or misspellings that your spell checker may have missed. (Remember, a spell checker will not flag a correctly spelled word that is used incorrectly.)

GRAMMAR IN CONTEXT

Contractions versus Possessive Pronouns

Be especially careful not to confuse the contractions *it's*, *who's*, *they're*, and *you're* with the possessive forms *its*, *whose*, *their*, and *your*.

INCORRECT	<u>Its</u> not always clear <u>who's</u> responsibility it is to promote green initiatives on campus.
CORRECT	<u>It's</u> not always clear <u>whose</u> responsibility it is to promote green initiatives on campus.

Choosing a Title

After you have edited and proofread your essay, you need to give it a title. Ideally, your title should create interest in your topic and give readers clear information about the subject of your essay. It should also be appropriate for your topic. A serious topic calls for a serious title, and a thoughtfully presented argument deserves a thoughtfully selected title.

A title does not need to surprise or shock readers. It also should not be long and wordy or something many readers will not understand. A simple statement of your topic ("Going Green") or of your position on the issue ("College Campuses Should Go Green") is usually all that is needed. If you like, you can use a quotation from one of your sources as a title ("Green Is Good").

➔ EXERCISE 7.15

Evaluate the suitability and effectiveness of the following titles for an argumentative essay on green campuses. Be prepared to explain the strengths and weaknesses of each title.

- Green Campuses

- It's Not Easy Being Green

- The Lean, Clean, Green Machine

- What Students Can Do to Make Their Campuses More Environmentally Responsible

- Why Campuses Should Be Green

- Planting the Seeds of the Green Campus Movement

- The Green Campus: An Idea Whose Time Has Come

Checking Format

Finally, make sure that your essay follows your instructor's guidelines for documentation style and manuscript format. (The student paper below follows MLA style and manuscript format. For additional sample essays illustrating MLA and APA documentation style and manuscript format, see Chapter 10 and Appendix B, respectively.)

The following student essay, "Going Green," argues that colleges should make every effort to create green campuses.

GOING GREEN

SHAWN HOLTON

1   Over the last few years, the pressure to go green has led colleges and universities to make big changes. The threats posed by global warming are encouraging campus leaders to push beyond early efforts, such as recycling, to become models of sustainability. Today, in the interest of reducing their environmental impact, many campuses are seeking to overhaul their entire infrastructure. Although many students, faculty, staff, and administrators are excited by these new challenges, some question this need to go green. Is it worth the money? Is it promoting "a moral and behavioral agenda rather than an educational one"? (Butcher). In fact, greening will ultimately save institutions money while providing their students with the educational opportunities necessary to help them solve the crisis of their generation. Colleges should make every effort to create green campuses because by doing so they will improve their own educational environment, ensure their own institution's survival, and help solve the global climate crisis.

Introduction

Thesis statement

2   Although the green movement has been around for many years, *green* has only recently become a buzzword. Green political parties and groups began forming in the 1960s to promote environmentalist goals ("Environmentalism"). These groups fought for "grassroots democracy, social justice, and nonviolence" in addition to environmental protections

Body paragraph: Background of green movement

and were "self-consciously activist and unconventional" in their strategies ("Environmentalism"). Today, however, *green* denotes much more than a political movement; it has become a catchall word for anything eco-friendly. People use *green* to describe everything from fuel-efficient cars to fume-free house paint. Green values have become more mainstream in response to evidence that human activities, particularly those that result in greenhouse-gas emissions, may be causing global warming at a dramatic rate ("Call for Climate Leadership" 4). To fight this climate change, many individuals, businesses, and organizations are choosing to go green, making sustainability and preservation of the environment a priority.

Body paragraph: Definition of *green* as it applies to colleges

Greening a college campus means moving toward a sustainable   3 campus that works to conserve the earth's natural resources. It means reducing the university's carbon footprint by focusing on energy efficiency in every aspect of campus life. This is no small task. Although replacing incandescent light bulbs with compact fluorescent ones and offering more locally grown food in dining halls are valuable steps, meaningful sustainability requires more comprehensive changes. For example, universities also need to invest in alternative energy sources, construct new buildings and remodel old ones, and work to reduce campus demand for nonrenewable products. Although these changes will eventually save universities money, in most cases, the institutions will need to spend money now to reduce costs in the long term. To achieve this transformation, many colleges are—individually or in cooperation with other schools—establishing formal "climate commitments," setting specific goals, and developing tools to track their investments and evaluate their progress.

Body paragraph: First argument in support of thesis

Despite these challenges, there are many compelling reasons to act   4 now. Saving money on operating costs, thus making the school more competitive in the long term, is an appealing incentive. In fact, many schools have made solid and sometimes immediate gains by greening some aspect of their campus. For example, by changing its parking and transit systems to encourage more carpooling, biking, and walking, Cornell University has saved 417,000 gallons of fuel and cut costs by $36 million over the last twelve years ("Call for Climate Leadership" 10). By putting in a "smart grid" that improves efficiency in energy distribution and use for three new buildings, Drexel University in Philadelphia is saving 20% on energy costs. By using a similar smart grid and by generating three megawatts of their own green power, Santa Clara University is working toward being entirely energy independent (McClure 64). Given the high cost of electricity in California, getting off the grid offers significant savings; as one university administrator puts it, "Those 3 megawatts allow us to stay open" (qtd. in McClure 64). And Oberlin College not only saves money by generating its own solar energy (as shown in Fig. 1) but also makes money by selling its excess electricity back to the local power company (Petersen). Many other schools have taken similar steps, with similarly positive results.

Fig. 1. Solar panels on the roof of the Adam Joseph Lewis Center for Environmental Studies, Oberlin College. 2008. Oberlin.edu.

5   Attracting the attention of the media, donors, and—most significantly—prospective students is another practical reason for schools to go green. As one researcher explains, "There is enough evidence nationwide to detect an arms-race of sorts among universities competing for green status" (Krizek et al. 27). The *Princeton Review* now includes a "green rating," and according to recent studies, more than two thirds of college applicants say that they consider green ratings when choosing a school (Krizek et al. 27). A school's commitment to the environment can also bring in large private donations. For example, Carnegie Mellon University attracted $1.7 million from the National Science Foundation for its new Center for Sustainable Engineering (Egan). The University of California, Davis, will be receiving up to $25 million from the Chevron Corporation to research biofuel technology ("Call for Climate Leadership" 10). While greening certainly costs money, a green commitment can also help a school remain financially viable.

Body paragraph: Second argument in support of thesis

6   In addition to these practical reasons for going green, universities also have another, perhaps more important, reason to promote and model sustainability: doing so may help solve the climate crisis.

Body paragraph: Third argument in support of thesis

Although an individual school's reduction of emissions may not noticeably affect global warming, its graduates will be in a position to make a huge impact. College is a critical time in most students' personal and professional development. Students are making choices about what kind of adults they will be, and they are also receiving the training, education, and experience that they will need to succeed in the working world. If universities can offer time, space, and incentives—both in and out of the classroom—to help students develop creative ways to live sustainably, these schools have the potential to change the thinking and habits of a whole generation.

Refutation of first opposing argument

Many critics of greening claim that becoming environmentally 7 friendly is too expensive and will result in higher tuition and fees. However, often a very small increase in fees, as little as a few dollars a semester, can be enough to help a school institute significant change. For example, at the University of Colorado–Boulder, a student-initiated $1 increase in fees allowed the school to purchase enough wind power to reduce its carbon emissions by 12 million pounds ("Call for Climate Leadership" 9). Significantly, the students were the ones who voted to increase their own fees to achieve a greener campus. Although university faculty and administrators' commitment to sustainability is critical for any program's success, few green initiatives will succeed without the enthusiastic support of the student body. Ultimately, students have the power. If they think their school is spending too much on green projects, then they can make a change or choose to go elsewhere.

Refutation of second opposing argument

Other critics of the trend toward greener campuses believe that 8 schools with commitments to sustainability are dictating how students should live rather than encouraging free thought. As one critic says, "Once [sustainability literacy] is enshrined in a university's public pronouncements or private articles, then the institution has diminished its commitment to academic inquiry" (Butcher). This kind of criticism overlooks the fact that figuring out how to achieve sustainability requires and will continue to require rigorous critical thinking and creativity. Why not apply the academic skills of inquiry, analysis, and problem solving to the biggest problem of our day? Not doing so would be irresponsible and would confirm the perception that universities are ivory towers of irrelevant knowledge. In fact, the presence of sustainability as both a goal and a subject of study has the potential to reaffirm academia's place at the center of civil society.

9   Creating a green campus is a difficult task, but universities must rise to the challenge or face the consequences. If they do not commit to changing their ways, they will become less and less able to compete for students and for funding. If they refuse to make a comprehensive commitment to sustainability, they also risk irrelevance at best and institutional collapse at worst. Finally, by not rising to the challenge, they will be giving up the opportunity to establish themselves as leaders in addressing the climate crisis. As the coalition of American College and University Presidents states in its Climate Commitment, "No other institution has the influence, the critical mass and the diversity of skills needed to successfully reverse global warming" ("Call for Climate Leadership" 13). Now is the time for schools to make the choice and pledge to go green.

Conclusion

Concluding statement

Works Cited

Butcher, Jim. "Keep the Green Moral Agenda off Campus." *Times Higher Education*. TSL Education, 19 Oct. 2007. Web. 12 Apr. 2012.

"A Call for Climate Leadership." *American College and University Presidents Climate Commitment*. Presidents Climate Commitment, Mar. 2007. Web. 15 Apr. 2012.

Egan, Timothy. "The Greening of America's Campuses." *New York Times*. New York Times, 8 Jan. 2006. Web. 12 Apr. 2012.

"Environmentalism." *Encyclopaedia Britannica Online*. Encyclopaedia Britannica, Inc., 2008. Web. 14 Apr. 2012.

Krizek, Kevin J., Dave Newport, James White, and Alan R. Townsend. "Higher Education's Sustainability Imperative: How to Practically Respond?" *International Journal of Sustainability in Higher Education* 13.1 (2012): 19–33. *Academic Search Complete*. Web. 8 Apr. 2012.

McClure, Ann. "The Power of Green: Campus Sustainability Policies and Practices That Make a Big Impact." *University Business* 14.6 (2011): 63–64. *Academic Search Complete*. Web. 8 Apr. 2012.

Petersen, John. "A Green Curriculum Involves Everyone on Campus." *Chronicle of Higher Education* 54.41 (2008): A25. *Academic Search Premier*. Web. 10 Apr. 2012.

⊙ EXERCISE 7.16

Find a visual that will strengthen your argument, and add it to your essay. Be sure to document it appropriately and to include a descriptive caption. Then, edit and proofread your paper, paying special attention to parenthetical documentation and your works-cited page. When you have finished, add a title, and print out a final copy of your essay.

4

Using Sources to Support Your Argument

8

Finding and Evaluating Sources

Do Social-Networking Sites Threaten Our Privacy?

Facebook currently has over 400 million users worldwide, and Twitter has over 100 million users. The longer people use these sites, the more comfortable they become, and the more information they reveal about themselves without thinking about the possible consequences. According to a 2010 *Consumer Reports* article, 25% of people using Facebook were unaware of privacy settings, and 40% posted their dates of birth online. Not surprisingly, social-networking sites have become the prime targets for those who seek to take advantage of people's willingness to share personal information: employers routinely use information from these sites to help them make hiring decisions, advertisers buy data to target consumers, and cybercriminals use information posted on social-networking sites to steal users' identities.

In response to complaints, the federal government has begun to focus on the issue of privacy on social-networking sites. As a result of pressure from the Federal Trade Commission, Facebook, Twitter, and Google have agreed to submit to privacy audits, and in response to complaints by users, Mark Zuckerberg, creator of Facebook, has repeatedly revised the site's privacy policies. Some critics, however, claim that actions like these do little to solve the problem and that the only way to ensure privacy is for people to disengage entirely from social media. Others disagree, saying that social networks are a fact of everyday life and that people have to learn to cope with them. They believe that people should be more realistic in their demands and should have no expectation of privacy when they post information about themselves online.

Later in this chapter, you will be asked to evaluate a number of research sources to determine if they are acceptable for an argumentative essay on the topic of whether social-networking sites threaten privacy. In Chapter 9,

(continued)

For comprehension quizzes,
see bedfordstmartins.com/practicalargument.

(continued)

you will learn how to integrate sources into an essay on this general topic. Finally, in Chapter 10, you will see an MLA paper on one aspect of the topic: whether it is ethical for employers to access information posted on job applicants' social-networking sites.

Finding Sources

In some argumentative essays, you can use your own ideas as evidence in support of your position. In many others, however, you have to do **research**—collect information (in both print and electronic form) from magazines, newspapers, books, journals, and other sources—to supplement your own ideas.

Finding Information in the Library

When most students do research, they immediately go to the Internet—or, more specifically, to the Web. Unfortunately, by doing this, they ignore the most reliable source of high-quality information available to them: their college library.

Your college library contains both print and electronic resources that you cannot find anywhere else. Although the Web gives you access to an almost unlimited amount of material, it does not offer the consistently high level of reliable information found in your college library. For this reason, you should always begin your research by surveying the resources of the library.

The best way to access your college library is to visit its Web site, which is the gateway to a great deal of information—for example, its online catalog, electronic databases, and reference works.

> **The Online Catalog:** The **online catalog** lists all the books, journals, newspapers, magazines, and other material housed in the library. Once you gain access to this catalog, you can type in keywords related to your topic. These will lead you to sources related to your topic.
>
> **Electronic Databases:** All college libraries subscribe to **electronic databases**—collections of digital information that you access through a keyword search. The library's electronic databases enable you to retrieve bibliographic citations as well as the full text of articles from hundreds of publications. Some of these databases—for example, *Expanded Academic Plus* and *Proquest Research Library*—provide information on a wide variety of topics. Others—for example, *Business Source Premier* and *Sociological Abstracts*—provide information on

a particular subject area. Before selecting a database, check with the reference librarian to determine which will be most useful for your topic.

Reference Works: All libraries contain **reference works**—sources of accurate and reliable information. These reference works are available both in print and in electronic form. **General encyclopedias**—such as the *New Encyclopaedia Britannica* and the *Columbia Encyclopedia*—provide general information on a wide variety of topics. **Specialized reference works**—such as *Facts on File* and the *World Almanac*—and **special encyclopedias**—such as the *Encyclopedia of Law and Economics*—offer detailed information on specific topics.

> **NOTE**
>
> Although a general encyclopedia can provide an overview of your topic, encyclopedia articles do not usually treat topics in enough depth for college-level research. Be sure to check your instructor's guidelines before you use a general encyclopedia in your research.

Finding Information on the Web

Although the Web gives you access to a vast amount of information, it has its limitations. For one thing, because anyone can publish on the Web, you cannot be sure if the information found there is trustworthy, timely, or authoritative. Of course, there are reliable sources of information on the Web. For example, Google Scholar provides links to some scholarly sources that are as good as those found in a college library's databases. Even so, you have to approach this material with caution; some articles accessed through Google Scholar are pay-per-view, and others are not current or comprehensive.

To carry out a Web search, you need a **browser**—such as Google Chrome or Microsoft Internet Explorer—that connects you to the Web. Once you connect to the Web, you need to use a **search engine**—such as Google or Yahoo!—to locate and to view documents that you search for with keywords. Different types of search engines are suitable for different purposes:

- **General-Purpose Search Engines: General-purpose search engines** retrieve information on a great number of topics. They cast the widest possible net and bring in the widest variety of information. The disadvantage of general-purpose search engines is that you get a great deal of irrelevant material. Because each search engine has its own unique characteristics, you should try a few of them to see which you prefer. The most popular general-purpose search engines are Ask, Bing, Excite, Google, Lycos, and Yahoo!

- **Specialized Search Engines: Specialized search engines** focus on specific subject areas or on a specific type of content. The advantage of specialized search engines is that they eliminate the need for you to wade through pages of irrelevant material. By focusing your Web search on a specific subject area, you are more likely to locate information on your particular topic. (You are able to narrow your search to a specific subject area when you use a general-purpose search engine, but a specialized search engine narrows your search for you.) You can find a list of specialized search engines on the Search Engine List (thesearchenginelist.com.)

- **Metasearch Engines:** Because each search engine searches the Web differently, results can (and do) vary. For this reason, if you limit yourself to a single search engine, you can miss a great deal of useful information. **Metasearch engines** solve this problem by taking the results of several search engines and presenting them in a simple, no-nonsense format. The most popular metasearch engines are Dogpile, Kartoo, Mamma, Metacrawler, Surfwax, and Vivisimo.

Evaluating Sources

Whenever you locate a source—print or electronic—you should always take the time to evaluate it. When you **evaluate** a source, you assess the objectivity of the author, the credibility of the source, and its relevance to your argument. (Although a librarian or an instructor has screened the print and electronic sources in your college library for general accuracy and trustworthiness, you cannot assume that all these sources are suitable for your particular writing project.)

Material that you access on the Internet presents particular problems. Because anyone can publish on the Internet, the information you find there has to be evaluated carefully for accuracy. Although some material on the Internet (for example, journal articles that are published in both print and digital format) is reliable, other material (for example, personal Web sites and blogs) may be totally unsuitable for your research.

To be reasonably certain that the information you are accessing is appropriate, you have to approach it critically. The pages that follow will give you some of the tools you will need to evaluate your sources.

Evaluating Print Sources

As you locate print sources, you need to evaluate them to make sure that they are suitable for your research. (Remember, if you use an untrustworthy source, you undercut your credibility.)

To evaluate print sources, you use the same process that you use when you evaluate anything else. For example, if you are thinking about buying a

Print sources must be evaluated carefully.

computer, you will decide on several criteria to help you make your decision—for example, price, speed, memory, reliability, and availability of technical support. The same is true for evaluating research sources. You can use the following criteria to decide whether a print source is appropriate for your research:

- Accuracy
- Credibility
- Objectivity
- Currency
- Comprehensiveness
- Authority

The illustrations on page 280 show where to find information that can help you evaluate a print source.

Accuracy   A print source is **accurate** when it is factual and free of errors. One way to judge the accuracy of a source is to compare the information it contains to that same information in several other sources. If a source has factual errors, then it probably includes other types of errors as well. Needless to say, errors in spelling and grammar should also cause you to question a source's general accuracy.

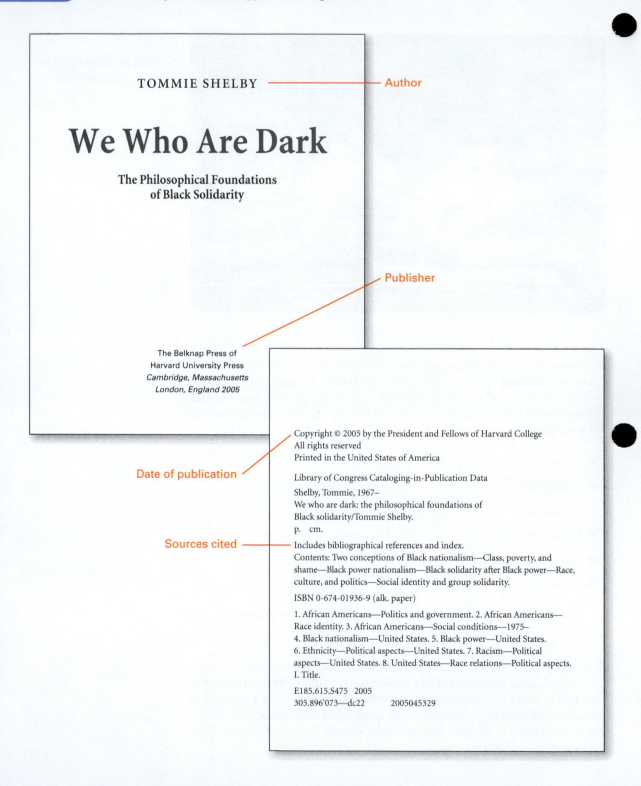

TOMMIE SHELBY ————————— Author

We Who Are Dark

**The Philosophical Foundations
of Black Solidarity**

The Belknap Press of
Harvard University Press
Cambridge, Massachusetts
London, England 2005

Publisher

Copyright © 2005 by the President and Fellows of Harvard College
All rights reserved
Printed in the United States of America

Library of Congress Cataloging-in-Publication Data

Shelby, Tommie, 1967–
We who are dark: the philosophical foundations of
Black solidarity/Tommie Shelby.
    p.   cm.

Date of publication

Includes bibliographical references and index.

Sources cited

Contents: Two conceptions of Black nationalism—Class, poverty, and
shame—Black power nationalism—Black solidarity after Black power—Race,
culture, and politics—Social identity and group solidarity.

ISBN 0-674-01936-9 (alk. paper)

1. African Americans—Politics and government. 2. African Americans—
Race identity. 3. African Americans—Social conditions—1975–
4. Black nationalism—United States. 5. Black power—United States.
6. Ethnicity—Political aspects—United States. 7. Racism—Political
aspects—United States. 8. United States—Race relations—Political aspects.
I. Title.

E185.615.S475   2005
305.896'073—dc22   2005045329

You can also judge the accuracy of a print source by checking to see if the author cites sources for the information that is discussed. Documentation can help readers determine both the quality of information in a source and the range of sources used. It can also show readers what sources a writer has failed to consult. (Failure to cite an important book or article should cause you to question the writer's familiarity with a subject.) If possible, verify the legitimacy of some of the books and articles that a writer cites by seeing what you can find out about them on the Web. If a print source has caused a great deal of debate or if it is disreputable, you will probably be able to find information about the source by researching it on Google.

Credibility A print source is **credible** when it is believable. You can begin checking a source's credibility by determining where a book or article was published. If a university press published the book, you can be reasonably certain that it was **peer reviewed**—read by experts in the field to confirm the accuracy of the information. If a commercial press published the book, you will have to consider other criteria—the author's reputation and the date of publication, for example—to determine quality. If your source is an article, see if it appears in a **scholarly journal**—a periodical aimed at experts in a particular field—or in a **popular magazine**—a periodical aimed at general readers. Journal articles are almost always acceptable research sources because they are usually documented, peer reviewed, and written by experts. (They can, however, be difficult for general readers to understand.) Articles in high-level popular magazines, such as the *Atlantic* and the *Economist*, may also be suitable—provided experts write them. However, articles in lower-level popular magazines—such as *Sports Illustrated* and *Time*—may be easy to understand, but they are seldom acceptable sources for research.

You can determine how well respected a source is by reading reviews written by critics. You can find reviews of books by consulting *Book Review Digest*—either in print or online—which lists books that have been reviewed in at least three magazines or newspapers and includes excerpts of reviews. In addition, you can consult the *New York Times Book Review* Web site—www.nytimes.com/pages/books/index.html—to access reviews printed by the newspaper since 1981. (Both professional and reader reviews are also available at Amazon.com.)

Finally, you can determine how well respected a source is by seeing how often other scholars in the field refer to it. **Citation indexes** indicate how often books and articles are mentioned by other sources in a given year. This information can give you an idea of how important a work is in a particular field. Citation indexes for the humanities, the social sciences, and the sciences are available online and in your college library.

Objectivity   A print source is **objective** when it is not unduly influenced by personal opinions or feelings. Ideally, you want to find sources that are objective, but to one degree or another, all sources are **biased**—prejudiced in favor of or against something. In short, all sources—especially those that take a stand on an issue—reflect the opinions of their authors, regardless of how hard they may try to be impartial. (Of course, an opinion is perfectly acceptable—as long as it is supported by evidence.)

As a researcher, you should recognize that bias exists and ask yourself whether a writer's assumptions are justified by the facts or are the result of emotion or preconceived ideas. You can make this determination by looking at a writer's choice of words and seeing if the language is slanted or by reviewing the writer's points and seeing if his or her argument is one-sided. Get in the habit of asking yourself whether you are being offered a legitimate point of view or simply being fed propaganda.

The covers of the liberal and conservative magazines shown here suggest different biases.

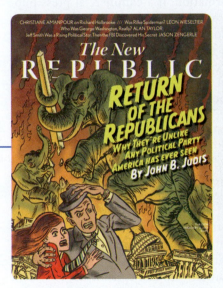
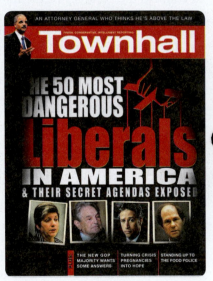

Currency   A print source is **current** when it is up-to-date. (For a book, you can find the date of publication on the same page that lists the publisher. For an article, you can find the date on the front cover of the magazine or journal.) If you are dealing with a scientific subject, the date of publication can be very important. Older sources might contain outdated information, so you want to use the most up-to-date source that you can find. For other subjects—literary criticism, for example—the currency of the information may not be as important as it is in the sciences.

Comprehensiveness A print source is **comprehensive** when it covers a subject in sufficient depth. The first thing to consider is whether the source deals specifically with your subject. (If it treats your subject only briefly, it will probably not be useful.) Does it treat your subject in enough detail? Does the source include the background information that you need to understand the discussion? Does the source mention other important sources that discuss your subject? Are facts and interpretations supported by the other sources you have read, or are there major points of disagreement? Finally, does the author include documentation?

How comprehensive a source needs to be depends on your purpose and audience as well as on your writing assignment. For a short essay for an introductory course, an editorial from the *New York Times* and a chapter in a book might give you enough information to support your argument. If you are writing a longer essay, however, you might need to consult journal articles (and possibly books) about your subject.

Authority A print source has **authority** when a writer has the expertise to write about a subject. Always try to determine if the author is a recognized authority or simply a person who has decided to write about a particular topic. For example, what other books or articles has the author written? Has your instructor ever mentioned the author's name? Is the author mentioned in your textbook? Has the author published other works on the same subject or on related subjects? (You can find this information on Amazon.com.)

You should also determine if the author has an academic affiliation. Is he or she a faculty member at a respected college or university? Do other established scholars have a high opinion of the author? You can often find this information by using a search engine such as Google or by consulting one of the following directories:

> *Biographies Plus Illustrated*
> *Contemporary Authors*
> *Directory of American Scholars*
> *International Who's Who*
> *National Faculty Directory*
> *Who's Who in America*

⊘ EXERCISE 8.1

Each of the following three print sources was found in a university library:

- Nicholas Thompson, "Bigger Brother: The Exponential Law of Privacy Loss"

- *USA Today* editorial board, "Time to Enact 'Do Not Track'"

- Maria Aspan, "How Sticky Is Membership on Facebook? Just Try Breaking Free"

Assume that you are preparing to write an argumentative essay on the topic of whether information posted on social-networking sites threatens privacy. Read the sources that follow, and evaluate each source for accuracy, credibility, objectivity, currency, and authority.

This essay appeared in the December 5, 2011, edition of the *New Yorker*.

BIGGER BROTHER: THE EXPONENTIAL LAW OF PRIVACY LOSS

NICHOLAS THOMPSON

This past Tuesday, Facebook made a deal with the F.T.C.: from now on, the social-networking company can no longer humbug us about privacy. If we're told that something we post on the site will be private, it will stay that way, unless we give Facebook permission to make it public. Or at least sort of. For a while. Facebook has been relentless in its effort to make more of what it knows about us—the music we listen to, the photos we take, the friends we have—available to more people, and it will surely figure out creative ways, F.T.C. or no F.T.C., to further that campaign. The company's leadership sincerely believes that the more we share the better the world will be. Mark Zuckerberg, the C.E.O., has said that in ten years we'll share a thousand times as much as we do now. That seems to be both an observation and a goal.

Meanwhile, Zynga has announced that it's going to raise about a billion dollars in an impending I.P.O. Zynga makes social games like *FarmVille*, in which people harvest and sell virtual tomatoes. The games sound inane to non-players, and Zynga employees claim that their workplace is run like a labor camp; yet the company is worth perhaps ten billion dollars. Why? Partly because they collect and analyze fifteen terabytes of data a day from their users. They watch carefully in order to learn how to hook people and what enticements to offer someone frustrated about his slow-growing tomato crop. (There's a segment from *Bloomberg West* in which an analyst compares Zynga to a drug dealer.) According to Zynga's recent S.E.C. filings, its total number of players is stagnant, but the amount of money it can extract from each one is growing. Data is the currency of the Web right now. Whoever has the most detailed data about you will get rich. Zynga has great data, and Zynga is about to get very rich.

> "Whoever has the most detailed data about you will get rich."

Last week also brought the news that a company called Carrier IQ has installed software on about a hundred and fifty million phones that lets it and its customers—such as Sprint, A.T. & T., and Apple—know an awful lot about you. It tracks location, stores the numbers you dial, and even records the Web sites you browse when you're not connected to a cell network. The point of the software is to help the phone companies improve their networks and serve you better. But this is done in a mysterious (and perhaps nefarious) way. Most people don't know they have it, and it's not easy to remove. It's also not clear exactly what it's recording, though a bevy of new lawsuits and government investigations will now try to figure that out. At the very least, there's one more company that you've never heard of that knows a heck of a lot about you. "The excuse proffered thus far—improved service—is at best feeble when compared to the extent of the potential invasion of privacy," Stephen Wicker, a professor in electrical and computer engineering at Cornell, told me.

These are just three stories from the past seven days. There'll surely be more soon. Together, they've made me think of something I'll call The Exponential Law of Privacy Loss (or TELPL, pronounced "tell people.") The more we do online, the better companies get at tracking us, and the more accurate and detailed the data they glean from us becomes. The amount of data that they have grows exponentially over time.

It's impossible to exactly measure what percent of our time is spent connected to the Internet: texting, shopping, surfing, browsing, sleeping. But, my best estimation is that, a few years ago, we lived roughly ten percent of our lives online, and companies captured about ten percent of what we did. Now it's about thirty percent, and the companies capture thirty percent of that—which means roughly nine times as much as a few years ago. Eventually, when we live seventy percent of our lives online, digital companies will capture and store about seventy percent of that. I'm not sure what will happen to the formula when we spend our entire lives online. Ideally, we won't get there.

This tracking isn't all bad; it may not even be mostly bad. People keep letting Facebook broadcast more of their preferences and habits, and they love it. The more that advertisers know about you, the more willing they are to do things like buy advertisements on Web sites, supporting journalism such as this. Carrier IQ makes our phones more efficient, and I have yet to hear of any specific harm done to any specific person by their system. Still, the Law is real. The F.T.C. can slow things down, but only a little. All of us are still becoming corporate data at an ever faster rate, for better and for worse.

This editorial was published in *USA Today* on December 11, 2011.

TIME TO ENACT "DO NOT TRACK"

USA TODAY EDITORIAL BOARD

Facebook's 800 million users are probably feeling a little more secure since the social media giant agreed to privacy measures forced by the Federal Trade Commission (FTC) late last month. But they'd be wise to stay cautious. Plenty of incentive for mischief remains, and not only on Facebook. 1

The agreement requires Facebook to stop letting users mark their profile information as private and then making it public without their permission. Facebook also promised that it will warn users of privacy policy changes before enacting them. 2

But the agreement won't stop Facebook from monitoring and sharing users' Web-browsing habits, which is a way for the company and others like it to make money. It's an unsatisfying ending to a two-year investigation, but more important, it's a marker of how difficult it will be to maintain privacy in an increasingly wired world. 3

The weakness in the FTC's agreement is that it didn't establish any guidelines about Internet tracking, the method by which Facebook collects data about its users even when they're not on the network itself. As company representatives recently acknowledged to *USA Today*, Facebook automatically compiles a log of every Web page its users visit that has a Facebook plug-in, such as the ubiquitous "like" button. 4

Other online giants, such as Google and Yahoo, use similar methods to monitor users' Web-browsing. This lets them tailor their pages and advertisements to appeal to different visitors. 5

Online tracking companies, which help sites compile these browsing records, claim that your personal details are not connected to your name, meaning your privacy is not compromised when they share information with advertisers or others. But as the *Wall Street Journal* discovered last year, at least one tracking company collected Web surfers' names and other personally identifiable information and passed it on to clients. 6

The implication is that tracking companies and advertisers could know your name, e-mail address, hometown, medical history, political affiliation, and more. Such information could be used in troubling ways. A health insurance company, for example, could guess your medical conditions. Or a potential employer could find out whether you spend your time gambling online. 7

> "Such information could be used in troubling ways."

If you don't like that prospect, your only option is to use a Web browser 8 that offers a "Do Not Track" mechanism, such as Mozilla Firefox or Internet Explorer 9. Once you activate the feature, it signals websites you visit indicating that you do not want your data tracked by third parties. But existing Do Not Track mechanisms can't control what websites do; they can only communicate your preference.

That's why the FTC has called for a tougher and more universal version of 9 Do Not Track, a move that the online advertising industry argues would hamper Internet innovation. These fears are overblown. Behavioral advertising, which targets viewers based on their Web-browsing history, is large and growing, but it still accounts for less than 5% of all online advertising. So ads that rely on tracking are hardly the Internet's only revenue stream.

Measures that would create a legally enforceable Do Not Track mechanism 10 or otherwise address privacy concerns are languishing in Congress. Lawmakers should give Web users more tools to control their personal information. Until that happens, your online habits will reveal much more about you than just what you put on your Facebook profile.

This article appeared in the February 11, 2008, *New York Times*.

HOW STICKY IS MEMBERSHIP ON FACEBOOK? JUST TRY BREAKING FREE

MARIA ASPAN

Are you a member of Facebook.com? You may have a lifetime contract. 1

Some users have discovered that it is nearly impossible to remove themselves entirely from Facebook, setting off a fresh round of concern over the popular social network's use of personal data.

While the Web site offers users the option to deactivate their accounts, 3 Facebook servers keep copies of the information in those accounts indefinitely. Indeed, many users who have contacted Facebook to request that their accounts be deleted have not succeeded in erasing their records from the network.

"It's like the Hotel California," said Nipon Das, 34, a director at a biotech- 4 nology consulting firm in Manhattan, who tried unsuccessfully to delete his account this fall. "You can check out any time you like, but you can never leave."

It took Mr. Das about two months and several e-mail exchanges with 5 Facebook's customer service representatives to erase most of his information from the site, which finally occurred after he sent an e-mail threatening legal action. But even after that, a reporter was able to find Mr. Das's empty profile on Facebook and successfully sent him an e-mail message through the network.

In response to difficulties faced by ex-Facebook members, a cottage in- 6
dustry of unofficial help pages devoted to escaping Facebook has sprung up
online—both outside and inside the network.

"I thought it was kind of strange that they save your information without 7
telling you in a really clear way," said Magnus Wallin, a 26-year-old patent
examiner in Stockholm who founded a Facebook group, "How to permanently
delete your Facebook account." The group has almost 4,300 members and is
steadily growing.

The technological hurdles set by Facebook have a business rationale: they 8
allow ex-Facebookers who choose to return the ability to resurrect their
accounts effortlessly. According to an e-mail message from Amy Sezak, a
spokeswoman for Facebook, "Deactivated accounts mean that a user can reacti-
vate at any time and their information will be available again just as they left it."

But it also means that disenchanted users cannot disappear from the site 9
without leaving footprints. Facebook's terms of use state that "you may remove
your user content from the site at any time," but also that "you acknowledge
that the company may retain archived copies of your user content."

Its privacy policy says that after someone 10
deactivates an account, "removed information may persist in backup copies for a reasonable period of time."

Facebook's Web site does not inform 11
departing users that they must delete information from their account in order to close
it fully—meaning that they may unwittingly leave anything from e-mail
addresses to credit card numbers sitting on Facebook servers.

> "'Removed information may persist in backup copies for a reasonable period of time.'"

Only people who contact Facebook's customer service department are 12
informed that they must painstakingly delete, line by line, all of the profile
information, "wall" messages, and group memberships they may have created
within Facebook.

"Users can also have their account completely removed by deleting all of 13
the data associated with their account and then deactivating it," Ms. Sezak said
in her message. "Users can then write to Facebook to request their account be
deleted and their e-mail will be completely erased from the database."

But even users who try to delete every piece of information they have ever 14
written, sent, or received via the network have found their efforts to permanently leave stymied. Other social networking sites like MySpace and
Friendster, as well as online dating sites like eHarmony.com, may require
departing users to confirm their wishes several times—but in the end they
offer a delete option.

"Most sites, even online dating sites, will give you an option to wipe your 15
slate clean," Mr. Das said.

Mr. Das, who joined Facebook on a whim after receiving invitations from 16
friends, tried to leave after realizing that most of his co-workers were also on

the site. "I work in a small office," he said. "The last thing I want is people going on there and checking out my private life."

"I did not want to be on it after junior associates at work whom I have to 17 manage saw my stuff," he added.

Facebook's quiet archiving of information from deactivated accounts has 18 increased concerns about the network's potential abuse of private data, especially in the wake of its fumbled Beacon advertising feature.

That application, which tracks and publishes the items bought by Facebook 19 members on outside Web sites, was introduced in November without a transparent, one-step opt-out feature. After a public backlash, including more than 50,000 Facebook users' signatures on a MoveOn.org protest petition, Facebook executives apologized and allowed such an opt-out option on the program.

Tensions remain between making a profit and alienating Facebook's users, 20 who the company says total about 64 million worldwide (MySpace has an estimated 110 million monthly active users).

The network is still trying to find a way to monetize its popularity, mostly 21 by allowing marketers access to its wealth of demographic and behavioral information. The retention of old accounts on Facebook's servers seems like another effort to hold onto—and provide its ad partners with—as much demographic information as possible.

"The thing they offer advertisers is that they can connect to groups of 22 people. I can see why they wouldn't want to throw away anyone's information, but there's a conflict with privacy," said Alan Burlison, 46, a British software engineer who succeeded in deleting his account only after he complained in the British press, to the country's Information Commissioner's Office and to the TRUSTe organization, an online privacy network that has certified Facebook.

Mr. Burlison's complaint spurred the Information Commissioner's Office, 23 a privacy watchdog organization, to investigate Facebook's data-protection practices, the BBC reported last month. In response, Facebook issued a statement saying that its policy was in "full compliance with U.K. data protection law."

A spokeswoman for TRUSTe, which is based in San Francisco, said its 24 account deletion process was "inconvenient," but that Facebook was "being responsive to us and they currently meet our requirements."

"I kept getting the same answer and really felt that I was being given the 25 runaround," Mr. Burlison said of Facebook's customer service representatives. "It was quite obvious that no amount of prodding from me on a personal level was going to make a difference."

Only after he sent a link to the video of his interview with Britain's 26 Channel 4 News to the customer service representatives—and Facebook executives—was his account finally deleted.

Steven Mansour, 28, a Canadian online community developer, spent two 27 weeks in July trying to fully delete his account from Facebook. He later wrote a blog entry—including e-mail messages, diagrams, and many exclamations of frustration—in a post entitled "2504 Steps to closing your Facebook account" (www.stevenmansour.com).

Mr. Mansour, who said he is "really skeptical of social networking sites," 28 decided to leave after a few months on Facebook. "I was getting tired of always getting alerts and e-mails," he said. "I found it very invasive."

"It's part of a much bigger picture of social networking sites on the Inter- 29 net harvesting private data, whether for marketing or for more sinister purposes," he said. His post, which wound up on the link-aggregator Digg.com, has been viewed more than 87,000 times, Mr. Mansour said, adding that the traffic was so high it crashed his server.

And his post became the touchstone for Mr. Wallin, who was inspired to 30 create his group, "How to permanently delete your Facebook account," after joining, leaving, and then rejoining Facebook, only to find that all of his information from his first account was still available.

"I wanted the information to be available inside Facebook for all the users 31 who wanted to leave, and quite a few people have found it just by using internal search," said Mr. Wallin. Facebook has never contacted Mr. Wallin about the group.

Mr. Wallin said he has heard through members that some people have suc- 32 cessfully used his steps to leave Facebook. But he is not yet ready to leave himself.

"I don't want to leave yet; I actually find it really convenient," he said. "But 33 someday when I want to leave, I want it to be simple."

❷ EXERCISE 8.2

Write a one- or two-paragraph evaluation of each of the three print sources you read for Exercise 8.1. Be sure to support your evaluation with specific references to the sources.

Evaluating Internet Sources

The Internet is like a freewheeling frontier town in the old West. Occasionally, a federal marshal may pass through, but for the most part, there is no law and order, so you are on your own. On the Internet, literally anything goes—exaggerations, misinformation, errors, and even complete fabrications. Some Web sites contain reliable content, but many do not. The main reason for this situation is that there is no authority—as there is in a college library—who evaluates sites for accuracy and trustworthiness. That job falls to you, the user.

Another problem is that Internet sources often lack some of the publication information that you find in print sources. For example, an article on a Web site may lack a date, a place of publication, or even a named author. For this reason, it is not always easy to evaluate the material you find online.

Most sources found in a college library have been evaluated by a reference librarian for their suitability as research sources.

When you evaluate an Internet source, you need to begin by viewing it skeptically—unless you know for certain that it is reliable. In other words, assume that its information is questionable until you establish that it is not. Then apply the same criteria you use to evaluate print sources—*accuracy, credibility, objectivity, currency, comprehensiveness,* and *authority*.

The Web page pictured on page 292 shows where to find information that can help you evaluate Internet sources.

Accuracy Information on a Web site is **accurate** when it is factual and free of errors. Information in the form of facts, opinions, statistics, and interpretations is everywhere on the Internet, and in the case of Wiki sites, this information is continuously being rewritten and revised. Given the volume and variety of this material, it is a major challenge to determine its accuracy. You can assess the accuracy of information on a Web site by asking the following questions:

- **Does the site contain errors of fact?** Factual errors—inaccuracies that relate directly to the central point of the source—should immediately disqualify a site as a reliable source.

- **Does the site contain a list of references or any other type of documentation?** Reliable sources indicate where their information comes from. The authors know that people want to be sure that the information they are using is accurate and reliable. If a site provides no documentation, you should not trust the information it contains.

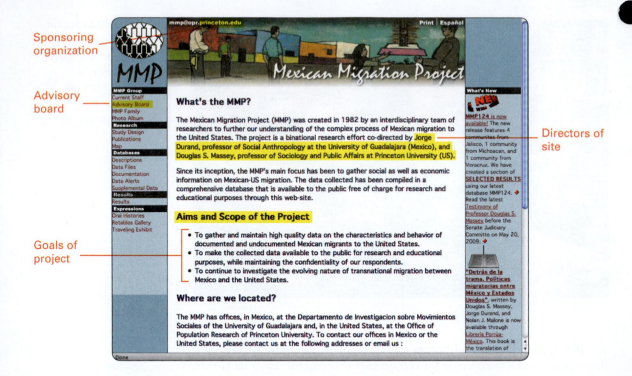

Sponsoring organization

Advisory board

Directors of site

Goals of project

- **Does the site provide links to other sites?** Does the site have links to reliable Web sites that are created by respected authorities or sponsored by trustworthy institutions? If it does, then you can conclude that your source is at least trying to maintain a certain standard of quality.

- **Can you verify information?** A good test for accuracy is to try to verify key information on a site. You can do this by checking it in a reliable print source or on a good reference Web site such as *Encyclopedia.com.*

Credibility   Information on a Web site is **credible** when it is believable. Just as you would not naively believe a stranger who approached you on the street, you should not automatically believe a site that you randomly encounter on the Web. You can assess the credibility of a Web site by asking the following questions:

- **Does the site list authors, directors, or editors?** Anonymity—whether on a Web site or on a blog—should be a red flag for a researcher who is considering using a source.

- **Is the site refereed?** Does a panel of experts or an advisory board decide what material appears on the Web site? If not, what standards are used to determine the suitability of content?

- **Does the site contain errors in grammar, spelling, or punctuation?** If it does, you should be on the alert for other types of errors. If the people maintaining the site do not care enough to make sure that the site is free of small errors, you have to wonder if they will take the time to verify the accuracy of the information presented.

- **Does an organization sponsor the site?** If so, do you know (or can you find out) anything about the sponsoring organization? Use a search engine such as Google to determine the purpose and point of view of the organization.

Objectivity Information on a Web site is **objective** when it limits the amount of **bias** that it displays. Some sites—such as those that support a particular political position or social cause—make no secret of their biases. They present them clearly in their policy statements on their home pages. Others, however, try to hide their biases—for example, by referring only to sources that support a particular point of view and not mentioning those that do not.

Keep in mind that bias does not automatically disqualify a source. It should, however, alert you to the fact that you are seeing only one side of an issue and that you will have to look further to get a complete picture. You can assess the objectivity of a Web site by asking the following questions:

- **Does advertising appear on the site?** If the site contains advertising, check to make sure that the commercial aspect of the site does not affect its objectivity. The site should keep advertising separate from content.

- **Does a commercial entity sponsor the site?** A for-profit company may sponsor a Web site, but it should not allow commercial interests to determine content. If it does, there is a clear conflict of interest. For example, if a site is sponsored by a company that sells organic products, it may include testimonials that emphasize the virtues of organic products and ignore information that is skeptical of their benefits.

- **Does a political organization or special-interest group sponsor the site?** Just as you would for a commercial site, you should make sure that the sponsoring organization is presenting accurate information. It is a good idea to check the information you get from a political site against information you get from an educational or a reference site—Ask.com or Encyclopedia.com, for example. Organizations have specific agendas, and you should make sure that they are not bending the truth to satisfy their own needs.

- **Does the site link to strongly biased sites?** Even if a site seems trustworthy, it is a good idea to check some of its links. Just as you can judge people by the company they keep, you can also judge Web sites by the sites they link to. Links to overly biased sites should cause you to reevaluate the information on the original site.

USING A SITE'S URL TO ASSESS ITS OBJECTIVITY

A Web site's **URL** (uniform resource locator) can give you information that can help you assess the site's objectivity.

Identify the site's purpose. Knowing who sponsors a site can help you determine whether a site is trying to sell you something or just trying to provide information.

Look at the domain name to identify sponsorship. The last part of a site's URL can tell you whether a site is a commercial site (.com and .net), an educational site (.edu), a nonprofit site (.org), or a governmental site (.gov, .mil, and so on).

See if the URL has a tilde (~) in it. A tilde in a site's URL indicates that information was published by an individual and is unaffiliated with the sponsoring organization. Individuals can have their own agendas, which may be different from the agenda of the site on which their information appears or to which it is linked.

AVOIDING CONFIRMATION BIAS

Confirmation bias is a tendency that people have to accept information that supports their beliefs and to ignore information that does not. For example, people see false or inaccurate information on Web sites, and because it reinforces their political or social beliefs, they forward it to others. Eventually, this information becomes so widely distributed that people assume that it is true. Numerous studies have demonstrated how prevalent confirmation bias is. Consider the following examples:

- A student doing research for a paper chooses sources that support her thesis and ignores those that take the opposite position.

- A district attorney interviews witnesses who establish the guilt of a suspect and overlooks those who do not.

- A researcher studying the effectiveness of a drug includes statistics that confirm his hypothesis and excludes statistics that do not.

When you write an argumentative essay, do not accept information just because it supports your thesis. Realize that we all have a tendency toward conformation bias and that you have an obligation to consider all sides of an issue, not just the side that reinforces your beliefs.

Currency Information on a Web site is **current** when it is up-to-date. Some sources—such as fiction and poetry—are timeless and therefore are useful whatever their age. Other sources, however—such as those in the hard sciences—must be current because advances in some disciplines can quickly make information outdated. For this reason, you should be aware of the shelf life of information in the discipline you are researching and choose information accordingly. You can assess the currency of a Web site by asking the following questions:

- **Does the Web site include the date when it was last updated?** As you look at Web pages, check the date on which they were created or updated. (Some Web sites automatically display the current date, so be careful not to confuse the date on which you are viewing the page with the date the page was last updated.)

- **Are all links on the site live?** If a Web site is properly maintained, all the links it contains will be **live**—that is, a click on the link will take you to other Web sites. If a site contains a number of links that are not live, you should question its currency.

- **Is the information on the Web site up-to-date?** A site might have been updated, but this does not necessarily mean that it contains the most up-to-date information. In addition to checking when a Web site was last updated, look at the dates of the individual articles that appear on the site to make sure they are not outdated.

Comprehensiveness Information on a Web site is **comprehensive** when it covers a subject in depth. A site that presents itself as a comprehensive source should include (or link to) the most important sources of information that you need to understand a subject. (A site that leaves out a key source of information or that ignores opposing points of view cannot be called comprehensive.) You can assess the comprehensiveness of a Web site by asking the following questions:

- **Does the site provide in-depth coverage?** Articles in professional journals—which are available both in print and online—treat subjects in enough depth for college-level research. Other types of articles—especially those in popular magazines and in general encyclopedias, such as *Wikipedia*—are often too superficial (or uneven) for college-level research.

- **Does the site provide information that is not available elsewhere?** The Web site should provide information that is not available from other sources. In other words, it should make a contribution to your knowledge and do more than simply repackage information from other sources.

■ **Who is the intended audience for this site?** Knowing the target audience for a Web site can help you to assess a source's comprehensiveness. Is it aimed at general readers or at experts? Is it aimed at high school students or at college students? It stands to reason that a site that is aimed at experts or college students will include more detailed information than one that is aimed at general readers or high school students.

Authority Information on a Web site has **authority** when you can establish the legitimacy of both the author and the site. You can determine the authority of a source by asking the following questions:

■ Is the author an expert in the professional or academic field that he or she is writing about? What credentials does the author have? Does he or she have the expertise to write about the subject? Sometimes you can find this information on the Web site itself. For example, the site may contain an "About the Author" section or links to other publications by the author. If this information is not available, you will have to do a Web search with the author's name as a keyword. If you cannot confirm the author's expertise (or if the site has no listed author), you should not use material from the site.

■ What do the links show? What information is revealed by the links on the site? Do they lead to reputable sites, or do they take you to sites that suggest that the author has a clear bias or a hidden agenda? Do other reliable sites link back to the site you are evaluating?

■ Is the site a serious publication? Does it include information that enables you to judge its legitimacy? For example, does it include a statement of purpose? Does it provide information that enables you to determine the criteria for publication? Does the site have a board of advisers? Are these advisers experts? Does the site include a mailing address and a phone number? Can you determine if the site is the domain of a single individual or the effort of a group of individuals?

■ Does the site have a sponsor? If so, is the site affiliated with a reputable institutional sponsor, such as a governmental, educational, or scholarly organization?

◯ EXERCISE 8.3

Consider the following two home pages—one from the *Chronicle of Higher Education*, a publication aimed at college instructors and administrators, and the other from *Parade*, a publication aimed at general readers. Assume that you have found articles about privacy and social-networking sites in both publications. Locate and label the information on each home page that would enable you to determine the suitability of using information from the site in your paper.

➲ EXERCISE 8.4

Here are the **mission statements**—statements of the organizations' purposes—from the *Chronicle of Higher Education* and *Parade,* whose home pages you considered in Exercise 8.3. What additional information can you get from these mission statements? How do they help you to evaluate the sites as well as the information that might appear on the sites?

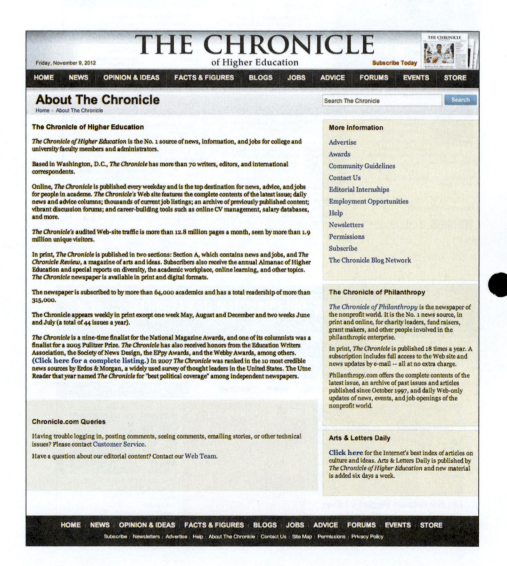

IMPORTANT INFORMATION

- **General Facts**
- **Mission Statement**
- **Brief History**

OUR TEAM

- **Management**
- **Newspaper Relations**
- **Business Contacts**

PARADE'S MISSION

PARADE needs no introduction to its 74 million readers, who value it for the fun and information of Personality Parade, for the challenge and wit of Ask Marilyn, the currency of ideas in Intelligence Report and, above all, for its relevance. PARADE begins with a single, powerful image that draws readers in and then holds them with stories that educate, entertain and empower. Joining the right writer to the right idea, PARADE consistently provides its readers with quality stories. That quality itself is defined by three elements: clarity, authority and substance. Each article must be clear in design and content and well researched and written with a voice of authority. It must also have substance, telling readers something they didn't know before and giving them an opportunity to effect change.

Source: MRI

⊖ EXERCISE 8.5

Each of the following sources was found on the Internet:

- Mark Zuckerberg, "Our Commitment to the Facebook Community"

- Facebook, "Facebook Principles"

- Ben Parr, "Is Facebook Trying to Kill Privacy?"

- Farhad Manjoo, "It's Not All Facebook's Fault"

Assume that you are preparing to write an essay on the topic of whether information posted on social-networking sites threatens privacy. First, visit the Web sites on which the articles appear, and evaluate each site for accuracy, credibility, objectivity, currency, comprehensiveness, and authority. Then, using the same criteria, evaluate each source.

This post was published on the *Facebook Blog* on November 29, 2011.

OUR COMMITMENT TO THE FACEBOOK COMMUNITY

MARK ZUCKERBERG

I founded Facebook on the idea that people want to share and connect with   1
people in their lives, but to do this everyone needs complete control over who they share with at all times.

This idea has been the core of Facebook since day one. When I built the first version of Facebook, almost nobody I knew wanted a public page on the Internet. That seemed scary. But as long as they could make their page private, they felt safe sharing with their friends online. Control was key. With Facebook, for the first time, people had the tools they needed to do this. That's how Facebook became the world's biggest community online. We made it easy for people to feel comfortable sharing things about their real lives.

We've added many new tools since then: sharing photos, creating groups, commenting on and liking your friends' posts, and recently even listening to music or watching videos together. With each new tool, we've added new privacy controls to ensure that you continue to have complete control over who sees everything you share. Because of these tools and controls, most people share many more things today than they did a few years ago.

Overall, I think we have a good history of providing transparency and control over who can see your information.

That said, I'm the first to admit that we've made a bunch of mistakes. In particular, I think that a small number of high-profile mistakes, like Beacon four years ago and poor execution as we transitioned our privacy model two years ago, have often overshadowed much of the good work we've done.

I also understand that many people are just naturally skeptical of what it means for hundreds of millions of people to share so much personal information online, especially using any one service. Even if our record on privacy were perfect, I think many people would still rightfully question how their information was protected. It's important for people to think about this, and not one day goes by when I don't think about what it means for us to be the stewards of this community and their trust.

Facebook has always been committed to being transparent about the information you have stored with us—and we have led the Internet in building tools to give people the ability to see and control what they share.

> "Facebook has always been committed to being transparent about the information you have stored with us."

But we can also always do better. I'm committed to making Facebook the leader in transparency and control around privacy.

As we have grown, we have tried our best to listen closely to the people who use Facebook. We also work with regulators, advocates, and experts to inform our privacy practices and policies. Recently, the U.S. Federal Trade Commission established agreements with Google and Twitter that are helping to shape new privacy standards for our industry. Today, the FTC announced a similar agreement with Facebook. These agreements create a framework for how companies should approach privacy in the United States and around the world.

For Facebook, this means we're making a clear and formal long-term commitment to do the things we've always tried to do and planned to keep doing—giving you tools to control who can see your information and then making sure only those people you intend can see it.

In the last 18 months alone, we've announced more than 20 new tools and   11
resources designed to give you more control over your Facebook experience. Some of the things these include are

- An easier way to select your audience when making a new post

- Inline privacy controls on all your existing posts

- The ability to review tags made by others before they appear on your profile

- Friend lists that are easier to create and that maintain themselves automatically

- A new groups product for sharing with smaller sets of people

- A tool to view your profile as someone else would see it

- Tools to ensure your information stays secure like double login approval

- Mobile versions of your privacy controls

- An easy way to download all your Facebook data

- A new apps dashboard to control what your apps can access

- A new app permission dialog that gives you clear control over what an app can do anytime you add one

- Many more privacy education resources

As a matter of fact, privacy is so deeply embedded in all of the devel-   12
opment we do that every day tens of thousands of servers worth of computational resources are consumed checking to make sure that on any webpage we serve, that you have access to see each of the sometimes hundreds or even thousands of individual pieces of information that come together to form a Facebook page. This includes everything from every post on a page to every tag in those posts to every mutual friend shown when you hover over a person's name. We do privacy access checks literally tens of billions of times each day to ensure we're enforcing that only the people you want see your content. These privacy principles are written very deeply into our code.

Even before the agreement announced by the FTC today, Facebook had   13
already proactively addressed many of the concerns the FTC raised. For example, their complaint to us mentioned our Verified Apps Program, which we canceled almost two years ago in December 2009. The same complaint also mentions cases where advertisers inadvertently received the ID numbers of

some users in referrer URLs. We fixed that problem over a year ago in May 2010.

In addition to these product changes, the FTC also recommended im- 14 provements to our internal processes. We've embraced these ideas, too, by agreeing to improve and formalize the way we do privacy review as part of our ongoing product development process. As part of this, we will establish a biennial independent audit of our privacy practices to ensure we're living up to the commitments we make.

Even further, effective today I am creating two new corporate officer roles to 15 make sure our commitments will be reflected in what we do internally—in the development of our products and the security of our systems—and externally— in the way we work collaboratively with regulators, government agencies, and privacy groups from around the world:

- Erin Egan will become Chief Privacy Officer, Policy. Erin recently joined Facebook after serving as a partner and co-chair of the global privacy and data security practice of Covington & Burling, the respected international law firm. Throughout her career, Erin has been deeply involved in legislative and regulatory efforts to address privacy, data security, spam, spyware, and other consumer protection issues. Erin will lead our engagement in the global public discourse and debate about online privacy and ensure that feedback from regulators, legislators, experts, and academics from around the world is incorporated into Facebook's practices and policies.

- Michael Richter will become Chief Privacy Officer, Products. Michael is currently Facebook's Chief Privacy Counsel on our legal team. In his new role, Michael will join our product organization to expand, improve, and formalize our existing program of internal privacy review. He and his team will work to ensure that our principles of user control, privacy by design, and transparency are integrated consistently into both Facebook's product development process and our products themselves.

These two positions will further strengthen the processes that ensure that 16 privacy control is built into our products and policies. I'm proud to have two such strong individuals with so much privacy expertise serving in these roles.

Today's announcement formalizes our commitment to providing you 17 with control over your privacy and sharing—and it also provides protection to ensure that your information is only shared in the way you intend. As the founder and CEO of Facebook, I look forward to working with the Commission as we implement this agreement. It is my hope that this agreement makes it clear that Facebook is the leader when it comes to offering people control over the information they share online.

Finally, I also want to reaffirm the commitment I made when I first 18 launched Facebook. We will serve you as best we can and work every day to provide you with the best tools for you to share with each other and the world. We will continue to improve the service, build new ways for you to share, and offer new ways to protect you and your information better than any other company in the world.

This statement is from facebook.com/principles.php.

FACEBOOK PRINCIPLES

FACEBOOK

We are building Facebook to make the world more open and transparent, which we believe will create greater understanding and connection. Facebook promotes openness and transparency by giving individuals greater power to share and connect, and certain principles guide Facebook in pursuing these goals. Achieving these principles should be constrained only by limitations of law, technology, and evolving social norms. We therefore establish these Principles as the foundation of the rights and responsibilities of those within the Facebook Service.

1. *Freedom to Share and Connect*. People should have the freedom to share whatever information they want, in any medium and any format, and have the right to connect online with anyone—any person, organization, or service—as long as they both consent to the connection.

2. *Ownership and Control of Information*. People should own their information. They should have the freedom to share it with anyone they want and take it with them anywhere they want, including removing it from the Facebook Service. People should have the freedom to decide with whom they will share their information, and to set privacy controls to protect those choices. Those controls, however, are not capable of limiting how those who have received information may use it, particularly outside the Facebook Service.

3. *Free Flow of Information*. People access all of the information made People should also have practical tools that make it easy, quick, and efficient to share and access this information.

> "People should have the freedom to access all of the information made available to them by others."

4. *Fundamental Equality.* Every person—whether individual, advertiser, developer, organization, or other entity—should have representation and access to distribution and information within the Facebook Service, regardless of the Person's primary activity. There should be a single set of principles, rights, and responsibilities that should apply to all People using the Facebook Service.

5. *Social Value.* People should have the freedom to build trust and reputation through their identity and connections, and should not have their presence on the Facebook Service removed for reasons other than those described in Facebook's Statement of Rights and Responsibilities.

6. *Open Platforms and Standards.* People should have programmatic interfaces for sharing and accessing the information available to them. The specifications for these interfaces should be published and made available and accessible to everyone.

7. *Fundamental Service.* People should be able to use Facebook for free to establish a presence, connect with others, and share information with them. Every Person should be able to use the Facebook Service regardless of his or her level of participation or contribution.

8. *Common Welfare.* The rights and responsibilities of Facebook and the People that use it should be described in a Statement of Rights and Responsibilities, which should not be inconsistent with these Principles.

9. *Transparent Process.* Facebook should publicly make available information about its purpose, plans, policies, and operations. Facebook should have a town hall process of notice and comment and a system of voting to encourage input and discourse on amendments to these Principles or to the Rights and Responsibilities.

10. *One World.* The Facebook Service should transcend geographic and national boundaries and be available to everyone in the world.

This essay was published on *Mashable.com* on September 23, 2011.

IS FACEBOOK TRYING TO KILL PRIVACY?

BEN PARR

Facebook has finally done it. It's just a few updates away now from euthanizing 1 the concept of privacy, already ailing on its network.

Timelines and Open Graph, introduced at this week's f8 conference, sit on 2 either edge of the sword that's just been run through privacy's heart. It is finished. It is done. This turn of events probably makes CEO Mark Zuckerberg happy. Let's look back:

> When I got started in my dorm room at Harvard, the question a lot of ₃ people asked was "Why would I want to put any information on the Internet at all? Why would I want to have a website?"
>
> And then in the last five or six years, blogging has taken off in a huge ₄ way and all these different services that have people sharing all this information. People have really gotten comfortable not only sharing more information and different kinds, but more openly and with more people. That social norm is just something that has evolved over time.

That was Zuckerberg's January 2010 argument that sharing is the new ₅ social norm. But that's only half of the sharing equation. Zuckerberg didn't talk about the other half: privacy.

Timeline: Showing the World Who You Are

The first big change Zuckerberg revealed on stage was Timeline, the completely ₆ overhauled version of profile pages. No longer is your Facebook profile about what you did recently—now it's about everything you've done on Facebook and beyond.

The Timeline interface lays out everything you've shared on Facebook. ₇ One of the new features, Map, lays out your checkins on a world map. My map is sparse because I primarily use Foursquare to share my location. But now that I see how sparse that map looks, I feel compelled to start sharing my location via Facebook.

In addition to laying out everything you already shared for the world to ₈ see, the Timeline encourages you to share more than ever about your life so far. Millions of people are likely to post their baby pictures so that the beginning of their Timelines—birth—isn't just an empty box.

The New Open Graph: Every Action Is Connected to Facebook

Timeline is just the appetizer. The second announcement, the launch of the ₉ new Facebook Open Graph, is what will forever transform the world's largest social network.

There are a couple of key changes that deserve mentioning. The first is ₁₀ the addition of customizable actions and gestures. No longer do apps prompt you just to "like" something on Facebook. Instead, you'll share that you "hiked a trail" or "rode your bike" or "kissed a girl" (and liked it). Any action can be shared via Facebook, and the only limit is the imagination of developers.

The second addition is the new permissions screen for giving apps access   11
to your Facebook account. It's more robust and explains exactly what an app
will be sharing with it. The result is that the prompt will only appear once.
Once you accept, the app can share exactly what you're doing to your Facebook
wall as you're doing it.

There is no longer a "Would you like to post this to Facebook?" prompt. It   12
just posts. When you run with Nike+, it gets posted. When you use your favorite cooking site to make a new dish, it gets posted. When you go to bed with a
device tracking your sleep patterns, it gets posted.

Everything can, and eventually will,
get posted. Facebook has done something
nobody has ever been able to do at scale:
It has enabled passive sharing.

> "Everything can, and
> eventually will, get
> posted."   13

Twisting the Knife

In 2009, Mashable's CEO and founder Pete Cashmore argued on CNN that   14
privacy was dead, and social media was holding the smoking gun:

> We're living at a time when attention is the new currency: With hun-   15
> dreds of TV channels, billions of Web sites, podcasts, radio shows, music
> downloads and social networking, our attention is more fragmented
> than ever before.
>
> Those who insert themselves into as many channels as possible   16
> look set to capture the most value. They'll be the richest, the most suc-
> cessful, the most connected, capable and influential among us. We're all
> publishers now, and the more we publish, the more valuable connections
> we'll make.

While I agree with his assertion that in an age where attention is king, pri-   17
vacy is simply an illusion, I disagree about the murderer. Sure, Twitter, Flickr,
Google, and others played a part in privacy's death, but Facebook made the
killing blow.

But thanks to what Facebook launched at f8, we're at the point of no   18
return. Facebook's passive sharing will change how we live our lives. More and
more, the things we do in real life will end up as Facebook posts. And while we
may be consoled by the fact that most of this stuff is being posted just to our
friends, it only takes one friend to share that information with his or her
friends to start a viral chain.

Sharing with just your friends doesn't protect your privacy. I know the   19
people at Facebook will disagree and argue that users can control what is
shared with whom. But this is simply an illusion that makes us feel better
about all the sharing we have done and are about to do.

We may not notice the impact on our lives immediately. But it won't be   20
long until your life is on display for all of your friends to see, and then we'll all
know what Facebook has wrought.

This article is from *Slate*, where it was published on November 30, 2011.

IT'S NOT ALL FACEBOOK'S FAULT

FARHAD MANJOO

Mark Zuckerberg wants you to know that Facebook has reformed. In the latest 1 installment of his recurring series of apologetic blog entries, Facebook's founder says that while the social network has always tried to protect its users' privacy, it has "made a bunch of mistakes" along the way.

Over the last year and a half, he explains, the company has instituted several 2 useful privacy features. Now, for instance, you can control who gets to see each individual item you post at the moment you post it. Facebook has also improved its methods for sharing items with subsets of friends—confusingly, the two methods are called Groups and Lists—and it has made its privacy settings panel slightly less confusing than it's been in the past. As of this week, Facebook is going even further: As part of a settlement with the Federal Trade Commission—the FTC charged the social network with "deceiv[ing] consumers by telling them they could keep their information on Facebook private, and then repeatedly allowing it to be shared and made public"—the company has agreed to institute a series of new internal controls. The settlement also requires Facebook to obtain a clean privacy bill of health from independent third-party auditors every two years, a requirement that will stay in place for the next two decades.

Facebook's settlement with the FTC—which is similar to agreements that 3 both Twitter and Google signed with the agency after their own privacy flare-ups—seems like a promising step for the company. The most obvious benefit for users is that Facebook will now have a rigorous process by which to examine the privacy implications of every new product or feature it rolls out. Zuckerberg says that he's appointed two senior privacy officers to oversee the company's commitments to the FTC. This will mark a change from the past, when Facebook's attitude toward privacy seemed to be to act first and apologize later. There was a logical, if cynical, rationale for that approach: Though we all moaned over the company's privacy violations, few of us ever made good on our vows to quit the site for good. Now, with the government watching everything it does, Facebook will have to be more careful.

But don't expect Facebook's deal with the government to turn the site into a safe haven for your private thoughts and photos. Facebook will never be "private"—indeed, the very idea of making

> "Facebook will never be 'private'—indeed, the very idea of making Facebook a more private place borders on the oxymoronic." 4

Facebook a more private place borders on the oxymoronic, a bit like expecting modesty at a strip club. I'm all for Facebook giving us more ways to retain control over what we post on the site. At the same time, I suspect that we expect more from the site vis-à-vis privacy than it can ever hope to deliver. Yes, Facebook has made some boneheaded privacy transgressions over the years. But the problem isn't only Facebook—it's also our misguided idea that we can control the audience for anything we post online. The entire point of Facebook is to allow us to connect and share stuff. It is thus, by its very nature, one of the most intrusive technologies ever built—and, for better or worse, we're stuck with it.

5   This might seem obvious: Facebook is on the Internet, and the Internet's main function is to distribute information—of course Facebook can't be private. That photo you just shared with "friends only"? Not only is it now stored on dozens of Facebook servers across the planet, but it has also lodged itself into each of your friends' browser caches. What's more, any of your "friends" is free to grab a screenshot of your image and spread it to the wider world. At best, then, the "privacy controls" on Facebook (or Google+, for that matter) should be regarded as aspirational, the most optimistic scenario for your data. Friends only, hopefully.

6   I don't think most Facebook users have internalized how leaky the site can be. At *Manners for the Digital Age*, the podcast that I co-host with my *Slate* colleague Emily Yoffe, we get Facebook privacy questions every day. A lot of listeners seem to be looking for a kind of privacy silver bullet—a foolproof way to keep their co-workers out of their Facebook profile, say. These people fundamentally misunderstand Facebook. The only sure way to keep something private on Facebook is not to post it to Facebook.

7   Mark Zuckerberg would never acknowledge this, but I think it will ultimately benefit both his site and its users if we adjusted our expectations about "privacy" there. You should approach Facebook as cautiously as you would approach your open bedroom window. However restrictive your privacy controls, you should imagine that everything that you post on Facebook will be available for public consumption forever. If you follow this simple rule, you'll never be blindsided.

8   Yes, anticipating the worst-case scenario of everything is kind of paranoid and more than a little frustrating. All you wanted to do was share pictures of your birthday dinner with a few friends—should you really have to think three times about the long-term implications of something so small?

9   Yes, you should. Facebook is a powerful tool, and the reason that so many people slip up on the site is that we fail to appreciate its power. It's time we all started taking it a bit more seriously. Sharing is fun. But if you don't plan on sharing with everyone, don't bother.

EXERCISE 8.6

Read the blog post and comments below, and then answer the questions on page 311.

This blog post, followed by a number of comments, first appeared on the Legal Blog Watch Web site on March 11, 2008.

DO EMPLOYERS USING FACEBOOK FOR BACKGROUND CHECKS FACE LEGAL RISKS?

CAROLYN ELEFANT

As employers increasingly turn to social networking sites like Facebook to [1] conduct background checks on job applicants and employees, a potential face-off is brewing regarding the legality of this practice, according to reports from *Financial Week* and the *New York Daily News*. Long ago, most employers stopped requiring applicants to submit photographs or inquiring about marital status or age to avoid accusations that they rejected a candidate for discriminatory reasons. Now, social networking profiles make this once off-limits information readily available, thus reopening the potential for liability. And demographic data isn't the only concern for employers. Facebook profiles may also include information about employees' political activities, a factor that employers are prohibited from considering under most states' laws.

A recent study suggests that in fact, many employers are taking advantage [2] of the treasure trove of information that social networking sites provide. A survey of 350 employers by the Vault found that 44% of employers use social networking sites to examine the profiles of job candidates, and 39% have looked up the profile of a current employee.

Despite increased employer use of social networking sites, most experts advise employers against the practice in light of the potential risks. Says Neal D. Mollen, an attorney with Paul Hastings, Janofsky & Walker, "I think it's unlikely employers are going to learn a good deal of job-related information from a Facebook page they won't learn in the context of a well-run interview, so the potential benefit of doing this sort of search is outweighed by the potential risk." And for those employers who can't resist peeking at social networking sites, Jennifer M. Bombard, an attorney with Morgan Brown & Joy,

> "Many employers are taking advantage of the treasure trove of information that social networking sites provide." [3]

recommends that they document a "legitimate business rationale for rejecting applicants" and make sure that hiring decisions are not motivated by information found on an applicant's social networking site. Yet even with these prophylactic° measures, a discrimination case will be "more problematic to defend" where an employer admits to having looked at a social networking site, says Gerald L. Maatman Jr., an attorney with Seyfarth Shaw.

Protective

If employers want to review social networking profiles to get a sense of 4 what a potential employee is like, I say let them (so long as they don't use the information to unlawfully discriminate against protected groups). But first, require them to disclose the practice to job applicants and employees. Just as the information that we post on Facebook says something about us, employers' use of Facebook to ferret out personal information about prospective or current employees conveys a lot about them.

Posted by Carolyn Elefant on March 11, 2008 at 12:45 PM | Comments (8)

Comments

I've never understood how employers are able to look at peoples' Facebook 5 profiles anyway, unless I'm Facebook-impaired. Can't you change your privacy settings so that only friends you've added can see your profile? I'm pretty sure that's the way mine's set. . . . not even people in my network can see my profile unless they're a friend.

Posted by: birdy | Mar 11, 2008 6:28:50 PM

It's true that you can set your Facebook privacy settings to only show your pro- 6 file to your friends, or even just your name and no location—but then nobody can find you on there, and you're typically on there to be findable. An employer can tell a lot from a picture—your race, whether you are attractive, whether you are overweight, if you are wearing a yarmulke or a veil. These are all bases for discrimination beyond what's on your resume. So, safer with no picture— but that also defeats the purpose of social contacts finding you.

Posted by: Carol Shepherd | Mar 12, 2008 9:19:03 AM

good post. I just put a copy on our employment screening blog: blog 7 .employeescreen.com.

Posted by: Jason Morris | Mar 14, 2008 10:02:09 AM

Tactics like utilizing searches on major social networking sites are very ques- 8 tionable. First, employee screening in general has a very subversive stigma associated with it b/c of what it does. Following stated regulated approaches as it relates to the FCRA and by being open about the type of information being requested will ensure a compliant employee background search. Using certified professionals and doing your home[work] by checking with Employee Screening resources should guide you properly.

Posted by: Bob Maxwell | Jun 27, 2008 10:32:50 PM

Hey! I am doing a legal research paper on this same topic for an independent 9
graduate study course and was wondering what your sources were. Also, can
you send me direction on how to find the Vault survey you referenced in the
blog? Thanks so much!

    Posted by Monica Dunham | July 3, 2008 12:10:19 PM

depends of the type of employment. . . . many jobs require applicants to con- 10
sent to a background check process.

    Posted by: | Sep. 15, 2008 8:56:56 PM

Questions

1. What steps would you take to determine whether Elefant's information is accurate?

2. How could you determine whether Elefant is respected in her field?

3. Is Elefant's blog written for an audience that is knowledgeable about her subject? How can you tell?

4. Do you think this blog post is a suitable research source? Why or why not?

5. What insights about this blog post do the comments that accompany it give you?

6. This blog post was written in 2008. Do you think it is still relevant today? Why or why not?

9

Summarizing, Paraphrasing, Quoting, and Synthesizing Sources

AT ISSUE

Do Social-Networking Sites Threaten Our Privacy? (continued)

In Chapter 8, you learned how to evaluate sources for an essay about the dangers of posting personal information on social-networking sites. In this chapter, you will learn how to take notes from various sources that address this issue.

As you saw in Chapter 8, before you can decide which material to use to support your arguments, you need to evaluate a variety of potential sources. After you decide what sources you will use, you can begin thinking about where you might use each source and about how to integrate the sources you have chosen into your essay in the form of *summary*, *paraphrase*, and *quotation*. When you actually write your argument, you will *synthesize* the sources into your paper, blending them with your own ideas and interpretations (as the student writer did when she wrote the MLA research paper in Chapter 10).

For comprehension quizzes, see bedfordstmartins.com/practicalargument.

Summarizing Sources

A **summary** restates the main idea of a passage (or even an entire book or article) in concise terms. Because a summary leaves out the examples, explanations, and stylistic devices of the source, it is always much shorter than the original. Usually, it is just a sentence or two.

WHEN TO SUMMARIZE

Summarize when you want to give readers a general sense of a source's position on an issue.

When you summarize information, you do not include your own opinions, but you do use your own words and phrasing, not those of your source. If you want to use a particularly distinctive word or phrase from your source, you may do so—but you must always place such words in quotation marks and **document** them. If you do not, you will be committing **plagiarism.** (See Chapter 10 for information on documenting sources; see Chapter 11 for information on avoiding plagiarism.)

The following paragraph is from a newspaper opinion essay.

ORIGINAL SOURCE

When everyone has a blog, a MySpace page, or Facebook entry, everyone is a publisher. When everyone has a cellphone with a camera in it, everyone is a paparazzo. When everyone can upload video on YouTube, everyone is a filmmaker. When everyone is a publisher, paparazzo, or filmmaker, everyone else is a public figure. We're all public figures now. The blogosphere has made the global discussion so much richer—and each of us so much more transparent. ("The Whole World Is Watching," Thomas L. Friedman, *New York Times*, June 27, 2007, 23)

The following effective summary conveys a general but accurate sense of the original paragraph without using the source's phrasing or including the writer's own opinions. (One distinctive and hard-to-reword phrase is placed in quotation marks.) Parenthetical documentation indicates the source of the material.

EFFECTIVE SUMMARY

The popularity of blogs, social-networking sites, cell phone cameras, and YouTube has enhanced the "global discussion" but made it very hard for people to remain anonymous (Friedman 23).

Notice that this summary is much shorter than the original passage and that it does not include all the original's examples. Still, it accurately communicates a general sense of the source's main idea.

The following summary is not acceptable because it uses the source's exact words without putting them in quotation marks or providing documentation. (This constitutes plagiarism.) The summary also expresses the student writer's opinion.

UNACCEPTABLE SUMMARY

It seems to me that blogs, social-networking sites, cell phone cameras, and YouTube are everywhere, and what this means is that we're all public figures now.

SUMMARIZING SOURCES

Do

- Convey the main idea of the original passage.
- Be concise.
- Use your own original words and phrasing.
- Place any words from your source in quotation marks.
- Include documentation.

Do not

- Include your own analysis or opinions.
- Include digressions.
- Argue with your source.
- Use your source's syntax or phrasing.

➲ EXERCISE 9.1

Write a two-sentence summary of the following passage. Then, edit your summary so that it is only one sentence long. Be sure your summary conveys the main idea of the original passage and includes proper documentation.

We're living at a time when attention is the new currency: with hundreds of TV channels, billions of Web sites, podcasts, radio shows, music downloads, and social networking, our attention is more fragmented than ever before.

Those who insert themselves into as many channels as possible look set to capture the most value. They'll be the richest, the most successful, the most connected, capable, and influential among us. We're all publishers now, and the more we publish, the more valuable connections we'll make.

Twitter, Facebook, Flickr, Foursquare, Fitbit, and the SenseCam give us a simple choice: participate or fade into a lonely obscurity. (Pete Cashmore, "Privacy Is Dead, and Social Media Hold Smoking Gun," CNN.com, October 28, 2009)

Paraphrasing Sources

A **paraphrase** is different from a summary. While a summary gives a general overview of the original, a paraphrase presents the source's ideas in detail, including its main idea, its key supporting points, and perhaps even its examples. For this reason, a paraphrase is longer than a summary. In fact, it may be as long as the original.

WHEN TO PARAPHRASE

Paraphrase when you want readers to understand a source's key points in specific terms.

Like a summary, a paraphrase uses your own words and phrasing, not the language and syntax of the original. Any words or phrases from your source must be placed in quotation marks. When you paraphrase, you may not always follow the order of the original source's ideas, but you should try to convey the writer's emphasis and most important points.

The following paragraph is from an editorial that appeared in a student newspaper.

ORIGINAL SOURCE

Additionally, as graduates retain their Facebook accounts, employers are increasingly able to use Facebook as an evaluation tool when making hiring decisions. Just as companies sometimes incorporate social functions into their interview process to see if potential hires can handle themselves responsibly, they may also check out a student's Facebook account to see how the student chooses to present him or herself. This may seem shady and underhanded, but one must understand that social networks are not anonymous; whatever one chooses to post will be available to all. Even if someone goes to great pains to keep an employer-friendly profile, his or her friends may still tag pictures of him or her which will be available to whoever wants to see them. Not only can unexpected Facebook members get information by viewing one's profile, but a user's personal information can also leak out by merely registering for the service. Both the user agreement and the privacy policy indicate that Facebook can give information to third parties and can supplement its data with information from newspapers, blogs and instant messages. ("Beware What You Post on Facebook," *The Tiger*, Clemson University, August 4, 2006)

The following paraphrase reflects the original paragraph's emphasis and communicates its key points.

EFFECTIVE PARAPHRASE

Because students keep their accounts at social-networking sites after they graduate, potential employers can use the information they find there to help them evaluate candidates' qualifications. This process is comparable to the way a company might evaluate an applicant in person in a social situation. Some people may see the practice of employers checking applicants' Facebook pages as "shady and underhanded," but these sites are not intended to be anonymous or private. For example, a person may try to maintain a profile that will be appropriate for employers, but friends may post inappropriate pictures. Also, people can reveal personal information not only in profiles but also simply by registering with Facebook. Finally, as Facebook states in its membership information, it can supply information to others as well as provide data from other sources. ("Beware")

Notice that this paraphrase includes many of the details presented in the original passage and quotes a key phrase, but its style and sentence structure are different from those of the original.

The following paraphrase is not acceptable because its phrasing and sentence structure are too close to the original. It also borrows words and phrases from the source without attribution or documentation.

UNACCEPTABLE PARAPHRASE

As more and more college graduates keep their Facebook accounts, employers are increasingly able to use them as evaluation tools when they decide whom to hire. Companies sometimes set up social functions during the interview process to see how potential hires handle themselves; in the same way, they can consult a Facebook page to see how an applicant presents himself or herself. This may seem underhanded, but after all, Facebook is not anonymous; its information is available to all. Many people try to keep their profiles employer friendly, but their friends sometimes tag pictures of them that employers will be able to see. Besides, students' personal information is available not just on their profiles but also in the form they fill out when they register. Finally, according to their user agreement and their privacy policy, Facebook can give information to third parties and also add data from other sources.

PARAPHRASING SOURCES

Do

- Convey the source's ideas fully and accurately.
- Use your own words and phrasing.
- Convey the emphasis of the original.
- Put any words borrowed from the source in quotation marks.
- Include documentation.

Do not

- Use the exact words or phrasing of your source (unless you are quoting).
- Include your own analysis or opinions.
- Argue with or contradict your source.
- Wander from the topic of the source.

➔ EXERCISE 9.2

Write a paraphrase of the passage you summarized in Exercise 9.1. How is your paraphrase different from your summary?

➔ EXERCISE 9.3

The following paragraph is from the same Clemson University student newspaper article that was excerpted on pages 316–317. Read the paragraph, and then write a paraphrase that communicates its key ideas. Before you begin, circle any distinctive word and phrases that might be difficult to paraphrase, and consider whether you should quote them. Be sure to include documentation.

> All these factors make clear the importance of two principles: Responsibility and caveat emptor. First, people should be responsible about how they portray themselves and their friends, and employers, authorities, and the owners must approach this information responsibly and fairly. Second, "let the buyer beware" applies to all parties involved. Facebook users need to understand the potential consequences of the information they share, and outside viewers need to understand that the material on Facebook is often only a humorous, lighthearted presentation of one aspect of a person. Facebook is an incredibly valuable communications tool that will link the college generation more tightly than any before it, but users have to understand that, like anything good in life, they have to be aware of the downsides.

Quoting Sources

When you **quote** words from a source, be sure that you are quoting accurately—that is, that every word and every punctuation mark in your quotation matches the source *exactly*. You also need to be sure that your quotation conveys the meaning its author intended and that you are not distorting the meaning by **quoting out of context** or by omitting a key part of the quotation.

WHEN TO QUOTE

Quote a source's words only in the following situations:

- Quote when your source's words are distinctive or memorable.

- Quote when your source's words are so direct and concise that a paraphrase would be awkward or wordy.

- Quote when your source's words add authority or credibility to your argument (for example, when your source is a well-known expert on your topic).

- Quote an opposing point when you will go on to refute it.

Remember, quoting from a source adds interest to your paper—but only when the writer's words are compelling. Too many quotations—especially long quotations—distract readers and make it difficult for them to follow your discussion. Quote only when you must. If you include too many quotations, your paper will be a patchwork of other people's words, not an original, unified whole.

QUOTING SOURCES

Do

- Enclose borrowed words in quotation marks.

- Quote accurately.

- Include documentation.

Do not

- Quote out of context.

- Distort the source's meaning.

- Include too many quotations.

⊘ EXERCISE 9.4

Read the following paragraphs from an essay that appeared in *New Scientist*. (The full text of this article begins below in Exercise 9.5.) If you were going to use these paragraphs as source material for an argumentative essay, which particular words or phrases do you think you might want to quote? Why?

> Cols likes a smoke and has tried many different drugs. He has three piercings and is in the process of tattooing his arm. He earns between $75,000 and $100,000 a year and doesn't see his dad.
>
> I know all about Cols even though I have never met him and probably never shall. Five years ago only a close friend of his would have known such personal details about him. Yet thanks to his profile on the social networking website MySpace, I even know the first thing he thinks about in the morning.
>
> There's nothing unusual about this. Millions of people share some of their most personal details with total strangers on the Internet via sites such as MySpace, Friendster, and Facebook. The dangers this can pose to children are well publicized, but it also has powerful if less well known implications for us all. The sheer volume of personal information that people are publishing online—and the fact that some of it could remain visible permanently—is changing the nature of personal privacy. Is this a good thing, or will the "MySpace generation" live to regret it? (Alison George, "Things You Wouldn't Tell Your Mother," *New Scientist*, September 16, 2006)

⊘ EXERCISE 9.5

Read the essay that follows, and highlight it to identify its most important ideas. (For information on highlighting, see Chapter 2.) Then, write a summary of one paragraph and a paraphrase of another paragraph. Assume that this essay is a source for a paper you are writing on the topic, "Do Social-Networking Sites Threaten Our Privacy?" Be sure to include documentation.

> This essay is from *New Scientist,* where it appeared on September 16, 2006.

THINGS YOU WOULDN'T TELL YOUR MOTHER

ALISON GEORGE

Cols likes a smoke and has tried many different drugs. He has three piercings and is in the process of tattooing his arm. He earns between $75,000 and $100,000 a year and doesn't see his dad.

I know all about Cols even though I have never met him and probably never shall. Five years ago only a close friend of his would have known such personal details about him. Yet thanks to his profile

> "I know all about Cols even though I have never met him." [2]

on the social networking website MySpace, I even know the first thing he thinks about in the morning.

There's nothing unusual about this. Millions of people share some of their [3] most personal details with total strangers on the Internet via sites such as MySpace, Friendster, and Facebook. The dangers this can pose to children are well publicized, but it also has powerful if less well known implications for us all. The sheer volume of personal information that people are publishing online—and the fact that some of it could remain visible permanently—is changing the nature of personal privacy. Is this a good thing, or will the "MySpace generation" live to regret it?

The change has been made possible by the way social networking sites are [4] structured. They allow users to create a profile of themselves for others to peruse, and to build networks with hundreds or thousands of people who share their interests or just like the look of their page. It's an opportunity to present yourself in a way you want others to see you. Many people reveal everything from their musical tastes and political and sexual orientation to their drinking and drug habits and their inner thoughts and feelings. And it's a very recent phenomenon. "There is no real-world parallel. You don't go walking round the mall telling people whether you are straight or gay," says Fred Stutzman, a researcher at the University of North Carolina at Chapel Hill who studies identity and social networks.

What's more, people can end up having multiple identities online. The [5] picture you present of yourself on the dating site Match.com, for instance, will likely be different to the one you give on Facebook, restricted mainly to universities and high schools. This can be confusing if someone is trying to find out more about you by searching on Google—if they're thinking of employing you, for example, or dating you. In recognition of this online identity crisis, Stutzman and his colleague Terrell Russell have set up a service called ClaimID (claimid.com) that allows you to track, verify, annotate, and prioritize the information that appears about you online, so that when someone searches you they get representative information.

Such a service could prove increasingly useful for people entering the [6] workforce with a few years of social networking behind them. Tasteless in-jokes are fine within the network, says Stutzman. "But when you're going for that job interview, they can really come back and bite people." A survey by the U.S. National Association of Colleges and Employers published in July found that 27 percent of employers have Googled their job candidates or checked their profiles on social networking sites. It is not just employers who are interested in your online revelations. U.S. college athletes who posted pictures of themselves behaving badly on their social networking profiles unwittingly found themselves on Bob Reno's badjocks.com site, which publishes stories about scandals in sport.

How does this happen? Offline, it is easy to compartmentalize the different 7 aspects of your life—professional, personal, family—but online, where social networks are so much larger and looser, the distinctions become blurred. These issues have not gone unnoticed by social network providers. They are reluctant to offer too much privacy because this makes it harder for users to communicate with people they don't know. Yet too little privacy means that users lose control over the information they post. "There is a fine balance between protecting and revealing—for users as well as providers," says Alessandro Acquisti of Carnegie Mellon University in Pittsburgh, Pennsylvania, who researches privacy and information security and is looking at the difference between online and offline behavior.

In everyday life, says Acquisti, we are better equipped to manage our 8 privacy—we are unlikely to give strangers our phone number and date of birth. So why do some people give out this information freely online? According to Acquisti, it's because people expect that the more information they give, the more they gain from the network. His research also shows that some users are not well informed about the reach of the network, and how their profile could potentially be viewed by millions of people. Internet researcher Steve Jones of the University of Illinois at Chicago agrees. "A social network where you create a circle of friends feels private," he says. "It's more of a feeling of a website shared with a small, closed group of people."

For those wishing to keep out prying eyes, most social networks do offer 9 additional privacy tools. Users of MySpace and Facebook can choose to reveal their profiles only to friends, for example. But recent research shows that many users don't make use of these tools, even if they are worried about privacy. A survey of Facebook users published in June by Acquisti and his colleague Ralph Gross found that even among users who were concerned about a stranger knowing their address or class schedule, 22 percent still gave their address on their Facebook profile, and 40 percent published their class schedule.

What can be done to prevent what Acquisti and Gross call "an eternal 10 memory of our indiscretions"? Some recommend drastic measures. "Anything you put on the Internet has the potential to be made public and you should treat it as such," says Jones. "If you put something on MySpace or Facebook ask yourself whether you would be comfortable shouting it out at a family reunion. If the answer is no, then don't put it up." As newspapers report more stories about students being kicked off their courses and bloggers being sacked because of their online revelations, users might well feel compelled to tighten up their online privacy. This semester, students moving into campus accommodation at the University of California, Berkeley, will even be required to attend a class in social networking to make them aware of the risks.

It could go another way, though. As people become more tolerant of 11 online openness, we could see a shift in attitudes and a rethinking of what we consider private. "People tend to adapt to new environments of revelations," says Acquisti. "The new generation may be used to people talking online about their drug use and sex lives."

Their attitudes may depend on what profession they end up in. Lindsey, a 12
law student in Philadelphia who we contacted, has noticed some interesting trends among her friends. "Friends who work as DJs, record-store owners, or graphic designers express themselves far more freely than friends who work in more traditional professions," she says. She has also noticed that most of her friends who are teachers don't have online profiles. "They've realized that there's nothing worse than walking in to teach your calculus class only to have them holding copies of the photograph of you on the beach."

Working Source Material into Your Argument

When you use source material in an argumentative essay, your goal is to integrate the material smoothly into your discussion, blending summary, paraphrase, and quotation with your own ideas.

To help readers follow your discussion, you need to indicate the source of your information clearly and distinguish your own ideas from those of your sources. Never simply drop source material into your discussion. Whenever possible, introduce quotations, paraphrases, and summaries with an **identifying tag** (sometimes called a *signal phrase*), a phrase that identifies the source, and always follow them with documentation. This practice helps readers identify the boundaries between your own ideas and those of your sources.

It is also important that you include clues to help readers understand why you are using a particular source and what the exact relationship is between your source material and your own ideas. For example, you may be using a source to support a point you are making or to disagree with another source.

Using Identifying Tags

Using identifying tags to introduce your summaries, paraphrases, or quotations will help you accomplish the goals discussed above (as well as avoid accidental plagiarism).

SUMMARY WITH IDENTIFYING TAG

According to Thomas L. Friedman, the popularity of blogs, social-networking sites, cell phone cameras, and YouTube has enhanced the "global discussion" but made it hard for people to remain anonymous (23).

Note that you do not always have to place the identifying tag at the beginning of the summarized, paraphrased, or quoted material. You can also place it in the middle or at the end:

IDENTIFYING TAG AT THE BEGINNING

<u>Thomas L. Friedman notes</u> that the popularity of blogs, social-networking sites, cell phone cameras, and YouTube has enhanced the "global discussion" but made it hard for people to remain anonymous (23).

IDENTIFYING TAG IN THE MIDDLE

The popularity of blogs, social-networking sites, cell phone cameras, and YouTube, <u>Thomas L. Friedman observes,</u> has enhanced the "global discussion" but made it hard for people to remain anonymous (23).

IDENTIFYING TAG AT THE END

The popularity of blogs, social-networking sites, cell phone cameras, and YouTube has enhanced the "global discussion" but made it hard for people to remain anonymous, <u>Thomas L. Friedman points out</u> (23).

TEMPLATES FOR USING IDENTIFYING TAGS

To avoid repeating phrases like *he says* in identifying tags, try using some of the following verbs to introduce your source material. (You can also use "According to . . . ," to introduce a source.)

For Summaries or Paraphrases

[Name of writer]	notes, acknowledges, proposes,	that [summary or paraphrase].
The writer	suggests, believes, observes,	
The article	explains, comments, warns,	
The essay	reports, points out, predicts,	
	implies, concludes, states	

For Quotations

As [name of writer]	notes, acknowledges, proposes,	"_____[quotation]_____."
As the writer	suggests, believes, observes,	
As the article	warns, reports, points out,	
As the essay	predicts, implies, concludes,	
	states, explains	

Working Quotations into Your Sentences

When you use quotations in your essays, you may need to edit them to provide context or to make them fit smoothly into your sentences. If you do edit a quotation, be careful not to distort the source's meaning.

Adding or Changing Words

When you add or change words in a quotation, use **brackets** to indicate your edits:

ORIGINAL QUOTATION
"Twitter, Facebook, Flickr, FourSquare, Fitbit, and the SenseCam give us a simple choice: participate or fade into a lonely obscurity." (Cashmore)

WORDS ADDED FOR CLARIFICATION
As Cashmore observes, "Twitter, Flickr, FourSquare, Fitbit, and the SenseCam [as well as similar social-networking sites] give us a simple choice: participate or fade into a lonely obscurity."

ORIGINAL QUOTATION
"The blogosphere has made the global discussion so much richer—and each of us so much more transparent" (Friedman 23).

WORDS CHANGED TO MAKE VERB TENSE LOGICAL
As Thomas Friedman explains, increased access to cell phone cameras, YouTube, and the like continues to "[make] the global discussion so much richer—and each of us so much more transparent" (23).

Deleting Words

When you delete words from a quotation, use **ellipses**—three spaced periods—to indicate your edits. However, never use ellipses to indicate a deletion at the beginning of a quotation:

ORIGINAL QUOTATION
"Just as companies sometimes incorporate social functions into their interview process to see if potential hires can handle themselves responsibly, they may also check out a student's Facebook account to see how the student chooses to present him or herself" ("Beware").

UNNECESSARY WORDS DELETED
"Just as companies sometimes incorporate social functions into their interview process, . . . they may also check out a student's Facebook account . . ." ("Beware").

MISREPRESENTING QUOTATIONS

Be careful not to distort a source's meaning when you add, change, or delete words from a quotation. In the following example, the writer intentionally deletes material from the original quotation that would weaken his argument.

Original Quotation

"This incident is by no means an isolated one. Connecticut authorities are investigating reports that seven girls were sexually assaulted by older men they met on MySpace" ("Beware").

Distorted

"This incident is by no means an isolated one. [In fact,] seven girls were sexually assaulted by older men they met on MySpace" ("Beware").

⊙ EXERCISE 9.6

Reread the summary you wrote for Exercise 9.1 and the paraphrase you wrote for Exercise 9.3. Add three different identifying tags to each, varying the verbs you use and the position of the tags. Then, check to make sure you have used correct parenthetical documentation. (If the author's name is included in the identifying tag, it should not also appear in the parenthetical citation.)

Synthesizing Sources

In a **synthesis**, you combine summary, paraphrase, and quotation from several sources with your own ideas to support an original conclusion. A synthesis sometimes identifies similarities and differences among ideas, indicating where sources agree and disagree and how they support or challenge one another's ideas. Transitional words and phrases identify points of similarity (*also*, *like*, *similarly*, and so on) or difference (*however*, *in contrast*, and so on). When you write a synthesis, you include identifying tags and parenthetical documentation to identify each piece of information you get from a source and to distinguish your sources' ideas from one another and from your own ideas.

The following effective synthesis is excerpted from the student paper in Chapter 10. Note how the synthesis blends information from three sources with the student's own ideas to support her point about how the Internet has affected people's concepts of "public" and "private."

EFFECTIVE SYNTHESIS

Student's original point

Paraphrase

Part of the problem is that the Internet has fundamentally altered our notions of "private" and "public" in ways that we are only just beginning to understand. As Alison George observes in *New Scientist* magazine, the enormous amount of personal information that appears (and remains) online poses a challenge to our notions of personal privacy (50). On sites like Facebook, people can reveal intimate details of their lives to millions of strangers. This situation is unprecedented and, at least for the foreseeable future, irreversible. As *New York Times* columnist Thomas L. Friedman observes, "When everyone has a blog, a MySpace page, or Facebook entry, everyone is a publisher. . . . When everyone is a publisher, paparazzo, or filmmaker, everyone else is a public figure." Given the changes in our understanding of privacy and the public nature of the Internet, the suggestion that we should live our lives by the same rules we lived by twenty years ago simply does not make sense. As Friedman notes, in the Internet age, more and more of "what you say or do or write will end up as a digital fingerprint that never gets erased" (23).

Student's own ideas

Quotation

Student's evaluation of source

Quotation

Compare the effective synthesis above with the following unacceptable synthesis.

UNACCEPTABLE SYNTHESIS

"The sheer volume of personal information that people are publishing online—and the fact that some of it could remain visible permanently—is changing the nature of personal privacy." On sites like Facebook, people can reveal the most intimate details of their lives to millions of total strangers. This development is unprecedented and, at least for the foreseeable future, irreversible. "When everyone has a blog, a MySpace page, or Facebook entry, everyone is a publisher. . . . When everyone is a publisher, paparazzo, or filmmaker, everyone else is a public figure" (Friedman 23). Given the changes in our understanding of privacy and the essentially public nature of the Internet, the analogy that Hall makes between a MySpace post and a private conversation seems of limited use. In the Internet age, more and more of "what you say or do or write will end up as a digital fingerprint that never gets erased."

Unlike the effective synthesis on pages 326–327, the unacceptable synthesis above does not begin with a topic sentence that states the point the source material in the paragraph will support. Instead, it opens with an out-of-context quotation whose source is not identified. This quotation could have been paraphrased—its wording is not particularly memorable—and, more important, it should have been accompanied by documentation. (If source information is not provided, the writer is committing plagiarism even if the borrowed material is set in quotation marks.) The second quotation, although it includes parenthetical documentation (Friedman 23), is dropped into the paragraph without an identifying tag; the third quotation, also from the Friedman article, is not documented at all, making it appear to be from Hall. All in all, the paragraph is not a smoothly connected synthesis but a string of unconnected ideas. It does not use sources effectively, and it does not cite them appropriately.

Documenting Sources: MLA

When you are building an argument, you use sources for support. To acknowledge the material you borrow and to help readers evaluate your sources, you need to supply documentation. In other words, you need to tell readers where you found your information. If you use documentation responsibly, you will also avoid **plagiarism**, an ethical offense with serious consequences. (See Chapter 11 for more on plagiarism.)

MLA documentation consists of two parts: **parenthetical references** in the text of your paper and a **works-cited list** at the end of the paper. (The references are keyed to the works-cited list.)

Using Parenthetical References

The basic parenthetical citation consists of the author's last name and a page number:

(Fielding 213)

If the author is referred to in the sentence, include only the page number in the parenthetical reference.

According to environmental activist Brian Fielding, the number of species affected is much higher (213).

Here are some other situations you may encounter:

- When referring to a work by two authors, include both authors' names.

(Stange and Hogarth 53)

- When citing a work with no listed author, include a short version of the title.

("Small Things" 21)

For comprehension quizzes, see bedfordstmartins.com/practicalargument.

- When citing a source that is quoted in another source, indicate this by including the abbreviation *qtd. in.*

  According to Kevin Kelly, this narrow approach is typical of the "hive mind" (qtd. in Doctorow 168).

- When citing two or more works by the same author, include a short title after the author's name.

  (Anderson, *Long Tail* 47)

- If a source does not include page numbers, or if you are referring to the entire source rather than to a specific page, cite the author's name in the text of your paper rather than in a parenthetical reference.

You must document *all* information that is not **common knowledge**, whether you are summarizing, paraphrasing, or quoting. (See p. 356 for an explanation of common knowledge.) With direct quotations, include the parenthetical reference and a period *after* the closing quotation marks.

  According to Doctorow, this is "authorship without editorship. Or authorship fused with editorship" (166).

When quoting a passage of more than four lines, introduce it with a complete sentence, followed by a colon. Indent the entire passage one inch from the left margin, and do not use quotation marks. Place the parenthetical reference *after* the final punctuation mark.

  Doctorow points out that *Wikipedia*'s history pages can be extremely informative:

  > This is a neat solution to the problem of authority—if you want to know what the fully rounded view of opinions on any controversial subject looks like, you need only consult its entry's history page for a blistering eyeful of thorough debate on the subject. (170)

Preparing the Works-Cited List

Start your works-cited list on a new page following the last page of your paper. Center the heading Works Cited at the top of the page. List entries alphabetically by the author's last name—or by the first word (other than an article such as *a* or *the*) of the title if an author is not given. Double-space within and between entries. Each entry should begin at the left-hand margin, with the other lines in the same entry indented one-half inch. (This format can be automatically generated if you use the "hanging indent" option in your word processing program.)

Here are some additional guidelines:

- Italicize all book and periodical titles.

- Use a short version of a publisher's name (Penguin rather than Penguin Books), and abbreviate *University Press* (as in Princeton UP or U of Chicago P).

- If you are listing more than one work by the same author, include the author's name in the first entry, and substitute three unspaced hyphens followed by a period for the second and subsequent entries.

- Put quotation marks around the title of a periodical article or a section of an edited book or anthology, and provide the inclusive page numbers: 44–99. For page numbers larger than 99, give the last two digits of the second number if the first is the same: 147–69 (but 286–301).

- Include the medium of publication—print, Web, CD, and so on—for all entries.

When you have completed your list, double-check your parenthetical references to make sure they match the items in your works-cited list.

The following models illustrate the most common kinds of references.

Periodicals

For periodical articles found online or through a full-text database, see page 341.

Guidelines for Citing a Periodical Article

To cite a print article in MLA style, include the following:

1. Author, last name first

2. Title of the article, in quotation marks

3. Title of the periodical, in italics

4. Volume and issue numbers

5. Date or year of publication

6. Page number(s) of the article

7. Medium of publication (Print)

┌─── 1 ───┐   ┌──────── 2 ────────┐
Carton, Evan. "American Scholars: Ralph Waldo Emerson, Joseph

┌──────────────── 2 ────────────────┐
Smith, John Brown, and the Springs of Intellectual Schism."

┌──────── 3 ────────┐ ┌─ 4 ─┐ ┌ 5 ┐ ┌─ 6 ─┐ ┌─ 7 ─┐
New England Quarterly 85.1 (2012): 5–37. Print.

Copyright Page

THE
NEW ENGLAND
QVARTERLY

A Historical Review of New England Life and Letters

Registered in the U.S. Patent and Trademark Office

EDITORS

Edmund S. Morgan   Robert L. Middlekauff
David Brion Davis   William M. Fowler Jr.
Andrew Delbanco   Robert D. Richardson
Bernard Bailyn   Daniel R. Coquillette
Louis Menand   Laura Dassow Walls
Mary Kelley   Richard D. Brown
Neil Harris   Michael Kammen
Nina Baym   Mary Loeffelholz

Editor
Linda Smith Rhoads

Editorial Assistant
Anna Kimball Williams

Volume LXXXV   Number 1
March 2012

Copyright 2012 by The New England Quarterly
ISSN 0028–4866

3. Title of periodical

4. Volume and issue number

5. Date of publication

2. Title of article

1. Author

First Page of Article

American Scholars: Ralph Waldo Emerson,
Joseph Smith, John Brown, and the Springs
of Intellectual Schism

EVAN CARTON

Every man, woman, and child was more or less a theologian.
—Harriet Beecher Stowe

THE literary intellectual, the Christian evangelical, and the political radical are, according to our contemporary civic understanding, denizens of distinctly separate spheres, spheres bounded and policed, to the extent that they come into contact at all, by mutual distrust or disdain. I propose to advance a counter-claim (for which I will begin to muster evidence and assess implications): to wit, that the seemingly divergent cultural icons of the American scholar, prophet, and revolutionary in fact share a common milieu and moment of origin in the social, spiritual, and epistemological ferment of the early nineteenth century. Thus, I contend, the icons' apparently incommensurable vocations and commitments are better viewed as variations on the volatile "American synthesis" of scriptural, rational, and ideological authority that historian of religion Mark Noll describes in his magisterial *America's God* or, rather, as schismatic expressions of what political scientist Hugh Heclo calls the "mutual and tensioned embrace between the democratic and Christian faiths."[1]

[1]Mark Noll, *America's God: From Jonathan Edwards to Abraham Lincoln* (New York: Oxford University Press, 2002), p. 9; Hugh Heclo, *Christianity and American Democracy* (Cambridge: Harvard University Press, 2007), p. 5.

The New England Quarterly, vol. LXXXV, no. 1 (March 2012). © 2012 by The New England Quarterly. All rights reserved.

6. Page numbers

5

Journals

Journals are periodicals published for experts in a field. Cite both volume number and issue number when available. In cases where only an issue number is available, cite just the issue.

> Minkler, Lanse. "Economic Rights and Political Decision-Making."
>
> > *Human Rights Quarterly* 31.2 (2009): 369–93. Print.
>
> Picciotto, Joanna. "The Public Person and the Play of Fact."
>
> > *Representations* 105 (2009): 85–132. Print.

Magazines

Magazines are periodicals published for a general audience. Do not include a magazine's volume and issue number, but do include the date (day, month, and year for weekly publications; month and year for those published less frequently). If pages are not consecutive, give the first page followed by a plus sign.

> Gladwell, Malcolm. "Open Secrets." *New Yorker* 8 Jan. 2007:
>
> > 44–53. Print.
>
> Rice, Andrew. "Mission from Africa." *New York Times Magazine*
>
> > 12 Apr. 2009: 30+. Print.

Newspapers

Include both the letter of the section and the page number. If an article continues on to another page, give just the first page followed by a plus sign.

> Darlin, Damon. "Software That Monitors Your Work, Wherever You
>
> > Are." *New York Times* 12 Apr. 2009: B2+. Print.

Editorial, Letter to the Editor, or Review

Include authors and titles where available as well as a descriptive label—for example Editorial, Letter, or Review. In the case of reviews, include the title and author of the work that is reviewed.

> Bernath, Dan. Letter. *Washington Post* 12 Apr. 2009: A16. Print.
>
> Franklin, Nancy. "Whedon's World." Rev. of *Dollhouse,* dir. Joss
>
> > Whedon. *New Yorker* 2 Mar. 2009: 45. Print.

"World Bank Responsibility." Editorial. *Wall Street Journal* 28 Mar.
    2009: A10. Print.

Political Cartoon or Comic Strip

Include the author and title (if available) of the cartoon or comic strip, followed by a descriptive label and publication information.

Adams, Scott. "Dilbert." Comic strip. *Chicago Tribune* 10 Mar.
    2009: C9. Print.

Pett, Joel. Cartoon. *Lexington Herald-Leader* 30 Apr. 2009: A12.
    Print.

Advertisement

Cite the name of the product or company that is advertised, followed by
the descriptive label and the publication information.

Rosetta Stone. Advertisement. *Atlantic* May 2009: 98. Print.

Books

Guidelines for Citing a Book

To cite a book in MLA style, include the following:

1. Author, last name first

2. Title, in italics

3. City of publication

4. Shortened form of the publisher's name

5. Date of publication

6. Medium of publication (Print).

1   2   3   4   5
Kahneman, Daniel. *Thinking, Fast and Slow*. New York: Farrar, 2011.
    6
    Print.

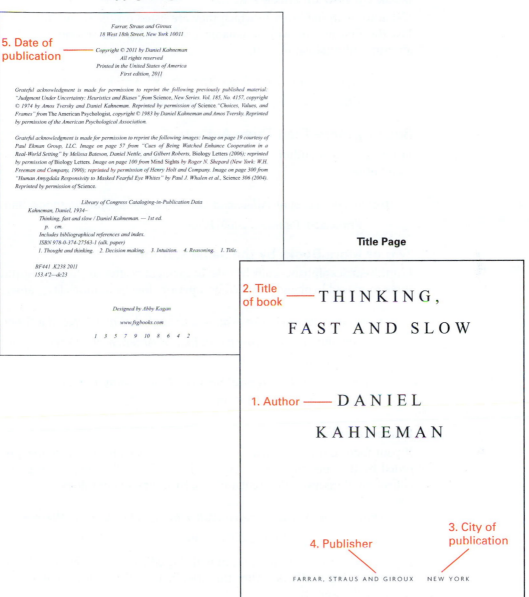

Copyright Page

Farrar, Straus and Giroux
18 West 18th Street, New York 10011

5. Date of publication — Copyright © 2011 by Daniel Kahneman
All rights reserved
Printed in the United States of America
First edition, 2011

Grateful acknowledgment is made for permission to reprint the following previously published material: "Judgment Under Uncertainty: Heuristics and Biases" from Science, New Series. Vol. 185, No. 4157, copyright © 1974 by Amos Tversky and Daniel Kahneman. Reprinted by permission of Science. "Choices, Values, and Frames" from The American Psychologist, copyright © 1983 by Daniel Kahneman and Amos Tversky. Reprinted by permission of the American Psychological Association.

Grateful acknowledgment is made for permission to reprint the following images: Image on page 19 courtesy of Paul Ekman Group, LLC. Image on page 57 from "Cues of Being Watched Enhance Cooperation in a Real-World Setting" by Melissa Bateson, Daniel Nettle, and Gilbert Roberts, Biology Letters (2006); reprinted by permission of Biology Letters. Image on page 100 from Mind Sights by Roger N. Shepard (New York: W.H. Freeman and Company, 1990); reprinted by permission of Henry Holt and Company. Image on page 300 from "Human Amygdala Responsivity to Masked Fearful Eye Whites" by Paul J. Whalen et al., Science 306 (2004). Reprinted by permission of Science.

Library of Congress Cataloging-in-Publication Data
Kahneman, Daniel, 1934–
   Thinking, fast and slow / Daniel Kahneman. — 1st ed.
      p.   cm.
   Includes bibliographical references and index.
   ISBN 978-0-374-27563-1 (alk. paper)
   1. Thought and thinking.   2. Decision making.   3. Intuition.   4. Reasoning.   1. Title.

BF441 .K238 2011
153.4'2—dc23

Designed by Abby Kagan

www.fsgbooks.com

1   3   5   7   9   10   8   6   4   2

Title Page

2. Title of book — THINKING, FAST AND SLOW

1. Author — DANIEL KAHNEMAN

4. Publisher — FARRAR, STRAUS AND GIROUX   **3. City of publication** — NEW YORK

Book by One Author

List the author, last name first, followed by the title (italicized). Include the city of publication and a short form of the publisher's name. End with the date of publication and the medium of publication.

Davidson, James West. *They Say: Ida B. Wells and the Reconstruction of Race.* New York: Oxford UP, 2009. Print.

Book by Two or Three Authors

List authors in the order in which they are listed on the book's title page. List the first author with last name first, but list the second and third authors with first names first.

> Singer, Peter, and Jim Mason. *The Way We Eat: Why Our Food
> Choices Matter*. Emmaus: Rodale, 2006. Print.

Book by More Than Three Authors

List only the first author, last name first, followed by the abbreviation et al. ("and others").

> Gould, Harvey, et al. *Advanced Computer Simulation Methods*. San
> Francisco: Pearson, 2009. Print.

Two or More Books by the Same Author

List the entries alphabetically by title. In each entry after the first, substitute three unspaced hyphens, followed by a period, for the author's last name.

> Friedman, Thomas L. *Hot, Flat, and Crowded: Why We Need a Green
> Revolution—and How It Can Renew America*. New York: Farrar,
> 2008. Print.
> ---. *The World Is Flat: A Brief History of the Twenty-First Century*.
> New York: Farrar, 2005. Print.

Edited Book

If your focus is on the *author*, include the editor's name after the title, preceded by the abbreviation Ed. (for "edited by"). If the book is an edited collection of essays by different authors, treat it as an anthology.

> Whitman, Walt. *The Portable Walt Whitman*. Ed. Michael Warner.
> New York: Penguin, 2004. Print.

If your focus is on the *editor*, begin with the editor's name followed by ed. (editor) or eds. (editors). After the title, include the author's name, preceded by the word By.

> Michael Warner, ed. *The Portable Walt Whitman*. By Walt Whitman.
> New York: Penguin, 2004. Print.

Translation

> Hernández Chávez, Alicia. *Mexico: A Brief History*. Trans. Andy Klatt.
> Berkeley: U of California P, 2006. Print.

Revised Edition

> Smith, Steven S., Jason M. Roberts, and Ryan J. Vander Weilen. *The*
> *American Congress*. 4th ed. Cambridge: Cambridge UP, 2006. Print.

Anthology

Include the name of the editor (or editors) of the anthology, followed by the abbreviation ed. (for "editor") or eds. (for "editors").

> Bob, Clifford, ed. *The International Struggle for New Human Rights*.
> Philadelphia: U of Pennsylvania P, 2009. Print.

Work in an Anthology

> Malone, Dan. "Immigration, Terrorism, and Secret Prisons."
> *Keeping Out the Other: Immigration Enforcement Today*.
> Ed. David C. Brotherton and Philip Kretsedemas. New York:
> Columbia UP, 2008. 44–62. Print.

More Than One Work in the Same Anthology

To avoid repeating the entire anthology entry, you may provide a cross-reference from individual essays to the entire anthology.

> Adelson, Glenn et al., eds. *Environment: An Interdisciplinary*
> *Anthology*. New Haven: Yale UP, 2008. Print.
> Lesher, Molly. "Seeds of Change." Adelson 131–37.
> Marshall, Robert. "The Problem of the Wilderness." Adelson 288–92.

Section or Chapter of a Book

> Leavitt, Steven D., and Stephen J. Dubner. "Why Do Drug Dealers
> Still Live with Their Moms?" *Freakonomics: A Rogue*
> *Economist Explores the Hidden Side of Everything*. New York:
> Morrow, 2006. 49–78. Print.

Introduction, Preface, Foreword, or Afterword

> Christiano, Thomas, and John Christman. Introduction.
> *Contemporary Debates in Political Philosophy*. Ed. Thomas
> Christiano and John Christman. Malden: Wiley, 2009. 1–20. Print.

Multivolume Work

> McNeil, Peter, ed. *Fashion: Critical and Primary Sources*. 4 vols.
> Oxford: Berg, 2009. Print.

Article in a Reference Work

If the entries in a reference work are arranged alphabetically, do not include page numbers or volumes. When citing a familiar encyclopedia that publishes new editions regularly, include only the edition (if given) and year. If the article's author is given, include that as well. For less well-known reference encyclopedias, include publication information.

"Human Rights." *Encyclopedia Americana*. 2003 ed. Print.

Sisk, David W. "Dystopia." *New Dictionary of the History of Ideas*. New York: Scribner's, 2005. Print.

> **NOTE**
>
> Keep in mind that many instructors do not consider encyclopedia articles acceptable research sources. Before including a citation for an encyclopedia article in your works-cited list, check with your instructor.

Audiovisual Sources

TV Show

"A Desperate Man." *NCIS*. By Nicole Mirante-Matthews. Dir. Leslie Libman. CBS. 10 Jan. 2012. Television.

Film

The Tree of Life. Dir. Terrance Malick. Perf. Brad Pitt, Sean Penn, and Jessica Chastain. Fox Searchlight, 2011. Film.

Internet Sources

Citing Web sources can be problematic because they sometimes lack basic information—for example, dates of publication or authors' names. When citing Internet sources, include all the information you can find.

- For sites that exist only on the Web, include (when available) the author, title, overall Web site title (if part of a larger project), version, sponsor of the site, date, medium (**Web**), and date of access.

- For sites that are online editions of printed works, include as much of the original print information as is available as well as the medium and the date accessed.

- For works that are accessed through a library database, include the name of the database.

It is not necessary to include a URL for a Web source unless your instructor requires it. In such cases, the URL should be placed in angle brackets (< >) followed by a period and set as the final element in the citation: <http://www.eff.org>.

Guidelines for Citing a Web Site

To cite a Web site in MLA style, follow these guidelines:

1. Author (if any)

2. Title (if any)

3. Publisher or sponsor (n.p. if none)

4. Date the site was last updated (n.d. if none)

5. Medium (**Web**)

6. Date you accessed the site

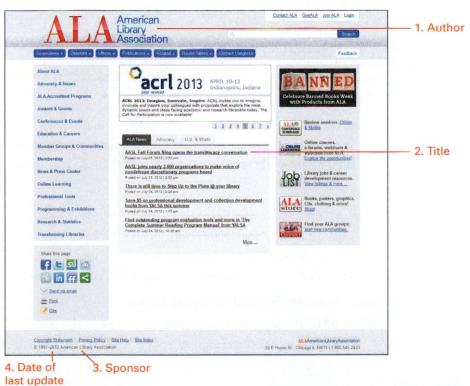

American Library Association. "AASL Fall Forum Ning Opens the Transliterary Conversation." American Library Association, 2012. Web. 13 Oct. 2012.

Entire Web Site

Include (if available) the author, title of the Web site, version, publisher or sponsor, date, medium (Web), and the date that the site was accessed. If the site has no title, use the designation Home page.

Document within a Web Site

"Uniform Impunity: Mexico's Misuse of Military Justice to Prosecute
    Abuses in Counternarcotics and Public Security Operations."
    Human Rights Watch. Human Rights Watch, Apr. 2009. Web.
    6 May 2012.

Online Video

Baggs, Amanda. "In My Language." *YouTube.* YouTube, 14 Jan.
    2007. Web. 21 May 2012.

Blog Posts and Blog Comments

Friedman, Kerim. "Information Foraging." *Savage Minds* 12 Apr.
    2009. Web. 14 May 2012.

McCreary, John. Weblog comment. *Savage Minds.* Your Name Here,
    12 Apr. 2009. Web. 14 May 2012.

Tweet

Begin with the author's real name, followed by the user name in parentheses. Include only the user name if the real name is unknown. Next, include the entire text of the tweet in quotation marks, followed by the date, the time, and the medium (Tweet).

Gates, Bill (@Billgates). "For those of us lucky enough to get to work
    with Steve, it's been an insanely great honor. I will miss Steve
    immensely. B-gat.es/qHXDsU." 5 Oct. 2011, 10:50 pm. Tweet.

Podcast

Glass, Ira. "Scenes from a Recession." *This American Life.* Chicago
    Public Radio, 27 Mar. 2009. Web. 10 May 2009.

Ogg, Erica. "Google Tries to Rehab Its Antitrust Image." *CNET News
    Daily Podcast.* CBS Interactive, 8 May 2009. Web. 12 May 2012.

Message from an Email Discussion Group

Kagan, Richard. "Mother's Day and Abortion." Message to
    H-Human-Rights Discussion. Michigan State U, 3 May 2009.
    Email. 12 May 2012.

Online Book

Doctorow, Cory. *Content: Selected Essays on Technology, Creativity,*
Copyright, and the Future of the Future. San Francisco: Tachyon,
2008. *Craphound.com.* Cory Doctorow. Web. 10 Apr. 2012.

Part of an Online Book

Zittrain, Jonathan L. "The Lessons of Wikipedia." *The Future of the*
Internet and How to Stop It. New Haven: Yale UP, 2008.
futureoftheinternet.org. Jonathan L. Zittrain. Web. 10 May 2012.

Article in an Online Scholarly Journal

Johnston, Rebecca. "Salvation or Destruction: Metaphors of the
Internet." *First Monday* 14.4 (2009): n. pag. Web. 15 Apr. 2012.

Magazine Article Accessed on the Web

Widdicombe, Lizzie. "You Belong with Me." *The New Yorker.* Condé
Nast, 10 Oct. 2011. Web. 19 Jan. 2012.

Article in an Online-only Magazine (an Ezine)

Leonard, Andrew. "A Chinese Lifeline for American Workers."
Salon.com. Salon Media Group, 15 Dec. 2011. Web. 19 Jan. 2012.

Newspaper Article Accessed on the Web

Possley, Maurice, and Ken Armstrong. "The Verdict: Dishonor."
Chicago Tribune. Tribune, 11 Jan. 1999. Web. 12 May 2012.

Article from a Library Database

Hartley, Richard D. "Sentencing Reform and the War on Drugs:
An Analysis of Sentence Outcomes for Narcotics Offenders
Adjudicated in the US District Courts on the Southwest
Border." *Criminal Justice Policy Review* 19.4 (2008): 414–37.
Sage Premier. Web. 12 May 2012.

Legal Case

When citing a court opinion, provide the plaintiffs' names, the legal citation (volume, abbreviation of the source, page numbers), the name of the
court, the year of the decision, and any relevant information about where
you found it. In many cases, online versions of the opinions will include

only the first page; in those cases, supply that page number followed by a plus sign.

> Miranda v. Arizona, 384 US 436+. Supreme Court of the US. 1966. *FindLaw*. Thompson Reuters, 2009. Web. 15 May 2012.

Government Document

Include the government agency or body issuing the document, followed by publication information.

> United States. Dept. of Homeland Security. *Estimates of the Unauthorized Immigrant Population Residing in the United States: January 2008.* Washington: Office of Immigration Policy, Feb. 2009. Web. 12 May 2012.

⬇ The following student research paper, "Should Data Posted on Social-Networking Sites Be 'Fair Game' for Employers?" by Erin Blaine, follows MLA documentation style as outlined in the preceding pages.

MLA PAPER GUIDELINES

- An MLA paper should have a one-inch margin all around and be double-spaced.

- Indent the first line of every paragraph. Number all pages, including the first, consecutively. Type your name, followed by the page number, in the upper right-hand corner.

- An MLA paper does not typically have a title page. Type the following information at the top of the paper, one inch from the left-hand margin:

  Name

  Instructor

  Course

  Date submitted

- Center the title of the paper. Capitalize all important words of the title, except prepositions, articles, coordinating conjunctions, and the *to* in infinitives—unless the word is the first or last word of the title. Titles should never be italicized, underlined, or followed by a period.

- Begin the **works-cited list** on a new numbered page, after the body of the paper. (See page 330 for a discussion of the works-cited list.)

- Citations should follow MLA documentation style.

Blaine 1

Erin Blaine

Professor Adams

Humanities 101

4 March 2012

Should Data Posted on Social-Networking Sites

Be "Fair Game" for Employers?

The popularity of social-networking sites such as [1]
Facebook and Twitter has increased dramatically over the last
several years, especially among college students and young
professionals. These sites provide valuable opportunities for
networking and for connecting socially. At the same time,
however, potential employers, human resources professionals,
and even college admissions officers routinely use these sites
to evaluate applicants. Because it is so easy to access social-
networking sites and because they provide valuable information,
this trend is certain to continue. Some people are concerned
about this development, arguing that social-networking sites
should be off-limits to potential employers because they do not
have the context they need to evaluate information. As long as
applicants have freely posted information in a public forum,
however, there is no reason for an employer not to consult this
information during the hiring process.

The number of employers and universities using social- [2]
networking sites to evaluate candidates is growing every year.
A recent survey found that 24% of college admissions officers
acknowledged visiting sites like Facebook to learn more about
applicants, and 12% said that the information they found "negatively impacted the applicant's admissions chances" ("Online
Behavior"). This practice also occurs in the business world,
where the numbers are even more striking. A recent study by
Reppler, a social-media monitoring service, found that 91% of
employers look at social-networking sites such as Facebook,
Twitter, and LinkedIn to help them evaluate potential employees

Parenthetical
reference
identifies the
source, which
is included in
the works-cited
list.

Blaine 2

("Potential Employers"). According to the *New York Times*, 75% of recruiters are required by their companies to research applicants online, and 70% of recruiters have rejected applicants because of information they found. The practice of checking social media is so common that some employers use outside companies, such as Social Intelligence Corp., to do Internet background checks on job candidates (Preston).

Because the article has no listed author, a shortened version of the title is included in the parenthetical documentation.

Not everyone is happy with this practice, though, and some have strong objections. Becca Bush, a college student in Chicago, argues that employers should not have the right to use social media to evaluate potential employees. "It's a violation of privacy," she says. "Twenty years ago, people still did the same things as now," but the information "wasn't as widespread" (qtd. in Cammenga). Marc S. Rotenberg, president of the Electronic Privacy Information Center, agrees, saying, "Employers should not be judging what people in their private lives do away from the workplace" (qtd. in Preston). Rotenberg goes on to say that privacy settings on sites like Facebook are often misunderstood. According to him, "People are led to believe that there is more limited disclosure than there actually is" (qtd. in Preston). Some people mistakenly think that looking at an applicant's Facebook page is illegal (Cammenga). Even though it is not, this practice can lead to discrimination, which *is* illegal. An online search can reveal characteristics that an applicant is not required to disclose to employers—for example, race, age, religion, sex, national origin, marital status, or disability (Preston).

Parenthetical documentation containing *qtd. in* indicates a source quoted in another source.

3

Given the realities of the digital age, however, admissions committees and job recruiters are acting reasonably when they access social-networking sites. As a practical matter, it would be almost impossible to prevent employers from reviewing online sites as part of informal background and reference

4

Blaine 3

checks. Moreover, those who believe that it is unethical for
recruiters to look at the online profiles of prospective job candidates seem willing to accept the benefits of social-networking
sites but unwilling to acknowledge that these new technologies
bring new responsibilities and liabilities. Finally, the problems
associated with employers' use of social-networking sites would
not be an issue in the first place if users of social-networking
sites took full advantage of the available measures to protect
themselves.

   Part of the problem is that the Internet has fundamentally   5
altered our notions of "private" and "public" in ways that we
are only just beginning to understand. As Alison George
observes in *New Scientist* magazine, the enormous amount of
personal information that appears (and remains) online poses a
challenge to our notions of personal privacy (50). On sites like
Facebook, people can reveal intimate details of their lives to
millions of strangers. This situation is unprecedented and, at
least for the foreseeable future, irreversible. As *New York Times*
columnist Thomas L. Friedman observes, "When everyone has
a blog, a MySpace page, or Facebook entry, everyone is a publisher. . . . When everyone is a publisher, paparazzo, or filmmaker, everyone else is a public figure." Given the changes in
our understanding of privacy and the public nature of the Internet, the suggestion that we should live our lives by the same
rules we lived by twenty years ago simply does not make
sense. As Friedman notes, in the Internet age, more and more
of "what you say or do or write will end up as a digital fingerprint that never gets erased" (23).

   Rather than relying on outdated notions of privacy, stu-   6
dents and job seekers should accept these new conditions and
take steps to protect themselves. Most college and career counseling services have easy-to-follow recommendations for how to

Because the
source is named
in an identifying
tag, only a page
number is
needed in the
parenthetical
documentation.

Ellipses
indicate that
words have
been left out of
a quotation.

Blaine 4

maintain a positive online reputation. First on almost everyone's list is the advice, "Adjust your privacy settings." Northwestern University's Career Services says it simply: "Use your settings wisely and employers will not have access to the contents of your sites" ("Using Social Networking"). Understanding and employing these settings is a user's responsibility; misunderstanding such protections is no excuse. As Mariel Loveland suggests, those who want extra help can hire an online reputation-management company such as Reputation.com or Integrity Defenders or use services such as those offered by Reppler. The "Reppler Image Score" enables social-networking users to identify questionable material "across different social networks" and to rate its "professionalism and consistency."

The most important way for people to protect themselves against others' possible misuse of personal information is for them to take responsibility for the information they post online. According to a recent article in *Education Week*, even middle school students should keep their future college and career plans in mind when they post information online ("Online Behavior"). In preparing students to apply for college, many high school counselors stress the "golden rule": "students should never post anything online they wouldn't want their parents to see" ("Online Behavior"). Students and job seekers must realize that a commonsense approach to the Internet requires that they develop good "digital grooming" habits (Bond). For example, one self-described "cautious Internet user" says that she "goes through the information on her [Facebook] account every few weeks and deletes statuses, messages, and other things" (Bond). She understands that a potential employer coming across an applicant's membership in a Facebook group such as "I Sold My Grandma for Crack-Cocaine!" or a picture of a student posing with an empty liquor

7

Internet source includes no page number in the parenthetical documentation.

Brackets indicate that a quotation has been edited for clarity.

Blaine 5

bottle may not understand the tone, the context, or the joke. Students should also be careful about "friends" who have access to their online social networks, asking themselves whether these people really know them and would have good things to say about them if a prospective employer contacted them for a reference. According to one high school principal, 75% of the students at his school admitted to accepting a friend request from someone they did not know ("Online Behavior"). Getting students to consider the repercussions of this kind of choice is central to many social-media education programs.

Although social-networking sites have disadvantages, they also have advantages. These sites provide an excellent opportunity for job seekers to connect with potential employers and to get their names and résumés in circulation. For example, a job seeker can search the LinkedIn networks of a company's executives or human resources staff for mutual connections. In addition, a job seeker can post information calculated to appeal to potential employers. Recruiters are just as likely to hire candidates based on social-media screening as they are to reject them. A recent article reports the following:

> Sixty-eight percent of recruiters have hired candidates based off positive aspects on their social networking profiles. . . . Employers have hired candidates based off positive impressions of their personality and organizational fit, profile supporting their professional qualifications, creativity, well-roundness, good references posted by others, and because of awards and accolades. ("Potential Employers")

In today's job market, people should think of their networks as extensions of themselves. They need to take an active role in shaping the image they want to project to future employers.

8

A quotation of more than four lines of text is double-spaced, indented one inch from the left margin, and typed as a block, without quotation marks. Parenthetical documentation comes after the final punctuation.

Blaine 6

As Thomas L. Friedman argues in his column, "The
Whole World Is Watching," access to information creates
opportunities as well as problems. Quoting Dov Seidman,
Friedman maintains that the most important opportunity may
be the one to "out-behave your competition." In other words,
just as the Internet allows negative information to travel
quickly, it also allows positive information to spread. So even
though students and job seekers should be careful when
posting information online, they should not miss the
opportunity to take advantage of the many opportunities that
social-networking sites offer.

Blaine 7

Works Cited

Bond, Michaelle. "Facebook Timeline a New Privacy Test." *USA Today*. USA Today, 2 Nov. 2011. Web. 2 Mar. 2012.

Cammenga, Michelle. "Facebook Might Be the Reason You Don't Get That Job." *Hub Bub*. Loyola University Chicago's School of Communication, 23 Feb. 2012. Web. 2 Mar. 2012.

Friedman, Thomas L. "The Whole World Is Watching." *New York Times* 27 June 2007: A23. Print.

George, Alison. "Things You Wouldn't Tell Your Mother." *New Scientist* 16 Sept. 2006: 50–51. Print.

Loveland, Mariel. "Reppler Launches 'Reppler Image Score,' Rates Social Network Profile Content for Potential Employers." *Scribbal*. PhoneDog Media Network, 27 Sept. 2011. Web. 2 Mar. 2012.

"Online Behavior Jeopardizing College Plans; Admissions Officers Checking Social-Networking Sites for Red Flags." *Education Week* 14 Dec. 2011: 11. *Academic One File*. Web. 2 Mar. 2012.

"Potential Employers Check Social Networks More Often Than You Think." *Office of Information Technology Blog*. West Virginia University, 28 Oct. 2011. Web. 2012.

Preston, Jennifer. "Social Media History Becomes a New Job Hurdle." *New York Times*. New York Times, 20 July 2011. Web. 1 Mar. 2012.

"Using Social Networking in Your Employment Search." *University Career Services*. Northwestern University, 2011. Web. 2 Mar. 2012.

The works-cited list includes full information for all sources cited in the paper.

Avoiding Plagiarism

AT ISSUE

Where Should We Draw the Line with Plagiarism?

In recent years, a number of high-profile plagiarism cases have put a spotlight on how much "borrowing" from other sources is acceptable. Some critics—and many colleges and universities—draw little distinction between intentional and unintentional plagiarism, arguing that any unattributed borrowing is theft. Others are more forgiving, accepting the fact that busy historians or scientists (or students) might not realize that a particular sentence in their notes was not their original idea or might accidentally incorporate a source's exact words (or its unique syntax or phrasing) into their own work without attribution.

In the age of the Internet, with its "cut-and-paste" culture, plagiarism has become easier to commit; however, with the development of plagiarism-detection software, it is also now much easier to detect. Still, some colleges and universities are uncomfortable with the idea of using such software, arguing that it establishes an atmosphere of distrust.

On college campuses, as in the professional world, questions like the following have arisen: What exactly constitutes plagiarism? How serious a matter is it? Is there a difference between intentional and unintentional plagiarism? Is plagiarizing a few sentences as bad as plagiarizing an entire paper? Why do people commit plagiarism? What should be done to prevent it? How should it be punished? What are its short- and long-term consequences?

These are some (although by no means all) of the questions that you might think about as you consider the sources at the end of this chapter. After reading these sources, you will be asked to write an argumentative essay that takes a position on the issue of what exactly constitutes plagiarism and how it should be dealt with.

For comprehension quizzes,
see bedfordstmartins.com/practicalargument.

Understanding Plagiarism

Plagiarism is the act of using the words or ideas of another person without attributing them to their rightful author—that is, presenting those borrowed words and ideas as if they are your own.

TWO DEFINITIONS OF PLAGIARISM

From *MLA Handbook for Writers of Research Papers,* Seventh Edition (2009)

Derived from the Latin word *plagiarius* ("kidnapper"), *to plagiarize* means "to commit literary theft" and to "present as new and original an idea or product derived from an existing source" (*Merriam-Webster's Collegiate Dictionary* [11th ed.; 2003; print]). Plagiarism involves two kinds of wrongs. Using another person's ideas, information, or expressions without acknowledging that person's work constitutes intellectual theft. Passing off another person's ideas, information, or expressions as your own to get a better grade or gain some other advantage constitutes fraud. Plagiarism is sometimes a moral and ethical offense rather than a legal one since some instances of plagiarism fall outside the scope of copyright infringement, a legal offense.

From *Publication Manual of the American Psychological Association,* Sixth Edition (2009)

Researchers do not claim the words and ideas of another as their own; they give credit where credit is due (APA Ethics Code Standard 8.11, Plagiarism). Quotation marks should be used to indicate the exact words of another. *Each time* you paraphrase another author (i.e., summarize a passage or rearrange the order of a sentence and change some of the words), you need to credit the source in the text.

The key element of this principle is that authors do not present the work of another as if it were their own work. This can extend to ideas as well as written words. If authors model a study after one done by someone else, the originating author should be given credit. If the rationale for a study was suggested in the Discussion section of someone else's article, that person should be given credit. Given the free exchange of ideas, which is very important to the health of intellectual discourse, authors may not know where an idea for a study originated. If authors do know, however, they should acknowledge the source; this includes personal communications.

For many people, defining plagiarism is simple: it is not "borrowing" but stealing, and it should be dealt with severely. For others, it is a more slippery term, seen as considerably more serious if it is intentional than if it is accidental (for example, the result of careless research methods). Most colleges and universities have guidelines that define plagiarism strictly and have penalties in place for those who commit it. To avoid committing unintentional plagiarism, you need to understand exactly what it is and why it occurs. You also need to learn how to use sources responsibly and to understand what kind of information requires documentation and what kind does not.

Avoiding Unintentional Plagiarism

Even if you do not intentionally misuse the words or ideas of a source, you are still committing plagiarism if you present the work of others as your own. The most common errors that lead to unintentional plagiarism—and how to avoid them—are listed below.

COMMON ERROR	HOW TO AVOID IT
No source information is provided for borrowed material (including statistics).	Always include full parenthetical documentation and a works-cited list that make the source of your information clear to readers. (See Chapter 10.)
A source's ideas are presented as if they are your own original ideas.	Keep track of the sources you consult, and always keep full source information with your sources. Never cut and paste material from an electronic source directly into your paper.
The boundaries of borrowed material are unclear.	Be sure to use an identifying tag *before* and parenthetical documentation *after* borrowed material. (See Chapter 9.)
The language of the paraphrases or summaries is still too close to that of the original source.	Be careful to use original phrasing and syntax when you write summaries and paraphrases. (See Chapter 9.)

(Continued)

COMMON ERROR	HOW TO AVOID IT
A friend's or tutor's words or ideas appear in your paper.	Any help you receive should be in the form of suggestions, not additions.
Material you wrote for another course is used in your paper.	Always get permission from *both* instructors if you want to reuse work you did for another course, and be sure the material you use is substantially revised.

Using Sources Responsibly

To avoid unintentional plagiarism, you need to take (and maintain) control over your sources, keeping track of all the material you use so that you remember where you found each piece of information.

As you take notes, be careful to distinguish your sources' ideas from your own. If you are copying a source's words into your notes, put them in quotation marks. (If you are taking notes by hand, circle the quotation marks; if you are typing your notes, put the quotation marks in boldface.) If you photocopy material, write the full source information on the first page, and staple the pages together. When you download sources from the Web, be sure the URL appears on every page. Finally, never cut and paste material from sources directly into your paper.

INTERNET SOURCES AND PLAGIARISM

The Internet presents a particular challenge for students as they try to avoid plagiarism. Committing plagiarism (intentional or unintentional) with electronic sources is easy because it is simple to cut and paste material from online sources into a paper. However, inserting even a sentence or two from an Internet source (including a blog, an email, or a Web site) into a paper without quotation marks and documentation constitutes plagiarism.

It is also not acceptable to use a visual (such as a graph, chart, table, or photograph) found on the Internet without acknowledging its source. Finally, even if an Internet source does not identify its author, the words or ideas you find there are not your own original material, so you must identify their source.

As you draft your paper, be sure to quote your sources' words accurately (even punctuation must be reproduced exactly as it appears in the source). Be careful not to quote out of context, and be sure that you are presenting your sources' ideas accurately when you summarize or paraphrase. (For information on quoting, paraphrasing, and summarizing source material, see Chapter 9.)

INTENTIONAL PLAGIARISM

Handing in other students' papers as your own or buying a paper from an Internet site is never acceptable. Such acts constitute serious violations of academic integrity. Creating your own original work is an important part of the educational experience, and misrepresenting someone else's work as your own undermines the goals of education.

Knowing What to Document

Documentation is the practice of identifying borrowed material and giving the proper bibliographic information for each source. Different academic disciplines require different formats for documentation—for example, English uses MLA, and psychology uses APA. For this reason, you should be sure to check with your instructor to find out what documentation style he or she requires. (For information on MLA and APA documentation formats, see Chapter 10 and Appendix B, respectively.)

Regardless of the discipline, the following kinds of information should always be documented:

- Quotations from a source

- Summaries or paraphrases of a source's original ideas

- Opinions, judgments, and conclusions that are not your own

- Statistics from a source

- Visuals from a source

- Data from charts or graphs in a source

The following kinds of information, however, do not require documentation:

- **Common knowledge**—that is, factual information that can be found in several different sources (for example, a writer's date of birth, a scientific fact, or the location of a famous battle)

- Familiar quotations—anything from proverbs to lines from Shakespeare's plays—that you expect readers will recognize

- Your own original opinions, judgments, and conclusions

◆ EXERCISE 11.1

Which of the following requires documentation, and why?

1. Doris Kearns Goodwin is a prize-winning historian.

2. Doris Kearns Goodwin's *The Fitzgeralds and the Kennedys* is a 900-page book with about 3,500 footnotes.

3. In 1994, Lynne McTaggart accused Goodwin of borrowing material from a book that McTaggart wrote.

4. My own review of the background suggests that Goodwin's plagiarism was unintentional.

5. Still, these accusations left Goodwin to face the "slings and arrows" of media criticism.

6. As Goodwin explains, "The more intensive and far-reaching a historian's research, the greater the difficulty of citation."

7. In her defense, Goodwin argued that the more research a historian does, the harder it is to keep track of sources.

8. Some people still remain convinced that Goodwin committed plagiarism.

9. Goodwin believes that her careful research methods, which she has described in exhaustive detail, should have prevented accidental plagiarism.

10. Goodwin's critics have concluded that her reputation as a historian was hurt by the plagiarism charges.

⊙ EXERCISE 11.2

Read the following editorial. If you were using it as a source, what information would you need to document, and what information would you *not* have to document? Identify two pieces of information you would need to document (for example, statistics). Then, identify two pieces of information you would *not* need to document (for example, common knowledge).

This unsigned newspaper editorial appeared on August 11, 2006.

CHEATERS NEVER WIN

AUSTIN AMERICAN-STATESMAN

1 We live in the era of cut and paste, thanks to the Internet, which provides students with countless materials to plagiarize.

2 If you think that's an exaggeration, do an Internet search of "free term papers." You'll find cheathouse.com, Cheater.com, Schoolsucks.com, echeat.com, and Free Essay Network (freeessay.com) among the 603 million results that turn up.

3 One site, 24hourtermpapers.com, even boasts of providing "custom term papers" within 24 hours (at $23.95 per page), targeting college students who put off writing papers until the 11th hour. A disclaimer warns that "these term papers are to be used for research purposes only. Use of these papers for any other purpose is not the responsibility of 24 Hour Term Papers." Funny that they say that, because the site provides the student with a nice package to hand directly to the professor: All term papers are "sent within the due date," with a bibliography page thrown in for no extra charge.

4 A student who pays such a steep price for a term paper is not likely to use it only as a resource. One of the perks of being a student today is unlimited access to a slew of research tools, from the library to an online research database the institution pays for the student to use.

5 Student Judicial Services at the University of Texas defines plagiarism as "representing as your own work any material that was obtained from another

source, regardless of how or where you acquired it." This includes borrowing ideas or even structure. And "by merely changing a few words or rearranging several words or sentences, you are not paraphrasing. Making minor revisions to borrowed text amounts to plagiarism," the Web site warns.

But those warnings go unheeded by many. The Center for Academic 6 Integrity found last year that more than 70 percent of college students admitted to having cheated at least once, more than 60 percent admitted to plagiarizing, and nearly 40 percent said they have plagiarized from the Internet.

Strict disciplinary action should follow students who are caught trying to 7 claim someone else's work as their own. The more it goes unnoticed, the easier it is for students to keep stealing. Educators should devote time and attention to properly educating students on what plagiarism is and why it's stupid to do it.

In the end, the plagiarizer has the most to lose, whether he or she gets 8 caught or not. Many of the online papers are not worthy of copying, especially if a student wants to excel in college. By stealing someone else's work and labeling it as their own, students forgo the opportunity to learn how to research, develop ideas, and translate them into quality writing. Not to mention tarnishing a reputation, if the student gets caught.

> "In the end, the plagiarizer has the most to lose."

Cheathouse.com and other sites like it might get students a passing grade 9 in a course, but it only puts them a step behind everyone else who is developing the skills needed to thrive in the workplace. Employers won't be as forgiving as teachers or disciplinary committees. The day will come when the "I'm a student. I'm still learning" excuse will fall on deaf ears.

Revising to Eliminate Plagiarism

As you revise your papers, scrutinize your work carefully to be sure you have not inadvertently committed plagiarism.

The following paragraph (from page 28 of Thomas L. Friedman's 2008 book *Hot, Flat and Crowded*) and the guidelines that follow it will help you to understand the situations in which accidental plagiarism is most likely to occur.

> So if you think the world feels crowded now, just wait a few decades. In 1800, London was the world's largest city with one million people. By 1960, there were 111 cities with more than one million people. By 1995 there were 280, and today there are over 300, according to

UN Population Fund statistics. The number of megacities (with ten million or more inhabitants) in the world has climbed from 5 in 1975 to 14 in 1995 and is expected to reach 26 cities by 2015, according to the UN. Needless to say, these exploding populations are rapidly overwhelming infrastructure in these megacities—nineteen million people in Mumbai alone—as well as driving loss of arable land, deforestation, overfishing, water shortages, and air and water pollution.

1. **Be sure you have identified your source and provided appropriate documentation.**

PLAGIARISM

The world is becoming more and more crowded, and some twenty-six cities are expected to have populations of over 10 million by 2015.

This student writer does not quote directly from Friedman's discussion, but her summary of his comments does not represent her original ideas and therefore needs to be documented.

The following correct use of source material includes both an **identifying tag** (a phrase that identifies Friedman as the source of the ideas) and a page number that directs readers to the exact location of the material the student is summarizing.

CORRECT

According to Thomas L. Friedman, the world is becoming more and more crowded, and twenty-six cities are expected to have populations of over 10 million by 2015 (28).

2. **Be sure you have placed quotation marks around borrowed words.**

PLAGIARISM

According to Thomas L. Friedman, the exploding populations of megacities around the world are overwhelming their infrastructure (28).

Although the passage above provides parenthetical documentation and includes an identifying tag indicating the source of its ideas, it uses Friedman's exact words without placing them in quotation marks.

To avoid committing plagiarism, the writer needs to either place quotation marks around Friedman's words or paraphrase his comments.

CORRECT (BORROWED WORDS IN QUOTATION MARKS)

According to Thomas L. Friedman, the "exploding populations" of large cities around the world are "rapidly overwhelming infrastructure in these megacities" (28).

CORRECT (BORROWED WORDS PARAPHRASED)

According to Thomas L. Friedman, the rapid rise in population of large cities around the world poses a serious threat to their ability to function (28).

3. **Be sure you have indicated the boundaries of the borrowed material.**

PLAGIARISM

The world is becoming more and more crowded, and this will lead to serious problems in the future. Soon, as many as twenty-six of the world's cities will have populations over 10 million. It is clear that "these exploding populations are rapidly overwhelming infrastructure in these megacities" (Friedman 28).

In the passage above, the student correctly places Friedman's words in quotation marks and includes appropriate parenthetical documentation. However, she does not indicate that other ideas in the passage, although not quoted directly, are also Friedman's.

To avoid committing plagiarism, the student needs to use identifying tags to indicate the boundaries of the borrowed material, which goes beyond the quoted words.

CORRECT

According to Thomas L. Friedman, the world is becoming more and more crowded, and this will lead to serious problems in the future. Soon, Friedman predicts, as many as twenty-six of the world's cities will have populations of over 10 million, and this rise in population will put a serious strain on the cities' resources, "rapidly overwhelming infrastructure in these megacities" (28).

4. **Be sure you have used your own phrasing and syntax.**

PLAGIARISM

If you feel crowded now, Thomas L. Friedman says, just wait twenty or thirty years. In 1800, London, with a million inhabitants, was the largest city in the world; over 111 cities had more than a million people by 1960. Thirty-five years later, there were 280; today, according to statistics provided by the UN Population Fund, there are more than 300. There were only five megacities (10 million people or more) in 1975 and fourteen in 1995. However, by 2015, the United Nations predicts, there might be twenty-six. These rapidly growing populations threaten to overwhelm the infrastructure of the megacities (Mumbai alone has 19 million people), destroying arable land, the forests, and fishing and causing water shortages and water and air pollution (28).

The student who wrote the passage on the preceding page does provide an identifying tag and parenthetical documentation to identify the source of the passage's ideas. Still, this passage is plagiarized because its phrasing and syntax are almost identical to Friedman's.

In the following paragraph, the writer correctly paraphrases and summarizes Friedman's ideas, quoting a few distinctive passages. (See Chapter 9 for information on paraphrase and summary.)

CORRECT

> As Thomas L. Friedman warns, the world has been growing more and more crowded and is likely to grow still more crowded in the years to come. Relying on UN population data, Friedman estimates that there will be some twenty more "megacities" (those with more than 10 million people) in 2015 than there were in 1975. (In 1800, in contrast, only one city in the world—London—had a million inhabitants.) Obviously, this is an alarming trend. Friedman believes that these rapidly growing populations are "overwhelming infrastructure in these megacities" and are bound to strain resources, leading to "loss of arable land, deforestation, [and] overfishing" and creating not only air and water pollution but water shortages as well (28).

NOTE

Do not forget to document statistics that you get from a source. For example, Thomas L. Friedman's statistics about the threat of rising population are the result of his original research, so you need to document them.

➲ EXERCISE 11.3

The following student paragraph synthesizes information from two different sources (which appear on pp. 362–363, after the student paragraph), but the student writer has not used sources responsibly. (For information on synthesis, see Chapter 9.) Read the sources and the paragraph, and then make the following changes:

- Insert quotation marks where the student has quoted a source's words.

- Edit paraphrased and summarized material if necessary so that its syntax and phrasing are not too close to those of a source.

- Add parenthetical documentation where necessary to acknowledge the use of a source's words or original ideas.

- Add identifying tags where necessary to clarify the scope of the borrowed material or to differentiate material from the two sources.

- Check every quoted passage once more to see if the quotation adds something vital to the paragraph. If it does not, summarize or paraphrase the source's words instead.

STUDENT PARAGRAPH

In recent years, psychologists have focused on the idea that girls (unlike boys) face a crisis of self-esteem as they approach adolescence. Both Carol Gilligan and Mary Pipher did research to support this idea, showing how girls lose their self-confidence in adolescence because of sexist cultural expectations. Women's groups have expressed concern that the school system favors boys and is biased against girls. In fact, boys are often regarded not just as classroom favorites but also as bullies who represent obstacles on the path to gender justice for girls. Recently, however, this impression that boys are somehow privileged while girls are shortchanged is being challenged.

Source 1

That boys are in disrepute is not accidental. For many years women's groups have complained that boys benefit from a school system that favors them and is biased against girls. "Schools shortchange girls," declares the American Association of University Women. . . . A stream of books and pamphlets cite research showing not only that boys are classroom favorites but also that they are given to schoolyard violence and sexual harassment.

In the view that has prevailed in American education over the past decade, boys are resented, both as the unfairly privileged sex and as obstacles on the path to gender justice for girls. This perspective is promoted in schools of education, and many a teacher now feels that girls need and deserve special indemnifying consideration. "It is really clear that boys are Number One in this society and in most of the world," says Patricia O'Reilly, a professor of education and the director of the Gender Equity Center, at the University of Cincinnati.

The idea that schools and society grind girls down has given rise to an array of laws and policies intended to curtail the advantage boys have and to redress the harm done to girls. That girls are treated as the second sex in school and consequently suffer, that boys are accorded privileges and consequently benefit—these are things everyone is presumed to know. But they are not true.

—Christina Hoff Sommers, "The War against Boys"

Source 2

Girls face an inevitable crisis of self-esteem as they approach adolescence. They are in danger of losing their voices, drowning, and facing a devastating dip in self-regard that boys don't experience. This is the picture that Carol Gilligan presented on the basis of her research at the Emma Willard School, a private girls' school in Troy, N.Y. While Gilligan did not refer to genes in her analysis of girls' vulnerability, she did cite both the "wall of Western culture" and deep early childhood socialization as reasons.

Her theme was echoed in 1994 by the clinical psychologist Mary Pipher's surprise best seller, *Reviving Ophelia* (Putnam, 1994), which spent three years on the *New York Times* best-seller list. Drawing on case studies rather than systematic research, Pipher observed how naturally outgoing, confident girls get worn down by sexist cultural expectations. Gilligan's and Pipher's ideas have also been supported by a widely cited study in 1990 by the American Association of University Women. That report, published in 1991, claimed that teenage girls experience a "free-fall in self-esteem from which some will never recover."

The idea that girls have low self-esteem has by now become part of the academic canon as well as fodder for the popular media. But is it true? No.

—ROSALIND C. BARNETT AND CARYL RIVERS, "MEN ARE FROM EARTH, AND SO ARE WOMEN. IT'S FAULTY RESEARCH THAT SETS THEM APART"

Where Should We Draw the Line with Plagiarism?

Reread the At Issue box on page 351. Then, read the sources on the following pages. As you read these sources, you will be asked to answer questions and to complete some activities. This work will help you to understand the content and structure of the material you read. When you have read the sources, you will be ready to write an argumentative essay in which you take a position on the topic, "Where Should We Draw the Line with Plagiarism?"

SOURCES

 Jack Shafer, "Sidebar: Comparing the Copy," p. 365

 Jack Shafer, "Eight Reasons Plagiarism Sucks," p. 368

 Lawrence M. Hinman, "How to Fight College Cheating," p. 371

 Trip Gabriel, "Plagiarism Lines Blur for Students in Digital Age," p. 374

 Elizabeth Minkel, "Too Hard *Not* to Cheat in the Internet Age?," p. 378

 Richard A. Posner, "The Truth about Plagiarism," p. 380

 Joshua Crawford, "It's Not All Plagiarism," p. 383

 Carolyn Foster Segal, "Copy This," p. 386

 Term Papers for Sale Advertisement (Web page), p. 390

For comprehension quizzes, see bedfordstmartins.com/practicalargument.

In this *Slate* article, Shafer accuses a *New York Times* reporter of plagiarism. As evidence, he presents the opening paragraphs from the source (a *Bloomberg News* story), the accused reporter's *New York Times* article, and—for contrast—two other newspaper articles that report the same story without relying heavily on the original source.

This article appeared in *Slate* on March 5, 2008.

SIDEBAR:° COMPARING THE COPY

JACK SHAFER

A short news story printed alongside a longer related article

1 How different can four news stories generated by the same assignment be? Compare the opening paragraphs of these pieces about the 2005 mad cow disease conference call: the *Bloomberg News* version; the *New York Times* version, which

> "How different can four news stories generated by the same assignment be?"

lifts passages from *Bloomberg* without attribution; and the starkly different pieces run by the globeandmail.com and the *Omaha World-Herald*.

Opening paragraphs from the July 15, 2005, *Bloomberg News* story by Daniel Goldstein:

2 The U.S. plans to resume imports of Canadian cattle, after an appellate court cleared the way to end a ban imposed two years ago because of mad-cow disease.° Cattle prices fell and shares of beef producer Tyson Foods Inc. surged.

3   The first shipments from Canada may arrive at U.S. slaughterhouses in days, U.S. Agriculture Secretary Mike Johanns said today in a conference call. "If things go well, it could very well be next week." USDA and Canadian officials are coordinating how to certify animals for shipment, he said.

A brain disease that can be transmitted to humans through consumption of contaminated beef

4   A U.S. appellate court° yesterday ruled in favor of the government, which argued Canadian cattle under 30 months of age don't pose a risk of mad-cow disease. Tyson's beef business had a loss of $19 million in the quarter ended April 2, as the lack of available cattle boosted costs and led to plant closings. Canada before the ban supplied about 5 percent of U.S. beef.

A higher court that hears appeals of rulings that were made by a lower court

Opening paragraphs from the July 16, 2005, *New York Times* story by Alexei Barrionuevo:

5 The United States Agriculture Department said on Friday that it planned to resume imports of Canadian cattle within days, after an appellate court lifted a two-year-old injunction imposed because of mad cow disease.

The first shipments from Canada could arrive at American slaughter- 6
houses as early as next week, Agriculture Secretary Mike Johanns said in a
conference call with reporters. Officials in Canada and the United States are
coordinating how to certify the animals for shipment, he said.

"We want to make sure everything is in place," he said. "If things go well, it 7
could very well be next week."

The news sent shares of the beef producer Tyson Foods and McDonald's 8
restaurants surging. Cattle prices fell. Shares of Tyson rose 7.5 percent in early
trading, and closed at $19.47 a share, a 5 percent increase, while McDonald's
closed at $30.99 a share, up 4.7 percent.

Tyson's beef business recorded a loss of $19 million in the quarter ended 9
April 2. The company was hurt by the ban on cattle from Canada, which
increased costs and led to temporary plant closings. Before the ban, Canada
supplied about 5 percent of the nation's beef.

A United States appeals court ruled on Thursday in favor of the govern- 10
ment, which had argued that Canadian cows under 30 months of age did not
pose a risk of bovine spongiform encephalopathy, or mad cow disease.

**Opening paragraphs from the July 15 *globeandmail.com* story by
Terry Weber, time stamped 12:28 p.m.:**

The United States is taking immediate steps to reopen the border to Canadian 11
cattle imports Agriculture Secretary Mike Johanns said Friday.

During a webcast, Mr. Johanns said that Washington has been in touch 12
with Ottawa and that the two sides are now going through the logistical steps
necessary to resume trade of live cattle for the first time since May, 2003.

"Our hope is we're talking about days and not weeks," he said. "If things 13
go well, it could very well be next week, but we have not set a specific date."

Late Thursday, a three-member U.S. appeal court panel in Seattle over- 14
turned a temporary injunction issued by Montana Judge Richard Cebull halt-
ing the U.S. Department of Agriculture's March plan to reopen the border.

Judge Cebull had sided with U.S. ranchers group R-Calf in its argument 15
that reopening the border exposed U.S. ranchers and consumers to unnecessary risks from mad-cow disease. The USDA had been planning to ease restrictions by allowing cattle younger than 30 months to be imported.

Mr. Johanns noted that Canadian officials had already anticipated the 16
ruling and taken steps to meet U.S. requirements, should Thursday's favor
reopening the border.

"It [the reopening] could be as early as next week, but we want to make 17
sure everything is in place," he said.

Those requirements, he said, including ensuring that animals being 18
imported into the U.S. meet minimal-risk rule criteria, getting documents to
U.S. customs to confirm the shipments are appropriate for entry.

Opening paragraphs from the July 15 *Omaha World-Herald* story by Chris Clayton:

Canadian cattle could start arriving at U.S. feedlots and meatpacking plants as early as next week, U.S. Agriculture Secretary Mike Johanns said Friday. 19

Thursday's unanimous decision by the 9th U.S. Circuit Court of Appeals lifting a lower court's injunction gives U.S. and Canadian officials a nearly two-week window to begin shipping live cattle from Canada before another court hearing, scheduled late this month in Montana. 20

No date has been set, but Johanns said he will move as "expeditiously as possible" to begin importing Canadian cattle once officials work out the ground rules. Canadian and USDA officials anticipated the requirements would be in place at whatever time the legal issues were resolved. 21

"Our hope is we are talking about days, not weeks," Johanns said. "It could be as early as next week, but we want to make sure everything is in place. . . . If things go well, it could very well be next week, but we haven't set a specific date" [*ellipsis in the original*]. 22

Johanns has lamented the closed border since becoming agriculture secretary in late January, saying that it hurts U.S. cattle feeders and meatpackers because the United States continued to import boxed beef from Canada. 23

Higher cattle prices because of tight supplies caused meatpackers to scale back production at U.S. facilities. Industry officials claim to have lost as many as 8,000 meatpacking jobs because of the closed border. 24

"I'm just worried that many of those jobs were impacted in a very permanent way," Johanns said. "My hope is that restructuring now will be abated and this industry can start getting back to a normal flow of commerce here." 25

About 1 million cattle were imported from Canada in the year before the border closed in May 2003 when Canada reported its first case of mad-cow disease, or bovine spongiform encephalopathy. 26

⊖ AT ISSUE: SOURCES FOR AVOIDING PLAGIARISM

1. Identify the passages in the *New York Times* story that you think are too close to the original *Bloomberg News* story.

2. Identify passages in the other two excerpts that convey the same information as the *Times* story (paraphrased or summarized).

3. In his introduction, Shafer says that the passages from the Toronto *Globe and Mail* and the *Omaha World-Herald* are "starkly different" from the *Bloomberg News* story. Do you agree?

4. Can you identify any passages in the *Globe and Mail* or *Omaha World-Herald* excerpts that you believe are too close to the original source?

5. On the basis of what you see here, do you agree with Shafer that the *New York Times* reporter is guilty of plagiarism? Explain your conclusion.

This article is from *Slate*, where it appeared on March 7, 2008.

EIGHT REASONS PLAGIARISM SUCKS

JACK SHAFER

Readers have stormed my inbox, accusing me of "picking nits" in the latest of my two columns about the plagiarism of *New York Times* reporter Alexei Barrionuevo (Feb. 27 and March 5). One reader found my charge "hyperactive." Another insisted that Barrionuevo's lifting from Bloomberg News was akin to "repeating the bus schedule," hence no foul. Another ridiculed me, saying I exist inside an "echo chamber" of journalists, academics, and bloggers who "care about this crap."

As I read that last note, I realized that I needed to explain in detail why plagiarism matters and why journalists, academics, and bloggers are right to care about it. In order of importance, here are my eight reasons plagiarism sucks:

It swindles readers. One of my correspondents mistakenly thought that what disturbed me most about plagiarism was that it robs other writers of their labors. That's the least of my problems. Plagiarism burns me up because it violates the implied warranty that comes with every piece of journalism. Unless qualified with citations or disclaimers such as "compiled from wire reports," news articles are supposed to be original work.

When a reporter appropriates the words of another without credit, he gives the reader the mistaken impression that he has independently verified the primary facts in his story. So, if the first reporter got stuff wrong—dates, names, places, events—the lazy and corrupt second reporter will end up cheating the reader out of the true story.

(Plagiarism aside, some editors discourage their reporters from milking Nexis for research not because they worry about their guys pinching but because they worry about their guys inadvertently retransmitting other guys' mistakes and clichés, setting them ever deeper in stone.)

Journalism is about truth, not lies. I cringe at writing those precious words, but like Samantha Power, I've released them and can't yank them back. A reporter who abducts the work of another reporter without giving credit tells a skeezy lie with every keyboard stroke. "I wrote that," he lies. The plagiarist's fraud dissolves the trust between his publication and its reader; it injures the reader (of course), the plagiarist's publication, the plagiarist's colleagues, and the plagiarist's profession. (Good lord, am I starting to sound like a weepy Committee of Concerned Journalists parishioner?)

> "Journalism is about truth, not lies."

It corrupts the craft. This is really a corollary of "Harms Readers" and "Truth, Not Lies." Every plagiarism bust reinforces the view of readers and viewers who already believe the profession is filled with lying, psychopathic scum. Bank robbers injure only the banks they rob. Plagiarists injure the entire journalism profession, even the most scrupulous and honest of practitioners.

It promotes the dishonest. One path to journalistic success is productivity. Another is writing deeply sourced stories. The industrious plagiarist combines both techniques, routinely out-producing his colleagues with stolen, excellent copy. When the time comes to appoint a new London bureau chief or a new deputy editor for metro, who is going to get the slot: the good reporter or the supercharged, not-yet-apprehended plagiarist. Nobody will deny that rewarding cheaters for cheating sucks. But again, the greatest injury isn't done to other journalists but to readers. When the less-talented fellow gets the better job, the paper (or magazine or Web site or broadcast) suffers, and that suffering is inflicted upon readers. 8

It denigrates the hard work of others. How often do convicted plagiarists or their apologists attempt to blot away the plagiarists' crimes by saying, "Oh, the borrowing was trivial." Or, "That was just a boilerplate story." They'll insist that there are only so many ways to write "Joe Doe, the famous rope climber, died in his bed last night from a gunshot wound," and that such news story similarities are inevitable. 9

The problem with the boilerplate excuse is that news stories written by nonplagiarists almost never overlap the way the stories written by plagiarists do. I thought I made this point in my last Barrionuevo story by publishing a sidebar that stacked the opening paragraphs from his "mad cow" story against those from the Bloomberg story he lifted from and the accounts published by the *globeandmail.com* and the *Omaha World-Herald*. Except for Barrionuevo, each journalist quoted in the sidebar brought to the alleged boilerplate their unique news judgment. 10

If you think it's easy to write compelling boilerplate, just try. 11

It's not what we paid for. No *New York Times* subscriber should have to pay in excess of $600 a year for rewritten Bloomberg News copy. 12

It's not theft—it's something worse. Lots of people hate plagiarism because they consider it theft. I'm not really a member of that party, even if I've used the words *theft, stealing, crime,* and the like in my plagiarism columns. There is no crime called "plagiarism." If somebody publishes an entire paragraph of mine without credit, you can't really say that he's *stolen* it from *Slate*. My words can still be found at the same old URL, and the local sheriff can't charge the perpetrator with felony theft even if he thinks the perp nicked my piece. (However, a word-thief can be served with a civil complaint alleging copyright infringement, or if the pilfering is grand enough, a U.S. attorney may decide to charge him with the felony of willful copyright infringement.) 13

The reason plagiarism is worse than theft is because the only real remedies for it are shame and ostracism, both of which have proved very poor deterrents. Most plagiarists find a way back into the business, as Trudy Lieberman reported in the *Columbia Journalism Review*. 14

It's vampiric. Before anybody points the plagiarism gun at me, please allow me to credit my *Slate* colleague David Plotz with that witty formulation. 15

369

"The plagiarist is, in a minor way, the cop who frames innocents, the doctor who kills his patients. The plagiarist violates the essential rule of his trade. He steals the lifeblood of a colleague," Plotz observed.

To put it in the modern vernacular, plagiarism sucks.

16

⊘ AT ISSUE: SOURCES FOR AVOIDING PLAGIARISM

1. Shafer presents his "eight reasons plagiarism sucks" in "order of importance" (para. 2). Do you agree with his ranking? Which of his reasons do you see as most important? Which do you see as least important? Why?

2. Which of Shafer's "eight reasons" apply to academic plagiarism? Which do not?

3. Shafer's essay responds directly to reader comments about an earlier article he wrote (which appears on p. 365). Do you consider "Eight Reasons Plagiarism Sucks" to be a **refutation** of these comments? Why or why not?

4. Do you think Shafer's irreverent title and informal style are appropriate for his subject matter? Why or why not?

5. What is your response to Shafer's concluding statement? Is it appropriate? Is it convincing?

6. Fill in the following template to express Shafer's thesis in one sentence. (Note that you should summarize his eight reasons, not list them all.)

    Plagiarism is a serious problem because _____

    _____.

7. Paragraph 5 is a one-sentence parenthetical comment. What purpose does this paragraph serve? How does it support Shafer's thesis? Is it necessary, or is it just a digression? Explain.

8. What is *boilerplate* (9–11)? What, according to Shafer, is wrong with "the boilerplate excuse"?

This essay appeared in the *Washington Post* on September 3, 2004.

HOW TO FIGHT COLLEGE CHEATING

LAWRENCE M. HINMAN

Recent studies have shown that a steadily growing number of students cheat or plagiarize in college—and the data from high schools suggest that this number will continue to rise. A study by Don McCabe of Rutgers University showed that 74 percent of high school students admitted to one or more instances of serious cheating on tests. Even more disturbing is the way that many students define cheating and plagiarism. For example, they believe that cutting and pasting a few sentences from various Web sources without attribution is not plagiarism. 1

Before the Web, students certainly plagiarized—but they had to plan ahead to do so. Fraternities and sororities often had files of term papers, and some high-tech term-paper firms could fax papers to students. Overall, however, plagiarism required forethought. 2

Online term-paper sites changed all that. Overnight, students could order a term paper, print it out, and have it ready for class in the morning—and still get a good night's sleep. All they needed was a charge card and an Internet connection. 3

One response to the increase in cheating has been to fight technology with more technology. Plagiarism-checking sites provide a service to screen student papers. They offer a color-coded report on papers and the original sources from which the students might have copied. Colleges qualify for volume discounts, which encourages professors to submit whole classes' worth of papers—the academic equivalent of mandatory urine testing for athletes. 4

The technological battle between term-paper mills and anti-plagiarism services will undoubtedly continue to escalate, with each side constructing more elaborate countermeasures to outwit the other. The cost of both plagiarism and its detection will also undoubtedly continue to spiral. 5

> "The cost of both plagiarism and its detection will also undoubtedly continue to spiral."

But there is another way. Our first and most important line of defense against academic dishonesty is simply good teaching. Cheating and plagiarism often arise in a vacuum created by routine, lack of interest, and overwork. Professors who give the same assignment every semester, fail to guide students in the development of their projects, and have little interest in what the students have to say contribute to the academic environment in which much cheating and plagiarism occurs. 6

Consider, by way of contrast, professors who know their students and who give assignments that require regular, continuing interaction with them about their projects—and who require students to produce work that is a meaningful 7 development of their own interests. These professors create an environment in which cheating and plagiarism are far less likely to occur. In this context, any plagiarism would usually be immediately evident to the professor, who would see it as inconsistent with the rest of the student's work. A strong, meaningful curriculum taught by committed professors is the first and most important defense against academic dishonesty.

The second remedy is to encourage the development of integrity in our 8 students. A sense of responsibility about one's intellectual development would preclude cheating and plagiarizing as inconsistent with one's identity. It is precisely this sense of individual integrity that schools with honor codes seek to promote.

Third, we must encourage our students to perceive the dishonesty of their 9 classmates as something that causes harm to the many students who play by the rules. The argument that cheaters hurt only themselves is false. Cheaters do hurt other people, and they do so to help themselves. Students cheat because it works. They get better grades and more advantages with less effort. Honest students lose grades, scholarships, recommendations, and admission to advanced programs. Honest students must create enough peer pressure to dissuade potential cheaters. Ultimately, students must be willing to step forward and confront those who engage in academic dishonesty.

Addressing these issues is not a luxury that can be postponed until a more 10 convenient time. It is a short step from dishonesty in schools and colleges to dishonesty in business. It is doubtful that students who fail to develop habits of integrity and honesty while still in an academic setting are likely to do so once they are out in the "real" world. Nor is it likely that adults will stand up against the dishonesty of others, particularly fellow workers and superiors, if they do not develop the habit of doing so while still in school.

❯ AT ISSUE: SOURCES FOR AVOIDING PLAGIARISM

1. In the first five paragraphs of this essay, Hinman provides background on how plagiarism by students has been changed by the Internet. Summarize the plagiarism situation before and after the development of the Internet.

2. The author's thesis appears in paragraph 6. Restate this thesis in your own words.

3. Does Hinman view plagiarism-detection sites as a solution to the problem of college cheating? What are the limitations of such sites?

4. According to Hinman, what steps can "committed professors" (7) take to eliminate academic dishonesty?

5. In paragraphs 8 and 9, Hinman suggests two additional solutions to the problem of plagiarism. What are these remedies? Given what you know about college students, do you think Hinman's suggestions are realistic? Explain.

6. Hinman does not address arguments that challenge his recommendations. What opposing arguments might he have presented? How would you refute these opposing arguments?

7. This essay was published in 2004. Do you think Hinman's observations and recommendations are still valid? Why or why not?

This article is from the August 1, 2010, edition of the *New York Times.*

PLAGIARISM LINES BLUR FOR STUDENTS IN DIGITAL AGE

TRIP GABRIEL

At Rhode Island College, a freshman copied and pasted from a Web site's frequently asked questions page about homelessness—and did not think he needed to credit a source in his assignment because the page did not include author information.

At DePaul University, the tip-off to one student's copying was the purple shade of several paragraphs he had lifted from the Web; when confronted by a writing tutor his professor had sent him to, he was not defensive—he just wanted to know how to change purple text to black.

And at the University of Maryland, a student reprimanded for copying from *Wikipedia* in a paper on the Great Depression said he thought its entries—unsigned and collectively written—did not need to be credited since they counted, essentially, as common knowledge.

Professors used to deal with plagiarism by admonishing students to give credit to others and to follow the style guide for citations, and pretty much left it at that.

But these cases—typical ones, according to writing tutors and officials responsible for discipline at the three schools who described the plagiarism—suggest that many students simply do not grasp that using words they did not write is a serious misdeed.

It is a disconnect that is growing in the Internet age as concepts of intellectual property, copyright, and originality are under assault in the unbridled exchange of online information, say educators who study plagiarism.

Digital technology makes copying and pasting easy, of course. But that is the least of it. The Internet may also be redefining how students—who came of age with music file-sharing, *Wikipedia*, and Web-linking—understand the concept of authorship and the singularity of any text or image.

"Now we have a whole generation of students who've grown up with information that just seems to be hanging out there in cyberspace and doesn't seem to have an author," said Teresa Fishman, director of the Center for Academic Integrity at Clemson University. "It's possible to believe this information is just out there for anyone to take."

Professors who have studied plagiarism do not try to excuse it—many are champions of academic honesty on their campuses—but rather try to understand why it is so widespread.

In surveys from 2006 to 2010 by Donald L. McCabe, a co-founder of the Center for Academic Integrity and a business professor at Rutgers University, about 40 percent of 14,000 undergraduates admitted to copying a few sentences in written assignments.

Perhaps more significant, the number who believed that copying from the 11
Web constitutes "serious cheating" is declining—to 29 percent on average in recent surveys from 34 percent earlier in the decade.

Sarah Brookover, a senior at the Rutgers campus in Camden, N.J., said 12
many of her classmates blithely cut and paste without attribution.

"This generation has always existed in a world where media and intellec- 13
tual property don't have the same gravity," said Ms. Brookover, who at 31 is older than most undergraduates. "When you're sitting at your computer, it's the same machine you've downloaded music with, possibly illegally, the same machine you streamed videos for free that showed on HBO last night."

Ms. Brookover, who works at the campus library, has pondered the differ- 14
ences between researching in the stacks and online. "Because you're not walking into a library, you're not physically holding the article, which takes you closer to 'this doesn't belong to me,'" she said. Online, "everything can belong to you really easily."

> "Online, 'everything can belong to you really easily.'"

A University of Notre Dame anthropolo- 15
gist, Susan D. Blum, disturbed by the high rates of reported plagiarism, set out to understand how students view authorship and the written word, or "texts" in Ms. Blum's academic language.

She conducted her ethnographic research among 234 Notre Dame under- 16
graduates. "Today's students stand at the crossroads of a new way of conceiving texts and the people who create them and who quote them," she wrote last year in the book *My Word! Plagiarism and College Culture*, published by Cornell University Press.

Ms. Blum argued that student writing exhibits some of the same qualities 17
of pastiche that drive other creative endeavors today—TV shows that constantly reference other shows or rap music that samples from earlier songs.

In an interview, she said the idea of an author whose singular effort cre- 18
ates an original work is rooted in Enlightenment ideas of the individual. It is buttressed by the Western concept of intellectual property rights as secured by copyright law. But both traditions are being challenged. "Our notion of authorship and originality was born, it flourished, and it may be waning," Ms. Blum said.

She contends that undergraduates are less interested in cultivating a unique 19
and authentic identity—as their 1960s counterparts were—than in trying on many different personas, which the Web enables with social networking.

"If you are not so worried about presenting yourself as absolutely unique, 20
then it's O.K. if you say other people's words, it's O.K. if you say things you don't believe, it's O.K. if you write papers you couldn't care less about because they accomplish the task, which is turning something in and getting a grade,"

Ms. Blum said, voicing student attitudes. "And it's O.K. if you put words out there without getting any credit."

The notion that there might be a new model young person, who freely 21 borrows from the vortex of information to mash up a new creative work, fueled a brief brouhaha earlier this year with Helene Hegemann, a German teenager whose best-selling novel about Berlin club life turned out to include passages lifted from others.

Instead of offering an abject apology, Ms. Hegemann insisted, "There's no 22 such thing as originality anyway, just authenticity." A few critics rose to her defense, and the book remained a finalist for a fiction prize (but did not win).

That theory does not wash with Sarah Wilensky, a senior at Indiana Uni- 23 versity, who said that relaxing plagiarism standards "does not foster creativity, it fosters laziness."

"You're not coming up with new ideas if you're grabbing and mixing and 24 matching," said Ms. Wilensky, who took aim at Ms. Hegemann in a column in her student newspaper headlined "Generation Plagiarism."

"It may be increasingly accepted, but there are still plenty of creative 25 people—authors and artists and scholars—who are doing original work," Ms. Wilensky said in an interview. "It's kind of an insult that that ideal is gone, and now we're left only to make collages of the work of previous generations."

In the view of Ms. Wilensky, whose writing skills earned her the role of 26 informal editor of other students' papers in her freshman dorm, plagiarism has nothing to do with trendy academic theories.

The main reason it occurs, she said, is because students leave high school 27 unprepared for the intellectual rigors of college writing.

"If you're taught how to closely read sources and synthesize them into your own original argument in middle and high school, you're not going to be tempted to plagiarize in college, and you certainly won't do so unknowingly," she said.

At the University of California, Davis, of the 196 plagiarism cases referred 29 to the disciplinary office last year, a majority did not involve students ignorant of the need to credit the writing of others.

Many times, said Donald J. Dudley, who oversees the discipline office on 30 the campus of 32,000, it was students who intentionally copied—knowing it was wrong—who were "unwilling to engage the writing process."

"Writing is difficult, and doing it well takes time and practice," he said. 31

And then there was a case that had nothing to do with a younger genera- 32 tion's evolving view of authorship. A student accused of plagiarism came to Mr. Dudley's office with her parents, and the father admitted that he was the one responsible for the plagiarism. The wife assured Mr. Dudley that it would not happen again.

⊘AT ISSUE: SOURCES FOR AVOIDING PLAGIARISM

1. Gabriel begins his article inductively, presenting three paragraphs of evidence before he states his thesis. Is this the best strategy, or should these examples appear later in his essay? Explain.

2. In paragraph 5, Gabriel notes that "many students simply do not grasp that using words they did not write is a serious misdeed." Is this his essay's thesis statement? Does this essay take a position, or is it strictly informational?

3. Why, according to this article, is plagiarism so widespread? Do you think the reasons Gabriel cites in any way excuse plagiarism—at least accidental plagiarism? Does Gabriel seem to think so?

4. What is *pastiche* (para. 17)? What is a collage (25)? How does the concept of pastiche or collage apply to plagiarism? Do you see the use of pastiche in TV shows or popular music (17) as different from its use in academic writing? Why or why not?

5. Summarize Sarah Wilensky's views (23–28) on the issue Gabriel discusses. Do you agree with her? Do you agree with Helene Hegemann's statement, "There's no such thing as originality anyway, just authenticity" (22)?

6. Do you think the anecdote in paragraph 32 is a strong ending for this article? Does the paragraph need a more forceful concluding statement? Explain.

This essay appeared on the *New Yorker*'s "Book Bench" blog on August 4, 2010.

TOO HARD *NOT* TO CHEAT IN THE INTERNET AGE?

ELIZABETH MINKEL

A deeply troubling article sat atop the *New York Times'* most-emailed list 1
yesterday (no, not the one about catching horrible diseases at the gym).
"Plagiarism Lines Blur for Students in Digital Age," the headline proclaimed,
pinpointing a problem, weaving a theory, and excusing youthful copycats in
one fell swoop. The story here is that a large number of college students today
are acting as college students always have—baldly lifting whole passages for
their term papers from other sources. But it's the Digital Age now, and between unverifiable, unattributed information sitting around online and the
general ease with which young people obtain, alter, and share creative content
on the Internet, students can't seem to figure out that cheating on a paper is
wrong. In fact, a lot of them can't even tell that they're cheating, and the
Internet is to blame.

Really? When I was in college (I graduated three years ago), I was well 2
aware of the necessity of avoiding minefields of unattributed—and often incorrect—information on the Web. *Wikipedia* was never an acceptable source,
perhaps because my professors knew they'd get students like the one from the
University of Maryland who, when "reprimanded for copying from *Wikipedia* . . .
said he thought its entries—unsigned and collectively written—did not need to
be credited since they counted, essentially, as common knowledge." There are
probably only two types of people pulling these excuses: the crafty, using the
Digital Age argument to their advantage, and the completely clueless, who, like
plenty in preceding generations, just don't understand the concept of plagiarism. The *Times* asked current students to weigh in (helpfully labelling them
"Generation Plagiarism"), and one wrote:

"I never 'copy and paste' but I will take information from the Internet and 3
change out a few words then put it in my paper. So far, I have not encountered
any problems with this. Thought [*sic*] the
information/words are technically mine because of a few undetectable word swaps, I
still consider the information to be that of
someone else."

The student goes on to say that, "In the
digital age, plagiarism isn't and shouldn't be
as big of a deal as it used to be when people
used books for research." The response leaves

> "I'm pretty
> convinced that he'd
> still be fuzzy on
> plagiarism if he'd
> lived back when
> people actually used
> books."

4

me just as confused as I believe he is, but I'm pretty convinced that he'd still be fuzzy on plagiarism if he'd lived back when people actually used books. But what I've found most frustrating in the ensuing debate is the assertion that these students are a part of some new *Reality Hunger*–type wave of open-source everything—if every song is sampled, why shouldn't writers do the same? The question is interesting, complicated, and divisive, but it has little bearing on a Psych 101 paper.

Excusing plagiarism as some sort of modern-day academic mash-up   5 won't teach students anything more than how to lie and get away with it. We should be teaching students how to produce original work—and that there's plenty of original thinking across the Internet—and leave the plagiarizing to the politicians.

⊃ AT ISSUE: SOURCES FOR AVOIDING PLAGIARISM

1. Minkel's essay is a refutation of Trip Gabriel's article (p. 374), whose head-line she accuses of "pinpointing a problem, weaving a theory, and excus-ing youthful copycats in one fell swoop" (para.1). Do you agree that Gabriel's article excuses plagiarism, or do you think it simply identifies a problem? Explain.

2. In paragraph 1, Minkel summarizes Gabriel's article. Is this a fair summary?

3. When Minkel quotes the student in paragraphs 3 and 4, is she setting up a **straw man**? Explain.

4. How would you characterize Minkel's tone? For example, is she angry? Frustrated? Condescending? Annoyed? Is this tone appropri-ate for her audience? (Note that this essay first appeared in the *New Yorker*, a magazine likely to be read by educated readers.)

5. In paragraph 2, Minkel identifies herself as a recent college graduate. Why? Is she appealing here to *ethos*, *pathos*, or *logos*?

6. Evaluate Minkel's last paragraph, particularly her concluding state-ment. Does this paragraph accurately express her reasons for criticiz-ing Gabriel's article? What, if anything, do you think she should add to her conclusion? Why?

This essay appeared in *Newsday* on May 18, 2003.

THE TRUTH ABOUT PLAGIARISM

RICHARD A. POSNER

Plagiarism is considered by most writers, teachers, journalists, scholars, and even members of the general public to be the capital intellectual crime. Being caught out in plagiarism can blast a politician's career, earn a college student expulsion, and destroy a writer's, scholar's, or journalist's reputation. In recent days, for example, the *New York Times* has referred to "widespread fabrication and plagiarism" by reporter Jayson Blair as "a low point in the 152-year history of the newspaper." 1

In James Hynes' splendid satiric novella of plagiarism, *Casting the Runes*, the plagiarist, having by black magic murdered one of the historians whom he plagiarized and tried to murder a second, is himself killed by the very same black magic, deployed by the widow of his murder victim. 2

There is a danger of overkill. Plagiarism can be a form of fraud, but it is no accident that, unlike real theft, it is not a crime. If a thief steals your car, you are out the market value of the car, but if a writer copies material from a book you wrote, you don't have to replace the book. At worst, the undetected plagiarist obtains a reputation that he does not deserve (that is the element of fraud in plagiarism). The real victim of his fraud is not the person whose work he copies, but those of his competitors who scruple to enhance their own reputations by such means. 3

> "There is a danger of overkill."

The most serious plagiarisms are by students and professors, whose undetected plagiarisms disrupt the system of student and scholarly evaluation. The least serious are those that earned the late Stephen Ambrose and Doris Kearns Goodwin such obloquy last year. Popular historians, they jazzed up their books with vivid passages copied from previous historians without quotation marks, though with footnote attributions that made their "crime" easy to detect. 4

(One reason that plagiarism, like littering, is punished heavily, even though an individual act of plagiarism usually does little or no harm, is that it is normally very difficult to detect—but not in the case of Ambrose and Goodwin.) Competing popular historians might have been injured, but I'm not aware of anyone actually claiming this. 5

Confusion of plagiarism with theft is one reason plagiarism engenders indignation; another is a confusion of it with copyright infringement. Wholesale copying of copyrighted material is an infringement of a property right, and legal remedies are available to the copyright holder. But the copying of brief passages, even from copyrighted materials, is permissible under the doctrine of "fair use," while wholesale copying from material that is in the public domain—material that never was copyrighted, or on which the copyright has expired—presents no copyright issue at all. 6

Plagiarism of work in the public domain is more common than otherwise. 7 Consider a few examples: *West Side Story* is a thinly veiled copy (with music added) of *Romeo and Juliet*, which in turn plagiarized Arthur Brooke's *The Tragicall Historye of Romeo and Juliet*, published in 1562, which in turn copied from several earlier Romeo and Juliets, all of which were copies of Ovid's story of Pyramus and Thisbe.

Paradise Lost plagiarizes the book of Genesis in the Old Testament. Classical 8 musicians plagiarize folk melodies (think only of Dvorak, Bartok, and Copland) and often "quote" (as musicians say) from earlier classical works. Edouard Manet's most famous painting, *Déjeuner sur l'herbe*, copies earlier paintings by Raphael, Titian, and Courbet, and *My Fair Lady* plagiarized Shaw's play *Pygmalion*, while Woody Allen's movie *Play It Again, Sam* "quotes" a famous scene from *Casablanca*. Countless movies are based on books, such as *The Thirty-Nine Steps* on John Buchan's novel of that name or *For Whom the Bell Tolls* on Hemingway's novel.

Many of these "plagiarisms" were authorized, and perhaps none was 9 deceptive; they are what Christopher Ricks in his excellent book *Allusions to the Poets* helpfully terms *allusion* rather than *plagiarism*. But what they show is that copying with variations is an important form of creativity, and this should make us prudent and measured in our condemnations of plagiarism.

Especially when the term is extended from literal copying to the copying of 10 ideas. Another phrase for copying an idea, as distinct from the form in which it is expressed, is dissemination of ideas. If one needs a license to repeat another person's idea, or if one risks ostracism by one's professional community for failing to credit an idea to its originator, who may be forgotten or unknown, the dissemination of ideas is impeded.

I have heard authors of history textbooks criticized for failing to document 11 their borrowing of ideas from previous historians. This is an absurd criticism. The author of a textbook makes no claim to originality; rather the contrary—the most reliable, if not necessarily the most exciting, textbook is one that confines itself to ideas already well accepted, not at all novel.

It would be better if the term *plagiarism* were confined to literal copying, 12 and moreover literal copying that is not merely unacknowledged but deceptive. Failing to give credit where credit is due should be regarded as a lesser, indeed usually merely venial, offense.

The concept of plagiarism has expanded, and the sanctions for it, though 13 they remain informal rather than legal, have become more severe, in tandem with the rise of individualism. Journal articles are no longer published anonymously, and ghostwriters demand that their contributions be acknowledged.

Individualism and a cult of originality go hand in hand. Each of us sup- 14 poses that our contribution to society is unique rather than fungible and so deserves public recognition, which plagiarism clouds.

This is a modern view. We should be aware that the high value placed on 15 originality is a specific cultural, and even field-specific, phenomenon, rather than an aspect of the universal moral law.

Judges, who try to conceal rather than to flaunt their originality, far from 16 crediting their predecessors with original thinking like to pretend that there is no original thinking in law, that judges are just a transmission belt for rules and principles laid down by the framers of statutes or the Constitution.

Resorting to plagiarism to obtain a good grade or a promotion is fraud 17 and should be punished, though it should not be confused with "theft." But I think the zeal to punish plagiarism reflects less a concern with the real injuries that it occasionally inflicts than with a desire on the part of leaders of professional communities, such as journalists and historians, to enhance their profession's reputation.

Postmodernism is a school of criticism that denies concepts such as scientific certainty and absolute truth.

Journalists (like politicians) have a bad reputation for truthfulness, and 18 historians, in this "postmodernist"° era, are suspected of having embraced an extreme form of relativism and of having lost their regard for facts. Both groups hope by taking a very hard line against plagiarism and fabrication to reassure the public that they are serious diggers after truth whose efforts, a form of "sweat equity," deserve protection against copycats.

Their anxieties are understandable; but the rest of us will do well to keep 19 the matter in perspective, realizing that the term *plagiarism* is used loosely and often too broadly; that much plagiarism is harmless and (when the term is defined broadly) that some has social value.

⊘ AT ISSUE: SOURCES FOR AVOIDING PLAGIARISM

1. According to Posner, how do most people define *plagiarism*? How is the definition he proposes different from theirs? Do you think this definition is too broad? Too narrow?

2. Why does Posner believe that the plagiarisms committed by students and professors are the most serious? Can you suggest an argument against this position?

3. How do the examples Posner cites in paragraphs 7 and 8 strengthen his argument? Do you agree that the examples he gives here constitute plagiarism? Why or why not?

4. Explain the connection the author makes in paragraph 16 between judges and plagiarism. (Note that Posner himself is a federal judge.)

5. Why, according to Posner, do journalists and historians think plagiarism should be punished severely?

6. According to Posner, "the truth about plagiarism" is that "much plagiarism is harmless and (when the term is defined broadly) that some has social value" (19). Does the evidence he presents in this essay support this conclusion? What connection do you see between this position and his comments about the rise of individualism and the "cult of originality" in paragraphs 13–15?

This opinion column was published in the *Diamondback*, the student newspaper of the University of Maryland, on February 5, 2009.

IT'S NOT ALL PLAGIARISM

JOSHUA CRAWFORD

Thanks to the class cancellations last Tuesday and Wednesday, almost the whole 1 first week of my semester was consumed with classes dedicated entirely to going over the syllabus. This process is usually fairly predictable. "Welcome to [insert class title here]." "My name is [insert professor's name here]." "We have a lot to get through this semester." Then comes a question about whether everyone has bought the textbook, then a quick preview of the schedule for the semester, then (if you're unlucky) an awkward and unnecessary round of forced introductions, and (if you're lucky) class is usually over by about that time.

This semester, however, one thing struck me as different: An inordinately 2 thorough, and threatening, focus on academic dishonesty policies. By this point, I think we're all more or less used to the speech about the honor pledge and not plagiarizing. But over the last week, my experience with this part of the syllabus went somewhat differently.

It began in a history discussion, when my teaching assistant informed us 3 that using the Internet to do research for a paper was prohibited. What happens if he thinks we've used the Internet, we asked. Nothing, he told us, except that he refers us to the professor, who will immediately refer us to the Student Honor Council, all apparently without even consulting us about his suspicions.

Then, in my next class, the academic dishonesty hardlining continued as my journalism teacher informed us that she wouldn't hesitate to refer us to the Honor Council and have us removed from the course with an XF for even the smallest of offenses. Having a roommate look over a draft before you submit it? Plagiarism. Asking a classmate for help on the third question on the homework? Academic dishonesty. Asking your neighbor how to spell a word? XF.

> "The academic dishonesty hardlining continued as my journalism teacher informed us that she wouldn't hesitate to refer us to the Honor Council." 4

Undoubtedly, I understand the need for strict policies in the face of the 5 plagiarism epidemic Jeremy Sullivan wrote about on Jan. 26. With the Internet at our fingertips and websites where you can actually pay a team of writers to write original term papers for you, cheating has the potential to be a more serious problem than ever before. And I commend the university for taking the steps it has to minimize the problem of academic dishonesty, namely through its use of the honor pledge and the Student Honor Council.

However, with such a highly public and oft-cited honor pledge, we run the 6 risk of over-applying terms such as "academic dishonesty" and "plagiarism." With such stringent penalties for violation of the honor code and all a professor interprets it to imply, we risk the "academic dishonesty" umbrella becoming too big. At what point does the penalty honestly no longer fit the crime?

If I pay for a term paper or copy the exam of the person beside me, I 7 would expect to receive an XF or to even be expelled from this university. But if I ask my neighbor whether or not *e-mail* is hyphenated in AP style, I seriously don't think it's an offense that calls for intervention by the Student Honor Council or the journalism school's dean.

It is undoubtedly important to abide by the classroom policies of a teach- 8 ing assistant, teacher, or professor. I fully intend to do all of my history research between the stacks of McKeldin Library; to read over my own journalism papers 10 times; and to clear up all spelling and capitalization inquiries without any outside assistance. But I question whether violating policies really merits punishment comparable to that received by someone who copies and pastes his final paper off the Internet.

At some point, "zero tolerance" becomes blind, irresponsible, totalitarian 9 enforcement of a blunt policy. The law doesn't treat jaywalkers and murderers as if their offenses are the same, and the university's academic dishonesty policies should not make similar generalizations.

⊖ AT ISSUE: SOURCES FOR AVOIDING PLAGIARISM

1. Crawford gives examples of different kinds of student plagiarism. List these types of plagiarism in order, from those he considers the most serious to those he considers the least serious. Do you agree with Crawford's assessments, or do you disagree with him about the seriousness of different violations? Can you think of other common examples of student plagiarism that Crawford omits? Where would you rank these on your list? Why?

2. Paraphrase Crawford's thesis by filling in the template below:

   Although universities are right to try to reduce academic dishonesty, _____
   _____.

3. This column first appeared in the University of Maryland's student newspaper. What different audiences might read this story? How would you expect each of these different kinds of readers to react to Crawford's argument?

4. Where does Crawford try to establish common ground with his readers? Where does he try to establish credibility? Is he successful?

5. In paragraph 5, Crawford summarizes an opposing argument. What is this argument? Do you think he does a good job of acknowledging the strengths of this argument? Of refuting it?

6. In his conclusion, Crawford compares the university policy of treating all levels of academic dishonesty the same way to the idea of treating "jaywalkers and murderers" alike. Is this analogy accurate? Is it logical? Is it fair? Is it convincing? Explain.

This essay first appeared on September 15, 2006, in the *Chronicle Review*.

COPY THIS

CAROLYN FOSTER SEGAL

Legal claims on creative products, such as computer codes or literary works

Not all plagiarists achieve fame and in-depth coverage by the *New York Times*, the *Wall Street Journal*, and the *Chronicle*; most are students toiling in relative obscurity, cutting and pasting or lifting in its entirety the work of others. Intellectual-property rights° in the 21st century may indeed be pre-empted by a return to the centuries-earlier, precopyright practice of "If I find a poem nailed to the church door, I can simply change the names and make it mine." In place of the church door, we have the global window of the computer. Technology has raised the crafty business of plagiarism and its detection to a whole new level.

My college has both an honor code and an ethics program. It also has an official but vague policy on plagiarism, which leaves the final determination of punitive measures up to the individual instructor; the college does ask instructors to file a report with the provost's office. In the first week of the semester, I hand out a syllabus with a description of and warning about plagiarism. I also spend time in that first week and throughout the semester describing ways to present secondary sources (direct quotation, paraphrase, summary); the categories of plagiarism (poor or lazy formatting of sources, unintentional, intentional); and the consequences of plagiarism (a grade of F for the paper, and, at my discretion, a grade of F for the course).

As I outline the categories of venal and mortal transgressions, I'm often reminded of Sister Mary Helen, my second-grade teacher, who drew an illustration of the soul on the backboard: a chalk circle, which she then filled with a snowstorm of dots representing our sins. A colleague of mine has created a marvelous high-tech version of his lecture on the sin of plagiarism, a Web site with allusions to Dante and the eighth circle of hell.° Neither threat of failure nor fear of everlasting damnation, however, seems to deter some students.

Dante Alighieri (1265–1321) was an Italian writer best known for The Divine Comedy, *which describes a journey through the afterlife, including a visit to hell.*

Even an emphasis on the process of writing—an earthly procedure more concrete than threats of divine retribution, involving drafts and peer-review sessions—does not stop some students, who will brazen their way through a barrage of probing questions in workshops. Their final papers usually feature blocks of silky-smooth contraband prose, interspersed with ungrammatical and unclear changes designed to cover up their theft.

For it is theft, plain and simple—or, more accurately, complex—as I tell my students. It is theft of another writer's ideas, work, and time; it is theft of their fellow students' time; it is theft of their own time, honor, and education; and it is theft of my time—minutes, hours, and days—that I'd rather spend reading, writing, or watching a softball game. And not only is it unethical, it's foolish. One of my husband's degrees is in library science—he once worked as a reference librarian—and I supported myself through most of graduate school by working in libraries. I teach research methods, for God's sake. I also have a tech wizard living in my basement—my 17-year-old daughter. "So just don't do it," I tell my students.

And most of them don't—not because of all my lectures, but because they are honest, love writing, and want to learn how to do it better. Over time, their hard work has made the plagiarism by the few all the more appalling to me.

The most recent incident involved a student's submitting a retitled appropriation of the poem "When We Two Parted," complete with "thee" and "thy," for her final project in "Creative Writing: Poetry." Charmed by a blogger's use of the lines, the student had apparently traced them to another blog created by someone who is a big fan of a writer he calls "George Gordon" (the poet formerly known as Lord George Gordon Byron). In another incident, in a nonfiction class, a student presented as her own work the text of a 2004 online human-resources guide. In terms of detection, this was a personal best: It took me 30 seconds to find the site after typing in one of the subheadings.

> "In terms of detection, this was a personal best: It took me 30 seconds."

On another occasion, I didn't have to search at all: After a creative-writing student ended her dramatic reading of her newest attempt, the student sitting next to her said, "Why am I thinking of *The Last Unicorn*?" As a quick click verified, she was thinking of Jimmy Webb's theme song for the animated film because the student had appropriated the lyrics.

The most outstanding act of plagiarism by a student I have encountered— an act of theft surrounded by a virtual web of lies—occurred two years ago in a nonfiction class, "Writing for Publication," and involved a woman who should have known better. G. was in her 40s and in her senior year; her major was information technology. At the beginning of the semester, I gave my usual lecture on the need for both students and professional writers to cite or handle sources responsibly. For the first workshop, G. brought a piece called "Ten Ways for Working Students to Cope with Stress." It was of nearly publishable quality, but there was something strange about it. Polished and professional, it lacked only one thing—or, more precisely, one part of speech. It contained no articles—the omission apparently a clever attempt to disguise the act of plagiarism.

I found "10 Ways the Working Student Can Cope with Stress" online in 10 minutes. The eighth listing of a search, the piece was a publication of the Counseling Center at the University of Pittsburgh. (I simply typed in the key words "ten ways cope stress," conscious of the fact that now I too had been reduced to eliminating all articles.) I e-mailed the student, asking her to meet with me before the next day's class; then I returned to the site, hoping to find some additional tips on stress.

The student had agreed to come in at 11 a.m. In preparation, I printed out 11 the online article and typed up a report. I made duplicate copies—of the article, the student's paper, my report, my assignment sheet, my rubric, the course's syllabus with the sections on plagiarism highlighted—for the chairman of my department, the acting provost, the student's adviser, and the director of the advising center. The student arrived at 12:30 p.m., an hour and a half late and just half an hour before our class was scheduled to meet. I asked G. to tell me about her process, and she began: She had to find a topic, make notes, and "get just the right words." I was tempted to jump up like Perry Mason, wave the printout of the original article, and say sternly, "And you got them right here, didn't you?" but I waited. "My only concern," she said, and then paused. I wanted her to tell me that she didn't "get" the assignment—really, both of our lives would have been simpler and happier, and I wouldn't have to send off all those packets of duplicates. "My only concern," she continued, "is that I didn't do the heading correctly, and so I won't get an A."

I explained that the format, while incorrect, was not my greatest worry, 12 and that, in fact, I had a far more serious concern—plagiarism. And so began the stages of plagiarism grief:

> Disbelief: How could I accuse her?
> Denial: This was her own original work.
> Astonishment: How could she and someone else have produced identical texts?
> Confusion, Part 1: She forgot to acknowledge her source.
> Confusion, Part 2: My assignment was not clear; she didn't realize that she actually had to produce her own original work.
> Plea No. 1: No one could ever produce original work on her topic (which had been her choice).
> Plea No. 2: Allow her to add a citation now.
> Plea No. 3: Allow her to redo the assignment and remain in the course.
> Plea No. 4: She didn't just cut and paste; she typed the entire essay herself.
> Plea No. 5: Change the grade for the paper to C, on the grounds of the above.
> Plea No. 6: All right, give the paper an F; just don't award a final grade of F.
> Defense: I never mentioned plagiarism in class.
> Accusation: I am mean and unfair.

My plagiarist tried—unsuccessfully—to withdraw from the course to 13 avoid her F and, when that didn't work, appealed my charges. Despite the student's protests and appeals, both my chairman and acting provost supported my decision to award the student a final grade of F for the course (possibly the earliest-recorded final grade in the history of academe). The following semester, G. repeated the course with another instructor in order to, as her adviser said, "*reclaim* [emphasis mine] her good name."

I've had work of my own used without my permission. One of my essays   14
appeared online both as part of a fundamentalist church's newsletter (the
theme of the issue was honesty) and as required reading for a journalism
course. In reply to my letter of complaint, the pastor of the church pointed
out—uncharitably—that he knew of two other Web sites where my pirated
work appeared and that "at least we included your name." The professor of the
journalism course never answered my letter. According to her home-page bio,
she had a degree in journalism ethics.

It's the brave/sad new world of the Internet, where every blogbaby can   15
have his or her Warholian 15 minutes of fame; it's a global market with everything ripe for the picking; it's the new frontier with no law and no order. On
one of the days that the grievance process with G. was tediously unwinding,
my in-house information specialist, my technology-savvy daughter, sent me an
e-mail message at work. She wanted me to check out a hit she had found on
Google: A term-paper company was selling essays about an article of mine on
student excuses.

⊝ AT ISSUE: SOURCES FOR AVOIDING PLAGIARISM

1. How does Segal define the word *plagiarism*? How have her personal
   and professional experiences shaped her view of plagiarism?

2. How is Segal's definition of the word *plagiarism* different from Richard A. Posner's (p. 380)? In what sense are the views she expresses in
   paragraph 4 a refutation of the comments Lawrence M. Hinman (p.
   371) makes about professors' responsibility to eliminate plagiarism?

3. Most of Segal's essay (paras. 7–13) consists of anecdotes about students who have committed plagiarism, Segal's discovery of their dishonesty, and her confrontations with them. How do these anecdotes
   support the sentiments she expresses in paragraph 6?

4. As a student, do you find Segal's essay mean-spirited? Do you think
   she should have balanced her negative examples with anecdotes
   about her other students—those who "are honest" and "love writing"
   (6)? Why or why not?

TERM PAPERS FOR SALE ADVERTISEMENT (*WEB PAGE*)

➲ AT ISSUE: SOURCES FOR AVOIDING PLAGIARISM

1. The Web page above is from a site that offers papers for sale to students. What argument does this Web page make? What counter-argument could you present?

2. Identify appeals to *logos*, *pathos*, and *ethos* on the TermPaperWriter .org page. Which appeal dominates?

3. Study the images of students on the page. What message do these images convey?

4. Unlike the TermPaperWriter.org page, many other sites that offer papers for sale include errors in grammar, spelling, and punctuation. Search the Web for some other sites that offer papers for sale. What errors can you find? Do such errors weaken the message of these ads, or are they irrelevant?

5. One site promises its papers are "100% plagiarism free." Does this promise make sense? Explain.

EXERCISE 11.4

Write a one-paragraph argument in which you take a position on where to draw the line with plagiarism. Follow the template below, filling in the blanks to create your argument.

TEMPLATE FOR WRITING AN ARGUMENT ABOUT PLAGIARISM

To many people, plagiarism is theft; to others, however, it is not that simple. For example, some define *plagiarism* as _____ _____; others see it as _____. Another thing to consider is _____ _____. In addition, _____ _____. Despite these differences of opinion, plagiarism is often dealt with harshly and can ruin careers and reputations. All things considered, _____ _____.

EXERCISE 11.5

Discuss your feelings about plagiarism with two or three of your class-mates. Consider how you define *plagiarism*, what causes it, whether there are degrees of dishonesty, and so on, but focus on the *effects* of plagiarism—on those who commit it and on those who are its victims. Then, write a paragraph that summarizes the key points of your discussion.

EXERCISE 11.6

Write an argumentative essay on the topic, "Where Should We Draw the Line with Plagiarism?" Begin by defining what you mean by *plagiarism*, and then narrow your discussion down to a particular group—for example, high school or college students, historians, scientists, or journalists. Cite the sources on pages 364–390, and be sure to document the sources you use and to include a works-cited page. (See Chapter 10 for information on documenting sources.)

EXERCISE 11.7

Review the four pillars of argument discussed in Chapter 1. Does your essay include all four elements of an effective argument? Add anything that is missing. Then, label the elements of your argument.

⊘ WRITING ASSIGNMENTS: AVOIDING PLAGIARISM

1. Write an argument in which you take a position on who (or what) is to blame for plagiarism among college students. Is plagiarism always the student's fault, or are other people (or other factors) at least partly to blame?

2. Write an essay in which you argue that an honor code will (or will not) eliminate (or at least reduce) plagiarism and other kinds of academic dishonesty at your school.

3. Reread the essays by Posner and Crawford in this chapter. Then, write an argument in which you argue that only intentional plagiarism should be punished.

4. Do you consider student plagiarism a victimless crime that is best left unpunished? If so, why? If not, how does it affect its victims—for example, the student who plagiarizes, the instructor, the class, and the school?

5

Strategies for Argument

In Chapter 1, you were introduced to the four pillars of argument—*thesis statement, evidence, refutation, and concluding statement*—the basic building blocks of an effective argumentative essay. The chapters that follow expand this discussion by illustrating and explaining different types of arguments.

Different purposes call for different argumentative strategies:

■ If you want to argue that something is (or is not) consistent with a particular definition, you can write a **definition argument**: "Is *Wikipedia* a legitimate research source?" **See Chapter 12.**

■ If you want your argument to take a stand on the causes or effects of an event or situation, you can write a **causal argument**: "Should the drinking age be lowered?" **See Chapter 13.**

■ If you want your argument to take a stand on the quality or worth of something, you can write an **evaluation argument**: "Are internships a good deal for college students?" **See Chapter 14.**

■ If you want your argument to recommend a solution to a problem, you can write a **proposal argument**: "Should the government do more to relieve the student-loan burden?" **See Chapter 15.**

■ If you want to argue that your position on an issue is valid because the situation you present is similar to another situation, you can write an **argument by analogy**: "Should college athletes be paid?" **See Chapter 16.**

■ If your purpose is to recommend a course of action because it is good or right (or argue against something because it is bad or wrong), you can write an **ethical argument**: "How far should colleges go to keep campuses safe?" **See Chapter 17.**

Definition Arguments

AT ISSUE

Is *Wikipedia* a Legitimate Research Source?

Wikipedia—the open-source online encyclopedia—is probably the most frequently used reference source on the planet. The use of this encyclopedia is not without controversy, however. Because anyone can write and edit entries, articles can—and do—contain errors. Over time, many errors get corrected, but some do not, perhaps because no one person or group is responsible for quality control. As a result, many college instructors question the reliability of *Wikipedia* as a research source. In fact, academic departments at some schools—for example, the history department at Middlebury College—have banned students from citing *Wikipedia* as a source. According to Don Wyatt, chair of the department, "Even though *Wikipedia* may have some value, particularly in leading students to citable sources, it is not itself an appropriate source for citation." Others disagree, pointing out that *Wikipedia* contains no more (and in some cases fewer) factual errors than traditional encyclopedias.

Later in this chapter, you will be asked to think more about this issue. You will be given several research sources to consider and asked to write a definition argument that takes a position on whether *Wikipedia* should be considered a legitimate research source.

For comprehension quizzes,
see **bedfordstmartins.com/practicalargument**.

What Is a Definition Argument?

When you write an argumentative essay that depends on your definition of a key term, it makes sense to structure your essay as a **definition argument**. In this type of essay, you will argue that something fits (or does not fit) the definition of a particular class of items. For example, to argue that *Wikipedia* is a legitimate research source, you have to define *legitimate research source* and then show that *Wikipedia* fits this definition.

Many arguments focus on definition. In fact, you encounter them so often that you probably do not recognize them for what they are. For example, consider the following questions:

- Is spanking child abuse?

- Should offensive speech be banned on campus?

- Should the rich pay more taxes than others?

- Are energy-efficient light bulbs bad for the environment?

- Is cheerleading a sport?

- Is *Wikipedia* a legitimate research source?

You cannot answer these questions without providing definitions. In fact, if you were writing an argumentative essay in response to one of these questions, much of your essay would be devoted to defining and discussing a key term.

QUESTION	KEY TERM TO BE DEFINED
Is spanking child abuse?	*child abuse*
Should offensive speech be banned on campus?	*offensive speech*
Should the rich pay more taxes than others?	*rich*
Are energy-efficient light bulbs bad for the environment?	*bad*
Is *Wikipedia* a legitimate research source?	*legitimate research source*

Many contemporary social and legal disputes involve definition arguments. For example, did a coworker's actions constitute *sexual harassment*? Is an individual trying to enter the United States a *political refugee* or an *illegal alien*? Is a combatant a *terrorist* or a *freedom fighter*? Is a person guilty of *murder* or of *manslaughter*? Did soldiers engage in *torture* or in *aggressive questioning*? Was the magazine cover *satirical* or *racist*? Is the punishment *just*, or is it *cruel and unusual*? The answers to these and many other questions hinge on definitions of key terms.

Keep in mind, however, that definitions can change as our thinking about certain issues changes. For example, fifty years ago the word *family* generally referred to one or more children living with two heterosexual married parents. Now, the term can refer to a wide variety of situations—children living with single parents, gay and lesbian couples, and unmarried heterosexual couples, for example. Our definition of what constitutes *cruel and unusual punishment* has also changed. Public hanging, a common method of execution for hundreds of years, is now considered barbaric.

The last public hanging in the United States (Owensboro, Kentucky, August 14, 1936)

Developing Definitions

Definitions explain terms that are unfamiliar to an audience. To make your definitions as clear as possible, avoid making them *too narrow*, *too broad*, or *circular*.

A definition that is **too narrow** leaves out information that is necessary for understanding a particular word or term. For example, if you define an *apple* as "a red fruit," your definition is too narrow since some apples are not red. To be accurate (and useful), your definition needs to be more inclusive and acknowledge the fact that apples can be red, green, or yellow.

A definition that is **too broad** includes things that should not be part of the definition. If, for example, you define *chair* as "something that people sit on," your definition includes things that are not chairs—stools, park benches, and even tree stumps. To be accurate, your definition needs to be much more specific: "A chair is a piece of furniture that has a seat, legs, arms, and a back and is designed to accommodate one person."

A **circular definition** includes the word being defined as part of the definition. For example, if you define *patriotism* as "the quality of being patriotic," your definition is circular. For the definition to work, you have to provide new information that enables readers to understand the term: "*Patriotism* is a belief characterized by love and support for one's country, especially its values and beliefs."

The success of a definition argument depends on your ability to define a term so that readers (even those who do not agree with your position) will see its validity. For this reason, the rhetorical strategies you use to develop your definitions are important.

NOTE

Sometimes you can clarify a definition by explaining how one term is different from another similar term. For example, consider the following definition:

Patriotism is different from *nationalism* because *patriotism* focuses on love for a country while *nationalism* assumes the superiority of one country over another.

Dictionary Definitions (Formal Definitions)

When most people think of definitions, they think of the formal definitions they find in a dictionary. Typically, a formal **dictionary definition** consists of the term to be defined, the general class to which the term belongs, and the qualities that differentiate the term from other items in the same class.

TERM	CLASS	DIFFERENTIATION
dog	a domesticated mammal	that has a snout, a keen sense of smell, and a barking voice
naturalism	a literary movement	whose followers believed that writers should treat their characters' lives with scientific objectivity

➔ EXERCISE 12.1

Write a one-sentence formal definition of each of the following words. Then, look each word up in a dictionary, and compare your definitions to the ones you found there.

Terrorism	Marriage
App	Blog
Tablet	Fairness

Extended Definitions

Although a definition argument may include a short dictionary definition, a brief definition is usually not enough to define a complex or abstract term. For example, if you were arguing that *Wikipedia* was a *legitimate research source*, you would have to include an **extended definition**, explaining to readers in some detail what you mean by this term and perhaps giving examples of other research sources that fit your definition.

Examples are often used to develop an extended definition in an argumentative essay. For instance, you could give examples to make the case that a particular baseball player, despite his struggles with substance abuse, is a great athlete. You could define *great athlete* solely in terms of athletic prowess, presenting several examples of other talented athletes and then showing that the baseball player you are discussing possesses the same qualities.

For your examples to be effective, they have to be relevant to your argument. Your examples also have to represent (or at least suggest) the full range of opinion concerning your subject. Finally, you have to make sure that your readers will accept your examples as typical, not unusual. For example, in the Declaration of Independence (p. 770), Thomas Jefferson presented twenty-five paragraphs of examples to support his extended definition of the king's tyranny. With these examples, he hoped to convince the world that the colonists were justified in breaking away from England. To accomplish his goal, Jefferson made sure that his examples supported his position, that they represented the full range of abuses, and that they were not unusual or atypical.

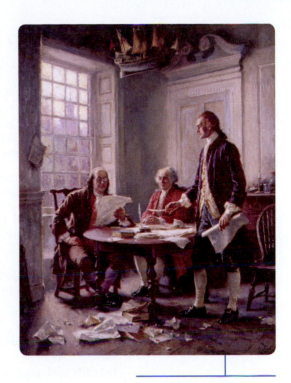

Writing the Declaration of Independence, 1776 by Jean Leon Gerome Ferris (Virginia Historical Society)

⊘ EXERCISE 12.2

Choose one of the terms you defined in Exercise 12.1, and write a paragraph-length definition argument that takes a position related to that term. Make sure you include two or three examples in your definition.

Operational Definitions

Whereas a dictionary definition tells what a term is, an **operational definition** defines something by telling how it acts or how it works. Thus, an operational definition transforms an abstract concept into something concrete, observable, and possibly measurable. Children instinctively understand the concept of operational definitions. When a parent tells them to *behave*, they know what the components of this operational definition are: clean up your room, obey your parents, come home on time, and do your homework. Researchers in the natural and social sciences must constantly come up with operational definitions. For example, if they want to study the effects of childhood obesity, they have to construct an operational definition of *obese*. Without such a definition, they will not be able to measure the various factors that make a person obese. For example, at what point does a child become obese? Does he or she have to be 10% above normal weight? More? Before researchers can carry out their study, they must agree on an operational (or working) definition.

Structuring a Definition Argument

In general terms, a definition argument can be structured as follows:

- **Introduction:** Establishes a context for the argument by explaining the need for defining the term; presents the essay's thesis

- **Evidence (first point in support of thesis):** Provides a short definition of the term as well as an extended definition (if necessary)

- **Evidence (second point in support of thesis):** Shows how the term does or does not fit the definition

- **Refutation of opposing arguments:** Addresses questions about or objections to the definition; considers and rejects other possible meanings (if any)

- **Conclusion:** Reinforces the main point of the argument; includes a strong concluding statement

The following student essay includes all the elements of a definition argument. The student who wrote this essay is trying to convince his university that he is a nontraditional student and is therefore entitled to the benefits such students receive.

WHY I AM A NONTRADITIONAL STUDENT
ADAM KENNEDY

Ever since I started college, I have had difficulty getting the extra   1
help I need to succeed. My final disappointment came last week when
my adviser told me that I could not take advantage of the programs the
school offers to nontraditional students. She told me that because I am
not old enough, I simply do not qualify. This is confusing to me because
I am anything but a "traditional" student. In fact, I am one of the most
nontraditional students I know. In spite of my age—I am twenty-two—
I have had experiences that separate me from most other students my

Thesis statement   age. The problem is that the school's definition of the term *nontraditional*
is so narrow that it excludes people like me who should be able to qualify.

2   According to researchers, the term *nontraditional student* is difficult to define. Studies show that a broad operational definition that acknowledges many factors is preferable to one that focuses on age alone. For example, the National Center for Educational Statistics bases its definition on whether or not a student has any of the following seven characteristics:

- Did not enter college right after high school
- Is a part-time student
- Does not depend on parents for money
- Has a full-time job
- Has children or a spouse
- Is a single parent
- Has a GED instead of a high school diploma (Kim et al. 405–6)

Evidence: Operational definition of nontraditional student

3   Many colleges use similar, or even broader, criteria to define *nontraditional student*. For example, the University of Arkansas provides special services for older students as well as for students with other work- or family-related responsibilities. In fact, the school has a special department—Non-Traditional Student Services—to meet these students' needs. The university Web site says that a nontraditional student is someone who meets just one of the criteria listed above ("Who"). In addition, the university recognizes other factors, like whether the student is a veteran, an active member of the military, or the first in his or her family to go to college ("Who").

Evidence: Other schools' definitions of nontraditional student

4   According to the criteria from the National Center for Educational Statistics (listed above), I would have no problem qualifying as a nontraditional student at the University of Arkansas. Our school, however, has a much narrower definition of the term. When I went to Non-Traditional Student Services, I was told that my case did not fit the definition that the school had established. Here, a nontraditional student is someone who is twenty-five or older, period. The person I spoke to said that the school's intention is to give special help to older students. I was then told that I could appeal and try to convince the dean of Non-Traditional Student Services that I do not fit the definition of a traditional student.

Evidence: Our school's definition of nontraditional student

5   By any measure, I am not a "traditional student." After getting married at seventeen, I dropped out of high school and got a full-time job. Soon, my wife and I began to resent our situation. She was still a

Evidence: How writer fits the definition of nontraditional student

high school student and missed being able to go out with her friends whenever she wanted to. I hated my job and missed being a student. Before long, we decided it was best to end our marriage. Instead of going back to high school, however, I enlisted in the Army National Guard. After two years, I had completed a tour in Iraq and earned my GED. As soon as I was discharged from active duty, I enrolled in college—all this before I turned twenty-one.

Refutation of opposing argument

I can see how someone could say that I am too young to be considered a nontraditional student. However, I believe that my life experiences should qualify me for this program. My marriage and divorce, time in the army, and reentry issues make me very different from the average first-year student. The special resources available to students who qualify for this program—tutors, financial aid, special advising, support groups, and subsidized housing—would make my adjustment to college a lot easier. I am only four years older than the average first-year students, but I am nothing like them. The focus on age to define *nontraditional* ignores the fact that students younger than twenty-five may have followed unconventional paths to college. Life experience, not age, should be the main factor in determining whether a student is nontraditional.

The university should expand the definition of *nontraditional* to include younger students who have followed unconventional career paths and have postponed college. Even though these students may be younger than twenty-five, they face challenges similar to those faced by older students. Students like me are returning to school in increasing numbers. Our situation is different from that of others our age, and that is exactly why we need all the help we can get.

Concluding statement

Works Cited

Kim, Karen A., Linda J. Sax, Jenny J. Lee, and Linda Serra Hagedorn. "Redefining Nontraditional Students: Exploring the Self-Perceptions of Community College Students." *Community College Journal of Research and Practice* 34 (2010): 402–22. *Academic Search Complete*. Web. 18 Apr. 2012.

"Who Is a Non-Traditional Student?" *Office of Campus Life*. U of Arkansas at Little Rock, 2012. Web. 18 Apr. 2012.

GRAMMAR IN CONTEXT

Avoiding *Is Where* and *Is When*

When you write a **definition argument**, you often include a **formal definition**, which is made up of the term that you are defining, the class to which the term belongs, and the characteristics that distinguish your term from other items in the same class.

In a formal definition, you may sometimes find yourself using the phrase *is where* or *is when*. If so, your definition is incomplete because it omits the term's class. The use of *is where* or *is when* signals that you are giving an example of the term, not a definition. You can avoid this problem by making sure that the verb *be* in your definition is always followed by a noun.

INCORRECT	The university Web site says that a nontraditional student **is when** you live off campus, commute from home, have children, are a veteran, and are over the age of twenty-five.
CORRECT	The university Web site says that a nontraditional student is **someone** who lives off campus, commutes from home, has children, is a veteran, and is over the age of twenty-five.

⊙ EXERCISE 12.3

The following essay, "They're Not Role Models" by Raina Kelley, includes the basic elements of a definition argument. Read the essay, and then answer the questions that follow it, consulting the outline on page 402 if necessary.

This essay was published in *Newsweek* on March 11, 2010.

THEY'RE NOT ROLE MODELS
RAINA KELLEY

Ben Roethlisberger is making controversial headlines again. So is Allen Iverson. The sports page has more scandal than *People* magazine. But so what? I have never in my life heard a grownup say his role model was an athlete. I've heard people pick Warren Buffett a bunch of times and Mandela, of course. When I ran with a more pretentious crowd, Bob Dylan and Holden Caulfield   1 were once offered up, but never Joe Namath or Magic Johnson. And you know why? Because any adult with a social IQ greater than a 10-year-old knows that athletes are hothouse flowers—worshiped, but isolated, from cradle to grave for their talent with a ball. In an interview with *Nerve.com*, Steven Ortiz, a sociology professor at Oregon State and the author of several published studies on athletes' bad behavior, explained:

> Spoiled-athlete syndrome begins early in sports socialization. From the time they could be picked out of a lineup because of their exceptional athletic ability, they've been pampered and catered to by coaches, classmates, teammates, family members and partners. As they get older, this becomes a pattern. Because they're spoiled, they feel they aren't accountable for their behaviors off the field. They're so used to people looking the other way.

But our sports-crazed society knew this long before Tiger became a wolf. Despite all the adulation and money they get, few professional athletes get elected to political office and fewer still inspire national holidays or granite monuments. I love the Dallas Cowboys but I wouldn't let them date my friends. A fan's love is intense but ultimately self-serving— we love athletes who win. But we're not loony enough to give them any real power after they retire. Why then do so many columnists waste time complaining that athletes aren't good role models? Who's asking for that? 2

> "I love the Dallas Cowboys but I wouldn't let them date my friends."

Sure, kids look up to sports heroes but that's because children can't help but conflate an athlete's behavior on the field with all the hagiography their sponsors offer. When allegations of Woods's cheating first became public, CNN reported that "A golfing phenomenon almost from the cradle, he inspired countless young people with his multicultural background and effortless athleticism. Nike, one of his major sponsors, seized on the theme for a commercial in which children of various ages and races uttered the phrase 'I'm Tiger Woods.'" But only a child would believe that Nike loves Tiger for his multicultural background. Nike loves him because he wins. 3

If sportswriters really wanted to do their readers a service, they would stop nagging the athletes to live up to childrens' expectations and start encouraging us fans to grow some scruples. Because that's what the big sports sponsors like Nike understand about our love of athletes that the media doesn't—a good image is better than a bad one, but it's talent that sells sneakers. Of course there are exceptions, O. J. Simpson being the most famous. But for the most part, fans will condone the criminal exploits of an athlete as long as he continues to perform on the field. As Stanley Teitelbaum, author of *Sports Heroes, Fallen Idols*, told *USA Today* in explaining why Tiger's reputation will heal, "We the fans have created that kind of climate. . . . It's what I call 'hero hunger.' It makes 4 people feel better about themselves if they latch onto a hero who does well." Which means we don't really care when athletes screw up—unless, that is, they screw up with the ball in their hands. Remember when all the pundits said fans would never accept Michael Vick back into the NFL after he served time in prison for running a dog-fighting ring? They did. I suspect Tiger will be greeted with open arms (platonic, of course) upon his return to golf despite the world wide web's consensus that's he's a cheating, lying creep with questionable taste in women. Indeed, stories bemoaning his absence (for the good of the game) are already popping up.

This is the kind of thing sportswriters should be chastising us for—I want   5
to be told there wouldn't be so many convicted felons in the NFL if the fans didn't write off all their bad behavior as a cost of winning. We know we're captive to a group of prima donnas who know they can get away with almost murder just because they can hit a 90 mph fastball out of the park. Not even diehard groupies confuse an athlete's statistics with the content of his character, but you need to remind us from time to time that such moral relativism isn't a good thing. Please, I'd forgive Tony Romo for mugging my mother if the Cowboys won the Super Bowl, but that doesn't make it right. What if one day we become unable to tell the difference between cosseting divas and suborning felons? And if Ben Roethlisberger has done even 20 percent of what he's been accused of doing, that day has already come.

Sports journalists should make it their mission to show sports fans our   6
part in all this. The average nonfan is appalled by the alleged exploits of athletes like Ben Roethlisberger or Tiger Woods. But aside from Bryant Gumbel and his team over at HBO Sports, you don't hear much from ESPN or *Sports Illustrated* about the dark side of this national obsession. More of them need to do just as Christopher Hitchens did here at *Newsweek* when he wrote, in a piece about the Olympics, "Whether it's the exacerbation of national rivalries that you want—as in Africa this year—or the exhibition of the most depressing traits of the human personality (guns in locker rooms, golf clubs wielded in the home, dogs maimed and tortured at stars' homes to make them fight, dope and steroids everywhere), you need only look to the wide world of sports for the most rank and vivid examples." So if we really want to create role models for our kids, why not start with ourselves? Because only children confuse sports stars with humanitarians; the rest of us know better.

Identifying the Elements of a Definition Argument

1. In your own words, summarize this essay's thesis.

2. Kelley does not include a formal definition of *role model*. Should she have? Where in the essay would you add such a definition?

3. According to Kelley, why are athletes not role models? What examples does she include to support this position? Do you think all these examples are effective? What additional examples could she have included?

4. Where does Kelley introduce possible objections to her idea of *role model*? Does she refute these objections convincingly? If not, how should she have addressed them?

5. Throughout her essay, Kelley discusses sports figures who are not role models. What does she accomplish with this strategy?

6. Following the template below, write your own one-sentence definition of *role model*.

   A *role model* is a _____ who _____

   _____

   _____.

7. Do you think this essay would be stronger if it included a picture such as the one below? Explain.

Ben Roethlisberger, a quarterback for the Pittsburgh Steelers, was involved in various scandals throughout his career.

⊘ EXERCISE 12.4

According to former First Lady Eleanor Roosevelt, "We gain strength, and courage, and confidence by each experience in which we really stop to look fear in the face. . . . We must do that which we think we cannot." Each of the two pictures on the facing page presents a visual definition of *courage*. Study the pictures, and then write a paragraph in which you argue that they are (or are not) consistent with Roosevelt's concept of courage.

Firefighters at Ground Zero after the World Trade Center terrorist attacks on September 11, 2001, in New York City

The Tuskegee Airmen, a group of African-American men who overcame tremendous odds to become U.S. Army pilots during World War II

Is *Wikipedia* a Legitimate Research Source?

Go back to page 397 and reread the At Issue box, which gives some background on the question of whether *Wikipedia* is a legitimate research source. As the following sources illustrate, this question suggests a variety of possible responses.

As you read the sources that follow, you will be asked to answer some questions and to complete some simple activities. This work will help you understand both the content and the structure of the sources. When you are finished, you will be ready to write a **definition argument** on the topic, "Is *Wikipedia* a Legitimate Research Source?"

SOURCES

 Timothy Messer-Kruse, "The 'Undue Weight' of Truth on *Wikipedia*," p. 411

 John Seigenthaler, "A False *Wikipedia* Biography," p. 414

 Randall Stross, "Anonymous Source Is Not the Same as Open Source," p. 417

 Wikipedia, "*Wikipedia*: About," p. 421; *Internet Encyclopedia of Philosophy*," About the *IEP*," p. 422

 Neil Waters, "Wikiphobia: The Latest in Open Source," p. 425

 The Stanford Daily, "*Wikipedia* with Caution," p. 428

 Wikipedia, "Revision History of 'Global Warming'," p. 430

 Wikipedia, "Global Warming (Differences between Two Revisions)," p. 433

 For comprehension quizzes,
see bedfordstmartins.com/practicalargument.

This essay was published on February 12, 2012, in the *Chronicle Review.*

THE "UNDUE WEIGHT" OF TRUTH ON *WIKIPEDIA*

TIMOTHY MESSER-KRUSE

For the past 10 years I've immersed myself in the details of one of the most famous events in American labor history, the Haymarket riot and trial of 1886. Along the way I've written two books and a couple of articles about the episode. In some circles that affords me a presumption of expertise on the subject. Not, however, on *Wikipedia.*

The bomb thrown during an anarchist rally in Chicago sparked America's first Red Scare, a high-profile show trial, and a worldwide clemency movement for the seven condemned men. Today the martyrs' graves are a national historic site, the location of the bombing is marked by a public sculpture, and the event is recounted in most American history textbooks. Its *Wikipedia* entry is detailed and elaborate.

A couple of years ago, on a slow day at the office, I decided to experiment with editing one particularly misleading assertion chiseled into the *Wikipedia* article. The description of the trial stated, "The prosecution, led by Julius Grinnell, did not offer evidence connecting any of the defendants with the bombing. . . ."

Coincidentally, that is the claim that initially hooked me on the topic. In 2001 I was teaching a labor-history course, and our textbook contained nearly the same wording that appeared on *Wikipedia.* One of my students raised her hand: "If the trial went on for six weeks and no evidence was presented, what did they talk about all those days?" I've been working to answer her question ever since.

I have not resolved all the mysteries that surround the bombing, but I have dug deeply enough to be sure that the claim that the trial was bereft of evidence is flatly wrong. One hundred and eighteen witnesses were called to testify, many of them unindicted coconspirators who detailed secret meetings where plans to attack police stations were mapped out, coded messages were placed in radical newspapers, and bombs were assembled in one of the defendants' rooms.

In what was one of the first uses of forensic chemistry in an American courtroom, the city's foremost chemists showed that the metallurgical profile of a bomb found in one of the anarchists' homes was unlike any commercial metal but was similar in composition to a piece of shrapnel cut from the body of a slain police officer. So overwhelming was the evidence against one of the defendants that his lawyers even admitted that their client spent the afternoon before the Haymarket rally building bombs, arguing that he was acting in self-defense.

So I removed the line about there being "no evidence" and provided a full explanation in *Wikipedia*'s behind-the-scenes editing log. Within minutes my changes were reversed. The explanation: "You must provide reliable sources for your assertions to make changes along these lines to the article."

That was curious, as I had cited the documents that proved my point, 8 including verbatim testimony from the trial published online by the Library of Congress. I also noted one of my own peer-reviewed articles. One of the people who had assumed the role of keeper of this bit of history for *Wikipedia* quoted the Web site's "undue weight" policy, which states that "articles should not give minority views as much or as detailed a description as more popular views." He then scolded me. "You should not delete information supported by the majority of sources to replace it with a minority view."

> "'You should not delete information supported by the majority of sources to replace it with a minority view.'"

The "undue weight" policy posed a problem. Scholars have been publish- 9 ing the same ideas about the Haymarket case for more than a century. The last published bibliography of titles on the subject has 1,530 entries.

"Explain to me, then, how a 'minority' source with facts on its side would 10 ever appear against a wrong 'majority' one?" I asked the Wiki-gatekeeper. He responded, "You're more than welcome to discuss reliable sources here, that's what the talk page is for. However, you might want to have a quick look at *Wikipedia*'s civility policy."

I tried to edit the page again. Within 10 seconds I was informed that my 11 citations to the primary documents were insufficient, as *Wikipedia* requires its contributors to rely on secondary sources, or, as my critic informed me, "published books." Another editor cheerfully tutored me in what this means: "*Wikipedia* is not 'truth,' *Wikipedia* is 'verifiability' of reliable sources. Hence, if most secondary sources which are taken as reliable happen to repeat a flawed account or description of something, *Wikipedia* will echo that."

Tempted to win simply through sheer tenacity, I edited the page again. My 12 triumph was even more fleeting than before. Within seconds the page was changed back. The reason: "reverting possible vandalism." Fearing that I would forever have to wear the scarlet letter of *Wikipedia* vandal, I relented but noted with some consolation that in the wake of my protest, the editors made a slight gesture of reconciliation—they added the word "credible" so that it now read, "The prosecution, led by Julius Grinnell, did not offer credible evidence connecting any of the defendants with the bombing. . . ." Though that was still inaccurate, I decided not to attempt to correct the entry again until I could clear the hurdles my anonymous interlocutors had set before me.

So I waited two years, until my book on the trial was published. "Now, at 13 last, I have a proper *Wikipedia* leg to stand on," I thought as I opened the page and found at least a dozen statements that were factual errors, including some that contradicted their own cited sources. I found myself hesitant to write, eerily aware that the self-deputized protectors of the page were reading over my shoulder, itching to revert my edits and tutor me in Wiki-decorum. I made a small edit, testing the waters.

My improvement lasted five minutes before a Wiki-cop scolded me, "I 14
hope you will familiarize yourself with some of *Wikipedia*'s policies, such as
verifiability and undue weight. If all historians save one say that the sky was
green in 1888, our policies require that we write 'Most historians write that the
sky was green, but one says the sky was blue.' . . . As individual editors, we're not
in the business of weighing claims, just reporting what reliable sources write."

I guess this gives me a glimmer of hope that someday, perhaps before 15
another century goes by, enough of my fellow scholars will adopt my views
that I can change that *Wikipedia* entry. Until then I will have to continue to
shout that the sky was blue.

⊘AT ISSUE: SOURCES FOR DEVELOPING A DEFINITION ARGUMENT

1. Throughout most of his essay, Messer-Kruse makes an appeal to
   ethos. What is this appeal? How does it strengthen his argument?

2. What misconception in the "Haymarket Affair" entry did Messer-
   Kruse try to correct? What changes did he make? What documents
   did he cite to support these changes?

3. What is *Wikipedia*'s "undue weight" policy? How did this policy
   cause the *Wikipedia* gatekeeper to reject Messer-Kruse's changes?
   What did the editor mean when he said, "*Wikipedia* is not 'truth,'
   Wikipedia is 'verifiability' of reliable sources" (para. 11)?

4. Do you think that Messer-Kruse's complaints about *Wikipedia* have
   merit, or do you think that the *Wikipedia* editors were right to reject
   his changes? Explain.

5. In a response to Messer-Kruse's article, one person posted the following:

   > On the Internet, no one knows that your [*sic*] a professor. If you're
   > used to deferential treatment, at your home institution, you'll be
   > treated like anyone else in the Wide Open Internet. This skepticism
   > is a good thing—after all, some prankster could easily create an
   > account using your name and pretend to be you.

   Do you think this statement points out *Wikipedia*'s strengths or its
   weaknesses? Explain.

6. How do you think Randall Stross (p. 417) would respond to Messer-
   Kruse's essay?

USA Today published this article on November 29, 2005.

A FALSE *WIKIPEDIA* BIOGRAPHY

JOHN SEIGENTHALER

> John Seigenthaler Sr. was the assistant to Attorney General Robert Kennedy in the early 1960s. For a brief time, he was thought to have been directly involved in the Kennedy assassinations of both John and his brother Bobby. Nothing was ever proven.
>
> —WIKIPEDIA

1   This is a highly personal story about Internet character assassination. It could be your story.

2   I have no idea whose sick mind conceived the false, malicious "biography" that appeared under my name for 132 days on *Wikipedia*, the popular, online, free encyclopedia whose authors are unknown and virtually untraceable. There was more:

> "Nothing was ever proven."

3   "John Seigenthaler moved to the Soviet Union in 1971, and returned to the United States in 1984," *Wikipedia* said. "He started one of the country's largest public relations firms shortly thereafter."

4   At age 78, I thought I was beyond surprise or hurt at anything negative said about me. I was wrong. One sentence in the biography was true. I was Robert Kennedy's administrative assistant in the early 1960s. I also was his pallbearer. It was mind-boggling when my son, John Seigenthaler, journalist with NBC News, phoned later to say he found the same scurrilous text on Reference.com and Answers.com.

5   I had heard for weeks from teachers, journalists, and historians about "the wonderful world of *Wikipedia*," where millions of people worldwide visit daily for quick reference "facts," composed and posted by people with no special expertise or knowledge—and sometimes by people with malice.

6   At my request, executives of the three websites now have removed the false content about me. But they don't know, and can't find out, who wrote the toxic sentences.

Anonymous Author

7   I phoned Jimmy Wales, *Wikipedia*'s founder, and asked, "Do you . . . have any way to know who wrote that?"

8   "No, we don't," he said. Representatives of the other two websites said their computers are programmed to copy data verbatim from *Wikipedia*, never checking whether it is false or factual.

Naturally, I want to unmask my "biographer." And, I am interested in letting 9 many people know that *Wikipedia* is a flawed and irresponsible research tool.

But searching cyberspace for the identity of people who post spurious 10 information can be frustrating. I found on *Wikipedia* the registered IP (Internet Protocol) number of my "biographer"—65-81-97-208. I traced it to a customer of BellSouth Internet. That company advertises a phone number to report "Abuse Issues." An electronic voice said all complaints must be e-mailed. My two-e-mails were answered by identical form letters, advising me that the company would conduct an investigation but might not tell me the results. It was signed "Abuse Team."

Wales, *Wikipedia*'s founder, told me that BellSouth would not be helpful. 11 "We have trouble with people posting abusive things over and over and over," he said. "We block their IP numbers, and they sneak in another way. So we contact the service providers, and they are not very responsive."

After three weeks, hearing nothing further about the Abuse Team investi- 12 gation, I phoned BellSouth's Atlanta corporate headquarters, which led to conversations between my lawyer and BellSouth's counsel. My only remote chance of getting the name, I learned, was to file a "John or Jane Doe" lawsuit against my "biographer." Major communications Internet companies are bound by federal privacy laws that protect the identity of their customers, even those who defame online. Only if a lawsuit resulted in a court subpoena would BellSouth give up the name.

Little Legal Recourse

Federal law also protects online corporations—BellSouth, AOL, MCI, 13 *Wikipedia*, etc.—from libel lawsuits. Section 230 of the Communications Decency Act, passed in 1996, specifically states that "no provider or user of an interactive computer service shall be treated as the publisher or speaker." That legalese means that, unlike print and broadcast companies, online service providers cannot be sued for disseminating defamatory attacks on citizens posted by others.

Recent low-profile court decisions document that Congress effectively has 14 barred defamation in cyberspace. *Wikipedia*'s website acknowledges that it is not responsible for inaccurate information, but Wales, in a recent C-Span interview with Brian Lamb, insisted that his website is accountable and that his community of thousands of volunteer editors (he said he has only one paid employee) corrects mistakes within minutes.

My experience refutes that. My "biography" was posted May 26. On 15 May 29, one of Wales' volunteers "edited" it only by correcting the misspelling of the word "early." For four months, *Wikipedia* depicted me as a suspected assassin before Wales erased it from his website's history Oct. 5. The falsehoods remained on *Answers.com* and *Reference.com* for three more weeks.

In the C-Span interview, Wales said *Wikipedia* has "millions" of daily 16 global visitors and is one of the world's busiest websites. His volunteer community runs the *Wikipedia* operation, he said. He funds his website through a non-profit foundation and estimated a 2006 budget of "about a million dollars."

And so we live in a universe of new media with phenomenal opportunities   17
for worldwide communications and research—but populated by volunteer vandals with poison-pen intellects. Congress has enabled them and protects them.

When I was a child, my mother lectured me on the evils of "gossip." She   18
held a feather pillow and said, "If I tear this open, the feathers will fly to the four winds, and I could never get them back in the pillow. That's how it is when you spread mean things about people."

For me, that pillow is a metaphor for *Wikipedia*.   19

● AT ISSUE: SOURCES FOR DEVELOPING A DEFINITION ARGUMENT

1. What specific points in the biographical sketch does Seigenthaler find objectionable?

2. What steps did Seigenthaler take to "unmask" his biographer?

3. Even though much of this article tells a story, it also makes a point. What point about *Wikipedia* does Seigenthaler want to make? How is his point similar to or different from the one Timothy Messer-Kruse makes (p. 411)?

4. What opposing arguments does Seigenthaler address? Are there other opposing arguments that he should have included?

5. Do you think this article is an argument? Why or why not?

6. At the end of the article, Seigenthaler tells a story about his mother. Why? What does he mean by "That pillow is a metaphor for *Wikipedia*"?

The *New York Times* published this essay on March 12, 2006.

ANONYMOUS SOURCE IS NOT THE SAME AS OPEN SOURCE

RANDALL STROSS

Wikipedia, the free online encyclopedia, currently serves up the following: Five billion pages a month. More than 120 languages. In excess of one million English-language articles. And a single nagging epistemological° question: Can an article be judged as credible without knowing its author?

Concerning the nature of knowledge

Wikipedia says yes, but I am unconvinced.

Dispensing with experts, the Wikipedians invite anyone to pitch in, writing an article or editing someone else's. No expertise is required, nor even a name. Sound inviting? You can start immediately. The system rests upon the belief that a collectivity of unknown but enthusiastic individuals, by dint of sheer mass rather than possession of conventional credentials,° can serve in the supervisory role of editor. Anyone with an interest in a topic can root out inaccuracies and add new material.

Qualifications such as a degree in a field

At first glance, this sounds straightforward. But disagreements arise all the time about what is a problematic passage or an encyclopedia-worthy topic, or even whether a putative correction improves or detracts from the original version.

The egalitarian nature of a system that accords equal votes to everyone in the "community"—middle-school student and Nobel laureate alike—has difficulty resolving intellectual disagreements.

Wikipedia's reputation and internal editorial process would benefit by having a single authority vouch for the quality of a given article. In the jargon of library and information science, lay readers rely upon "secondary epistemic criteria," clues to the credibility of information when they do not have the expertise to judge the content.

Once upon a time, *Encyclopaedia Britannica* recruited Einstein, Freud, Curie, Mencken, and even Houdini as contributors. The names helped the encyclopedia bolster its credibility. *Wikipedia*, by contrast, provides almost no clues for the typical article by which reliability can be appraised. A list of edits provides only screen names or, in the case of the anonymous editors, numerical Internet Protocol addresses. Wasn't yesterday's practice of attaching "Albert Einstein" to an article on "Space-Time" a bit more helpful than today's "71.240.205.101"?

> "What does *Wikipedia*'s system offer in place of an expert authority?"

What does *Wikipedia*'s system offer in place of an expert authority willing to place his or her professional reputation on the line with a signature attached to an article?

When I asked Jimmy Wales, the founder of *Wikipedia*, last week, he 9 discounted the importance of individual contributors to *Britannica*. "When people trust an article in *Britannica*," he said, "it's not who wrote it, it's the process." There, a few editors review a piece and then editing ceases. By contrast, *Wikipedia* is built with unending scrutiny and ceaseless editing.

He predicts that in the future, it will be *Britannica*'s process that will 10 seem strange: "People will say, 'This was written by one person? Then looked at by only two or three other people? How can I trust that process?'"

The Wikipedian hive is capable of impressive feats. The English-language 11 collection recently added its millionth article, for example. It was about the Jordanhill railway station, in Glasgow. The original version, a few paragraphs, appeared to say all that a lay reader would ever wish to know about it. But the hive descended and in a week, more than 640 edits were logged.

If every topic could be addressed like this, without recourse to specialized 12 learning—and without the heated disputes called flame wars—the anonymous hive could be trusted to produce work of high quality. But the Jordanhill station is an exception.

Biographical entries, for example, are often accompanied by controversy. 13 Several recent events have shown how anyone can tamper with someone else's entry. Congressional staff members have been unmasked burnishing articles about their employers and vandalizing those of political rivals. (Sample addition: "He likes to beat his wife and children.")

Mr. Wales himself ignored the encyclopedia's guidelines about "Dealing 14 with Articles about Yourself" and altered his own *Wikipedia* biography; when other editors undid them, he reapplied his changes. The incidents, even if few in number, do not help *Wikipedia* establish the legitimacy of a process that is reluctant to say no to anyone.

It should be noted that Mr. Wales is a full-time volunteer, and that neither 15 he nor the thousands of fellow volunteer editors has a pecuniary interest in this nonprofit project. He also deserves accolades for keeping *Wikipedia* operating without the intrusion of advertising, at least so far.

Most winningly, he has overseen a system that is gleefully candid in its 16 public self-examination. If you're seeking a well-organized list of criticisms of *Wikipedia*, you won't find a better place than *Wikipedia*'s coverage of itself. *Wikipedia* also provides a taxonomy of no fewer than 23 different forms of vandalism that strike it.

It is easy to forget how quickly *Wikipedia* has grown; it began only in 2001. 17 With the passage of a little more time, Mr. Wales and his associates may come around to the idea that identifying one person as a given article's supervising editor would enhance the encyclopedia's reputation.

Mr. Wales has already responded to recent negative articles about 18 vandalism at the site with announcements of modest reforms. Anonymous visitors are no longer permitted to create pages, though they still may edit existing ones.

To curb what Mr. Wales calls "drive-by pranks" that are concentrated on   19
particular articles, he has instituted a policy of "semi-protection." In these
cases, a user must have registered at least four days before being permitted to
make changes to the protected article. "If someone really wants to write
'George Bush is a poopy head,' you've got to wait four days," he said.

When asked what problems on the site he viewed as most pressing,   20
Mr. Wales said he was concerned with passing along the Wikipedian culture to
newcomers. He sounded wistful when he spoke of the days not so long ago
when he could visit an article that was the subject of a flame war and would
know at least some participants—and whether they could resolve the dispute
tactfully.

As the project has grown, he has found that he no longer necessarily   21
knows anyone in a group. When a dispute flared recently over an article related
to a new dog breed, he looked at the discussion and asked himself in frustration, "Who are these people?"

Isn't this precisely the question all users are bound to ask about contributors?   22

By wide agreement, the print encyclopedia in the English world reached   23
its apogee in 1911, with the completion of *Encyclopaedia Britannica*'s 11th edition. (For the fullest tribute, turn to *Wikipedia*.) But the *Wikipedia* experiment
need not be pushed back in time toward that model. It need only be pushed
forward, so it can catch up to others with more experience in online collaboration: the open-source software movement.

Wikipedia and open-source projects like Linux are similarly noncommer-   24
cial, intellectual enterprises, mobilizing volunteers who will probably never
meet one another in person. But even though Wikipedians like to position
their project under the open-source umbrella, the differences are wide.

Jeff Bates, a vice president of the Open Source Technology Group who   25
oversees SourceForge.net, the host of more than 80,000 active open-source
projects, said, "It makes me grind my teeth to hear *Wikipedia* compared to
open source." In every open-source project, he said, there is "a benevolent dic-
tator" who ultimately takes responsibility, even though the code is contributed
by many. Good stuff results only if "someone puts their name on it."

Wikipedia has good stuff, too. These have been designated "featured arti-   26
cles." But it will be a long while before all one-million-and-counting entries
have been carefully double-checked and buffed to a high shine. Only 923 have
been granted "featured" status, and the consensus-building process is presently
capable of adding only about one a day.

Mr. Wales is not happy with this pace and seems open to looking again at   27
the open-source software model for ideas. Software development that relies on
scattered volunteers is a two-step process: first, a liberal policy encourages the
contributions of many, then a restrictive policy follows to stabilize the code in
preparation for release. *Wikipedia*, he said, has "half the model."

There's no question that *Wikipedia* volunteers can address many more   28
topics than the lumbering, for-profit incumbents like *Britannica* and *World
Book*, and can update entries swiftly. Still, anonymity blocks credibility. One

thing that Wikipedians have exactly right is that the current form of the encyclopedia is a beta test. The quality level that would permit speaking of Version 1.0 is still in the future.

◗ AT ISSUE: SOURCES FOR DEVELOPING A DEFINITION ARGUMENT

1. In paragraph 3, Stross presents the *Wikipedia* philosophy. In your own words, summarize this philosophy.

2. At what points in his essay does Stross refute the *Wikipedia* philosophy? What aspects of this philosophy does he seem to disagree with most?

3. Do you think Stross should have provided formal definitions of the terms *anonymous source* and *open source*? Why or why not?

4. Where in the essay does Stross acknowledge *Wikipedia*'s strengths? Do you think that the encyclopedia's strengths outweigh its weaknesses? Explain.

5. Do you agree with Jimmy Wales, founder of *Wikipedia*, that in the future, *Britannica*'s process "will seem strange" (para. 10)? Why or why not?

6. What does Stross mean when he says, "Version 1.0 is still in the future" (28)?

WIKIPEDIA: ABOUT

WIKIPEDIA

From *Wikipedia*, the free encyclopedia ₁

A general introduction for visitors to *Wikipedia*. The project also has an ₂ encyclopedia article about itself, *Wikipedia*, and some introductions for aspiring contributors.

For *Wikipedia*'s formal organi- ₃ zational structure, see *Wikipedia*: Formal organization.

Wikipedia (◄ⁱ/ˌwɪkɨˈpiːdi.ə/ or ₄ ◄ⁱ/ˌwɪkiˈpiːdi.ə/ *WIK-i-PEE-dee-ə*) is a multilingual, web-based, free-content encyclopedia project based on an openly editable model. The name *Wikipedia* is a portmanteau of the words *wiki* (a technology for creating collaborative websites, from the Hawaiian word *wiki*, meaning "quick") and *encyclopedia*. *Wikipedia*'s articles provide links to guide the user to related pages with additional information.

> ## English *Wikipedia* right now
>
> *Wikipedia* is running MediaWiki version 1.18wmf1 (r109351).
>
> It has 3,859,117 content articles, and 26,106,710 pages in total.
>
> There have been 513,565,315 edits.
>
> There are 797,211 uploaded files.
>
> There are 16,163,858 registered users, including
>
> 1,507 administrators.
>
> This information is correct as of 18:50, 30 January 2012 (UTC).

Wikipedia is written collaboratively by largely anonymous Internet volun- ₅ teers who write without pay. Anyone with Internet access can write and make changes to *Wikipedia* articles (except in certain cases where editing is restricted to prevent disruption or vandalism). Users can contribute anonymously, under a pseudonym, or with their real identity, if they choose.

The fundamental principles by which *Wikipedia* operates are the five pil- ₆ lars. The *Wikipedia* community has developed many policies and guidelines to improve the encyclopedia; however, it is not a formal requirement to be familiar with them before contributing.

Since its creation in 2001, *Wikipedia* has grown rapidly into one of the ₇ largest reference websites, attracting 400 million unique visitors monthly as of March 2011 according to ComScore. There are more than 82,000 active contributors (http://en.wikipedia.org/wikistats/EN/TablesWikipediansEditsGt5 .htm) working on more than 19,000,000 articles in more than 270 languages. As of today, there are 3,859,117 articles in English. Every day, hundreds of thousands of visitors from around the world collectively make tens of thousands of edits and create thousands of new articles to augment the knowledge held by the *Wikipedia* encyclopedia. (See also *Wikipedia*: Statistics.)

People of all ages, cultures, and backgrounds can add or edit article 8 prose, references, images, and other media here. What is contributed is more important than the expertise or qualifications of the contributor. What will remain depends upon whether it fits within *Wikipedia*'s policies, including being verifiable against a published reliable source, so excluding editors' opinions and beliefs and unreviewed research, and is free of copyright restrictions and contentious material about living people. Contributions cannot damage *Wikipedia* because the software allows easy reversal of mistakes and many experienced editors are watching to help ensure that edits are cumulative improvements. Begin by simply clicking the *edit* link at the top of any editable page!

Wikipedia is a live collaboration differing from paper-based reference 9 sources in important ways. Unlike printed encyclopedias, *Wikipedia* is continually created and updated, with articles on historic events appearing within minutes, rather than months or years. Older articles tend to grow more comprehensive and balanced; newer articles may contain misinformation, unencyclopedic content, or vandalism. Awareness of this aids obtaining valid information and avoiding recently added misinformation (see Researching with *Wikipedia*).

This Web page was accessed on April 24, 2012.

ABOUT THE *IEP*

INTERNET ENCYCLOPEDIA OF PHILOSOPHY

The *Internet Encyclopedia of Philosophy* (*IEP*) (ISSN 2161-0002) was founded 1 in 1995 as a non-profit organization to provide open access to detailed, scholarly information on key topics and philosophers in all areas of philosophy. The *Encyclopedia* receives no funding, and operates through the volunteer work of the editors, which consists of editors, authors, volunteers, and technical advisers. At present the *IEP* is visited by over 500,000 persons per month.

Most of the articles in the *IEP* are original contributions by specialized 2 philosophers; these are identifiable by the author's name at the foot of the article. Others are temporary, or "proto articles," and have largely been adapted from older sources. They are identifiable by the inclusion of the initials "*IEP*" at the close and will in time be replaced by original articles.

Statement of Purpose

The purpose of the *IEP* is to provide detailed, scholarly information on key
topics and philosophers in all areas of philosophy. The *Encyclopedia* is free of
charge and available to all users of the Internet world-wide. The present staff
of 25 editors and approximately
300 authors hold doctorate degrees
and are professors at colleges and
universities around the world, most
notably from the United States,
Great Britain, and Australia. The
submission and review process of
articles is the same as that with
printed philosophy journals, books, and reference works. The authors are specialists in the areas in which they write and are frequently leading authorities.
Submissions are peer reviewed by specialists according to strict criteria.

> "The purpose of the *IEP*
> is to provide detailed,
> scholarly information on
> key topics and philosophers
> in all areas of philosophy."

3

Scholarly Standards

Our peer review process is rigorous and meets high academic standards.
Authors submit their articles to a specific *IEP* area editor, who reads through
the article and makes an initial judgment about its overall quality. Many submissions are rejected at this stage. The area editor then sends the promising
submission to qualified referees. Usually there are two referees per article. The
area editor evaluates the reviews from the referees, makes a decision whether to
publish, and sends a recommendation to the author. Most submissions are then
revised, in either their form or substance. In some cases more rounds of revision are required, and we sometimes must reject entries because of inadequate
revision. More commonly, any problems with entries are fixed with revision—
as one might expect when well-qualified people are recruited to write entries.
This is a common pattern for scholarly journal articles and reference works.

4

Consequently, the quality of our articles is at the same level as that of the best
multi-volume encyclopedias of philosophy which appear in print. However, an
article published in our *Encyclopedia* surveys its field and so is not equivalent to a
journal article that advances the field. Nevertheless, it is also the case that journals
from time to time publish or commission review articles that do not necessarily
have this function and that *IEP* articles can be considered as comparable to such
review articles. For additional information, please contact the general editors.

5

Citing Entries

Here is a suggested way to cite our articles in your own writing:

6

"Naturalistic Epistemology," by Chase B. Wrenn, *The Internet Encyclopedia
of Philosophy*, ISSN 2161-0002, http://www.iep.utm.edu/, today's date.

As the *Encyclopedia* is regularly updated, we archive earlier versions for
our own records; earlier versions are publicly available at archive.org. Teachers

7

and scholars with special needs—such as authenticating quotations and detecting plagiarism—may be provided copies of an earlier version of an article upon request to the General Editor.

⊘ AT ISSUE: SOURCES FOR DEVELOPING A DEFINITION ARGUMENT

1. According to the "About" sections of these two online encyclopedias, how is *The Internet Encyclopedia of Philosophy* different from *Wikipedia*? Do you think both encyclopedias are aimed at the same audience?

2. Who is able to add to or edit *Wikipedia* articles? Who is able to make changes to *The Internet Encyclopedia of Philosophy*? Who is *not* able to make changes?

3. How do the editors of each online encyclopedia try to maintain the quality of their articles? Which encyclopedia do you think is more successful at doing this?

4. Both *Wikipedia* and *The Internet Encyclopedia of Philosophy* give users access to earlier versions of articles. Why do they do this? What can users gain by looking at these earlier versions?

5. In your opinion, which is the more reliable source, *The Internet Encyclopedia of Philosophy* or *Wikipedia*? Why?

This essay was published in the *Middlebury Campus*, the student weekly newspaper of Middlebury College, on April 11, 2007.

WIKIPHOBIA: THE LATEST IN OPEN SOURCE

NEIL WATERS

It seemed like a no-brainer. Several students in one of my classes included the same erroneous information in final examination essays. Google whisked me immediately to *Wikipedia*, where I found the source of the erroneous information in under a minute. To prevent recurrences of the problem, I wrote a policy for consideration by the history department, in less than two minutes:

> 1) Students are responsible for the accuracy of information they provide, and they cannot point to *Wikipedia* or any similar source that may appear in the future to escape the consequences of errors. 2) *Wikipedia* is not an acceptable citation, even though it may lead one to a citable source.

I brought up this modest policy proposal, suitably framed in whereases and be it resolved, at the next meeting of the department, and it was passed within about three minutes, and we moved on to more pressing business. And that, I thought, was that—a good six minutes' worth of work, culminating in clear guidelines for the future. Some colleagues felt I was belaboring the obvious, and they were right. The history department always has held students responsible for accuracy, and does not consider general encyclopedias of the bound variety to be acceptable for citation either. But *Wikipedia* seemed worth mentioning by name because it is omnipresent and because its "open-source" method of compilation makes it a different animal from, say, the *Encyclopedia Britannica*.

The *Campus* published an article on the departmental policy, and the rest, as they say, is history. Alerted by the online version of the *Campus* Tim Johnson of the *Burlington Free* Press interviewed me and a spokesman for *Wikipedia* who agreed with the history department's position, and published an article. Several college newspapers followed suit, and then Noam Cohen of the *New York Times* interviewed Don Wyatt, chair of the history department, and me, and published the story. Within a day it received more online "hits" than any other *New York Times* feature. Another interview followed with the *Asahi Shimbun* in Tokyo, and additional articles appeared in *El Pais* in Spain, the *Guardian* in England, and then in literally hundreds of newspapers in the U.S. and abroad. Along with other members of the history department, I found myself giving interviews almost daily—to radio stations, newspaper reporters, inquisitive high school students, WCAX television news in Burlington, and even to the *NBC Nightly News*, which sent correspondent Lisa Daniels to Middlebury to interview me and students in my History of Modern Japan class. A stream of phone calls and e-mails from a wide range of people, from *Wikipedia* disciples

1

2

3

to besieged librarians who felt free at last to express their *Wikipedia* misgivings, continues to the present. Somehow the modest policy adoption by the history department at Middlebury College hit a nerve.

Why this overwhelming spate of interest? I can think of three reasons 4 immediately: 1) Timing. *Wikipedia* has existed since 2001, but it has expanded exponentially, and reached a critical mass in the last couple of years. With over 1.6 million entries in its English language edition, *Wikipedia* has something to say about almost everything. Its popularity has soared with its comprehensiveness and ease of use, and its ease of use in turn has been enhanced by popularity-driven algorithms; Google lists a *Wikipedia* article in first or second place more often than not. 2) Passion. There is something exciting about the growth and development of an entity to which anyone can contribute.

At its best, *Wikipedia* works wonders. Anonymous editors actually improve 5 entries over time, including new material, editing away mistakes, polishing the writing. Accordingly, some of *Wikipedia*'s defenders approach their task with near-religious zeal. But *Wikipedia* at its worst excites similarly intense passions, because anonymous, non-accountable editors can include, through ignorance or malice, misinformation that may or may not get "fixed." Further, thousands of high school teachers as well as college professors who try mightily to induce a measure of critical thinking in their students' approach to sources for research grow quietly furious because the very ubiquity of *Wikipedia* tempts people to use it in lieu of other, more reliable sources of information. 3) Scandals. The *Wikipedia* entry for John Seigenthaler, Sr., in 2004 contained spurious accusations that he was a suspect in the assassinations of both John F. Kennedy and Robert Kennedy. The entry was unaltered for four months (thereafter authors of new entries, but not editors of existing entries, had to register their names with *Wikipedia*). A *Wikipedia* "policeman" turned out to have bogus credentials. Sinbad was declared dead (he has since risen again). All this keeps the pot boiling.

In the final analysis, *Wikipedia*'s greatest strength is also its greatest weakness. Anonymous, unaccountable, unpaid, often non-expert yet passionate editors built *Wikipedia*, but their anonymity and lack of accountability assures that *Wikipedia* cannot be considered an authoritative source. And yet it is frequently used as if it were, *Wikipedia*'s own disclaimers notwithstanding. College professors and high school teachers alike need to remember that the impressive computer acumen of their students does not automatically translate into impressive levels of critical thought, particularly when it comes to evaluating the reliability of the new tools at their disposal, and of the information those tools provide. The Internet has opened up new highways of information, but we need to know how to spot the potholes.

> "In the final analysis, *Wikipedia*'s greatest strength is also its greatest weakness." 6

⊜AT ISSUE: SOURCES FOR DEVELOPING
A DEFINITION ARGUMENT

1. In paragraph 1, Waters, who teaches at Middlebury, lists the two policies he proposed to the history department. Do you think these policies make sense? Are they fair? Explain.

2. Why do you think Waters's "modest policy proposal" (para. 2) attracted so much interest not only on campus but also around the world?

3. Do you think Waters oversimplifies the issue of using *Wikipedia* as a source? What additional points could he have discussed?

4. Where does Waters acknowledge the arguments in favor of using *Wikipedia* as a research source? How does he refute these arguments?

5. Summarize Waters's reasons for concluding that *Wikipedia* is not an acceptable research source. Does he convince you?

6. How do you suppose Waters would respond to "*Wikipedia* with Caution," an editorial in the *Stanford Daily* (p. 428)?

This editorial appeared in the *Stanford Daily* on March 8, 2007.

WIKIPEDIA WITH CAUTION

THE STANFORD DAILY

It is difficult not to love *Wikipedia*, the free online encyclopedia to which any- 1
one can contribute (www.wikipedia.org). With 1,674,086 articles in English
alone, it provides anyone with Internet access the ability to get fast, free information on anything from the New Orleans Mint (operational until 1909), to
the biography of Weird Al Yankovic (he started accordion lessons at age seven).

In February, the Department of History at Middlebury College forbade 2
students from citing *Wikipedia* as a source in history papers and tests, also giving notice that students would not be given any breaks for mistaken knowledge
they derived from the site.

The department's decision received national attention, including a 3
February 21 article in the *New York Times*, and much of the response has been
negative. One op-ed printed in the *Middlebury Campus*, the school newspaper,
likened the move to "censorship" and condemned the professors who advocated the ban.

We have a hard time understanding what all of the fuss is about. Middle- 4
bury's new rule is hardly censorship. Students are not prohibited from viewing,
discussing, or disseminating anything from *Wikipedia*. Rather, history students
have simply been officially told what should already be obvious: *Wikipedia*,
however useful, is not something that should be cited in a serious academic
context, and if it is used, it could reflect poorly on students' work.

Most university-level students should be able to discern between *Wiki-* 5
pedia and more reliable online sources like government databases and online
periodicals. To be fair, some of *Wikipedia*'s entries are specific enough to be
extremely valuable in studying or researching, but others are shallow, short,
and occasionally completely inaccurate. There are many Web sites that can
provide credible resources, but *Wikipedia* is not one of them, nor does it pur-
port to be. Jimmy Wales, one of the founders of *Wikipedia*, told the *Times* that
he does not even consider Middlebury's action "a negative thing."

Naturally, because it is a user-generated Web site, the articles are not 6
always perfect, and should not be relied on as much as actual class materials.
Wikipedia has even introduced a
citation function where contributors
can direct readers to other more
well-established sources.

> "The articles are not always perfect."

Yet even as we point out that college students ought to know better than to 7
rely completely on *Wikipedia*, Middlebury's ban seems a bit overzealous. Students are also supposed to use proper grammar and spelling in assignments,
but rather than having an official policy against poor writing, most schools
simply tell students what the standards are ahead of time.

It is the role of teachers to advise students what is acceptable; for some 8
assignments it is conceivable that referencing *Wikipedia* as an example, rather
than an authoritative source, might be useful. Instead of totally banning *Wiki-pedia* as an information source departmentally, history professors at Middle-bury should have stressed or continued to stress that using it could hurt an
individual's performance in the class. Much like spelling and grammar, if stu-dents already know what is expected in terms of citations, any deviation from
expectations will make grading easier for professors.

There was a point in time where all Internet sources were suspect for most 9
academic uses. Thankfully, that is no longer the case. Research has certainly
become easier and more accessible with online help, but some sites, like some
books, are better than others. We still love *Wikipedia* and admit that it can be
great for a quick definition or fact, but we won't be citing it in any papers any-time soon.

⊃ AT ISSUE: SOURCES FOR DEVELOPING A DEFINITION ARGUMENT

1. In paragraph 4, the editorial says that *Wikipedia* "is not something
   that should be cited in a serious academic context." Later, in para-graph 7, the editorial says, "Middlebury's ban seems a bit over-zealous." Do these two statements contradict each other? Explain.

2. Based on your reading of this editorial, write a one-paragraph
   definition of *acceptable source*.

3. In paragraph 8, the editorial makes a distinction between "referencing
   Wikipedia as an example" and citing it as "an authoritative source."
   What is this distinction? Do you think it is valid?

4. This editorial was written by students at a prestigious university.
   Do you think their position on the issue makes sense for all college
   students? For high school students? For scholars?

This Web page was accessed from *Wikipedia* on January 24, 2012.

REVISION HISTORY OF "GLOBAL WARMING"*

WIKIPEDIA

View logs for this page   1

(latest | earliest) View (newer 50 | older 50) (20 | 50 | 100 | 250 | 500)   2

Browse history From year (and earlier): From month (and earlier): Tag 3
filter: Deleted only

For any version listed below, click on its date to view it. For more help, see 4
Help:Page history and Help:Edit summary.

External tools: Revision history statistics · Revision history search · 5
Contributors · User edits · Number of watchers · Page view statistics (cur) =
difference from current version, (prev) = difference from preceding version, m = minor edit, → = section edit, ← = automatic edit summary

Compare selected versions   6

(cur | prev) 17:21, 26 January 2012 Nirvana2013 (talk | contribs) . . 7
(144,239 bytes) (+17) . . (→Related information: Add template)

(cur | prev) 22:10, 24 January 2012 NewsAndEventsGuy (talk | contribs) . . 8
(144,222 bytes) (-19) . . (Revert ambiguous temporal reference; See talk thread
on time)

(cur | prev) 22:08, 24 January 2012 NewsAndEventsGuy (talk | contribs) . . 9
(144,241 bytes) (-102) . . (revert redundancy; see WP:COPYEDIT)

(cur | prev) 19:51, 24 January 2012 Scott Illini (talk | contribs) . . (144,343 10
bytes) (+121) . . (adding back babies removed with bathwater, please see Talk
regarding choosing a date for "since when")

(cur | prev) 12:37, 24 January 2012 KimDabelsteinPetersen (talk | con- 11
tribs) (144,222 bytes) (Reverted to revision 472952964 by William M. Connolley: rv 1850 seems randomly picked. re:Academies - one ref is chosen != only
one ref exists. Nat. Geo? On this timescale? No!. using TW)

(cur | prev) 11:09, 24 January 2012 Scott Illini (talk | contribs) (144,389 12
bytes) (adding ref)

(cur | prev) 11:05, 24 January 2012 Scott Illini (talk | contribs) (144,314 13
bytes) (Undid revision 472952964 by William M. Connolley (talk) 1850
matches date used in "retreat of glaciers", refactor of geo context)

---

*By clicking on "(*cur*)" or "(*prev*)" next to each entry, you can see the current version of a
text or the previous version of the text before it was edited. By clicking on the "Compare
selected versions" button near the top of the page, you can view the changes in the context
of the article. Readers can access the revision history by clicking on the "View History" box
at the beginning of an article. This history gives readers a sense of how extensively revised
the article is.

(cur | prev) 09:43, 24 January 2012 William M. Connolley (talk | contribs) (144,222 bytes) (Undid revision 472948675 by Scott Illini (talk) thanks but No. LIA is ~wrong, interglacial is wonr/doesn't belong)

> "Undid revision 472948675 by Scott Illini (talk) thanks but No." [14]

(cur | prev) 08:58, 24 January 2012 Scott Illini (talk | contribs) (144,384 bytes) (several adds) [15]

(cur | prev) 16:24, 23 January 2012 William M. Connolley (talk | contribs) (144,222 bytes) (Undid revision 472807783 by Originalwana (talk) not in the lede, shirley?) [16]

(cur | prev) 14:53, 23 January 2012 Originalwana (talk | contribs) (144,430 bytes) (+vid) [17]

(cur | prev) 23:01, 19 January 2012 Dave souza (talk | contribs) (144,222 bytes) (Undid revision 472134759 by Dave souza (talk) oops, new file uploaded with same name) [18]

(cur | prev) 21:57, 19 January 2012 Dave souza (talk | contribs) (144,222 bytes) (Undid revision 472129107 by Simplex1swrhs (talk) not what it says on the tin) [19]

(cur | prev) 20:50, 19 January 2012 Clay (talk | contribs) (144,222 bytes) (replace dead links) [20]

(cur | prev) 20:51, 17 January 2012 J. Johnson (talk | contribs) m (144,266 bytes) (→ Climate models: minor correction) [21]

(cur | prev) 00:54, 17 January 2012 Srich32977 (talk | contribs) m (144,296 bytes) (spaced en dashes & hyphen fixes) [22]

(cur | prev) 16:36, 14 January 2012 Tpbradbury (talk | contribs) (144,336 bytes) (add dead link tags) [23]

(cur | prev) 14:51, 14 January 2012 Tpbradbury (talk | contribs) m (143,949 bytes) (clear refs) [24]

(cur | prev) 23:55, 10 January 2012 FrescoBot (talk | contribs) m (143,974 bytes) (Bot: link syntax/spacing) [25]

(cur | prev) 11:56, 10 January 2012 AnomieBOT (talk | contribs) m (143,974 bytes) (Dating maintenance tags: {{Clarify}}) [26]

(cur | prev) 11:35, 10 January 2012 Tpbradbury (talk | contribs) (143,956 bytes) (the term "4C world" is introduced without explanation and does not appear to ever be mentioned again in the article) [27]

(cur | prev) 11:14, 10 January 2012 Tpbradbury (talk | contribs) (143,844 bytes) (standardise US spelling) [28]

(cur | prev) 10:46, 10 January 2012 Tony Sidaway (talk | contribs) (143,923 bytes) (Is this in keeping with our usual policy on cats? Please discuss. Undid revision 470572795 by Alan Liefting (talk)) [29]

(cur | prev) 06:49, 10 January 2012 Alan Liefting (talk | contribs) (143,895 bytes) (removed Category:Climate change using HotCat) [30]

(cur | prev) 18:07, 8 January 2012 Ocdnctx (talk | contribs) (143,923 bytes) (→ See also: link wp art.: * Environmental impact of the coal industry) [31]

⮞ AT ISSUE: SOURCES FOR DEVELOPING A DEFINITION ARGUMENT

1. Above is an excerpt from a long list of revisions to a *Wikipedia* article on global warming. What information about the revision process do you learn from this excerpt?

2. How does the information on the revision-history pages affect your opinion of *Wikipedia*?

3. Why do you think the editors of *Wikipedia* make this kind of information available to readers?

This Web page was accessed from *Wikipedia* on January 30, 2012.

GLOBAL WARMING (DIFFERENCES BETWEEN TWO REVISIONS)

WIKIPEDIA

Revision as of 05:20, 30 January 2012 (view source)

Mann jess (talk | contribs)

(Reverted 1 edit by Scott Illini (talk): Stop edit warring please. (TW))

← Previous edit

Latest revision as of 06:13, 30 January 2012 (view source)

NewsAndEventsGuy (talk | contribs)

(Undid revision 473984594 by Mann jess (talk) He wasn't.... did you miss [Talk:Global_warming#Breakout_discussion_of_.27 projected_continuation.27 this grammar discussion]?)

Line 10:

|caption4=Fossil fuel related C02 emissions compared to five of IPCC's emissions scenarios. The dips are related to global recessions. Data from [http://www.ipcc.ch/ipccreports/sres/emission/data/aIlsc en.xls IPCC SRES scenarios]; [http://www.iea.org/co2highlights/co2High lights.XLS Data spreadsheet included with International Energy Agency's "CO2 Emissions from Fuel Combustion 2010 – Highlights"]; and [http://www.guardian.co.uk/environment/2011/may/29/carbon-emissions-nuclearpower Supplemental IEA data]. Image source: [[Skeptical Science]]}}

Line 10:

|caption4=Fossil fuel related CO2 emissions compared to five of IPCC's emissions scenarios. The dips are related to global recessions. Data from [http://www.ipcc.ch/ipccreports/sres/emission/data/allsc en.xls IPCC SRES scenarios]; [http://www.iea.org/co2highlights/co2Higlights.XLS Data spreadsheet included with International Energy Agency's "CO2 Emissions from Fuel Combustion 2010 – Highlights"]; and [http://www.guardian.co.uk/environment/2011/may/29/carbon-emissions-nuclearpower Supplemental IEA data]. Image source: [[Skeptical Science]]}}

"'Global warming'" refers to the **rising** [[Instrumental temperature record|average temperature]] of [[Earth]]'s atmosphere and oceans and its projected continuation. In the last 100 years, Earth's average surface temperature increased by about {{convert|0.8|C-change|F-change|1}} with about two thirds of the increase occurring over just the last three decades.<ref name= "Americas-ClimateChoices-2011-FullReport"/> Warming of the [[climate]] system is unequivocal, and scientists are more than 90% certain most of it is caused by increasing concentrations of [[greenhouse

"'Global warming'" refers to the **current rise in the** [[Instrumental temperature record|average temperature]] of [[Earth]]'s atmosphere and oceans and its projected continuation. In the last 100 years, Earth's average surface temperature increased by about {{convert|0.8|C-change |F-change|l}} with about two thirds of the increase occurring over just the last three decades.<ref name="AmericasClimateChoices-2011-FullReport"/> Warming of the [[climate]] system is unequivocal, and scientists are more than 90% certain most of it is caused by increasing

433

gas]]es produced by human activities such as [[deforestation]] and burning [[fossil fuel]]s. <ref>"Warming of the climate system is unequivocal, as is now evident from observations of increases in global average air and ocean temperatures, widespread melting of snow and ice and rising global average sea level." IPCC, [http://www.ipcc.ch/publications_and_data/ar4/syr/en/main.html Synthesis Report], [http://www.ipcc.ch/publications_and_data/ar4/syr/en/mainsl.html Section 1.1: Observations of climate change], in {{Harvnb|IPCC AR4 SYR|2007}}.</ref> <ref> "Three different approaches are used to describe uncertainties each with a distinct form of language. * * * Where uncertainty in specific outcomes is assessed using expert judgment and statistical analysis of a body of evidence (e.g. observations or model results), then the following likelihood ranges are used to express the assessed probability of occurrence: virtually certain >99%; extremely likely >95%; very likely >90%......" IPCC, [http://www.ipcc.ch/publications_and_data/ar4/syr/en/main.html Synthesis Report], [http://www.ipcc.ch/publications_and_data/ar4/syr/en/mainssyr-introduction.html Treatment of Uncertainty], in {{Harvnb|IPCC AR4 SYR|2007}}.</ref><ref>IPCC, [http://www.ipcc.ch/publications_and_data/ar4/syr/en/main.html Synthesis Report], [http://www.ipcc.ch/publications_and_data/ar4/syr/en/mains2-4.html Section 2.4: Attribution of climate change], in {{Harvnb|IPCC AR4 SYR|2007}}.</ref> <ref name="AmericasClimateChoices-2010-SciPanel"/> These findings are recognized by the national science academies of all the major industrialized countries.<ref name="SciAcademy Statement"/>{{Cref2|A}}

concentrations of [[greenhouse gas]]es produced by human activities such as [[deforestation]] and burning [[fossil fuel]]s. <ref>"Warming of the climate system is unequivocal, as is now evident from observations of increases in global average air and ocean temperatures, widespread melting of snow and ice and rising global average sea level." IPCC, [http://www.ipcc.ch/publications_and_data/ar4/syr/en/main.html Synthesis Report], [http://www.ipcc.ch/publications_and_data/ar4/syr/en/mains1.html Section 1.1: Observations of climate change], in {{Harvnb|IPCC AR4 SYR|2007}}.</ref> <ref> "Three different approaches are used to describe uncertainties each with a distinct form of language. * * * Where uncertainty in specific outcomes is assessed using expert judgment and statistical analysis of a body of evidence (e.g. observations or model results), then the following likelihood ranges are used to express the assessed probability of occurrence: virtually certain >99%; extremely likely >95%; very likely >90%......" IPCC, [http://www.ipcc.ch/publications_and_data/ar4/syr/en/main.html Synthesis Report], [http://www.ipcc.ch/publications_and_data/ar4/syr/en/mainssyr-introduction.html Treatment of Uncertainty], in {{Harvnb|IPCC AR4 SYR|2007}}.</ref> <ref>IPCC, [http://www.ipcc.ch/publications_and_data/ar4/syr/en/main.html Synthesis Report], [http://www.ipcc.ch/publications_and_data/ar4/syr/en/mains2-4.html Section 2.4: Attribution of climate change], in {{Harvnb|IPCC AR4 SYR|2007}}.</ref> <ref name="AmericasClimateChoices-2010-SciPanel"/> These findings are recognized by the national science academies of all the major industrialized countries.<refname="SciAcademy Statement"/>{{Cref2|A}}

[[Climate model]] projections are summarized in the 2007 [[IPCC Fourth Assessment Report|Fourth Assessment Report]] (AR4) by the [[Intergovernmental Panel on Climate Change]] (IPCC). They indicate that during the 21st century the global surface temperature is likely to rise a further {{convert|1.1|to|2.9|C-change|F-change|1}} for their lowest [[Special Report on Emissions Scenarios|emissions scenario]] and {{convert|2.4|to|6.4|C-change|F-change|1}} for their highest.<ref>Meehl "et al.", [http://www.ipcc.ch/publications_and_data/ar4/wg1/en/ch10.html Chap. 10: Global Climate Projections], [http://www.ipcc.ch/publications_and_data/ar4/wg1/en/ch10s10-es-l-mean-temperature.html Sec. 10.ES: Mean Temperature], in {{Harvnb|IPCC AR4 WG1|2007}}. </ref> The ranges of these estimates arise from the use of models with differing [[climate sensitivity|sensitivity to greenhouse gas concentrations]].<ref>{{cite journal

[[Climate model]] projections are summarized in the 2007 [[IPCC Fourth Assessment Report|Fourth Assessment Report]] (AR4) by the [[Intergovernmental Panel on Climate Change]] (IPCC). They indicate that during the 21st century the global surface temperature is likely to rise a further {{convert|1.1|to|2.9|C-change|F-change|1}} for their lowest [[Special Report on Emissions Scenarios|emissions scenario]] and {{convert|2.4|to|6.4|C-change|F-change|1}} for their highest.<ref>Meehl "et al.", [http://www.ipcc.ch/publications_and_data/ar4/wg1/en/ch10.html Chap. 10: Global Climate Projections], [http://www.ipcc.ch/publications_and_data/ar4/wg1/en/ch10s10-es-l-mean-temperature.html Sec. 10.ES: Mean Temperature], in {{Harvnb|IPCC AR4 WG1|2007}}. </ref> The ranges of these estimates arise from the use of models with differing [[climate sensitivity|sensitivity to greenhouse gas concentrations]] .<ref>{{cite journal

⊘ AT ISSUE: SOURCES FOR DEVELOPING A DEFINITION ARGUMENT

1. Pages 433–435 compare two versions of a passage (boxed) from the *Wikipedia* article on global warming. What is the nature of the revision it illustrates? Do you think the revision is an improvement over the original?

2. Does the fact that the editor is identified by name affect your assessment of the changes?

3. Look up the term *global warming* on *Wikipedia*. Then, access its revision history. Look at specific revisions, and compare them. How would you characterize these revisions? Are they minor, or do you think they actually improve the entry?

4. Based on the nature of the revisions you see in the global warming entry, do you think *Wikipedia* is a legitimate research source?

⊙ **EXERCISE 12.5**

Write a one-paragraph definition argument in which you take a position on the topic, "Is *Wikipedia* a Legitimate Research Source?" Follow the template below, filling in the blanks to create your argument.

TEMPLATE FOR WRITING A DEFINITION ARGUMENT

Many people are questioning the use of *Wikipedia* as a legitimate research source. A *legitimate source* can be defined as a source that _____ _____ _____.

According to this definition, *Wikipedia* _____ _____ _____. Not everyone agrees, however. Some people say that *Wikipedia* _____ _____ _____ _____. Others say that _____ _____ _____.

Although these points make sense, it is clear that _____ ___ _____ _____ _____. In conclusion, *Wikipedia* _____ _____ _____ _____.

⊙ **EXERCISE 12.6**

Ask two or three of your instructors whether they consider *Wikipedia* a legitimate research source. Then, revise the draft of the paragraph you wrote for Exercise 12.5 so that it includes your instructors' opinions.

⊙ **EXERCISE 12.7**

Write a definition argument on the topic, "Is *Wikipedia* a Legitimate Research Source?" Make sure that you define the term *legitimate research source* and that you give examples to develop your definition. (If you like, you may incorporate the material you developed in Exercises 12.5 and 12.6 into your essay.) Cite the readings on pages 410–435, and be sure to document the sources you use and to include a works-cited page. (See Chapter 10 for information on documenting sources.)

⬈ EXERCISE 12.8

Review the four pillars of argument discussed in Chapter 1. Does your essay include all four elements of an effective argument? Add anything that is missing. Then, label the key elements of your essay.

⬈ WRITING ASSIGNMENTS: DEFINITION ARGUMENTS

1. On most campuses, instructors have the right to pursue, teach, and discuss ideas without restriction. This principle is called *academic freedom*. Do you think that instructors should have academic freedom, or do you believe that this principle should be restricted? For example, are there any subjects or ideas an instructor should *not* be allowed to discuss? Write a definition argument in which you define *academic freedom* and take a position on this issue.

2. Many colleges require students to perform community service before they graduate. Do you think that college students should have to do community service? Before you begin your argument, find a definition of the term *community service*. Be sure your argument focuses on the definition of this term.

3. Take detailed notes about the food and service in your campus cafeteria. Then, write an argumentative essay in which you rate the cafeteria as *excellent, good, bad,* or *poor*. Keep in mind that you are presenting *operational definitions* of these terms (see p. 401) and that you will have to explain the factors you examined to form your assessment.

Causal Arguments

Should the Drinking Age Be Lowered?

In 1984, the National Minimum Drinking Age Act encouraged states to raise the drinking age to twenty-one by reducing the federal highway appropriation for any state that did not do so. This act effectively created a national minimum drinking age of twenty-one. The intent was to reduce reckless driving among young adults, thereby preventing injuries and deaths caused by drunk driving. (The problem of teenage drinking was exacerbated by young people driving to neighboring states with lower drinking ages.)

In 2008, more than one hundred college presidents, joining together in a group called the Amethyst Initiative, released a statement calling for a "public debate" on the issue of lowering the federal drinking age from twenty-one to eighteen. The statement argues that the current drinking age encourages binge drinking among college students as well as disrespect for the law. Critics of this position, led by Mothers Against Drunk Driving, have called the proposal irresponsible, accusing college presidents of trying to sidestep the difficult task of cracking down on underage drinking. Others have pointed out that the higher drinking age has had beneficial effects—for example, reducing drunken driving deaths among eighteen- to twenty-year-olds—that lowering the drinking age would most likely eliminate.

The question of lowering the drinking age is more complicated than it may seem. For example, did raising the drinking age to twenty-one actually *cause* the rise in binge drinking? If so, is it the most important cause?

(continued)

For comprehension quizzes, see **bedfordstmartins.com/practicalargument.**

(*continued*)

And even if the higher drinking age is the main cause of the problem, will lowering the age once again to eighteen eliminate the problem? And might it create other problems? These are some of the questions that you will be asked to think about as you read the research sources that appear later in this chapter. After reading these selections, you will be asked to write a causal argument that takes a position on whether the drinking age should be lowered.

What Is a Causal Argument?

Causal arguments attempt to find causes (Why don't more Americans vote?) or identify possible effects (Does movie violence cause societal violence?). A causal argument identifies the causes of an event or situation and takes a stand on what actually caused it. Alternatively, a causal argument can focus on effects, taking a position on what a likely outcome is, has been, or will be.

Many of the arguments that you read and discuss examine causes and effects. In an essay on one of the topics listed below, you would search for the causes of an event or a situation, examining a number of different possible causes before concluding that a particular cause was the most likely one. You also could consider the possible outcomes or results of a given event or situation and conclude that one possible effect would most likely occur:

- Are designated bicycle lanes really safer for cyclists?
- Is autism caused by childhood vaccines?
- Is fast food making Americans fat?
- Is human activity responsible for climate change?
- Does the death penalty discourage crime?
- Do charter schools improve students' academic performance?
- Does profiling decrease the likelihood of a terrorist attack?

⬢ EXERCISE 13.1

Each of the following visuals takes a stand on an issue related to public health and safety. Look at the visuals, and consider the causes and effects you might discuss if you were writing a causal argument developing the position each one takes. List as many possible causes and effects as you can.

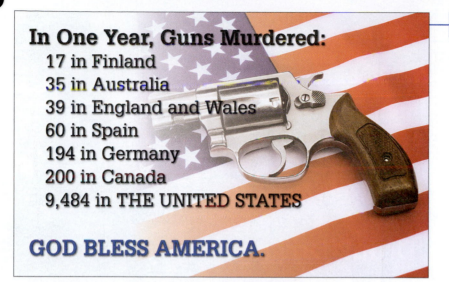

Advertisement promoting gun safety

In One Year, Guns Murdered:
17 in Finland
35 in Australia
39 in England and Wales
60 in Spain
194 in Germany
200 in Canada
9,484 in THE UNITED STATES

GOD BLESS AMERICA.

Surgeon general's warnings

SURGEON GENERAL'S WARNING: Smoking Causes Lung Cancer, Heart Disease, Emphysema, And May Complicate Pregnancy.

·SURGEON GENERAL'S WARNING: Smoking By Pregnant Women May Result in Fetal Injury, Premature Birth, And Low Birth Weight.

Public-service ad
cautioning against
driving after drinking
alcohol

⬤ EXERCISE 13.2

Bumper-sticker slogans frequently make causal arguments that suggest
the consequences of ignoring the message or the positive results of
following the slogan's advice. Choose three of the bumper stickers pictured
on the facing page, and explain the causal argument each slogan makes.

Bumper stickers

Understanding Cause-and-Effect Relationships

Before you can write a causal argument, you need to understand the nature of cause-and-effect relationships, some of which can be very complex. For one thing, a single event or situation can have many possible results, and not all of these will be equally significant. In the same way, identifying

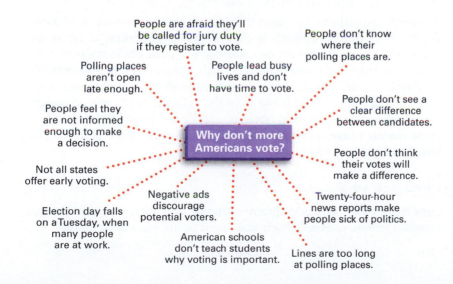

causes can be particularly challenging because an event or situation can have more than one cause. For example, many factors might explain why more Americans do not vote. (The diagram on the previous page illustrates some possible causes.)

Main and Contributory Causes

In a causal argument, your focus is on identifying what you believe is the most important cause and presenting arguments that convince readers *why* it is the most important (and why other causes are not as important).

The most important cause is the **main cause**; the less important causes are **contributory causes**. Typically, you will present the main cause as your key argument in support of your thesis, and you will identify the contributory causes elsewhere in your argument. (You may also identify factors that are *not* causes and explain why they are not.)

Identifying the main cause is not always easy; the most important cause may not always be the most obvious one. However, you need to figure out which cause is most important so you can structure and support your essay with this emphasis in mind.

⊙ EXERCISE 13.3

Look at the diagram on page 443. Which causes do you see as the most and least important? Why? Do you think that any of the factors presented in the diagram are not really causes? Can you suggest any additional causes? If you were writing a causal argument taking a position on the topic of why many Americans do not vote, which cause would you focus on? What kind of evidence would you use to support your argument?

Immediate and Remote Causes

As mentioned earlier, one reason that identifying the main cause of a particular effect can be difficult is that the most important cause is not necessarily the most obvious one. Usually, the most obvious cause is the **immediate cause**—the one that occurs right before an event. For example, a political scandal that erupts the day before an election might cause many disillusioned voters to stay home from the polls. However, this immediate cause, although it is the most obvious, may be less important than one or more **remote causes**—factors that occurred further in the past but may have had a greater impact.

⊙ EXERCISE 13.4

Look once more at the diagram on page 443. Which causes do you consider remote causes? Which one might be the immediate cause?

Causal Chains

A **causal chain** is a sequence of events in which one event causes the next, which in turn causes the next, and so on. For example, the problem of Americans who do not vote can be presented as a causal chain.

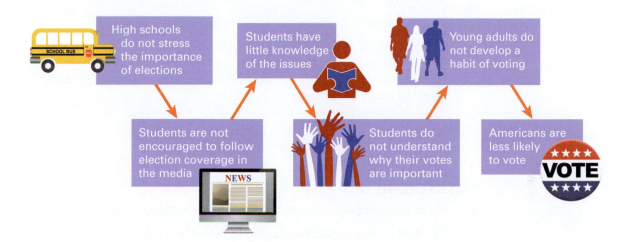

When you write a causal argument, you can organize your essay as a causal chain, as the following outline illustrates.

Thesis statement: U.S. secondary education is at fault for Americans' failure to see voting as a civic duty.

- High schools do not stress the importance of elections.

- As a result, students do not follow election coverage in the media.

- Because they do not follow election coverage, students have little knowledge of the issues.

- With little knowledge of the issues, students do not understand that it is important to vote.

- Because they do not see voting as important, young adults do not develop a habit of regular voting.

- As a result, American adults are less likely to vote.

Concluding statement: Because the habit of voting is established early, high schools need to take responsibility for encouraging students to vote.

KEY WORDS FOR CAUSAL ARGUMENT

When you write causal arguments, choose verbs that indicate causal connections:

bring about	create	lead to	encourage
influence	contribute to	originate in	cause

Be sure to use transitional words and phrases such as *consequently* and *as a result* to help readers follow your argument. You should also try to repeat words like *cause*, *effect*, *outcome*, and *result* to help identify individual causes and effects.

⊝ EXERCISE 13.5

Fill in the templates to create a causal chain for each of these sequences:

1. Restaurants should be required to list fat and calorie content on their menus. If they do so, _____. As a result, _____. Eventually, _____.

2. Abstinence programs should be instituted in high schools. One immediate result would be _____. This could bring about _____. This in turn might lead to _____. Ideally, the result would be _____.

3. Taxes on cigarettes should be raised. If this step is taken, the first result would be _____. This might encourage _____. In a few years' time, the outcome might be _____.

Post Hoc Reasoning

Post hoc reasoning is the incorrect assumption that because an event precedes another event, it has caused that event. For example, you may notice that few of your friends voted in a recent election, and you may realize that many of your friends had previously decided to become science majors. This does not mean, of course, that their decision to choose careers in science has made them nonvoters. In fact, a scientist can be very interested in electoral politics. As you develop your causal argument, be careful not to assume that every event that precedes another event has somehow caused it. (For information on avoiding post hoc fallacies, see Chapter 5.)

⊘ EXERCISE 13.6

The following excerpt from a humorous essay takes a lighthearted look at the concept of post hoc reasoning. Identify the cause and the result discussed in each paragraph. Then, list several more plausible causes for each effect.

This essay appeared in the *New York Times* on January 13, 2008.

THE CHICKEN SOUP CHRONICLES

NORA EPHRON

The other day I felt a cold coming on. So I decided to have chicken soup to ward off the cold. Nonetheless I got the cold. This happens all the time: you think you're getting a cold; you have chicken soup; you get the cold anyway. So: is it possible that chicken soup gives you a cold?

> "So: is it possible that chicken soup gives you a cold?"

I will confess a bias: I've never understood the religious fervor that surrounds breast-feeding. There are fanatics out there who believe you should breast-feed your child until he or she is old enough to unbutton your blouse. Their success in conning a huge number of women into believing this is one of the truly grim things about modern life. Anyway, one of the main reasons given for breast-feeding is that breast-fed children are less prone to allergies. But children today are far more allergic than they were when I was growing up, when far fewer women breast-fed their children. I mean, what is it with all these children dropping dead from sniffing a peanut? This is new, friends, it's brand-new new, and don't believe anyone who says otherwise. So: is it possible that breast-feeding causes allergies?

It's much easier to write a screenplay on a computer than on a typewriter. Years ago, when you wrote a screenplay on a typewriter, you had to retype the entire page just to make the smallest change; now, on the computer, you can make large and small changes effortlessly, you can fiddle with dialogue, you can change names and places with a keystroke. And yet movies are nowhere near as good as they used to be. In 1939, when screenwriters were practically still using quill pens, the following movies were among those nominated for best picture: *Gone with the Wind*, *The Wizard of Oz*, *Mr. Smith Goes to Washington*, *Wuthering Heights*, and *Stagecoach*, and that's not even the whole list. So: is it possible that computers are responsible for the decline of movies?

There is way too much hand-washing going on. Someone told me the 4 other day that the act of washing your hands is supposed to last as long as it takes to sing the song "Happy Birthday." I'm not big on hand-washing to begin with; I don't even like to wash fruit, if you must know. But my own prejudices aside, all this washing-of-hands and use of Purell before picking up infants cannot be good. (By the way, I'm not talking about hand-washing in hospitals, I'm talking about everyday, run-of-the-mill hand-washing.) It can't possibly make sense to keep babies so removed from germs that they never develop an immunity to them. Of course, this isn't my original theory—I read it somewhere a few weeks ago, although I can't remember where. The *New York Times*? The *Wall Street Journal*? Who knows? Not me, that's for sure. So: is it possible that reading about hand-washing leads to memory loss?

Structuring a Causal Argument

Generally speaking, a causal argument can be structured in the following way:

- **Introduction:** Establishes a context for the argument by explaining the need to examine causes or consider effects; states the essay's thesis

- **Evidence (first point in support of thesis):** Discusses less important causes or effects

- **Evidence (second point in support of thesis):** Discusses major causes or effects

- **Refutation of opposing arguments:** Considers and rejects other possible causes or effects

- **Conclusion:** Reinforces the argument's main point; includes a strong concluding statement

Other organizational patterns are also possible. For example, you might decide to refute opposing arguments *before* you have discussed

arguments in support of your thesis. You might also include a background paragraph (as the student writer whose essay begins below
does). Finally, you might decide to organize your essay as a **causal chain**
(see p. 445).

The following student essay illustrates one possible structure for a
causal argument. (Note, for example, that the refutation of opposing arguments precedes the evidence.) The student writer argues that, contrary to
popular opinion, texting is not causing damage to the English language
but is a creative force with the power to enrich and expand the language.

TEXTING: A BOON, NOT A THREAT, TO LANGUAGE

KRISTINA MIALKI

1   Certain technological developments of the last two decades have a
lot of people worrying about the state of the English language.
Emailing, blogging, instant-messaging, tweeting, and texting are
introducing new ways of writing and communicating, and the fear is
that these technologies will encourage a sloppy, casual form of written
English that will eventually replace "proper" English altogether.
Texting, in particular, has people concerned because it encourages the
use of a specialized, nonstandard form of English. However, the effects
of this new "textese" are misunderstood. Texting is not destroying the   Thesis statement
English language; in fact, it is keeping the language alive.

2   Texting has become extremely popular because sending text   Background
messages is instant, mobile, and silent. To make texting more efficient,
texters have developed a shorthand—an abbreviated form of English
that uses numbers and symbols in addition to letters. In textese,
common phrases such as "see you later" or "talk to you later" become
"cul8r" and "T2YL." Feelings and phrases are also expressed with
emoticons, such as "*:-o" (meaning "alarmed") or ">:-<" (meaning
"angry"). Today, texting is the preferred method of communication for
millions of people—especially young people, who are the most

enthusiastic users of this technology. Not surprisingly, unwarranted fears that texting will destroy the language often focus on this group.

Refutation of opposing argument

Some people say texting will destroy the English language because it encourages the use of an overly simplified form of written English that does not follow standard rules of spelling, grammar, and punctuation. The implication is that people who text, particularly children and teens, will not learn standard written English. However, there is no evidence that texting is having or will have this effect. In fact, Australian researchers Nenagh Kemp and Catherine Bushnell at the University of Tasmania recently found just the opposite to be true. They demonstrated that students who were good at texting were also strong in reading, writing, and spelling (Rock). If, in fact, young people's language skills are weakening, researchers should look for the real cause for this decline rather than incorrectly blaming texting.

Evidence: First point in support of thesis

Despite what its critics charge, texting is a valuable way of communicating that actually encourages more writing and reading. Texters often spend hours each day engaged with language. This is time that would otherwise probably be spent on the phone, not reading or writing. Textese may not be standard written English, but it is a rich and inventive form of communication, a creative modification of English for a particular purpose. For this reason, standard English is not in danger of being destroyed or replaced by textese. Just as most young people know not to talk to their teachers the way they talk to their friends, they know not to write essays the way they write text messages. Texting simply broadens young people's exposure to the written word.

Evidence: Second point in support of thesis

Another reason texting is valuable is that it encourages creative use of language. The 140-character limit requires texters to be inventive, so the need for new and clever abbreviations is constant. Texters are continually playing with words and coming up with new ways of expressing themselves. Texting does not, as some fear, encourage sloppy, thoughtless, or careless writing. On the contrary, it rewards ingenuity and precision. One ongoing study by Canadian researchers aims to prove this point. They have already been able to demonstrate that texters are "creative and efficient at communicating" and use "novel forms of communications" (Shaw). Nenagh Kemp has also observed how texting encourages word play. Kemp maintains that texting shows "language is fluid and flourishing, rather than in a sad state of decline" (Rock). In other words, researchers recognize that texting is not damaging the English language but actually enriching it and keeping it alive.

According to a Pew Research Center report on Americans' text messaging habits, eighteen- to twenty-four-year-olds now send and receive an average of 110 texts a day (Smith). The exceptional popularity of texting and its fast growth over the last ten years explain why it is attracting attention. It is not, however, the threat that some believe it to be. It is neither destroying the language nor deadening people's thoughts and feelings. It is a lively, original, and creative way for people to play with words and stay connected.

6

Concluding statement

Works Cited

Rock, Margaret. "Texting May Improve Literacy." *Mobiledia*. 12 Sept. 2011. Web. 19 Apr. 2012.

Shaw, Gillian. "Researchers Study Text Messages as Language Form." *Vancouver Sun*. 18 Jan. 2012. Web. 19 Apr. 2012.

Smith, Aaron. "Americans and Text Messaging." *Pew Internet and American Life Project*. Pew Research Center, 19 Sept. 2011. Web. 19 Apr. 2012.

GRAMMAR IN CONTEXT

Avoiding "The Reason Is Because"

When you write a **causal argument**, you connect causes to effects. In the process, you might be tempted to use the ungrammatical phrase *the reason is because*. However, the word *because* means "for the reason that"; therefore, it is redundant to say "the reason is because" (which actually means "the reason is for the reason that"). Instead, use the grammatical phrase "the reason is *that*."

INCORRECT   Another <u>reason</u> texting is so valuable <u>is because</u> it encourages creative use of language.

CORRECT   Another <u>reason</u> texting is so valuable <u>is that</u> it encourages creative use of language.

⊝ **EXERCISE 13.7**

The following essay, "Should the World of Toys Be Gender-Free?" by Peggy Orenstein, is a causal argument. Read the essay carefully, and then answer the questions that follow it, consulting the outline on page 448 if necessary.

This opinion column is from the December 29, 2011, *New York Times*.

SHOULD THE WORLD OF TOYS BE GENDER-FREE?

PEGGY ORENSTEIN

Now that the wrapping paper and the infernal clamshell packaging have been relegated to the curb and the paying off of holiday bills has begun, the toy industry is gearing up—for Christmas 2012. And its early offerings have ignited a new debate over nature, nurture, toys, and sex. 1

Hamleys, which is London's 251-year-old version of F.A.O. Schwarz, recently dismantled its pink "girls" and blue "boys" sections in favor of a gender-neutral store with red-and-white signage. Rather than floors dedicated to Barbie dolls and action figures, merchandise is now organized by types (Soft Toys) and interests (Outdoor). 2

That free-to-be gesture was offset by Lego, whose Friends collection, aimed at girls, will hit stores this month with the goal of becoming a holiday must-have by the fall. Set in fictive Heartlake City (and supported by a $40 million marketing campaign), the line features new, pastel-colored, blocks that allow a budding Kardashian, among other things, to build herself a cafe or a beauty salon. Its tasty-sounding "ladyfig" characters are also taller and curvier than the typical Legoland denizen. 3

So who has it right? Should gender be systematically expunged from playthings? Or is Lego merely being realistic, earnestly meeting girls halfway in an attempt to stoke their interest in engineering? 4

> "Should gender be systematically expunged from playthings?"

Among the "10 characteristics for Lego" described in 1963 by a son of the founder was that it was "for girls and for boys," as Bloomberg Businessweek reported. But the new Friends collection, Lego says, was based on months of anthropological research revealing that—gasp!—the sexes play differently. 5

While as toddlers they interact similarly with the company's Duplo blocks, by preschool girls prefer playthings that are pretty, exude "harmony," and allow them to tell a story. They may enjoy building, but they favor role play. So it's 6 bye-bye Bionicles, hello princesses. In order to be gender-fair, today's executives insist, they have to be gender-specific.

As any developmental psychologist will tell you, those observations are, 7 to a degree, correct. Toy choice among young children is the Big Kahuna of sex differences, one of the largest across the life span. It transcends not only culture but species: in two separate studies of primates, in 2002 and 2008, researchers found that males gravitated toward stereotypically masculine toys (like cars and balls) while females went ape for dolls. Both sexes, incidentally, appreciated stuffed animals and books.

Human boys and girls not only tend to play differently from one 8 another—with girls typically clustering in pairs or trios, chatting together more than boys, and playing more cooperatively—but, when given a choice, usually prefer hanging with their own kind.

Score one for Lego, right? Not so fast. Preschoolers may be the self- 9 appointed chiefs of the gender police, eager to enforce and embrace the most rigid views. Yet, according to Lise Eliot, a neuroscientist and the author of *Pink Brain, Blue Brain*, that's also the age when their brains are most malleable, most open to influence on the abilities and roles that traditionally go with their sex.

Every experience, every interaction, every activity—when they laugh, cry, 10 learn, play—strengthens some neural circuits at the expense of others, and the younger the child the greater the effect. Consider: boys from more egalitarian homes are more nurturing toward babies. Meanwhile, in a study of more than 5,000 3-year-olds, girls with older brothers had stronger spatial skills than both girls and boys with older sisters.

At issue, then, is not nature or nurture but how nurture becomes nature: 11 the environment in which children play and grow can encourage a range of aptitudes or foreclose them. So blithely indulging—let alone exploiting— stereotypically gendered play patterns may have a more negative long-term impact on kids' potential than parents imagine. And promoting, without forcing, cross-sex friendships as well as a breadth of play styles may be more beneficial. There is even evidence that children who have opposite-sex friendships during their early years have healthier romantic relationships as teenagers.

Traditionally, toys were intended to communicate parental values and 12 expectations, to train children for their future adult roles. Today's boys and girls will eventually be one another's professional peers, employers, employees, romantic partners, co-parents. How can they develop skills for such collaborations from toys that increasingly emphasize, reinforce, or even create, gender differences? What do girls learn about who they should be from Lego kits with beauty parlors or the flood of "girl friendly" science kits that run the gamut from "beauty spa lab" to "perfume factory"?

The rebellion against such gender apartheid may have begun. Consider 13 the latest cute-kid video to go viral on YouTube: "Riley on Marketing" shows a little girl in front of a wall of pink packaging, asking, "Why do all the girls have to buy pink stuff and all the boys have to buy different-color stuff?" It has been viewed more than 2.4 million times.

Perhaps, then, Hamleys is on to something, though it will doubtless meet   14
with resistance—even rejection—from both its pint-size customers and multi-
national vendors. As for me, I'm trying to track down a poster of a 1981 ad for
a Lego "universal" building set to give to my daughter. In it, a freckle-faced girl
with copper-colored braids, baggy jeans, a T-shirt, and sneakers proudly holds
out a jumbly, multi-hued Lego creation. Beneath it, a tag line reads, "What it is
is beautiful."

Identifying the Elements of a Causal Argument

1. Where does Orenstein answer the question her title asks? How would
   you answer this question?

2. Orenstein's discussion of toys is based on the assumption that the
   world would be a better place if children were raised in a gender-
   neutral environment, but she does not offer any evidence to support
   this implied idea. Should she have? Is she **begging the question**?

3. In paragraph 7, Orenstein reports on two studies of primates. What
   conclusion does this evidence support? What conclusion does Lise
   Eliot's research (para. 9) support?

4. How do you react to Orenstein's use of the term "gender apartheid"
   (13)? What does this term mean? What connotations does it have?
   Given these connotations, do you think her use of this term is appropriate? Why or why not?

5. According to Orenstein, what effects do stereotyped toys have on
   children? Does she support her claims?

6. Orenstein's thesis seems to leave no room for compromise. Given
   the possibility that some of her readers might disagree with her,
   should she have softened her position? What compromise position
   might she have proposed?

7. This essay traces a causal chain. The first link in this chain is the
   "anthropological research revealing that . . . the sexes play differently" (5). Complete the causal chain by filling in the template below.

Anthropological research _____→
_____→
_____→
_____→

Should the Drinking Age Be Lowered?

Reread the At Issue box on pages 439–440. Then, read the sources on the pages that follow.

As you read each of these sources, you will be asked to respond to a series of questions and complete some simple activities. This work will help you to understand the content and structure of the material you read. When you are finished, you will be prepared to write a **causal argument** in which you take a position on the topic, "Should the Drinking Age Be Lowered?"

SOURCES

For comprehension quizzes, see bedfordstmartins.com/practicalargument.

The Amethyst Initiative is an organization composed of presidents and chancellors of colleges that has called for a revision of alcohol policy in the United States. This position paper is from its Web site.

STATEMENT
AMETHYST INITIATIVE

It's Time to Rethink the Drinking Age

In 1984 Congress passed the National Minimum Drinking Age Act, which imposed a penalty of 10% of a state's federal highway appropriation on any state setting its drinking age lower than 21. 1

Twenty-four years later, our experience as college and university presidents convinces us that . . . 2

> "Twenty-one is not working."

Twenty-One Is Not Working

A culture of dangerous, clandestine "binge-drinking"—often conducted off-campus—has developed. 3

Alcohol education that mandates abstinence as the only legal option has not resulted in significant constructive behavioral change among our students. 4

Adults under 21 are deemed capable of voting, signing contracts, serving on juries, and enlisting in the military, but are told they are not mature enough to have a beer. 5

By choosing to use fake IDs, students make ethical compromises that erode respect for the law. 6

How Many Times Must We Relearn the Lessons of Prohibition?

We call upon our elected officials: 7

To support an informed and dispassionate public debate over the effects of the 21-year-old drinking age.

To consider whether the 10% highway fund "incentive" encourages or inhibits that debate.

To invite new ideas about the best ways to prepare young adults to make responsible decisions about alcohol.

We pledge ourselves and our institutions to playing a vigorous, constructive role as these critical discussions unfold. 8

To Sign:

1. Review and print statement 9
2. Sign, indicating your name and institution

3. Return by mail to:

   The Amethyst Initiative
   PO Box 507
   Middlebury, VT 05753

   Or by fax to: 802-398-2029

   Currently, membership in the Amethyst Initiative is limited to college and uni-   10
   *versity presidents and chancellors. If you are not a president or chancellor, but would
   like to become part of this larger effort, please sign-up at chooseresponsibility.org.*

   Amethyst Initiative
   PO Box 507 Middlebury, VT 05753 802.398.2024
   info@amethystinitiative.org

⊘AT ISSUE: SOURCES FOR DEVELOPING A CAUSAL ARGUMENT

1. Two of the headings in this position paper—"It's Time to Rethink the Drinking Age" and "Twenty-One Is Not Working"—together express the college presidents' position. Combine these two headings to create a one-sentence thesis statement that expresses this opinion. To construct your thesis statement, use one of the following templates:

   ■ Because _____ ,
   _____ .

   ■ _____ ; therefore,
   _____ .

2. Read the argument in paragraph 5. Then, write a one-sentence refutation of this argument.

3. Does the college presidents' statement actually call for lowering the drinking age, or does it take a different position? Explain.

4. What does the statement ask of elected officials? What does it pledge that college presidents will do?

5. How do the writers of this statement establish their credibility? Do you think they need to do more?

This article is from FoxNews.com, where it appeared on August 25, 2008.

AMETHYST INITIATIVE'S DEBATE ON DRINKING A WELCOME ALTERNATIVE TO FANATICISM

RADLEY BALKO

1 It's been nearly 25 years since Congress blackmailed the states to raise the minimum drinking age to 21 or lose federal highway funding. Supporters of the law have hailed it as an unqualified success, and until recently, they've met little resistance.

2 For obvious reasons, no one wants to stand up for teen drinking. The alcohol industry won't touch the federal minimum drinking age, having been sufficiently scolded by groups like Mothers Against Drunk Driving and federal regulators. So the law's miraculous effects have generally gone unchallenged.

3 But that may be changing. Led by John McCardell, the soft-spoken former president of Middlebury in Vermont, a new group called the Amethyst Initiative is calling for a new national debate on the drinking age. And McCardell and his colleagues ought to know. The Amethyst Group consists of current and former college and university presidents, and they say the federal minimum drinking age has contributed to an epidemic of binge drinking, as well as other excessive, unhealthy drinking habits on their campuses.

4 This makes perfect sense. Prohibitions have always provoked overindulgence. Those of us who have attended college over the last 25 years can certainly attest to the fact that the law has done nothing to diminish freshman and sophomore access to alcohol. It has only pushed underage consumption underground. It causes other problems, too. Underage students, for example, may be reluctant to obtain medical aid for peers who have had too much to drink, out of fear of implicating themselves for drinking illegally, or for contributing to underage drinking.

> "It has only pushed underage consumption underground."

5 More than 120 college presidents and chancellors have now signed on to the Amethyst Initiative's statement, including those from Duke, Tufts, Dartmouth, Johns Hopkins, Syracuse, Maryland, and Ohio. Over the last few years several states, including Wisconsin, Montana, Minnesota, Kentucky, South Carolina, and Vermont, have also considering lowering their drinking ages back to 18.

6 All of this has the usual suspects predictably agitated. Mothers Against Drunk Driving, not accustomed to striking a defensive posture, calls the Amethyst Initiative's request for an "informed debate" on the issue "deeply

disappointing," and has even raised the possibility that parents shouldn't send their kids to colleges who have signed on to the measure.

Acting National Transportation Safety Board Chairman Mark Rosenker 7 says it would be a "national tragedy" to, for example, allow 19- and 20-year-old men and women returning from Iraq and Afghanistan to have a beer in celebration of completing their tours of duty.

Supporters of the 21 minimum drinking age have long credited the law 8 with the dramatic reduction in traffic fatalities they say took place after it was passed. But a study released last July may pull the rug out from their strongest argument.

The working paper by economic researchers Jeffrey Miron and Elina 9 Tetelbaum finds that the bulk of studies on highway fatalities since the federal minimum drinking age went into effect erroneously include data from 12 states that had already set their drinking ages at 21, without federal coercion. That, Miron and Tetelbaum conclude, may have skewed the data, and indicated a national trend that may not actually exist.

While it's true that highway fatalities have dropped since 1984, it isn't nec- 10 essarily because we rose the drinking age. In fact, the downward trend actually began in 1969, just as many states began *lowering* their drinking ages in recognition of the absurdity of prohibiting servicemen returning from Vietnam from enjoying a beer (the 1984 law was a backlash against those states). As Miron and Tetelbaum explain, 1969 was the year when "several landmark improvements were made in the accident avoidance and crash protection features of passenger cars," a more likely explanation for the drop than a law passed 15 years later.

Miron and Tetelbaum also credit advances in medical technology and 11 trauma treatment for the decline in fatalities, which makes sense, given that we've seen improvements in just about every other area of human development over the same period, including life expectancy, and both incidence and survival rates of major medical conditions like heart disease, cancer, and stroke—none of which have much to do with teen drinking.

The U.S. has the highest minimum drinking age in the world (save for 12 countries where it's forbidden entirely). In countries with a low or no national minimum drinking age, teens are introduced to alcohol gradually, moderately, and under the supervision of their parents.

U.S. teens, on the other hand, tend to first try alcohol in unsupervised 13 environments—in cars, motels, or outdoor settings in high school, or in dorm rooms, fraternity parties, or house parties when they leave home to go to college. During alcohol prohibition, we saw how adults who imbibed under such conditions reacted—they drank way too much, way too fast. It shouldn't be surprising that teens react in much the same way.

Anti-alcohol organizations like MADD and the American Medical Asso- 14 ciation oppose even allowing parents to give minors alcohol in supervised settings, such as a glass of wine with dinner, or a beer on the couch while watching the football game. They've pushed for prison time for parents who throw supervised parties where minors are given access to alcohol, even though those parties probably made the roads safer than they otherwise would have been (let's face it—if the kids hadn't been drinking at the supervised party, they'd have been drinking at an unsupervised one). They advocate a "not one drop until 21" policy that's not only unrealistic, it mystifies and glorifies alcohol by making the drug a forbidden fruit—a surefire way to make teens want to taste it.

McCardell and the academics who have signed on to the Amethyst Initiative are asking only for a debate—an honest discussion based on data and common sense, not one tainted by Carry Nation–style fanaticism. In today's hyper-cautious, ban-happy public health environment, that's refreshing. The group comprises serious academics who have collectively spent thousands of years around the very young people these laws are affecting. The nation's policy makers would be foolish to dismiss their concerns out of hand.   15

❍ AT ISSUE: SOURCES FOR DEVELOPING A CAUSAL ARGUMENT

1. Write a thesis statement for Balko's argument. Where would you locate this thesis statement? Why?

2. In paragraph 4, Balko summarizes two problems that he says have been caused by the higher drinking age. In your own words, summarize these two problems. If you can, list one or two additional problems.

3. What, according to Balko, is the Amethyst Initiative's position on the drinking age? Where does he summarize this position? Is his interpretation of the group's position accurate? (Refer to the Amethyst Initiative's statement on p. 456.)

4. How do Miron and Tetelbaum's findings (summarized in paras. 9–11) challenge the arguments of those who support the current minimum drinking age? Does Balko cite any other experts to support his position? What additional kinds of supporting evidence do you think would be helpful?

5. Consider each of the following words and expressions: *fanaticism* (title), *blackmailed* (1), *scolded* (2), *the usual suspects* (6). Do you think any of this language is inflammatory? Can you find examples of slanted language elsewhere in the article? Do you think that more neutral language would be more appropriate (and just as effective) here, or do you see this strong language as necessary?

The *Arkansas Democrat-Gazette* published this editorial on August 31, 2008.

SAVE US FROM YOUTH

BRADLEY R. GITZ

It was Ralph Waldo Emerson who wrote, "A foolish consistency is the hobgoblin 1 of little minds." Seldom has anything so stupid been said by someone so smart.

Far from a reflection of deficient thinking, consistency is the most impor- 2 tant and elusive quality in politics, if only because without it we are left with nothing but sheer randomness. For our laws to make sense they must be based on discernible political principles free of the kind of internal contradictions that consistency irons out.

A modest case of inconsistency arose recently with newspaper reports that a 3 growing number of American college presidents are agitating for a reduction in the drinking age from 21. A petition they have circulated to that effect has already drawn fire from Mothers Against Drunk Driving and various public safety experts (whatever that means) who have conjured up the usual horror stories of the carnage on our roads that would supposedly flow from such a change.

The complaint of the college presidents is a reasonable if hardly decisive 4 one—that it has become too difficult to police the thing because their students are going to drink anyway, with such difficulties contribut- ing to a shift toward surreptitious behavior that undermines respect for the law.

> "Students are going to drink anyway."

The interesting part of the spat, and that which brings the consistency 5 angle into play, is the part that is missing: any discussion of whether it is mor- ally acceptable to deny a certain group of legal adults, in this case those between 18 and 21, things that other legal adults are not denied.

Ultimately, the most important issue at stake with respect to the drinking age 6 is not whether 18-year-olds are responsible enough to consume alcohol, or even the consequences of such consumption in legal vs. illegal circumstances, but whether those who are old enough to be sued in a court of law, carry a gun into combat on behalf of their fellow citizens, and participate in our democratic process by stepping into a voting booth should be prevented from occupying a bar stool.

Clearly, even those skeptical of the maturity of 18- and 19-year-olds must 7 recognize that a significant percentage of the military personnel defending their freedom to drink liquor and do lots of other things is of such age. Indeed, it takes a rather extraordinary amount of chutzpah for Party A to tell Party B, who happens to be risking his life on the battlefield on behalf of Party A, that he is not mature enough to legally enjoy the things in life that Party A gets to enjoy. Amer- ican soldiers who have served their country by braving the suicide bombers and snipers in places like Iraq and Afghanistan would seem to deserve better.

All of this becomes more bizarre still when we encounter enthusiastic 8 campaigns to increase the voting rates of those 18 to 21 on the assumption that they don't vote as often as they should. For some inexplicable reason, we feel that such young people are capable of making the kinds of political distinctions compatible with democratic governance but are thoroughly untrustworthy when it comes to a six-pack of Budweiser.

The point here is not that the drinking age should be 18, as opposed to 21 9 or even 40; rather, it is that consistency should prevail so that it is not different from the age of consensual adult behavior in other realms, including serving in the military and voting. No one should be treated with the respect accorded an adult in some areas but not others.

In short, it matters less what the drinking age is than that it corresponds to 10 and is compatible with the other standards of adulthood. So if the idea of 18-year-olds flooding into the bars alarms us, as well it might, then the better solution might be to raise the age requirement for lots of other things to 21 or wherever, thereby providing the logical heft that only consistency can provide to an argument.

The current disparity in age requirements carries with it not only incon- 11 sistency but the implicit assumption that certain activities, such as military service and voting, require less maturity and matter less than the ability to safely consume a glass of cheap wine.

For some of us, the specter of college students at a fraternity keg party is a 12 great deal less terrifying than the fact that a fair number of 18-year-olds who don't know who the vice president is or whether Mexico is to our north or south will be handed ballots on the first Tuesday in November.

⊙ AT ISSUE: SOURCES FOR DEVELOPING A CAUSAL ARGUMENT

1. Gitz develops his thesis in paragraphs 6, 9, and 10. State this thesis in one sentence.

2. Why does Gitz begin with a quotation from Emerson and a commentary on that quotation? Is this an effective opening strategy? What does it tell you about how Gitz sees his audience?

3. In paragraph 3, Gitz refers to a statement by college presidents (which appears on p. 456) who recommend that the drinking age be reconsidered. Does he agree with their position? Do you think he would agree with their reasoning? Explain.

4. In what respects is Gitz's editorial an **argument by analogy**? Are the analogies he draws valid? Are they convincing?

This editorial appeared in the January 12, 2006, edition of the *Christian Science Monitor.*

THERE'S NO BENEFIT TO LOWERING THE DRINKING AGE

ROBERT VOAS

After nearly four decades of exacting research on how to save lives and reduce injuries by preventing drinking and driving, there is a revanchist attempt afoot to roll back one of the most successful laws in generations: the minimum legal drinking age of 21.

This is extremely frustrating. While public health researchers must produce painstaking evidence that's subjected to critical scholarly review, lower-drinking-age advocates seem to dash off remarks based on glib conjecture and self-selected facts.

It's startling that anybody—given the enormous bodies of research and data—would consider lowering the drinking age. And yet, legislation is currently pending in New Hampshire and Wisconsin to lower the drinking age for military personnel and for all residents in Vermont. Just as bad are the arguments from think-tank writers, various advocates, and even academics (including at least one former college president) that ignore or manipulate the real evidence and instead rely on slogans.

> "It's startling that anybody—given the enormous bodies of research and data—would consider lowering the drinking age."

I keep hearing the same refrains: "If you're old enough to go to war, you should be old enough to drink," or "the drinking-age law just increases the desire for the forbidden fruit," or "lower crash rates are due to tougher enforcement, not the 21 law," or "Europeans let their kids drink, so they learn how to be more responsible," or finally, "I did it when I was a kid, and I'm OK."

First, I'm not sure what going to war and being allowed to drink have in common. The military takes in youngsters particularly because they are not yet fully developed and can be molded into soldiers. The 21 law is predicated on the fact that drinking is more dangerous for youth because they're still developing mentally and physically, and they lack experience and are more likely to take risks. Ask platoon leaders and unit commanders, and they'll tell you that the last thing they want is young soldiers drinking.

As for the forbidden fruit argument, the opposite is true. Research shows that back when some states still had a minimum drinking age of 18, youths in those states who were under 21 drank more and continued to drink more as adults in their early 20s. In states where the drinking age was 21, teenagers drank less and continue to drink less through their early 20s.

And the minimum 21 law, by itself, has most certainly resulted in fewer accidents, because the decline occurred even when there was little enforcement and tougher penalties had not yet been enacted. According to the National Highway Traffic Safety Administration, the 21 law has saved 23,733 lives since states began raising drinking ages in 1975.

Do European countries really have fewer youth drinking problems? No, that's a myth. Compared to American youth, binge drinking rates among young people are higher in every European country except Turkey. Intoxication rates are higher in most countries; in Britain, Denmark, and Ireland they're more than twice the U.S. level. Intoxication and binge drinking are directly linked to higher levels of alcohol-related problems, such as drinking and driving.

But, you drank when you were a kid, and you're OK. Thank goodness, because many kids aren't OK. An average of 11 American teens die each day from alcohol-related crashes. Underage drinking leads to increased teen pregnancy, violent crime, sexual assault, and huge costs to our communities. Among college students, it leads to 1,700 deaths, 500,000 injuries, 600,000 physical assaults, and 70,000 sexual assaults each year.

Recently, New Zealand lowered its drinking age, which gave researchers a good opportunity to study the impact. The result was predictable: The rate of alcohol-related crashes among young people rose significantly compared to older drivers.

I've been studying drinking and driving for nearly 40 years and have been involved in public health and behavioral health for 53 years. Believe me when I say that lowering the drinking age would be very dangerous; it would benefit no one except those who profit from alcohol sales.

If bars and liquor stores can freely provide alcohol to teenagers, parents will be out of the loop when it comes to their children's decisions about drinking. Age 21 laws are designed to keep such decisions within the family where they belong. Our society, particularly our children and grandchildren, will be immeasurably better off if we not only leave the minimum drinking age law as it is, but enforce it better, too.

⊘ AT ISSUE: SOURCES FOR DEVELOPING A CAUSAL ARGUMENT

1. Voas, a research scientist, addresses the "consistency" argument advanced by Bradley R. Gitz (p. 461). Does he do a satisfactory job of presenting arguments against this position? Why or why not?

2. How does Voas view people who favor lowering the drinking age? How can you tell? Do you agree with his characterizations?

3. In paragraph 11, Voas establishes himself as an expert on the issue. Should he have presented his credentials earlier? If so, where?

The *Deseret Morning News* published this editorial on May 29, 2011.

LOWER DRINKING AGE TO EIGHTEEN? LOOK AT COSTS

JAY EVENSEN

Any time you talk about setting age limits for behavior, you've got a fight on your hands. 1

You can drive in most states at age 16, fight for your country and vote at 18, but not drink until 21. Some people don't see this as logical, which is why clear-eyed and sober (pun intended) examinations are so important. 2

Thankfully, we got some of that on the alcohol front recently. 3

Three years have passed since a lot of college presidents and chancellors flashed on the national stage by signing the Amethyst Initiative, which encouraged the nation to rethink the 21-year-old age limit for legally consuming alcohol. 4

I use the word *flash* because that's how the media works these days. A few stories (elections, war) have staying power. The rest, whether it be nuclear meltdowns in Japan or tornadoes in the Midwest, flash momentarily if they have enough of what it takes to get people to raise eyebrows and talk for a while. Then they quickly disappear back into the darkness. 5

We're lucky the Amethyst Initiative just flashed, even though it continues as a cause. So far, the number of signers is up to 136, which is just a few more than the 115 when I first wrote about this in 2008 (Westminster College President Michael Bassis was the only local college president to sign). 6

Why are we lucky? A new study by a pair of economists, Christopher Carpenter of the University of California at Irvine and Carlos Dobkin at the University of California at Santa Cruz, adds a bit of perspective. 7

The college presidents believe that the 21-year-old limit, in the words of the initiative's web site, "is not working, and, specifically, that it has created a culture of dangerous binge drinking on their campuses." 8

Because under-aged college students have to go into the shadows to drink, the thinking goes, they tend to do so irresponsibly. Lower the age to 18 and you also would reduce binge drinking and save lives. 9

Which may sound good, except that it probably isn't true. Carpenter and Dobkin found instead the result likely would be an increase in deaths among people in the 18-to-20 age group. Their study, "The minimum legal drinking age and public health," was published in the spring issue of the *Journal of Economic Perspectives*. (To read the full report, go to pubs.aeaweb.org/doi/pdfplus/10.1257/jep.25.2.133). 10

> "The result likely would be an increase in deaths among people in the 18-to-20 age group."

They use a variety of public data, including mortality rates from the '70s 11 and '80s when some states temporarily lowered their drinking age. Being economists, they put a unique twist on the issue by figuring out how much lowering the age would add to the cost of a drink, if the bartender was forced to include everything.

Their conclusion? The hidden mortality costs would add more than $15 12 per drink, which they believe is a conservative estimate given the injuries, lost productivity, and health problems that would result. Add another $2.63 for the costs borne by other people who might be killed or harmed by the drinker. They estimate drinking would increase by 6.1 percent among people aged 18-20.

The lesson here is that laws can affect behavior, which is quite different 13 from the idea that kids always are going to act a certain way regardless of the rules.

Yes, binge drinking remains a problem among college students. According 14 to the Centers for Disease Control and Prevention, college students aren't the nation's biggest binge problem—70 percent of excessive drinking episodes happen among those 26 and older. But among people under 21 who drink, 90 percent binge.

I can't fault college presidents for wanting to explore ways to tackle that 15 problem. But allowing younger people to legally buy alcohol isn't the way to do it.

No matter how popular the thinking, there really is no logical connection 16 between being old enough to qualify as a fit and effective soldier and making mature drinking decisions. Rental car companies understand this, which is why they generally don't trust their cars to anyone under 25.

❯ AT ISSUE: SOURCES FOR DEVELOPING A CAUSAL ARGUMENT

1. Paraphrase Evensen's thesis by filling in the template below:

    The drinking age should not be lowered to eighteen because

    _____.

2. Evensen's commentary is a **refutation** of a statement by the Amethyst Initiative, a group of university presidents, that recommends reconsidering the drinking age (see p. 456). Which of the following points made by Evensen most effectively (and least effectively) refutes the Amethyst Initiative's statement?

    - In the three years since the statement was issued, not many additional college presidents have signed on.

    - A study found that lowering the drinking age would increase deaths of those between eighteen and twenty-one.

- A study found that lowering the drinking age would increase the cost of an alcoholic drink.

- Binge drinking is more common among those age twenty-six and older than among younger people.

- Rental car companies require customers to be over twenty-five.

3. Do all of the points listed above support Evensen's position on the issue? Should he have deleted any of them?

4. In paragraph 13, Evensen says, "The lesson here is that laws can affect behavior, which is quite different from the idea that kids are always going to act a certain way regardless of the rules." Based on your reading of the Amethyst Initiative statement, do you think Evensen is creating a **straw man**, or do you think he is accurately summarizing their argument?

5. What two analogies does Evensen make in his conclusion? Are they both valid? Are they both convincing? What might Bradley R. Gitz (p. 461) say about these analogies?

The *San Jose Mercury News* published this essay on May 23, 2011.

KEEP DRINKING AGE AT TWENTY-ONE: TEENS AREN'T MATURE ENOUGH TO HANDLE CONSEQUENCES

JOYCE ALCANTARA

We do crazy things when we are drunk. 1

We do crazy things when we are young. 2

What if we were young and drunk at the same time? 3

It seems as if the United States is the last country to reduce its drinking 4 age. Unlike our friends across the pond, Americans younger than 21 do not have the privilege of consuming alcohol. This policy has inspired countless debates. It goes something like this: Eighteen-year-olds can vote, marry, drive, and serve in the Army, so why can't they legally drink alcohol?

This may seem like a valid line of reasoning. However, the "Old enough to 5 fight, old enough to drink" argument is not as clever as it sounds. Alcohol is one of the most used and abused drugs among teenagers in the U.S. According to one survey, young people who begin drinking before age 15 are four times more likely to develop alcoholism than those who begin drinking at 21. On top of that, more than 25,000 lives have been saved in the U.S. thanks to the 21 minimum legal drinking age, according to Mothers Against Drunk Driving.

> "Alcohol is one of the most used and abused drugs among teenagers in the U.S."

If we lowered the drinking age to 18, we would be allowing alcohol prob- 6 lems to increase among our youths. Eighteen-year-olds heavily influence those younger who look up to them. An 18-year-old easily could make a purchase at the liquor store for a 16-year-old, giving that younger teen more opportunities to hurt himself. Let's also remember that many 18-year-olds are still high school students living at home with their parents.

The effects of alcohol on the body are not always acknowledged. Accord- 7 ing to the U.S. Department of Health and Human Services, one of the primary factors in how much alcohol affects the brain is the age that a person begins drinking. These effects include blackout and memory lapse, brain shrinkage, and the brain disorder Wernicke Korsakoff Syndrome. Drinking at an earlier age also increases the possibility of liver diseases like cirrhosis, which results from excessive alcohol consumption.

Eighteen-year-olds are not mature enough and wise enough to handle the 8 negative consequences of drinking. It is doubtful that one could emotionally handle a drunken driving incident. Alcohol can lower inhibitions and lead to choices that a sober person might not ordinarily make such as sex, which can lead to teen pregnancy. Other issues alcohol can be a factor in include date rape and suicide.

The depictions of teen drinking in pop culture bolster my argument. On programs such as *Gossip Girl*, *One Tree Hill*, and other shows and films, it seems like obtaining alcohol is easier than getting soda from a vending machine. We see teens get wasted, but the underage characters are seldom seen suffering any consequences, which makes the action all the more appealing. In real life, abusing alcohol can have life-altering effects. I've seen the damage alcohol can do. I know people who have been arrested for drunken quarrels and people whose licenses have been suspended because of underage drinking and driving. These incidents are 100 percent preventable.

Though there is only a three-year difference between 18 and 21, there's a world of difference in maturity level. At 21 or older, with a few years of college and independent living under their belts, young adults have enough sense and maturity to think thoroughly before making decisions.

It's cliché, but true: "Our youths today are the leaders of tomorrow." We have to protect our future.

⊙ AT ISSUE: SOURCES FOR DEVELOPING A CAUSAL ARGUMENT

1. Outline Alcantara's essay, making sure to include her thesis state-ment, evidence, refutation of opposing arguments, and conclusion. (Follow the outline for structuring a causal argument on p. 448.) Does she include all the elements of a causal argument? Should anything be added or deleted?

2. Why, according to Alcantara, is the "'Old enough to fight, old enough to drink' argument . . . not as clever as it sounds" (para. 5)? Is her refutation of this argument effective?

3. In paragraph 6, Alcantara says, "Eighteen-year-olds heavily influence those younger who look up to them." Why does she make this state-ment? Do you think it supports her position? Summarize the causal chain developed in this paragraph.

4. In paragraph 9, Alcantara says, "The depictions of teen drinking in pop culture bolster my argument." Do you agree that movies and TV shows seldom show the negative consequences of teenage drinking? Can you refute her statement?

5. Alcantara is a teen correspondent for the *San Jose Mercury News*, where this commentary appeared. Does this information add to or detract from her credibility?

6. In her last paragraph, Alcantara acknowledges that her concluding statement is a cliché. Rewrite this paragraph, including a more origi-nal (and memorable) concluding statement.

This commentary appeared on August 22, 2007, on *BG Views*, a Web site for Bowling Green State University and the citizens of its community.

RAISE THE DRINKING AGE TO TWENTY-FIVE

ANDREW HERMAN

As a new school year begins, as dorms fill with new and returning students alike, a single thought frequents the minds of every member of our population: newfound freedom from a summer of jobs and familial responsibilities. 1

But our return to school coexists with a possibly lethal counterpart: college drinking. 2

Nearly everyone is exposed to parties during college, and one would be hard pressed to find a college party without alcohol. Most University students indicate in countless surveys they have used alcohol in a social setting before age 21. 3

It is startling just how ineffective current laws have been at curbing underage drinking. 4

> "It is startling just how ineffective current laws have been."

A dramatic change is needed in the way society addresses drinking and the way we enforce existing laws, and it can start with a simple change: making the drinking age 25. 5

Access and availability are the principal reasons underage drinking has become easy to do. Not through direct availability, but through access to legal-aged "friends." 6

In a college setting, it is all but impossible not to know a person who is older than 21 and willing to provide alcohol to younger students. Even if unintentional, there is no verification that each person who drinks is of the appropriate age. 7

However, it should be quite easy to ensure underage individuals don't have access to alcohol. In reality, those who abstain from alcohol are in the minority. Countless people our age consider speeding tickets worse than an arrest for underage consumption. 8

Is it truly possible alcohol abuse has become so commonplace, so acceptable, that people forget the facts? 9

Each year, 1,400 [college students] die from drinking too much. 600,000 are victims of alcohol-related physical assault and 17,000 are a result of drunken driving deaths, many being innocent bystanders. 10

Perhaps the most disturbing number: 70,000 people, overwhelmingly female, are annually sexually assaulted in alcohol-related situations. 11

These numbers are difficult to grasp for the sheer prevalence of alcoholic destruction. Yet, we, as college students, are responsible for an overwhelming portion of their incidence. It is difficult to imagine anyone would wish to 12 assume the role of rapist, murderer, or victim. We all assume these things could never happen to us, but I am certain victims in these situations thought the same. The simple truth is that driving under the influence is the leading cause of death for teens. For 10- to 24-year-olds, alcohol is the fourth-leading cause of death, made so by factors ranging from alcohol poisoning to alcohol-related assault and murder.

For the sake of our friends, those we love, our futures, and ourselves, we 13
must take a stand and we must do it now.

Advocates of lowering the drinking age assert only four countries world- 14
wide maintain a "21 standard," and a gradual transition to alcohol is useful in reducing the systemic social problems of substance abuse.

If those under the age of 21 are misusing alcohol, it makes little sense to 15
grant free rein to those individuals to use it legally. A parent who observes their children abusing the neighbor's dog would be irresponsible to get one of their own without altering such dangerous behavior.

Increasing the drinking age will help in the search for solutions to griev- 16
ous alcoholic problems, making it far more difficult in college environments to find legal-aged providers.

By the time we are 25, with careers and possibly families of our own, there 17
is no safety net to allow us to have a "Thirsty Thursday." But increasing the legal age is not all that needs to be done. Drinking to get drunk needs to exist as a social taboo rather than a doorway to popularity.

Peer pressure can become a tool to change this. What once was a factor 18
greatly contributing to underage drinking can now become an instrument of good, seeking to end such a dangerous practice as excessive drinking. Laws on drinking ages, as any other law, need to be enforced with the energy and vigor each of us should expect.

Alcohol is not an inherently evil poison. It does have its place, as do all 19
things in the great scheme of life.

But with alcohol comes the terrible risk of abuse with consequences many 20
do not consider. All too often, these consequences include robbing someone of his life or loved one. All communities in the country, our own included, have been touched by such a tragedy.

Because of this, and the hundreds of thousands of victims each year in 21
alcohol-related situations, I ask that you consider the very real possibility of taking the life of another due to irresponsible drinking.

If this is not enough, then take time to think, because that life could very 22
well be your own.

⊘ AT ISSUE: SOURCES FOR DEVELOPING A CAUSAL ARGUMENT

1. The writer is a college student. Given his position on the issue, does his status as a student increase or decrease his credibility?

2. How does Herman try to establish common ground with his readers?

3. In paragraph 14, Herman mentions an opposing argument. How does he refute it? Do you think his refutation is strong enough? If not, how would you expand or reword it?

4. Herman proposes raising the drinking age to twenty-five. Why doesn't he support keeping the drinking age at twenty-one? Do you think most of his readers would be likely to support this position rather than the position advocated by Joyce Alcantara (p. 468)? Do you see Herman's position as realistic, or do you consider it extreme? Do you think he is serious?

This opinion column was published by the *St. Paul Pioneer Press* on June 9, 2011.

HOW BEST TO BALANCE THE BENEFITS AND RESPONSIBILITIES OF ADULTHOOD?

CARYN SULLIVAN

On a January night in 2006, 18-year-old Fabrizio Montermini drank Gatorade 1 and vodka, drove more than 100 mph, T-boned another car, abandoned his unconscious passengers in a dark church parking lot, and fled the scene. Last month, he was convicted of the third-degree murder of his 18-year-old passenger, who suffered a traumatic brain injury in the crash. Montermini's case, while extraordinary, illuminates an issue plaguing many parents of teens and young adults.

In 1984, the federal government raised the legal drinking age to 21. By 2 1988, all 50 states had opted to comply, rather than forfeit federal highway funds. Although many states have since lowered the drinking age, Minnesota has not. The proper age for legal drinking persists as a quandary involving reasoned positions but no easy solution.

This time of year, high school students begin the transition from their 3 parents' home to independent living, unencumbered by school rules designed to deter drinking. Meanwhile, college students are returning after living out of their parents' view for much of the year. When both the temptation and the opportunity to imbibe are present, parents are challenged to monitor behavior of those who consider themselves adults, and reasonably so.

Thus, discussions about the drinking age abound. 4

Mothers Against Drunk Driving correlates the higher drinking age with 5 reduction in alcohol-related driving deaths. MADD asserts teens get drunk twice as fast as adults and they binge-drink more often.

MADD characterizes as a "myth" arguments that because Europeans 6 expose children to alcohol at a younger age they have fewer drinking problems. The earlier children drink the more likely they are to be perpetrators or victims of violence, to drop out of school, or have unprotected or unplanned sex, the argument goes.

Those who favor a lower drinking age point to the disparity between laws 7 governing drinking and other rites of passage into adulthood. At 18, adults can marry, vote, and join the military. Yet, they'll have three years of college behind them before they can legally drink a beer. Better to introduce alcohol at a younger age at home where we can supervise and inform, the argument goes. This argument favors the European approach—accept moderation, punish abuse harshly. Putting a year's distance between high school graduation and legal drinking makes sense, they say, so 19 is a more reasonable drinking age.

In contrast to their parents' *Brady Bunch* entertainment experience, today's 8 youth have grown up in an instant gratification, girls-and-boys-gone-wild era, in which alcohol is often portrayed as an ingredient in life's recipe for fun. Reality TV features graphic and coarse behavior a la drunken coeds having a blast at wet t-shirt parties. In the popular *Hangover II* movie, a male bonding experience involves mixing pills and booze. The dudes awaken with a tattooed face and shaved head, no memory of how they got that way, but happy.

In real life, a hangover or blackout is anything but funny. Dr. Jim Thomp- 9 son, medical director for emergency services at the University of Minnesota, has observed how students often consume alcohol with a purpose, sometimes with life-threatening results. On weekends, it's not uncommon for one-fourth of the emergency room to house students with drinking-related issues, he says. They can require six to eight hours of monitoring for alcohol poisoning or, occasionally, intensive-care treatment with ventilators. During one Spring Jam, so many students were admitted with alcohol-related problems the emergency room closed to additional ambulance admissions.

> "In real life, a hangover or blackout is anything but funny."

Lt. Troy Buhta of the University of Minnesota Police Department sees the 10 forbidden-fruit phenomenon in action. Kids come to college for the first time and, without Mom and Dad there, they want to do it all and do it in a hurry, he says. In each of the past two years, his department issued well more than 300 underage-drinking citations. So far this year, they've cited 109.

MADD cites the reduction in drinking and driving as a reason to keep the 11 drinking age at 21. The higher drinking age may have yielded benefits, but it has also caused unintended consequences. Individuals who are otherwise law-abiding citizens either break the law by drinking or turn a blind eye to their grown children's illegal behavior.

Students I've surveyed acknowledge the effectiveness of the graphic and 12 realistic campaign against drinking and driving. Many embrace the message: the price of drinking and driving is too high. Yet, other consequences of drinking—until they hit home—may be more difficult for young people to comprehend.

The world has changed since the drinking age was raised in 1984. It's time 13 for an honest reassessment. Are restorative justice programs or educational curricula such as DARE a successful antidote to Hollywood's potent depiction of the alcohol fun factor? Does it make sense to allow an 18- or 19-year-old to go to war but prohibit him from drinking a beer with his buddies? Wouldn't we better align adult benefits and responsibilities if the drinking age were 19?

If the drinking and driving curriculum offered to students is largely effec- 14 tive, perhaps they need a comparable high impact lesson on additional real-life consequences of irresponsible drinking. Imagine the power of a testimonial from Fabrizio Montermini entitled "My Life as a Felon—the Unintended Consequence of Excessive Drinking, Driving, and Horrific Choices."

⊘ AT ISSUE: SOURCES FOR DEVELOPING A CAUSAL ARGUMENT

1. In paragraphs 5–6, Sullivan summarizes MADD's objections to lowering the drinking age; in paragraph 7, she summarizes arguments for changing the legal drinking age to eighteen or nineteen. Based on what you have read in the other At Issue essays in this chapter, do you think Sullivan's summaries are accurate? Do you think they are comprehensive enough?

2. In paragraphs 8–9, Sullivan contrasts the "real-life" consequences of drinking with the portrayal of the consequences in films and in reality TV. How are they different? How are her observations similar to and different from those made by Joyce Alcantara on this point (p. 468)?

3. Sullivan cites the expert opinion of Dr. Jim Thompson (para. 9), police officer Troy Buhta (10), and MADD (11); in paragraph 1, she summarizes an event that had tragic consequences; and in paragraph 12, she refers to "students I've surveyed." What kind of appeal is she making in each case? Which of these appeals do you find most and least convincing? Why?

4. In paragraphs 7 and 13, Sullivan mentions the option of changing the drinking age to nineteen. Do you think this is a better option than a legal drinking age of eighteen or twenty-one? If so, why? If not, why not?

5. Sullivan's purpose, as indicated in her title, is not to take a position on the issue but to consider both sides and recommend "an honest reassessment" (13) of the problem. Do you think she is successful? Does her essay present a balanced view of the issue, or does the evidence presented on one side outweigh the evidence presented on the other side? Explain.

This graph is from the Federal Trade Commission's "Don't Serve Teens" Web site.

HIGH SCHOOL SENIORS' ALCOHOL USE DECLINES

FEDERAL TRADE COMMISSION

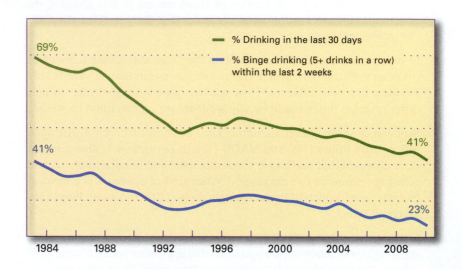

◉ AT ISSUE: SOURCES FOR DEVELOPING A CAUSAL ARGUMENT

1. Summarize the information presented in the graph above. What effect does the graph focus on? What possible causes might have led to this effect?

2. Could you use the information in the graph to support a position in favor of lowering the drinking age? Could you use the same data to support the opposite position? Which position do you think the data could support more convincingly? Why?

3. This graph appears on the Federal Trade Commission's "Don't Serve Teens" Web site under the heading "21 Is the Legal Drinking Age." Visit this site, and try to determine who its intended audience is.

4. How do you think high school seniors would react to the information presented in this graph? How might their parents react?

This advertisement was created by Mothers Against Drunk Driving (MADD).

17,000 KILLED IN SENSELESS ACT

MADD

> **Rational Report**
>
> ## 17,000 killed in senseless act
>
> ### Authorities search for answers on a day of sadness
>
> A nation is in mourning as thousands were suddenly killed yesterday all across the country by people who had been drinking and driving. Traffic was backed up in all 50 states making it difficult for emergency vehicles to reach the victims. Hospitals in every city remain overwhelmed with thousands of critically injured patients. . . . the help of National Gua. . .
>
> simply are not enough resources to meet the demands of this catastrophe. The president spoke early this morning at an emergency press conference expressing his condolences to the friends and families of those who were lost. One official in DeBeau County called this "the most devastating moment in American history." In some places, entire families were killed, leaving many to wonder how something like this could happen in our country today. In a show of support, long lines of volunteers have formed at the . . . of blood and . . . enters . . . to . . .
>
> If this were today's headline, would you notice? Last year, drinking and driving actually did kill about 17,000 people. It injured half a million more. But because it happened over a year rather than in a single day, it's not always front-page news. It's a growing problem, with a simple answer. If you drink, find a safe way home. And do your part to keep drunk driving out of the headlines.
>
> **MADD.**
> Activism : Victim Services : Education
> www.madd.org

➲ AT ISSUE: SOURCES FOR DEVELOPING A CAUSAL ARGUMENT

1. Does this public-service ad, prepared by Mothers Against Drunk Driving, seem to be addressed to a specific audience or to anyone who might read it? Who is the "you" the text of the ad refers to?

2. The newspaper clipping shown in this ad, particularly the headline, is intended to shock. Does it have the intended effect on you? Why or why not?

3. What causal argument does the MADD ad present? Is the newspaper clipping also a causal argument? Explain.

4. Does this ad use appeals to *logos*, *pathos*, or *ethos*—or does it use all three kinds of appeals? Which appeal is most powerful in this argument? Why?

➔ EXERCISE 13.8

Write a one-paragraph causal argument in which you take a position on whether lowering the drinking age to eighteen will solve the problem of binge drinking among college students. Follow the template below, filling in the blanks to create your argument.

TEMPLATE FOR WRITING A CAUSAL ARGUMENT

In 1984, the federal drinking age was raised to twenty-one. Since that time, there have been many positive results, such as _____ _____ _____. However, there have also been some negative effects. As over 100 college presidents who favor reconsidering the federal drinking age point out, _____ _____ _____. For these reasons, they suggest the drinking age might be lowered. MADD and others, however, argue against lowering the drinking age, noting that _____ _____. Granted, _____ _____. Still, _____ _____ _____ _____. All things considered, the drinking age (should/should not) be lowered.

➔ EXERCISE 13.9

Working with a group of two or three of your classmates, discuss your experiences with alcohol as a high school student and as a college student. What negative behavior have you observed at parties where alcohol was served? What problems have you observed with teenage drivers and alcohol? Do you and your classmates believe that these problems were caused or exacerbated by the current drinking age? Write a paragraph that summarizes your group's impressions.

➲ EXERCISE 13.10

Write a causal argument on the topic, "Should the Drinking Age Be Lowered?" Begin by considering all possible problems associated with teenage drinking and deciding which factors are most to blame for the situation. Then, consider whether a change in the drinking age will have a positive effect on the problem. (If you like, you may incorporate the material you developed for Exercises 13.8 and 13.9 into your essay.) Cite the readings on pages 455–478, and be sure to document the sources you use and to include a works-cited page. (See Chapter 10 for information on documenting sources.)

➲ EXERCISE 13.11

Review the four pillars of argument discussed in Chapter 1. Does your essay include all four elements of an effective argument? Add anything that is missing. Then, label the key elements of your essay.

➲ WRITING ASSIGNMENTS: CAUSAL ARGUMENTS

1. What could your school do to encourage students to adopt healthier lifestyles? Write an editorial for your college newspaper in the form of a causal argument. In your editorial, take one of these two positions:

   - If the university takes steps to encourage healthier lifestyles, students will benefit greatly.

   - If the university does not take steps to encourage students to adopt healthier lifestyles, the consequences could be serious.

2. Look at pictures of female celebrities online, and consider the likely effects of these images on teenage girls. Then, write an essay arguing for or against the charge that images such as these help to encourage poor self-esteem, risky behavior, or eating disorders. Include some of the images in your essay, and analyze the impact of their visual elements as well as the effect of the words in the accompanying articles or captions.

3. In recent years, young children's lives have become more and more structured. Instead of the free play that their parents enjoyed, many of today's children are busy with scheduled sports, lessons, and play dates. Write an essay structured as a causal chain that traces the

probable causes of this change as well as its likely effects on children and on their families. In your thesis statement, indicate whether you consider the effects positive or negative.

"We have an opening for a part-time unpaid intern, which could lead to a full-time unpaid internship."

Evaluation Arguments

AT ISSUE

Are Internships a Good Deal for College Students?

Internships are a vital part of the college experience for many students. In fact, approximately 75% of students currently enrolled in U.S. four-year colleges will have internships before they graduate. An intern typically works for a summer or a semester, sometimes receiving college credit, a small stipend, or—in fewer than half of internships—a salary.

Proponents of internships (students, employers, and college placement staff) argue that although many student interns perform entry-level tasks—photocopying, running errands, and so on—they also gain useful work experience and may make valuable business contacts as well as find mentors. Moreover, internships enable students to determine whether a particular career is right for them.

Those who are critical of internships concede that internships, particularly those related to a student's field of study, can prepare them for the world of work and help them find jobs after they graduate. However, they contend that low-paid or unpaid internships exploit students, requiring them to work hard for little, if any, financial gain. Moreover, internships tend to favor financially well-off students and discriminate against those who cannot afford to work for little or no pay. Upper-income students can also afford to relocate, to pay their own living expenses, or to give up a higher-paying job to take an internship.

Later in this chapter, you will return to this topic as you explore readings on both sides of this issue. You will then be asked to write an **evaluation argument** that takes a position on whether internships are a good deal for college students.

For comprehension quizzes,
see **bedfordstmartins.com/practicalargument**.

What Is an Evaluation Argument?

When you **evaluate**, you make a value judgment about something or someone—for example, a product, service, program, performance, work of literature or art, or candidate for public office.

Evaluation is part of your daily life. Before you make any decision, you need to evaluate your options. For example, you evaluate clothing and electronic equipment before you make a purchase, and you evaluate films, concerts, and TV shows before you decide how to spend your evening. Before you decide to go to a party, you evaluate its positive and negative qualities—who will be there, what music you are likely to hear, and what kind of food and drink will probably be on hand. You also evaluate your teachers, your classes, and even your friends. Without evaluation, you would be unable to function in your day-to-day life.

When constructing an **evaluation argument**, you have several options: you can make a positive or negative judgment, you can assert that someone else's positive or negative judgment is not accurate or justified, or you can write a comparative evaluation, in which you demonstrate that one thing is (or is not) superior to another.

As a college student, you might read (or write) evaluation arguments based on topics like the following:

- Is the college bookstore doing its best to serve students?

- Is a vegan diet really a healthy option?

- Is *Moby-Dick* the great American novel?

- Is New Orleans still a rewarding tourist destination?

- Is the SAT a valid testing instrument?

- Are portable e-book readers really better than print books?

- Are Crocs a marvel of comfort and design or just ugly shoes?

- Are hybrid cars worth the money?

- Were the Beatles the most important band of the twentieth century?

⊝ EXERCISE 14.1

List ten additional topics that would be suitable for evaluation arguments.

MAKING EVALUATIONS

When you write an evaluation, you use terms like the following to express judgments and indicate the relative merits of two items:

Superior/inferior	Important/trivial
Useful/useless	Original/trite
Efficient/inefficient	Innovative/predictable
Effective/ineffective	Interesting/dull
Successful/unsuccessful	Inspiring/depressing
Deserving/undeserving	

⊝ EXERCISE 14.2

Choose one word in each of the word pairs listed above, and use each word in a sentence that evaluates a service or program at your school.

IDENTIFYING BIAS

Everyone has biases, and these are likely to show up in evaluations, where strong opinions may overcome objectivity. As you read and write evaluation arguments, be on the lookout for evidence of bias:

- When you *read* evaluation arguments, carefully consider what the writer reveals (or actually states) about his or her values, beliefs, and opinions. Also be alert for evidence of bias in a writer's language and tone as well as in his or her choice of examples. (See "Detecting Bias in Your Sources" in Chapter 7 for more on this issue.)

- When you *write* evaluation arguments, focus on trying to make a fair assessment of your subject. Be particularly careful not to distort or slant evidence, quote out of context, or use unfair appeals or logical fallacies. (See "Being Fair" in Chapter 7 for more on how to avoid bias in your writing.)

Criteria for Evaluation

When you evaluate something, you cannot simply state that it is good or bad, useful or useless, valuable or worthless, or superior or inferior to something else. You need to explain *why* this is so. Before you can begin to develop a thesis and gather supporting evidence for your argument, you need to decide what **criteria for evaluation** you will use: to support a *positive* judgment, you need to show that something has value because it satisfies certain criteria; to support a *negative* judgment, you need to show that something lacks value because it does not satisfy those criteria.

To make any judgment, then, you need to select the specific criteria you will use to assess your subject. For example, in an evaluation of a college bookstore, will you base your evaluation on the friendliness of its service? Its prices? The number of books it stocks? Its return policy? The efficiency or knowledge of the staff? Your answers to these questions will help you begin to plan your evaluation.

The criteria that you establish will help you decide how to evaluate a given subject. For example, if your criteria for evaluating rock bands focus on their influence on other musicians, you may be able to support the thesis that the Beatles were the most influential group of the twentieth century. If, however, your criteria for evaluation are singing ability and complexity of musical arrangements, your case may be less compelling. Similarly, if you are judging health-care systems on the basis of how many individuals have medical coverage, you may be able to demonstrate that the Canadian system is superior to the U.S. system. If your criteria are referral time and government support for medical research, your evaluation argument might support a different position. Whatever criteria you decide on, a bookstore (or band or health-care system) that satisfies them will be seen as superior to one that does not.

Consider another example. Suppose you want to evaluate the government's Head Start program, which was established in 1964 to provide preschool education to children from low-income families. The program also provides medical coverage and social services to the children enrolled, and in recent years it has expanded to cover children of migrant workers and children in homeless families. On what basis would you evaluate this program? Would you evaluate only the children's educational progress or also consider the program's success in providing health care? In considering educational progress, would you focus on test scores or on students' performance in school? Would you measure long-term effects—for example, Head Start students' likelihood of attending college and their annual earnings as adults? Or would you focus on short-term results—for example, students' performance in elementary school? Finally, would you evaluate only the children or also their families? Depending on the criteria you select for your evaluation, the Head Start program could be considered a success or a failure—or something in between.

⬦ EXERCISE 14.3

Choose one of the topics you listed in Exercise 14.1, and list five possible criteria for an evaluation argument on that topic.

⬦ EXERCISE 14.4

By what criteria do you evaluate the textbooks for your college courses? Design? Content? Clarity? Comprehensiveness? Cost? Work with another student to decide on the most important criteria, and then write a paragraph in which you evaluate this textbook.

Structuring an Evaluation Argument

In general terms, an evaluation argument can be structured like this:

- **Introduction:** Establishes the criteria by which you will evaluate your subject; states the essay's thesis

- **Evidence (first point in support of thesis):** Supplies facts, opinions, and so on to support your evaluation in terms of one of the criteria you have established

- **Evidence (second point in support of thesis):** Supplies facts, opinions, and so on to support your evaluation in terms of one of the criteria you have established

- **Evidence (third point in support of thesis):** Supplies facts, opinions, and so on to support your evaluation in terms of one of the criteria you have established

- **Refutation of opposing arguments:** Presents others' evaluations and your arguments against them

- **Conclusion:** Reinforces the main point of the argument; includes a strong concluding statement

The following student essay includes all the elements of an evaluation argument. The student who wrote the essay was evaluating a popular Web site, RateMyProfessors.com.

EVALUATION OF A WEB SITE: RATEMYPROFESSORS.COM

KEVIN MURPHY

Since 1999, both students and professors have been writing, reading, defending, and criticizing the content on RateMyProfessors.com (RMP). With over 13 million student-written reviews and over 4 million visitors a month, RMP continues to be the most popular site of its kind ("About RateMYProfessors.com"). However, the fact that a Web site is popular does not mean that it is reliable. Certainly RMP may be interesting and entertaining (and even, as *New York Times* writer Virginia Heffernan recently wrote, "engrossing"), but is it useful? Will it help students to make informed decisions about the schools they choose to attend and the classes they choose to take? Are the ratings—as well as the site itself—trustworthy? Is the information about professors and schools comprehensive enough to be meaningful? No student wants to waste time in a course that is poorly taught by a teacher who lacks enthusiasm, knowledge, or objectivity. However, an evaluation of the reviews on RateMyProfessors.com suggests that the site is not trustworthy or comprehensive enough to help college students make the right choices about the courses they take.

Thesis statement

Evidence: First point in support of thesis

The first question to ask about the reviews on RMP is, "Who is writing them?" All reviews on the site are anonymous, and although anonymity protects the writers' privacy and may encourage them to offer honest feedback, it is also a red flag. There is no guarantee that the reviews are written by students. In fact, anyone—even the professors themselves—can create RMP accounts and post reviews, and there is no way of knowing who is writing or what a writer's motivations and biases are. In addition, the percentage of students who actually write reviews is small. According to one recent survey, only 8% of students have ever written a review for an online professor-rating site; in other words, "a vocal minority" is running the show (Arden). Furthermore, the ratings for each individual professor vary greatly in number, quality, and currency. Even in the rare cases where a professor has hundreds of recent ratings, the score may represent the views of only a small percentage of that professor's students. This means that getting a representative sample is highly unlikely. Unless the Web site's managers institute rules and restrictions to ensure the legitimacy of the writer and the size of the sample, the RMP ratings will continue to be untrustworthy.

Evidence: Second point in support of thesis

The second question to ask is, "Who controls RMP's content?" Although RMP posts "Site Guidelines" with a "Do" list and a "Do Not" list, these lists are merely suggestions. The RMP Site Moderation Team will remove obscene or unlawful posts, but it has no way to enforce other guidelines. For instance, one of the items on the "Do Not" list asks users not to "post a rating if you have not taken a class with the professor" ("Site Guidelines"). However, to sign up for an RMP account, a user does not have to identify his or her university or list the courses he or she has taken. The site asks only for a name, a birth date, and the right to share the user's personal information with its partner companies. This last question is a reminder that RMP is ultimately a commercial venture. The site is not owned by students or by their universities; it is owned by mtvU, a TV network that in turn is owned by

media giant Viacom. The fact that each page of RMP content is surrounded
on three sides by advertisements reminds users that the primary purpose of
this site is to make money. When that fact is combined with the fact that the
company has "the right to delete, re-format and/or change your Postings in
any manner that we may determine," it indicates that RMP does not warrant
students' trust ("Terms of Use"). A for-profit corporation, not the student
reviewers, controls all of the information on the site and may modify content
to increase traffic and impress advertisers.

4   The last question to ask is, "Does RMP offer students the right kind
of information—and enough in-depth information to give them a
comprehensive understanding of a professor's effectiveness as a
teacher?" In fact, the site offers ratings in only four categories:
"Helpfulness," "Clarity," "Easiness," and "Hotness." As one highly rated
professor points out, "None of the dimensions [of RMP's rating system]
directly addresses how much students felt they learned" (qtd. in Arden).
Moreover, no category addresses the professor's knowledge of the subject
matter. The ratings tend to focus attention on superficial qualities rather
than on substance, apparently assuming that most students are looking
for "easy A" classes taught by attractive, pleasant instructors. For students
who are trying to make informed decisions about which classes to take,
these criteria are inadequate. As one frustrated student user explains,
"One of my professors had a really negative rating and comments, but he
came to be one of my favorites. . . . his way of teaching matched me
perfectly" (qtd. in Ross). The focus of RateMyProfessors.com is not on
giving substantial feedback about teaching effectiveness or information
about the educational value of a class. Perhaps these kinds of feedback do
not attract advertisers; feedback about a professor's "Hotness"—the least
important measure of effectiveness—apparently does.

5   Students who argue that RMP is a "useful resource" say that the site
helps them decide which professors to take and which to avoid (Davis). For
example, one community college student says that checking professors'
scores on RMP "helps me choose a professor who will suit my needs" (qtd.
in Davis). Committed RMP users also say that they are able to sift through
the superficial comments and find useful information about professors'
teaching styles. As one junior at Baruch College in New York City says, "It's
all about perspective, and you need to be aware of this when you use the

Evidence: Third point in support of thesis

Refutation of opposing arguments

site" (qtd. in Ross). Users claim that they can read reviews and understand that "even though [a particular student] doesn't seem to like the professor, it sounds like I might" (qtd. in Davis). This ability to read between the lines, however, does not change the fact that the information on RMP is neither verifiable nor comprehensive. RMP's reviews are anonymous, and some of them are almost certainly not written by students who have taken the professors' classes. Professors' "Overall Quality" scores, which so many students rely on, are based on ratings by these untrustworthy reviewers. Furthermore, these "overall" ratings are based on only two factors: "Helpfulness" and "Clarity" ("Rating Categories"). A rating that is calculated on the basis of very limited information from questionable sources can hardly be a "useful resource." On balance, then, RMP does not give students the information they need to make informed decisions.

On RMP's homepage, the site managers encourage visitors to "join the 6 fun!" ("About RateMyProfessors.com"). "Fun" is ultimately all users can hope to find at RMP. As Virginia Heffernan recommends, "Read it like a novel, watch it like MTV, study it like sociology. Just don't base any real decisions on it." Real students' honest and thorough reviews of professors are invaluable, but sites like RMP do not provide this kind of helpful feedback. When deciding between a commercial Web site and old-fashioned word of mouth, anyone who thinks that RMP offers more useful information should keep in mind who writes and controls the site's content. Because visitors to the site know almost nothing about the reviewers, they cannot know if their comments and ratings are trustworthy. Moreover, because they do know something about the site's owners, they should know enough to be wary of their motives. If students are looking for useful advice about which classes to take, they should look no further than their own campuses.

Concluding statement

Works Cited

"About RateMyProfessors.com." *Rate My Professors.* MTV Networks, 2011. Web. 13 Mar. 2012.

Arden, Patrick. "Rate My Professors Has Some Academics Up in Arms." *Village Voice.* Village Voice, 26 Oct. 2011. Web. 13 Mar. 2012.

Davis, Mandi. "Rate My Professor Gains Popularity with MCCC Students." *Agora.* Monroe County Community College, 7 Dec. 2011. Web. 13 Mar. 2012.

Heffernan, Virginia. "The Prof Stuff." *New York Times.* New York Times, 11 Mar. 2010. Web. 12 Mar. 2012.

"Rating Categories." *Rate My Professors.* MTV Networks, 2011. Web.

> 13 Mar. 2012.

Ross, Terrance. "Professor Evaluation Website Receives Mixed Reviews."

> *Ticker.* Baruch College, City U of New York, 12 Sept. 2011. Web.
>
> 12 Mar. 2012.

"Site Guidelines." *Rate My Professors.* MTV Networks, 20 June 2011.

> Web. 13 Mar. 2012.

"Terms of Use." *Rate My Professors.* MTV Networks, 20 June 2011. Web.

> 13 Mar. 2012.

GRAMMAR IN CONTEXT

Comparatives and Superlatives

When you write an **evaluation argument**, you make judgments, and these judgments often call for comparative analysis—for example, arguing that one thing is better than another or the best of its kind.

When you compare two items or qualities, you use a **comparative** form: *bigger, better, more interesting, less realistic.* When you compare three or more items or qualities, you use a **superlative** form: *the biggest, the best, the most interesting, the least realistic.* Be careful to use these forms appropriately.

- **Do not use the comparative when you are comparing more than two things.**

  INCORRECT Perhaps these kinds of feedback do not attract advertisers; feedback about a professor's "Hotness"—<u>the less important measure</u> of effectiveness—apparently does.

  CORRECT Perhaps these kinds of feedback do not attract advertisers; feedback about a professor's "Hotness"—<u>the least important measure</u> of effectiveness—apparently does.

- **Do not use the superlative when you are comparing only two things.**

  INCORRECT When deciding between a commercial Web site and old-fashioned word of mouth, anyone who thinks that RMP offers <u>the most useful information</u> should keep in mind who writes and controls the site's content.

  CORRECT When deciding between a commercial Web site and old-fashioned word of mouth, anyone who thinks that RMP offers <u>more useful information</u> should keep in mind who writes and controls the site's content.

⊃ EXERCISE 14.5

The following commentary, "Nothing Pretty in Child Pageants," includes the basic elements of an evaluation argument. Read the essay, and then answer the questions that follow it, consulting the outline on page 487 if necessary.

This article was published in the *Lexington Herald-Leader* on August 14, 2011.

NOTHING PRETTY IN CHILD PAGEANTS

VERNON R. WIEHE

Toddlers and Tiaras is a televised beauty pageant for very young children 1 which appears weekly ironically on The Learning Channel. The Web site for the show describes it this way: "On any given weekend, on stages across the country, little girls and boys parade around wearing makeup, false eyelashes, spray tans, and fake hair to be judged on their beauty, personality, and costumes. *Toddlers and Tiaras* follows families on their quest for sparkly crowns, big titles, and lots of cash."

A TV viewer will see the program's feeble attempts at Las Vegas–like glam- 2 our and glitz in a rented hotel ballroom or school auditorium with primarily little girls in adult-like pageant attire parading in front of a small audience consisting largely of participants' families. The tots' attire includes makeup, hair extensions, and "flippers" to hide missing teeth. Mothers, often overweight, engage in silly antics coaching the children in every move of their routines with the hope of winning a trophy taller than the child, a rhinestone crown, the title of "Ultimate Grand Supreme," and possibly some cash.

The viewer will also be taken behind the scenes to witness temper tan- 3 trums from children resisting the role into which they are being put. On a recent show, a 2-year-old cried the entire time on stage; in another show, a mother literally dragged the child around the stage supposedly putting the child through her routine.

It raises questions for the viewer: Whose idea is this—the child's or the 4 adult's? Is participating in such pageants age-appropriate behavior for a small child? Might such participation even represent a potential danger for the child's emotional development?

The potential impact of child beauty pageants may be viewed in terms of 5 the fallacious arguments most frequently cited in support of this activity:

All Little Girls Like to Play Dress-Up at Some Time

Dress-up, a sign of a child identifying with or mimicking the mother, is signifi- 6 cantly different from organized child beauty pageants.

First, dress-up play generally is an activity engaged in by a young girl alone or 7
with a group of playmates at home rather than on a stage in front of an audience.

Second, competition, an important element in child beauty pageants, 8
ranks contestants, with one child becoming a winner and the others losers.

Third, dress-up involves little girls wearing their mothers' cast-off clothing 9
or cosmetics in a way the child perceives mother uses these objects. Participants
in *Toddlers and Tiaras* spend hundreds and even thousands of dollars for costumes, cosmetics, and even beauty consultants.

Parents certainly have a right to spend their money on children as they 10
wish, but if this expenditure of money and effort is for the ultimate goal of the
child winning the contest and the child fails to do so, what is the emotional
cost to the child? What happens to the child's self-esteem?

Children's Beauty Pageants Teach Poise and Self-Confidence

Even if the pageants do foster the development of these attributes, the question 11
must be raised whether poise and self-confidence stemming from beauty pageants is age appropriate for the child. One of the most dangerous aspects of
these pageants is the sexualization of young girls.

Sexualization occurs through little girls wearing adult women's clothing in 12
diminutive sizes, the use of makeup which often is applied by makeup consultants, spray tanning the body, the dying of hair and the use of hair extensions,
and assuming provocative postures more appropriate for adult models.

The sexualization of young children sends a conflicting message to the 13
child and a dangerous message to adults. To the child, a message is given that
sexuality—expressed in clothing, makeup, and certain postures—is appropriate
and even something to exploit. The message to adults, especially pedophiles, is
one condoning children as sexual objects. Research on child sexual abuse shows
that the sexualization of children is a contributing factor to their sexual abuse.

Children Enjoy Participating in Beauty Pageants

While young children may express enjoyment in participating in pageants, 14
children are eager to please adults. Sleeping with their hair in curlers, having to
sit quietly while their hair is being tinted or rolled, fake nails being applied, or
their body being spray tanned hardly seems like activities very young girls
would choose over having fun with friends in age-appropriate play. The negative reactions of many of the participants in *Toddlers and Tiaras* testify to this.

Participation in Beauty Pageants Is No Different from Participating in Athletic or Suzuki Music Education Programs

Children's athletic programs and music education programs teach skills appro- 15
priate to the developmental stage of the child upon which the child can build
later in life rather than emphasizing the beauty of the human body that can
change significantly with time. In Suzuki recitals, for example, the unique
contribution of each child is recognized and no child loses.

Do child beauty pageants constitute child abuse? 16

"Do child beauty pageants constitute child abuse?" 17

This question must be answered on an individual basis. Parents who force their children to participate in pageants, as well as in athletic and music education programs, can be emotionally and even physically abusive, if participation is meeting parental needs rather that the needs of the child.

The risk for such abuse to occur is perhaps greatest when children are not 18 recognized for what they are—children—but rather are forced to assume miniature adult roles.

Play is an important factor in children's early development because, 19 through play, they learn skills for adulthood.

After all, what is the rush to become an adult? 20

Identifying the Elements of an Evaluation Argument

1. Wiehe does not state his thesis directly. Write a thesis statement for this essay by filling in the template below. (Hint: Try answering the questions Wiehe asks in paragraph 4.)

   Because _____

   _____, beauty pageants

   are bad for children.

2. What criteria does Wiehe use to evaluate child beauty pageants? If he wanted to make the opposite case, what criteria might he use instead?

3. In his essay's boldface headings, Wiehe identifies four opposing arguments. Which of these opposing arguments do you think presents the strongest challenge to Wiehe's position? Why?

4. Do you think Wiehe expects his readers to have seen the program *Toddlers and Tiaras*? Does he expect them to have strong feelings about child beauty pageants? How can you tell?

5. After he has refuted arguments against his position, Wiehe (a professor emeritus of social work) begins a discussion of whether "child beauty pageants constitute child abuse" (para. 16). Should he have done more to prepare readers for this discussion? Explain.

6. Do you think Wiehe's concluding statement would have a greater impact if it were in the form of a statement rather than a question? Write a new sentence that could serve as a strong concluding statement for this essay.

Are Internships a Good Deal for College Students?

"We have an opening for a part-time unpaid intern, which could lead to a full-time unpaid internship."

Reread the At Issue box on page 483, which provides background on the question of whether internships truly benefit college students. Then, read the sources on the pages that follow.

As you read these sources, you will be asked to respond to some questions and complete some activities. This work is designed to help you understand the content and structure of the selections. When you are finished, you will be ready to decide on the criteria you will use to write an **evaluation argument** on the topic, "Are Internships a Good Deal for College Students?"

SOURCES

 Ryan Burkey, "In Tough Economic Times, Internships Provide More Than Money," p. 496

 Ross Perlin, "Unpaid Interns, Complicit Colleges," p. 499

 Anya Kamenetz, "Take This Internship and Shove It," p. 502

 John Stossel, "Unpaid Interns Are Exploited?," p. 505

 Jennifer Wheary, "Only One Option for Young Job Seekers," p. 508

 Danielle Connor, "The Real Intern Scandal: Working without Pay Privileges the Privileged," p. 510

 The Onion, "Fill This, Intern" (photograph), p. 513

For comprehension quizzes,
see bedfordstmartins.com/practicalargument.

This article was published in the *Easterner*, the student newspaper of Eastern Washington University, on April 1, 2009.

IN TOUGH ECONOMIC TIMES, INTERNSHIPS PROVIDE MORE THAN MONEY

RYAN BURKEY

With the economy lagging, many people are struggling to find jobs. And for college students who are already strapped thanks to increased tuition, higher housing costs, and outrageously priced textbooks, the economic downturn is hitting especially hard. This has many college students discouraged and a bit cynical. 1

"Trying to get the money to pay for anything essential in this economy is like drinking soup with a hole in your spoon—you get a little, but never enough," said Jessica Motley, a sophomore at Eastern Washington University. 2

But while the feeble economy is making money more obscure and jobs hard to find, internships are relatively easy to land. Although not as lucrative or glamorous as outright jobs, internships are much more available, and some do pay. Most universities, including EWU, allow students to take internships for credit. 3

"An internship can save you years' worth of grief," Career Adviser Virginia "Ginny" Hinch recently told a group of EWU students. 4

More specifically, she means that internships allow students to experiment with different career fields before declaring a major and spending years pursuing a career they may regret later.

> "Internships allow students to experiment with different career fields before declaring a major."

Internships also give students experience, which is crucial for future employment. 6

"[Internships] will give you a lot of confidence," Hinch said, adding that employers see experience as "a critical element before they hire you. GPA is some of it, but really what nails it for the employer is experience." 7

It's not just the career advisers who are advocating internships, however. Students are as well. 8

Kelly Darrah, chief copy editor for *The Easterner*, also shared the benefits of her internship with her EWU peers. 9

"I would definitely encourage people to try an internship," Darrah said. "I can guarantee you'll learn more than anything you learn in class." 10

Darrah, a journalism major at EWU, is currently undertaking an internship at the Indiana branch of Planned Parenthood in Spokane, the nation's largest sexual and reproductive health care organization. 11

"I chose my internship because that's my passion, women's issues," she said. 12

Working at Planned Parenthood has had great benefits for Darrah, who 13 often flits back and forth from her internship in Spokane to her main job at *The Easterner* in Cheney. Not only does she get on-the-job experience, she also gets to see her work in action.

"I did see my letter to the editor in *The Spokesman*, and I thought that was 14 cool," she said at a question-and-answer session, referring to some of her regular duties at Planned Parenthood, which include writing letters to the editor, press releases, and op-ed pieces in local publications.

For Darrah, the internship at Planned Parenthood has solidified her pas- 15 sion and confirmed her career choice.

"I would just love to work at this company forever. That would be nice," 16 she said.

A group of three other Eastern students expressed similar sentiments 17 about the benefits of internships at a panel discussion earlier in the quarter. Panelists Elli McHugh, Allison Lyons, and Mark Proulx said their internships at a pharmacy, a physical therapy clinic, and a semi-pro football club, respectively, helped show them that the careers they were leaning toward were not what they wanted.

These personal stories, and the advice of advisers like Hinch, combine for 18 an overwhelming consensus on internships: they are important.

"When you're in the field, you just learn more," said Darrah. 19

Hinch reiterated that internships provide valuable work experience that 20 can help students in the future.

"What this is all about is you standing out in the crowd." 21

That's something everyone needs in these unfriendly economic times. 22 Jobs may not be easy to find right now, but having an internship experience— paid or unpaid—is a huge asset when seeking a job. As Hinch puts it, students should be using "everything available to you that you could possibly have to your advantage."

⊖AT ISSUE: SOURCES FOR DEVELOPING AN EVALUATION ARGUMENT

1. Burkey takes a strong stand in favor of internships. Paraphrase the writer's thesis statement by filling in the following template:

   Internships are valuable because_____

   _____.

2. To support his thesis, Burkey quotes several Eastern Washington University students who were happy with their internships. What appeals do these quotations make? What other evidence does Burkey cite? Do you think he needs additional evidence to make a convincing case?

3. What criteria does Burkey use to evaluate student internships? If you were taking the opposite position, what criteria would you use?

4. Burkey does not refute (or even acknowledge) opposing arguments. Should he have? Why or why not?

5. Would the other writers whose essays appear in this chapter agree with Burkey's basic position? Which writers, if any, do you think would say he makes too positive a case for internships?

This opinion column appeared in the *New York Times* on April 2, 2011.

UNPAID INTERNS, COMPLICIT COLLEGES

ROSS PERLIN

On college campuses, the annual race for summer internships, many of them 1
unpaid, is well under way. But instead of steering students toward the best opportunities and encouraging them to value their work, many institutions of higher
learning are complicit in helping companies skirt a nebulous area of labor law.

Colleges and universities have become cheerleaders and enablers of the 2
unpaid internship boom, failing to inform young people of their rights or protect them from the miserly calculus of employers. In hundreds of interviews
with interns over the past three years, I found dejected students resigned to
working unpaid for summers, semesters, and even entire academic years—
and, increasingly, to paying for the privilege.

For the students, the problems are less philosophical and legal than practi- 3
cal. In 2007, for instance, Will Batson, a Colgate University student from Augusta,
Ga., and a son of two public-interest lawyers, worked as an unpaid, full-time
summer intern for WNBC and had to scramble for shelter in New York City.

"It definitely hurt my confidence," Mr. Batson told me. He recalled crash- 4
ing on more than 20 floors and couches, being constantly short on cash, and
fearing he would have to quit and go home. His father, he said, felt like a failure
for not being able to help him rent an apartment.

What makes WNBC—whose parent company, General Electric, is valued 5
at more than $200 billion—think it can get away with this? In Mr. Batson's
case, a letter from Colgate, certifying that he was receiving credit for doing the
internship. (Now 24, he gave up on journalism and is at a technology start-up.
NBC calls its internship program "an important recruiting tool.")

The uncritical internship fever on college campuses—not to mention the 6
exploitation of graduate student instructors, adjunct faculty members, and
support staff—is symptomatic of a broader malaise. Far from being the liberal,
pro-labor bastions of popular image, universities are often blind to the realities
of work in contemporary America.

In politics, film, fashion, journalism, and book publishing, unpaid intern- 7
ships are seen as a way to break in. (The *New York Times* has paid and unpaid
interns.) But the phenomenon goes beyond fields seen as glamorous.

Three-quarters of the 10 million students enrolled in America's four-year 8
colleges and universities will work
as interns at least once before graduating, according to the College
Employment Research Institute.
Between one-third and half will get

"Between one-third and half
will get no compensation
for their efforts."

499

no compensation for their efforts, a study by the research firm Intern Bridge found. Unpaid interns also lack protection from laws prohibiting racial discrimination and sexual harassment.

The United States Department of Labor says an intern at a for-profit company may work without pay only when the program is similar to that offered in a vocational school, benefits the student, does not displace a regular employee, and does not entitle the student to a job; in addition, the employer must derive "no immediate advantage" from the student's work, and both sides must agree that the student is not entitled to wages. 9

Employers and their lawyers appear to believe that unpaid interns who get academic credit meet those criteria, but the law seems murky; the Labor Department has said that "academic credit alone does not guarantee that the employer is in compliance." 10

Fearing a crackdown by regulators, some colleges are asking the government, in essence, to look the other way. In a letter last year, 13 university presidents told the Labor Department, "While we share your concerns about the potential for exploitation, our institutions take great pains to ensure students are placed in secure and productive environments that further their education." 11

Far from resisting the exploitation of their students, colleges have made academic credit a commodity. Just look at Menlo College, a business-focused college in northern California, which sold credits to a business called Dream Careers. Menlo grossed $50,000 from the arrangement in 2008, while Dream Careers sold Menlo-accredited internships for as much as $9,500. 12

To meet the credit requirement of their employers, some interns have essentially had to pay to work for free: shelling out $2,700 to the University of Pennsylvania in the case of an intern at NBC Universal and $1,600 to New York University by an intern at *The Daily Show*, to cite two examples from news reports. 13

Charging students tuition to work in unpaid positions might be justifiable in some cases—if the college plays a central role in securing the internship and making it a substantive academic experience. But more often, internships are a cheap way for universities to provide credit—cheaper than paying for faculty members, classrooms, and equipment. 14

A survey of more than 700 colleges by the National Association of Colleges and Employers found that 95 percent allowed the posting of unpaid internships in campus career centers and on college Web sites. And of those colleges, only 30 percent required that their students obtain academic credit for those unpaid internships; the rest, evidently, were willing to overlook potential violations of labor law. 15

Campus career centers report being swamped; advisers I spoke to flatly denied being able to "monitor and reassess" all placements or even postings, as the 13 university presidents claim to do—their ability to visit students' workplaces, for instance, is almost nil. They described feeling caught between the demands of employers and interns and scrambling to make accommodations: issuing vague letters of support for interns to show employers; offering sketchy "internship transcript notations" or "internship certificates"; and even handing out "0.0 credit"—a mysterious work-around by which credit both is and isn't issued. 16

Is there a better way? Cooperative education, in which students alternate 17 between tightly integrated classroom time and paid work experience, represents a humane and pragmatic model.

Colleges shouldn't publicize unpaid internships at for-profit companies. 18 They should discourage internship requirements for graduation—common practice in communications, psychology, social work, and criminology. They should stop charging students to work without pay—and ensure that the currency of academic credit, already cheapened by internships, doesn't lose all its value.

To be sure, the unpaid internship is only part of a phenomenon that 19 includes the growing numbers of temps, freelancers, adjuncts, self-employed "entrepreneurs," and other low-wage or precariously employed workers who live gig by gig. The academy should critique, not amplify, those trends.

While higher education has tried to stand for fairness in the past few 20 decades through affirmative action and financial aid, the internship boom gives the well-to-do a foot in the door while consigning the less well-off to dead-end temporary jobs. Colleges have turned internships into a prerequisite for the professional world but have neither ensured equal access to these opportunities nor insisted on fair wages for honest work.

⊖ AT ISSUE: SOURCES FOR DEVELOPING AN EVALUATION ARGUMENT

1. The subject of Perlin's column is what he calls "the uncritical internship fever on college campuses" (para. 6). What does he mean by "uncritical"? By "fever"? Do your own observations support this characterization of students' attitudes toward internships?

2. In paragraph 2, Perlin criticizes colleges for having become "cheerleaders and enablers of the unpaid internship boom." Where else does he use strongly critical language to advance his position? Do such statements strengthen or weaken his argument? Explain.

3. What problems with internships does Perlin identify? Whom does he blame for these problems? What solutions does he propose?

4. Perlin objects not to internships but to the fact that colleges are charging students tuition for the right to work without pay. How might Ryan Burkey (p. 496) or John Stossel (p. 505) respond to Perlin's objection?

5. Perlin supports his position by describing one student's negative experience (3–5) and by citing statistics (8) and U.S. Department of Labor guidelines (9–10); he also gives examples of colleges "selling" academic credits (12–13). What other evidence does he provide? Which evidence do you find most convincing? Why?

6. Who does Perlin think is more culpable—the colleges for charging students or the employers for not paying them? Do you agree?

This opinion essay appeared in the *New York Times* on May 30, 2006.

TAKE THIS INTERNSHIP AND SHOVE IT

ANYA KAMENETZ

1 My younger sister has just arrived in New Orleans for the summer after her freshman year at Yale. She will be consuming daily snowballs, the local icy treat, to ward off the heat, volunteering to help clean up neighborhoods damaged by Hurricane Katrina, and working part time, for pay, at both a literary festival and a local restaurant. Meanwhile, most of her friends from college are headed for the new standard summer experience: the unpaid internship.

2 Instead of starting out in the mailroom for a pittance, this generation reports for business upstairs without pay. A national survey by Vault, a career information Web site, found that 84 percent of college students in April planned to complete at least one internship before graduating. Also according to Vault, about half of all internships are unpaid.

3 I was an unpaid intern at a newspaper from March 2002, my senior year, until a few months after graduation. I took it for granted, as most students do, that working without pay was the best possible preparation for success; parents usually agree to subsidize their offspring's internships on this basis. But what if we're wrong?

4 What if the growth of unpaid internships is bad for the labor market and for individual careers?

5 Let's look at the risks to the lowly intern. First there are opportunity costs. Lost wages and living expenses are significant considerations for the two-thirds of students who need loans to get through college. Since many internships are done for credit and some even cost money for the privilege of placement overseas or on Capitol Hill, those students who must borrow to pay tuition are going further into debt for internships.

6 Second, though their duties range from the menial to quasi-professional, unpaid internships are not jobs, only simulations. And fake jobs are not the best preparation for real jobs.

> "Unpaid internships are not jobs, only simulations."

7 Long hours on your feet waiting tables may not be particularly edifying, but they teach you that work is a routine of obligation, relieved by external reward, where you contribute value to a larger enterprise. Newspapers and business magazines are full of articles expressing exasperation about how the Millennial-generation employee supposedly expects work to be exciting immediately, wears flip-flops to the office, and has no taste for dues-paying. However true this stereotype may be, the spread of the artificially fun internship might very well be adding fuel to it.

By the same token, internships promote overidentification with employers: 8
I make sacrifices to work free; therefore, I must love my work. A sociologist at
the University of Washington, Gina Neff, who has studied the coping strategies
of interns in communications industries, calls the phenomenon "performative
passion." Perhaps this emotion helps explain why educated workers in this
country are less and less likely to organize, even as full-time jobs with benefits
go the way of the Pinto.

Although it's not being offered this year, the A.F.L.-C.I.O.'s Union Summer 9
internship program, which provides a small stipend, has shaped thousands of
college-educated career organizers. And yet interestingly, the percentage of
young workers who hold an actual union card is less than 5 percent, compared
with an overall national private-sector union rate of 7.8 percent. How are
twentysomethings ever going to win back health benefits and pension plans
when they learn to be grateful to work for nothing?

So an internship doesn't teach you everything you need to know about 10
coping in today's working world. What effect does it have on the economy as a
whole?

The Bureau of Labor Statistics does not identify interns or track the 11
economic impact of unpaid internships. But we can do a quick-and-dirty
calculation: according to Princeton Review's *Internship Bible*, there were 100,000
internship positions in 2005. Let's assume that out of those, 50,000 unpaid
interns are employed full time for 12 weeks each summer at an average minimum wage of $5.15 an hour. That's a nearly $124 million yearly contribution to
the welfare of corporate America.

In this way, unpaid interns are like illegal immigrants. They create an over- 12
supply of people willing to work for low wages, or in the case of interns, literally
nothing. Moreover, a recent survey by Britain's National Union of Journalists
found that an influx of unpaid graduates kept wages down and patched up the
gaps left by job cuts.

There may be more subtle effects as well. In an information economy, pro- 13
ductivity is based on the best people finding the jobs best suited for their talents, and interns interfere with this cultural capitalism. They fly in the face of
meritocracy—you must be rich enough to work without pay to get your foot
in the door. And they enhance the power of social connections over ability to
match people with desirable careers. A 2004 study of business graduates at a
large mid-Atlantic university found that the completion of an internship
helped people find jobs faster but didn't increase their confidence that those
jobs were a good fit.

With all this said, the intern track is not coming to an end any time soon. 14
More and more colleges are requiring some form of internship for graduation.
Still, if you must do an internship, research shows you will get more out of it if
you find a paid one.

A 1998 survey of nearly 700 employers by the Institute on Education and 15
the Economy at Columbia University's Teachers College found: "Compared to
unpaid internships, paid placements are strongest on all measures of internship

quality. The quality measures are also higher for those firms who intend to hire their interns." This shouldn't be too surprising—getting hired and getting paid are what work, in the real world, is all about.

⊘ AT ISSUE: SOURCES FOR DEVELOPING AN EVALUATION ARGUMENT

1. In paragraph 4, Kamenetz asks, "What if the growth of unpaid internships is bad for the labor market and for individual careers?" Answer this question in the form of a thesis statement for this essay.

2. What "risks to the lowly intern" (para. 5) does Kamenetz identify in paragraphs 5–9? According to Kamenetz, what risks do internships pose for the economy?

3. In paragraph 12, Kamenetz compares unpaid interns to illegal immigrants. On what basis does she compare these two groups? Do you think this is an appropriate analogy? Why or why not?

4. The title of Kamenetz's column is an allusion to the song "Take This Job and Shove It." Does she expect readers to recognize the allusion? Do they have to? Watch Johnny Paycheck performing this song on YouTube, or find the lyrics on CowboyLyrics.com or another site. Do you think this allusion makes sense?

5. In paragraph 6, Kamenetz says, "fake jobs are not the best preparation for real jobs." Do you agree with her that unpaid internships are "fake jobs" and that paid jobs (even waiting tables) are more "real"? Explain.

This article was distributed in *Creators Syndicate* on May 4, 2010.

UNPAID INTERNS ARE EXPLOITED?

JOHN STOSSEL

Do you employ unpaid student interns—college students who work in 1
exchange for on-the-job training?

If so, President Obama's Labor Department says that you're an exploiter. 2
The government says an internship is OK only if it meets six criteria, among
them that the employer must get "no immediate advantage" from the intern's
activities. In fact, the employer's work "may be impeded."

Impeded? No immediate advantage? 3

I'm in trouble, then. I have an intern at Fox Business News, and I'm get- 4
ting immediate advantages from her work all the time. I've had interns my
whole career and gotten lots of immediate advantage from them. Occasionally,
I've been impeded—but the better interns did the research that made my work
possible. I'd asked my TV bosses to pay for research help, but they said, "You
think we're made of money?"

So I asked colleges if students wanted internships. Many did, and from 5
then on I got much of my best help from unpaid college students.

Did I exploit them? Obama's Labor Department says it's hired 250 new 6
investigators to catch exploiters like me. I tried to get the department to answer
my questions, but it declined.

So I spoke with *Village Voice* writer Anya Kamenetz, who wrote a column 7
titled "Take This Internship and Shove It" in the *New York Times* (http://
tinyurl.com/2anss9s).

"We have minimum wage laws in this country for a very good reason," she 8
replied. "We had them to avoid exploitation like child labor."

But what's wrong with a free 9
internship if a student learns something about the career he wants to
pursue?

> "But what's wrong with a
> free internship if a student
> learns something about the 10
> career he wants to pursue?"

I was a little stunned by Kamenetz's answer: "Employers could say
we cannot afford to pay anybody, so
why should we be forced to pay the guy who cleans the floors?"

Because they wouldn't get people to clean floors if they didn't pay. But I 11
guess I shouldn't expect a New York writer to understand markets.

"Interns are people that come in and work for below minimum wage," she 12
said. "They pull the bottom out of the labor market, and it's less fair for everybody."

So it should be banned? 13

"There are a lot of ways to fill in the need for interns and the need for col- 14
lege students to get experience. One way is for colleges to pay stipends."

But they won't. 15

"They will if the law is enforced. Another way is for companies to hire stu- 16
dents that are eligible for federal work-study."

Oh, I see. The taxpayers should pay for my interns. 17

"Nobody is saying that these interns should go away," Kamenetz added. 18
"What they're saying is a company should put money in their budgets to pay
people the minimum wage to work for them, and that is just the basic issue of
fairness. If you start working for free, where's it going to end?"

Give me a break. It would end when the interns have the skills to earn 19
market salaries. Minimum-wage law and union rules already killed off appren-
tice jobs on construction sites. Contractors say: If I must pay high union wages,
I'll hire experienced workers. I'd lose money if I hired a kid and helped him
learn on the job.

My interns often told me that working—unpaid—at WCBS or ABC was 20
the best learning experience of their lives: "I learned more from you than at college, and I didn't have to pay tuition!" It was good for them and good for me.

Kamenetz said, "Studies show that when companies pay their interns, they 21
design the internships better."

Please. A few years ago, my old employer, ABC, started paying our interns. 22
That was good for well-connected students who got internships, but bad for
those who were turned down. ABC cut the number of interns by more than
half. There's no free lunch.

What's happened to the rights of contract and free association? If student 23
and employer come to an agreement, both expect to benefit or it wouldn't happen. The student is no indentured servant. If the employer "exploits" the student,
the student can quit. The contract ought to be nobody's business but theirs.

Butt out, federal bullies. Grown-ups can take care of ourselves. 24

◐ AT ISSUE: SOURCES FOR DEVELOPING AN EVALUATION ARGUMENT

1. Stossel's article is a refutation of comments made by Anya Kamenetz
   (p. 502). Which of her arguments does he refute? Do you think his
   refutations are successful? Why or why not?

2. Stossel asks a number of questions in his article—for example, in his title
   and in paragraphs 1, 3, 9, and 13. Does he answer these questions? Should
   he have? Do you find these questions thought provoking? Distracting?
   Annoying?

3. Consider the following statements:

   ■ "But I guess I shouldn't expect a New York writer to understand
   markets." (para. 11)

- "Oh, I see. The taxpayers should pay for my interns." (17)

- "Give me a break." (19)

- "Please." (22)

- "Butt out, federal bullies." (24)

Are these statements appropriate? Fair? Condescending? Sarcastic? Mean-spirited? Inflammatory? Explain your reaction to each statement's tone and content.

4. Stossel, a libertarian, supports a political party whose motto is "Minimum Government, Maximum Freedom." How might his political philosophy have shaped his attitude toward internships?

5. Evaluate the logic of these statements:

   - "My interns often told me that working—unpaid—at WCBS or ABC was the best learning experience of their lives." (20)

   - "If the employer 'exploits' the student, the student can quit." (23)

6. What criteria does Stossel use to evaluate internships? Are these the same criteria used by Anya Kamenetz?

This opinion column was published in *Newsday* on August 3, 2011.

ONLY ONE OPTION FOR YOUNG JOB SEEKERS

JENNIFER WHEARY

How do you get a job without experience? And how do you get experience 1 without a job? For today's young workers, the answer is get an internship. More than half of this year's college graduates did just that at some point before earning their degrees, according to a survey just released by the National Association of Colleges and Employers.

Internships are nothing new. But as the employment picture for recent 2 college graduates has grown more bleak, the number of young workers feeling the pressure to do internships has increased. More students getting early professional experience sounds like a great thing, but it also has its pitfalls.

About 90 percent of members of the college classes of 2006 and 2007 3 found employment within a year of graduating, according to a survey conducted this spring by the John J. Heldrich Center for Workforce Development at Rutgers University. For the class of 2010, that figure dropped to just 56 percent. The jobs that are available for recent grads also pay about 10 percent less than those won by the class of 2006.

In this dismal climate, the class of 2011 and those following them have the 4 feeling that, for future hirability, there's no option but to do a pre-graduation internship.

Marianna Savoca, director of the Career Center at Stony Brook University, 5 says, "Employers have the luxury of setting high expectations for their newly graduated hires." In fact, she says, "Students in pre-professional academic programs like journalism, engineering, and business know they need an internship to be competitive."

But even as they are becoming a de facto requirement, not all internships are created equal. About half are unpaid. That

> "Not all internships are created equal. About half are unpaid." 6

means options are limited for students whose parents aren't able to foot the bill while they work for free—and already established economic disparities are exacerbated.

Dolores Ciaccio, director of the Career Development Center at Farming- 7 dale State College, told me about the gap she sees between students who can afford to intern without pay and those who cannot: "Most of our students have part-time jobs to support their expenses, and if they were to take an unpaid internship in lieu of the job it would leave them in a negative situation financially. So this creates somewhat of a conflict."

Students who are worse off economically either have to make sure they 8 find increasingly rare paid internships, or they're forced to work a side job while interning. When done right, internships are an excellent learning experience—but learning happens best when you have time to process, reflect on, and draw lessons from the experience. Students who are struggling at a second or third job have less opportunity to do that.

When it comes to getting a job after graduation, an unpaid internship is better than none—though not much. According to the National Association of Colleges and Employers survey, only 33 percent of students who failed to do any type of internship had a job offer at time of graduation. In comparison, 38 percent of those who completed an unpaid internship were employed. But those with paid internships under their belt blew these other groups away. Of this group, 61 percent had a job offer by graduation day. 9

The take-away for college students seems to be: Shoot for a paid internship, but get any one you can and make it work out. Heather Huhman, a career consultant and author of "Lies, Damned Lies, and Internships," says that "Every internship teaches you something . . . even bad ones." 10

Maybe you'll learn that your chosen field isn't really for you. Maybe you'll understand what it's like to work for a bad boss. Maybe you'll walk away with valuable contacts or a new appreciation for earning a salary. Maybe you'll do nothing more than acquire a line that every employer expects to see on your resume. 11

Whatever the circumstances, the bottom line remains the same: Embrace the internship, young workers. Because—at least until the economy recovers—it's here to stay. 12

⊙ AT ISSUE: SOURCES FOR DEVELOPING AN EVALUATION ARGUMENT

1. Fill in the template below to create a thesis statement for this essay.

   Although _____

   _____ ,

   students should seek out internships because they are becoming a requirement for jobs in many fields.

2. In paragraph 6, Wheary observes that "not all internships are created equal." Why not? Why is this situation a problem? How would Danielle Connor (p. 510) respond to this criticism of internships?

3. Wheary states that in terms of helping college graduates get jobs, "an unpaid internship is better than none—though not much" (para. 9). What does she mean by "not much"? In general, how does her evaluation of paid internships differ from her evaluation of unpaid internships?

4. According to Wheary, what are the benefits of internships? Why do you suppose she mentions these benefits late in her discussion? Should she have presented them earlier? Why or why not?

5. Do you think the advice Wheary gives readers in her conclusion is cynical or just realistic? Is this paragraph's tone appropriate for her purpose and audience? Explain.

This opinion column appeared in the *Christian Science Monitor* on April 8, 2010.

THE REAL INTERN SCANDAL: WORKING WITHOUT PAY PRIVILEGES THE PRIVILEGED

DANIELLE CONNOR

Internships are becoming a joke. Once a coveted form of apprenticeship, 1
they're now a cynical way for companies to trim labor costs.

During this great recession, more and more students and young people are 2
accepting unpaid internships because there simply aren't paying gigs available.

Some employers are taking advantage of this, deceiving young people and 3
offering shallow experiences that won't actually help them develop professional skills.

Now the Obama administration wants to crack down on these abusive 4
practices.

"If you're a for-profit employer or you want to pursue an internship with a 5
for-profit employer, there aren't going to be many circumstances where you
can have an internship and not be paid and still be in compliance with the law,"
a Labor Department official told the *New York Times* this week.

Such accountability is welcome, but 6
there's a deeper issue at stake: the way
internships today privilege the privileged.

> "This great recession may end up providing a further boost to the prep-school crowd."

In an environment where getting a good 7
job requires a long stint as an unpaid intern,
only those with substantial savings can get
ahead. So rather than act as a leveler, this
great recession may end up providing a further boost to the prep-school crowd.

It seems the more competitive the field, the higher the entry fee. Aspiring 8
lawyers and doctors who weren't born into wealth are cornered into immense
debt situations, making the idea of pro bono work unrealistic to many even if
that's why they started. Writers and filmmakers, among other artists and performers, are looking at enormous entry fees that might require years of low or
unpaid work.

This all was news to me. I was raised with the idea that if you are willing to 9
work and study hard you will make it. If you invest in your education by taking
out student loans you will wind up in a higher pay bracket. If you want to
work, there will be a job for you. That's the story, anyway.

We take on debt because of the promise of upward mobility and attend 10
expensive private colleges to gain edge.

When we get there, we meet students who have been bouncing from one 11
enrichment program to the next and taking advantage of every summer opportunity. They've traveled around the world and developed a sexy skill set.

If it's worth nothing more, they've got the advantage at awkward network- 12
ing parties. They've always made small talk with fancy people, whether while
answering phones for a high-powered attorney their dad became friends with
on a transatlantic flight or sitting around their own dinner table.

Class issues aren't new, though access to education for middle-class fami- 13
lies is. Working-class kids go to private schools and learn to run faster.

If you can't afford not to have an internship, and you can't afford not to 14
have a job, you do both—and the stakes are high on either end because if
either operation fails you are left in the lurch with no safety net.

The technical term for this in my family is "building character," and it's 15
filed alongside stories about walking to school uphill, both ways.

In the fundamental first several years out of college many young people 16
are forced to decide whether it is possible to pursue their dreams or not.
Unfortunately, if there's no family money to keep you afloat, you are forced to
take jobs miles away from your desired path. College passions become foolish
ideals and the class system wins.

I was grateful to have the support of college funding to make my internship 17
possible.

I can remember working at high noon in Patagonia, Ariz., on the border 18
of Mexico at a seed conservation farm. There wasn't a cloud in the sky. I was
hoeing beans. I was an unpaid intern, and I cared about my job.

Everyone at Mount Holyoke College seemed to have summer opportuni- 19
ties like this. The air there made me believe anything was possible, and I was
willing to go for it with little or no money in my pocket.

Through financial aid in the form of the Frances Perkins Program, the col- 20
lege funded three years of summer internships as part of my research to fulfill
my independent major. Without that funding, I would never have been able to
accept the volunteer positions.

These experiences are still opening doors for me. They provided the nar- 21
rative for my first articles and video projects, building the portfolio to get the
contracts I make my living with today.

Those internships granted me the privilege of "experience." 22

The issues we face, from war to poverty and environmental catastrophe, 23
require serious skills and creativity in developing solutions. What ever happened
to mentorship? Who's going to step up and offer interns some real learning
opportunities that will result in innovative leadership for the next generation?

Students must remember that the benefit of these internships is your per- 24
sonal narrative—who you are, where you've been, what you've worked on. People
get the impression that you are committed to your work. In some circles it's a
credibility badge—a key. The tragedy lies in keys being passed between the same
people with every generation. We have the collective resources to change this fate.

If it weren't for my unpaid internships, I highly doubt I would be in a posi- 25
tion today to make my living as a freelance writer, producer, and campaign consultant. It was the internships that qualified me for my first couple important
entry-level jobs in the nonprofit world, which have given me the skills and experience to do what I want now.

⊙ AT ISSUE: SOURCES FOR DEVELOPING AN EVALUATION ARGUMENT

1. In her evaluation of internships, Connor discusses both positive and negative aspects. List the statements she makes on both sides of this issue. All things considered, does she present internships for the most part in positive or negative terms?

2. Based on your answer to question 1, write a thesis statement for Connor's essay, following one of these two templates:

   Although _____

   _____ , internships are

   a good deal for most college students.

   Although internships can be valuable, their drawbacks, such

   as _____

   _____ , suggest that they are not

   always a good deal for college students.

3. What details about her personal life does Connor reveal to readers? How have her experiences shaped her position on the issue of the value of internships? What kind of appeal does her life story make to readers? Is this appeal effective?

4. In paragraph 6, Connor observes that "internships today privilege the privileged"; in paragraph 7, she says that "rather than act as a leveler, this great recession may end up providing a further boost to the prep-school crowd." Would you describe the attitude she expresses in these comments as realistic, resentful, resigned, matter-of-fact, or hostile?

5. How might John Stossel (p. 505) respond to Connor's position—in particular to the fact that she welcomes the federal government's intervention?

6. In paragraph 24, Connor says, "Students must remember that the benefit of these internships is your personal narrative—who you are, where you've been, what you've worked on." Do you think this sentence would make a more powerful concluding statement than the current one? Is there another sentence in the essay that might work even better?

This image is from the *Onion* store page, store.theonion.com.

FILL THIS, INTERN

THE ONION

⊙ AT ISSUE: SOURCES FOR DEVELOPING AN EVALUATION ARGUMENT

1. What argument does this visual make? In what sense is it an evaluation argument?

2. What other slogans could be written on the cup to make the same argument?

3. Write a slogan for this coffee cup that makes the opposite argument.

⊕ EXERCISE 14.6

Write a one-paragraph evaluation argument in which you take a position on whether internships are a good deal for college students. Follow the template below, filling in the blanks to create your argument.

TEMPLATE FOR WRITING AN EVALUATION ARGUMENT

Depending on the criteria used for evaluation, student internships can be seen in a largely positive or negative light. If they are judged on the basis of _____, it seems clear that they (are/are not) a good deal for college students. Some people say that _____

_____. They also

point out that _____

_____.

Others disagree with this position, claiming that _____

_____.

However, _____

_____.

All things considered, _____

_____.

⊕ EXERCISE 14.7

In a group of three or four students, discuss your own opinions (or those of your friends or siblings) about the value of student internships. Do you think they can be a rewarding experience? Do you think they exploit students? What problems do you see? (If you have had an internship, be sure to discuss your own experiences.) Write a paragraph that summarizes your group's conclusions.

⊕ EXERCISE 14.8

Write an evaluation argument on the topic, "Are Internships a Good Deal for College Students?" Begin by establishing the criteria by which you will evaluate student internships. Then, consider how well internships meet these criteria. (If you like, you may incorporate the material you developed for Exercises 14.6 and 14.7 into your essay.) Cite the sources on pages 495–513, and be sure to document the sources you use and to include a works-cited page. (See Chapter 10 for information on documenting sources.)

EXERCISE 14.9

Review the four pillars of argument discussed in Chapter 1. Does your essay include all four elements of an effective argument? Add anything that is missing. Then, label the key elements of your essay.

WRITING ASSIGNMENTS: EVALUATION ARGUMENTS

1. As a college student, you have probably had to fill out course-evaluation forms. Now, you are going to write an evaluation of one of your courses in the form of an argumentative essay that takes a strong stand on the quality of the course. Before you begin, decide on the criteria by which you will evaluate it—for example, what practical skills it provided to prepare you for your future courses or employment, whether you enjoyed the course, or what you learned. (If you can download an evaluation form, you can use it to help you brainstorm.)

2. Write an evaluation argument challenging a popular position on the quality of a product or service that you know or use. For example, you can defend a campus service that most students criticize or criticize a popular restaurant or film. Be sure you establish your criteria for evaluation before you begin. (You do not have to use the same criteria used by those who have taken the opposite position.)

3. Write a comparative evaluation—an essay in which you argue that one thing is superior to another. You can compare two teachers, two advertisements, two part-time jobs, or any other two subjects you feel confident you can write about. In your thesis, take the position that one of your two subjects is superior to the other. As you would with any evaluation, begin by deciding on the criteria you will use.

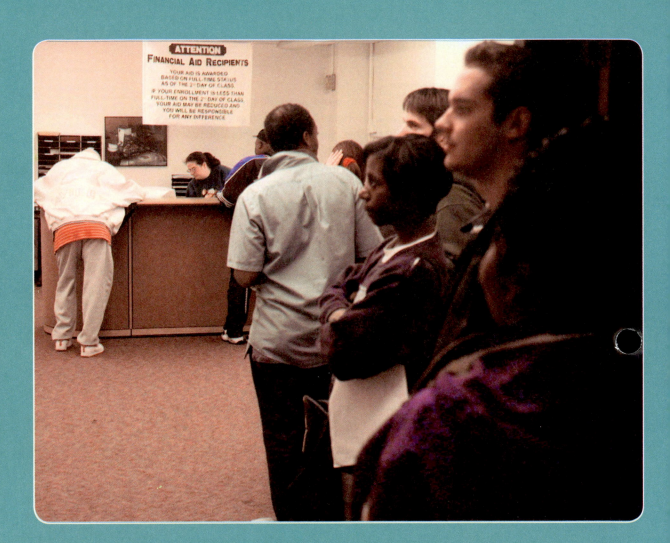

Proposal Arguments

Should the Government Do More to Relieve the Student-Loan Burden?

In 2011, the protest movement called Occupy Wall Street began in New York City's Zucotti Park. The protestors' focus was on issues such as social and economic inequality, high unemployment, and lack of affordable health care. As the movement spread, other issues came to the forefront, including a demand for student-loan forgiveness. Perhaps in response to the wide attention attracted by the protests, President Barack Obama announced a program of student-loan relief. Acknowledging that student debt was excessive—it exceeded $1 trillion in 2012—the president reduced the maximum required payment on student loans from 15% to 10% of a borrower's annual income and instituted a policy of debt forgiveness after twenty years.

Needless to say, the president's actions did not satisfy everyone. Some critics pointed out that the reforms did not address the root cause of the student-loan problem—the ever-increasing cost of tuition. (For example, in academic year

2010–11, in-state tuition and fees at public four-year colleges rose 8.3%, and tuition at private nonprofit four-year colleges rose 4.4%.) To address this problem, critics called for sweeping reforms of the student-loan program and proposed a total restructuring of federal aid to colleges and universities. Those against government involvement in the student-loan program pointed out that most students receive enough financial aid to offset tuition; according to them, the situation is not as dire as some have made it out to be. Others who objected to government involvement pointed out that a student loan is a contract, and students (like other borrowers) should be required to fulfill the terms to which they agreed.

Later in this chapter, you will be asked to think more about this issue. You will be given several sources to consider and asked to write a **proposal argument** that takes a position on whether the government should do more to relieve the student-loan burden.

For comprehension quizzes, see bedfordstmartins.com/practicalargument.

Many college students apply for loans.

What Is a Proposal Argument?

When you write a **proposal argument**, you suggest a solution to a problem. The purpose of a proposal argument is to convince people that a problem exists and that your solution is both practical and worthwhile.

Proposal arguments are the most common form of argument. You see them every day on billboards and in advertisements, editorials, and letters to the editor. The problems proposal arguments address can be local:

- What steps should the community take to protect its historic buildings?
- Should the mayor be limited to two terms in office?
- How can the city promote the use of public transportation?
- What can the township do to help the homeless?
- What should be done to encourage recycling on campus?
- How can community health services be improved?

Many proposals try to influence behavior.

The problems addressed in proposal arguments can also be more global:

- Should the United States cut its military budget?
- What should be done to increase domestic energy production?
- What is the best way to lower the federal deficit?
- How can we solve the problem of childhood obesity?
- What can countries do to protect themselves against terrorist attacks?
- What should be done to decrease gun violence?

Stating the Problem

When you write a proposal argument, you should begin by demonstrating that a problem exists. In some cases, readers will be familiar with the problem, so you will not have to explain it in great detail. For example, it would not take much to convince students at your university that tuition is high or that some classrooms are overcrowded. Most people also know about the need to provide health care to the uninsured and to reduce the rising level of student debt and are aware of other problems that have received a good deal of media attention.

Other, less familiar issues need more explanation—sometimes a great deal of explanation. In these cases, you should not assume that readers will accept (or even understand) the importance of the problem you are discussing. For example, why should readers care about the high dropout rate at a local high school? You can answer this question by demonstrating that this problem affects not only the students who drop out but others as well:

- Students who do not have high school diplomas earn substantially less than those who do.

- Studies show that high school dropouts are much more likely to live in poverty than students who complete high school.

- Taxpayers pay for the social services that dropouts often require.

- Federal, state, and local governments lose the taxes that dropouts would pay if they had better jobs.

When you explain the situation in this way, you show that a problem that appears to be limited to just a few individuals actually affects society as a whole.

How much background information you need to provide about a problem depends on how much your readers already know about it. In many cases, a direct statement of a problem is not enough: you need to explain the context of the problem and then discuss it with this context in mind. For example, you cannot simply say that the number of databases to which your college library subscribes needs to be increased. Why does it need to be increased? How many new databases should be added? Which ones? What benefits would result from increasing the number of databases? What will happen if the number is not increased? Without answers to these questions, readers will not be able to understand the full extent of the problem. (Statistics, examples, personal anecdotes, and even visuals can also help you demonstrate the importance of finding a solution to the problem.) By presenting the problem in detail, you draw readers into your discussion and motivate them to want to solve it.

Proposing a Solution

After you have established that a problem exists, you have to propose a solution. Sometimes the solution is self-evident, so that you do not need to explain it in much detail. For example, if you want to get a new computer for the college newspaper, you do not have to give a detailed account of how you intend to purchase it. On the other hand, if your problem is more complicated—for example, proposing that your school should sponsor a new student organization—you will have to go into more detail, possibly listing the steps that you will take to implement your plan as well as the costs associated with it.

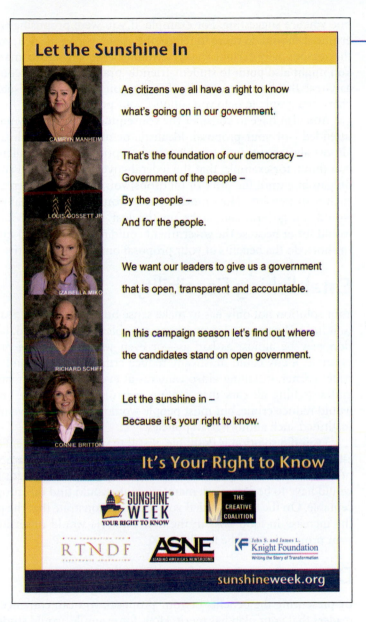

Advocacy groups
frequently publish
proposals.

Demonstrating That Your Solution Will Work

When you present a solution to a problem, you have to support it with **evidence**—facts, examples, and so on from your own experience and from research. You can also point to successful solutions that are similar to the one you are suggesting. For example, if you were proposing that the government should do more to relieve the student-loan burden, you could list the reasons why certain changes would be beneficial for many students. You might also point to student-friendly practices in other countries, such as Great Britain and Australia. Finally, you could use a visual, such as a chart or a graph, to help you support your position.

You also have to consider the consequences—both intended and unintended—of your proposal. Idealistic or otherwise unrealistic proposals almost always run into trouble when skeptical readers challenge them. If you think, for example, that the federal government should suspend taxes on gasoline until the price of oil drops, you should consider the effects of such a suspension. How much money would drivers actually save? How would the government make up the lost tax revenue? What programs would suffer because the government could no longer afford to fund them? In short, do the benefits of your proposal outweigh its negative effects?

Establishing Feasibility

Your solution not only has to make sense but also has to be **feasible**—that is, it has to be practical. Sometimes a problem can be solved, but the solution may be almost as bad as—or even worse than—the problem. For example, a city could drastically reduce crime by putting police on every street corner, installing video cameras at every intersection, and stopping and searching all cars that contain two or more people. These actions would reduce crime, but most people would not want to live in a city that instituted such authoritarian policies.

Even if a solution is desirable, it still may not be feasible. For example, although expanded dining facilities might improve life on campus, the cost of a new student cafeteria would be high. If paying for it means that tuition would have to be increased, many students would find this proposal unacceptable. On the other hand, if you could demonstrate that the profits from the increase in food sales in the new cafeteria would offset its cost, then your proposal would be feasible.

Discussing Benefits

By presenting the benefits of your proposal, you can convince undecided readers that your plan has merit. How, for example, would students benefit from an expansion of campus parking facilities? Would student morale improve because students would get fewer parking citations? Would lateness to class decline because students would no longer have to spend time looking for a parking spot? Would the college earn more revenue from additional parking fees? Although not all proposals list benefits, many do. This information can help convince readers that your proposal has merit and is worth implementing.

Refuting Opposing Arguments

You should always assume that any proposal—no matter how strong—will be objectionable to some readers. Moreover, even sympathetic readers will have questions that they will want answered before they accept your ideas. That is why you should always anticipate and refute possible objections to your proposal. For example, if the federal government did more to relieve the student-loan burden, would some students try to take advantage of the program by borrowing more than they need? Would all students be eligible for help, even those from wealthy families? Would students who worked while attending school be eligible? If any objections are particularly strong, concede them: admit that they have merit, but point out their shortcomings. For instance, you could concede that some students might try to abuse the program, but you could then point out that only a small minority of students would do this and recommend steps that could be taken to address possible abuses.

An image of an overcrowded campus parking lot can help convince your audience to see the merits of a proposal to make more parking available.

⊖ EXERCISE 15.1

List the evidence you could present to support each of these thesis statements for proposal arguments.

1. Because many Americans are obese, the government should require warning labels on all sugared cereals.

2. The United States should ban all gasoline-burning cars in ten years.

3. Candidates for president should be required to use only public funding for their campaigns.

4. Teachers should carry handguns to protect themselves and their students from violence.

5. To reduce prison overcrowding, states should release all nonviolent offenders.

⊖ EXERCISE 15.2

Review the proposals in Exercise 15.1, and list two problems that each one could create if implemented.

⊙ EXERCISE 15.3

Look at the following ad, which is designed to promote recycling. In what sense is it a proposal argument? For example, what problem does it identify? What solution does it propose? What arguments does it present to support this solution? How does the image in the ad help to support the proposal?

An ad to encourage recycling

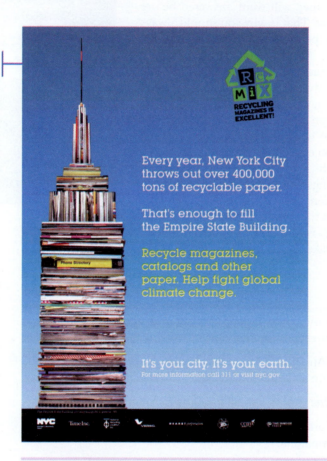

⊙ EXERCISE 15.4

Read the following opinion column, "Teach Your Teachers Well" by Susan Engel. What problem does Engel discuss? How does she propose to solve this problem? What benefits does she expect her solution to have? Note that Engel does not refute possible objections to her proposal. What objections could she have mentioned? What evidence could she have added to strengthen her proposal?

This opinion column was published in the *New York Times* on November 2, 2009.

TEACH YOUR TEACHERS WELL

SUSAN ENGEL

Arne Duncan, the secretary of education, recently called for sweeping changes to the way we select and train teachers. He's right. If we really want good schools, we need to create a critical mass of great teachers. And if we want smart, passionate people to become these great educators, we have to attract them with excellent programs and train them properly in the substance and practice of teaching. 1

Our best universities have, paradoxically, typically looked down their noses at education, as if it were intellectually inferior. The result is that the strongest students are often in colleges that have no interest in education, while the most inspiring professors aren't working with students who want to teach. This means that comparatively weaker students in less intellectually rigorous programs are the ones preparing to become teachers. 2

So the first step is to get the best colleges to throw themselves into the fray. If education was a good enough topic for Plato, John Dewey, and William James, it should be good enough for 21st-century college professors. 3

These new teacher programs should be selective, requiring a 3.5 undergraduate grade point average and an intensive application process. But they should also be free of charge, and admission should include a stipend for the first three years of teaching in a public school. 4

> "If education was a good enough topic for Plato, John Dewey, and William James, it should be good enough for 21st-century college professors."

Once we have a better pool of graduate students, we need to train them differently from how we have in the past. Too often, teaching students spend their time studying specific instructional programs and learning how to handle mechanics like making lesson plans. These skills, while useful, are not what will transform a promising student into a good teacher. 5

First, future teachers should continue studying the subject they hope to teach, with outstanding professors. It makes no sense at all to stop studying the thing you want to teach at the very moment you begin to learn how. 6

Meanwhile, students should learn their craft the way a surgeon learns to operate: by intense supervision in a real setting with expert mentors. Student-teachers are usually observed only twice during a semester and then given a written evaluation. But young teachers, like young doctors, should work side by side with skilled mentors, getting plenty of feedback, having plenty of opportunities to observe, and taking on greater and greater responsibility as they improve. 7

Teacher training can also learn from family therapy programs. Therapists 8 spend a great deal of time watching videotapes of themselves in action, reflecting on their sessions and discussing the most difficult moments with senior therapists to explore other ways they might have responded. In much the same way, young teachers need to record their daily encounters with their classrooms and then, with mentors and peers, have serious, open-minded conversations about what's working and what isn't.

Teachers must also learn far more about children: typically, teaching students are provided with fairly static and superficial overviews of developmental stages but learn little about how to watch children, using research and theory to understand what they are seeing. As James Comer, a professor of child psychiatry at Yale, has argued for years, if we disregard the developmental needs of our students, it's unlikely we'll succeed in teaching them. 9

One more thing is required—give as many public schools as possible the 10 financial incentives to hire these newly prepared teachers in groups of seven or more. This way, talented eager young teachers won't languish or leave teaching because they felt bored, inept, isolated, or marginalized. Instead, they will feel part of a robust community of promising professionals. They will struggle and learn together. Good teachers need good colleagues.

To fix our schools, we need teaching programs that are as rich in resources, 11 interesting, high-reaching, and thoughtful as the young people we want to attract to the profession. Show me a school where teachers are smart, well-educated, skilled, and happy to be there, and I'll show you a group of children who are getting a good education.

⊘ EXERCISE 15.5

Write a paragraph or two in which you argue for or against the recommendations Engel proposes in "Teach Your Teachers Well." Be sure to present a clear statement of the problems she is addressing as well as the strengths or weaknesses of her proposal.

Structuring a Proposal Argument

In general, a proposal argument can be structured in the following way:

- **Introduction:** Establishes the context of the proposal and presents the essay's thesis

- **Explanation of the problem:** Identifies the problem and explains why it needs to be solved

- **Explanation of the solution:** Proposes a solution and explains how it will solve the problem

- **Evidence in support of the solution:** Presents support for the proposed solution (this section is usually more than one paragraph)

- **Benefits of the solution:** Explains the positive results of the proposed course of action

- **Refutation of opposing arguments:** Addresses objections to the proposal

- **Conclusion:** Reinforces the main point of the proposal; includes a strong concluding statement

The following student essay contains all the elements of a proposal argument. The student who wrote this essay is trying to convince the college president that the school should adopt an **honor code**—a system of rules that defines acceptable conduct and establishes procedures for handling misconduct.

COLLEGES NEED HONOR CODES

MELISSA BURRELL

1   Today's college students are under a lot of pressure to do well in school, to win tuition grants, to please teachers and family, and to compete in the job market. As a result, the temptation to cheat is greater than ever. At the same time, technology, particularly the Internet, has made cheating easier than ever. Colleges and universities have tried various strategies to combat this problem, from increasing punishments to using plagiarism-detection tools such as Turnitin.com. However, the most comprehensive and effective solution to the problem of academic dishonesty is an honor code, a campuswide contract that spells out and enforces standards of honesty. To fight academic dishonesty, colleges should institute and actively maintain honor codes.

2   Although the exact number of students who cheat is impossible to determine, two out of three students in one recent survey admitted to cheating (Grasgreen). Some students cheat by plagiarizing entire papers or stealing answers to tests. Many other students commit so-called

Thesis statement

Explanation of the problem: Cheating

lesser offenses, such as collaborating with others when told to work alone, sharing test answers, cutting and pasting material from the Internet, or misrepresenting data. All of these acts are dishonest; all amount to cheating. Part of the problem, however, is that many students simply do not understand what the rules are (Chace 24). Unclear about expectations and overwhelmed by the pressure to succeed, students can easily justify their own acts of dishonesty.

Explanation of the solution: Institute an honor code

An honor code solves these problems by clearly presenting the rules and by establishing honesty, trust, and academic honor as shared values. According to recent research, "setting clear expectations, and repeating them early and often, is crucial" (Grasgreen). Schools with honor codes require *every* student to sign a pledge to uphold the honor code. Ideally, students write and manage the honor code themselves, with the help of faculty and administrators. According to Timothy M. Dodd, however, to be successful, the honor code must be more than a document; it must be a way of thinking. To accomplish this, all first-year students should receive copies of the school's honor code at orientation. At the beginning of each academic year, students should be required to reread the honor code and renew their pledge to uphold its values and rules. In addition, students and instructors need to discuss the honor code in class. (Some colleges post the honor code in every classroom.) In other words, Dodd believes, the honor code must be part of the fabric of the school. It should be present in students' minds, guiding their actions and informing their learning and teaching.

Evidence in support of the solution

Studies show that serious cheating is 25% to 50% lower at schools with honor codes (Dodd). With an honor code in place, students cannot say that they do not know what constitutes cheating or that they do not understand what will happen to them if they cheat. Studies also show that in schools with a strong honor code, instructors are more likely to take action against cheaters. One study shows that professors frequently do not confront students who cheat because they are not sure the university will back them up (Vandehey, Diekhoff, and LaBeff 469). When a school has an honor code, however, instructors can be certain that both the students and the school will support their actions.

Benefits of the solution

When a school institutes an honor code, a number of positive results will occur. First, an honor code creates a set of basic rules that

3

4

5

students can follow. Students know in advance what is expected of them and what will happen if they commit an infraction. In addition, an honor code promotes honesty, placing more responsibility and power in the hands of students and encouraging them to act according to a higher standard. As a result, schools with honor codes often permit unsupervised exams that require students to monitor one other. Finally, according to Timothy M. Dodd, honor codes encourage students to act responsibly. They assume that students will not take unfair advantage of each other or undercut the academic community. Thus, as Dodd concludes, plagiarism (and cheating in general) becomes a concern for everyone—students as well as instructors—in schools with honor codes.

6   Some people argue that plagiarism-detection tools such as Turnitin.com are simpler and more effective at preventing cheating than honor codes. However, such tools focus on catching individual acts of cheating, not on preventing a culture of cheating. When schools use these tools, they are telling students that their main concern is not to avoid cheating but to avoid getting caught. Thus, these tools do not deal with the real problem: the decision to be dishonest. Rather than trusting students, schools that use plagiarism-detection tools assume that all students are cheating. Unlike plagiarism-detection tools, honor codes fight dishonesty by promoting a culture of integrity, fairness, and accountability. By assuming that most students are trustworthy and punishing only those who are not, schools with honor codes set high standards for students and encourage them to rise to the challenge.

Refutation of opposing arguments

7   The only long-term, comprehensive solution to the problem of cheating is campuswide honor codes. No solution will be completely effective in preventing dishonesty, but honor codes go a long way toward addressing the root causes of this problem. The goal of an honor code is to create a campus culture that values and rewards honesty and integrity. By encouraging students to do what is expected of them, honor codes help create a confident, empowered, and trustworthy student body.

Concluding statement

Works Cited

Chace, William M. "A Question of Honor." *American Scholar* 81.2 (2012): 20-32. *Academic OneFile.* Web. 22 Apr. 2012.

Dodd, Timothy M. "Honor Code 101: An Introduction to the Elements of Traditional Honor Codes, Modified Honor Codes and Academic Integrity Policies." *Center for Academic Integrity.* Clemson U, 2010. Web. 22 Apr. 2012.

Grasgreen, Allie. "Who Cheats, and How." *Inside Higher Ed.* Inside Higher Ed, 16 Mar. 2012. Web. 22 Apr. 2012.

Vandehey, Michael, George Diekhoff, and Emily LaBeff. "College Cheating: A Twenty-Year Follow-Up and the Addition of an Honor Code." *Journal of College Student Development* 48.4 (2007): 468–80. *Academic OneFile.* Web. 21 Apr. 2012.

GRAMMAR IN CONTEXT

Will versus *Would*

Many people use the helping verbs *will* and *would* interchangeably. When you write a proposal, however, keep in mind that these words express different shades of meaning.

Will expresses certainty. In a list of benefits, for example, *will* indicates the benefits that will occur if the proposal is accepted.

First, an honor code will create a set of basic rules that students can follow.

In addition, an honor code will promote honesty.

Would expresses probability. In a refutation of an opposing argument, for example, *would* indicates that another solution is likely to be more effective than the one being proposed.

Some people argue that a plagiarism-detection tool such as Turnitin.com would be simpler and a more effective way of preventing cheating than an honor code.

⊃ EXERCISE 15.6

The following essay, "My Plan to Escape the Grip of Foreign Oil" by T. Boone Pickens, includes the basic elements of a proposal argument. Read the essay, and answer the questions that follow it, consulting the outline on pages 526–527 if necessary.

This opinion column appeared in the *Wall Street Journal* on July 9, 2008.

MY PLAN TO ESCAPE THE GRIP OF FOREIGN OIL

T. BOONE PICKENS

One of the benefits of being around a long time is that you get to know a lot about certain things. I'm 80 years old and I've been an oilman for almost 60 years. I've drilled more dry holes and also found more oil than just about anyone in the industry. With all my experience, I've never been as worried about our energy security as I am now. Like many of us, I ignored what was happening. Now our country faces what I believe is the most serious situation since World War II. 1

The problem, of course, is our growing dependence on foreign oil—it's extreme, it's dangerous, and it threatens the future of our nation. 2

Let me share a few facts: Each year we import more and more oil. In 1973, the year of the infamous oil embargo, the United States imported about 24% of our oil. In 1990, at the start of the first Gulf War, this had climbed to 42%. Today, we import almost 70% of our oil. 3

This is a staggering number, particularly for a country that consumes oil the way we do. The U.S. uses nearly a quarter of the world's oil, with just 4% of the population and 3% of the world's reserves. This year, we will spend almost $700 billion on imported oil, which is more than four times the annual cost of our current war in Iraq. 4

In fact, if we don't do anything about this problem, over the next 10 years we will spend around $10 trillion importing foreign oil. That is $10 trillion leaving the U.S. and going to foreign nations, making it what I certainly believe will be the single largest transfer of wealth in human history. 5

Why do I believe that our dependence on foreign oil is such a danger to our country? Put simply, our economic engine is now 70% dependent on the energy resources of other countries, their good judgment, and most importantly, their good will toward us. Foreign oil is at the intersection of America's three most important issues: the economy, the environment and our national security. We need an energy plan that maps out how we're going to work our way out of this mess. I think I have such a plan. 6

> "Our economic engine is now 70% dependent on the energy resources of other countries."

Consider this: The world produces about 85 million barrels of oil a day, but global demand now tops 86 million barrels a day. And despite three years of record price increases, world oil production has declined every year since 2005. 7

Meanwhile, the demand for oil will only increase as growing economies in countries like India and China gear up for enhanced oil consumption.

Add to this the fact that in many countries, including China, the government has a great deal of influence over its energy industry, allowing these countries to set strategic direction easily and pay whatever price is needed to secure oil. The U.S. has no similar policy, because we thankfully don't have state-controlled energy companies. But that doesn't mean we can't set goals and develop an energy policy that will overcome our addiction to foreign oil. I have a clear goal in mind with my plan. I want to reduce America's foreign oil imports by more than one-third in the next five to 10 years. 8

How will we do it? We'll start with wind power. Wind is 100% domestic, it is 100% renewable, and it is 100% clean. Did you know that the midsection of this country, that stretch of land that starts in West Texas and reaches all the way up to the border with Canada, is called the "Saudi Arabia of the Wind"? It gets that name because we have the greatest wind reserves in the world. In 2008, the Department of Energy issued a study that stated that the U.S. has the capacity to generate 20% of its electricity supply from wind by 2030. I think we can do this or even more, but we must do it quicker. 9

My plan calls for taking the energy generated by wind and using it to replace a significant percentage of the natural gas that is now being used to fuel our power plants. Today, natural gas accounts for about 22% of our electricity generation in the U.S. We can use new wind capacity to free up the natural gas for use as a transportation fuel. That would displace more than one-third of our foreign oil imports. Natural gas is the only domestic energy of size that can be used to replace oil used for transportation, and it is abundant in the U.S. It is cheap and it is clean. With eight million natural-gas-powered vehicles on the road world-wide, the technology already exists to rapidly build out fleets of trucks, buses, and even cars using natural gas as a fuel. Of these eight million vehicles, the U.S. has a paltry 150,000 right now. We can and should do so much more to build our fleet of natural-gas-powered vehicles. 10

I believe this plan will be the perfect bridge to the future, affording us the time to develop new technologies and a new perspective on our energy use. In addition to the plan I have proposed, I also want to see us explore all avenues and every energy alternative, from more R&D into batteries and fuel cells to development of solar, ethanol, and biomass to more conservation. Drilling in the outer continental shelf should be considered as well, as we need to look at all options, recognizing that there is no silver bullet. 11

I believe my plan can be accomplished within 10 years if this country takes decisive and bold steps immediately. This plan dramatically reduces our dependence on foreign oil and lowers the cost of transportation. It invests in the heartland, creating thousands of new jobs. It substantially reduces America's carbon footprint and uses existing, proven technology. It will be accomplished solely through private investment with no new consumer or corporate taxes or government regulation. It will build a bridge to the future, giving us the time to develop new technologies. 12

The future begins as soon as Congress and the president act. The govern- 13
ment must mandate the formation of wind and solar transmission corridors, and
renew the subsidies for economic and alternative energy development in areas
where the wind and sun are abundant. I am also calling for a monthly progress
report on the reduction in foreign oil imports, as well as a monthly progress
report on the state of development of natural gas vehicles in this country.

We have a golden opportunity in this election year to form bipartisan sup- 14
port for this plan. We have the grit and fortitude to shoulder the responsibility
of change when our country's future is at stake, as Americans have proven
repeatedly throughout this nation's history.

We need action. Now. 15

Identifying the Elements of a Proposal Argument

1. What is the essay's thesis statement? How effective do you think it is?

2. Where in the essay does Pickens identify the problem he wants to solve?

3. According to Pickens, what are the specific ways dependence on foreign oil threatens the United States?

4. Where does Pickens present his solutions to the problem he identifies?

5. Where does Pickens discuss the benefits of his proposal? What other benefits could he have addressed?

6. Pickens does not address possible arguments against his proposal. Should he have? What possible arguments might he have addressed? How would you refute each of these arguments?

7. Evaluate the essay's concluding statement.

Should the Government Do More to Relieve the Student-Loan Burden?

Reread the At Issue box on page 517, which gives background on whether the government should do more to relieve the student-loan burden. Then, read the sources on the following pages.

As you read this material, you will be asked to answer questions and to complete some simple activities. This work will help you understand both the content and structure of the selections. When you are finished, you will be ready to write a **proposal argument** that makes a case for or against having the government do more to relieve the student-loan burden.

SOURCES

 Jesse Jackson, "We Bail Out Banks, but Not Desperate Students," p. 535

 SovereignDollar.com, "Student Debt Crisis Solution" (Editorial Cartoon), p. 538

 Richard Vedder, "Forgive Student Loans?," p. 539

 Mark Kantrowitz, "Five Myths about Student Loans," p. 542

 Kevin Carey, "The U.S. Should Adopt Income-Based Loans Now," p. 546

 Mary Kate Cary, "Why the Government Is to Blame for High College Costs," p. 550

 Robert Zaller, "Higher Education's Coming Crisis," p. 553

 For comprehension quizzes,
see **bedfordstmartins.com/practicalargument**.

This article appeared in the *Chicago Sun-Times* on October 25, 2011.

WE BAIL OUT BANKS, BUT NOT DESPERATE STUDENTS

JESSE JACKSON

The sign at the Occupy Wall Street demonstration revealed the struggles of 1
America's young: "A B.A., $30,000 in student debt, and no job." Young people
are graduating from college into the worst jobs market since the 1930s while
carrying record levels of student debt. The sad truth of Occupy Wall Street is
that for many of the young activists, Wall Street occupied them first.

Students are borrowing twice what they did a decade ago, even adjusting 2
for inflation. Debt has doubled in just five years. Student debt is likely to exceed
$1 trillion over the next year.

As states cut back on college support and grants, college tuitions have risen 3
faster than the cost of homes, health care, or energy. Americans believe a college
education is key to their children's future, so more and more borrow what
they can.

Students are now graduating with 4
average debts of over $24,000. When I
speak to families in mining towns in
Appalachia, I ask how many have lost a
job, how many face foreclosure, how
many face costly medical bills. Many

> "Students are now graduating with average debts of over $24,000."

hands go up. But when I ask how many worry about student loans, the biggest
portion of the audience stands up. It is working families—families stretching
to give their children the chance that they never had—who are taking on the
greatest debt and are at the greatest risk.

The banking industry has used its clout to make these loans the harshest 5
of all debt. They survive bankruptcy. The lenders have broad collection powers, far greater than with a mortgage or a credit card. They can garnish wages
or even Social Security payments. When payments are missed, penalties are
brutal. Students who graduate and then lose their job suddenly find themselves owing twice what they signed up for.

The debt constricts normal life events. Students must put off moving out 6
from their parents' home, buying a car, or saving for a home or retirement.
They delay getting married or having children.

Defaults have soared. In 2008, more than 238,000 defaulted on their loans. 7
The number of loans that went into forbearance or deferment (when borrowers receive temporary relief from payments) rose to 22 percent in 2007.

President Obama and his wife, Michelle, struggled to pay off student debts 8
long after they graduated. The president increased Pell grants and provided
relief that would link government loan payments to income and provide

potential forgiveness for those taking public service jobs. But despite the largest increase of student aid since the GI Bill, the debts keep getting bigger.

The debt not only enslaves the borrowers, it threatens the economy. With millions of young people burdened by debt, demand for apartments, homes, cars, and discretionary goods is reduced.   9

Occupy Wall Street can ask these hard questions: 10

Banks corrupted Congress with campaign contributions to facilitate their fleecing of the most vulnerable of students with the most onerous of provisions.   11

Why should big banks be able to get virtually interest-free money from the Federal Reserve, while students are forced to pay far higher interest rates? Why should bankruptcy courts be able to rewrite mortgages on the vacation homes of the wealthy while student loans are untouchable? Students need legislation to allow their loans to be refinanced in bankruptcy court or forgiven. Why don't we provide students with the grants or low-cost loans the banks get?   12

Many young people forgo college. Others drop out, unwilling to rack up debt. If there is anything that is too big and too important to fail, it is our next generation.   13

⊘ AT ISSUE: SOURCES FOR DEVELOPING A PROPOSAL ARGUMENT

1. At the end of paragraph 1, Jackson uses the word *occupy* twice in one sentence: "The sad truth of Occupy Wall Street is that for many of the young activists, Wall Street occupied them first." What does each use of *occupy* mean? What is Jackson trying to get across in this play on words? Is he successful?

2. Paraphrase Jackson's thesis statement by filling in the following template.

   The government should help students with their loans because

   _____

   _____.

3. Jackson begins his essay by discussing the student-debt problem. Is his explanation of this problem clear? Does he present enough facts and figures to put the problem in context?

4. Jackson devotes four paragraphs to defining *debt*. Why does he do this? Do you think this extended definition is necessary? Why does Jackson assume that his readers do not know what *debt* is?

5. What assumptions does Jackson believe are self-evident and need no proof? Do you agree that these assumptions are self-evident? If not, what evidence do you think Jackson should have included?

6. In paragraph 12, Jackson compares banks that borrow money from the Federal Reserve to students who take out loans. Is this comparison accurate? Is it fair? Does this analogy strengthen or weaken Jackson's case?

7. Does Jackson see students as innocent victims or as something else? Do you agree or disagree with his characterization? How would Richard Vedder (p. 539) respond to Jackson's portrayal of students?

This editorial cartoon was adapted from an illustration in the *Atlantic Monthly*.

STUDENT DEBT CRISIS SOLUTION

⊙ AT ISSUE: SOURCES FOR DEVELOPING A PROPOSAL ARGUMENT

1. The editorial cartoon above shows Minerva, an ancient Roman goddess. Consult an encyclopedia to find out more about Minerva. Why do you think this mythical figure is used in this visual?

2. Why are Minerva's wrists chained? Why does she have a sign hanging from her neck? What point is the creator of this image trying to make?

3. How could you use this visual to support an argument about student loans? What position do you think it could support?

4. What argument does this editorial cartoon make?

The blog entry was posted to *National Review Online* on October 11, 2011.

FORGIVE STUDENT LOANS?

RICHARD VEDDER

As the Wall Street protests grow and expand beyond New York, growing 1 scrutiny of the nascent movement is warranted. What do these folks want? Alongside their ranting about the inequality of incomes, the alleged inordinate power of Wall Street and large corporations, the high level of unemployment, and the like, one policy goal ranks high with most protesters: the forgiveness of student-loan debt. In an informal survey of over 50 protesters in New York last Tuesday, blogger and equity research analyst David Maris found 93 percent of them advocated student-loan forgiveness. An online petition drive advocating student-loan forgiveness has gathered an impressive number of signatures (over 442,000). This is an issue that resonates with many Americans.

Economist Justin Wolfers recently opined that "this is the worst idea ever." 2 I think it is actually the second-worst idea ever—the worst was the creation of federally subsidized student loans in the first place. Under current law, when the feds (who have basically taken over the student-loan industry) make a loan, the size of the U.S. budget deficit rises, and the government borrows additional funds, very often from foreign investors. We are borrowing from the Chinese to finance school attendance by a predominantly middle-class group of Americans.

But that is the tip of the iceberg: Though the ostensible objective of the 3 loan program is to increase the proportion of adult Americans with college degrees, over 40 percent of those pursuing a bachelor's degree fail to receive one within six years. And default is a growing problem with student loans.

Further, it's not clear that college imparts much of value to the average 4 student. The typical college student spends less than 30 hours a week, 32 weeks a year, on all academic matters—class attendance, writing papers, studying for exams, etc. They spend about half as much time on school as their parents spend working. If Richard Arum and Josipa Roksa (authors of *Academically Adrift*) are even roughly correct, today's students typically learn little in the way of critical learning or writing skills while in school.

Moreover, the student-loan program has proven an ineffective way to 5 achieve one of its initial aims, a goal also of the Wall Street protesters: increasing economic opportunity for the poor. In 1970, when federal student-loan and -grant programs were in their infancy, about 12 percent of college graduates came from the bottom one-fourth of the income distribution. While people from all social classes are more likely to go to college today, the poor haven't gained nearly as much ground as the rich have: With the nation awash in nearly a trillion dollars in student-loan debt (more even than credit-card obligations), the proportion of bachelor's-degree holders coming from the bottom one-fourth of the income distribution has fallen to around 7 percent.

> "The sins of the loan program are many. Let's briefly mention just five."

The sins of the loan program are many. Let's briefly mention just five.

6

First, artificially low interest rates are set by the federal government—they are fixed by law rather than market forces. Low-interest-rate mortgage loans resulting from loose Fed policies and the government-sponsored enterprises Fannie Mae and Freddie Mac spurred the housing bubble that caused the 2008 financial crisis. Arguably, federal student financial assistance is creating a second bubble in higher education.

Second, loan terms are invariant, with students with poor prospects of graduating and getting good jobs often borrowing at the same interest rates as those with excellent prospects (e.g., electrical-engineering majors at MIT).

Third, the availability of cheap loans has almost certainly contributed to the tuition explosion—college prices are going up even more than health-care prices.

Fourth, at present the loans are made by a monopoly provider, the same one that gave us such similar inefficient and costly monopolistic behemoths as the U.S. Postal Service.

Fifth, the student-loan and associated Pell Grant programs spawned the notorious FAFSA form that requires families to reveal all sorts of financial information—information that colleges use to engage in ruthless price discrimination via tuition discounting, charging wildly different amounts to students depending on how much their parents can afford to pay. It's a soak-the-rich scheme on steroids.

Still, for good or ill, we have this unfortunate program. Wouldn't loan forgiveness provide some stimulus to a moribund economy? The Wall Street protesters argue that if debt-burdened young persons were free of this albatross, they would start spending more on goods and services, stimulating employment. Yet we demonstrated with stimulus packages in 2008 and 2009 (not to mention the 1930s, Japan in the 1990s, etc.) that giving people more money to spend will not bring recovery. But even if it did, why should we give a break to this particular group of individuals, who disproportionately come from prosperous families to begin with? Why give them assistance while those who have dutifully repaid their loans get none? An arguably more equitable and efficient method of stimulus would be to drop dollars out of airplanes over low-income areas.

7

Moreover, this idea has ominous implications for the macro economy. Who would take the loss from the unanticipated non-repayment of a trillion dollars? If private financial institutions are liable for some of it, it could kill

8

them, triggering another financial crisis. If the federal government shoulders the entire burden, we are adding a trillion or so more dollars in liabilities to a government already grievously overextended (upwards of $100 trillion in liabilities counting Medicare, Social Security, and the national debt), almost certainly leading to more debt downgrades, which could trigger investor panic. This idea is breathtaking in terms of its naïveté and stupidity.

The demonstrators say that selfish plutocrats are ruining our economy 9 and creating an unjust society. Rather, a group of predominantly rather spoiled and coddled young persons, long favored and subsidized by the American taxpayer, are complaining that society has not given them enough—they want the taxpayer to foot the bill for their years of limited learning and heavy partying while in college. Hopefully, this burst of dimwittery should not pass muster even in our often dysfunctional Congress.

⊘AT ISSUE: SOURCES FOR DEVELOPING A PROPOSAL ARGUMENT

1. According to Vedder, forgiveness of student debt is "the second-worst idea ever" (para. 2). Why? What is the worst idea?

2. In paragraphs 3 through 6, Vedder examines the weaknesses of the federally subsidized student-loan program. List some of the weaknesses he identifies.

3. Why do you think Vedder waits until paragraph 7 to discuss debt forgiveness? Should he have discussed it sooner?

4. Summarize Vedder's primary objection to forgiving student debt. Do you agree with him? How would you refute his objection?

5. Throughout his essay, Vedder uses rather strong language to characterize those who disagree with him. For example, in paragraph 8, he calls the idea of forgiving student loans "breathtaking in terms of its naïveté and stupidity." In paragraph 9, he calls demonstrators "spoiled and coddled young persons" and labels Congress "dysfunctional." Does this language help or hurt Vedder's case? Would more neutral words and phrases have been more effective? Why or why not?

6. How would Vedder respond to Jesse Jackson's assessment (p. 535) of the student-loan crisis? Are there any points that Jackson makes with which Vedder might agree?

This opinion column appeared in the *St. Paul Pioneer Press* on November 20, 2011.

FIVE MYTHS ABOUT STUDENT LOANS

MARK KANTROWITZ

Many of the Occupy Wall Street protesters are struggling to repay student loans and want their debt to go away. An online petition calling for cancellation of all student loans has gathered more than 600,000 signatures over the past 11 weeks. President Obama responded, in part, last month with an improved income-based repayment plan, but most of the protesters and petitioners will not qualify for it. The increased attention on education debt has also brought attention to many misconceptions about how people borrow to pay for school.

1. Forgiving student loan debt would help stimulate the economy. People who want all student loan debt forgiven argue that getting rid of monthly loan payments would lead to increased consumer spending, thereby providing a quick boost to the struggling U.S. economy. However, only about 40 percent of all outstanding student loan debt is actively being repaid. The remaining borrowers are still in school or otherwise not paying their loans back, so they wouldn't immediately benefit from forgiveness.

And a "forgiveness stimulus" would have a limited impact. According to my calculations based on data from the Education Department's Direct Loan Program, annual payments and default collections total about 5.6 percent of these outstanding direct loans. If this proportion is similar for other kinds of education debt, then forgiving the nearly $1 trillion in outstanding student debt would inject at most $56 billion per year. Not a paltry sum, but certainly small compared with more significant stimulus efforts.

2. All education debt is good debt. Certainly, taking out loans to pay for college is an investment in your future and a key to a better-paying job. So it's good debt. But too much of a good thing can be bad for you.

> "So it's good debt. But too much of a good thing can be bad for you."

Students who graduate with high debt often must abandon certain career aspirations. I've spoken to hundreds of borrowers who are behind on their student loans, and they tell me they have delayed major life events, such as buying a car or a home, getting married, having children, or saving for their children's college education or for retirement. According to a recent survey by Monster Learning, about a third of recent college graduates have to move back in with their parents to save on living expenses.

A good rule of thumb is that students' total debt at graduation should be ₆ less than their expected starting salary—ideally, a lot less. This will allow them to repay their loans in 10 years. Otherwise, they will need to use an alternate repayment plan, which reduces the monthly loan payment by stretching it out over 20, 25, or even 30 years. This means that when their own children start college, some of these people will still be paying off their old loans.

3. If you declare bankruptcy, your student loans go away. Neither federal nor ₇ private student loans can be discharged in a bankruptcy unless the borrower files an "undue hardship" petition—which often involves a very harsh and high standard that was set in a New York state case more than 20 years ago. It requires that the borrower cannot maintain a minimal standard of living while repaying the loans, that the circumstances that prevent repayment will probably persist for most of the life of the loans, and that the borrower made a good-faith effort to repay the loans. In the words of one bankruptcy judge, a successful undue hardship petition requires a "certainty of hopelessness."

According to the Educational Credit Management Corp., a guarantee ₈ agency that manages the student loans of federal borrowers with an active bankruptcy filing, about 72,000 federal student loan borrowers filed for bankruptcy in 2008, but only 29 succeeded in obtaining a full or partial discharge of their loans. That's 0.04 percent. You're more likely to die of cancer or in a car crash than to have your loans discharged in bankruptcy.

4. Widespread defaults on federal student loans would worsen the govern- ₉ **ment's deficit.** Some people argue that the student loan "bubble" could be the next to pop. Yet despite the recent increase in default rates to nearly 9 percent, federal education loans remain profitable for the government.

And the government has strong powers to compel repayment on defaulted ₁₀ loans. For example, it can garnish up to 15 percent of take-home pay without a court order for a borrower who is 12 months behind on student loan payments. The government can also intercept federal and state income tax refunds and lottery winnings and offset up to 15 percent of Social Security disability and retirement benefit payments. Default rates would have to more than triple for the government to lose money on federal education loans.

5. The federal government should get out of the student loan business—the ₁₁ **private sector can do it better.** Private loans make up a relatively small percentage of total education debt. Some private loans currently offer lower interest rates than federal education loans—but most of those rates are variable and restricted to borrowers with excellent credit or with a creditworthy co-signer (usually a parent). Interest rates are unusually low now, but the rates on variable loans are likely to start increasing soon.

The federal government, on the other hand, seeks to increase access to a higher education in addition to earning a profit. The federal Stafford loan is available to all students without regard to the borrower's credit history. The federal PLUS loan requires that borrowers not have an "adverse credit history," but this is a weaker standard than the ones used by private lenders.

But there's more the federal government can do. The Consumer Financial Protection Bureau and the Education Department have proposed a plan to standardize financial aid award letters, so that they provide better disclosures of college costs and aid. College is becoming less affordable. Tuition rates at public colleges are growing at above-average rates, and low- and moderate-income students are increasingly being priced out of a higher education. Families need federal and private student loans to help pay for college, but they also need clear, correct, and comparable information about college costs and financial aid so they can make informed decisions about affordability, and so students can graduate without crippling loan debt.

AT ISSUE: SOURCES FOR DEVELOPING A PROPOSAL ARGUMENT

1. Even though this opinion column is essentially a list of "myths," it does make an argument. Using the template below, write a thesis statement that expresses the main idea of the essay.

   When you examine people's attitudes about student debt, it is

   clear that _____

   _____.

2. Kantrowitz addresses five misconceptions that he assumes readers have about student loans. How effectively does he refute these misconceptions? Does he ever concede that readers may be at least partially right?

3. Does Kantrowitz provide enough evidence to support his position? What points—if any—does he assume are self-evident and need no proof?

4. Which does Kantrowitz think is better equipped to deal with the student-loan problem—the federal government or the private sector? According to Kantrowitz, what benefits can the government offer borrowers that the private sector cannot? What problems could government involvement in the loan program cause?

5. Do a Web search to find out more about Mark Kantrowitz. What qualifications does he have? Does he ever allude to his qualifications in his essay? Should he have done more to establish his credibility? Explain.

6. This essay lacks a strong concluding statement. Why do you think Kantrowitz chose not to include one? Would his essay have been more convincing if he had done so? Write a sentence that could serve as the concluding statement of Kantrowitz's essay.

7. How would Kantrowitz respond to Robert Zaller's claim in "Higher Education's Coming Crisis" (p. 553) that "there is a single driving force behind" the rise in college costs?

This commentary was published in the *Chronicle of Higher Education* on October 23, 2011.

THE U.S. SHOULD ADOPT INCOME-BASED LOANS NOW

KEVIN CAREY

A new generation of student debtors has seized the public stage. While the demands of the Occupy Wall Street movement are many, college lending reform is near the top of every list. Decades of greed, inattention, and failed policy have created a growing class of young men and women with few prospects of landing jobs good enough to bear the weight of their crushing college loans.

Some activists have called for wholesale student-loan forgiveness—a kind of 21st-century jubilee. That's unlikely. But there's something the federal government can do right now to help students caught by our terribly unjust higher-education financing system: End all federal student-loan defaults forever by moving to income-contingent loans.

The concept is simple. Right now, students pay back their loans on a fixed schedule, typically amortized over 10 years. Since people usually make less money early in their careers, their fixed monthly loan bill is hardest to manage in the first years after graduating (or not) from college. People unlucky enough to graduate during horrible recessions are even more likely to have bad jobs or no jobs and struggle paying back their loans. Not coincidentally, the U.S. Department of Education recently announced a sharp rise in loan defaults.

Under an income-contingent loan system, like those in Australia and Britain, students pay a fixed percentage of their income toward their loans. Payments are automatically deducted from their paychecks by the IRS, just like income-tax withholding. Self-employed workers pay in quarterly installments, just as they do with their taxes. If borrowers earn a lot, their payments rise accordingly, and their loans are retired quickly. If their income falls below a certain level—say, the poverty line—they pay nothing. After an extended time period of 20 or 30 years, any remaining debt is forgiven.

> "Under an income-contingent loan system, ...students pay a fixed percentage of their income toward their loans."

In other words, nobody ever defaults on a federal student loan again. The whole concept of "default" is expunged from the system. No more collection agencies hounding people with 10 phone calls a night. No more ruined credit and dashed hopes of home-ownership. People who want to enter virtuous but lower-paid professions like social work and teaching won't be deterred by unmanageable debt.

And by calibrating interest and payment rates, the federal government can make the program no more expensive than the current cost of subsidizing loans and writing off unpaid debt. The only losers are the repo men.

The concept has been proven to work—Australia and Britain have used it for years—and both liberals and conservatives have reason to get on board. The Nobel Prize–winning economist Milton Friedman proposed the idea all the way back in 1955.

Indeed, income-contingent loans are such a good idea, one might wonder why they don't exist already. Historically, administrative complications have been a major culprit. Until last year, the federal government managed most student loans by paying private banks to act as lenders and then guaranteeing their losses. The IRS would have had to maintain relationships with scores of different lenders, relying on banks for notification of who owes how much and disbursing money hither and yon. Income-contingent loans would have created a huge bureaucratic headache.

But in 2010, Congress abolished the old system, cutting out private banks. Now the federal government originates all federal loans. The IRS would have to deal with only one lender: the U.S. Department of Education. In other words, there is a new opportunity to overhaul the way students repay their college debt that didn't exist until this year.

It's true that students who pay over long periods of time will pay more interest and that the taxpayers will bear the cost of partially forgiven loans. But under the current system the federal government is already eating the cost of defaulted loans, and low-income students who can't repay loans are often hit with fines and penalties that dwarf the cost of extra interest.

When federal loans were first created, nobody imagined they would become standard practice for financing college. As late as 1993, most undergraduates didn't borrow. Now, two-thirds take on debt, and most of those loans are federal. The average debt load increased over 50 percent during that time.

Nor is repayment an isolated problem. One recent study found that the majority of American borrowers—56 percent—struggled with loan payments in the first five years after college. In Britain, by contrast, 98 percent of borrowers are meeting their obligations.

Because student loans can almost never be discharged in bankruptcy, defaulted loans can haunt students for a lifetime. Some senior citizens theoretically could have their Social Security checks garnished to make good on old student debt. That is insane.

A similar-sounding federal program, called income-based repayment, is now on the books and is scheduled to become somewhat more generous starting in 2014. But the program is administratively complicated, involving income-eligibility caps and requiring students to reapply every year. This points to another major advantage of income-contingent loans: simplicity.

Even with the government as the sole source of federal loans, many graduates still have to navigate a thicket of different rates, terms, lenders, consolidation options, and schedules in order to meet their obligations. Some fall behind not because they're unwilling or unable to pay, but because they can't get the right check to the right place at the right time. An income-contingent system would remove all of that hassle, making repayment simple and automatic, and setting college graduates free to get on with the important business of starting their lives.

The student-loan system has grown into an out-of-control monster tearing at the fabric of civil society. In Chile, student anger over an inequitable, unaffordable, profit-oriented higher-education system led to nationwide protests and violent confrontation just months ago. Now the seeds of similar unrest are sprouting here. 16

Income-contingent loans won't solve the escalating college prices, state disinvestment in higher education, and overall economic weakness that are driving more students into debt. But they offer a simpler, fairer, more efficient, and more humane way of allowing students to repay loans that aren't disappearing from the higher-education landscape anytime soon. They could be put in place quickly at no extra cost to the taxpayer. In a dismal fiscal environment, there are few deals this good. 17

The students at the barricades are right to be angry. They didn't run the economy into the ditch. They didn't create the system in which a college degree is all but mandatory to pursue a good career, and loans are often unavoidable. But they have to live with it. Income-contingent loans are one way to give them the help they need. 18

⊘ AT ISSUE: SOURCES FOR DEVELOPING A PROPOSAL ARGUMENT

1. Carey blames the current student-loan problem on years of "greed, inattention, and failed policy" (para. 1). Is he right to assume his readers will agree with him, or should he have provided evidence to support this statement? Explain.

2. In paragraph 2, Carey says that income-contingent loans would end "forever" all student-loan defaults. After reading Carey's explanation, how would you define *income-contingent loans*?

3. What evidence does Carey present to support his proposal? If income-contingent loans are such a good idea, why hasn't the government tried them before?

4. What kind of appeal does Carey make in paragraph 7? In your opinion, how effective is this appeal?

5. Where does Carey address arguments against his proposal? List these arguments. Which argument do you think presents the most effective challenge to Carey's position? Why?

6. In paragraph 16, Carey calls the student-loan system "an out-of-control monster tearing at the fabric of civil society." In paragraph 18, he says, "The students at the barricades are right to be angry." Do you think he is exaggerating, or is this strong language justified?

7. In paragraph 17, Carey lists problems that income-contingent loans will *not* solve. Does this paragraph undercut (or even contradict) his statement in paragraph 2 that income-contingent loans would end student-loan defaults? Explain.

This opinion column is from the November 23, 2011, issue of *U.S. News & World Report*.

WHY THE GOVERNMENT IS TO BLAME FOR HIGH COLLEGE COSTS

MARY KATE CARY

1 Last month President Obama, facing increasingly violent Occupy Wall Street protests nationwide, announced executive action to help alleviate the heavy burden of student debt faced by many of the young, unemployed protesters. Although many of the protesters are blaming private banks and corporate "fat cats" for the financial pickle they're in, the president thought he'd calm them down by easing the terms of repayment and forgiveness. What Obama didn't tell them is that it's really the federal government they should blame.

2 A year ago, the president signed legislation ending subsidies for private banks giving federally guaranteed student loans—making the federal government, not banks, the lender of choice for most students. You can still get private bank loans for your college education, but since they no longer are backed by the U.S. government, private loans aren't as good a deal anymore; most are variable rate loans that require a co-signer and are difficult to qualify for. So it doesn't take a rocket scientist to see why most kids take out federal student loans from the Department of Education now, and leave the bank loans as a last resort.

3 Back in the mid-1980s when I went to college, there was a $2,500 limit on the amount of federal student loans you could take out in a year. I graduated with $10,000 of debt and worked three jobs to pay it off. That's all changed. The limit on federal loans for most students is now $31,000 for four years. These days, the average college senior who had loans graduates with $25,250 in student debt, a new record, with some high-tuition colleges averaging double that, at over $55,000 per student. Unemployment has hit a new high among young people, and their median incomes are falling. Many of them are having trouble finding a job and making their loan payments. A whole generation of middle-class students is being crushed by student debt.

4 It all goes back to two well-intentioned federal goals: first, that a college education should be within the reach of every American, and second, that if students borrow money from the federal government, they should repay it. Most of us would agree that both are noble goals. But the consequences of both have been stunning.

5 As a result of the first, the money began to flow; over the last 30 years, inflation-adjusted federal financial aid has quadrupled. Total student debt has now reached the $1 trillion mark, more than the credit card debt of every American combined. The federal deficit in the recently ended fiscal year totaled $1.3 trillion; the debt load carried by college grads now stands at more than two thirds of our nation's massive budget shortfall. According to the College Board, over half of all full-time undergrads at public colleges and universities

are now full-time borrowers. At private nonprofit schools, a whopping two thirds have loans.

The more money the federal government pumps into financial aid, the 6 more money the colleges charge for tuition. Inflation adjusted tuition and fees have tripled over those same 30 years while aid quadrupled; the aid is going up faster than the tuition. Thanks to the federal government, massive sums of money are available to pay for massive tuitions.

> "Thanks to the federal government, massive sums of money are available to pay for massive tuitions."

This has nothing to do with costs. 7 According to Neal McCluskey's research at the Cato Institute, it costs roughly $8,000 a year to educate an undergraduate at an average residential college. Yet the average college bill—including room and board—charged at a private four-year university is $37,000, and $16,000 at a public one. For a long time, college tuition has been rising faster than the inflation rate, which certainly has hurt middle-class families. Colleges can raise tuition with impunity because colleges know they'll get paid no matter what.

That brings us to that second well-intentioned federal goal, that all 8 student loans must be repaid. In 1976 federal law was changed to state that student loans would no longer be "dischargeable," or covered by bankruptcy. Along the way, the federal government also removed the requirement that college students have parents or grandparents co-sign for federal loans, making young students solely responsible for payment in full.

This means that if you owe the government money for college and don't 9 pay it back, filing bankruptcy isn't going to help you. You will still owe the government. All you can do is default on the loan or seek early forgiveness. And that's exactly what's happening. According to the Department of Education, the national default rate has increased every year for the last four years, and has nearly doubled since 2005. As the administration forgives more loans and defaults keep climbing, the cost to taxpayers keeps going up.

It's not crazy to talk about making student loans dischargeable again, or 10 even capping the number of federally guaranteed loans so that private banks can compete for more borrowers. But the bigger challenge is reducing the cost of tuition in the first place. Tuitions are artificially high directly because of federal financial aid. "It's a vicious cycle," McCluskey recently explained in a speech. "Students tell the politicians, 'We don't want to pay this much for college,' and politicians respond by throwing more money at them, and colleges respond by increasing costs."

While critics charge that gradually cutting back on federal financial aid is 11 "heartless," doing so would actually be one of the most compassionate things we can do in the long run for middle-class families. Going to college is a big part of the American Dream for many young people, but well-meaning "help" from the federal government is driving up costs, creating massive debt, and, in some cases, ruining lives.

⊘ AT ISSUE: SOURCES FOR DEVELOPING A PROPOSAL ARGUMENT

1. What misconception does Cary assume readers have about student-debt forgiveness? Do you think she is correct?

2. Do you think her thesis statement at the end of paragraph 1 will encourage readers to want to read on, or do you think it might discourage them? Explain.

3. In paragraph 3, Cary discusses her own student loans. Why does she include this material? What point is she trying to make? Is she successful?

4. According to Cary, how is the federal government responsible for the student-debt crisis? What evidence does she provide to support her position? Do you think she needs to supply more evidence? Explain.

5. In paragraph 4, Cary says that there are "two well-intentioned federal goals." What are they? Why does she think these goals are misguided? Do you agree?

6. In her conclusion, Cary notes that critics say that reducing federal aid to students is "heartless." How does she refute this charge? Why do you think Cary decided to end her essay in this way? Would another concluding strategy have been more convincing? Explain.

7. Make an outline of Cary's essay. Then, decide if it includes all the elements of an effective proposal argument. (You may want to look at the outline on p. 526–527.) What sections—if any—are missing? Do you think Cary should have included them? Why or why not?

8. Except for Robert Zaller's essay (p. 553), all of the essays in this section refer to Occupy Wall Street—a protest group that demonstrates against social and economic inequality. What points does Occupy Wall Street help each writer make? Visit the Occupy Wall Street Web site to research its goals. How accurately does each writer represented here portray this group?

This opinion essay was published in the *Triangle*, the student newspaper of Drexel University, on February 3, 2012.

HIGHER EDUCATION'S COMING CRISIS

ROBERT ZALLER

A few years ago, walking around an upper-middle-class neighborhood in southern California, I noticed that home sale prices were near the seven-figure range. Looking at the houses themselves and imagining the income levels of their occupants, my thought was: This can't last. It's unreal. 1

So it was. The housing market soon crashed. Now, looking at the costs of private higher education, typically in the range of $40,000–$50,000 per year, it seems clear that they, too, have become unsustainable. Like the housing market, the market for higher education—already undercut by online education factories—is headed for collapse. For a long time, both markets were propped up by debt, but that has reached a saturation point in education as it did in housing. Student loans, once mainly confined to pricey medical and law school programs, have now become the largest single source of private indebtedness in the United States. That isn't just impossible to sustain. It's an outrage and a disgrace, and it points to a general systemic crisis that transcends the academy. Affordable housing, health care, and education are the three prerequisites of a functioning society. At present, we provide none of them to a growing segment of our population. 2

> "Like the housing market, the market for higher education . . . is headed for collapse."

In each of these areas, costs have been rising in excess of the general inflation rate for decades; in health care and higher education, they still are. When a product costs more on the market, it is supposed to be the result of either a scarcity of supply or a surplus in demand. Neither is the case in academia. The national population is growing only very modestly, and there is no shortage of universities. The principal cost factor in higher education—productive labor—is actually declining. In real dollar terms, my own salary is less than it was when I came to Drexel 25 years ago, and I am sure my situation is not unique among the faculty. But labor costs have been driven down far more radically by the transformation of the academy itself. Whereas a quarter century ago it still consisted largely of tenured faculty, a majority of courses are now taught by a nontenured proletariat whose salaries and benefits (if any) are sharply lower than those of their older and fast-disappearing tenured colleagues, whose classroom workloads are higher and who are, for the most part, subject to dismissal at pleasure. This means, in bureaucratic terms, a cheaper and more disposable workforce. Add to this the proliferation of online courses (particularly popular at Drexel), which require next to no 3 investment in physical plant and support services, and you have a lean and very mean academic delivery system whose costs should be going down, not up.

There is no single explanation for the actual rise in college costs, but there is a single driving force behind them. Lest you distrust me as a source, I refer you to Mark G. Yudof, who, as president of the University of California system, is the preeminent bureaucrat in academia today. Yudof, interviewed recently on PBS, offered one flat reason for the price explosion in higher education: "Administration."

This will, of course, come as no surprise to anyone who has spent time in academia. In 1975 there was one administrator per 84 students and one non-academic staff member per 50. By 2005 these ratios were 50 and 21, respectively. At the same time, faculty-to-student ratios remained constant while per-unit costs, as explained above, declined. Put another way: In 1975 there were 178,000 more faculty than administrators and support staff. In 2005 there were 181,000 more administrators and staff than faculty. That, to put it mildly, is crazy. It is also expensive.

The American university was not underbureaucratized in 1975; it is super-bureaucratized today. The explanation lies in the corporatization of the modern university. It is not simply that corporate values have come to dominate the academy, but that a corporate management structure has replaced the older system in which administrators, typically drawn from and ultimately returning to faculty ranks, shared governance responsibilities with faculty representatives and senates, with whom they negotiated faculty salaries, benefits, and working conditions (though not their own). This model, while far from perfect, did function after a fashion. It has almost completely vanished today. A professional administrative class has grown up with no experience of teaching or research and scant respect for accomplishment in either, except as it can be quantified as contributing to "profit centers." This class has feathered its nest handsomely and redefined the work of the university in terms of what it does—compile reports, attend meetings, and engross itself in mission statements and five-year plans, which always entail the need for more administration.

Not only has the number of administrators grown exponentially, but so have their salaries, particularly at higher levels. Drexel made national headlines recently with the revelation that it paid out $4.9 million in compensation and benefits to the estate of President Papadakis. This kind of Caesarean largesse was not long ago inconceivable in higher education, but of course, it is only modest compared to the payouts of other corporate executives. Welcome to the world of what one observer has called "the all-administrative university."

Academia has become, in fact, a sweetheart racket for its beneficiaries. Universities have partnered with private businesses in profit-sharing enterprises while they themselves retain tax-exempt status. The corporatized university has also become the commoditized one, as we witness the chastity belt of businesses and private apartments growing up around Creese and MacAlister on our own campus. And, of course, universities that specialize in sports programs, like a certain neighbor in Happy Valley, reap neofeudal profits from athletic serfs who get room, board, and emergency medical attention but are barred from earning a penny off the millions their labor generates. Like the Egyptian military, American higher education has branched out into areas of civil activity it was never designed for and—so far—enjoys privileges and exemptions denied to others with whom it competes. That state of affairs cannot last indefinitely. Nor should it.

President Obama has fired a shot across the bows of higher education in warning that if college costs continue to go up, government subvention will go down. This may not be an idle threat, and it signals that public patience is wearing thin. The problem is that education for participation in a democratic society has been so weakened, disenfranchised, and compromised that it is hardly up to the task of defending itself, let alone engaging a wider community. That has been the tragedy of academia in my generation. When the reckoning comes, though, faculty and administration may find themselves in the same boat. They will then have no one to blame but each other.

⊘ AT ISSUE: SOURCES FOR DEVELOPING A PROPOSAL ARGUMENT

1. Zaller, a college professor, begins his essay by drawing an analogy between the housing crisis and the cost of private higher education. According to Zaller, how are these two markets similar? How are they different? Is this comparison accurate? Is it fair?

2. In paragraph 2, Zaller states his thesis: "Affordable housing, health care, and education are three prerequisites of a functioning society. At present we provide none of them to a growing segment of our population." Does he discuss all three of these "prerequisites"? Should he have limited his thesis statement to education? Why or why not?

3. According to Zaller, why should the cost of college be going down instead of up? What force keeps costs rising?

4. In paragraph 6, Zaller uses the terms *superbureaucratized* and *corporatization*. In paragraph 8, he uses the term *commoditized*. What do these terms mean? Considering that this essay appeared in a student newspaper, should he have used different language instead? Explain.

5. In his essay, Zaller uses some forceful language. For example, in paragraph 2, he calls the burden of student loans "an outrage and a disgrace." Find other examples of this kind of language. Do you think this language strengthens or weakens Zaller's argument? Explain.

6. What different appeals does Zaller make in his essay? Are there any appeals that he should have made but did not? Explain.

7. What does Zaller mean in his conclusion when he says that when the reckoning comes, faculty and administration will "have no one to blame but each other"? What do you think Mary Kate Cary (p. 550) would have to say about this statement?

⊘ EXERCISE 15.7

Write a one-paragraph proposal argument in which you consider the topic, "Should the Government Do More to Relieve the Student-Loan Burden?" Follow the template below, filling in the blanks to create your proposal.

TEMPLATE FOR WRITING A PROPOSAL ARGUMENT

The current federal student-loan program has some problems that must be addressed. For example, _____ _____. In order to address this situation, _____.

First, _____ _____ _____. Second, _____ _____ _____. Finally, _____ _____ _____.

Not everyone agrees that this is the way to solve these problems, however. Some say _____ _____ _____. Others point out that _____ _____.

These objections make sense, but _____ _____ _____. All in all, _____ _____ _____ _____.

⊘ EXERCISE 15.8

Ask several of your instructors and your classmates whether they think the government should do more to relieve the student-loan burden. Then, add their responses to the paragraph you wrote for Exercise 15.7.

⊖ EXERCISE 15.9

Write a proposal arguing that the government should do more to relieve the student-loan burden. Be sure to present examples from your own experience to support your arguments. (If you like, you may incorporate the material you developed for Exercises 15.7 and 15.0 into your essay.) Cite the readings on pages 534–555, and be sure to document your sources and include a works-cited page. (See Chapter 10 for information on documenting sources.)

⊖ EXERCISE 15.10

Review the four pillars of argument discussed in Chapter 1. Does your essay include all four elements of an effective argument? Add anything that is missing.

⊖ WRITING ASSIGNMENTS: PROPOSAL ARGUMENTS

1. Each day, students at college cafeterias throw away hundreds of pounds of uneaten food. A number of colleges have found that by simply eliminating the use of trays, they can cut out much of this waste. At one college, for example, students who did not use trays wasted 14.4% less food for lunch and 47.1% less for dinner than those who did use trays. Write a proposal to your college or university in which you recommend eliminating trays from dining halls. Use your own experiences as well as information from your research and from interviews with other students to support your position. Be sure to address one or two arguments against your position.

2. Look around your campus, and find a service that you think should be improved. It could be the financial aid office, the student health services, or the writing center. Then, write an essay in which you identify the specific problem (or problems) and suggest a solution. If you wish, interview a few of your friends to get some information that you can use to support your proposal.

3. Assume that your college or university has just received a million-dollar donation from an anonymous benefactor. Your school has decided to solicit proposals from both students and faculty on ways to spend the money. Write a proposal to the president of your school in which you identify a good use for this windfall. Make sure you identify a problem, present a solution, and discuss the advantages of your proposal. If possible, address one or two arguments against your proposal—for example, that the money could be put to better use somewhere else.

16

Argument by Analogy

Should College Athletes Be Paid?

Current National Collegiate Athletic Association (NCAA) regulations make it illegal for colleges to pay student athletes, whom they consider to be amateurs. Recently, however, critics have argued that because some athletics programs bring millions of dollars to their schools, student athletes should share the wealth.

Many questions surround this debate. For example, those who oppose salaries for players believe that college sports will be less open to corruption if student athletes retain their amateur status. Others cite practical concerns, asking where financially strapped schools will get the money to compensate athletes. Still others point out that student athletes are already being compensated—by athletic scholarships that cover tuition, room and board, and incidentals. Questions also arise about *which* athletes should be paid—all student athletes or just those (such as football players) whose sports bring big money to

their schools? Since Title IX forbids gender discrimination in college athletics programs, would paying a salary to male basketball players require schools to compensate female basketball players as well? And how much should players be paid: A small stipend? A salary? A salary plus bonuses based on performance? Finally, if student athletes are paid, would they still be seen as students, or would they be treated as professional athletes—that is, as workers employed by their schools?

Central to this debate is the mission of the university. If its primary mission is to educate, do extensive (and expensive) athletics programs undermine that mission?

These are some of the questions that you should think about as you read the sources at the end of this chapter. After reading this material, you will be asked to write an **argument by analogy** in which you take a position on the issue of whether college athletes should be paid.

e For comprehension quizzes,
see bedfordstmartins.com/practicalargument.

What Is Analogy?

An **analogy** is an extended comparison between two items, situations, or concepts on the basis of a number of shared characteristics. Unlike a traditional comparison, however, an analogy explains a difficult or unfamiliar concept in terms of something familiar. For example, trying to define an electronic database to elderly readers who are not familiar with electronic communication might be a challenge, but if you begin by telling them that a telephone book is a kind of database, you will be able to get the concept across.

When you set out to develop an analogy, you have a number of options. You can draw an analogy with a historical event—making the case, for example, that a current political campaign, military action, act of legislation, or Supreme Court decision is like an earlier one. You can also compare two current situations that are alike in some respects—two school systems, two fashion trends, two kinds of energy-conservation measures. In each case, you would use a familiar concept to explain a less familiar one.

KEY WORDS FOR ANALOGY

When you develop an analogy, you use words and phrases such as the following to emphasize the parallels between the unfamiliar subject you are explaining and the familiar subject to which it is similar.

like	similarly	in the same way	just as
in comparison	likewise	also	

What Is Argument by Analogy?

When you construct an **argument by analogy**, you make the case that your position about an issue is valid because it is analogous to a comparable position on another issue (a position you expect your readers to accept). For example, most people would agree that laws should protect citizens from danger—speeding cars, epidemics, criminals, and so on. Based on this premise, someone who considers dogs a danger could develop an argument by analogy by saying that it is the government's responsibility to protect its citizens from dogs. Like speeding cars, dogs that are not controlled can injure or even kill someone. For this reason, the government should license dog owners just as it licenses drivers.

Such an argument, however (like all arguments by analogy), has its limitations. For one thing, most dogs are not dangerous, and there is a big difference between a pit bull bred to fight and a toy poodle bred to be a companion. For another, uncontrolled dogs and speeding cars obviously have significant differences. These weaknesses highlight the major limitation of any argument by analogy: an item that is similar to another item in some respects is not necessarily similar in all (or even most) respects. Because no two items, concepts, or situations are exactly alike, an analogy alone, no matter how convincing, cannot be a substitute for evidence.

> **NOTE**
>
> Brief analogies are often included in argumentation essays regardless of their overall structure or purpose. For example, in a definition argument, you might draw an analogy to support your definition. In this chapter, however, we focus on analogy as a strategy for an entire argumentative essay.

AVOIDING WEAK ANALOGIES

Whether you are using a brief analogy as an example in a support paragraph or an extended analogy to structure an entire essay, be sure it is strong enough to carry the weight of your argument. Be careful not to construct a **weak analogy**—one that is comparable to something else in only a few respects. Remember, the more similar the two items you are comparing, the stronger your analogy will likely be. (See Chapter 5 for more on weak analogies.)

When you write an argument by analogy, you might consider topics such as the following:

- Should sugary soft drinks be taxed?
- Should religious institutions' employee health insurance be required to cover birth control?
- Should cyberbullying be treated as a crime?
- Should SUV owners have to pay an energy surcharge?
- Is it acceptable for parents to spank their children?
- Should felons lose the right to vote?
- Should disabled people be barred from adopting children?

⊖ EXERCISE 16.1

Explain how a position on each of the above topics might be supported by an analogy. Begin by identifying a possible analogy. (For example, in responding to the first topic, you might say that sugary soft drinks are analogous to tobacco products.) Then, consider how the situation presented in each topic is like and unlike the analogous situation. Finally, draft a possible thesis statement for an argument by analogy on each topic.

Favorable and Unfavorable Analogies

In an argument by analogy, you can make either favorable or unfavorable comparisons, using either positive or negative examples to help you make your case.

Suppose you were assigned to write an argumentative essay taking a position on the topic, "Should government-issued identity cards be required for all U.S. citizens?" You might decide to structure your essay as an argument by analogy. To make the case that such cards *should* be required, you would use positive examples, drawing favorable analogies with other relatively routine and harmless documents, such as driver's licenses, voter registration cards, and social security cards. To make the case that such cards *should not* be required, you would use negative examples, drawing unfavorable analogies with identity cards issued to citizens of the former Soviet Union.

Of course, no analogy will actually prove your case. Identity cards are not completely harmless; after all, they are designed in part to identify legal residents (and therefore to identify undocumented immigrants). However, they are not inherently evil or dangerous, either. The truth lies somewhere in between. Finally, remember that an analogy is simply a persuasive strategy; it does not constitute evidence.

⊘ EXERCISE 16.2

Write two thesis statements—one using a favorable analogy and one using an unfavorable analogy—for each of the following templates. (Hint: In each case, begin by identifying various ways in which the given item— bicycles, restaurants, or motorcyclists—is like some other item.)

- Bicycles should have to be licensed because _____
  _____.

- Bicycles should not have to be licensed because _____
  _____.

- Restaurants should be required to post calorie counts for all their foods because _____
  _____.

- Restaurants should not be required to post calorie counts for all their foods because _____
  _____.

- Motorcyclists should be required to wear helmets because _____
  _____.

- Motorcyclists should not be required to wear helmets because _____
  _____.

Structuring an Argument by Analogy

Generally speaking, an argument by analogy can be structured as follows:

- **Introduction:** Establishes the context for the argument by explaining the central analogy that will be developed

- **Evidence (first point in support of thesis):** Presents one respect in which the current situation is analogous to another situation

- **Evidence (second point in support of thesis):** Presents another respect in which the current situation is analogous to another situation

- **Refutation of opposing arguments:** Explains why the analogy is valid (despite some limitations)

- **Conclusion:** Reinforces the essay's main point; includes a strong concluding statement

The following student essay illustrates one possible way of organizing an argument by analogy. The student writer argues that separate housing for minority students should be permitted, just as other kinds of special-interest living arrangements are.

DOES SEPARATE HOUSING FOR MINORITY STUDENTS MAKE SENSE?

ANTHONY LUU

1   Students come to college to learn, to expand their horizons, and to become independent adults, but this process is difficult when they do not feel comfortable in their surroundings. Some eighteen-year-olds, especially members of minority groups, may actually do better if they live in like-minded communities that can give them the support and confidence they need to succeed. Although some people see "affinity housing" as controversial, this option can help minority students get the most out of college and help more of them graduate.

Thesis statement

2   The idea of allowing students to choose to live with other students who share their values and backgrounds is not new. Most schools offer a variety of living options to undergraduates, including single-sex dorms,

First point in support of thesis: Analogy with other kinds of affinity housing

fraternities and sororities, honors colleges, and dorms based on common interests, such as foreign-language study or environmental activism. Just as women students can choose to live in all-female dorms and students who pledge to abstain from alcohol, tobacco, and recreational drugs can opt to live in substance-free housing, minority students should be able to live in a "safe space" where they will not be seen as different or be constantly asked to explain or defend their values and traditions. Such housing can give them the support they need to survive—and thrive—in school.

Background

Because minority students are underrepresented at most colleges, they can often feel isolated from the general campus culture. Without adequate support, these students will continue to graduate at lower rates than their white peers. As Charles Dervarics reports, studies show that minority students are far less likely than white students to graduate from college. In fact, recent data reveal that the "college completion gap" is growing, not shrinking. African-American students are 20% less likely than white students to graduate from college; Hispanic students are 26% less likely (6). This is a problem that schools must address, and one way to address it is to create supportive affinity groups for minority students. 3

Second point in support of thesis (paras. 4–5): Analogy with short-term "living and learning communities"

To help minority students adjust to college, many universities have set up short-term living and learning communities that are analogous to affinity housing. For example, Florida State University's "summer bridge" program targets at-risk applicants, many of whom are members of ethnic and racial minorities. Here, these students "have the opportunity to meet the university president and senior faculty during a weeklong orientation, followed by six weeks where roughly 300 students live together in a residence hall staffed by hand-picked upperclassman counselors" (Carey 3). By living in a self-contained community where they can relate to and encourage each other, these students form close bonds. In six years, as Jay Mathews of the *Washington Post* points out, this program has "raised Florida State's six-year graduation rate for black students to 72 percent, higher than its white graduation rate." By raising minority students' comfort level and giving them a community in which to grow and learn together, this program (and many others like it) aids retention and student success among minorities. 4

Using a similar program that includes creating first-year "learning communities," the University of Alabama has raised its graduation rates 5 eleven percentage points. The school explains its commitment to these learning communities in this way:

> [F]reshmen at big universities can feel lost and anonymous as they struggle alone to contend with disconnected courses taught in depersonalized settings along with hundreds of their peers. Learning communities provide more connected individualized instruction, allowing students to form strong academic relationships with their fellow students, share knowledge, and work together to succeed in school. (Carey 7)

Research is beginning to show that fostering connections among minority students improves retention. As Clarence V. Reynolds explains, programs like the Student African-American Brotherhood, which has chapters on many college campuses, are helping "boost the number of African-American and Latino males who graduate from college by creating a positive peer community." Students in these programs support each other through "student-to-student, or peer-to-peer, mentoring," Reynolds reports. Minority dorms are in many ways comparable to these learning communities because they permit members of minority groups to form separate nurturing communities within their universities.

6   Opponents of minority dorms argue that because students need to learn to live together, racial and ethnic groups should not isolate themselves from the population at large. After all, college is a place for students to meet many different kinds of people—people whose traditions, values, politics, and cultures may be very different from their own. In fact, a *New York Times* opinion piece about housing at Cornell University, "Separate Is Never Equal," calls affinity housing "irrational" and uses the term "Balkanization"—the division of an area into small, hostile units—to describe the way various ethnic groups have chosen their own living spaces on campus (Clark and Meyers). This dramatic language makes the situation seem much more dire than it is. Unlike the warring Balkan states, minority students and white students do interact—in classes, in clubs, on sports teams, and in other public spaces. They do not have to live together for four years to get to know each other or to benefit from their campus's diversity.

> Refutation of opposing argument

7   The idea of allowing students to live in minority dorms is often seen as more controversial than other kinds of affinity housing, but it should not be.

As temporary "living and learning communities" on many campuses have recognized, first-year students are especially vulnerable to letting feelings of alienation drive them away from higher education. Among schools that are attempting to raise their minority graduation rates, there is a "broad movement to focus on the first year of college, when students are most likely to drop out" (Carey 8). It is crucial to offer these particularly vulnerable entering students the option of living in communities with people whom they consider their allies—those similarly situated students who understand the challenges of being outnumbered on campus. Building on the mutual support of their early years, they will learn to feel like insiders, they will stay enrolled—and they will graduate.

Concluding statement

Works Cited

Carey, Kevin. "Graduation Rate Watch: Making Minority Student Success a Priority." *Education Sector*. Education Sector, Apr. 2008. Web. 14 Sept. 2012.

Clark, Kenneth B., and Michael Meyers. "Separate Is Never Equal." *New York Times*. New York Times, 1 Apr. 1995. Web. 9 Sept. 2012.

Dervarics, Charles. "College Completion Gaps Widening, Data Show." *Diverse: Issues In Higher Education* 28.10 (2011): 6. *Academic Search Complete*. Web. 28 Apr. 2012.

Mathews, Jay. "Raising Minority Graduation Rates in College." *Washington Post*. Washington Post, 16 June 2008. Web. 14 Sept. 2012.

Reynolds, Clarence V. "No Man Left Behind." *Chronicle of Higher Education* (2012): 20–28. *Academic Search Complete*. Web. 29 Apr. 2012.

GRAMMAR IN CONTEXT

Using *Like* and *As*

When you write an argument by analogy, you may use *like* or *as* to express your comparison. When you do so, be sure to use these two words correctly.

- Use *like* only as a preposition.

  CORRECT Separate college dorms for members of minority groups are in many ways like separate dorms for women.

- Use *as* only to introduce a complete clause.

  INCORRECT Students must learn to live together in college like they do in the rest of their lives.

  CORRECT Students must learn to live together in college as they do in the rest of their lives.

⊙ EXERCISE 16.3

The following essay, "How to Take American Health Care from Worst to First" by Billy Beane, Newt Gingrich, and John Kerry, is an argument by analogy. Read the essay, and then answer the questions that follow it, consulting the outline on page 563 if necessary.

The *New York Times* published this opinion column on October 24, 2008.

HOW TO TAKE AMERICAN HEALTH CARE FROM WORST TO FIRST

BILLY BEANE, NEWT GINGRICH, AND JOHN KERRY

In the past decade, baseball has experienced a data-driven information revolution. Numbers-crunchers now routinely use statistics to put better teams on the field for less money. Our overpriced, underperforming health care system needs a similar revolution. 1

Data-driven baseball has produced surprising results. Michael Lewis writes in *Moneyball* that the Oakland A's have won games and division titles at one-sixth the cost of the most profligate teams. This season, the New York Yankees, Detroit Tigers, and New York Mets—the three teams with the highest payrolls, a combined $486 million—are watching the playoffs on television, while the Tampa Bay Rays, a franchise that uses a data-driven approach and has the second-lowest payroll in baseball at $44 million, are in the World Series (a sad reality for one of us). 2

Remarkably, a doctor today can get more data on the starting third baseman on his fantasy baseball team than on the effectiveness of life-and-death medical procedures. Studies 3

"Most health care is not based on clinical studies of what works best."

have shown that most health care is not based on clinical studies of what works best and what does not—be it a test, treatment, drug, or technology. Instead, most care is based on informed opinion, personal observation, or tradition.

It is no surprise then that the United States spends more than twice as 4 much per capita on health care compared to almost every other country in the world—and with worse health quality than most industrialized nations. Health premiums for a family of four have nearly doubled since 2001. Starbucks pays more for health care than it does for coffee. Nearly 100,000 Americans are killed every year by preventable medical errors. We can do better if doctors have better access to concise, evidence-based medical information.

Look at what's happened in baseball. For decades, executives, managers, 5 and scouts built their teams and managed games based on their personal experiences and a handful of dubious statistics. This romantic approach has been replaced with a statistics-based creed called *sabermetrics*.

These are not the stats we studied as children on the backs of baseball 6 cards. Sabermetrics relies on obscure statistics like WHIP (walks and hits per inning pitched), VORP (value over replacement player), or runs created—a number derived from the formula [(hits + walks) x total bases]/(at bats + walks). Franchises have used this data to answer some of the key questions in baseball: When is an attempted steal worth the risk? Whom should we draft, and in what order? Should we re-sign an aging star player and run the risk of paying for past performance rather than future results?

Similarly, a health care system that is driven by robust comparative clinical 7 evidence will save lives and money. One success story is Cochrane Collaboration, a nonprofit group that evaluates medical research. Cochrane performs systematic, evidence-based reviews of medical literature. In 1992, a Cochrane review found that many women at risk of premature delivery were not getting corticosteroids, which improve the lung function of premature babies.

Based on this evidence, the use of corticosteroids tripled. The result? A 8 nearly 10 percentage point drop in the deaths of low-birth-weight babies and millions of dollars in savings by avoiding the costs of treating complications.

Another example is Intermountain Healthcare, a nonprofit health care sys- 9 tem in Utah, where 80 percent of the care is based on evidence. Treatment data is collected by electronic medical records. The data is analyzed by researchers, and the best practices are then incorporated into the clinical process, resulting in far better quality care at a cost that is one-third less than the national average. (Disclosure: Intermountain Healthcare is a member of Mr. Gingrich's organization.)

Evidence-based health care would not strip doctors of their decision- 10 making authority nor replace their expertise. Instead, data and evidence should complement a lifetime of experience, so that doctors can deliver the best-quality care at the lowest possible cost.

Working closely with doctors, the federal government and the private sec- 11 tor should create a new institute for evidence-based medicine. This institute would conduct new studies and systematically review the existing medical literature to help inform our nation's over-stretched medical providers. The government should also increase Medicare reimbursements and some liability protections for doctors who follow the recommended clinical best practices.

America's health care system behaves like a hidebound, tradition-based ball   12
club that chases after aging sluggers and plays by the old rules: we pay too much and get too little in return. To deliver better health care, we should learn from the successful teams that have adopted baseball's new evidence-based methods. The best way to start improving quality and lowering costs is to study the stats.

Identifying the Elements of an Argument by Analogy

1. This opinion column develops an analogy between Major League Base-ball and the U.S. health-care system. In what respects is the health-care system comparable to baseball? In what respects are they different?

2. Given the obvious differences between health care and baseball, is the writers' central analogy still valid? Explain.

3. What is the "romantic approach" (para. 5) to sports management? What is "sabermetrics" (6)? What is the basic difference between these two approaches? How do they apply to health care?

4. In addition to their central analogy, what other analogies do the writ-ers make? How do these comparisons help you to understand their position?

5. The writers' central analogy is based on the assumption that most readers will know more about baseball than about health care. Do you think this is a reasonable assumption? Do you think the success of this analogy depends on readers' knowing a lot about baseball? Why or why not?

6. This column has three authors—the general manager of the Oakland Athletics, the former Republican Speaker of the U.S. House of Repre-sentatives, and a Democratic U.S. senator (now secretary of state). What does each author contribute to the argument's credibility?

7. Consider the column's title. Do you think the writers really believe that the American health-care system is the "worst"? What do they want the title to suggest to readers?

8. State this column's thesis in the form of a one-sentence argument by analogy, filling in the template below:

> Just as data-driven baseball management has improved teams'
>
> performance, _____
>
> _____.

Should College Athletes Be Paid?

Reread the At Issue box on page 559, which gives background on the question of whether college athletes should be paid. Then, read the sources on the following pages.

As you read these sources, you will be asked to respond to questions and to complete various activities. This work will help you to understand the content and structure of the material you read. When you are finished, you will be ready to write an **argument by analogy** on the topic, "Should College Athletes Be Paid?"

SOURCES

 David Brooks, "The Amateur Ideal," p. 571

 Los Angeles Times, "College Sports: Boola Boola vs. Moola Moola," p. 574

 Kristi Dosh, "The Problems with Paying College Athletes," p. 577

 Mark Cassell, "College Athletes Should Be Able to Negotiate Compensation," p. 580

 Allen Sack, "Should College Athletes Be Paid?, p. 583?

 For comprehension quizzes,
see **bedfordstmartins.com/practicalargument**.

This opinion column appeared in the *New York Times* on September 23, 2011.

THE AMATEUR IDEAL

DAVID BROOKS

The 1910s and 1920s were the golden age of the amateur ideal. On the golf courses, Bobby Jones, the greatest amateur golfer of all time, won a string of major championships.

He served as a moral exemplar as well. In the 1925 U.S. Open, he accidentally nudged his ball while setting up for a shot. He asked the marshals and members of the gallery if they had noticed. None had. Nevertheless, he assigned himself a two-stroke penalty, which cost him the tournament as he lost by one stroke. When complimented for his sense of fairness, Jones replied, "You may as well praise a man for not robbing a bank."

At Princeton, Hobey Baker was the glittering star of college sports, dominating in both football and hockey. He was also famous for his sportsmanship. He had only one penalty called on him his entire college hockey career. After each game, he went to the opposing locker room to thank his opponents for a good match. He was acutely modest when people spoke of his triumphs.

There were two sides to the amateur ideal. On the one hand, it was meant to serve as a restraint on some of the more brutal forces of the day. Social Darwinism was in full flower, with its emphasis on ruthless competition and survival of the fittest. Capitalism was rough and raw. The amateur ideal was a restraining code that emphasized fair play and honor. It held that those blessed with special gifts have a special responsibility to hew to a chivalric code. The idea was to make sport a part of the nation's moral education.

On the other hand, the amateur code was elitist. It was designed to separate the affluent sports from the working-class sports, to create a refined arena that only the well-bred and well-born could enter.

Today's left-leaning historians generally excoriate the amateur ideal for its snobbery and the hypocrisy it engendered. The movie *Chariots of Fire* popularized their critique. In the film, the upholders of the amateur ideal are snobbish, anti-Semitic reactionaries. The heroes are unabashedly commercial and practical. Modern and free-thinking, they pay people so they can win.

Thus did the left-wing critique welcome the corporate domination of sport.

Over the decades, the word *amateur* changed its meaning. It used to convey a moral sensibility, but now it conveys an economic one: not getting paid. As many universities have lost confidence in their ability to instill character, the moral mission of the university has withered.

> "The moral mission of the university has withered."

571

Commercialism and professionalism have filled the void. Taylor Branch's 9 superb cover article in the current issue of the *Atlantic*, "The Shame of College Sports," shows how financial concerns have come to dominate college athletics. Everybody makes money except the players. College football coaches at public universities make more than $2 million on average, according to the article, and even assistant coaches sometimes make nearly $1 million.

Quarterback Cam Newton was investigated for violating the amateur 10 rules. Meanwhile, there were at least 15 corporate logos on the uniform he wore every week. A. J. Green, a wide receiver, was punished for selling his jersey. While he was serving his suspension, the school continued selling replicas of his No. 8 jersey for $39.95 and up.

Branch shows the brutal ways the N.C.A.A. and its member schools protect 11 and advance their financial interests. For example, one of the reasons schools fight to keep the student-athlete tag on their players is to keep from having to pay workman's compensation if they get hurt. Kent Waldrep, a running back, was paralyzed while playing for Texas Christian. He sued to get some compensation for his sacrifice for the university. T.C.U. fought him in court and won.

Branch concludes that it is time to give up on the amateur code entirely. 12 Pay the players and get over it. At this late date, he may be right, but there are two concerns.

The first is practical. How exactly would you pay them? Would the stars get 13 millions while the rest get hardly nothing? Would you pay the wrestling team, or any of the female athletes? Only 7 percent of Division I athletic programs make money, according to the N.C.A.A.; where would the salary dollars come from?

The other is moral and cultural. A competitive society requires a set of social institutions that restrain naked self-interest and shortsighted greed. The amateur ideal, though faded and worn, still imposes some restraints. It forces athletes, seduced by Michael Jordan fantasies, to at least think of themselves partially as students. It forces coaches, an obsessively competitive group, to pay homage to academic pursuits. College basketball is more thrilling than pro basketball because the game is still animated by amateur passions, not coldly calculating professional interests.

The commercial spirit is strong these days. But people seem to do best when 15 they have to wrestle between commercial interests and value systems that counteract them. The lingering vestiges of the amateur ideal are worth preserving.

➲ AT ISSUE: SOURCES FOR DEVELOPING AN ARGUMENT BY ANALOGY

1. Why does Brooks begin his column with an overview of "the golden age of the amateur ideal" (para. 1)? Do you think he is romanticizing this "golden age"? Why or why not?

2. How, according to Brooks, have "left-leaning historians" (6) brought about the decline of the amateur ideal in sports? What does he claim

that these historians object to in the amateur ideal? Do you think he should have identified these historians? Do you think he needs to offer evidence to support his claim?

3. According to Brooks, how has the meaning of the word *amateur* changed over the years? Does he see this change in meaning as good or bad for college sports? Why?

4. In paragraph 9, Brooks begins a discussion of a long article in the *Atlantic* by Taylor Branch, which is also discussed by the editors of the *Los Angeles Times* (p. 574). How are Brooks's comments about the *Atlantic* article different from the discussion of this article in the *Los Angeles Times*?

5. In paragraphs 13 and 14, Brooks expresses his concerns about paying college athletes. The first concern is "practical"; the second is "moral and cultural." Which of these two kinds of concerns does Brooks think is more important? How can you tell? Which do you think is more important? Why?

The *Los Angeles Times* published this editorial on October 18, 2011.

COLLEGE SPORTS: BOOLA BOOLA VS. MOOLA MOOLA

LOS ANGELES TIMES

Thousands of college football fans had their pick of games Saturday—historic rivals Michigan and Michigan State and Oklahoma State and the University of Texas faced off in anticipated games, while top-ranked LSU took on the Tennessee Volunteers. On Sunday, the National Football League drew fans in similar legions, crowding stadiums in Detroit and Chicago, New England and Green Bay; millions more watched from couches across America. 1

Both days are sports extravaganzas, and lucrative ones. Millions are spent 2 on advertising during telecasts of the games; logos cover the stadiums and team uniforms. The coaches and staffs play to win, and those who do stand to make millions of dollars a year.

But the money flows unevenly. Sunday's games were played by millionaires— 3 a top NFL player can make more than $10 million a year. Saturday's were played by amateurs, whose efforts make their schools and sports leagues rich but who themselves are compensated only with scholarships.

That disparity has long been the subject of debate, and it has been re- 4 energized in recent weeks by Taylor Branch's powerful essay in this month's *Atlantic* magazine. Titled "The Shame of College Sports," it is a thorough indictment of the state of college athletics. Branch's conclusions are sobering. "I once . . . shuddered instinctively at the notion of paid college athletes," he acknowledges.

"But after an inquiry that took me into locker rooms and ivory towers 5 across the country, I have come to believe that sentiment blinds us to what's before our eyes. Big-time college sports are fully commercialized. Billions of dollars flow through them each year. The NCAA makes money, and enables universities and corporations to make money, from the unpaid labor of young athletes."

> "Big-time college sports are fully commercialized."

Branch's essay has stoked a long-running conversation about how best 6 to reconcile the competing impulses of college athletics. His descriptions of transparent injustices—athletes who lose their ability to play over trivial NCAA rules violations, the lack of insurance coverage for student athletes, scholarships voided for athletes who are hurt or lose their touch, legal waivers that allow the NCAA to control the likenesses of college stars long after they have graduated—have touched a nerve among educators and sports officials. And though opinion is sharply divided over Branch's proposed remedy—paying the athletes—many officials acknowledge that a wholesale review of the NCAA's rules is long overdue.

There are some basic reforms that would address problems discussed by 7 Branch and acknowledged by college athletic directors and administrators:

- It is unfair to bring poor students to campuses to play ball and to waive their tuition but then to expect them to survive without money. For Branch, the remedy is to professionalize college sports altogether by offering the players a salary. That's appealing, but it creates tensions of its own. Would football and basketball stars rake in millions while Olympic-caliber college athletes in water polo or track got nothing? Many coaches and athletic directors are advocating "cost of attendance" scholarships—stipends that would cover tuition, room and board, and some reasonable payment for incidentals such as books, travel, and spending money. Students who work in libraries or school newspapers as teaching assistants are allowed to earn modest sums of spending money. Why not athletes for their work? Cost-of-attendance scholarships would be a valuable innovation.

- Today's student athletes lack the most basic worker protections. If a student working in a library is injured by a book falling on her head, she is covered by workers' compensation or by college insurance. If a student is crippled on the playing field, she is not. The NCAA should extend insurance protection to athletes, treating sports as more akin to work-study and offering death benefits to the families of those who perish in practice or during games. In addition to offering basic security for players, requiring the NCAA to insure them might also encourage development of safety measures.

- Scholarships should not be revocable. For too many students, education comes to an end when their eligibility expires or they are injured or cut from a team. Schools that lure athletes to their campuses with the promise of free education should be good to their word. Once accepted, a scholarship must be binding, whether the athlete completes that degree in four years or comes back to finish his education at some later point.

- The NCAA's rights to an athlete's likeness should end at graduation. Hard as it is to believe, college athletes today are required to permanently waive their rights to their own images as players as a condition of participating in college sports. That means that the NCAA continues to profit from images of Michael Jordan playing for the University of North Carolina or Jackie Robinson at UCLA. Athletes make their own careers; the NCAA should not be allowed to profit from those achievements forever.

Even if adopted in their entirety, these proposals would not cleanse college 8 sports of their commercialism. At major campuses, sports are and would remain multimillion-dollar-a-year businesses, fervidly backed by alumni and awash in revenue from sponsorships and television contracts, as well as ticket sales and souvenirs. For some, the disparity between the wealth of those programs and the unpaid labor of their stars will remain intolerable and continue to fuel calls for paying athletes outright.

Lawsuits challenging aspects of that disparity already threaten to upend 9 the NCAA's current system—one is challenging the requirement that athletes give up the rights to their images, for instance, and another is taking on the notion that scholarships can be revoked if a player is injured or cut from a team.

Recognizing that, the NCAA's governing board would be wise to tackle 10 reform before others take the matter into their own hands. These reforms offer an opportunity to eliminate some of the system's more egregious inequities while preserving its essence as an amateur endeavor.

❯AT ISSUE: SOURCES FOR DEVELOPING AN ARGUMENT BY ANALOGY

1. This editorial opens with descriptions of two different days of football games. How does the comparison developed here support the editorial's purpose?

2. Does this editorial state a position on the issue of whether college athletes should be paid? If so, what is it? If not, what position do you think the writers have? Express this position in the form of a thesis statement by filling in the template below.

   Because _____

   _____,

   college athletes (should/should not) be paid.

3. What specific reforms does this editorial propose? What other reforms can you suggest?

4. The first two reforms listed in paragraph 7 develop an argument by analogy. What is the analogy? How convincing is it?

5. Like David Brooks (p. 571), the writers of this editorial favor preserving the amateur status of college athletes. Are their reasons for taking this position similar to Brooks's reasons? Explain.

6. In paragraph 8, the editorial concedes that problems would remain even after the proposed reforms were instituted. Does this admission weaken the editorial's argument (suggesting, for example, that it does not go far enough), or does it add a sense of urgency to its recommendations? Explain.

This essay was published in *Forbes* on June 9, 2011.

THE PROBLEMS WITH PAYING COLLEGE ATHLETES

KRISTI DOSH

I recently attended a conference where I heard a very intelligent attorney contradict himself over the course of an afternoon. His diametrically opposed opinions are ones I think are not uncommon amongst college football fans. Early on in the day, he admonished college athletic departments for relying on direct institutional support and state government subsidies in order to operate in the black. Later that afternoon, he made the case for why college athletes should be paid.   1

I'm not sure you can have it both ways.   2

The first question I ask people when they say college athletes should be paid is: where is the money going to come from? If you're unaware, the NCAA released data showing that only 14 programs are turning a profit without having to rely on institutional support (like student fees or a check cut directly from the university coffers).   3

> "Where is the money going to come from?"

Although the NCAA did not list the 14 schools turning a net profit, Notre Dame is one of them. Athletic Director Jack Swarbrick has revealed that Notre Dame actually pours money back *into* the college's coffers, to the tune of about $10 million in 2009. LSU tells me they are also one of the 14, having sent about $8 million back to the university last year.   4

Other schools that have been confirmed to be among the 14: Alabama, University of Missouri, University of Texas, University of Florida, University of Tennessee, Ohio State University, and Nebraska. BYU's athletic director also recently confirmed that BYU has operated in the black for the past three years.   5

I recently revealed Ohio State's line item budget. It showed that OSU needs over $22 million from the booster club, interest off their endowment, and royalty fees in order to balance the budget. Could they get more from these sources of income and find the money to pay players? Of course.   6

But what about a school like Western Kentucky? They already spend $5.6 million on grants-in-aid, and it takes $8.2 million from the university to balance their budget. How do they afford to pay players?   7

I use Western Kentucky as an example because I have their budget in front of me, but there are plenty of programs in AQ conferences who rely on assistance. Virginia, for example, relies on over $12 million in student fees to balance their budget. Florida State? $6.9 million. How do those programs afford to pay players? And if they can't find a way to afford it, how do they recruit against the programs who can?   8

So, where is the money supposed to come from to pay these athletes?   9

Even if we could get past this issue, I see a number of other problems. 10
Here are some of my questions:

How do you decide which athletes are paid? Is it just in revenue-producing 11
sports? Is it every athlete playing in those sports or just the elite?

Here is the second big problem. Actually, it's probably the first, but I chose 12
to focus on the issue of finances first. You cannot pay players without invoking
Title IX. Safely assuming that any pay-for-play plan would include paying male
football and basketball players, you run into huge issues with federal law.

The bottom line is that more money will have to be devoted to women's 13
sports, and it's highly likely it's men's sports outside of football and basketball
that will suffer. And, again, where is all this money going to come from?

Even if Title IX weren't an issue (and let me just say, without revision to 14
these federal laws, college athletes will never be paid), there are plenty of other
problems standing between college athletes and their big pay day:

How much do you pay players? Is it one set amount for every athlete no 15
matter the sport or the school in order to keep things fair? At least within a
sport I think it has to be the same, otherwise schools with more money will
have the advantage.

If you let athletes get paid for endorsements (which could avoid the first 16
problem I outlined above), will it give some programs an unfair advantage?
Playing for Alabama or Ohio State is bound to give you more endorsement
opportunities (and more lucrative ones) than playing for Tulsa.

I see the same problem with allowing athletes to profit off merchandise 17
sold with their name or number, like jerseys. Playing for Florida is going to
give you greater opportunity to make money off merchandise than playing for
Western Michigan.

Another way to pay players and avoid the first problem I outlined is to 18
allow agents to pay players. Darren Heitner over at the Sports Agent Blog
recently wrote a post advocating the lifting of all regulations against agents paying players. Heitner believes there would be no harm to the athletes from this
situation and that it would allow the market to dictate what a player is worth.

Aside from the initial concerns I have regarding the influence these agents 19
would have and the types of promises they could elicit from players about
being paid back in the future, I have another, bigger concern. Could these
agents pay a player to choose a specific school? And what's to stop a big car
dealership run by an alumnus in Athens from slipping money to an agent so he
can encourage a player to attend the University of Georgia?

Will sports that pay athletes have to break from the NCAA? I think so. 20
Tack on new administrative costs as those sports are forced to form new
leagues to manage their sport.

There are far too many serious questions to answer for me to jump on the 21
pay-college-athletes bandwagon. Without even getting into whether college
athletes *should* be paid, I just don't see a scenario where college athletes can be
paid without allowing the gap to grow between the haves and have-nots.

578

AT ISSUE: SOURCES FOR DEVELOPING AN ARGUMENT BY ANALOGY

1. What reservations does Dosh have about paying college athletes? Are these reservations largely practical, or are they primarily moral or ethical? How do her reservations compare with the concerns expressed by David Brooks in paragraphs 13–14 of "The Amateur Ideal" (p. 571)?

2. In paragraph 18, Dosh discusses a plan to permit agents to pay players. What concerns does she have about this plan?

3. Dosh assumes that schools that compensate student athletes will have to "break from the NCAA" (20). How would the writers of the *Los Angeles Times* editorial (p. 574) respond to this assumption?

4. In her conclusion, Dosh states that paying college athletes would widen the gap between "the haves and have-nots." What does she mean? Does her essay explain this consequence? Should it?

5. Dosh's essay was published in *Forbes*, a business magazine. Still, she writes in a generally informal style, using the pronoun *I* and contractions. Why do you think she uses this informal style?

This editorial is from the *Columbus Dispatch*, where it was published on November 16, 2011.

COLLEGE ATHLETES SHOULD BE ABLE TO NEGOTIATE COMPENSATION

MARK CASSELL

Last year, the National Collegiate Athletic Association imposed a five-game 1 suspension on Terrelle Pryor, Ohio State's star quarterback, for getting tattoos in exchange for autographs and memorabilia. Pryor earned millions of dollars for the university, the NCAA, the many corporations that tattooed his body with their logos during each game. Not only was Pryor prohibited from receiving a penny of the revenues he generated; he could not even get a break on a tattoo.

Welcome to the NCAA, an all-powerful, unaccountable cartel that over- 2 sees a multibillion-dollar industry. In true paternalistic fashion, the NCAA claims singular authority to know what is best for athletes, schools, and college sports. What is best includes limiting compensation to the athletic workers on the field (or on the court) to no more than a scholarship. Coaches, athletic directors, university presidents, and every other actor involved in college sports, on the other hand, are free to negotiate any compensation the market will bear. And, it turns out, the market bears a lot.

> "The NCAA claims singular authority to know what is best."

Average compensation for head football coaches at public universities is 3 more than $2 million. Top college basketball coaches pull in more than $4 million. Even assistant coaches earn sizeable salaries: 26 assistant football coaches earned over $400,000 in 2010. Why the generous packages? Because these workers are free to negotiate their compensation and because college sports is big business. CBS Sports recently paid the NCAA $771 million to air March Madness. The Big Ten and SEC are expected to receive a billion dollars in revenues each next year. Given the size of the market, why shouldn't coaches and athletic directors earn the big bucks?

Can you imagine the state legislature capping coaches' salaries at 4 $100,000 for the good of the game? Or capping university presidents' salaries at $100,000 for the good of the university? Yet, when even more Draconian rules are applied to the very workers who create the value for college sports, there is no outcry. On the contrary, athletic workers like Pryor are condemned for seeking even a token compensation for their efforts on the field. The recent NCAA proposal to give schools the ability to offer athletic workers a $2,000 grant is an insult akin to a monarch throwing peasants some crumbs to keep them happy.

So why, in the most market-oriented society in the world, does such a relic   5
continue? Three reasons:

- Race. Ninety percent of the revenue of NCAA sports is produced by 1 percent
  of the athletes. And of the 1 percent, nearly all the star players are African-
  American.

- Collective-action problems. Without a union or an organization to represent their interests, athletic workers have little chance to fight against the
  NCAA, which holds all the cards. Although, imagine if before the final
  game of the NCAA basketball tournament, the 10 starting players decided
  at the last minute to hold a work stoppage.

- Everyone else benefits, so why rock the system? Coaches and the other
  sports administrators profit from the system, but so do the 99 percent of
  other NCAA athletes whose activities are subsidized by the revenues of
  the 1 percent. And let's not forget professional leagues, such as the National
  Football League, that benefit from a crop of newly trained recruits every
  year.

So what would happen if athletic workers could negotiate their compen-   6
sation freely like everyone else in the college sports industry? Since most
NCAA athletes are not on scholarship, the majority of players would see little
change. A small percentage of athletes—the star players—likely would see their
compensation grow in much the same way Olympic athletes saw their incomes
rise after the International Olympic Committee eliminated its amateur rule.

But the most important change that would come from allowing athletes to   7
negotiate compensation is that universities would be forced to re-evaluate
whether multimillion-dollar athletic programs that no longer can rely on the
free labor of the athletic workers are consistent with the core academic mission
of institutions of higher learning.

⊙ AT ISSUE: SOURCES FOR DEVELOPING
AN ARGUMENT BY ANALOGY

1. This editorial takes a strong position in favor of paying college athletes. According to Cassell, why should college athletes "be able to
   negotiate compensation"?

2. In paragraph 2, Cassell refers to the NCAA as "an all-powerful, unaccountable cartel that oversees a multibillion-dollar industry." Why
   is it essential that he establish that the NCAA is a business?

3. Central to Cassell's argument is the idea that college athletes are
   "athletic workers" (para. 4). For example, in paragraphs 2–4, he discusses the generous compensation packages of others involved in
   college sports, explaining that "these workers [unlike college athletes]

are free to negotiate their compensation" (3). Which of the other writers in this At Issue section do you think would consider college athletes to be workers? Which would not?

4. What factors does Cassell believe are to blame for the current state of affairs in college sports? Which of the factors he lists do you think are most important? Why?

5. According to Cassell, how does race explain why college athletes are not paid? What is he implying but not saying?

6. Why doesn't Cassell address opposing arguments in this editorial? Should he have done so?

7. Cassell's concluding paragraph describes the result that he believes his proposals would achieve. What kind of appeal does this paragraph make?

This article appeared in the *Christian Science Monitor* on March 7, 2008.

SHOULD COLLEGE ATHLETES BE PAID?

ALLEN SACK

As the NCAA's season-ending basketball tournament approaches, talk of the future of college sports is hot. One of the most controversial questions: Should the college athletes who are the main attraction at this multibillion-dollar March Madness tournament be paid? As a longtime supporter of amateur sport, my answer is no. The amateur model embraced by the founding fathers of the National Collegiate Athletic Association (NCAA) in 1905 remains the best fit for the academic mission of higher education.

However, if the NCAA doesn't change the status quo—which is on a fast course toward building a sports entertainment empire—how could they *not* pay athletes or at least extend workers' rights?

There would be good reasons for supporting the prohibition against paying college athletes *if* the NCAA's claim were true that big-time college athletes—like those who will electrify the crowds at this year's Final Four—are merely "amateurs" engaged in sport during their free time. That claim, though, has absolutely no support in recent history, aside from some Division III exceptions.

When I played football for Notre Dame in the 1960s, the NCAA had already compromised its half-century commitment to amateur principles. In 1957, after years of intense internal debate, the NCAA caved under pressure to subsidize athletes and voted to allow athletic scholarships. It was at this point that commercialized college sports started down the slippery slope toward open professionalism.

At first, NCAA rules allowed these scholarships to be awarded for four years, as I was assured mine would be when I was recruited in the 1960s—regardless of my performance on the athletic field. Unfortunately, since I graduated, scholarships have taken on the trappings of an employment contract.

At the height of student revolts on college campuses in 1967, the association adopted rules that allowed the immediate termination of scholarship aid to athletes who challenge the authority of a coach or withdraw from sports voluntarily. In 1973, four-year scholarships were relegated to the scrap heap. Today, scholarships are awarded on a year-to-year basis. Athletes who have been injured or who turn out to be recruiting mistakes can be fired.

During the past four decades, the NCAA has crafted a payment system that provides a relatively cheap and steady supply of blue-chip athletes for the burgeoning business of collegiate sports and gives coaches the kind of control over them that employers have over employees. It is little wonder that a recent survey of college athletes by the NCAA found that the majority of those polled identify themselves more as athletes than as students.

> "The majority of those polled identify themselves more as athletes than as students."

8

At schools that award no athletic scholarships, such as those in the Ivy League or the NCAA's Division III, athletes are students first, and even though athletes get a break in admissions, scandals like those that plague big-time college sports are rare.

However, athletes who are recruited and subsidized to provide commercial entertainment for millions of Americans are a very different matter. Because they are already essentially paid to play, they deserve the same rights and benefits as other employees, including medical benefits, workers' compensation when injured, and the right to use their God-given talents to build some financial security for their families while still in college. The denial of these rights is morally unconscionable.

9

At present, a fairly small number of athletes, many of them African-American football and basketball players, produce much of the revenue that keeps entire athletic programs afloat. Because most athletic programs run deficits, paying these athletes a salary of some kind would be a stretch. At the very least, however, the athletes who put fans in the seats and in front of TV sets deserve a genuine opportunity to receive the education they were promised and a stipend to cover the full cost of their education.

10

These athletes also need players' associations to bargain for better medical benefits and the right to engage in the same kinds of entrepreneurial ventures that are the stock and trade of celebrity coaches. Scholarship athletes should be able to endorse products, accept pay for speaking engagements, and get a cut of the profits universities make by marketing their images. They should also be allowed to have agents to help them plan their financial futures.

11

In past decades, the NCAA substituted a counterfeit version of amateurism for the real thing. It happened so slowly that most people did not notice. As college sports moves into the second decade of the new millennium, athletes will undoubtedly organize to demand a bigger share of the money. When this occurs, one can only hope that the NCAA will abandon its present course toward building a sports entertainment empire and consider a return to bona-fide amateurism.

12

➲ AT ISSUE: SOURCES FOR DEVELOPING AN ARGUMENT BY ANALOGY

1. In paragraph 2, Sack asks, "if the NCAA doesn't change the status quo . . . how could they *not* pay athletes or at least extend workers' rights?" Does he think college athletes should be paid?

2. In paragraph 1, Sack characterizes himself as "a longtime supporter of amateur sport"; in paragraph 4, he mentions that he once played college football. Why does he include these two details?

3. What is the significance of each of the following pieces of information:

   ▪ Athletes no longer get four-year scholarships; they can be "fired."

   ▪ Most college athletes see themselves more as athletes than as students.

   ▪ Ivy League schools do not give athletic scholarships.

   How does each of the above statements support Sack's argument?

4. In paragraph 10, Sack mentions that many of the football and basketball players who generate large amounts of revenue for their schools are African American. Why does he mention this fact? Should he have discussed this point further? Why or why not?

5. What specific proposals does Sack make for improving the way college athletes are treated? Do these suggestions seem feasible? Do you have other suggestions?

6. How is the "bona-fide amateurism" that Sack mentions in his conclusion like (and unlike) the "amateur ideal" discussed by David Brooks (p. 571)?

⊘ **EXERCISE 16.4**

Write a one-paragraph argument by analogy that takes a position on the issue of whether college athletes should be paid. Follow the template below, filling in the blanks to create your argument.

TEMPLATE FOR WRITING AN ARGUMENT BY ANALOGY

Being a student athlete is like being a _____

_____. Both student athletes and _____ are _____

_____.

In addition, both student athletes and _____ are

_____

_____. Finally, both student athletes and _____ are

_____

_____. Of course, there are some differences. For one thing,

_____.

Also, _____. Even so,

like _____, student athletes are _____

_____. For

this reason, they (should/should not) be paid.

⊘ **EXERCISE 16.5**

In a group of four students, discuss the advantages and disadvantages of paying college athletes. What problems might this create? For example, how would it change the way student athletes are viewed by their peers? By their professors? Which athletes should be paid, and which should not be? Why? Write a paragraph that expresses your group's opinions.

⊘ **EXERCISE 16.6**

Write an argument by analogy on the topic, "Should College Athletes Be Paid?" Begin by establishing an analogy between college athletes and other students or between college athletes and professional athletes. Then, use this analogy to help you support your thesis. (If you like, you may include material from the paragraphs you wrote for Exercises 16.4 and 16.5.) Cite the sources on pages 570–585, and be sure to document the sources you use and to include a works-cited page. (See Chapter 10 for information on documenting sources.)

EXERCISE 16.7

Review the four pillars of argument discussed in Chapter 1. Does your essay include all four elements of an effective argument? Add anything that is missing. Then, label the key elements of your essay.

● WRITING ASSIGNMENTS: ARGUMENT BY ANALOGY

1. Many college campuses are now smoke-free, but some people argue that the laws banning smoking on campus are too strict. Write an argument by analogy in which you take a position on the issue of whether smoking should be permitted on college campuses.

2. Do you believe that college administrators should be able to censor your school's student newspaper? If so, under what circumstances? If not, why not? Establish an analogy between the school newspaper and another campus service (or another kind of media outlet), and use this analogy to help you develop your argument.

3. Should your school mandate community service as a requirement for graduation? Write an argument by analogy in which you take a position on this issue.

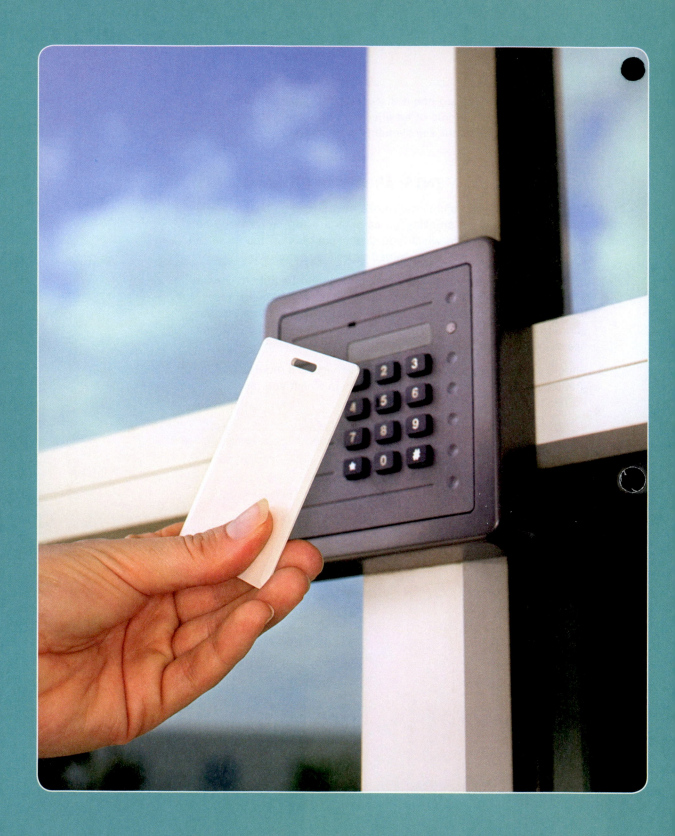

CHAPTER 17

17

Ethical Arguments

AT ISSUE

How Far Should Colleges Go to Keep Campuses Safe?

As the 2007 Virginia Tech massacre tragically illustrated, college campuses are no longer the safe, open environments they once were. In fact, some campuses have become downright dangerous. It is no longer unusual to read reports of shootings, robberies, and muggings (and even murders) on campuses—both urban and rural. As a result, students, parents, and educators have called for more security. In response, colleges have increased the number of blue-light phones and campus guards, installed card-access systems in dorms and labs, and placed surveillance cameras in parking garages and public areas. Many colleges also use text messages, automated phone calls, and emails to alert students and faculty to emergency situations.

Not everyone is happy about this emphasis on security, however. Some faculty members point out that colleges are supposed to be places of free thought and that a high level of security undercuts this freedom by limiting access to campus and sanitizing the college experience. Students complain about having to wait in long lines to get into campus buildings as security guards examine and scan IDs. They also complain about having to register guests in advance and having to accompany them to dorm rooms. They point out that colleges tell them they are adults but treat them like children.

Later in this chapter, you will be asked to think more about this issue. You will be given several research sources to consider and asked to write an **ethical argument** discussing how far colleges should go to keep students safe.

For comprehension quizzes,
see bedfordstmartins.com/practicalargument.

589

What Is an Ethical Argument?

Ethics is the field of philosophy that studies the standards by which actions can be judged as right or wrong or good or bad. To make such judgments, we either measure actions against some standard (such as a moral rule like "Thou shall not kill") or consider them in terms of their consequences. Usually, making ethical judgments means examining abstract concepts such as *good*, *right*, *duty*, *obligation*, *virtue*, *honor*, and *choice*. **Applied ethics** is the field of philosophy that applies ethics to real-life issues, such as abortion, the death penalty, animal rights, and doctor-assisted suicide.

An **ethical argument** focuses on whether something should be done because it is good or right (or not done because it is bad or wrong). For example, consider the following questions:

- Should teenagers ever be tried as adults?

- Is torture ever justified?

- Should terrorists be tried in civilian courts?

- Should gay and lesbian couples be allowed to marry?

- Is the death penalty ever justified?

- Do animals have rights?

Ethical arguments that try to answer questions like these usually begin with a clear statement that something is right or wrong and then go on to show how a religious, philosophical, or ethical principle supports this position. Consider how the last three questions on the list above can be examined in ethical arguments:

- **Should gay and lesbian couples be allowed to marry?** You could begin your ethical argument by pointing out that marriage stabilizes society and is therefore good. You could go on to demonstrate how both individuals and society as a whole would be better off if gay and lesbian couples were permitted to marry.

- **Is the death penalty ever justified?** You could begin your ethical argument by pointing out that because killing in any form is immoral, the death penalty is morally wrong. You could go on to demonstrate that despite its usefulness—it rids society of dangerous criminals—the death penalty hurts all of us. You could conclude by saying that because the death penalty is so immoral, it has no place in a civilized society.

- **Do animals have rights?** You could begin your ethical argument by pointing out that like all thinking beings, animals have certain basic rights. You could go on to discuss the basic rights that all thinking beings have—for example, the right to respect, a safe environment, and a dignified death. You could conclude by saying that the inhumane

One could make an ethical argument in favor of gay marriage.

treatment of animals should not be tolerated, whether those animals are pets, live in the wild, or are raised for food.

Stating an Ethical Principle

The most important part of an ethical argument is the **ethical principle**— a general statement about what is good or bad, right or wrong. It is the set of values that guide you to an ethically correct conclusion.

- **You can show that something is good or right** by establishing that it conforms to a particular moral law or will result in something good for society. For example, you could argue for a policy restricting access to campus by saying that such a policy will reduce crime on campus or will result in a better educational experience for students.

- **You can show that something is bad or wrong** by demonstrating that it violates a moral law or will result in something bad for society. For example, you could argue against the use of torture by saying that respect for individual rights is one of the basic principles of American society and that by ignoring this principle we undermine our Constitution and our way of life.

Whenever possible, you should base your ethical argument on an ethical principle that is **self-evident**—one that needs no proof or explanation. (By doing so, you avoid having to establish the principle that is the basis for your essay.) Thomas Jefferson uses this strategy in the Declaration of Independence (p. 770). When he says, "We hold these truths to be self-evident," he is saying that the ethical principle that supports the rest of his argument is so basic (and so widely accepted) that it requires no proof—in other words, that it is self-evident. If readers accept Jefferson's assertion, then the rest of his argument—that the thirteen original colonies owe no allegiance to England—will be much more convincing. (Remember, however, that the king of England, George III, would not have accepted Jefferson's assertion. For him, the ethical argument made in the Declaration of Independence was not at all self-evident.)

Keep in mind that an ethical principle has to be self-evident to most of your readers—not just to those who agree with you or hold a particular set of religious or cultural beliefs. Using a religious doctrine as an ethical principle has its limitations, and doctrines that cut across religions and cultures are more suitable than those that do not. For example, every culture prohibits murder and theft. But some other doctrines—such as the Jehovah's Witness prohibition against blood transfusion or the Muslim dietary restrictions—are not universally accepted. In addition, an ethical principle must be stated so that it applies universally. For example, not all readers will find the statement, "As a Christian, I am against killing and therefore against the death penalty" convincing. A more effective statement would be, "Because it is morally wrong, the death penalty should be abolished" or "With few exceptions, taking the life of another person is never justified, and there should be no exception for the government."

Ethics versus Law

Generally speaking, an ethical argument deals with what is right and wrong, not necessarily with what is legal or illegal. In fact, there is a big difference between law and ethics. **Laws** are rules that govern a society and are enforced by its political and legal systems. **Ethics** are standards that determine how human conduct is judged.

Keep in mind that something that is legal is not necessarily ethical. As Socrates, St. Augustine, Henry David Thoreau, and Martin Luther King Jr. have all pointed out, there are just laws, and there are unjust laws. For example, when King wrote his famous "Letter from Birmingham Jail" (p. 799), segregation was legal in many Southern states. According to King, unjust laws—such as those that institutionalized segregation—are out of harmony with both moral law and natural law. As King wrote, "We should never forget that everything Adolf Hitler did in Germany was 'legal.'" For King, the ultimate standard for deciding what is just or unjust is morality, not legality.

Women march for the right to vote, New York, 1913,

There are many historical examples of laws that most people would now consider unjust:

- **Laws against woman suffrage:** In the late eighteenth century, various states passed laws prohibiting women from voting.

- **Jim Crow laws:** In the mid-nineteenth century, laws were passed in the American South that restricted the rights of African Americans.

For decades in America, African Americans were treated unfairly due to unjust laws.

German Jews being sent to concentration camps

- **Nuremberg laws:** In the 1930s, Nazi Germany passed a series of laws that took away the rights of Jews living in Germany.

- **Apartheid laws:** Beginning in 1948, South Africa enacted laws that defined and enforced racial segregation. These laws stayed in effect until 1994, when Nelson Mandela was elected South Africa's first black president.

Today, virtually everyone would agree that these laws were wrong and should never have been enacted. Still, many people obeyed these laws, with disastrous consequences. These consequences illustrate the importance of doing what is ethically right, not just what is legally right.

The difference between ethics and law can be seen in many everyday situations. Although we have no legal obligation to stop a drunk friend from driving, most people would agree that we should. In addition, although motorists (or even doctors) have no legal obligation to help at the scene of an accident, many people would say that it is the right thing to do.

An example of a person going beyond what is legally required occurred in Lawrence, Massachusetts, in 1995, when fire destroyed Malden Mills, the largest employer in town. Citing his religious principles, Aaron Feuerstein, the owner of the mill and inventor of Polartec fleece, decided to rebuild in Lawrence rather than move his business overseas as many of his competitors had done. In addition, he decided that for sixty days, all employees would receive their full salaries—even though the mill was closed. Feuerstein was not required by law to do what he did, but he decided to do what he believed was both ethical and responsible.

Understanding Ethical Dilemmas

Life decisions tend to be somewhat messy, and it is often not easy to decide what is right or wrong or what is good or bad. In many real-life situations, people are faced with **dilemmas**—choices between alternatives that seem equally unfavorable. An **ethical dilemma** occurs when there is a conflict between two or more possible actions—each of which will have a similar consequence or outcome.

The classic ethical dilemma is the so-called lifeboat dilemma. In this hypothetical situation, a ship hits an iceberg, and survivors are crowded into a lifeboat. As a storm approaches, the captain realizes that he is faced with an ethical dilemma. If he does nothing, the overloaded boat will capsize, and all the people will drown. If he throws some of the passengers overboard, he will save those in the boat, but those he throws overboard will drown.

Another ethical dilemma occurs in William Styron's 1979 novel *Sophie's Choice.* The novel's narrator is fascinated by the story of Sophie,

Aaron Feuerstein at Malden Mills

A scene from Alfred Hitchcock's *Lifeboat* (1944)

In the 1982 film *Sophie's Choice,* a mother (played by Meryl Streep) is forced to make a terrible decision.

a woman who was arrested by the Nazis and sent along with her two children to the Auschwitz concentration camp. When she arrived, she was given a choice by a sadistic guard: one of her children would go to the gas chamber and one would be spared, but she had to choose which one. If she did not choose, both children would be murdered.

Ethical dilemmas are not just the stuff of fiction; people confront them every day. For example, an owner of a business who realizes that costs must be cut faces an ethical dilemma. If the owner takes no action, the business will fail, and all the employees will lose their jobs. If the owner lays off some employees, they will be hurt, but the business might be saved and so might the jobs of the remaining workers. A surgeon who has to separate conjoined twins who share a heart also faces an ethical dilemma. If the surgeon does nothing, both twins will die, but if the surgeon operates, one of the twins might live although the other will be sacrificed.

Often, the only way to resolve an ethical dilemma is to choose the lesser of two evils. Simple "right or wrong" or "good versus bad" prescriptions will not work in such cases. For example, killing may be morally, legally, and ethically wrong, but what if it is done in self-defense? Stealing is also wrong, but what if a person steals food to feed a hungry child? Although it may be tempting to apply clear ethical principles, you should be careful not to oversimplify the situations you are writing about.

⊙ EXERCISE 17.1

Consider the following topics for ethical arguments. Then, decide what ethical principle you could use for each argument. For example, if you were going to argue that doctors should not participate in doctor-assisted suicide, you could use the principles mentioned in the Hippocratic Oath as the basis for your argument.

- The United States should (or should not) prohibit the use of animals in scientific experiments.

- Students with special needs should (or should not) get preference in college admissions.

- Homeless people should (or should not) be forcibly removed from city streets.

- Everyone should (or should not) be required to sign an organ-donor card.

- A witness to academic cheating should (or should not) report the cheater.

⊛ EXERCISE 17.2

Make a list of some rules or laws that you think are unjust. Then, next to each item on your list, write down the ethical principle on which you based your conclusion.

⊛ EXERCISE 17.3

Look at the following two images. In what sense do they make ethical arguments? What ethical principle underlies each image?

⊙ EXERCISE 17.4

Read the following poem. What ethical dilemma does the poem present?
Does the poem resolve this dilemma?

ETHICS

LINDA PASTAN

In ethics class so many years ago   1
our teacher asked this question every fall:
If there were a fire in a museum
which would you save, a Rembrandt painting
or an old woman who hadn't many   5
years left anyhow? Restless on hard chairs
caring little for pictures or old age
we'd opt one year for life, the next for art
and always half-heartedly. Sometimes
the woman borrowed my grandmother's face
leaving her usual kitchen to wander
some drafty, half imagined museum.
One year, feeling clever, I replied
why not let the woman decide herself?
Linda, the teacher would report, eschews   15
the burdens of responsibility.
This fall in a real museum I stand
before a real Rembrandt, old woman,
or nearly so, myself. The colors
within this frame are darker than autumn,   20
darker even than winter—the browns of earth,
though earth's most radiant elements burn
through the canvas. I know now that woman
and painting and season are almost one
and all beyond saving by children.   25

How would you resolve the ethical dilemma that Pastan presents in her poem? Write a paragraph or two in which you discuss the dilemma as well as the ethical principle on which you based your conclusion.

Structuring an Ethical Argument

In general, an ethical argument can be structured in the following way.

- **Introduction:** Establishes the ethical principle and states the essay's thesis

- **Background:** Gives an overview of the situation

- **Ethical analysis:** Explains the ethical principle and analyzes the particular situation on the basis of this principle

- **Evidence:** Presents points that support the thesis

- **Refutation of opposing arguments:** Addresses arguments against the thesis

- **Conclusion:** Restates the ethical principle as well as the thesis; includes a strong concluding statement

The following student essay contains all the elements of an ethical argument. The student takes the position that colleges should do more to help nontraditional students succeed.

ARE COLLEGES DOING ENOUGH FOR NONTRADITIONAL STUDENTS?

CHRIS MUÑOZ

Colleges and universities are experiencing an increase in the   1
number of nontraditional students, and this number is projected to rise. Although these students enrich campus communities and provide new opportunities for learning, they also present challenges. Generally, nontraditional students are older, attend school part-time, and are

Ethical principle
established

Thesis statement

Background: Gives an
overview of the situation

Ethical analysis: Presents
the ethical principle and
analyzes the situation on
the basis of this principle

self-supporting. With their years of life experience, they tend to have different educational goals from other students. While many schools recognize that nontraditional students have unique needs, most schools ignore these needs and unfairly continue to focus on the "typical" student. As a result, nontraditional students frequently do not have the same access to educational opportunities as their younger counterparts. To solve this problem, universities need to do more to ensure equitable treatment of nontraditional students.

Most people's assumptions about who is enrolled in college are out of date. According to the educational policy scholar Frederick Hess, only 15% of all undergraduates attend a four-year college and live on campus. In other words, so-called typical college students are in the minority. In fact, 38% of today's undergraduates are over age twenty-five, 37% attend part-time, 32% work full-time, and many are responsible for dependents. In addition, real-world responsibilities cause many nontraditional students to delay starting school, to take a break in the middle, or to drop out entirely. According to Alan Tripp, nearly two thirds of all nontraditional students drop out of college. Although some argue that schools already provide extra help, such as advising and tutoring, others point out that asking nontraditional students to adapt to an educational model that focuses on the traditional student is a form of discrimination against them. These people recommend that schools institute policies that reflect the growing number of nontraditional students on campus and address the challenges that these students face every day.

Most people would agree that diversity is highly valued on college campuses. In fact, most universities go to great lengths to admit a diverse group of students—including nontraditional students. However, as Jacqueline Muhammad points out, universities do not serve these students well after they are enrolled. By asking nontraditional students to assimilate into the traditional university environment, colleges marginalize them, and this is not ethical. Evidence of this marginalization is not difficult to find. As one college student acknowledges, "These students have a lot to offer, but often they don't feel included" (qtd. in Muhammad). This lack of inclusion is seen in many areas of campus life, including access to classes and services, availability of relevant programs and courses, and use of fair and appropriate classroom practices. To be fair, a university should ensure that all of its students have equal access to a meaningful and fulfilling education. By maintaining policies and approaches that are not inclusive, colleges marginalize nontraditional students.

4   To ensure the fair treatment of nontraditional students, colleges need to remove the barriers those students face. One of the first barriers that nontraditional students face is difficulty gaining access to classes and student services. Academic schedules, including the academic calendar and class times, frequently exclude working adults and parents. As Frederick Hess explains, "A semester system . . . works well for 19-year-olds used to the rhythms of high school, but that's hugely frustrating for workers." In addition, unless classes and services are available in the evening, on weekends, or online, they are inaccessible to many students. As one professional advocate for nontraditional students explains, "Most nontraditional students have obligations during the day that make it difficult to access on-campus resources that are only open during business hours" (qtd. in Muhammad). This situation makes it difficult (and sometimes impossible) for nontraditional students to schedule required courses or to get extra help, such as tutoring. As long as these barriers to equal access exist, nontraditional students will always be "second-class citizens" in the university.

Evidence: First point in support of the thesis

5   Schools also need to stop devaluing the kinds of programs that nontraditional students tend to enroll in. Research shows that older students "view education as an opportunity to continue on their other life pursuits" (Scott and Lewis 1). Many are earning degrees in order to return to work, change careers, or improve their chances for a promotion. According to Hess, although the greatest demand is for associate's degrees or certificates—over 50% of nontraditional students are seeking one of these "subbaccalaureate" credentials—a clear bias against these programs remains. As Hess demonstrates, these "subbaccalaureate programs continue to be regarded as marginal," even in community colleges. One reason for this situation is that most schools still judge their own worth by factors—such as academic ranking or grant money— that have little to do with career skills. By devaluing practical training, these schools are undermining the educational experience that many nontraditional students want.

Evidence: Second point in support of the thesis

Finally, universities need to do more to encourage inclusive teaching 6
approaches. According to Joshua L. Carreiro and Brian P. Kapitulik, most
educators assume their students are "traditional"—that they are recent
high school graduates from middle-class backgrounds with little work
experience (232). As a result, nontraditional students "may experience
hostile or uncomfortable learning environments that impede their
learning opportunities" (Scott and Lewis 8). Carreiro and Kapitulik
conclude that these assumptions result in "an exclusive classroom
environment" that excludes and marginalizes nontraditional students
(246). One way of addressing this problem is for universities to expand
online education offerings. Online courses enable nontraditional
students to gradually assimilate into the college environment and to
work at their own pace without fear of ridicule. Universities can also
encourage instructors to develop new teaching approaches. If instructors
want to be more inclusive, they can acknowledge diversity by engaging
students in diverse ways of thinking and learning (Hermida). For
example, they can ask students to relate course material to their own
experiences, and they can bring in guest speakers from a variety of
backgrounds. By acknowledging the needs of nontraditional students,
instructors can provide a better education for all students.

Not everyone believes that colleges and universities need to
change their basic assumptions about education. Some educators
maintain that schools should not have to change the way they operate.
They concede that nontraditional students might need extra support, but
they say that these students are adults and should be able to fend for
themselves. Students' commitments outside of school—for instance,
children or a full-time job—should not be a concern for colleges and
universities. If these students need help, they can get support from one
another, or they can turn to student-led organizations, such as the
Association of Nontraditional Students in Higher Education (Scott and
Lewis 9). Even those educators who are sympathetic to nontraditional
students suggest that extra mentoring or advising is all that is
necessary. However, the problems faced by these students need to be
addressed, and according to Hermida, by ignoring institutional barriers
and biases, colleges and universities are essentially burying their
heads in the sand (22). To be more welcoming to nontraditional

students, universities must fundamentally change the structures and practices that have traditionally defined them. Ultimately, everyone—the schools, the communities, and the students—will benefit from these adjustments.

8   According to Hermida, many of today's students are nontraditional (20). Most of the current research suggests that inclusion is their most pressing concern. As this population continues to grow, say Scott and Lewis, "administrators will be confronted with new challenges to make sure their [nontraditional students'] experiences are equitable to other student populations" (1). Giving preferential treatment to some students while ignoring others who have different needs is ethically wrong, so schools need to work harder to end discrimination against this increasingly large group of learners.

Concluding statement

Works Cited

Carreiro, Joshua L., and Brian P. Kapitulik. "Budgets, Board Games, and Make Believe: The Challenge of Teaching Social Class Inequality with Nontraditional Students." *American Sociologist* 41.3 (2010): 232–48. *Academic Search Complete*. Web. 22 Mar. 2012.

Hermida, Julian. "Inclusive Teaching: An Approach for Encouraging Nontraditional Student Success." *International Journal of Research and Review* 5.1 (2010): 19–30. *Academic Search Complete*. Web. 22 Mar. 2012.

Hess, Frederick. "Old School: College's Most Important Trend Is the Rise of the Adult Student." *The Atlantic*. The Atlantic Monthly Group, 28 Sept. 2011. Web. 24 Mar. 2012.

Muhammad, Jacqueline. "New Coordinator to Address Nontraditional Student Needs." *Daily Egyptian*. Southern Illinois University, Carbondale, IL, 8 Dec. 2011. Web. 24 Mar. 2012.

Scott, Lakia M., and Chance W. Lewis. "Nontraditional College Students: Assumptions, Perceptions, and Directions for a Meaningful Academic Experience." *International Journal of Interdisciplinary Social Sciences* 6.4 (2012): 1–10. *Academic Search Complete*. Web. 22 Mar. 2012.

Tripp, Alan. "Guest Post: Nontraditional Students Key to College Completion Goal." *Washington Post*. Washington Post, 25 Mar. 2011. Web. 24 Mar. 2012.

GRAMMAR IN CONTEXT

Subordination and Coordination

When you write an argumentative essay, you need to show readers the logical and sequential connections between your ideas. You do this by using *coordinating conjunctions* and *subordinating conjunctions*—words that join words, phrases, clauses, or entire sentences. Be sure to choose conjunctions that accurately express the relationship between the ideas they join.

Coordinating conjunctions—*and, but, for, nor, or, so,* and *yet*—join ideas of equal importance. In compound sentences, they describe the relationship between the ideas in the two independent clauses and show how these ideas are related.

- "Colleges and universities are experiencing an increase in the number of nontraditional students, and this number is projected to rise." (*And* indicates addition.) (para. 1)

- "These students have a lot to offer, but often, they don't feel included." (*But* indicates contrast or contradiction.) (3)

- "For example, they can ask students to relate course material to their own experiences, and they can bring in guest speakers from a variety of backgrounds." (*And* indicates addition.) (6)

Subordinating conjunctions—*after, although, because, if, so that, where,* and so on—join ideas of unequal importance. In complex sentences, they describe the relationship between the ideas in the dependent clause and the independent clause and show how these ideas are related.

- "Although these students enrich campus communities and provide new opportunities for learning, they also present challenges." (*Although* indicates a contrast.) (1)

- "While many schools recognize that nontraditional students have unique needs, most schools continue to focus on the 'typical' student." (*While* indicates a contrast.) (1)

- "As long as these barriers to equal access exist, nontraditional students will always be 'second-class citizens' in the university." (As long as indicates a causal relationship.) (4)

- "If instructors want to be more inclusive, they can acknowledge diversity by engaging students in diverse ways of thinking and learning." (*If* indicates condition.) (6)

⊃ EXERCISE 17.6

The following speech includes the basic elements of an ethical argument. Read the essay, and then answer the questions that follow it, consulting the outline on page 599 if necessary.

This speech was delivered in the East Room of the White House on April 12, 1999.

THE PERILS OF INDIFFERENCE
ELIE WIESEL

Mr. President, Mrs. Clinton, members of Congress, Ambassador Holbrooke, 1 Excellencies, friends: Fifty-four years ago to the day, a young Jewish boy from a small town in the Carpathian Mountains woke up, not far from Goethe's beloved Weimar, in a place of eternal infamy called Buchenwald. He was finally free, but there was no joy in his heart. He thought there never would be again.

Liberated a day earlier by American soldiers, he remembers their rage at 2 what they saw. And even if he lives to be a very old man, he will always be grateful to them for that rage, and also for their compassion. Though he did not understand their language, their eyes told him what he needed to know— that they, too, would remember, and bear witness.

And now, I stand before you, Mr. President—Commander-in-Chief of the 3 army that freed me, and tens of thousands of others—and I am filled with a profound and abiding gratitude to the American people.

Gratitude is a word that I cherish. Gratitude is what defines the humanity 4 of the human being. And I am grateful to you, Hillary—or Mrs. Clinton—for what you said, and for what you are doing for children in the world, for the homeless, for the victims of injustice, the victims of destiny and society. And I thank all of you for being here.

We are on the threshold of a new century, a new millennium. What will 5 the legacy of this vanishing century be? How will it be remembered in the new millennium? Surely it will be judged, and judged severely, in both moral and metaphysical terms. These failures have cast a dark shadow over humanity: two World Wars, countless civil wars, the senseless chain of assassinations— Gandhi, the Kennedys, Martin Luther King, Sadat, Rabin—bloodbaths in Cambodia and Nigeria, India and Pakistan, Ireland and Rwanda, Eritrea and Ethiopia, Sarajevo and Kosovo; the inhumanity in the gulag and the tragedy of Hiroshima. And, on a different level, of course, Auschwitz and Treblinka. So much violence, so much indifference.

What is indifference? Etymologically, the word means "no difference." A 6 strange and unnatural state in which the lines blur between light and darkness, dusk and dawn, crime and punishment, cruelty and compassion, good and evil.

What are its courses and inescapable consequences? Is it a philosophy? Is there a philosophy of indifference conceivable? Can one possibly view indifference as a virtue? Is it necessary at times to practice it simply to keep one's sanity, live normally, enjoy a fine meal and a glass of wine, as the world around us experiences harrowing upheavals? [7]

Of course, indifference can be tempting—more than that, seductive. It is so much easier to look away from victims. It is so much easier to avoid such rude interruptions to our work, our dreams, our hopes. It is, after all, awkward, troublesome, to be involved in another person's pain and despair. Yet, for the person who is indifferent, his or her neighbors are of no consequence. And, therefore, their lives are meaningless. Their hidden or even visible anguish is of no interest. Indifference reduces the other to an abstraction. [8]

> "Indifference can be tempting—more than that, seductive."

Over there, behind the black gates of Auschwitz, the most tragic of all prisoners were the "Muselmanner," as they were called. Wrapped in their torn blankets, they would sit or lie on the ground, staring vacantly into space, unaware of who or where they were, strangers to their surroundings. They no longer felt pain, hunger, thirst. They feared nothing. They felt nothing. They were dead and did not know it. [9]

Rooted in our tradition, some of us felt that to be abandoned by humanity then was not the ultimate. We felt that to be abandoned by God was worse than to be punished by Him. Better an unjust God than an indifferent one. For us to be ignored by God was a harsher punishment than to be a victim of His anger. Man can live far from God—not outside God. God is wherever we are. Even in suffering? Even in suffering. [10]

In a way, to be indifferent to that suffering is what makes the human being inhuman. Indifference, after all, is more dangerous than anger and hatred. Anger can at times be creative. One writes a great poem, a great symphony, one does something special for the sake of humanity because one is angry at the injustice that one witnesses. But indifference is never creative. Even hatred at times may elicit a response. You fight it. You denounce it. You disarm it. Indifference elicits no response. Indifference is not a response. [11]

Indifference is not a beginning, it is an end. And, therefore, indifference is always the friend of the enemy, for it benefits the aggressor—never his victim, whose pain is magnified when he or she feels forgotten. The political prisoner in his cell, the hungry children, the homeless refugees—not to respond to their plight, not to relieve their solitude by offering them a spark of hope is to exile them from human memory. And in denying their humanity we betray our own. [12]

Indifference, then, is not only a sin, it is a punishment. And this is one of the most important lessons of this outgoing century's wide-ranging experiments in good and evil. [13]

In the place that I come from, society was composed of three simple catego- 14
ries: the killers, the victims, and the bystanders. During the darkest of times,
inside the ghettoes and death camps—and I'm glad that Mrs. Clinton mentioned
that we are now commemorating that event, that period, that we are now in the
Days of Remembrance—but then, we felt abandoned, forgotten. All of us did.

And our only miserable consolation was that we believed that Auschwitz 15
and Treblinka were closely guarded secrets; that the leaders of the free world
did not know what was going on behind those black gates and barbed wire;
that they had no knowledge of the war against the Jews that Hitler's armies and
their accomplices waged as part of the war against the Allies.

If they knew, we thought, surely those leaders would have moved heaven 16
and earth to intervene. They would have spoken out with great outrage and
conviction. They would have bombed the railways leading to Birkenau, just the
railways, just once.

And now we knew, we learned, we discovered that the Pentagon knew, the 17
State Department knew. And the illustrious occupant of the White House then,
who was a great leader—and I say it with some anguish and pain, because,
today is exactly 54 years marking his death—Franklin Delano Roosevelt died
on April the 12th, 1945, so he is very much present to me and to us.

No doubt, he was a great leader. He mobilized the American people and 18
the world, going into battle, bringing hundreds and thousands of valiant and
brave soldiers in America to fight fascism, to fight dictatorship, to fight Hitler.
And so many of the young people fell in battle. And, nevertheless, his image in
Jewish history—I must say it—his image in Jewish history is flawed.

The depressing tale of the *St. Louis* is a case in point. Sixty years ago, its 19
human cargo—maybe 1,000 Jews—was turned back to Nazi Germany. And
that happened after the Kristallnacht, after the first state-sponsored pogrom,
with hundreds of Jewish shops destroyed, synagogues burned, thousands of
people put in concentration camps. And that ship, which was already on the
shores of the United States, was sent back.

I don't understand. Roosevelt was a good man, with a heart. He understood 20
those who needed help. Why didn't he allow these refugees to disembark? A
thousand people—in America, a great country, the greatest democracy, the most
generous of all new nations in modern history. What happened? I don't understand. Why the indifference, on the highest level, to the suffering of the victims?

But then, there were human beings who were sensitive to our tragedy. 21
Those non-Jews, those Christians, that we called the "Righteous Gentiles,"
whose selfless acts of heroism saved the honor of their faith. Why were they so
few? Why was there a greater effort to save SS murderers after the war than to
save their victims during the war?

Why did some of America's largest corporations continue to do business 22
with Hitler's Germany until 1942? It has been suggested, and it was documented,
that the Wehrmacht could not have conducted its invasion of France without oil
obtained from American sources. How is one to explain their indifference?

And yet, my friends, good things have also happened in this traumatic 23
century: the defeat of Nazism, the collapse of communism, the rebirth of Israel
on its ancestral soil, the demise of apartheid, Israel's peace treaty with Egypt,
the peace accord in Ireland. And let us remember the meeting, filled with
drama and emotion, between Rabin and Arafat that you, Mr. President, con-
vened in this very place. I was here and I will never forget it.

And then, of course, the joint decision of the United States and NATO to 24
intervene in Kosovo and save those victims, those refugees, those who were
uprooted by a man whom I believe that because of his crimes, should be
charged with crimes against humanity. But this time, the world was not silent.
This time, we do respond. This time, we intervene.

Does it mean that we have learned from the past? Does it mean that soci- 25
ety has changed? Has the human being become less indifferent and more
human? Have we really learned from our experiences? Are we less insensitive to
the plight of victims of ethnic cleansing and other forms of injustices in places
near and far? Is today's justified intervention in Kosovo, led by you, Mr. President, a lasting warning that never again will the deportation, the terrorization
of children and their parents be allowed anywhere in the world? Will it discourage other dictators in other lands to do the same?

What about the children? Oh, we see them on television, we read about 26
them in the papers, and we do so with a broken heart. Their fate is always the
most tragic, inevitably. When adults wage war, children perish. We see their
faces, their eyes. Do we hear their pleas? Do we feel their pain, their agony?
Every minute one of them dies of disease, violence, famine. Some of them—so
many of them—could be saved.

And so, once again, I think of the young Jewish boy from the Carpathian 27
Mountains. He has accompanied the old man I have become throughout these
years of quest and struggle. And together we walk towards the new millennium, carried by profound fear and extraordinary hope.

Identifying the Elements of an Ethical Argument

1. Look up the definition of *indifference* in a few different dictionaries.
   How is Wiesel's definition different from the ones you found?

2. What ethical principle does Wiesel apply in his speech? At what point
   in the speech does he state this principle? Why do you think he states
   it where he does?

3. What is the thesis of this speech? In your own words, write it on the
   lines in the template below.

   Despite the events of the previous century, _____

   _____

   _____.

4. In his speech, Wiesel employs all three appeals—*logos*, *pathos*, and *ethos*. Locate examples of each appeal. How effective is each? Explain.

5. Throughout this speech, Wiesel supports his thesis with examples of the "perils of indifference" in the twentieth century. In paragraph 23, however, he shifts his focus to some good things that happened in the twentieth century. What point is Wiesel making with this shift? Does this shift weaken his argument in any way? Why or why not?

6. What ideas are emphasized in the speech's conclusion? Do you think the conclusion is effective? Explain.

7. How would "The Perils of Indifference" be different if Wiesel had structured it as a proposal argument?

How Far Should Colleges Go to Keep Campuses Safe?

Go back to page 589, and reread the At Issue box, which gives background on how far colleges should go to keep their students safe. Then, read the sources on the pages that follow.

As you read this source material, you will be asked to answer some questions and to complete some simple activities. This work will help you understand both the content and the structure of the selections. When you are finished, you will be ready to write an **ethical argument** that takes a position on the topic, "How Far Should Colleges Go to Keep Campuses Safe?"

SOURCES

 Brett A. Sokolow, "How Not to Respond to Virginia Tech—II," p. 611

 Jesus M. Villahermosa Jr., "Guns Don't Belong in the Hands of Administrators, Professors, or Students," p. 615

 Timothy Wheeler, "There's a Reason They Choose Schools," p. 618

 Isothermal Community College, "Warning Signs: How You Can Help Prevent Campus Violence" (brochure), p. 621

 Amy Dion, "Gone but Not Forgotten" (poster), p. 625

 For comprehension quizzes, see **bedfordstmartins.com/practicalargument**.

Inside Higher Ed published this essay on May 1, 2007.

HOW NOT TO RESPOND TO VIRGINIA TECH—II

BRETT A. SOKOLOW

If you believe the pundits and talking heads in the aftermath of the Virginia Tech tragedy, every college and university should rush to set up text-message-based early warning systems, install loudspeakers throughout campus, perform criminal background checks on all incoming students, allow students to install their own locks on their residence hall room doors, and exclude from admission or expel students with serious mental health conditions. We should profile loners, establish lockdown protocols, and develop mass-shooting evacuation plans. We should even arm our students to the teeth. In the immediate aftermath, security experts and college and university officials have been quoted in newspapers and on TV with considering all of these remedies, and more, to be able to assure the public that WE ARE DOING SOMETHING.

Since when do we let the media dictate to us our best practices? Do we need to do something? Do we need to be doing all or some of these things? Here's what I think. These are just my opinions, informed by what I have learned so far in the reportage on what happened at Virginia Tech. Because that coverage is inaccurate and incomplete, please consider these my thoughts so far, subject to revision as more facts come to light.

> "Since when do we let the media dictate to us our best practices?"

We should not be rushing to install text-message-based warning systems. At the low cost of $1 per student per year, you might ask what the downside could be? Well, the real cost is the $1 per student that we don't spend on mental health support, where we really need to spend it. And, what do you get for your $1? A system that will send an emergency text to the cell phone number of every student who is registered with the service. If we acknowledge that many campuses still don't have the most current mailing address for some of our students who live off-campus, is it realistic to expect that students are going to universally supply us with their cell phone numbers? You could argue that students are flocking to sign up for this service on the campuses that currently provide it (less than 50 nationally), but that is driven by the panic of current events. Next fall, when the shock has worn off, apathy will inevitably return, and voluntary sign-up rates will drop. How about mandating that students participate? What about the costs of the bureaucracy we will need to collect and who will input this data? Who will track which students have yet to give us their numbers, remind them, and hound them to submit the information?

Who will update this database as students switch cell numbers mid-year, which many do? That's more than a full-time job, with implementation already costing more than the $1 per student. Some students want their privacy. They won't want administrators to have their cell number. Some students don't have cell phones. Many students do not have text services enabled on their phones. More added cost. Many professors instruct students to turn off their phones in classrooms.

Texting is useless. It's useless on the field for athletes, while students are 4 swimming, sleeping, showering, etc. And, perhaps most dangerously, texting an alert may send that alert to a psychopath who is also signed-up for the system, telling him exactly what administrators know, what the emergency plan is, and where to go to effect the most harm. Would a text system create a legal duty that colleges and universities do not have, a duty of universal warning? What happens in a crisis if the system is overloaded, as were cellphone lines in Blacksburg? What happens if the data entry folks mistype a number, and a student who needs warning does not get one? We will be sued for negligence. We need to spend this time, money, and effort on the real problem: mental health.

We should consider installing loudspeakers throughout campus. This 5 technology has potentially better coverage than text messages, with much less cost. Virginia Tech used such loudspeakers to good effect during the shootings.

We should not rush to perform criminal background checks (CBCs) on 6 **all incoming students.** A North Carolina task force studied this issue after two 2004 campus shootings and decided that the advantages were not worth the disadvantages. You might catch a random dangerous applicant, but most students who enter with criminal backgrounds were minors when they committed their crimes, and their records may have been sealed or expunged. If your student population is largely of non-traditional age, CBCs may reveal more, but then you have to weigh the cost and the question of whether you are able to perform due diligence on screening the results of the checks if someone is red-flagged. How will you determine which students who have criminal histories are worthy of admission and which are not? And, there is always the reality that if you perform a check on all incoming students and the college across the street does not, the student with the criminal background will apply there and not to you. If you decide to check incoming students, what will you do about current students? Will you do a state-level check, or a 50-state and federal check? Will your admitted applicants be willing to wait the 30 days that it takes to get the results? Other colleges who admitted them are also waiting for an answer. The comprehensive check can cost $80 per student. We need to spend this time, money, and effort on the real problem: mental health.

We should not be considering whether to allow students to install their 7 **own locks on their dormitory room doors.** Credit *Fox News Live* for this deplorably dumb idea. If we let students change their locks, residential life and campus law enforcement will not be able to key into student rooms when they overdose on alcohol or try to commit suicide. This idea would prevent us from saving lives, rather than help to protect members of our community. The Virginia Tech killer could have shot through a lock, no matter whether it was the original or a retrofit. This is our property, and we need to have access to it. We need to focus our attention on the real issue: mental health.

Perhaps the most preposterous suggestion of all is that we need to relax 8 **our campus weapons bans so that armed members of our communities can defend themselves. We should not allow weapons on college campuses.** Imagine you are seated in Norris Hall, facing the whiteboard at the front of the room. The shooter enters from the back and begins shooting. What good is your gun going to do at this point? Many pro-gun advocates have talked about the deterrent and defense values of a well-armed student body, but none of them have mentioned the potential collateral criminal consequences of armed students: increases in armed robbery, muggings, escalation of interpersonal and relationship violence, etc. Virginia, like most states, cannot keep guns out of the hands of those with potentially lethal mental health crises. When we talk about arming students, we'd be arming them too. We need to focus our attention on the real issue: mental health.

We should establish lockdown protocols that are specific to the nature 9 **of the threat.** Lockdowns are an established mass-protection tactic. They can isolate perpetrators, insulate targets from threats, and restrict personal movement away from a dangerous line-of-fire. But, if lockdowns are just a random response, they have the potential to lock students in with a still-unidentified perpetrator. If not used correctly, they have the potential to lock students into facilities from which they need immediate egress for safety reasons. And, if not enforced when imposed, lockdowns expose us to the potential liability of not following our own policies. We should also establish protocols for judicious use of evacuations. When police at Virginia Tech herded students out of buildings and across the Drill Field, it was based on their assessment of a low risk that someone was going to open fire on students as they fled out into the open, and a high risk of leaving the occupants of certain buildings in situ, making evacuation from a zone of danger an appropriate escape method.

We should not exclude from admission or expel students with mental 10 **health conditions, unless they pose a substantial threat of harm to themselves or others.** Section 504 of the Rehabilitation Act prohibits colleges and universities from discrimination in admission against those with disabilities. It also prohibits colleges and universities from suspending or expelling disabled students, including those who are suicidal, unless the student is deemed to be a direct threat of substantial harm in an objective process based on the most current medical assessment available. Many colleges do provide health surveys to incoming students, and when those surveys disclose mental health conditions, we need to consider what appropriate follow-up should occur as a result. The Virginia Tech shooter was schizophrenic or mildly autistic, and identifying those disabilities early on and providing support, accommodation—and potentially intervention—is our issue.

We should consider means and mechanisms for early intervention with 11 **students who exhibit behavioral issues, but we should not profile loners. At**

the University of South Carolina, the Behavioral Intervention Team makes many early catches of students whose behavior is threatening, disruptive, or potentially self-injurious. By working with faculty and staff at opening communication and support, the model is enhancing campus safety in a way that many other campuses are not. In the aftermath of what happened at Virginia Tech, I hope many campuses are considering a model designed to help raise flags for early screening and intervention. Many students are loners, isolated, withdrawn, pierced, tattooed, dyed, Wiccan, skate rats, fantasy gamers, or otherwise outside the "mainstream." This variety enlivens the richness of college campuses, and offers layers of culture that quilt the fabric of diverse communities. Their preferences and differences cannot and should not be cause for fearing them or suspecting them. But, when any member of the community starts a downward spiral along the continuum of violence, begins to lose contact with reality, goes off their medication regimen, threatens, disrupts, or otherwise gains our attention with unhealthy or dangerous patterns, we can't be bystanders any longer. Our willingness to intervene can make all the difference.

All of the pundits insist that random violence can't be predicted, but many 12 randomly violent people exhibit a pattern of detectable disintegration of self, often linked to suicide. People around them perceive it. We can all be better attuned to those patterns and our protocols for communicating our concerns to those who have the ability to address them. This will focus our attention on the real issue: mental health.

⊘ AT ISSUE: SOURCES FOR DEVELOPING AN ETHICAL ARGUMENT

1. Why does Sokolow begin his essay by discussing what "pundits and talking heads" think should be done to stop campus violence? Is this an effective opening strategy?

2. In paragraph 2, Sokolow says, "Here's what I think. These are just my opinions." Do these two statements undercut or enhance his credibility? Why do you suppose he includes them?

3. How does Sokolow propose to make campuses safer? Do you agree with his suggestions? Why or why not?

4. Is Sokolow's argument a refutation? If so, what arguments is he refuting?

5. In what sense is this essay an ethical argument?

6. In his concluding statement, Sokolow says that the real issue is "mental health." What does he mean? Do you agree?

This essay is from the April 18, 2008, issue of the *Chronicle of Higher Education*.

GUNS DON'T BELONG IN THE HANDS OF ADMINISTRATORS, PROFESSORS, OR STUDENTS

JESUS M. VILLAHERMOSA JR.

In the wake of the shootings at Virginia Tech and Northern Illinois University, a number of state legislatures are considering bills that would allow people to carry concealed weapons on college campuses. I recently spoke at a conference on higher-education law, sponsored by Stetson University and the National Association of Student Personnel Administrators, at which campus officials discussed the need to exempt colleges from laws that let private citizens carry firearms and to protect such exemptions where they exist. I agree that allowing guns on campuses will create problems, not solve them.

I have been a deputy sheriff for more than 26 years and was the first certified master defensive-tactics instructor for law-enforcement personnel in the state of Washington. In addition, I have been a firearms instructor and for several decades have served on my county sheriff's SWAT team, where I am now point man on the entry team. Given my extensive experience dealing with violence in the workplace and at schools and colleges, I do not think professors and administrators, let alone students, should carry guns.

Some faculty and staff members may be capable of learning to be good shots in stressful situations, but most of them probably wouldn't practice their firearms skills enough to become confident during an actual shooting. Unless they practiced those skills constantly, there would be a high risk that when a shooting situation actually occurred, they would miss the assailant. That would leave great potential for a bullet to strike a student or another innocent bystander. Such professors and administrators could be imprisoned for manslaughter for recklessly endangering the lives of others during a crisis.

Although some of the legislative bills have been defeated, they may be reintroduced, or other states may introduce similar measures. Thus, colleges should at least contemplate the possibility of having armed faculty and staff members on their campuses, and ask themselves the following questions:

- Is our institution prepared to assume the liability that accompanies the lethal threat of carrying or using weapons? Are we financially able and willing to drastically increase our liability-insurance premium to cover all of the legal ramifications involved with allowing faculty and staff members to carry firearms?

- How much time will each faculty and staff member be given each year to spend on a firing range to practice shooting skills? Will we pay them for that time?

615

- Will their training include exposing them to a great amount of stress in order to simulate a real-life shooting situation, like the training that police officers go through?

- Will the firearm that each one carries be on his or her person during the day? If so, will faculty and staff members be given extensive defensive-tactics training, so that they can retain their firearm if someone tries to disarm them?

- The fact that a college allows people to have firearms could be publicized, and, under public-disclosure laws, the institution could be required to notify the general public which faculty or staff members are carrying them. Will those individuals accept the risk of being targeted by a violent student or adult who wants to neutralize the threat and possibly obtain their weapons?

- If the firearms are not carried by faculty and staff members every day, where and how will those weapons be secured, so that they do not fall into the wrong hands?

- If the firearms are locked up, how will faculty and staff members gain access to them in time to be effective if a shooting actually occurs?

- Will faculty and staff members who carry firearms be required to be in excellent physical shape, and stay that way, in case they need to fight someone for their gun?

- Will weapons-carrying faculty and staff members accept that they may be shot by law-enforcement officers who mistake them for the shooter? (All the responding officers see is a person with a gun. If you are even close to matching the suspect's description, the risk is high that they may shoot you.)

- Will faculty and staff members be prepared to kill another person, someone who may be as young as a teenager?

> "Will faculty and staff members be prepared to kill another person?"

- Will faculty and staff members be prepared for the possibility that they may miss their target (which has occurred even in police shootings) and wound or kill an innocent bystander?

- Will faculty and staff members be ready to face imprisonment for manslaughter, depending on their states' criminal statutes, if one of their bullets does, in fact, strike an innocent person?

- Even if not criminally charged, would such faculty and staff members be prepared to be the focus of a civil lawsuit, both as a professional working for the institution and as an individual, thereby exposing their personal assets?

If any of us in the law-enforcement field were asked these questions, we 5
could answer them all with absolute confidence. We have made a commitment
to train relentlessly and to die, if we have to, in order to protect others. Experienced officers have typically fired tens of thousands of rounds practicing for
the time when they might need those skills to save themselves or someone else
during a lethal situation. We take that commitment seriously. Before legislators
and college leaders make the decision to put a gun in the hands of a professor
or administrator, they should be certain they take it seriously, too.

⊘ AT ISSUE: SOURCES FOR DEVELOPING AN ETHICAL ARGUMENT

1. What is Villahermosa's thesis? Where does he state it?

2. What is Villahermosa trying to establish in paragraph 2? Do you think this paragraph is necessary?

3. In the bulleted list in paragraph 4, Villahermosa poses a series of ques-tions. What does he want this list to accomplish? Is he successful?

4. What arguments does Villahermosa include to support his thesis? Which of these arguments do you find most convincing? Why?

5. Do you think Villahermosa is making an ethical argument here? If so, on what ethical principle does he base his argument?

6. What points does Villahermosa emphasize in his conclusion? Should he have emphasized any other points? Explain.

7. Both Villahermosa and Timothy Wheeler (p. 618) deal with the same issue—guns on campus. Which writer do you think makes the stron-ger case? Why?

This article is from the October 11, 2007, issue of *National Review*.

THERE'S A REASON THEY CHOOSE SCHOOLS

TIMOTHY WHEELER

Wednesday's shooting at yet another school has a better outcome than most in recent memory. No one died at Cleveland's Success Tech Academy except the perpetrator. The two students and two teachers he shot are in stable condition at Cleveland hospitals. 1

What is depressingly similar to the mass murders at Virginia Tech and Nickel Mines, Pennsylvania, and too many others was the killer's choice of venue—that steadfastly gun-free zone, the school campus. Although murderer Seung-Hui Cho at Virginia Tech and Asa Coon, the Cleveland shooter, were both students reported to have school-related grudges, other school killers have proved to be simply taking advantage of the lack of effective security at schools. The Bailey, Colorado, multiple rapes and murder of September 2006, the Nickel Mines massacre of October 2006, and Buford Furrow's murderous August 1999 invasion of a Los Angeles Jewish day-care center were all committed by adults. They had no connection to the schools other than being drawn to the soft target a school offers such psychopaths. 2

This latest shooting comes only a few weeks after the American Medical Association released a theme issue of its journal *Disaster Medicine and Public Health Preparedness*. This issue is dedicated to analyzing the April 2007 Virginia Tech shootings, in which 32 people were murdered. The authors are university officials, trauma surgeons, and legal analysts who pore over the details of the incident, looking for "warning signs" and "risk factors" for violence. They rehash all the tired rhetoric of bureaucrats and public-health wonks, including the public-health mantra of the 1990s that guns are the root cause of violence. 3

Sheldon Greenberg, a dean at Johns Hopkins, offers this gem: "Reinforce a 'no weapons' policy and, when violated, enforce it quickly, to include expulsion. Parents should be made aware of the policy. *Officials should dispel the politically driven notion that armed students could eliminate an active shooter*" (emphasis added). Greenberg apparently isn't aware that at the Appalachian School of Law in 2002 another homicidal Virginia student was stopped from shooting more of his classmates when another student held him at gunpoint. The Pearl High School murderer Luke Woodham was stopped cold when vice principal Joel Myrick got his Colt .45 handgun out of his truck and pointed it at the young killer. 4

Virginia Tech's 2005 no-guns-on-campus policy was an abject failure at deterring Cho Seung-Hui. Greenberg's audacity in ignoring the obvious is typical of arrogant school officials. What the AMA journal authors studiously 5 avoid are on one hand the repeated failures of such feel-good steps as no-gun policies, and on the other hand the demonstrated success of armed first responders. These responders would be the students themselves, such as the trained and licensed law student, or their similarly qualified teachers.

> "Virginia Tech's . . . no-guns-on-campus policy was an abject failure." 6

In Cleveland this week and at Virginia Tech the shooters took time to walk the halls, searching out victims in several rooms, and then shooting them. Virginia Chief Medical Examiner Marcella Fierro describes the locations of the dead in Virginia Tech's Norris Hall. Dead victims were found in groups ranging from 1 to 13, scattered throughout 4 rooms and a stairwell. If any one of the victims had, like the Appalachian School of Law student, used armed force to stop Cho, lives could have been saved.

The people of Virginia actually had a chance to implement such a plan last 7 year. House Bill 1572 was introduced in the legislature to extend the state's concealed-carry provisions to college campuses. But the bill died in committee, opposed by the usual naysayers, including the Virginia Association of Chiefs of Police and the university itself. Virginia Tech spokesman Larry Hincker was quoted in the *Roanoke Times* as saying, "I'm sure the university community is appreciative of the General Assembly's actions because this will help parents, students, faculty, and visitors feel safe on our campus."

It is encouraging that college students themselves have a much better 8 grasp on reality than their politically correct elders. During the week of October 22–26 Students for Concealed Carry on Campus will stage a nationwide "empty holster" demonstration (peaceful, of course) in support of their cause.

School officials typically base violence-prevention policies on irrational 9 fears more than real-world analysis of what works. But which is more horrible, the massacre that timid bureaucrats fear might happen when a few good guys (and gals) carry guns on campus, or the one that actually did happen despite Virginia Tech's progressive violence-prevention policy? Can there really be any more debate?

AMA journal editor James J. James, M.D., offers up this nostrum: 10

> We must meaningfully embrace all of the varied disciplines contributing to preparedness and response and be more willing to be guided and informed by the full spectrum of research methodologies, including not only the rigid application of the traditional scientific method and epidemiological and social science applications but also the incorporation of observational/empirical findings, as necessary, in the absence of more objective data.

Got that?

I prefer the remedy prescribed by self-defense guru Massad Ayoob. When 11 good people find themselves in what he calls "the dark place," confronted by the imminent terror of a gun-wielding homicidal maniac, the picture becomes clear. Policies won't help. Another federal gun law won't help. The only solution is a prepared and brave defender with the proper lifesaving tool—a gun.

⮞ AT ISSUE: SOURCES FOR DEVELOPING AN ETHICAL ARGUMENT

1. According to Wheeler, what is "depressingly similar" about the mass murders committed on campuses (para. 2)?

2. What is Wheeler's attitude toward those who said that "guns are the root cause of violence" (3)? How can you tell?

3. Why, according to Wheeler, do college administrators and bureaucrats continue to ignore the answer to the problem of violence on campus? How does he refute their objections?

4. Do you find Wheeler's argument in support of his thesis convincing? What, if anything, do you think he could have added to strengthen his argument?

5. How does Wheeler's language reveal his attitude toward his subject? (For example, consider his use of "gem" in paragraph 4 and "politically correct" in paragraph 8.) Can you give other examples of language that conveys his point of view?

6. How would you characterize Wheeler's opinion of guns? How is his opinion different from Villahermosa's (p. 615)?

7. How do you think Wheeler would respond to the ideas in "Warning Signs: How You Can Help Prevent Campus Violence" (p. 621)? Which suggestions do you think he would support? Which would he be likely to oppose? Explain.

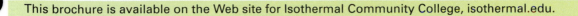

This brochure is available on the Web site for Isothermal Community College, isothermal.edu.

WARNING SIGNS: HOW YOU CAN HELP PREVENT CAMPUS VIOLENCE

ISOTHERMAL COMMUNITY COLLEGE

2 ....

Things to

LOOK OUT FOR . . .

- Any direct statement about the intention to harm him/her self or other members of the community

- "Hints" that the individual intends to harm him/her self or other members of the community: For example, "I might not be around after this weekend;" "It would be a good idea for you to stay out of the cafeteria tomorrow;" "People might get hurt, if they're not careful"

- Extreme difficulty adjusting to college life; for example, the student is isolated, depressed, and/or very angry with peers

- Significant changes in behavior, appearance, habits, mood, or activities

- Statements from individuals about access to firearms and suggestions that they may be bringing them to the campus or may already have them on campus

- Behaviors that indicate that the individual is settling his/her affairs, which may include telling people goodbye, giving possessions away, and/or making statements about what they would like to have done should something happen to them

- Fascination with violence, including some types of video games and music, and/or focusing on or admiring violent "role models"

- Your own "gut feeling" that someone that you know intends to harm him/her self or others

Campus Security – 289-1393
Isothermal Community College
Improve Life Through Learning
www.isothermal.edu

At Isothermal Community College, we want all of our students, faculty, and staff to be safe and secure on campus.

In light of the tragic shootings at Virginia Tech and other recent events on college campuses and in schools around the country, it has become clear that friends, classmates, and acquaintances of troubled students may be the most likely individuals to be aware of potentially dangerous and/or self-destructive situations.

However, students often are not certain about what kinds of warning signs they should take seriously and/or whether reporting the signs to faculty or staff members is the right thing to do.

The tips in this brochure are aimed at helping you identify potential problems and behaviors that could lead to incidents of campus violence.

If you ever feel endangered or threatened at any time on campus, we ask that you immediately contact Isothermal security, an instructor, or an employee of the college for assistance.

Campus security can be reached at 289-1393. To contact the switchboard operator, dial **0** on any campus phone. You should also report any threatening activity to local law enforcement by dialing **911**. Don't forget to dial **9** for an outside line if using the campus phone system.

A lockdown procedure is in place for Isothermal Community College. Faculty and staff members periodically practice the procedure. **If you are informed of a lockdown situation, please cooperate with the proper authorities.** Leaving the classroom or the building in such a situation may put you at greater risk.

POTENTIAL FOR VIOLENCE
Warning Signs in Others

Often people who act violently have trouble controlling their feelings. They may have been hurt by others and may think that making people fear them through violence or threats of violence will solve their problems or earn them respect. This isn't true. People who behave violently lose respect. They find themselves isolated or disliked, and they still feel angry and frustrated.

If you see these immediate warning signs, violence is a serious possibility:

- Loss of temper on a daily basis
- Frequent physical fighting
- Significant vandalism or property damage
- Increase in use of drugs or alcohol
- Increase in risk-taking behavior
- Detailed plans to commit acts of violence
- Announcing threats or plans for hurting others
- Enjoying hurting animals
- Carrying a weapon

4 •

If you notice the following signs over a period of time, the potential for violence exists:

- A history of violent or aggressive behavior
- Serious drug or alcohol use
- Gang membership or strong desire to be in a gang
- Access to or fascination with weapons, especially guns
- Threatening others regularly
- Trouble controlling feelings like anger
- Withdrawal from friends and usual activities
- Feeling rejected or alone
- Having been a victim of bullying
- Poor school performance
- History of discipline problems or frequent run-ins with authority
- Feeling constantly disrespected
- Failing to acknowledge the feelings or rights of others

Source: American Psychological Association

⮫ AT ISSUE: SOURCES FOR DEVELOPING AN ETHICAL ARGUMENT

1. This brochure is designed to help students recognize people who have the potential to commit campus violence. What warning signs does the brochure emphasize?

2. What additional information do you think should have been included in this brochure? Why?

3. Are there any suggestions in this brochure that could possibly violate a person's right to privacy? Explain.

4. What additional steps do you think students should take to prevent campus violence?

This poster is from the UCDA Campus Violence Poster Project show at Northern Illinois University.

GONE BUT NOT FORGOTTEN

AMY DION

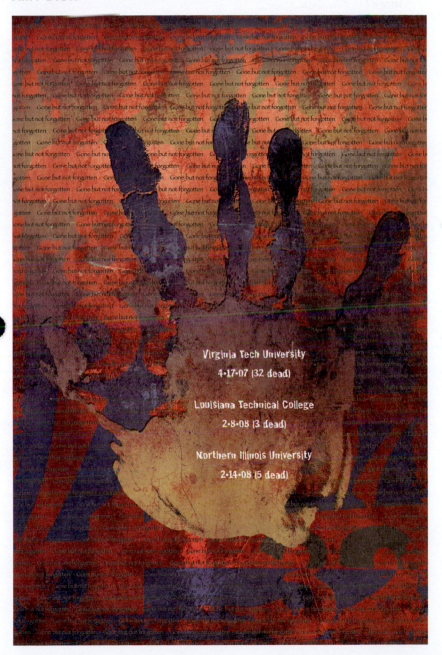

⊙ AT ISSUE: SOURCES FOR DEVELOPING AN ETHICAL ARGUMENT

1. This poster shows a handprint on a background that repeats the phrase "Gone but not forgotten." What argument does the poster make?

2. What other images does the poster include? How do these images reinforce its message?

3. Do you think posters like this one can really help to combat campus violence? Can they serve any other purpose? Explain.

⊙ EXERCISE 17.7

Write a one-paragraph ethical argument in which you answer the question, "How far should colleges go to keep campuses safe?" Follow the template below, filling in the blanks to create your argument.

TEMPLATE FOR WRITING AN ETHICAL ARGUMENT

Recently, a number of colleges have experienced violence on their campuses. For example, _____

_____. Many colleges have gone too far (or not far enough) in trying to prevent violence because _____

_____

_____. One reason _____

_____.

Another reason _____

_____. Finally, _____

_____

_____. If colleges really want to remain safe, _____

_____

_____

_____.

⊙ EXERCISE 17.8

Ask your friends and your teachers whether they think any of the steps your school has taken to prevent campus violence are excessive—or whether they think these measures don't go far enough. Then, revise the paragraph you wrote for Exercise 17.7 so that it includes their opinions.

⊙ EXERCISE 17.9

Write an ethical argument in which you consider the topic, "How far should colleges go to keep campuses safe?" Make sure you include a clear analysis of the ethical principle that you are going to apply. (If you like, you may incorporate the material you developed for Exercises 17.7 and 17.8 into your essay.) Cite the readings on pages 610–625, and document the sources you use, and be sure to include a works-cited page. (See Chapter 10 for information on documenting sources.)

➲ EXERCISE 17.10

Review the four pillars of argument discussed in Chapter 1. Does your essay include all four elements of an effective argument? Add anything that is missing. Then, label the key elements of your essay.

➲ WRITING ASSIGNMENTS: ETHICAL ARGUMENTS

1. Write an ethical argument in which you discuss whether hate groups have the right to distribute material on campus. Be sure to explain the ethical principle you are applying and to include several arguments in support of your position. (Don't forget to define and give examples of what you mean by *hate groups*. Remember to address arguments against your position.)

2. Should English be made the official language of the United States? Write an ethical argument in which you take a position on this topic.

3. Many people think that celebrities have an ethical obligation to set positive examples for young people. Assume that you are a celebrity, and write an op-ed piece in which you support or challenge this idea. Be sure to identify the ethical principle on which you base your argument.

Part 5 Review: Combining Argumentative Strategies

In Chapters 12–17, you have seen how argumentative essays can use different strategies to serve particular purposes. The discussions and examples in these chapters highlighted the use of a single strategy for a given essay. However, many (if not most) argumentative essays combine several different strategies.

For example, an argument recommending that the United States implement a national sales tax could be largely a **proposal argument**, but it could present a **causal argument** to illustrate the likely benefits of the proposal, and it could also use an **argument by analogy** to suggest parallels with state sales taxes that have successfully raised money to fund education or programs for the elderly.

The following two essays—"Get the Lead out of Hunting" and "Why Medical School Should Be Free"—illustrate how various strategies can work together in a single argument. Note that both essays include the four pillars of argument—*thesis statement*, *evidence*, *refutation*, and *concluding statement*. (The first essay includes marginal annotations that identify the different strategies the writer uses to advance his argument.)

This opinion essay is from the December 15, 2010, *New York Times*.

GET THE LEAD OUT OF HUNTING

ANTHONY PRIETO

I've hunted elk, deer, and wild pigs in the American West for 25 years. Like many hunters, I follow several rules: Respect other forms of life, take only what my family can eat and the ecosystem can sustain, and leave as little impact on the environment as possible. [1]

Causal argument
Ethical argument

That's why I hunt with copper bullets instead of lead. We've long known about the collateral damage caused by lead ammunition. When bald and golden eagles, vultures, bears, endangered California condors, and other scavengers eat the innards, called gutpiles, that hunters leave in the field after cleaning their catch or the game that hunters wound but don't capture, they can ingest poisonous lead fragments. Most sicken, and many die. [2]

Causal argument

When I began hunting, I buried the lead-laden gutpiles. It would help if more hunters did this, but it's not enough. Scavengers often dig gutpiles up anyway. And the meat that hunters take home to their families could be tainted. I've seen X-rays of shot game showing dust-sized lead particles spread throughout the meat, far away from the bullet hole. The best solution is to stop using lead ammunition altogether. [3]

Proposal argument

So last summer conservationists—along with the organization I run—formally petitioned the Environmental Protection Agency to ban lead bullets and shot nationwide (there are limited bans for some hunting areas and game). The E.P.A. rejected the petition, and we've since filed a lawsuit to get the agency to address the problem. [4]

Unfortunately, there is vocal opposition to any ammunition regulation from groups like the National Rifle Association and the National Shooting Sports Foundation, which see the campaign as an attack on hunting rights and fear that the cost of non-lead ammunition would drive hunters away from the sport. [5]

Argument by analogy

But this campaign has nothing to do with revoking hunting rights; if it did, I would not be involved. It's an issue of using non-toxic materials. Was the removal of lead paint from children's toys a plot to do away with toys? Did the switch to unleaded gas hide an ulterior motive of removing vehicles from our roads? [6]

Argument by analogy

And although copper bullets can be more expensive than lead ones, the cost of ammunition is a small fraction of what I spend on hunting, which includes gear, optics, food, gas, and licenses. No one will quit hunting over spending a few more quarters per bullet. Besides, the more hunters switch to copper, the faster prices will come down. Back in the '90s, before pre-loaded copper cartridges could be bought over the counter, I had to hand-load my copper bullets. But already it's easy to find them in many calibers, including those for my Browning .270 and my Winchester .300. [7]

8   The dozen friends I hunt with love shooting non-lead bullets, and it's not just because they're doing something

> "Copper kills cleanly."

Evaluation argument

good for the environment. The ballistics are better. I've killed more than 80 pigs and 40 deer shooting copper. These bullets travel up to 3,200 feet per second and have about a 98 percent weight retention—meaning they don't fragment as easily as lead. Copper kills cleanly. It can help keep our hunting grounds clean as well.

◑ REVIEW EXERCISE 1

1. Prieto uses various argument strategies in "Get the Lead out of Hunting," which are identified in the annotations. Why is each strategy used?

2. How does each strategy support the argument the writer makes?

3. Does one particular strategy seem to dominate the essay—that is, do you see it as largely a proposal argument, an ethical argument, or something else?

4. Where, if anywhere, could Prieto have used a definition argument? What might this strategy have added to this essay?

This opinion essay is from the May 28, 2011, *New York Times*.

WHY MEDICAL SCHOOL SHOULD BE FREE

PETER B. BACH AND ROBERT KOCHER

Doctors are among the most richly rewarded professionals in the country. The 1
Bureau of Labor Statistics reports that of the 15 highest-paid professions in the
United States, all but two are in medicine or dentistry.

Why, then, are we proposing to make medical school free?   2

Huge medical school debts—doctors now graduate owing more than 3
$155,000 on average, and 86 percent have some debt—are why so many doctors
shun primary care in favor of highly paid specialties, where there are incentives
to give expensive treatments and order expensive tests, an important driver of
rising health care costs.

Fixing our health care system will be impossible without a larger pool of 4
competent primary care doctors who can make sure specialists work together in
the treatment of their patients—not in isolation, as they often do today—and
keep track of patients as they move among settings like private residences, hospitals, and nursing homes. Moreover, our population is growing and aging; the
American Academy of Family Physicians has estimated a shortfall of 40,000
primary care doctors by 2020. Given the years it takes to train a doctor, we need
to start now.

Making medical school free would relieve doctors of the burden of student 5
debt and gradually shift the work force away from specialties and toward primary care. It would also attract college graduates who are discouraged from
going to medical school by the costly
tuition.

We estimate that we can make medical school free for roughly $2.5 billion per
year—about one-thousandth of what we
spend on health care in the United States
each year. What's more, we can offset most if not all of the cost of medical school
without the government's help by charging doctors for specialty training.

> "We can make medical
> school free for roughly
> $2.5 billion per year."   6

Under today's system, all medical students have to pay for their training, 7
whether they plan to become pediatricians or neurosurgeons. They are then
paid salaries during the crucial years of internship and residency that turn them
into competent doctors. If they decide to extend their years of training to
become specialists, they receive a stipend during those years, too.

But under our plan, medical school tuition, which averages $38,000 per 8
year, would be waived. Doctors choosing training in primary care, whether they
plan to go on later to specialize or not, would continue to receive the stipends
they receive today. But those who want to get specialty training would have to
forgo much or all of their stipends, $50,000 on average. Because there are nearly

as many doctors enrolled in specialty training in the United States (about 66,000) as there are students in United States medical schools (about 67,000), the forgone stipends would cover all the tuition costs.

While this may seem like a lot to ask of future specialists, these same doctors will have paid nothing for medical school and, through their specialty training, would be virtually assured highly lucrative jobs. Today's specialists earn a median of $325,000 per year by one estimate, 70 percent more than the $190,000 that a primary care doctor makes. (Although a large shift away from specialty training may weaken the ability of our plan to remain self-financed, the benefits would make any needed tuition subsidies well worth it.)

Our proposal is not the first to attempt to shift doctors toward primary care, but it's the most ambitious. The National Health Service Corps helps doctors repay their loans in exchange for a commitment to work in an underserved area, but few doctors sign up. The National Institutes of Health offers a similar program to promote work in research and public health, but this creates more researchers, not more practitioners.

Many states have loan forgiveness programs for doctors entering primary care. The health care reform law contains incentive programs that will include bonuses for primary care doctors who treat Medicare patients and help finance a small increase in primary care training positions.

Our proposal is certain to raise objections. Because some hospitals that provide training to specialists are not associated with medical schools, we will need a system to redistribute the specialty training fees and medical school subsidies. Several entities that have not collaborated before, including the organizations that license specialty training programs and medical school associations, would have to work together to manage this. For the plan to work, it will also be critical that medical schools do not start raising tuitions just because people other than their students are footing the bill.

Our plan would not directly address the chronic wage gap between primary care providers and specialists. But efforts to equalize incomes have been stymied for decades by specialists, who have kept payment rates for procedures higher than those for primary care services. When Medicare has stepped in, most of the increases given to primary care have been diluted by byzantine budgetary rules that cap total spending.

Nothing in our plan would diminish the quality of medical school education. If anything, free tuition would increase the quality of the applicants. Neither would our approach quash the creativity of medical schools in developing curriculums. Medical students would still be required to pass the various licensing examinations and complete patient care rotations as they are today.

Critics might object to providing free medical education when students have to pay for most other types of advanced training. But the process of training doctors is unlike any other, and much of the costs are already borne by others. Hospitals that house medical residents and specialist trainees receive payments from the taxpayer, through Medicare. Patients give of their time and of their bodies in our nation's teaching hospitals so that doctors in training can become skilled practitioners.

We need a better way of paying for medical training, to address the loom- 16 ing shortage of primary care doctors, and to better match the costs of specialty training to the income it delivers. Taking the counterintuitive step of making medical education free, while charging those doctors who want to gain specialty training, is a straightforward way of achieving both goals.

⊘ REVIEW EXERCISE 2

1. What proposal argument do Bach and Kocher make in "Why Medical School Should Be Free"?

2. Where do the writers argue by analogy? What does the analogy compare? Is the analogy valid? Is it convincing?

3. Where do the writers make an ethical argument?

4. Where do the writers make causal arguments? What causes and effects do they identify?

5. How does each strategy contribute to the overall effectiveness of the argument?

6

Debates, Casebooks, and Classic Arguments

Should "Study Drugs" Be Banned?

Many researchers over the past decade have examined the use of so-called study drugs on college campuses. For example, a 2009 National Survey on Drug Use and Health indicated that college students used Adderall at twice the rate of eighteen- to twenty-two-year olds who did not attend college. According to a 2009 survey in the *Journal of Attention Deficit Disorders*, 56% of students with legitimate attention deficit hyperactivity disorder (ADHD) prescriptions reported having been asked to give or sell their medication to other students. The anecdotal evidence is disturbing as well. In "A Ban on Brain-Boosting Drugs Is Not the Answer" (p. 640), Matt Lamkin describes two student journalists who walk into the University of Wisconsin library, tap a random undergraduate on the shoulder, and are "connected with an Adderall supply in less than a minute." In some cases, people even fake the symptoms of ADHD to obtain a prescription.

Why are such drugs so popular? What are their dangers? What should be done to regulate them? The first two questions have relatively simple answers; the last question, however, is more difficult. Drugs like Ritalin and Adderall can help students focus and improve concentration. Essentially, these medications function as performance-enhancing steroids for the brain. However, their use also has downsides. When taken by healthy people, drugs like Adderall can cause insomnia, high blood pressure, and paranoia as well as other problems. Moreover, in most states, distributing or using another person's prescription is a felony. In addition, study drugs raise ethical issues along with legal questions: some colleges, for example, view the use of these medications as a form of academic cheating. On the other hand, how are they different from stimulants such as caffeine, energy drinks, or products like Five-Hour Energy? And, if so-called study drugs really improve cognitive functioning, might it make more sense to *encourage* their use, as several scientists proposed in a 2008 issue of the prestigious journal *Nature*?

The popularity of study drugs suggests an irony, too: substance abuse on college campuses is usually associated with escapism and recreation.

For comprehension quizzes,
see bedfordstmartins.com/practicalargument.

What does it say about contemporary students—and about our society as a whole—that their new drug of choice enhances cognitive functions rather than numbs them? The two writers whose essays appear in this debate try to answer such questions. David Alpert sees the use of study drugs as an "unmistakable wrong" and argues that colleges must discourage them through honor codes. Matt Lamkin agrees that these drugs are a problem but contends that the proper way to handle them is not to ban them outright but to reaffirm the value of an education and to discourage students from seeing the college experience as a "competition for credentials."

This article is from the January 20, 2012, edition of *USA Today College*.

CHANGE HONOR CODES TO INCLUDE ABUSE OF NONPRESCRIPTION DRUGS

DAVID ALPERT

1 Universities should use their respective honor codes to prohibit the abuse of performance-enhancing drugs in order to stem a growing epidemic among college students.

2 Last September, the Duke University Office of Student Conduct amended the Academic Integrity Policy to ban the abuse of academic performance-enhancing drugs without a prescription. The use of drugs like Adderall, Ritalin, Concerta, and others intended for sufferers of ADD and ADHD without a proper prescription is already against the law—so, why would Duke altering its honor code make any sort of impact on the abuse of these study drugs? And why should other universities follow suit?

3 To answer this question, and refute any possible counter-arguments, it's important to consider honor systems in greater detail. While honor codes vary broadly across institutions of higher education, there are some basic central tenets shared across the board:

4 Honor systems are aspirational, seeking to foster a community of trust and instill individuals with recognized institutional values—they do this mainly by prohibiting lying, cheating, and stealing. They rely on elected or appointed students to enforce honor systems.

5 Honor codes and systems also differ significantly from the legal system.

6 Between speeding, underage drinking, and the recreational use of drugs like marijuana, many college-aged students show varying degrees of respect for the law. While

> "Many college-aged students show varying degrees of respect for the law."

these behaviors may be as commonplace as cheating on a test or plagiarizing a paper, they don't come with the same stain on a student's character. This is in part because students were born into a legal system, while they chose to enter into an institution with an honor system. This subtle distinction is an important one, as the college experience is prone to allow, if not spark, some behavioral and intellectual rebellion against a student's origins.

These characteristics of honor systems make them a useful first step 7 towards combating the illegal usage of prescription drugs. The use of these drugs without a proper prescription unequivocally constitutes cheating. While Adderall and Ritalin abusers often see their use as a "victimless crime," there are, in fact, many victims, and they are all around the abuser. The abuser's inflated grades unfairly skew grading curves and grade point averages. Those who abstain from taking the drugs may end up with lesser grades, which in turn hurt their chances of securing everything from graduate school acceptances to internships and post-grad employment.

Student enforcement of honor systems will push the issue of prescription drug abuse from its current moral grey area to a more unmistakable wrong. Without overstating the importance of honor codes, or the amount of purchase they hold on a college campus, there is a stigma that accompanies violating a shared honor code that does not always come with breaking the law.

An honor code provision also seems to be the best way to limit the use 9 of these drugs by students who are "legally abusing" them; procuring prescriptions by either faking the symptoms of ADD/ADHD or seeking out physicians with a known proclivity for dishing out the meds. While technically these students would not be in violation of the honor code ban, they may still feel certain pressures to better align their behaviors with the values of their university.

Some argue that the stories of prescription study aid abuse are overblown 10 and sensationalized. However, research from the University of Kentucky suggests that 34% of all undergrads there have used study aids illegally, and that percentage is almost doubled among upperclassmen.

Others may counter that the honor code is not the best avenue through 11 which to attack this problem. However, it seems to be the most balanced approach. Unlike more extreme measures, like random drug testing, an honor code ban on the abuse of these drugs is feasible, because it is neither a significant financial drain, nor does it stir any privacy concerns. More moderate policy choices by a university administration, such as issuing some sort of advisory to students and families about the dangers and legalities of the drugs, would also be less costly, but they would not go far enough in instilling the cultural change in institutional values so critical to the re-leveling of the academic playing field. And until other universities follow Duke's lead by recognizing their moral responsibility to take charge of this issue, the stain of suspicion could blemish all our records.

⊜ READING ARGUMENTS

1. Alpert points out that honor codes "differ significantly from the legal system" (para. 5). How are such codes different from laws? Why is this ethical distinction important to Alpert's argument?

2. According to Alpert, those who use study drugs see their use as a "victimless crime" (7). Does he agree with them? Do you? Why or why not?

3. In what sense is Alpert's essay a causal argument?

4. Where does Alpert address arguments against his position? How effectively does he present and refute them?

This essay is from the *Chronicle of Higher Education*. It was published on February 27, 2011.

A BAN ON BRAIN-BOOSTING DRUGS IS NOT THE ANSWER

MATT LAMKIN

The Wisconsin Center for Investigative Journalism recently described an 1 experiment in which two student journalists at the University of Wisconsin at Madison tested how quickly they could "score" Adderall—a prescription stimulant designed to treat attention-deficit disorders but often used by healthy students as a study aid. The reporters walked into a campus library, tapped a studying stranger on the shoulder, and were connected to an Adderall supply in less than one minute.

> "The reporters . . . were connected to an Adderall supply in less than one minute."

While rates of drinking among college students have been relatively steady 2 in recent years, nontherapeutic use of prescription drugs has soared—now second only to marijuana as a form of illicit drug use. Research by Alan D. DeSantis, a professor of communication at the University of Kentucky who has studied ADHD-stimulant use in fraternities, suggests that 34 percent of the university's undergraduates have used stimulants like Ritalin and Adderall as study aids. According to DeSantis, that number rises the longer students are in college, and nearly 60 percent of Kentucky's juniors and seniors have used "neuroenhancers."

Concerned observers of this trend, most notably at Britain's Academy of 3 Medical Sciences, have characterized the use of "study drugs" as a form of cheating, akin to the use of steroids in sports. Having diagnosed the problem as an issue of unfair competition, the academy has called on universities to consider banning the use of cognition-enhancing drugs by healthy students. This past October, Wesleyan University did just that, amending its student code of conduct to recognize "misuse" of prescription drugs as a violation of the college's prohibition against receiving "improper assistance" in completing academic work.

The sense that this practice qualifies as "cheating" reflects an intuitive dis- 4 comfort with healthy students' using drugs to improve their academic performance. But the instinct to view the problem as a form of unfair competition is itself a manifestation of the debased educational culture that has rendered these drugs so attractive to students. Simply calling the use of study drugs "unfair" tells us nothing about why colleges should ban them. If such drugs really do improve academic performance among healthy students (and the evidence is scant), shouldn't colleges put them in the drinking water instead? After all, it would be unfair to permit wealthy students to use them if less privileged students can't afford them.

If our key concern is fairness, making study drugs available to all students 5 could actually do more to promote that goal than banning them. Of course, to the extent that such drugs pose health risks, it's prudent to restrict their use. But that seems like an argument about safety, not fairness. While safety is a valid concern, it is one that might be overcome by better drug design. If we are still troubled by the idea of a study drug that is safe and universally available, we have to look for other sources of our discomfort.

The word "cheating" has another meaning, one that has nothing to do 6 with competition. When someone has achieved an end through improper means, we might say that person has "cheated herself" out of whatever rewards are inherent in the proper means. The use of study drugs by healthy students could corrode valuable practices that education has traditionally fostered. If, for example, students use such drugs to mitigate the consequences of procrastination, they may fail to develop mental discipline and time-management skills.

On the other hand, Ritalin might enable a student to engage more deeply 7 in college and to more fully experience its internal goods—goods she might be denied without that assistance. The distinction suggests that a blanket policy, whether of prohibition or universal access, is unlikely to be effective.

Instead, colleges need to encourage students to engage in the practice of 8 education rather than to seek shortcuts. Instead of ferreting out and punishing students, universities should focus on restoring a culture of deep engagement in education, rather than just competition for credentials.

Students take cues about what to value—what types of achievements and 9 undertakings are worthwhile, which elements of character are important, which modes of behavior are honorable—from the cultures of their colleges and in the wider society. We live in a society that exalts competition and its monetary rewards. High-school students compete for college admissions.

College students compete for grades, then for jobs. Employees compete for promotions, and their employers compete for market share. Within that context, "just saying no" to drugs that might confer a competitive edge can start to look crazy—or at best apathetic.

If our goal is to promote students' engagement in education, we should 10 realign student incentives with the appreciation of education's internal benefits, so that students are not rewarded for taking shortcuts. In drug-policy terms, this is a "demand reduction" strategy that works by draining study drugs of their value.

It is not an undertaking that can be accomplished in one fell swoop. 11 Rather, it requires a series of smaller steps that gradually reshape the character of higher education over time—by, for example, de-emphasizing standardized-test scores in admissions decisions in favor of criteria that reflect deeper forms of student engagement, like essay writing and participation in internships, clinics, practicum courses, and extracurriculars. Adderall may raise test scores, but it is unlikely to help students develop interesting résumés.

If universities instead choose to enact blanket prohibitions on the use of 12 study drugs by healthy students, it would be more sensible to enforce such a policy through honor codes than through measures such as urine testing, as the Academy of Medical Sciences has proposed. Unlike a policing approach, honor codes ask students to internalize values that are important to education and to character in general. Although students who violate honor codes face sanctions, the primary aim is not to deter improper conduct with threats but to persuade students that to breach the code is to betray themselves. If colleges believe that enhancing cognition with drugs deprives students of the true value of education, they must encourage students to adopt that value as their own.

⊙READING ARGUMENTS

1. What purpose do Lamkin's first two paragraphs serve?

2. In part, Lamkin's essay is a response to researchers who have compared the use of study drugs to "the use of steroids in sports" (para. 3). Is this a valid analogy? Explain.

3. Lamkin devotes several paragraphs to defining the word *cheating*. How does he use this definition to make his case against banning study drugs?

4. In what sense is this essay a proposal argument? What does Lamkin propose? How realistic are his proposals?

⊘ AT ISSUE: SHOULD "STUDY DRUGS" BE BANNED?

1. In making their arguments, both Alpert and Lamkin try to establish that study drugs are a legitimate problem. Why do they need to do this? How does each writer establish this premise? Which writer do you think makes the more convincing case? Why?

2. Both Alpert and Lamkin want to reduce the abuse of study drugs. In what respects are both of their essays ethical arguments?

3. Lamkin writes, "If such drugs really do improve academic performance among healthy students (and the evidence is scant), shouldn't colleges put them in the drinking water instead?" (para. 4). Does this seemingly frivolous question make a serious point? If so, what is this point?

⊘ WRITING ARGUMENTS: SHOULD "STUDY DRUGS" BE BANNED?

Both Alpert and Lamkin suggest that cultural change is necessary to reduce the use of study drugs. However, Alpert focuses on individual students and honor codes, while Lamkin focuses on academic culture and a "society that exalts competition and its monetary rewards" (para. 9). What do you think are the causes of study-drug abuse? Which writer's analysis seems more accurate? Do you see this problem as an issue of individual responsibility or as a symptom of a society that gives the wrong "cues" about the value of an education? Write an essay that presents your position on this issue.

CHAPTER 19

Should Controversial Sports Mascots Be Replaced?

As Mark Hyman notes in "So Sioux Me" (p. 648), the controversy over sports mascots that some perceive as offensive is not new. The National Congress of American Indians began a campaign against these stereotypes in 1968—encouraged by the civil rights era's increasing emphasis on tolerance, equality, and diversity. In the late 1960s, Dartmouth College became one of the first colleges to drop its Indian mascot. The school was responding to its Native American undergraduates, who found the war-paint-and-feathers imagery offensive, and to the Dartmouth board of trustees, who considered this symbolism "inconsistent with the present institutional and academic objectives of the college." Not everyone supported that view, however. For some Dartmouth faculty, undergraduates, and alumni, the school's disavowal of its Indian mascot undermined tradition and represented a drift toward hypersensitive identity politics. Their resistance led to a "Bring Back the Indian" campaign at Dartmouth in the 1970s and 1980s.

Since that time, many college athletic programs and sports organizations have dropped their Native American mascots. Others have not, including professional teams such as the Atlanta Braves, the Cleveland Indians, and the Washington Redskins. The broad contours of the debate have remained the same throughout the decades. For their detractors, these mascots evoke offensive, dehumanizing ethnic stereotypes and the specter of historical oppression. Viewed in this light, the Cleveland Indians' red-faced "Chief Wahoo" logo insults Indian people the "same way that little black Sambo offended African Americans," according to the National Coalition on Racism in Sports and Media. In contrast, supporters of these mascots argue that they capture the collective spirit of a college community, support sports traditions, and even honor the heritage of Native Americans. According to them, at the college and professional levels, team logos are integral to regional sports identities as well as to the giant merchandizing industry.

The two writers in the debate that follows explore the larger issues of this issue. Jack Shakely acknowledges that the subject may seem "trivial" on the surface, but he argues that these stereotypes inflict real damage on human dignity. For Mark Hyman, the controversy around Indian mascots suggests an attack on common sense—and the excesses of the hypersensitive "PC police."

This essay was published in the *Los Angeles Times* on August 25, 2011.

INDIAN MASCOTS—YOU'RE OUT

JACK SHAKELY

I got my first lesson in Indians portrayed as sports team mascots in the early 1950s when my father took me to a Cleveland Indians–New York Yankees game. Dad gave me money to buy a baseball cap, and I was conflicted. I loved the Yankees, primarily because fellow Oklahoman Mickey Mantle had just come up and was being touted as rookie of the year. But being mixed-blood Muscogee/Creek, I felt a (misplaced) loyalty to the Indians. So I bought the Cleveland cap with the famous Chief Wahoo logo on it. 1

When we got back to Oklahoma, my mother took one look at the cap with its leering, big-nosed, buck-toothed redskin caricature just above the brim, jerked it off my head, and threw it in the trash. She had been fighting against Indian stereotypes all her life, and I had just worn one home. I was only 10 years old, but the look of betrayal in my Creek mother's eyes is seared in my memory forever. 2

So maybe I shouldn't have been surprised when half a century later, a *Los Angeles Times* editorial about legislators in North Dakota struggling over whether the University of North Dakota should be forced to change its team name and mascot from the Fighting Sioux provoked such a strong reaction. It was an irritant, like a long-forgotten piece of shrapnel working its way to the surface. 3

Most stories about sports teams and their ethnic mascots are treated like tempests in a teacup. The *Times'* editorial writer, however, while noting that the solons probably had better things to do, understood the sensitivity and pain that can accompany such a seemingly trivial subject. It is a small matter, perhaps, but far from trivial. 4

> "It is a small matter, perhaps, but far from trivial."

Many of the fights over team names and mascots cover familiar territory. Usually the team name in question has been around so long as to lose a good bit of its meaning. The University of Illinois' Fighting Illini, for example, refers 5 to an Indian nation, but now that its Chief Illiniwek mascot has been abandoned, few people make the connection. Nor do they think twice about what the Atlanta Braves or Edmonton Eskimos or Florida State Seminoles represent other than sports franchises. But that doesn't necessarily make the brands benign. And the irony that the football team in our nation's capital is called the Redskins is not lost on a single Native American.

The controversy over changing ethnocentric mascot names is not a simple 6 matter of stodgy white alums holding on to college memories. Indians, too, are conflicted. In a 2002 study on the subject, *Sports Illustrated* reported that 84% of Native Americans polled had no problem with Indian team names or mascots. Although the methods used by the magazine to reach these figures were later criticized, that misses the point. If 16% of a population finds something offensive, that should be enough to signal deep concern. There are many things in this country that are subject to majority rule; dignity and respect are not among them.

And it is dignity and respect we are talking about. Since the creation of the 7 National Coalition on Racism in Sports and Media in 1991, that group of Native American organizations has been protesting negative portrayals of Indians, hammering away at what's behind our discomfort with Indian sports mascots. Many of these mascots—maybe most of them—act like fools or savage cutthroats.

When I went to an Atlanta Braves game in the 1970s, the Braves name 8 wasn't the biggest problem. It was that cringe-worthy Chief Noc-A-Homa who came stomping and war-dancing his way out of a tepee in center field every time the Braves hit a home run that got to me. He was dressed in a Plains Indian chief's eagle bonnet and acted like a village idiot. To their credit, the Braves retired Chief Noc-A-Homa and his girlfriend Princess Win-A-Lot in 1983, amid assertions by the Braves' home office that the protesters were over-dramatizing the issue.

Few people complain about Florida State University calling itself the Sem- 9 inoles. But its war-painted and lance-threatening mascot Chief Osceola is intended to be menacing, and that's the take-away many children will have. Such casual stereotyping can breed callousness. In the "only good Indian" category, in 1999 the *New York Post* entitled an editorial about the pending New York–Cleveland baseball playoffs, "Take the Tribe and Scalp 'Em."

It isn't easy or inexpensive to remove ethnic and racial stereotypes from 10 college and professional sports. When Stanford University changed from the Indians to the Cardinals in 1972, recriminations were bitter. Richard Lyman, a friend of mine, was president of Stanford at the time. He said the university lost millions of alumni dollars in the short run, but it was the right thing to do.

In 21st-century America, to name a sports team after an African American, 11 Asian, or any other ethnic group is unthinkable. So why are Native Americans still fair game? As benign as monikers like Fighting Sioux and Redskins or mascots like Chief Osceola may seem, they should take their place with the

Pekin, Ill., Chinks and the Atlanta Black Crackers in the dust bin of history. It is the right thing to do.

⊙READING ARGUMENTS

1. How does Shakely incorporate personal narrative and anecdotal evidence into his argument? Do you find this kind of material convincing? Explain.

2. What point does Shakely make in his fourth paragraph? How is this point related to his thesis?

3. In what sense is this essay an ethical argument?

4. In paragraph 6, Shakely cites a poll that indicated that 84% of Native Americans "had no problem with Indian team names or mascots." How does he use this evidence to reinforce his own position? How might this evidence also support a counterargument?

5. Where does Shakely make a causal argument? Where does he argue by analogy?

This article appeared in the *American Spectator Online* on November 23, 2009.

SO SIOUX ME

MARK HYMAN

A North Dakota judge will hear arguments next month in a case of political 1 correctness that has embroiled the state university for a number of years.

In 2005, the National Collegiate Athletic Association announced a complete 2 ban on hosting post-season competition by 18 colleges that were using Indian mascots, logos, or nicknames. The ban was to become effective in February 2006.

The NCAA made an assumption, 3 jumped to a conclusion, and adopted the politically correct viewpoint that using Indian heritage in such a manner was "hostile and abusive." The problem, it appears, is that no one bothered to check with the assumed aggrieved parties to determine if they were truly offended.

> "No one bothered to check with the assumed aggrieved parties to determine if they were truly offended."

Since the original announcement, the NCAA's political correctness offensive encountered the stiff defense of several universities and common sense.

The college sports governing body backed off its strident and absolute 4 demand after learning that some Native American groups endorsed use of their tribal names by their adoptive schools. The NCAA relented and gave the go-ahead for Florida State, the University of Utah, and Central Michigan University to continue using Seminole, Ute, and Chippewa, respectively, without the risk of facing the post-season ban.

Sensitivity toward the use of Native American symbols goes back a few 5 decades. In the early 1970s, Stanford University and Dartmouth College jettisoned the nickname "Indians." Stanford chose as its replacement mascot the innocuous color, Cardinal. Dartmouth went so far as to select a dark shade of green formally known as PMS 349 and frequently referred to as Dartmouth Green as its official school color to complement its nickname of the Big Green.

As an aside, the legitimacy of the Ivy League school's color could be called 6 into question. Would crayon-maker Crayola give a legal release to Dartmouth to poach Forest Green and claim the color as its own?

After more than 35 years, the Big Green nickname remains wildly unpop- 7 ular and the college's student body has instead given unofficial approval to an animated beer keg as the school mascot. Now here is a healthy alternative to a school's politically incorrect use of a Native American mascot—glorification of alcohol.

What is not yet known is how the NCAA will measure Native American 8 approval or displeasure of a school's use of a generic nickname such as Indian, Redman, or Brave in contrast to a more specific tribal name such as Seminole. Bradley University and the University of North Carolina–Pembroke both use the nickname "Brave," yet Bradley is on the NCAA banned list and UNC–Pembroke got a free pass. San Diego State was given NCAA okay for that school's use of Aztec for still unexplained reasons. Perhaps it is because Aztec represents not just an Indian tribe but is instead an entire civilization.

The NCAA signaled moral outrage at the University of North Dakota's 9 Fighting Sioux nickname. Yet the association has remained silent on the fact that the school is (as are both the states of North and South Dakota) named after the Dakota tribe.

The NCAA's battle with UND has been raging for more than four years. 10 Criticizing the Fighting Sioux nickname as racist, offensive, and derogatory have been groups such as the school's faculty Senate and the state Board of Higher Education. They are seemingly undeterred by one significant group that wants the university to retain the nickname and logo. That is the Spirit Lake Sioux tribe, the nearby tribe from whom the school nickname is derived. The most absurd aspect of this politically correct ruckus is that non-native Americans are lecturing Native Americans on what should offend them. A hearing on the matter is scheduled in a county courtroom in early December.

Then there is the case of South Dakota's Huron College. The school was   11
purchased in 2001 by the Cheyenne River Sioux Tribe, and was renamed
Si Tanka University, another American Indian name. The school closed its
doors in early 2005 due to financial difficulties. Rumors have been rampant
that the school may eventually be sold to a group anxious to reopen the college
under its former name, Huron, which is another tribal name. Where to draw
the line? Let's see: Native American school name—good; Native American
school nickname—bad.

The imbroglio over Indian names is not limited to college sports. A   12
recent decision by the U.S. Supreme Court appears to have finally closed the
door on a 17-year-old lawsuit against the National Football League's Washington Redskins for that team's logo. It was a New Mexico man who originally
claimed the Redskins mascot and logo "is damaging to Native American peoples." However, according to *Playboy* magazine, 90 percent of Native Americans who were polled responded they were not offended by the Redskins
mascot. Is disapproval by a single individual sufficient to terminate the use of
a Native American symbol or does majority rule? More importantly, one
could argue it has been this year's lackluster play and dismal won-loss record
by the Redskins that is more damaging to its fan base than any nickname the
team could use.

Perhaps a more comprehensive poll could be taken of American Indian   13
attitudes and views on the use of Indian names. The NCAA could commission
the Quinnipiac University Polling Institute to complete the task although an
apparent conflict of interest exists since the school is named after a Connecticut area tribe.

It is entirely possible that before long we will hear from other interested
parties who will protest the use of school mascots and nicknames they find
offensive. Will the People for the Ethical Treatment of Animals protest the use
of Wildcats at the University of Kentucky? How do Satan worshippers feel
about the Duke University Blue Devils? It may not be surprising if the
National Education Association were to announce its opposition to Virginia
Military Institute's misspelling of "cadets" as Keydets. Finally, could descendants of the sixth century B.C. Peloponnesians criticize Michigan State's use
of Spartan?

Perhaps it is time for the PC police to take a long, deep breath and relax   15
before contemplating any further action. Maybe all parties could sit down and
calmly discuss the matter during a lunchtime meeting. I suggest a menu of
German bologna and Swiss cheese on Jewish rye, with a helping of Amish sau-
erkraut, a slice of kosher pickle, a Greek salad with Italian dressing on the side,
followed by a Danish pastry for dessert with a hot cup of Colombian coffee.
After all, everyone should be reasonable about this and avoid using any racial,
ethnic, or national origin in a manner that any single person might decide is
offensive and derogatory.

⊙ READING ARGUMENTS

1. Where does Hyman use inductive reasoning? Why do you think he uses inductive as opposed to deductive reasoning here?

2. Hyman accuses the NCAA of engaging in a logical fallacy. To what error in reasoning does he refer? How does his response to this fallacy help him to structure his essay?

3. In paragraph 14, Hyman writes, "It is entirely possible that before long we will hear from other interested parties who will protest the use of school mascots and nicknames they find offensive." He then provides hypothetical examples. Do you find these examples convincing? Is Hyman committing the **slippery-slope** fallacy? Why or why not?

4. Evaluate the essay's final paragraph. What is Hyman's tone here? Given his subject matter and audience, is this tone appropriate? Explain.

⊙ AT ISSUE: SHOULD CONTROVERSIAL SPORTS MASCOTS BE REPLACED?

1. Both Shakely and Hyman refer to the principle of "majority rule," but they differ about how it should be applied in the debate over sports mascots. Summarize each writer's position on this principle. Which seems more persuasive? Why?

2. Hyman makes several references to "political correctness" in his essay; he also abbreviates it in the expression "PC police" (para. 15). What does *political correctness* mean? What connotations does it have? Do you think political correctness is a problem, as Hyman implies it is? Explain.

3. According to Shakely, "casual stereotyping can breed callousness" (9). What do you think he means by this, particularly in light of his use of the adjective "casual"? Do you agree that "casual stereotyping" leads to "callousness," or do you think it is essentially harmless? Explain.

⊙ WRITING ARGUMENTS: SHOULD CONTROVERSIAL MASCOTS BE REPLACED?

Write an essay that takes a position on the issue of controversial sports mascots. Should they be replaced at the professional, college, or high school levels?

Should the Names of Sex Offenders Continue to Be Made Public?

Both of the essays that follow refer to the 1994 sexual assault and murder of a seven-year-old New Jersey girl, Megan Kanka, a case that transcended the private grief of one family and led to public outrage. The murderer had been convicted twice previously for sexually assaulting a child, but local residents were unaware of his past when he moved into their neighborhood. Soon after the crime, New Jersey—and then other states—passed laws requiring that local communities be notified when convicted sexual offenders move to the area. These notification laws vary by state. However, the Internet has provided a broad, convenient platform for collecting this information, both locally and nationally. The United States Department of Justice now maintains a national sex-offender Web site, and many similar sites allow users to locate the photographs, addresses, and conviction records of sex offenders.

Although online databases make information easily available, the practice of community notification predates the use of technology. For example, before Megan's Law, Oregon enacted legislation that mandated placing highly visible signs in the windows of homes occupied by convicted sex offenders. In 1992, Louisiana passed a so-called Scarlet Letter Law, which required sex offenders to send postcards to their neighbors, listing their names, their crimes, and their addresses. The allusion to Nathaniel Hawthorne's *The Scarlet Letter* is revealing: set in seventeenth-century Puritan New England, Hawthorne's 1850 novel focuses on the public shaming of its protagonist. The allusion also evokes some of the potential problems with public notification laws. Certainly the information can be useful, especially in the case of so-called tier-three sex offenders, who pose a genuine risk of repeating their crimes. Some critics, however, believe that these laws can also be harmful. According to the American Civil Liberties Union, harsh sex-offender restrictions and the stigma of public registries constitute an unfair punishment, especially for low-risk, tier-one offenders. These people can lose their jobs or be forbidden to see their own children—consequences that are disproportionate to their crimes and to the threat they pose to the public. Moreover, information on public registries may be inaccurate and out-of-date.

This is a highly emotional issue, as is evident in the laws named after specific victims: "Megan's Law," "the Adam Walsh Act," the "Dru Sjodin National Sex Offender Public Website." As *Philadelphia Magazine* editor Sandy Hingston once asked, "What legislator would vote against a dead child?" The writers in this debate weigh the value of public information and public safety against the potential overreach of—and outright harm done by—sex-offender laws. For the editors of the *Economist* (below), "sensible sex laws are better than vengeful ones." For Rick Schneider, publisher and editor of the *Eastern Arizona Courier* (p. 657), "It's the duty of this newspaper to alert the community about the whereabouts of high-risk sex offenders."

This editorial is from the August 6, 2009, edition of the *Economist*.

AMERICA'S UNJUST SEX LAWS

THE ECONOMIST

1   It is an oft-told story, but it does not get any less horrific on repetition. Fifteen years ago, a pedophile enticed seven-year-old Megan Kanka into his home in New Jersey by offering to show her a puppy. He then raped her, killed her, and dumped her body in a nearby park. The murderer, who had recently moved into the house across the street from his victim, had twice before been convicted of sexually assaulting a child. Yet Megan's parents had no idea of this. Had they known he was a sex offender, they would have told their daughter to stay away from him.

2   In their grief, the parents started a petition, demanding that families should be told if a sexual predator moves nearby. Hundreds of thousands signed it. In no time at all, lawmakers in New Jersey granted their wish. And before long, "Megan's laws" had spread to every American state.

3   America's sex-offender laws are the strictest of any rich democracy. Convicted rapists and child-molesters are given long prison sentences. When released, they are put on sex-offender registries. In most

> "America's sex-offender laws are the strictest of any rich democracy."

states this means that their names, photographs, and addresses are published online, so that fearful parents can check whether a child-molester lives nearby. Under the Adam Walsh Act of 2006, another law named after a murdered child, all states will soon be obliged to make their sex-offender registries public. Such rules are extremely popular. Most parents will support any law that promises to keep their children safe. Other countries are following America's example, either importing Megan's laws or increasing penalties: after two little girls were murdered by a school caretaker, Britain has imposed multiple conditions on who can visit schools.

Which makes it all the more important to ask whether America's approach 4 is the right one. In fact, its sex-offender laws have grown self-defeatingly harsh. They have been driven by a ratchet effect. Individual American politicians have great latitude to propose new laws. Stricter curbs on pedophiles win votes. And to sound severe, such curbs must be stronger than the laws in place, which in turn were proposed by politicians who wished to appear tough themselves. Few politicians dare to vote against such laws, because if they do, the attack ads practically write themselves.

A Whole Wyoming of Offenders

In all, 674,000 Americans are on sex-offender registries—more than the popu- 5 lation of Vermont, North Dakota, or Wyoming. The number keeps growing partly because in several states registration is for life and partly because registries are not confined to the sort of murderer who ensnared Megan Kanka. According to Human Rights Watch, at least five states require registration for people who visit prostitutes, 29 require it for consensual sex between young teenagers, and 32 require it for indecent exposure. Some prosecutors are now stretching the definition of "distributing child pornography" to include teens who text half-naked photos of themselves to their friends.

How dangerous are the people on the registries? A state review of one 6 sample in Georgia found that two-thirds of them posed little risk. For example, Janet Allison was found guilty of being "party to the crime of child molestation" because she let her 15-year-old daughter have sex with a boyfriend. The young couple later married. But Ms. Allison will spend the rest of her life publicly branded as a sex offender.

Several other countries have sex-offender registries, but these are typically 7 held by the police and are hard to view. In America it takes only seconds to find out about a sex offender: some states have a "click to print" icon on their websites so that concerned citizens can put up posters with the offender's mugshot on trees near his home. Small wonder most sex offenders report being harassed. A few have been murdered. Many are fired because someone at work has Googled them.

Registration is often just the start. Sometimes sex offenders are barred 8 from living near places where children congregate. In Georgia no sex offender may live or work within 1,000 feet (300 meters) of a school, church, park, skating rink, or swimming pool. In Miami an exclusion zone of 2,500 feet has helped create a camp of homeless offenders under a bridge.

Make the Punishment Fit the Crime

There are three main arguments for reform. First, it is unfair to impose harsh 9 penalties for small offenses. Perhaps a third of American teenagers have sex before they are legally allowed to, and a staggering number have shared revealing photographs with each other. This is unwise but hardly a reason for the law to ruin their lives. Second, America's sex laws often punish not only the offender but also his family. If a man who once slept with his 15-year-old girlfriend is barred forever from taking his own children to a playground, those children suffer.

Third, harsh laws often do little to protect the innocent. The police complain that having so many petty sex offenders on registries makes it hard to keep 10 track of the truly dangerous ones. Cash that might be spent on treating sex offenders—which sometimes works—is spent on huge indiscriminate registries. Public registers drive serious offenders underground, which makes them harder to track and more likely to reoffend. And registers give parents a false sense of security: most sex offenders are never even reported, let alone convicted.

It would not be hard to redesign America's sex laws. Instead of lumping all 11 sex offenders together on the same list for life, states should assess each person individually and include only real threats. Instead of posting everything on the Internet, names could be held by the police, who would share them only with those, such as a school, who need to know. Laws that bar sex offenders from living in so many places should be repealed, because there is no evidence that they protect anyone: a predator can always travel. The money that a repeal saves could help pay for monitoring compulsive molesters more intrusively—through ankle bracelets and the like.

In America it may take years to unpick this. However practical and just the 12 case for reform, it must overcome political cowardice, the tabloid media, and parents' understandable fears. Other countries, though, have no excuse for committing the same error. Sensible sex laws are better than vengeful ones.

⊕READING ARGUMENTS

1. According to the writers, why is it important to ask whether America's approach to sex-offender laws is the right one?

2. What causal connections do the writers identify between the political self-interest of public officials and America's "self-defeatingly harsh" sex laws (para. 4)?

3. In what respects is this essay an evaluation argument? In what respects is it a proposal argument?

4. In paragraph 6, the writers discuss the case of Janet Allison, who "will spend the rest of her life publicly branded as a sex offender."

What general point do they make by using this example? Is this example convincing in itself, or do the writers need to include more evidence?

5. The writers argue that these harsh sex-offender laws "often do little to protect the innocent" (10). How do they support this claim?

6. This editorial was published in the *Economist*, a British magazine that targets educated, politically knowledgeable readers. Does this information weaken (or strengthen) the writers' credibility, or is it irrelevant?

This essay appeared in the *Eastern Arizona Courier* on February 7, 2011.

PROTECT YOURSELF, FAMILY FROM SEX OFFENDERS

RICK SCHNEIDER

Arizona passed a community notification law in 1996 based on Megan's law,   1
named after a 7-year-old girl assaulted and murdered by a neighbor who was a recently released sex offender.

After a sex offender is released from prison or probation, the probation   2
agency or the Department of Corrections is required to enter that person's information into a state database that includes the person's risk assessment. This indicates the offender's potential for repeating the crime. Sex offenders are rated as to whether they're a low, medium, or high risk.

The state requires that the community notify schools, day cares, community   3
groups, surrounding homes, and prospective employers of high-risk offenders.

The *Courier* started releasing the names and addresses of high-risk and   4
intermediate-risk offenders in our community in about 2002. Shortly after that, a woman who lived with one of the offenders called. She was furious because she said he'd served his time and thought it was "horribly unfair" to identify where he lived.

I explained that we felt it was important to let the community know about   5
the sex offenders who live in our community so that parents can take proper precautions.

Sex offenders should not be harassed after they've served their sentences, but they need to be monitored because they often strike again.

> "They need to be monitored because they often strike again."   6

People feeling sorry for the sex offenders we identified in 2002 should   7
have heard the torment and grief expressed to me from two sexual assault
victims.

One woman explained how she'd been brutally beaten, knifed, and raped.   8
She said she now sleeps with a pistol under her pillow. Isn't it "horribly unfair"
that this woman must live in terror for the rest of her life?

Another person called and asked why a sex offender she knew about was   9
not included on the list of sexual predators in our community. I explained that
we publish only the names of those the state says pose a reasonable risk of
repeating their crimes.

One caller said a sex offender we listed was proven innocent and exoner-   10
ated of his crime. I said that was highly unlikely and that if the state had listed
a name incorrectly, that person would have called and threatened to sue the
newspaper for libel. I explained that he may have been exonerated of the particular crime she was referring to, but that he probably had been convicted of
other sex crimes.

She said this guy played with her children and was a close friend of the family.   11

I told her sex offenders are listed on the Arizona Department of Safety   12
Web site, www.azsexoffender.org. I said she needed to check it out for the safety
of her children. She did and learned that this creep was, indeed, a sexual predator. She called and thanked the *Courier* for making her aware of this. It was
only a matter of time before he'd have molested her children.

Courier assistant editor Jon Johnson recently reported that a sex offender   13
convicted in 2000 for sexual conduct with a minor was back in jail on new
sexual abuse charges.

Safford officers were dispatched to an apartment Jan. 26 in regard to an   14
assault. An elderly female victim said a Level 3 sex offender had climbed into
her bed while she was sleeping and sexually abused her.

The victim said the sex offender lived in another apartment in the com-   15
plex and frequently visited and watched television. She said he also walks her
dog for her and performs the same service for two other women in the complex. Sound familiar?

This is another example of how dangerous sex offenders gain their next   16
victims' trust before striking again. A typical comment after a sex offender is
caught is, "He seemed like the nicest guy in the world."

We will continue to publish names and pictures of high-risk sex offenders   17
in our community. I don't feel sorry for them because of the lifetime of hurt
and shame they caused their victims.

I get tired of reading about people who have been raped, mutilated, and   18
killed. When you get to the end of these stories, you usually learn the perpetrator was a repeat sex offender.

It's the duty of this newspaper to alert the community about the where-   19
abouts of high-risk sex offenders, and I'd never forgive myself if a child was
raped and killed because the child's parents didn't know that a sexual predator
lived near them.

⊜ READING ARGUMENTS

1. What is the purpose of the first three paragraphs of Schneider's essay? Why are they important to his overall argument?

2. What evidence does Schneider provide to support his position? Is it sufficient? Why or why not? What other kinds of evidence might he have included?

3. Where does Schneider address arguments that challenge his position? What is his attitude toward those who disagree with him? How effectively does he refute their claims?

4. In what sense does this essay present an ethical argument?

⊜ AT ISSUE: SHOULD THE NAMES OF SEX OFFENDERS CONTINUE TO BE MADE PUBLIC?

1. The subject of sexual offenders—especially those who commit crimes against children—lends itself to arguments with strong emotional appeals. Accordingly, both the writers in this debate use appeals to *pathos*, but they do so in different ways. How does each writer appeal to *pathos*? Which approach is more effective? Explain.

2. In the concluding paragraph of "America's Unjust Sex Laws," the writers assert that America must "overcome political cowardice." What do they mean by "political cowardice"? What role does it play in this debate? How does "political cowardice" affect other important issues in our society?

3. Schneider writes: "Sex offenders should not be harassed after they've served their sentences, but they need to be monitored because they often strike again" (para. 6). Do you think this distinction makes sense? What is Schneider's view of sex offenders who have "served their sentences" (6)? Do you agree with him?

⊜ WRITING ARGUMENTS: SHOULD THE NAMES OF SEX OFFENDERS CONTINUE TO BE MADE PUBLIC?

According to the editorial from the *Economist*, a significant majority of those listed on sex registries do not pose a significant risk to the community. Still, Rick Schneider argues for the public's right to know the names and addresses of high- and intermediate-risk offenders. Write an essay that explains your own views on this issue. How should we balance the public's "right to know" against the potential damage to individuals who are branded (some unjustly) as sex offenders?

DEBATE

Do the Benefits of Bottled Water Outweigh the Costs?

Three decades ago, the bottled-water industry barely existed in the United States. Although imports such as sparkling Perrier had snob appeal and cult status, most Americans saw water as a public utility that flowed from a tap. But sales of bottled water soared in the 1990s, and brands like Evian and Poland Spring became more than sources of hydration: they emerged as fashion accessories and markers of personal taste. As a 1996 *New York Times* article noted, "for every jogging Bill Clinton cradling a bottle of Mountain Valley, there is a Princess of Wales exiting her gym clutching Evian." In 2011, Americans bought 9 billion gallons of bottled water; every year, the $22 billion industry grows by over 5%.

This growth has its benefits. In a country that favors soft drinks and struggles with obesity, the popularity of a healthy, convenient, calorie-free alternative to sugary soda is a good thing. But critics of bottled water have become increasingly vocal. They cite the environmental effects of manufacturing and disposing of billions of plastic containers. They note the expense of bottled water compared to its low-cost alternative from the tap. They also argue that bottled water's marketing and advertising obscure the reality that tap water is generally held to higher health and safety standards than its bottled counterpart. These critics are active as well as vocal: numerous U.S. colleges, including Washington University and the University of Vermont, now ban the sale of plastic bottles of water on their campuses. Of course, the bottled-water industry has responded with its own campaign, which seeks to correct (in the words of the International Bottled Water Association) "misinformation" and the "highly emotional and incorrect" claims of critics.

The two writers in this debate have different perspectives on the issue. Business and technology writer Tom Standage sees the popularity of

e For comprehension quizzes,
see bedfordstmartins.com/practicalargument.

bottled water as a "fashionable" but "illogical" phenomenon; he views the issue in a global context, pointing out that "more than one billion people lack reliable access to safe drinking water." For International Bottled Water Association representative Thomas J. Lauria, misguided restrictions on bottled water do nothing to improve the environment or the health of consumers.

This essay appeared in the *New York Times* on August 1, 2005.

BAD TO THE LAST DROP

TOM STANDAGE

It's summertime, and odds are that at some point during your day you'll reach 1 for a nice cold bottle of water. But before you do, you might want to consider the results of an experiment I conducted with some friends one summer evening last year. On the table were 10 bottles of water, several rows of glasses, and some paper for recording our impressions. We were to evaluate samples from each bottle for appearance, odor, flavor, mouth, feel, and aftertaste—and our aim was to identify the interloper among the famous names. One of our bottles had been filled from the tap. Would we spot it?

We worked our way through the samples, writing scores for each one. 2 None of us could detect any odor, even when swilling water around in large wine glasses, but other differences between the waters were instantly apparent. Between sips, we cleansed our palates with wine. (It seemed only fair, since water serves the same function at a wine tasting.)

The variation between waters was wide, yet the water from the tap did not 3 stand out: only one of us correctly identified it. This simple experiment seemed to confirm that most people cannot tell the difference between tap water and bottled water. Yet they buy it anyway—and in enormous quantities.

In 2004, Americans, on average, drank 24 gallons of bottled water, making 4 it second only to carbonated soft drinks in popularity. Furthermore, consumption of bottled water is growing more quickly than that of soft drinks and has more than doubled in the past decade. This year, Americans will spend around $9.8 billion on bottled water, according to the Beverage Marketing Corporation.

Ounce for ounce, it costs more than gasoline, even at today's high gasoline 5 prices; depending on the brand, it costs 250 to 10,000 times more than tap water. Globally, bottled water is now a $46 billion industry. Why has it become so popular?

It cannot be the taste, since most people cannot tell the difference in a 6 blind tasting. Much bottled water is, in any case, derived from municipal water supplies, though it is sometimes filtered or has additional minerals added to it.

Nor is there any health or nutritional benefit to drinking bottled water over tap water. In one study, published in the *Archives of Family Medicine*, researchers compared bottled water with tap water from Cleveland and found that nearly a quarter of the samples of bottled water had significantly higher levels of bacteria. The scientists concluded that "use of bottled water on the assumption of purity can be misguided." Another study carried out at the University of Geneva found that bottled water was no better from a nutritional point of view than ordinary tap water.

Admittedly, both kinds of water suffer from occasional contamination problems, but tap water is more stringently monitored and tightly regulated than bottled water. New York City tap water, for example, was tested 430,600 times during 2004 alone.

What of the idea that drinking bottled water allows you to avoid the chemicals that are sometimes added to tap water? Alas, some bottled waters contain the same chemicals anyway—and they are, in any case, unavoidable.

Researchers at the University of Texas found that showers and dishwashers liberate trace amounts of chemicals from municipal water supplies into the air. Squirting hot water through a nozzle, to produce a fine spray, increases the surface area of water in contact with the air, liberating dissolved substances in a process known as "stripping." So if you want to avoid those chemicals for some reason, drinking bottled water is not enough. You will also have to wear a gas mask in the shower and when unloading the dishwasher.

Bottled water is undeniably more fashionable and portable than tap water. The practice of carrying a small bottle, pioneered by supermodels, has become commonplace. But despite its association with purity and cleanliness, bottled water is bad for the environment. It is shipped at vast expense from one part of the world to another, is then kept refrigerated before sale, and causes huge numbers of plastic bottles to go into landfills.

Of course, tap water is not so abundant in the developing world. And that is ultimately why I find the illogical enthusiasm for bottled water not simply peculiar but distasteful. For those of us in the developed world, safe water is now so abundant that we can afford to shun the tap water under our noses and drink bottled water instead: our choice of water has become a lifestyle option. For many people in the developing world, however, access to water remains a matter of life or death.

> "Our choice of water has become a lifestyle option."

More than 2.6 billion people, or more than 40 percent of the world's population, lack basic sanitation, and more than one billion people lack reliable access to safe drinking water. The World Health Organization estimates that 80 percent of all illness in the world is due to water-borne diseases, and that at any given time, around half of the people in the developing world are suffering from diseases associated with inadequate water or sanitation, which kill around five million people a year.

Widespread illness also makes countries less productive, more depen- 14 dent on outside aid, and less able to lift themselves out of poverty. One of the main reasons girls do not go to school in many parts of the developing world is that they have to spend so much time fetching water from distant wells.

Clean water could be provided to everyone on earth for an outlay of 15 $1.7 billion a year beyond current spending on water projects, according to the International Water Management Institute. Improving sanitation, which is just as important, would cost a further $9.3 billion per year. This is less than a quarter of global annual spending on bottled water.

I have no objections to people drinking bottled water in the developing 16 world; it is often the only safe supply. But it would surely be better if they had access to safe tap water instead. The logical response, for those of us in the developed world, is to stop spending money on bottled water and to give the money to water charities.

If you don't believe me about the taste, then set up a tasting, and see if you 17 really can tell the difference. A water tasting is fun, and you may be surprised by the results. There is no danger of a hangover. But you may well conclude, as I have, that bottled water has an unacceptably bitter taste.

⊖ READING ARGUMENTS

1. In paragraphs 1–5, Standage presents a long introduction about an experiment that he conducted. How does this introduction prepare readers for his thesis?

2. In your own words, summarize the opposing arguments Standage presents in paragraphs 8–12. How does he refute these arguments? Why doesn't he wait to refute opposing arguments until after he makes his case?

3. In paragraphs 13–15, Standage presents the arguments in support of his thesis. What are these arguments?

4. Standage does not state his thesis until paragraph 16. In your own words, restate this thesis. Why does he wait so long to state his thesis? Do you think presenting it this late is a mistake?

5. In your own words, summarize Standage's concluding statement. How does the phrase "bitter taste" (para. 17) strengthen this statement?

This letter to the editor was published in the *Harvard Crimson*, the student newspaper of Harvard University, on October 21, 2010.

IN DEFENSE OF BOTTLED WATER

THOMAS J. LAURIA

To the editors: 1

Bottled water and its role on campuses has become a topic of great interest—   2
and sometimes, heated debate. The *Crimson*'s Oct. 13, 2010, editorial "Bottle It
Up," which advocated for a ban of this healthful beverage choice, showed that
Harvard University is no exception. I hope to provide some much needed clarification on the issue from a viewpoint you may not have heard yet.

In an age when American adults con-   3
sume 450 calories a day from beverages and
68 percent of those 20 years old and older are
classified as overweight or obese, bottled
water provides a healthy choice when tap
water is not accessible, preferred, or convenient. But if bottled water is not available,
consumer research shows that more than
one-half of people would choose soda instead.

> "Bottled water provides a healthy choice when tap water is not accessible."

This means a ban on bottled water would have the unintended consequence of
driving people to consume more unhealthy beverages that add calories and
sugar to their diets.

While few can argue about the health benefits of "water," college students   4
and administrators may question the impact of "the bottle." To better understand the environmental impact of bottled water and other beverage options,
Nestlé Waters, a member of the International Bottled Water Association where I
work, commissioned a first-of-its-kind, peer-reviewed life cycle assessment. This
LCA found that bottled water has the lightest environmental footprint of all
packaged beverages. This means that every time people choose bottled water
instead of a packaged beverage such as soda or a sports drink, they are choosing
a beverage that uses less water and energy. So banning bottled water is not only
the wrong move for our health, but also the wrong move for the environment.

It's also important to note that bottled water is not an either/or decision   5
for most consumers; 70 percent of bottled water drinkers also drink from the
tap. Simply put, people want access to clean, high-quality drinking water as
part of their daily lives, and that is a good thing. Bottled water is an important
choice in situations where there is a lack of water fountains or concern about
water quality. You may recall bottled water's key role during the boil water alert
last May, which impacted about two million people in Massachusetts.

In sum, banning bottled water does not address the challenges students or other activists seek to resolve by demanding such a measure. Such bans do not improve water conservation practices, nor do they increase the diversion of plastic beverage containers from landfills. Rather, these bans succeed only in removing one of the most healthful beverage choices and replacing it with less healthy options that require more plastic and more water to produce than bottled water.

I hope you will reference this information and consider all the facts when evaluating whether or not any type of bottled water ban is in the best interest of your student community.

Thomas J. Lauria
Alexandria, Va.
Oct. 18, 2010

➡ READING ARGUMENTS

1. This letter was written by Thomas J. Lauria, a bottled-water executive, and published in a college newspaper. What does Lauria hope to accomplish by publishing this letter? What assumptions does he have about his audience's views on the issue and about how they are likely to respond?

2. In what sense is this letter a causal argument? Is it also an evaluation argument? Explain.

3. Lauria believes that opponents of bottled water may be engaging in a logical fallacy. Which fallacy does he identify in their reasoning? Do you agree with his assessment?

4. Would you classify Lauria's letter as a **Rogerian argument**? Why or why not?

➡ AT ISSUE: DO THE BENEFITS OF BOTTLED WATER OUTWEIGH THE COSTS?

1. Both Standage and Lauria write about the health and environmental issues surrounding bottled water. Are there any ethical questions in this debate? Do either of these writers make ethical arguments? Explain.

2. Lauria writes as a representative of the International Bottled Water Association, an organization that characterizes itself as the "leading voice of the bottled water industry," which "serves to protect the

interests of bottled water bottlers, distributors, and suppliers." Should this industry connection affect your evaluation of the writer's *ethos* and arguments? Why or why not?

3. Although Standage concedes that bottled water is "undeniably more fashionable and portable than tap water" (para. 11), he finds its popularity "illogical" (12). Why? What does the word *fashionable* connote here? Are there good reasons for the prevalence of bottled water— reasons that Standage downplays or ignores altogether?

⊘ WRITING ARGUMENTS: DO THE BENEFITS OF BOTTLED WATER OUTWEIGH THE COSTS?

Many U.S. colleges are curbing, banning, or restricting the sale and use of bottled water in plastic containers. Would you support such restrictions, either on your campus or at your workplace? Why or why not? What do you see as the most pressing issues in this debate? Write an essay in which you take a stand on this issue.

Should Every American Go to College?

Since Harvard College was founded in 1636, the history of American higher education has been closely intertwined with the history of the United States—economically, socially, and culturally. Both have generally been associated with expanding opportunity, as colleges and universities have become less a privilege of an elite few and more of a training ground for Americans of all backgrounds, as well as for many foreign students. The nineteenth century witnessed the development of the state university system, which educated many engineers, teachers, agricultural experts, and other professionals who participated in the country's industrial boom—especially after the Civil War. In the post–World War I era, the City College of New York provided a free quality college education to many working-class people (including immigrants) at a time when they were effectively barred from attending most colleges. But perhaps the most significant expansion in American higher education occurred after World War II, when millions of returning veterans attended college with the support of federal funding from the 1944 GI Bill. Enrollment skyrocketed—and many credit this bill with helping to create postwar economic prosperity and a large middle class in the United States.

In the decades since the first GI Bill was passed, the number of colleges and universities has increased steadily: there are now over 4,000 such institutions in the United States. Public policy has been shaped to make higher education more accessible—for example, by supporting publicly funded community colleges and creating federal student-loan programs. But in recent years, the cost of a four-year degree has increased faster than the rate of inflation, even as more and more people see college as a necessity.

Between 28% and 30% of Americans now have college degrees; roughly two-thirds of high school graduates enroll in college after graduation. Labor statistics show that those with bachelor's degrees earn an average of $20,000 more annually than their counterparts with only a high school diploma. This financial reality, along with the need for a highly educated and competitive workforce in an increasingly global marketplace, has led some to argue that the federal government should do more than it already does to make sure that more—and perhaps even all—Americans attend college. Such proposals raise fundamental questions about the nature of higher education. How should colleges maintain academic standards even as they admit more students? How should such institutions control costs? Is higher education really a right in the same way that a high school education is? Should everyone go to college?

The following four essays address these and other questions from starkly different points of view. For example, in "On 'Real Education,'" Robert T. Perry argues that the United States needs more college-educated workers than ever. In contrast, Charles Murray believes that too many people are going to college. All four writers explore the nature and significance of a college degree in important contexts—and all of the writers suggest new ways of viewing postsecondary education as the United States looks to the future.

This essay appeared on InsideHigherEd.com on August 21, 2008.

ON "REAL EDUCATION"

ROBERT T. PERRY

Bell Curve author Charles Murray takes direct aim at higher education in his 1 new book *Real Education* by asserting that we are wasting our time trying to educate too many people. Murray contends that only 10 to 20 percent of those enrolled in four-year degree programs should actually be there. His pessimistic view of people's ability to learn ignores not just good evidence to the contrary but the real pressures the American economy is facing. Removing some 80–90 percent of our students in my state or just about any state would interrupt the pipeline of skilled workers, making it nearly impossible to meet the needs of a society that has defined postsecondary credentials as an entry point for most professions.

Consider the following: 2

- The U.S. Department of Labor reports that the country needs more graduates if we are to keep up with, let alone lead, other nations in the global economy.

- By the end of the next president's first term, there will be three million more jobs requiring bachelor's degrees and not enough college graduates to fill them.

■ 90 percent of the fastest growing job categories, including software engineers, physical therapists, and preschool teachers, 60 percent of all new jobs, and 40 percent of manufacturing jobs, will all require some form of postsecondary education.

We need *more*, not fewer university and community college graduates, even 3
in rural states like mine. South Dakota's aging population will require 30 percent more health care workers in the coming decades—and those workers will require degrees. We're also facing a teacher shortage; educators of all levels need postsecondary education to successfully command and manage a classroom, let alone impart wisdom on elementary and secondary students. Our state also lacks accountants, and the industry has informed us that tomorrow's professionals will require 150 hours of postsecondary education to successfully complete the Certified Public Accountant's exam.

> "We need *more*, not fewer university and community college graduates."

Those left out of higher education would have fewer employment options 4
than they do today. Low-wage, low-skill careers are disappearing rapidly, as manufacturing jobs head overseas and American companies are looking for new ways to compete. Those workers who hope to maintain their current standard of living must have some sort of postsecondary credential—participation in the knowledge-based economy demands it. Without some type of degree, their ability to pay for basics like housing, food, and gas will diminish greatly.

We cannot survive in an international economy by simply working 5
cheaper, as there will always be companies overseas who are willing and able to use unskilled work at a lower cost. If we are to work smarter, our workforce needs to acquire more knowledge and skills that are adaptable in a constantly changing world. The people who have proven to be the most knowledgeable, skilled, and adaptable are those with postsecondary credentials. Murray's suggestions are completely contrary to this. Dummying down our workforce would result in a lower standard of living for most Americans.

The United States has long enjoyed the enviable position as the leader in 6
educational attainment—just a decade ago, we led all other industrialized nations in this area. That's no longer the case. Now, we rank tenth behind other nations in the percentage of young adults with postsecondary credentials. The National Center for Higher Education Management Systems indicates that the U.S. will need to produce 63.1 million degrees to match leading nations Canada, Japan, and South Korea in the percentage of adults with a college degree by 2025. At our current pace, we would fall short of that threshold by 16 million degrees.

Educating a larger percentage of the population does not amount to 7
"educational romanticism," as Murray contends. It simply makes sense—both economically and socially. Higher education allows people of all backgrounds to hone their writing, reading, cognitive, and critical thinking skills that enable

them to actively participate as citizens. Not everyone who completes a four-year degree will be able to write like William Faulkner—and some may argue that's a good thing. But the papers students have to research and write in college are valuable and marketable experiences to future employers who need workers who can craft memos, reports, and strategic plans, all valuable skills in the knowledge economy. Moreover, people with postsecondary degrees also tend to be healthier, are more productive throughout their work lives, are more engaged in their communities, more philanthropic, and are less likely to be involved in crime.

The State Higher Education Executive Officers are calling on political 8 leaders to make college access and success a national priority. To heed this call, SHEEO believes we need to take immediate action by

- Targeting low-income and first-generation students (populations who are historically least likely to succeed in college and complete their degree programs), by allocating greater public resources to community colleges and regional four-year institutions, while also providing adequate need-based financial aid.

- Overhauling the notoriously complex financial aid system. We can start by making most of the required data for the Free Application for Federal Student Aid directly transferable from the federal income tax form. Also, Pell Grants should be pegged to students' basic living costs, rather than tuition, to highlight the responsibility of states and colleges to moderate tuition and fees and to provide grants for tuition to low-income students.

- Developing information systems to better track students' progress and determine whether they are at risk of dropping out.

In South Dakota, we're committed to raising our graduation rates by 9 20 percent by 2010, so we can be competitive both nationally and internationally. To do so, the state is reaching out to nontraditional adult learners by offering more university classes in urban centers. The state's public institutions are opening our doors to more out-of-state students by cutting our non-resident tuition rates in half. So far, the increase in students has offset any potential revenue shortfall. The state is also providing $5,000 scholarships to students who take more rigorous courses in high school, maintain a B average, receive a 24 on their ACT, and pursue their education in South Dakota. We also want to make sure that those students who start college, finish college. To that end, our Board of Regents has tied retention rates to a pool of performance dollars; retention rates are on the rise.

To Murray's point, people do vary in academic ability, and not everyone 10 can handle the rigors of a postsecondary degree program. I'm not suggesting that everyone needs to spend four years at a flagship state institution or even two years at their local community college. However, everyone should have at least the option to participate successfully in some form of postsecondary experience—be it a Ph.D. program or a short-term certificate program for dental assistants. Educators need to help more average Americans *and* educational elite succeed. It's common sense. And our future depends on it.

⊙ READING ARGUMENTS

1. This essay is a refutation of ideas expressed in *Real Education*, a 2008 book by Charles Murray (also see p. 676). What ideas of Murray's is Perry refuting? Is his refutation convincing?

2. In paragraph 4, Perry refers to the demands of a "knowledge-based economy." What is a knowledge-based economy?

3. Perry argues that the United States needs more college-educated workers, not fewer. How does he use causal argument to make this case?

4. According to Perry, why does higher education benefit people of all backgrounds? What benefits does it provide for the average citizen?

This essay is from the January–February 2008 issue of *Change*.

THE PRIVILEGES OF THE PARENTS

MARGARET A. MILLER

The apple doesn't fall far from the tree.

—FOLK SAYING

Paul Barton and Anthony Carnevale, in their articles in this issue, are in fundamental disagreement about the economy's need for college-educated workers. What they don't disagree about, though, are the benefits that accrue to individuals from having a college education. Barton and Carnevale focus on the economic benefits—the wage differentials between those with a high-school education or even some college and those with a bachelor's degree or higher (which is one reason we need to graduate students, not just admit them). But when it comes to the private benefits of higher education, possibly even more important is how advanced intellectual abilities help people navigate contemporary life.

We have to do so many things that other people used to do for us, from making our own plane reservations to making choices about our health to planning for our security in old age (someone has called this the "democratization of risk," although with a $30 trillion shortfall projected for Social Security and Medicare, it's more like the "privatization of risk"). We have to be able to hop from job to job without loss of momentum as we acquire new skills and knowledge. We have to deal with a wider variety of people in this country and in an increasingly constricted world. We need to fill out FAFSA forms for our children (there, even a doctorate may not be enough!).

So I was aware of the stakes when my daughter-in-law told me about a 3 friend of hers who hasn't been to college—indeed, hasn't been in this country for long. This friend, while having no collegiate ambitions for herself, is very ambitious for her son and is determined that he will go to college. But when they spend the afternoon together, Beth notices a difference between herself and the other mother. "She tells him to study," Beth says, "but she can't help him with the content, and she doesn't know that she needs to really push him to do his homework for a certain amount of time after school every day."

I thought of that story when I opened a chart recently produced by Tom 4 Mortenson, which shows the correlation between parental education and children's grades. Sure enough, the more highly educated the parents, the higher the grades of their children: 60.6 percent of children whose parents have advanced degrees get mostly A's, whereas only 27.8 percent of high-school dropouts' children do.

That differential comes about in innumerable small, intangible ways. For 5 instance, educated parents use a wider vocabulary in speaking to their infants than their less-educated counterparts do. According to ETS's recently released *The Family: America's Smallest School*, "by age 4, the average child in a professional family hears about 20 million more words than the average child in a working-class family." Children of educated mothers are also almost twice as likely to be read to as those with less-educated mothers. And if my family is any indication, they are also apt to participate in sustained conversations, even debates (in our household, these periodically featured loud-voiced uncles), which help immeasurably when it comes to writing papers in school and college.

With their sense of entitlement, more highly educated parents are more 6 likely to fight for their children in school, and they know what privileges to fight for. They make sure that their children start algebra in the 8th grade, that they take a college-prep curriculum, that they are placed among the "gifted and talented" students who absorb a disproportionate share of school resources, and that they see college as a realistic possibility and worth taking out loans for (indeed, they may be in a position to subsidize those loans). Having been through the system, they are more knowledgeable about its twists and turns and better able to help their children navigate them.

And they continue to hover over their college-going children. However 7 annoying it may be to us, their involvement has, as the most recent National Survey of Student Engagement (NSSE) reveals, a remarkably good effect on their children's engagement and satisfaction with college, and hence on their ultimate success.

In short, a college education has benefits that ripple down through the generations. Children inherit not just the "sins of the fathers" but their privileges. That's why it is so important that we focus all our intelligence and resources on attracting to our colleges and universities not the children of the privileged (they will come anyway) but first-generation students, whose success we then must do our best to ensure.

> "A college education has benefits that ripple down through the generations."

8

In this country we've prided ourselves on a system of higher education by which we, as Carnevale puts it, "mediate opportunity [and] expand merit-based success without surrendering individual responsibility." But with college-going rates stagnating, completion rates a disgrace, and income gaps widening (consider: the richest one percent of Americans hold a third of the nation's wealth), we are becoming as caste-bound a society as any in the Old World. 9

The children of the less educated will be an increasingly large proportion of the college-going pool. Their parents are equally, if not more, determined to see them succeed than those for whom college is a family tradition, but they can't help them adequately. We need to do for those children what our parents did for us—smooth the way for them to get into college, and once they're there, make sure that they have the same kinds of experiences that help more-privileged students succeed. Again, the NSSE data are revelatory: First-generation students are less likely than the average student to participate in collegiate activities that lead to student success (learning communities, research with faculty members, study abroad, or capstone experiences). We're the ones who can steer them towards those experiences the way the "helicopter parents" guide their children. This gives a whole new meaning to "in loco parentis." 10

This attention to the success of first-generation students will entail turning many of higher education's lived values on their heads. Instead of pursuing "the best and brightest," we'll need to look out for the most promising first-generation students; instead of running the rankings race, we'll need to tighten our belts to keep ourselves affordable and spend the resources we have on practices like those that Charles Reed described in the previous issue of *Change* to attract and retain these students. But we need to get better at this job, and fast, because as Carnevale points out, "ultimately, of course, there are no 'other people's children'"—or children's children, for that matter. We need to want the son of Beth's friend to succeed as much as his mother does, for his own, his children's, and our sakes. 11

⊖ READING ARGUMENTS

1. Miller believes that recent shifts in society make the benefits of higher education more valuable than ever before. What societal changes does she mention? How are these changes related to the need for "advanced intellectual abilities" (para. 1)?

2. In paragraph 4, Miller cites statistics illustrating the correlation between parental education and children's grades. How does she use these statistics to support her argument?

3. According to Miller, the United States is "becoming as caste-bound a society as any in the Old World" (9). What does she mean? How does she support this statement?

4. In what respects is this essay a proposal argument?

The *Wall Street Journal* published this opinion piece on January 17, 2007.

WHAT'S WRONG WITH VOCATIONAL SCHOOL?

CHARLES MURRAY

The topic yesterday was education and children in the lower half of the intelligence distribution. Today I turn to the upper half, people with IQs of 100 or higher. Today's simple truth is that far too many of them are going to four-year colleges.

Begin with those barely into the top half, those with average intelligence. To have an IQ of 100 means that a tough high-school course pushes you about as far as your academic talents will take you. If you are average in math ability, you may struggle with algebra and probably fail a calculus course. If you are average in verbal skills, you often misinterpret complex text and make errors in logic.

These are not devastating shortcomings. You are smart enough to engage in any of hundreds of occupations. You can acquire more knowledge if it is presented in a format commensurate with your intellectual skills. But a genuine college education in the arts and sciences begins where your skills leave off.

In engineering and most of the natural sciences, the demarcation between high-school material and college-level material is brutally obvious. If you cannot handle the math, you cannot pass the courses. In the humanities and social sciences, the demarcation is fuzzier. It is possible for someone with an IQ of 100 to sit in the lectures of Economics 1, read the textbook, and write answers in an examination book. But students who cannot follow complex arguments accurately are not really learning economics. They are taking away a mishmash of half-understood information and outright misunderstandings that probably leave them under the illusion that they know something they do not.

(A depressing research literature documents one's inability to recognize one's own incompetence.) Traditionally and properly understood, a four-year college education teaches advanced analytic skills and information at a level that exceeds the intellectual capacity of most people.

There is no magic point at which a genuine-college-level education 5
becomes an option, but anything below an IQ of 110 is problematic. If you want to do well, you should have an IQ of 115 or higher. Put another way, it makes sense for only about 15% of the population, 25% if one stretches it, to get a college education. And yet more than 45% of recent high school graduates enroll in four-year colleges. Adjust that percentage to account for high-school dropouts, and more than 40% of all persons in their late teens are trying to go to a four-year college—enough people to absorb everyone down through an IQ of 104.

No data that I have been able to find tell us what proportion of those stu- 6
dents really want four years of college-level courses, but it is safe to say that few people who are intellectually unqualified yearn for the experience, any more than someone who is athletically unqualified for a college varsity wants to have his shortcomings exposed at practice every day. They are in college to improve their chances of making a good living. What they really need is vocational training. But nobody will say so, because "vocational training" is second class. "College" is first class.

Large numbers of those who are intellectually qualified for college also 7
do not yearn for four years of college-level courses. They go to college because their parents are paying for it and college is what children of their social class are supposed to do after they finish high school. They may have the ability to understand the material in Economics 1 but they do not want to. They, too, need to learn to make a living—and would do better in vocational training.

Combine those who are unqualified with those who are qualified but 8
not interested, and some large proportion of students on today's college campuses—probably a majority of them—are looking for something that the four-year college was not designed to provide. Once there, they create a demand for practical courses, taught at an intellectual level that can be handled by someone with a mildly above-average IQ and/or mild motivation. The nation's colleges try to accommodate these new demands. But most of the practical specialties do not really require four years of training, and the best way to teach those specialties is not through a residential institution with the staff and infrastructure of a college. It amounts to a system that tries to turn out televisions on an assembly line that also makes pottery. It can be done, but it's ridiculously inefficient.

Government policy contributes to the problem by making college scholar- 9
ships and loans too easy to get, but its role is ancillary. The demand for college is market-driven, because a college degree does, in fact, open up access to jobs that are closed to people without one. The fault lies in the false premium that our culture has put on a college degree.

For a few occupations, a college degree still certifies a qualification. For example, employers appropriately treat a bachelor's degree in engineering as a requirement for hiring engineers. But a bachelor's degree in a field such as sociology, psychology, economics, history, or literature certifies nothing. It is a screen-

> "A bachelor's degree in a field such as sociology, psychology, economics, history, or literature certifies nothing."

ing device for employers. The college you got into says a lot about your ability, and that you stuck it out for four years says something about your perseverance. But the degree itself does not qualify the graduate for anything. There are better, faster, and more efficient ways for young people to acquire credentials to provide to employers.

The good news is that market-driven systems eventually adapt to reality, and signs of change are visible. One glimpse of the future is offered by the nation's two-year colleges. They are more honest than the four-year institutions about what their students want and provide courses that meet their needs more explicitly. Their time frame gives them a big advantage—two years is about right for learning many technical specialties, while four years is unnecessarily long.

Advances in technology are making the brick-and-mortar facility increasingly irrelevant. Research resources on the Internet will soon make the college library unnecessary. Lecture courses taught by first-rate professors are already available on CDs and DVDs for many subjects, and online methods to make courses interactive between professors and students are evolving. Advances in computer simulation are expanding the technical skills that can be taught without having to gather students together in a laboratory or shop. These and other developments are all still near the bottom of steep growth curves. The cost of effective training will fall for everyone who is willing to give up the trappings of a campus. As the cost of college continues to rise, the choice to give up those trappings will become easier.

A reality about the job market must eventually begin to affect the valuation of a college education: The spread of wealth at the top of American society has created an explosive increase in the demand for craftsmen. Finding a good lawyer or physician is easy. Finding a good carpenter, painter, electrician, plumber, glazier, mason—the list goes on and on—is difficult, and it is a seller's market. Journeymen craftsmen routinely make incomes in the top half of the income distribution while master craftsmen can make six figures. They have work even in a soft economy. Their jobs cannot be outsourced to India. And the craftsman's job provides wonderful intrinsic rewards that come from mastery of a challenging skill that produces tangible results. How many white-collar jobs provide nearly as much satisfaction?

Even if forgoing college becomes economically attractive, the social cachet of a college degree remains. That will erode only when large numbers of high-status, high-income people do not have a college degree and don't care. The information technology industry is in the process of creating that class, with Bill Gates and Steve Jobs as exemplars. It will expand for the most natural of reasons: A college education need be no more important for many high-tech occupations than it is for NBA basketball players or cabinet-makers. Walk into Microsoft or Google with evidence that you are a brilliant hacker, and the job interviewer is not going to fret if you lack a college transcript. The ability to present an employer with evidence that you are good at something, without benefit of a college degree, will continue to increase, and so will the number of skills to which that evidence can be attached. Every time that happens, the false premium attached to the college degree will diminish.

Most students find college life to be lots of fun (apart from the boring 15 classroom stuff), and that alone will keep the four-year institution overstocked for a long time. But, rightly understood, college is appropriate for a small minority of young adults—perhaps even a minority of the people who have IQs high enough that they could do college-level work if they wished. People who go to college are not better or worse people than anyone else; they are merely different in certain interests and abilities. That is the way college should be seen. There is reason to hope that eventually it will be.

⊘ READING ARGUMENTS

1. Construct a syllogism for the deductive argument Murray uses in his opening paragraphs. Do you find this argument persuasive? Why or why not?

2. Murray makes a distinction between engineering and the natural sciences (on the one hand) and the humanities and social sciences (on the other). What difference does he identify? Why is this difference important to his argument?

3. Murray claims that too many people are going to four-year colleges. What causal arguments does he use to support this claim? How do these arguments support his position on the issue?

4. More than once in his essay, Murray notes that the "intellectually unqualified" probably do not want to attend a four-year college, and he implies that if given the chance, they would choose not to. Do you think this is true? Do you believe Murray's emphasis on personal choice strengthens his argument? Explain.

5. According to Murray, more people should go to vocational schools. What advantages does he see for those who choose careers in trades and crafts?

This essay appeared in an AssociatedContent.com blog posting dated April 25, 2007.

IS COLLEGE FOR EVERYONE?

PHARINET

"You won't get anywhere without your education." We hear this refrain from the time we are in elementary school. This may be true, but is college for everyone? More and more individuals are enrolling in two- and four-year postsecondary schools, but why? Often, a desire for learning is not what drives students to attend college. Factors that determine reasons for attending college vary from personal to professional. These factors are the key to our discussion.

There is no doubt that education is important. There is also no doubt that every person has the right to an education. However, not every person should attend college. There are too many students enrolled in school who simply don't belong there. Though drop-out rates vary, it is estimated that in the U.S., approximately 50% of students who begin college never graduate. There exist students who are not yet ready for the academic and financial challenges of college. There exist students who do not have the desire for college or learning. Some students may be better suited for a different type of education, if any.

> "There are too many students enrolled in school who simply don't belong there."

The student who is not yet ready for the academic and financial challenges of college is the most common. While the cost of college can be offset by grants, scholarships, and work-study programs, too many students find themselves in desperate financial situations by the end of their first semester. The cost of books can run several hundred dollars per semester. There are living expenses that students may not have planned for, including the cost of food, rent, gasoline, spending money, and supplies other than books. Students find themselves working full-time jobs while attending school full-time, and their minds, bodies, and grades end up suffering. While it may take a while longer to graduate, many students who find themselves in a position where they must work may do better to drop themselves to part-time student status, taking fewer classes. This lowers the cost of education each semester (though requires a longer-term commitment) and increases the chances of classroom success. There is more time to dedicate to coursework without overloading and over-scheduling. Perhaps, certain individuals should consider a different life choice, as the long-term responsibility of repaying student loans can be overwhelming. However, the best financial planning in the world will not prepare a student for the academic challenges that await them.

Believe it or not, there are students who cannot read [but who are] attending college. While this is an extreme case, it is symptomatic of the problems with the idea that "college is for everyone." If college is for everyone, why do we rely on SAT scores and high school transcripts? Why doesn't every school have an open admissions policy? Quite simply, because not everyone should attend college. If individuals are unable to read, they benefit more from a literacy program than a college course. There are also plenty of literate students who are not up for the challenge. They may have graduated from a high school that did not expect much from them, academically. They may not have the maturity necessary to dedicate themselves to the coursework. For many, this is the first time they have had personal freedom and responsibility without their parents. They aren't necessarily prepared to be "grown ups" yet. College prep courses don't often teach students about being responsible. Teaching responsibility and time and stress management may prepare some students for their college experience, but many will still fall victim to their first taste of "freedom."

"C's get degrees." One of my own students said this to me when inquiring 5 about his progress this semester. Unfortunately, this is an all too common mentality among college students. There is no real desire for learning. Students are "going through the motions" to earn their degrees, hoping to settle into a comfortable job that will pay them well because that "C degree" hangs on their wall. Motivating students to learn is the biggest challenge most educators face. While it may be possible to ignite a spark in some, most students who don't wish to learn simply won't learn. What good is there, then, in attending college? None. What happens when this type of student enters the workforce? Do they exhibit the same lack of motivation in their careers? If so, what type of value is actually attached to that degree?

Once upon a time, college was a place you went when you wished to 6 learn. Now, college is the place you go when you want to get a good job, or appease your parents, or because you are "finding yourself." While admissions representatives and administration share some of the blame (college is a business, after all), it is important to examine other reasons why students who don't belong in college end up there anyway. Students and parents need to examine their options. Is it really going to benefit you (or your child) to attend college? What other options exist? Is a trade school the best option? Perhaps allowing yourself to take a year or two to carefully consider who you are and what you want will save you time and money, and better prepare you should you decide to attend college. Society, too, plays a part in pushing students into college classrooms. We need to start distinguishing between the right to an education, and the benefit of an education. College does not benefit everyone. Not everyone should attend college. It is OK to say this! It is OK to believe this! You are not putting anyone down by saying these things. You may be doing them a favor by letting them know that it is OK not to attend college. Higher education is not the key to happiness and success for every person.

Many people have found happiness in careers that do not require a college 7 education. If we continue to tell everyone to acquire a college degree, we lessen the pool of people who will do the jobs that keep our world running smoothly. There are jobs that do not require a college education. Some work can be learned on the job or from a trade school. We need fork lift drivers, factory workers, sales clerks, and cashiers. What would we do without tractor-trailer drivers, mail carriers, and construction workers? Refuse to accept the political correctness that says all of our citizens should receive a higher education. Embrace the reality that college is not for everyone.

⊙ READING ARGUMENTS

1. In her second paragraph, the writer claims that there is "no doubt that every person has the right to an education" but also asserts that "not every person should attend college." Why is this distinction important to her argument? Is it in any sense a contradiction?

2. In her conclusion, the writer advises, "Refuse to accept the political correctness that says all of our citizens should receive a higher education." Do you agree that "college for everyone" has its roots in "political correctness"?

3. According to the writer, what is the biggest challenge that educators face?

⊙ AT ISSUE: SHOULD EVERY AMERICAN GO TO COLLEGE?

1. Margaret A. Miller suggests that access to higher education is a way of increasing opportunity and equality as well as of expanding "merit-based success" (para. 9). Do you agree? How does widening access to a college or university education keep the United States from being "caste-bound" (9)?

2. Charles Murray bases his argument on "intelligence distribution" (1) in the general population. Why? What are the strengths and limitations of his premises?

3. Pharinet writes, "Once upon a time, college was a place you went when you wished to learn," whereas now people go "to get a good job, or appease [their] parents," or find themselves (6). Do you believe she is correct? If so, do you see this shift as a problem? Explain.

⊘ WRITING ARGUMENTS: SHOULD EVERY AMERICAN GO TO COLLEGE?

1. After reading and thinking about the four essays in this casebook, do you think more people should be encouraged to attend college, or do you think some people should be discouraged from attending? Do you see higher education as a right (and a necessity) for most—or even all—citizens? Write an argumentative essay that answers these questions.

2. Pharinet writes, "Motivating students to learn is the biggest challenge most educators face" (para. 5). Based on your own observations, what is the biggest challenge—or challenges—that most *students* face as they make their way through postsecondary education?

Should We Eat Meat?

According to the Vegetarian Resource Group, over 4 million vegetarians and vegans live in the United States. Indeed, as health experts increasingly worry about heart disease and obesity, this seems to be an especially good time for Americans to evaluate the merits of meat-eating. However, the issue goes well beyond health and nutrition. People become vegetarians for a variety of reasons—nutritional, ethical, environmental, and religious. Thus, these choices are not only personal but also cultural. As Jonathan Safran Foer writes in "Let Them Eat Dog," "Food is not rational. Food is culture, habit, craving, and identity."

Our culture seems obsessed with healthy eating, as shown by the increasing popularity of organic and locally grown food and by the popularity of books and films such as *The Omnivore's Dilemma*, *Fast Food Nation*, and *Slaughterhouse: The Labor behind the Profit*. Of course, dietary controversies are not new—and neither is vegetarianism, which has long been associated with certain religious traditions (Jainism and various sects of Hinduism, for example). Western philosophers from Pythagoras to Jean-Jacques Rousseau and René Descartes also advocated forms of vegetarianism. In the eighteenth and nineteenth centuries, a vegetarian diet was associated with radical politics. The English Romantic poet Percy Shelley endorsed the practice—and even blamed some of the excesses of the French Revolution on meat-eating. In the United States, vegetarianism has had strong advocates dating back to the founding of the country. Presbyterian minister and dietary reformer Sylvester Graham, for example, helped found the American Vegetarian Society in 1850. He touted the benefits of a high-fiber diet of fruits and vegetables—the staple of which was the "Graham cracker," made of whole-wheat flour and bran.

For the zealous Graham, who attracted a sizable following, a meatless diet improved both health and personal morality. Although the language and aims of vegetarians may have changed, many still see the choice to eat—or not eat—meat as a profoundly moral and ethical decision, not just a matter of personal choice. All the writers in this casebook agree that social or environmental dimensions are involved in being an omnivore. Laura Fraser argues that human beings are ultimately omnivores and that people must consider the realities of human society when making dietary choices. Modeling his essay on Jonathan Swift's famous satire "A Modest Proposal" (p. 763), Jonathan Safran Foer highlights the logical and ethical inconsistency of those who justify consuming animals such as chickens, pigs, and cows for food even though they would be horrified by killing and eating domesticated dogs and cats. Rancher Nicolette Hahn Niman addresses the connection between food production and climate change but corrects some common misperceptions about the relative environmental effects of vegetarianism and meat-eating. A longtime vegetarian, Laurel Gladden still feels a "larger responsibility" for the ethical treatment of animals within our food system.

This essay first appeared on January 7, 2000, on Salon.com.

WHY I STOPPED BEING A VEGETARIAN

LAURA FRASER

Until a few months ago, I had been a vegetarian for 15 years. Like most people 1 who call themselves vegetarians (somewhere between 4 and 10 percent of us, depending on the definition; only 1 percent of Americans are vegans, eating no animal products at all), I wasn't strict about it. I ate dairy products and eggs, as well as fish. That made me a pesco-ovo-lacto-vegetarian, which isn't a category you can choose for special meals on airlines.

About a year ago, in Italy, it dawned on me that a little pancetta was 2 really good in pasta, too. After failing to convince myself that pancetta was a vegetable, I became a pesco-ovo-lacto-pancetta-vegetarian, with a "Don't Ask, Don't Tell" policy about chicken broth. It was a slippery slope from there.

Nevertheless, for most of those 15 years, hardly a piece of animal flesh 3 crossed my lips. Over the course of that time, many people asked me why I became a vegetarian. I came up with vague answers: my health, the environment, the impracticality and heartlessness of killing animals for food when we can survive perfectly well on soy burgers. It was political, it was emotional, and it made me special, not to mention slightly morally superior to all those bloodthirsty carnivores out there.

The truth is, I became a vegetarian in college for two reasons. One was 4 that meat was more expensive than lentils, and I was broke, or broke enough to choose to spend my limited budget on other classes of ingestibles. The other was that I was not a lesbian.

This is not to say that all lesbians are carnivores; in fact, there's probably a 5 higher percentage of vegetarians among lesbians than most other groups. But there was a fair amount of political pressure to be something in those days. Since, as a privileged white girl from suburban Denver, I couldn't really identify with any oppressed minority group, I was faced with becoming a lesbian in order to prove my political mettle. I had to decide between meat and men, and for better or worse, I became a vegetarian.

The identity stuck, even though the political imperative for my label 6 faded. It wasn't an identity that ever really fit: My friends thought it odd that such an otherwise hedonistic woman should have that one ascetic streak. It was against my nature, they said. But by then, I'd started to believe the other arguments about vegetarianism.

First was health. There's a lot of evidence that vegetarians live longer, have 7 lower cholesterol levels, and are thinner than meat-eaters. This is somewhat hard to believe, since for the first few years of not eating meat, I was basically a cheesetarian. Try leafing through some of those vegetarian recipe books from the early '80s: You added three cups of grated cheddar to everything but the granola. Then vegetarianism went through that mathematical phase where you had to figure out which proteins you had to combine with which in order to get a complete protein. Since many nutritionists will tell you people don't need that much protein anyway, I gave up, going for days and days without so much as contemplating beans or tofu.

For whatever haphazard combination of proteins I ate, being a vegetarian 8 did seem to have a stunning effect on my cholesterol level. This, of course, could be genetic. But when I had a very involved physical exam once at the Cooper Institute for Aerobic Fitness in Dallas, my total cholesterol level was a super-low 135, and my ratio of HDL (good) cholesterol to LDL (evil) was so impressive that the doctor drawled, "Even if you had heart disease, you would be reversing it." This good news, far from reassuring me that I could well afford a few barbecued ribs now and then, spurred me on in my vegetarianism, mainly because my cholesterol numbers effectively inoculated me against the doctor's advice that I also needed to lose 15 pounds.

"Why?" I asked. "Don't you lose weight to lower your cholesterol?"   9

He couldn't argue with that. Whether or not most vegetarians are 10 leaner than carnivores, in my case I was happy to more than make up the calories with carbohydrates, which, perhaps not coincidentally, I always craved.

After the health rationale came the animal rights one. Like most vegetari- 11 ans, I cracked Peter Singer's philosophical treatise on animal rights, and bought his utilitarian line that if you don't have to kill animals, and it potentially causes suffering, you shouldn't do it. (Singer, now at Princeton, has recently come under attack for saying that if a human being's incapacitated life causes more suffering than good, it is OK to kill him.)

It's hard to know where to stop with utilitarianism. Do I need a cashmere 12 sweater more than those little shorn goats need to be warm themselves? Do animals really suffer if they have happy, frolicking lives before a quick and painless end? Won't free-range do?

My animal rights philosophy had a lot of holes from the start. First of all, 13 I excluded fish from the animal kingdom—not only because fish taste delicious grilled with a little butter and garlic, but also because they make it a lot easier to be a vegetarian when you go out to restaurants. Now that's utilitarian. Besides, as soon as you start spending your time fretting about the arguments that crowd the inner pens of animal rights philosophy—do fish think?—then you know you're experiencing a real protein deficiency.

I rationalized the fish thing by telling myself I would eat anything I would 14 kill myself. I had been fly-fishing with my dad and figured a few seconds of flopping around was outweighed by the merits of trout almondine. (Notice that I, not the fish, was doing the figuring.) But who was I kidding? If I were hungry enough, I'd kill a cow in a heartbeat. I'd practically kill a cow just for a great pair of shoes.

Which brings me to the leather exception. As long as other people are 15 eating cow, I decided, I might as well recycle the byproducts and diminish the harm by wearing leather jackets and shoes. When everyone stopped eating meat, I'd stop buying leather jackets and shoes. In the meantime, better stock up.

Then there's the environmental rationale. There is no doubt, as Frances 16 Moore Lappe first pointed out in her 1971 book *Food First*, that there is a huge loss of protein resources going from grain to meat, and that some animals, especially cattle and Americans, use up piggish amounts of water, grain, and crop land.

But the problem really isn't meat, but too much meat—over-grazing, over-fishing, and over-consumption. If Americans just ate less meat—like driving cars less often—the problem could be allevi- 17

> "But the problem really isn't meat, but too much meat."

ated without giving up meat entirely. That approach has worked for centuries, and continues to work in Europe.

All my deep vegetarian questioning was silenced one day when a friend 18 ordered roasted rosemary chicken for two. I thought I'd try "just a bite," and then I was ripping into it like a starving hyena. Roasted chicken, I realized, is wonderful. Meat is good.

From a culinary point of view, that's obvious. Consider that most vegetar- 19 ians live in America and England, places tourists do not visit for the food. You don't find vegetarians in France, and rarely in Italy. Enough said.

As for health, if nutritionists are always telling you to "listen to your body," 20 mine was definitely shouting for more meat. One roasted bird unleashed 15 years' worth of cravings. All of a sudden I felt like I had a bass note playing in my body to balance out all those soprano carbohydrates. Forget about winning the low-cholesterol Olympics. For the first time in a long time, I felt satisfied.

As a vegetarian, not only had I denied myself something I truly enjoyed, 21 I had been anti-social. How many times had I made a hostess uncomfortable by refusing the main course at a dinner party, lamely saying I'd "eat around it"?

How often did my vegetarianism cause other people to go to extra trouble to make something special for me to eat, and why did it never occur to me that that was selfish? How about the time, in a small town in Italy, when the chef had presented me with a plate of very special local sausage, since I was the American guest—and I had refused it, to the mortification of my Italian friends? Or when a then-boyfriend, standing in the meat section of the grocery store, forlornly told a friend, "If only I had a girlfriend who ate meat"? If eating is a socially conscious act, you have to be conscious of the society of your fellow homo sapiens along with the animals. And we humans, as it happens, are omnivores.

⊙ READING ARGUMENTS

1. What were some of Fraser's motives for becoming a vegetarian? Why does she explain these motives in her essay?

2. In paragraphs 7 and 8, Fraser discusses the health benefits of vegetarianism, using examples from her own life experiences. What point is she making here? Does she need additional evidence to support this point? Why or why not?

3. Fraser refers to "utilitarianism" and the "utilitarian" arguments in favor of vegetarianism. What is *utilitarianism*?

4. More than once in her essay, Fraser makes some strong statements in favor of eating meat—for example, "Roasted chicken, I realized, is wonderful. Meat is good" (para. 18). How convincing are such statements? Why does Fraser include them? Should she have used more balanced, less opinionated language? Why or why not?

This essay is from the October 31, 2009, *Wall Street Journal*.

LET THEM EAT DOG

JONATHAN SAFRAN FOER

Despite the fact that it's perfectly legal in 44 states, eating "man's best friend" is 1
as taboo as a man eating his best friend. Even the most enthusiastic carnivores won't eat dogs. TV guy and sometimes cooker Gordon Ramsay can get pretty macho with lambs and piglets when doing publicity for something he's selling, but you'll never see a puppy peeking out of one of his pots. And though he once said he'd electrocute his children if they became vegetarian, one can't help but wonder what his response would be if they poached the family pooch.

Dogs are wonderful, and in many ways unique. But they are remarkably 2 unremarkable in their intellectual and experiential capacities. Pigs are every bit as intelligent and feeling, by any sensible definition of the words. They can't hop into the back of a Volvo, but they can fetch, run and play, be mischievous, and reciprocate affection. So why don't they get to curl up by the fire? Why can't they at least be spared being tossed on the fire? Our taboo against dog eating says something about dogs and a great deal about us.

The French, who love their dogs, sometimes eat their horses.   3

The Spanish, who love their horses, sometimes eat their cows.   4

The Indians, who love their cows, sometimes eat their dogs.   5

While written in a much different context, George Orwell's words (from 6 *Animal Farm*) apply here: "All animals are equal, but some animals are more equal than others."

So who's right? What might be the reasons to exclude canine from the 7 menu? The selective carnivore suggests:

Don't eat companion animals. But dogs aren't kept as companions in all 8 of the places they are eaten. And what about our petless neighbors? Would we have any right to object if they had dog for dinner?

OK, then: Don't eat animals with significant mental capacities. If by "sig- 9 nificant mental capacities" we mean what a dog has, then good for the dog. But such a definition would also include the pig, cow, and chicken. And it would exclude severely impaired humans.

> "Properly cooked, dog meat poses no greater health risks than any other meat."   10

Then: It's for good reason that the eternal taboos—don't fiddle with your crap, kiss your sister, or eat your companions—are taboo. Evolutionarily speaking, those things are bad for us. But dog eating isn't a taboo in many places, and it isn't in any way bad for us. Properly cooked, dog meat poses no greater health risks than any other meat.

Dog meat has been described as "gamey," "complex," "buttery," and "floral." 11 And there is a proud pedigree of eating it. Fourth-century tombs contain depictions of dogs being slaughtered along with other food animals. It was a fundamental enough habit to have informed language itself: the Sino-Korean character for "fair and proper" (yeon) literally translates into "as cooked dog meat is delicious." Hippocrates praised dog meat as a source of strength. Dakota Indians enjoyed dog liver, and not so long ago Hawaiians ate dog brains and blood. Captain Cook ate dog. Roald Amundsen famously ate his sled dogs. (Granted, he was really hungry.) And dogs are still eaten to overcome bad luck in the Philippines; as medicine in China and Korea; to enhance libido in Nigeria; and in numerous places, on every continent, because they taste good. For centuries, the Chinese have raised special breeds of dogs, like the black-tongued chow, for chow, and many European countries still have laws on the books regarding postmortem examination of dogs intended for human consumption.

Of course, something having been done just about everywhere is no kind   12
of justification for doing it now. But unlike all farmed meat, which requires the
creation and maintenance of animals, dogs are practically begging to be eaten.
Three to four million dogs and cats are euthanized annually. The simple disposal
of these euthanized dogs is an enormous ecological and economic problem. But
eating those strays, those runaways, those not-quite-cute-enough-to-take and
not-quite-well-behaved-enough-to-keep dogs would be killing a flock of birds
with one stone and eating it, too.

In a sense it's what we're doing already. Rendering—the conversion of ani-   13
mal protein unfit for human consumption into food for livestock and pets—
allows processing plants to transform useless dead dogs into productive members of the food chain. In America, millions of dogs and cats euthanized in
animal shelters every year become the food for our food. So let's just eliminate
this inefficient and bizarre middle step.

This need not challenge our civility. We won't make them suffer any more   14
than necessary. While it's widely believed that adrenaline makes dog meat taste
better—hence the traditional methods of slaughter: hanging, boiling alive,
beating to death—we can all agree that if we're going to eat them, we should
kill them quickly and painlessly, right? For example, the traditional Hawaiian
means of holding the dog's nose shut—in order to conserve blood—must be
regarded (socially if not legally) as a no-no. Perhaps we could include dogs
under the Humane Methods of Slaughter Act. That doesn't say anything about
how they're treated during their lives, and isn't subject to any meaningful oversight or enforcement, but surely we can rely on the industry to "self-regulate," as
we do with other eaten animals.

Few people sufficiently appreciate the colossal task of feeding a world of   15
billions of omnivores who demand meat with their potatoes. The inefficient use
of dogs—conveniently already in areas of high human population (take note,
local-food advocates)—should make any good ecologist blush. One could argue
that various "humane" groups are the worst hypocrites, spending enormous
amounts of money and energy in a futile attempt to reduce the number of
unwanted dogs while at the very same time propagating the irresponsible no-
dog-for-dinner taboo. If we let dogs be dogs, and breed without interference, we
would create a sustainable, local meat supply with low energy inputs that would
put even the most efficient grass-based farming to shame. For the ecologically
minded it's time to admit that dog is realistic food for realistic environmentalists.

For those already convinced, here's a classic Filipino recipe I recently came   16
across. I haven't tried it myself, but sometimes you can read a recipe and just
know.

Stewed Dog, Wedding Style

First, kill a medium-sized dog, then burn off the fur over a hot fire. Carefully remove the skin while still warm and set aside for later (may be used
in other recipes). Cut meat into 1" cubes. Marinate meat in mixture of
vinegar, peppercorn, salt, and garlic for 2 hours. Fry meat in oil using a

large wok over an open fire, then add onions and chopped pineapple and sauté until tender. Pour in tomato sauce and boiling water, add green pepper, bay leaf, and Tabasco. Cover and simmer over warm coals until meat is tender. Blend in purée of dog's liver and cook for additional 5–7 minutes.

There is an overabundance of rational reasons to say no to factory-farmed meat: It is the No. 1 cause of global warming, it systematically forces tens of billions of animals to suffer in ways that would be illegal if they were dogs, it is a decisive factor in the development of swine and avian flus, and so on. And yet even most people who know these things still aren't inspired to order something else on the menu. Why?   17

Food is not rational. Food is culture, habit, craving, and identity. Responding to factory farming calls for a capacity to care that dwells beyond information. We know what we see on undercover videos of factory farms and slaughterhouses is wrong. (There are those who will defend a system that allows for occasional animal cruelty, but no one defends the cruelty, itself.) And despite it being entirely reasonable, the case for eating dogs is likely repulsive to just about every reader of this paper. The instinct comes before our reason, and is more important.   18

⊙ READING ARGUMENTS

1. Several times in his essay, Foer uses the term *taboo,* as when he refers to the "eternal taboos" in paragraph 10. What is a taboo? Why do you think he uses this term rather than a neutral word, such as "rule"?

2. In what sense is Foer's essay an argument by analogy?

3. In what sense is Foer's essay a proposal argument?

4. What is Foer's thesis? Where is it located? Do you agree with his position on the issue? Why or why not?

This opinion essay is from the October 31, 2009, edition of the *New York Times.*

THE CARNIVORE'S DILEMMA

NICOLETTE HAHN NIMAN

Is eating a hamburger the global warming equivalent of driving a Hummer? This week an article in the *Times* of London carried a headline that blared: "Give Up Meat to Save the Planet." Former Vice President Al Gore, who has made climate change his signature issue, has even been assailed for omnivorous eating by animal rights activists.   1

It's true that food production is an important contributor to climate ₂ change. And the claim that meat (especially beef) is closely linked to global warming has received some credible backing, including by the United Nations and University of Chicago. Both institutions have issued reports that have been widely summarized as condemning meat-eating.

But that's an overly simplistic conclusion to draw from the research. To a ₃ rancher like me, who raises cattle, goats, and turkeys the traditional way (on grass), the studies show only that the prevailing methods of producing meat—that is, crowding animals together in factory farms, storing their waste in giant lagoons, and cutting down forests to grow crops to feed them—cause substantial greenhouse gases. It could be, in fact, that a conscientious meat eater may have a more environmentally friendly diet than your average vegetarian.

So what is the real story of meat's connection to global warming? Answer- ₄ ing the question requires examining the individual greenhouse gases involved: carbon dioxide, methane, and nitrous oxides.

Carbon dioxide makes up the majority ₅ of agriculture-related greenhouse emissions. In American farming, most carbon dioxide emissions come from fuel burned to operate vehicles and equipment. World agricultural carbon emissions, on the other hand, result primarily from the clearing of woods for crop growing and livestock grazing. During the 1990s, tropical deforestation in Brazil, India, Indonesia, Sudan, and other developing countries caused 15 percent to 35 percent of annual global fossil fuel emissions.

> "So what is the real story of meat's connection to global warming?"

Much Brazilian deforestation is connected to soybean cultivation. As ₆ much as 70 percent of areas newly cleared for agriculture in Mato Grosso State in Brazil is being used to grow soybeans. Over half of Brazil's soy harvest is controlled by a handful of international agribusiness companies, which ship it all over the world for animal feed and food products, causing emissions in the process.

Meat and dairy eaters need not be part of this. Many smaller, traditional ₇ farms and ranches in the United States have scant connection to carbon dioxide emissions because they keep their animals outdoors on pasture and make little use of machinery.

Moreover, those farmers generally use less soy than industrial operations ₈ do, and those who do often grow their own, so there are no emissions from long-distance transport and zero chance their farms contributed to deforestation in the developing world.

In contrast to traditional farms, industrial livestock and poultry facilities ₉ keep animals in buildings with mechanized systems for feeding, lighting, sewage flushing, ventilation, heating, and cooling, all of which generate emissions. These factory farms are also soy guzzlers and acquire much of their feed overseas. You can reduce your contribution to carbon dioxide emissions by avoiding industrially produced meat and dairy products.

Unfortunately for vegetarians who rely on it for protein, avoiding soy 10 from deforested croplands may be more difficult: as the Organic Consumers Association notes, Brazilian soy is common (and unlabeled) in tofu and soy-milk sold in American supermarkets.

Methane is agriculture's second-largest greenhouse gas. Wetland rice 11 fields alone account for as much as 29 percent of the world's human-generated methane. In animal farming, much of the methane comes from lagoons of liquefied manure at industrial facilities, which are as nauseating as they sound.

This isn't a problem at traditional farms. "Before the 1970s, methane 12 emissions from manure were minimal because the majority of livestock farms in the U.S. were small operations where animals deposited manure in pastures and corrals," the Environmental Protection Agency says. The E.P.A. found that with the rapid rise of factory farms, liquefied manure systems became the norm and methane emissions skyrocketed. You can reduce your methane emissions by seeking out meat from animals raised outdoors on traditional farms.

Critics of meat-eating often point out that cattle are prime culprits in 13 methane production. Fortunately, the cause of these methane emissions is understood, and their production can be reduced.

Much of the problem arises when livestock eat poor-quality forages, 14 throwing their digestive systems out of balance. Livestock nutrition experts have demonstrated that by making minor improvements in animal diets (like providing nutrient-laden salt licks) they can cut enteric methane by half. Other practices, like adding certain proteins to ruminant diets, can reduce methane production per unit of milk or meat by a factor of six, according to research at Australia's University of New England. Enteric methane emissions can also be substantially reduced when cattle are regularly rotated onto fresh pastures, researchers at University of Louisiana have confirmed.

Finally, livestock farming plays a role in nitrous oxide emissions, which 15 make up around 5 percent of this country's total greenhouse gases. More than three-quarters of farming's nitrous oxide emissions result from manmade fertilizers. Thus, you can reduce nitrous oxide emissions by buying meat and dairy products from animals that were not fed fertilized crops—in other words, from animals raised on grass or raised organically.

In contrast to factory farming, well-managed, non-industrialized animal 16 farming minimizes greenhouse gases and can even benefit the environment. For example, properly timed cattle grazing can increase vegetation by as much as 45 percent, North Dakota State University researchers have found. And grazing by large herbivores (including cattle) is essential for well-functioning prairie ecosystems, research at Kansas State University has determined.

Additionally, several recent studies show that pasture and grassland areas 17 used for livestock reduce global warming by acting as carbon sinks. Converting croplands to pasture, which reduces erosion, effectively sequesters significant amounts of carbon. One analysis published in the journal *Global Change*

Biology showed a 19 percent increase in soil carbon after land changed from cropland to pasture. What's more, animal grazing reduces the need for the fertilizers and fuel used by farm machinery in crop cultivation, things that aggravate climate change.

Livestock grazing has other noteworthy environmental benefits as well. 18 Compared to cropland, perennial pastures used for grazing can decrease soil erosion by 80 percent and markedly improve water quality, Minnesota's Land Stewardship Project research has found. Even the United Nations report acknowledges, "There is growing evidence that both cattle ranching and pastoralism can have positive impacts on biodiversity."

As the contrast between the environmental impact of traditional farming 19 and industrial farming shows, efforts to minimize greenhouse gases need to be much more sophisticated than just making blanket condemnations of certain foods. Farming methods vary tremendously, leading to widely variable global warming contributions for every food we eat. Recent research in Sweden shows that, depending on how and where a food is produced, its carbon dioxide emissions vary by a factor of 10.

And it should also be noted that farmers bear only a portion of the blame 20 for greenhouse gas emissions in the food system. Only about one-fifth of the food system's energy use is farm-related, according to University of Wisconsin research. And the Soil Association in Britain estimates that only half of food's total greenhouse impact has any connection to farms. The rest comes from processing, transportation, storage, retailing, and food preparation. The seemingly innocent potato chip, for instance, turns out to be a dreadfully climate-hostile food. Foods that are minimally processed, in season and locally grown, like those available at farmers' markets and backyard gardens, are generally the most climate-friendly.

Rampant waste at the processing, retail, and household stages compounds 21 the problem. About half of the food produced in the United States is thrown away, according to University of Arizona research. Thus, a consumer could measurably reduce personal global warming impact simply by more judicious grocery purchasing and use.

None of us, whether we are vegan or omnivore, can entirely avoid foods 22 that play a role in global warming. Singling out meat is misleading and unhelpful, especially since few people are likely to entirely abandon animal-based foods. Mr. Gore, for one, apparently has no intention of going vegan. The 90 percent of Americans who eat meat and dairy are likely to respond the same way.

Still, there are numerous reasonable ways to reduce our individual contri- 23 butions to climate change through our food choices. Because it takes more resources to produce meat and dairy than, say, fresh locally grown carrots, it's sensible to cut back on consumption of animal-based foods. More important, all eaters can lower their global warming contribution by following these simple rules: avoid processed foods and those from industrialized farms; reduce food waste; and buy local and in season.

⊙ READING ARGUMENTS

1. Where does Niman use an appeal to *ethos*? What role does this appeal play in her argument?

2. Where does Niman address arguments against her position? Are her refutations of these opposing arguments effective? Why or why not? How would you characterize her attitude toward those who disagree with her?

3. What kinds of specific evidence does Niman use to support her points? What other kinds of evidence could she use?

4. According to Niman, how can we "reduce our individual contributions to climate change" (23)?

5. What different argumentative strategies does Niman use in this essay? For example, in what respects is this essay a proposal argument? What other strategies does she use?

This essay is from the *Santa Fe New Mexican* of March 3, 2010.

THE ETHICAL EPICURE; ANOTHER LOOK AT MEAT

LAUREL GLADDEN

Two Saturday nights ago, I did something I haven't done since I was a teenager: 1 I ate a big plate of meat.

The summer I was 16, I worked in a small swanky café in the affluent sub- 2 urb where I grew up. One of my jobs was to make industrial-size batches of the café's popular fancy chicken salad. My "aha" moment happened one afternoon when I pulled a bowl of tannish-pink boiled chicken from the cooler, preparing to chop it into bite-size bits.

Something made me look at the meat differently that day, though, and 3 suddenly all I could think was, "Those used to be chickens! With feet and feathers and beaks and stuff." I just couldn't stomach the idea of eating something when I could envision the ingredients strutting around the barnyard. By that fall, I'd switched to a completely meat-free diet, and by the time I was 20, I'd gone vegan.

The occasion that inspired my first seriously meat-centric outing since the 4 '80s was a tasting of heritage meats sponsored by Slow Food Santa Fe. Chefs

Joel Coleman, Charles Dale, Tom Kerpon, Kim Müller, and Andrew Nichols prepared a variety of dishes using beef, pork, and lamb from local suppliers Pecos Valley Grassfed Beef and Talus Wind Ranch, as well as Heritage Meats USA, a national organization dedicated to promoting "genetic diversity, small family farms, and a fully traceable food supply" and "to making sustainably produced heritage foods available to all Americans."

Heritage Foods' philosophy has an appealing ring. "The farms and foods 5 that once sustained our forefathers are now endangered," declares the organization's Web site. "Farms are going belly up every day and the foods small farms raise are being lost forever because they are ignored by industrial agriculture." In an article in *Miller-McCune* magazine, Emily Badger adds fuel to the fire: "If we would just eat endangered crops and livestock now, restoring their role in the food supply, we could save them from extinction."

Though the "eat it to save it" argument is intriguing, it's hard to dispute that 6 people and the planet would be better off if we ate less meat. Practically speaking, though, no one can declare, "Vegetarianism for everyone!" and leave it at that. Americans love their meat. As Tara Austen-Weaver says in her book, *The Butcher and the Vegetarian: One Woman's Romp through a World of Men, Meat, and Moral Crisis*, "No one wants to be told that the American dream is over and we're all going to have to eat lentils now."

> "Americans love their meat."

Some of us find it easy to pass on the critter. Some people wag their fingers 7 while they munch righteously on brown rice and tofu, ignoring how meat ends up on their neighbors' plates. Don't we have a larger responsibility, though?

Hugh Fearnley-Whittingstall, author of *The River Cottage Meat Book*, 8 thinks all of us have ethical accountability as the stewards of domesticated farm animals. "We control almost every aspect of their lives," he insists. "Their suffering or lack of it, their animal happiness, or animal misery, are down to us. This dependency would not be suspended if we all became vegetarians. We would remain their custodians, with full moral responsibility for their welfare." He continues, "The vast majority of our food animals are now raised under methods that are systematically abusive. This isn't husbandry. It's persecution. In the face of such abuse, the moral defense of meat eating is left in tatters."

That's why, whether we choose to eat meat or not, we need to ensure that 9 animals are raised and treated ethically and humanely. The best way to have an impact is to choose sustainable meat purchased from small—if possible, local—farmers and to support the stores and restaurants that sell their products rather than those of factory farms.

Chef and caterer Louisa Shafia, who did a stint at San Francisco's well- 10 known vegan restaurant Millennium, has done much to promote vegetarian diets, but you'll still find recipes for meat-based dishes in her new cookbook, Lucid Food. "Many of my favorite vendors at the farmers' market are suppliers of eggs, chicken, fish, cheese, and meat," she admits. "It is vital to support small, ethical suppliers of animal products so that there remains a viable alternative to factory farms."

698

To eat or not to eat meat is a personal decision. For several of my friends, 11
eating "nose to tail" is a way of respecting an animal by not wasting a single
part of it; but it could be a long, long time before I'm ready to sit down with a
plate of offal from a locally raised pig. Still, I'd rather do that than purchase
unrecognizable meat Cling-Wrapped to a Styrofoam tray.

"Are you among the millions of consumers putting pressure on farmers 12
to produce mountains of cheap meat of dubious quality, by dubious means?"
asks Fearnley-Whittingstall. "Ultimately, the only person who is going to
make any significant difference in the way meat is produced, sold, and
cooked is you."

⊖ READING ARGUMENTS

1. Paraphrase Gladden's thesis. How do you react to her position?

2. Do you consider this essay a **Rogerian argument**? Explain.

3. What is the purpose of paragraph 8? How does it strengthen Gladden's argument?

4. What is the "eat it to save it" argument (para. 6)? What is Gladden's response to this argument?

5. In paragraph 11, Gladden refers to the practice of eating "nose to tail." What does this mean? How is this practice related to the ethics of meat-eating?

⊖ AT ISSUE: SHOULD WE EAT MEAT?

Gladden quotes the writer Tara Austen-Weaver, who says, "No one wants
to be told that the American dream is over and we're all going to have to
eat lentils now" (para. 6). How do you interpret Austen-Weaver's
statement? What does meat-eating have to do with the American dream?
Does the consumption of meat have anything to do with status, affluence,
and national—or personal—identity?

⊘ WRITING ARGUMENTS: SHOULD WE EAT MEAT?

All essays in this casebook consider the ethics of eating. For example, Laura Fraser writes that, as a "pesco-vegetarian," she would eat anything that she would kill herself (para. 14) Jonathan Safran Foer examines a number of standards that supposedly guide food choices—for instance, "Don't eat animals with significant mental capacities" (9). Nicolette Hahn Niman considers the environmental consequences of eating meat, with an implied ethical assumption that people should reduce their "individual contributions to climate change" (23). Finally, Laurel Gladden writes about the need to "ensure that animals are raised and treated ethically and humanely" (9). Do you think it is morally and ethically acceptable to eat meat? Write an argumentative essay in which you take a position on this issue. Be sure to address opposing arguments presented by the writers in this casebook.

CHAPTER 24

Is America Safer Now Than before 9/11?

In a speech on the tenth anniversary of the September 11, 2001, terrorist attacks, former New York mayor Rudolph W. Giuliani said, "As with Pearl Harbor and the John F. Kennedy assassination, these defining events have a big impact on a nation because they're not just a shared experience; they're a shared memory." There is no doubt that the attacks profoundly affected our country's policies, politics, economy, society, and even collective psychology. Moreover, in addition to sharing the immediate experience of September 11, Americans have dealt with its consequences in the years since.

In the immediate aftermath of 9/11, the United States heightened security at home and applied military force overseas. In Afghanistan, the United States toppled the ruling Taliban (a regime that provided sanctuary for al Qaeda) and in 2003 began the politically contentious Iraq war. President George W. Bush claimed that these engagements were part of an international "War on Terror" that would ensure that we would not have to face terrorists "at home." Although the war in Iraq officially ended in 2011, American forces are scheduled to remain in Afghanistan through 2014, and the United States continues to be engaged in military operations in other regions, such as Yemen and Pakistan. Many people question whether these foreign interventions have made America safer.

Most Americans experienced the long-term effects of 9/11 at home through the actions of new agencies, such as the Transportation Security Administration and the Department of Homeland Security, as well as the provisions of the Patriot Act. For example, Americans have grown used to removing their shoes and submitting to invasive searches at airport security checkpoints. Beyond these obvious responses to the threat of terrorism, however, a large, complex, expensive, and largely hidden security apparatus has come into being. According to a 2010 *Washington Post* report, "some 1,271 government organizations and 1,931 private companies work on programs related to counterterrorism, homeland security, and intelligence in about

For comprehension quizzes,
see **bedfordstmartins.com/practicalargument**.

10,000 locations across the United States." All this comes at considerable cost—over $1 trillion since the 9/11 attacks. Given that at least thirty planned terrorist attacks have been thwarted since that time, many argue that the government's actions are justified. Others worry about excessive—and possibly unconstitutional—infringements of privacy and civil liberties in the name of national security.

The four essays in this casebook evaluate America's long-term responses to the September 11, 2001, attacks. In "Ten Years after 9/11, We're Still in the Dark," Omar Ashmawy, an attorney and U.S. Air Force veteran, examines America's misunderstandings of Muslims as well as the country's approach to interrogating and detaining suspected terrorists. In an essay published just prior to the tenth anniversary of 9/11, Pulitzer Prize–winning columnist Charles Krauthammer evaluates America's responses at home and abroad. Assessing national security efforts domestically and internationally, Obama administration Attorney General Eric Holder, Secretary of Homeland Security Janet Napolitano, and Director of National Intelligence James Clapper contend that "We're Safer Post-9/11." Conversely, Charles C. Mann questions the effectiveness of our costly "nationwide safety upgrade," suggesting that much of it is designed merely "to make the government look like it is on the job."

This essay was published in the Washington Post on September 9, 2010.

TEN YEARS AFTER 9/11, WE'RE STILL IN THE DARK

OMAR ASHMAWY

I joined the U.S. military after law school to help my country defend itself 1 against the threat of Islamic extremism. My final assignment in my eight years in the Air Force was as a war crimes prosecutor in Guantanamo Bay, Cuba. With access to our nation's most intimate secrets, I shuttled between Guantanamo and the Pentagon from the summer of 2007 to the winter of 2009. I learned many lessons, but on the anniversary of the Sept. 11 attacks, the most important lesson I can share is the most alarming: After so many years and so much sacrifice, nothing has changed.

Our greatest weakness remains today what it was 10 years ago, and what it 2 was eight years before that, when the World Trade Center was bombed in 1993. We don't understand Islam or Arab culture, and that ignorance prevents us from accurately predicting our relationship with Arab and Muslim countries and identifying our enemies.

From our government to the front lines, individuals are making decisions 3 based on inaccurate, biased information. The White House's August announcement on combating radical Islam acknowledged this reality. Our soldiers, agents, and analysts don't have the facts they need to make informed decisions about whom to trust, what to believe, and how to keep the threat at bay.

Whether it's the FBI recommending its agents read books by a known anti-Muslim author, misplaced anxiety over "sharia law," the near absence of linguistic and cultural training in the military, or our government's collective surprise at the Arab Spring, the effect of what we don't know reverberates through U.S. policy. But the result is the same: We are caught off guard by events we should have anticipated, or, worse, we confuse our enemy's propaganda with knowledge.

> "We are caught off guard by events we should have anticipated." 4

As an American Muslim born and raised in New Jersey, I am frustrated 5 that America still struggles with the basics: We don't understand the difference between Islam and Islamic extremism or that Arab culture is not the same as the religion. We divide Muslims into secularists and extremists and can't tell the devout from the radical, the sympathizer from the opportunist.

Two of the most enduring examples are the military commissions and 6 Guantanamo Bay—intractable problems that will never be resolved to anyone's satisfaction. They're once and future disasters built by people who should have known better—people America trusted to know more. Both were operated and sustained by individuals so uninformed of our enemy's religion, language, and culture that they could not accurately process the information available to them. Attorneys couldn't tell good cases from bad ones, and the agents assigned to the commissions didn't know what questions to ask detainees.

I saw it firsthand. From lawyers to interrogators, the vacuum was enormous. It filled Guantanamo Bay with men who did not need to be there and barred their release. It was fuel on a fire set by a legal process that initially conflated the mutually exclusive missions of intelligence-gathering and the rendering of justice. The absence of knowledge and leadership permitted the worst of what happened—reports of the abuse of prisoners, the desecration of holy books, the legal pantomimes—and continues to prevent a resolution to the human drama playing out on that island.

We cannot close Guantanamo because the trials of the detainees who 8 remain would be tainted by evidence from botched interrogations and because the men there are now radicalized—the result of decisions based in an ignorance tantamount to racism.

This ignorance is a degenerative disease that debilitates our efforts to protect our nation. It was tempting to think that with Osama bin Laden's death we could end this conflict, if only we could end the wars in Iraq and Afghanistan. While those wars must be concluded, neither their end nor the death of any individual terrorist will secure us against another attack by Islamic extremists. We're not fighting a single enemy but a decentralized patchwork of groups that adhere to the same twisted, bankrupt ideology. Whether it is Jemaah Islamiah in Southeast Asia or al-Shabab in Somalia, our enemies are motivated and wait—patiently—until we forget.

As we honor the past, we must also commit to the future. This commit- 10 ment must include an expectation that all Americans responsible for protecting us possess the education and knowledge to do so and be committed to accuracy and learning. A good place to start would be language and culture training for our soldiers, and training in Islam and Arab culture and history for policy- makers. Similar education should be made available to local law enforcement and community leaders. At the height of the Cold War, we encouraged our best and brightest to study Russian language and history. Ten years after Sept. 11, this is a basic but necessary step. Ignorance is our vulnerability, and we must begin somewhere. Those individuals we remember Sunday deserve better. We all do.

⊖READING ARGUMENTS

1. In what sense is this essay an evaluation argument? In what sense is it a proposal argument? Identify the specific elements of each argumentative strategy.

2. According to Ashmawy, what is the United States' "greatest weakness" (para. 2) in dealing with the threat of terrorism?

3. Ashmawy uses first-person plural pronouns (such as *we* and *our*) in this essay, particularly in paragraphs 2–5. Why do you think he does this? How does this choice strengthen his argument?

4. Where in this essay does Ashmawy appeal to *ethos*? Why is his personal background important to his argument?

The following opinion essay was published in the *Washington Post* on September 8, 2011.

THE 9/11 "OVERREACTION"? NONSENSE.

CHARLES KRAUTHAMMER

The new conventional wisdom on 9/11: We have created a decade of fear. We 1 overreacted to 9/11—al-Qaeda turned out to be a paper tiger; there never was a second attack—thereby bankrupting the country, destroying our morale and sending us into national decline.

The secretary of defense says that al-Qaeda is on the verge of strategic 2 defeat. True. But why? Al-Qaeda did not spontaneously combust. Yet, in a decade Osama bin Laden went from the emir of radical Islam, jihadi hero after whom babies were named all over the Muslim world—to pathetic old recluse, almost incommunicado, watching shades of himself on a cheap TV in a bare room.

What turned the strong horse into the weak horse? Precisely the massive 3
and unrelenting American war on terror, a systematic worldwide campaign
carried out with increasing sophistication, efficiency and lethality—now so
cheaply denigrated as an "overreaction."

First came the Afghan campaign, once so universally supported that Dem- 4
ocrats for years complained that President Bush was not investing enough
blood and treasure there. Now, it is reduced to a talking point as one of "the two
wars" that bankrupted us. Yet Afghanistan was utterly indispensable in defeat-
ing the jihadis then and now. We think of Pakistan as the terrorist sanctuary. We
fail to see that Afghanistan is our sanctuary, the base from which we have freedom of action to strike Jihad Central in Pakistan and the border regions.

Iraq, too, was decisive, though not in the way we intended. We no more 5
chose it to be the central campaign in the crushing of al-Qaeda than Eisenhower chose the Battle of the Bulge as the locus for the final destruction of the
German war machine.

Al-Qaeda, uninvited, came out to fight us in Iraq, and it was not just 6
defeated but humiliated. The local population—Arab, Muslim, Sunni, under the
supposed heel of the invader—joined the infidel and rose up against the jihadi in
its midst. It was a singular defeat from which al-Qaeda never recovered.

True, in both wars there was much trial, error and tragic loss. In Afghani- 7
stan, too much emphasis on nation-building. In Iraq, the bloody middle years
before we found our general and our strategy. But cannot the same be said of,
for example, the Civil War, the terrible years before Lincoln found his general?
Or the Pacific campaign of World War II, with its myriad miscalculations, its
often questionable island-hopping, that cost infinitely more American lives?

In the end: 10 years, no second attack (which everyone assumed would 8
come within months). That testifies to the other great achievement of the decade:
the defensive anti-terror apparatus hastily constructed from scratch after 9/11 by
President Bush, and then continued by President Obama. Continued why?
Because it worked. It kept us safe—the warrantless wiretaps, the Patriot Act,
extraordinary rendition, preventive detention and, yes, Guantanamo.

Perhaps, says the new conventional wisdom, but these exertions have 9
bankrupted the country and led to our current mood of despair and decline.

Rubbish. The total cost of "the two wars" is $1.3 trillion. That's less than 10
1/11th of the national debt, less than one year of Obama deficit spending.
During the golden Eisenhower 1950s of robust economic growth averaging 5
percent annually, defense spending was 11 percent of GDP and 60 percent of
the federal budget. Today, defense spending is 5 percent of GDP and 20 percent
of the budget. So much for imperial overstretch.

Yes, we are approaching bankruptcy. But this has as much to do with the 11
war on terror as do sunspots. Looming insolvency comes not from our shrinking defense budget but from the explosion of entitlements. They devour nearly
half the federal budget.

As for the Great Recession and financial collapse, you can attribute it to 12
misguided federal policy pushing homeownership through risky subprime
lending. To Fannie and Freddie. To greedy bankers, unscrupulous lenders,

naive (and greedy) home buyers. To computer-enabled derivatives so complicated and interwoven as to elude control. But to the war on terror? Nonsense.

9/11 was our Pearl Harbor. This
time, however, the enemy had no

> "9/11 was our Pearl Harbor." 13

home address. No Tokyo. Which is
why today's war could not be wrapped up in a mere four years. It was unconventional war by an unconventional enemy embedded within a worldwide
religious community. Yet in a decade, we largely disarmed and defeated it, and
developed the means to continue to pursue its remnants at rapidly decreasing
cost. That is a historic achievement.

Our current difficulties and gloom are almost entirely economic in origin, 14
the bitter fruit of misguided fiscal, regulatory and monetary policies that had
nothing to do with 9/11. America's current demoralization is not a result of the
war on terror. On the contrary. The denigration of the war on terror is the
result of our current demoralization, of retroactively reading today's malaise
into the real—and successful—history of our 9/11 response.

❯ READING ARGUMENTS

1. What is Krauthammer's thesis? Restate it in your own words.

2. Where does Krauthammer anticipate and refute possible objections
   to his argument?

3. How does Krauthammer support the claims he makes in paragraph 3?
   What evidence does he use? Do you find this evidence persuasive?
   Why or why not?

4. Does Krauthammer appeal primarily to *ethos*, *pathos*, or *logos*? Why
   do you think he chose the appeal he did?

The following opinion essay was published on the Web site of *USA Today* on
September 8, 2011.

WE'RE SAFER POST-9/11

ERIC HOLDER, JANET NAPOLITANO, AND JAMES CLAPPER

All of us who are old enough remember exactly where we were on Septem- 1
ber 11, 2001, at the moment we first learned that terrorists had taken control
of commercial jetliners and crashed them into the World Trade Center in
Manhattan, the Pentagon, and a field in Shanksville, Pa.

On that day, our lives, our country, and our world fundamentally changed. 2

Today, a decade later, we remember the loss of the nearly 3,000 innocent 3 victims of the attacks, honor the firefighters, police, and many other first responders, who showed such courage and conviction on that tragic day, and take stock of the fundamental changes that have reshaped our country and improved security for all Americans. While there are no guarantees—and there never will be—we have accomplished much to minimize the risk that a successful terror attack like 9/11 will ever occur on American soil.

Ten years ago, our intelligence and law enforcement communities were 4 aware of potential threats to the homeland from terrorist organizations such as al-Qaeda, but we lacked the focus necessary to anticipate and prevent the attack. Sharing essential information to confront this threat was impeded by long-standing cultural, legal, and institutional barriers, stove-piped government organizations, and a lack of coordination and cooperation.

In the decade since 9/11, an unprecedented international partnership has 5 emerged. Together, the United States and our allies have captured or killed most of those responsible for the events of 9/11; we continue to pursue those who remain at large; and the organization that orchestrated these attacks, while still a serious threat, has been significantly weakened.

Today, we are working together as never before to share information, tac- 6 tics, and training to fight terrorists and prevent them from putting their plans into practice, while affirming our support for security, prosperity, and universal rights around the globe. We owe a great debt to our men and women in uniform who are working tirelessly and effectively in many places around the world to protect us from harm.

At home, we have made equally important strides to build the capacity to 7 protect our country and the American people in an age of rapidly evolving threats, and we have made critical enhancements to our nation's counterterrorism capabilities.

New federal agencies like the Director of National Intelligence and the 8 National Counterterrorism Center, and a robust information-sharing environment, have strengthened analysis, improved terrorist watch lists and databases, and created a "need to share" culture, leading to enhanced coordination, tools, and capabilities. Indeed, the entire Intelligence Community is producing better intelligence than at any time in history.

In 2009 and 2010, as a result of investigations by the Department of Jus- 9 tice and the Federal Bureau of Investigation, more defendants were charged in federal court with the most serious terrorism violations than in any two-year period in our history. And the Department of Homeland Security, created in 2003 as part of the largest reorganization of the federal government since the start of the Cold War, is working daily with its federal, state, local, tribal, and private-sector partners to enhance the security of communities across the country. One recent study found that between 1999 and 2009, 86 terrorist plots against Americans have been foiled.

Our nation has continued to strengthen and expand information sharing, intelligence, and public awareness efforts since 9/11. We have supported the creation of 72 state and local fusion centers, where information about threats can be gathered, analyzed, and shared among federal, state, local, tribal, territorial, and private-sector partners. We have expanded the number of Joint Terrorism Task Forces (JTTFs) around the country from 35 to 104 and increased the number of JTTF personnel from roughly 1,000 to nearly 4,500. In addition, the Justice Department has implemented a series of far-reaching legal, structural, and cultural changes over the past decade, including the creation of the Department's National Security Division and the FBI's National Security Branch, to more effectively combat national security threats through intelligence.

We have established a new Nationwide Suspicious Activity Reporting Initiative, which trains law enforcement across our country to recognize behaviors and indicators related to terrorism-related crime. It also standardizes how those observations are documented, analyzed, and shared.

We have worked to engage the broadest possible set of partners in security by expanding the "If You See Something, Say Something™" campaign, a nationwide effort originally implemented by New York City's Metropolitan Transportation Authority, to increase public awareness and the reporting of suspicious activity to the authorities.

In short, we have created a much stronger framework for managing threats to our nation. The capabilities that we have today are far greater than what existed 10 years ago, and they have helped us thwart numerous terrorist plots, from the attempt to bomb New York City subways to the foiled attacks against air cargo, Times Square, and a parade in Seattle. And these capabilities continue to contribute to the security of the American people every day.

> "We have created a much stronger framework for managing threats to our nation."

Make no mistake: Our nation is stronger and more secure than it was on 9/11, better prepared to confront the challenges we face, and more resilient than ever before. But despite these improvements, we do not have the luxury to rest on our laurels. There are still terrorist groups around the world who wish us ill and are plotting attacks against us.

Our success in confronting these threats in the future will depend on those who work on the frontlines, day and night, at home and abroad, to keep us safe. As important, it will depend on the American people and our collective determination to stand firm against threats, united in our resolve, free from fear, and resilient should we be attacked again.

⊝ READING ARGUMENTS

1. What do you think the writers hoped to accomplish in this essay? Does their status as political appointees affect your response to their argument? If so, how? If not, why not?

2. How does paragraph 4 set up the essay's main arguments? Is this paragraph actually necessary?

3. According to the writers, the "entire Intelligence Community is producing better intelligence than at any time in history" (para. 8). How do they support this claim? Do you find their evidence convincing?

4. Describe the writers' style and tone. Does the essay have a distinctive voice? For example, how would you characterize the language in paragraph 7?

This essay was published on December 20, 2011, in *Vanity Fair*.

SMOKE SCREENING

CHARLES C. MANN

Not until I walked with Bruce Schneier toward the mass of people unloading 1 their laptops did it occur to me that it might not be possible for us to hang around unnoticed near Reagan National Airport's security line. Much as upscale restaurants hang mug shots of local food writers in their kitchens, I realized, the Transportation Security Administration might post photographs of Schneier, a 48-year-old cryptographer and security technologist who is probably its most relentless critic. In addition to writing books and articles, Schneier has a popular blog; a recent search for "TSA" in its archives elicited about 2,000 results, the vast majority of which refer to some aspect of the agency that he finds to be ineffective, invasive, incompetent, inexcusably costly, or all four.

As we came by the checkpoint line, Schneier described one of these 2 aspects: the ease with which people can pass through airport security with fake boarding passes. First, scan an old boarding pass, he said—more loudly than necessary, it seemed to me. Alter it with Photoshop, then print the result with a laser printer. In his hand was an example, complete with the little squiggle the T.S.A. agent had drawn on it to indicate that it had been checked. "Feeling safer?" he asked.

Ten years ago, 19 men armed with utility knives hijacked four airplanes and within a few hours killed nearly 3,000 people. At a stroke, Americans were thrust into a menacing new world. "They are coming after us," C.I.A. director George Tenet said of al-Qaeda. "They intend to strike this homeland again, and we better get about the business of putting the right structure in place as fast as we can."

The United States tried to do just that. Federal and state governments embarked on a nationwide safety upgrade. Checkpoints proliferated in airports, train stations, and office buildings. A digital pan-opticon of radiation scanners, chemical sensors, and closed-circuit television cameras audited the movements of shipping containers, airborne chemicals, and ordinary Americans. None of this was or will be cheap. Since 9/11, the U.S. has spent more than $1.1 trillion on homeland security.

> "Since 9/11, the U.S. has spent more than $1.1 trillion on homeland security."

To a large number of security analysts, this expenditure makes no sense. The vast cost is not worth the infinitesimal benefit. Not only has the actual threat from terror been exaggerated, they say, but the great bulk of the post-9/11 measures to contain it are little more than what Schneier mocks as "security theater": actions that accomplish nothing but are designed to make the government look like it is on the job. In fact, the continuing expenditure on security may actually have made the United States less safe.

The first time I met Schneier, a few months after 9/11, he wanted to bet me a very expensive dinner that the United States would not be hit by a major terrorist attack in the next 10 years. We were in Washington, D.C., visiting one of the offices of Counterpane Internet Security, the company he had co-founded in 1999. (BT, the former British Telecom, bought Counterpane seven years later; officially, Schneier is now BT's chief security technology officer.) The bet seemed foolhardy to me. Defense Secretary Donald Rumsfeld had just told the *Washington Times* that al-Qaeda was dispersing its killers all over the world.

From an airplane-hijacking point of view, Schneier said, al-Qaeda had used up its luck. Passengers on the first three 9/11 flights didn't resist their captors, because in the past the typical consequence of a plane seizure had been "a week in Havana." When the people on the fourth hijacked plane learned by cell phone that the previous flights had been turned into airborne bombs, they attacked their attackers. The hijackers were forced to crash Flight 93 into a field. "No big plane will ever be taken that way again, because the passengers will fight back," Schneier said. Events have borne him out. The instigators of the two most serious post-9/11 incidents involving airplanes—the "shoe bomber" in 2001 and the "underwear bomber" in 2009, both of whom managed to get onto an airplane with explosives—were subdued by angry passengers.

Schneier's sanguine views had little resonance at a time when the fall of the   8
twin towers was being replayed nightly on the news. Two months after 9/11, the
Bush administration created the Transportation Security Agency, ordering it to
hire and train enough security officers to staff the nation's 450 airports within a
year. Six months after that, the government vastly expanded the federal sky-
marshal program, sending thousands of armed lawmen to ride planes undercover. Meanwhile, the T.S.A. steadily ratcheted up the existing baggage-screening
program, banning cigarette lighters from carry-on bags, then all liquids (even,
briefly, breast milk from some nursing mothers). Signs were put up in airports
warning passengers about specifically prohibited items: snow globes, printer cartridges. A color-coded alert system was devised; the nation was placed on "orange
alert" for five consecutive years. Washington assembled a list of potential terror targets that soon swelled to 80,000 places, including local libraries and
miniature-golf courses. Accompanying the target list was a watch list of potential
suspects that had grown to 1.1 million names by 2008, the most recent date for
which figures are available. Last year, the Department of Homeland Security,
which absorbed the T.S.A. in 2003, began deploying full-body scanners, which
peer through clothing to produce nearly nude images of air passengers.

Bruce Schneier's exasperation is informed by his job-related need to spend a   9
lot of time in Airportland. He has 10 million frequent-flier miles and takes about
170 flights a year; his average speed, he has calculated, is 32 miles an hour. "The
only useful airport security measures since 9/11," he says, "were locking and reinforcing the cockpit doors, so terrorists can't break in, positive baggage matching"—ensuring that people can't put luggage on planes, and then not board
them—"and teaching the passengers to fight back. The rest is security theater."

Remember the fake boarding pass that was in Schneier's hand? Actually, it   10
was mine. I had flown to meet Schneier at Reagan National Airport because I
wanted to view the security there through his eyes. He landed on a Delta flight
in the next terminal over. To reach him, I would have to pass through security.
The day before, I had downloaded an image of a boarding pass from the Delta
Web site, copied and pasted the letters with Photoshop, and printed the results
with a laser printer. I am not a photo-doctoring expert, so the work took me
nearly an hour. The T.S.A. agent waved me through without a word. A few
minutes later, Schneier deplaned, compact and lithe, in a purple shirt and with
a floppy cap drooping over a graying ponytail.

The boarding-pass problem is hardly the only problem with the check-   11
points. Taking off your shoes is next to useless. "It's like saying, Last time the
terrorists wore red shirts, so now we're going to ban red shirts," Schneier says.
If the T.S.A. focuses on shoes, terrorists will put their explosives elsewhere.
"Focusing on specific threats like shoe bombs or snow-globe bombs simply
induces the bad guys to do something else. You end up spending a lot on the
screening and you haven't reduced the total threat."

As I waited at security with my fake boarding pass, a T.S.A. agent had   12
darted out and swabbed my hands with a damp, chemically impregnated cloth:
a test for explosives. Schneier said, "Apparently the idea is that al-Qaeda has

never heard of latex gloves and wiping down with alcohol." The uselessness of the swab, in his view, exemplifies why Americans should dismiss the T.S.A.'s frequent claim that it relies on "multiple levels" of security. For the extra levels of protection to be useful, each would have to test some factor that is independent of the others. But anyone with the intelligence and savvy to use a laser printer to forge a boarding pass can also pick up a stash of latex gloves to wear while making a bomb. From the standpoint of security, Schneier said, examining boarding passes and swabbing hands are tantamount to performing the same test twice because the person you miss with one test is the same person you'll miss with the other.

After a public outcry, T.S.A. officers began waving through medical sup-   13
plies that happen to be liquid, including bottles of saline solution. "You fill one of them up with liquid explosive," Schneier said, "then get a shrink-wrap gun and seal it. The T.S.A. doesn't open shrink-wrapped packages." I asked Schneier if he thought terrorists would in fact try this approach. Not really, he said. Quite likely, they wouldn't go through the checkpoint at all. The security bottlenecks are regularly bypassed by large numbers of people—airport workers, concession-stand employees, airline personnel, and T.S.A. agents themselves (though in 2008 the T.S.A. launched an employee-screening pilot study at seven airports). "Almost all of those jobs are crappy, low-paid jobs," Schneier says. "They have high turnover. If you're a serious plotter, don't you think you could get one of those jobs?"

⊖ READING ARGUMENTS

1. Where does Mann state his thesis? Why do you think he chose to state it where he does?

2. Is this essay a causal argument? Why or why not?

3. Throughout his essay, Mann appeals to the authority of security expert Bruce Schneier. How does he establish Schneier's credibility?

4. According to Bruce Schneier, what are "the only useful airport security measures [put into place] since 9/11" (para. 9)? Do you think Schneier has a point, or does he seem to be overstating his case?

5. Mann discusses the problem of fake boarding passes early in his essay and returns to the subject again later on. Why is the boarding-pass problem significant? What role does it play in his argument?

⊘ AT ISSUE: IS AMERICA SAFER NOW THAN BEFORE 9/11?

1. Omar Ashmawy is critical of the U.S. government's approach to capturing, detaining, and interrogating suspects after 9/11: "It was fuel on a fire set by a legal process that initially conflated the mutually exclusive missions of intelligence-gathering and the rendering of justice" (para. 7). What distinction is Ashmawy suggesting here? Why is this distinction important? Do you agree that these two "missions" should be "mutually exclusive"? Why or why not?

2. Eric Holder, Janet Napolitano, and James Clapper were all members of a Democratic presidential administration when they wrote "We're Safer Post-9/11." Do you think the writers' political affiliations shape their argument in any way? Can you find specific examples in the essay that suggest partisanship?

3. In paragraph 5 and elsewhere, Charles C. Mann refers to "security theater." What connotations does this phrase have? Could such "theater" be useful in its own right? What are your own opinions of TSA procedures? Has reading Mann's essay changed your view?

⊘ WRITING ARGUMENTS: IS AMERICA SAFER NOW THAN BEFORE 9/11?

1. The authors of "We're Safer Post-9/11" argue that "our lives, our country, and our world fundamentally changed" after the attacks (para. 2). Do you agree that the United States changed in some fundamental or essential way after 9/11? Or, do you believe that the changes have mostly been superficial, temporary, or consistent with America's identity before the attacks? In an argumentative essay, take a stand on this issue.

2. After reading these four selections, do you think America is safer now than before 9/11? Write an argumentative essay that presents your position on this issue.

CHAPTER 25

Is the Glass Ceiling a Myth or a Reality?

Decades after the beginning of the women's liberation movement, women still face obstacles to advancement within the professional world. Law may prohibit overt sexism and gender discrimination, but women can find their careers blocked by a subtle, often unseen barrier in the organizational hierarchy—the so-called glass ceiling. Although the origins of the term *glass ceiling* are debatable, writer and editor Gay Bryant is often credited with coining it in her 1985 book *The Working Woman Report: Succeeding in Business in the 80's.* The metaphor has survived because of its power to evoke a vivid image.

Few people dispute the advancements of women over the last half century—especially their progress in the white-collar world. In 2010, women became a majority in the American workforce. They now hold over half of all managerial and professional jobs and continue to gain on men in fields such as law, medicine, and accounting. Women also earn more undergraduate and master's degrees than their male counterparts, a trend that indicates a long-term social and economic ascent. As Hanna Rosin argues in her controversial 2010 *Atlantic Monthly* article, "The End of Men," "Of the 15 job categories projected to grow the most in the next decade in the U.S., all but two are occupied primarily by women. Indeed, the U.S. economy is in some ways becoming a kind of traveling sisterhood: upper-class women leave home and enter the workforce, creating domestic jobs for other women to fill."

Despite these advances, major disparities between men and women in the workplace persist. According to the Bureau of Labor Statistics, women's salaries remain only 81% of men's. This pay gap begins immediately after college, when women with undergraduate degrees earn 17% less than men with the same education. Compounded over a lifetime, that difference can add up to millions of dollars. Moreover, while women hold an increasing number of management positions, their career ladders often do not reach the executive suite: only 3% of Fortune 500 CEOs are female, for example.

 For comprehension quizzes, see bedfordstmartins.com/practicalargument.

Observers disagree about the reasons for these disparities. For some, the gaps suggest the persistence of the "old boy network" and lingering prejudices about the place of women. For others, the disparity indicates that women lack the assertiveness, negotiating skills, or commitment to their careers that they need to get to higher executive positions. Still others think women hit a glass ceiling when colleagues perceive them as too assertive (although assertiveness is valued in men).

The writers whose essays appear in this casebook offer a cross-section of opinions on the glass ceiling. Susan M. Kochanowski's "Women in Leadership: Persistent Problems or Progress?" brings a scholarly approach to the issue; the writer assesses the "progress women have made toward advancement into top leadership positions" and examines the "issues impacting this advancement by reviewing current literature." Kochanowski also questions the usefulness of the term "glass ceiling." In "Are We There Yet?," *Newsweek* writers Jessica Bennett, Jesse Ellison, and Sarah Ball reevaluate the notion that the "fight for equality [is] history" even as they present a historical account of feminist progress at their own magazine. In "The Real Reason So Few Women Are in the Boardroom," Marty Nemko focuses on the choices that women make rather than on institutional barriers to their progress. Finally, Lisa Quast, in "Debunking the Myths of Gender Equality," contends that gender disparities in education and the workplace are largely the result of women's own personal choices.

This report was published in the Summer 2010 issue of *Forum on Public Policy: A Journal of the Oxford Round Table*.

WOMEN IN LEADERSHIP: PERSISTENT PROBLEMS OR PROGRESS?

SUSAN M. KOCHANOWSKI

Introduction

In the world of work, there is a scarcity of women in top leadership. Despite the   1 documented progress of women in the workplace demonstrating that women now hold more that 40% of all managerial positions in the United States, there remains a paucity of women in executive roles and on corporate boards of directors (Eagly and Carli 2007; Wolfman 2007). A growing body of research suggests that women add value to companies when holding executive and board positions (Hillman, Harris, Cannella, and Bellinger 1998; Adler 2001; Carter, Simkins, and Simpson 2003; Richard 2000). However, in 2008 women held only 15.7 percent of corporate officer positions at Fortune 500 companies. The number of companies with no women corporate officers increased from 74 in 2007 to 75 in 2008. The number of companies with three or more women corporate officers also increased from 203 in 2007 to 206 in 2008.

Similarly, in 2008, women held 15.2 percent of directorships at Fortune 500 companies; this number was 14.8 percent in 2007. The number of companies with no women board directors increased from 59 in 2007 to 66 in 2008, representing an average increase of only 0.5 percent annually over the last 10 years. It seems that little progress is being made in the United States toward parity with men in top leadership positions.

These numbers are even bleaker in other countries. The top 300 European companies now have 9.7 percent of women on their boards, up from 8.5 percent in 2006 and 8 percent in 2004. Norway's impressive 44.2 percent women on boards is a result of quota legislation. Without Norway, the European growth average growth rate of around 0.5 percentage points over each two-year period from 2004 onwards parallels that of the United States (European Professional Women's Network website).

This problem of women's scarcity in top leadership positions first gained attention in 1977 when the nonprofit organization Catalyst, instituting a corporate board service to help introduce professional and business women to corporations, reported their findings that there were only 147 women directors represented on the 1,300 largest U.S. public companies' boards of directors (Schwartz 1980; Wolfman 2007). At the time, there was little data on the role of women in the workplace and this number caught the attention of many interested people.

The purpose of this paper is to assess the progress women have made toward advancement into top leadership positions and to examine the issues impacting this advancement by reviewing the current literature. Toward this end, a 1980 *Harvard Business Review* article by Felice Schwartz, founder of Catalyst, provides some important baseline observations as a starting place from which to measure advancement. In this article, Schwartz (1980) begins by reporting the tentatively optimistic increase in the number of women directors from 147 in 1976 to 300 in 1979. However, while this represented an impressive overall increase, the ratio of women to men on boards remained very small with 300 women as directors on 365 of the Fortune 1,300 boards to about 16,000 men on these boards (Schwartz 1980).

In an effort to understand the qualifications chairmen were seeking in potential board members, Schwartz (1980) reports that chief executive officers (CEO's) were the most desirable board members. This was due to the perception that, with experienced CEO's on a board, their combined experiences would cover most problems, challenges, and opportunities that might possibly arise. Noting that there were only two women CEO's of major corporations in the United States at that time and that only about twenty-four women had CEO-equivalent level of experience, Schwartz (1980) points out that "thus it will very likely take two decades for the number of women in upper management to assume significant proportions and another five to ten years after that for these women to acquire experience and move up to the officer level, where they can obtain the broad perspective that is so desirable for the corporate board's planning function" (p. 7).

The connection between top executive positions, often referred to as C-Suite positions (Eagly and Carli 2007), and board positions is clear. In order for there to be more women directors of large corporations, there must also be more women in top executive positions in large corporations. In this 1980 article, Schwartz expressed optimism that women would continue to progress into these top leadership ranks.

Two decades later, at the time Schwartz (1980) predicted that women would be reaching parity with men in terms of top leadership positions, Judith Oakley (2000) observed in her article "Gender-Based Barriers to Senior Management Positions: Understanding the Scarcity of Female CEO's" that, although the number of women in middle management has rapidly grown, the number of female CEO's in large corporations continues to be extremely low. In this article, Oakley (2000) examines what has been described as "the glass ceiling," which is conceptualized as an invisible employment barrier impeding women's career progression from reaching the highest ranks of the corporate structures.

Glass Ceiling

The term *glass ceiling* was first used in a 1986 *Wall Street Journal* article written by Hymowitz and Schellhardt. Subsequently, this "glass ceiling" phenomenon has generated a large body of research affirming the existence of an impediment to women's career progression into top leadership ranks as well as exploring the nature of the barrier (Eisner and Harvey 2009). Subsequent to much of this research, a Federal Glass Ceiling Commission was created in 1991. In 1992 the Federal Glass Ceiling Commission, after a year of research and investigation, agreed that the glass ceiling does exist.

Studies exploring the issues comprising the glass ceiling suggest that this barrier is not a single obstacle but multiple obstacles (Kilian, Hukai, and McCarty 2005; MacRae 2005; Oakley 2000). Researchers demonstrate some consistency and overlap regarding their findings of what constitutes the glass ceiling as well as some unique findings. There is, however, more agreement than not.

> "This barrier is not a single obstacle but multiple obstacles."

Oakley (2000) lists the glass ceiling barriers as including: lack of line management experience; inadequate career opportunities; gender differences in socialization and linguistic styles; gender-based stereotypes; the old boy network persisting at the top of organizations; and tokenism. According to MacRae (2005), these barriers include: the common perception that men are leaders while women are supportive followers; lack of strong female role models; the existence of the "good ole boy" network; the issue of family responsibility; and the need for women to develop a professional style with which male counterparts would be comfortable. Similarly, Kilian, Hukai, and

McCarty's (2005) list includes: lack of mentors and role models; exclusion from informal networks of communication; stereotyping and preconception of roles and abilities; lack of significant line experience; and commitment to personal and family responsibilities.

Kottke and Agars (2005) condense these overlapping lists into what they argue are four basic underlying processes: social cognitions, justice, threat, and utility. In this model, the authors present the concept of social cognitions arguing that change is a social process. As such, efforts to implement policies and practices related to the advancement of women are embedded in complex social schemas. Among the most critical of these social factors are gender stereotypes and social identity (Kottke and Agars 2005). [12]

Justice is also a complex process that ironically hinders advancement initiatives. Problems in this process realm include issues of negative perceptions around family-friendly policies because they disproportionately address women's needs. This perception of injustice leads both men and women to resist the implementation of gender initiatives in organizations because of the attention they draw to differences rather than neutralizing differences as they are intended (Kottke and Agars 2005; Kilian et al. 2005). [13]

The theory of tokenism, first presented by Rosabeth Moss Kanter (1977), predicts this justice paradox by suggesting that individuals whose social category is underrepresented will face negative experiences such as increased visibility and social isolation. A very recent study by King, Hebl, George, and Matusik (2010) found that women's token status, especially in the top management ranks, is associated with their perceptions of an inequitable gender climate in their organizations. Additionally, these perceptions of inequity were related to job satisfaction, affective commitment, helping behaviors and were positively associated with turnover intentions and job stress. [14]

According to Kottke and Agars (2005), threat-rigidity theory argues that where there is a perceived threat there will be a rigid response that relies upon previously dominant responses. This theory predicts that at an individual level, any perceived threat will increase both genders' reliance upon gender stereotypes. At the organizational level, this threat will increase the organization's reliance on formalized practices and policies, resulting in an unwillingness to emphasize developmental efforts (Kottke and Agars 2005). [15]

Utility refers to the cost-effectiveness of an organizational endeavor. Kottke and Agars (2005) state that utility is pertinent for effectively every organizational decision, and that attempts to understand the barriers obstructing women's advancement to top leadership positions would be incomplete if the utility perceptions were not addressed. While there is research evidence of the value that women bring to corporate leadership, this evidence is largely based on correlational studies, which leaves causation still in question (Kottke and Agars 2005; Hillman et al. 1998; Adler 2001; Carter et al. 2003; Richard 2000). Kottke and Agars (2005) suggest that the lack of adequately explored utility is one reason why organizations are not compelled to proceed with initiatives that will effectively close the gender gap at top leadership levels. [16]

The Role of Family

One of the multiple issues comprising the glass ceiling that has received atten- 17 tion from numerous researchers is the role of family and its impact on women's competing demands (Brizendine 2008; Hoobler, Wayne, and Lemmon 2009; Kilian et al. 2005; MacRae 2005; Oakley 2000). According to MacRae (2005), the pressure on women to perform multiple roles in paid and unpaid work persists. In her ten-year retrospective of women and work, MacRae (2005) underscores this problem when she states that "the single issue that has gained more prominence is the role of family, how it affects paid work choices, and how women balance their often competing demands" (p. 331).

Many of the issues identified as comprising the glass ceiling such as per- 18 sistent stereotyping, lack of line experience, and exclusion from informal networks (Kilian et al. 2005; MacRae 2005; Oakley 2000) are issues related to this somewhat overarching issue of family responsibilities. Researchers have suggested that women's traditional roles as family caregivers and nurturers have created a double bind for women based on a complex blend of some real and some perceived differences between male and female managers. This double bind based on gender stereotypes puts women in a position where they are unassociated with management effectiveness because that label is associated with male characteristic and they are associated with nurturing communal roles (Hoober et al. 2009; Oakley 2000). The issue is not whether women are one or the other but that variation exists and women can be either or both.

Louann Brizendine (2008) is a neuropsychiatrist who studies brain gender 19 differences. In her article "One Reason Women Don't Make It to the C-Suite," Brizendine (2008) states that ". . . women in childbearing years undergo changes that intensify their focus on the viability of offspring. It's a passing phenomenon, but ill-timed for those with career ambitions" (36). Brizendine's observations underscore what many other researchers have noted. Specifically that due to childbearing, childrearing, and other caretaking responsibilities, women enter and leave the workforce more than men and that women accept part-time work at double the rate of men (Kilian et al. 2005) often in efforts to balance paid and unpaid work responsibilities (MacRae 2005). This non-linear, interrupted career path hinders women at a time when many managers have gained the knowledge and perspective needed to begin taking on greater responsibility in business (Brizendine 2008).

While research demonstrates that caretaking responsibilities often compete 20 for time and priority in women's lives, there is also research challenging the underlying stereotype that all women have caretaking responsibilities (Greenhaus and Powell 2006; Hoobler et al. 2009). Research conducted on women who are highly career focused found little difference in work and family interference between men and women. Byron (2005) conducted a meta-analysis on work-family conflict and found that gender has a weak to near zero relationship with work-family interferences.

Hoobler, Wayne, and Lemmon (2009) hypothesized that the subconscious 21 stereotyping of all women into these caretaking roles helps to explain the differences between men and women's upward progress in organizations. Based on person categorization and social role theory, Hoobler et al. (2009) examined whether bosses perceive women as having greater family-work conflict, thereby viewing them as less well matched to their organizations and less promotable. Results of this study supported the model that bosses' perceptions of family-work conflict mediated the relationship between subordinate gender and perceptions of fit. In turn, these perceptions were related to issues of development and promotability to line management and executive management positions (Hoobler et al. 2009).

Leadership Styles

The gender differences in management and leadership styles have been the 22 topic of much research demonstrating that the problems of gender stereotypes impact the leadership styles of men and women. Several studies have identified women's leadership styles to be more interactive and transformational whereas men's style has been identified as more directive (Gardiner and Tiggemann 1999; Grisoni and Beeby 2007; MacRae 2005). Based on their research findings that women in organizations with higher ratios of males to females adopted more male-associated leadership styles, Eagly and Johnson (1990) postulated that women adopt more masculine styles in certain environments so as not to lose authority and position.

These findings are consistent with the research conducted by Oakley 23 (2000), who found that women's linguistic styles may be misinterpreted or devalued by men. The less aggressive styles of many women may be perceived as unacceptable in the upper echelons of most organizations. However, in adopting a more traditionally masculine leadership communication style, women risk being perceived as too aggressive because of the inconsistency with female interaction stereotypes (Oakley 2000).

Gardiner and Tiggemann (1999) explored the relationship between dominant leadership styles and mental health. Although there were no overall differences between men and women's general mental health, the researchers did find that women in male-dominated industries reported worse mental health when they utilized more traditionally female-oriented leadership styles. This research helps to uncover stress-related barriers to women working in senior management roles in male-dominated industries.

> "Women in male-dominated industries reported worse mental health." 24

Similarly, Grisoni and Beeby (2007) conducted an experiment examining 25 the extent to which leadership as a sense-making process is impacted by gender. Results indicated that groups of all female, all male, and mixed male and female managers quickly resorted to traditional male-dominated styles of decision-making when under a time pressure. There were expressions of frustration in the single-gendered teams that more creativity was not used in exploring a decision-making style. The researchers concluded that both genders need to be aware that the behavioral legacy of male-dominated command and control cultures is deeply embedded and may limit the emergence of more horizontal working relationships.

The Metaphor Barrier

For more than two decades, the barrier impeding women's progress toward   26
executive leadership positions has been referred to as the *glass ceiling* (Eisner and Harvey 2009). Although this is the dominant metaphor used to understand women's career path obstacles to top leadership, the research has indicated that the idea of a singular transparent barrier existing at a point in time near the top of career advancement is too simplistic of a concept. The glass ceiling is instead comprised of many intertwined and complex barriers that obstruct career advancement at various points along a career path. Eagly and Carli (2007) suggest that the glass-ceiling metaphor itself has become one of the obstacles.

Positing that the glass-ceiling metaphor misdiagnoses the problem,   27
thereby leading to ineffective remedies, Eagly and Carli (2007) suggest that a more appropriate metaphor would be a labyrinth. This new metaphor captures more of what research has shown to be true about women's career advancement obstacles. More specifically, it addresses the problem that there is not one absolute unvarying barrier at a high level in organizations. It also addresses the misperception that women and men have equal entry access in organizations. The labyrinth metaphor additionally captures more of the complexity of a journey toward a goal acknowledging inherent obstacles without being discouraging (Eagly and Carli 2007).

Conclusion

The growing body of literature exploring the value that women bring to corpo-   28
rate leadership elucidates some of the implications of women's scarcity in these positions. There is research correlating board and corporate management diversity with good corporate governance practices as well as with superior economic performance. Other studies have focused on the importance of women's perspectives in determining the strategic direction of organizations (Hillman et al. 1998; Adler 2001; Carter et al. 2003; Richard 2000; Wolfman 2007).

Women represent an important economic group in the changing compo-   29
sition of the marketplace and the global economy. In fact, women are a dominant force in the marketplace. In the United States alone, women represent the overwhelming majority of consumers and a growing segment of women-owned or women-controlled businesses generating trillions of dollars in sales and employing millions of people (Wolfman 2007).

In the 1980 *Harvard Business Review* article serving as the baseline for this   30
review, Felice Schwartz expressed optimism regarding women's future advancement into top leadership positions. Despite this optimism, a review of

the recent literature regarding women's advancement into leadership positions indicates that women have made little progress toward parity with men in holding positions of top leadership. The issues are complex and deeply embedded in attitudes, assumptions, social processes, and structures as well as in business imperatives. Future research and efforts toward progress may require new approaches and paradigms as researchers and practitioners seek to understand and address this ongoing problem.

References

Adler, R. D. "Women in the Executive Suite Correlate to High Profits." *Harvard Business Review* 79, no. 10 (2001).

Brizendine, Louann. "One Reason Women Don't Make It to the C-Suite." *Harvard Business Review* 86, no. 6 (2008): 36.

Byron, K. "A Meta-Analytic Review of Work-Family Conflict and Its Antecedents." *Journal of Vocational Behavior* 67 (2005): 169–198.

Carter, D. A., B. J. Simkins, and W. G. Simpson. "Corporate Governance Board Diversity and Firm Performance." *The Financial Review* 38, no. 1 (2003): 33–53.

Eagly, Alice H., and Linda L. Carli. "Women and the Labyrinth of Leadership." *Harvard Business Review* 85, no. 9 (2007): 63–71.

Eagly, A. H., and B. T. Johnson. "Gender and Leadership Style: A Meta-Analysis." *Psychological Bulletin* 108, no. 2 (1990): 233–256.

Eisner, S. P., and M. Harvey. "C-Change? Generation Y and the Glass Ceiling." *SAM Advanced Management Journal* 74, no. 1 (2009): 13–28.

European Professional Women's Network. Retrieved from http://www.europeanpwn.net.

Federal Glass Ceiling Commission of 1992. Retrieved from http:www.theglassceiling.com.

Gardiner, M., and M. Tiggemann. "Gender Differences in Leadership Style, Job Stress and Mental Health in Male and Female-Dominated Industries." *Journal of Occupational and Organizational Psychology* 72, no. 3 (1999): 301–315.

Greenhaus, J. H., and G. Powell. "When Work and Family Are Allies: A Theory of Work-Family Enrichment." *Academy of Management Review* 31, no. 1 (2006): 72–92.

Grisoni, L., and M. Beeby. "Leadership, Gender and Sense-Making." *Gender, Work and Organization* 14, no. 3 (2007): 190–209.

Hillman, A. J., I. C. Harris, A. A. Cannella, and L. Bellinger. "Diversity and the Bottom Line." *Journal of Commerce* September (1998).

Hoobler, J. M., S. J. Wayne, and G. Lemmon. "Bosses' Perceptions of Family-Work Conflict and Women's Promotability: Glass Ceiling Effects." *Academy of Management Journal* 52, no. 5 (2009): 939–957.

Kanter, R. M. "Some Effects of Proportions on the Group Life: Skewed Sex Ratios and Responses to Token Women." *American Journal of Sociology* 82 (1977): 965–990.

Kilian, C. M., D. Hukai, and C. E. McCarty. "Building Diversity in the Pipeline to Corporate Leadership." *Journal of Management Development* 24, no. 2 (2005): 155–168.

King, Eden B., Michelle R. Hebl, Jennifer M. George, and Sharon F. Matusik. "Understanding Tokenism: Antecedents and Consequences of a Psychological Climate of Gender Inequity." *Journal of Management* 36, no. 2 (2010): 482–510.

Kottke, Janet, L., and Mark D. Agars. "Understanding the Processes That Facilitate and Hinder Efforts to Advance Women in Organizations." *Career Development International* 10, no 3 (2005): 190–202.

Oakley, J. D. "Gender-Based Barriers to Senior Management Positions: Understanding the Scarcity of Female CEO's." *Journal of Business Ethics* 27, no. 4 (2000): 321–334.

Richard, O. "Racial Diversity, Business Strategy, and Firm Performance: A Resource-Based View." *Academy of Management Journal* 43, no. 2 (2000): 164–177.

Schwartz, Felice N. "'Invisible' Resource: Women for Boards." *Harvard Business Review* 58, no. 2 (1980): 6–18.

Wolfman, Toni G. "The Face of Corporate Leadership." *New England Journal of Public Policy* 22, no. 1/2 (2007): 37–72.

↪ READING ARGUMENTS

1. Kochanowski uses a number of analogies in this report. Point to instances where she analyzes or develops an analogy. How does this strategy help her to achieve her purpose?

2. Who is Kochanowski's intended audience? How can you tell?

3. Where does Kochanowski use inductive reasoning to make inferences and draw conclusions? Identify an example of this strategy, and explain how the evidence supports a general conclusion.

4. What is Kochanowski's thesis? What kind of evidence does she use to support this thesis? Is all of this evidence convincing? Explain.

5. In her discussion of women in the workplace, Kochanowski refers to the "justice paradox" (para. 14). What does she mean by this term? According to her, why is the "justice paradox" a problem for women seeking leadership positions in business?

This essay was published in the *Daily Beast* on March 18, 2010.

ARE WE THERE YET?

JESSICA BENNETT, JESSE ELLISON, AND SARAH BALL

They were an archetype: independent, determined young graduates of Seven 1
Sisters colleges, fresh-faced, new to the big city, full of aspiration. Privately,
they burned with the kind of ambition that New York encourages so well. Yet
they were told in job interviews that women could never get to the top, or even
the middle. They accepted positions anyway—sorting mail, collecting newspaper clippings, delivering coffee. Clad in short skirts and dark-rimmed glasses,
they'd click around in heels, currying favor with the all-male management,
smiling softly when the bosses called them "dollies." That's just the way the
world worked then. Though each quietly believed she'd be the one to break
through, ambition, in any real sense, wasn't something a woman could talk
about out loud. But by 1969, as the women's movement gathered force around
them, the dollies got restless. They began meeting in secret, whispering in the
ladies' room or huddling around a colleague's desk. To talk freely they'd head
to the Women's Exchange, a 19th-century relic where they could chat discreetly
on their lunch break. At first there were just three, then nine, then ultimately
46—women who would become the first group of media professionals to sue
for employment discrimination based on gender under Title VII of the Civil
Rights Act. Their employer was *Newsweek* magazine.

Until six months ago, when sex- and gender-discrimination scandals hit 2
ESPN, David Letterman's *Late Show*, and the *New York Post*, the three of us—all
young *Newsweek* writers—knew virtually nothing of these women's struggle.
Over time, it seemed, their story had faded from the collective conversation.
Eventually we got our hands on a worn copy of *In Our Time*, a memoir written
by a former *Newsweek* researcher, Susan Brownmiller, which had a chapter on
the uprising. With a crumpled Post-it marking the page, we passed it around,
mesmerized by descriptions that showed just how much has changed, and how
much hasn't.

Forty years after *Newsweek*'s women rose up, there's no denying our cohort 3
of young women is unlike even the half-generation before us. We are post–Title
IX women, taught that the fight for equality was history; that we could do, or
be, anything. The three of us were valedictorians and state-champion athletes;
we got scholarships and were the first to raise our hands in class. As young
professionals, we cheered the third female Supreme Court justice and, nearly,
the first female president. We've watched as women became the majority of
American workers, prompting a Maria Shriver–backed survey on gender,
released late last year, to proclaim that "the battle of the sexes is over."

The problem is, for women like us, the victory dance feels premature. 4
Youthful impatience? Maybe. But consider this: U.S. Department of Education
data show that a year out of school, despite having earned higher college GPAs
in every subject, young women will take home, on average across all professions, just 80 percent of what their male colleagues do. Even at the top end,
female M.B.A.s make $4,600 less per year in their first job out of business
school, according to a new Catalyst study. Motherhood has long been the
explanation for the persistent pay gap, yet a decade out of college, full-time
working women who haven't had children still make 77 cents on the male dollar. As women increasingly become the breadwinners in this recession, bringing home 23 percent less bacon hurts families more deeply than ever before.
"The last decade was supposed to be the 'promised one,' and it turns out it
wasn't," says James Turley, the CEO of Ernst & Young, a funder of the recent
M.B.A. study. "This is a wake-up call."

In countless small ways, each of us has felt frustrated over the years, as if 5
something was amiss. But as products of a system in which we learned that the
fight for equality had been won, we didn't identify those feelings as gender-
related. It seemed like a cop-out, a weakness, to suggest that the problem was
anybody's fault but our own. It sounds naive—we know—especially since our
own boss Ann McDaniel climbed the ranks to become *Newsweek*'s managing
director, overseeing all aspects of the company. Compared with the *Newsweek*
dollies, what did we have to complain about? "If we judge by what we see in the
media, it looks like women have it made," says author Susan Douglas. "And if
women have it made, why would you be so ungrateful to point to something
and call it sexism?"

Yet the more we talked to our friends
and colleagues, the more we heard the
same stories of disillusionment, regardless of profession. No one would dare say
today that "women don't write here," as
the *Newsweek* women were told 40 years
ago. But men wrote all but six of *Newsweek*'s 49 cover stories last year—and two

> "The more we talked
> to our friends and
> colleagues, the more we
> heard the same stories
> of disillusionment." 6

of those used the headline "The Thinking Man." In 1970, 25 percent of *Newsweek*'s editorial masthead was female; today that number is 39 percent. Better?
Yes. But it's hardly equality. (Overall, 49 percent of the entire company, the
business and editorial sides, is female.) "Contemporary young women enter
the workplace full of enthusiasm, only to see their hopes dashed," says historian Barbara J. Berg. "Because for the first time they're slammed up against
gender bias."

We should add that we are proud to work at *Newsweek*. (Really, boss, we 7
are!) We write about our magazine not because we feel it's worse here, but
because *Newsweek* was once ground zero for a movement that was supposed to
break at least one glass ceiling. Just as our predecessors' 1970 case didn't happen in a vacuum, *Newsweek* today is neither unique nor unusual. Female

bylines at major magazines are still outnumbered by seven to one; women are just 3 percent of Fortune 500 CEOs and less than a quarter of law partners and politicians. That imbalance even applies to the Web, where the founder of a popular copywriting Web site, Men with Pens, revealed late last year that "he" was actually a she. "I assumed if I chose a male name, [I'd] be viewed as somebody who runs a company, not a mom sitting at home with a child hanging off her leg," the woman says. It worked: her business doubled once she joined the boys' club.

We know what you're thinking: we're young and entitled, whiny and humorless—to use a single, dirty word, feminists! But just as the first black president hasn't wiped out racism, a female at the top of a company doesn't eradicate sexism. In fact, those contradictory signs of progress—high-profile successes that mask persistent inequality—are precisely the problem. Douglas describes those mixed messages as "enlightened sexism": the idea that because of all the gains women have made, biases that once would have been deemed sexist now get brushed off. Young women, consequently, are left in a bind: they worry they'll never be taken as seriously as the guys, yet when they're given the opportunity to run the show, they balk. A recent Girl Scouts study revealed that young women avoid leadership roles for fear they'll be labeled "bossy"; another survey found they are four times less likely than men to negotiate a first salary. As it turns out, that's for good reason: a Harvard study found that women who demand higher starting salaries are perceived as "less nice," and thus less likely to be hired. "This generation has had it ingrained in them that they must thrive within a 'yes, but' framework: Yes, be a go-getter, but don't come on too strong. Yes, accomplish, but don't brag about it," says Rachel Simmons, author of *The Curse of the Good Girl*. "The result is that young women hold themselves back, saying, 'I shouldn't say this, ask for this, do this—it will make me unlikable, a bitch, or an outcast.'"

Somewhere along the road to equality, young women like us lost their voices. So when we marched into the workforce and the fog of subtle gender discrimination, it was baffling and alien. Without a movement behind us, we had neither the language to describe it nor the confidence to call it what it was. "It's so much easier when you're the generation that gets to fight against [specific] laws than it is to deal with these more complicated issues," says Gail Collins, the *New York Times* columnist. In a highly sexualized, post-PC world, navigating gender roles at work is more confusing than ever. The sad truth is that when we do see women rise to the top, we wonder: was it purely their abilities, or did it have something to do with their looks? If a man takes an interest in our work, we can't help but think about the male superior who advised "using our sexuality" to get ahead, or the manager who winkingly asked one of us, apropos of nothing, to "bake me cookies." One young colleague recalls being teased about the older male boss who lingered near her desk. "What am I supposed to do with that? Assume that's the explanation for any accomplishments? Assume my work isn't valuable?" she asks. "It gets in your head, which is the most insidious part."

Recognizing that sexism still exists despite its subtlety is one of the chal- 10
lenges of the new generation—though it doesn't hold a candle to what the dollies of 1970 pulled off. When they filed their legal complaint, the bottom tiers
of the *Newsweek* masthead were filled almost exclusively by women. "It was a
nice place—especially if you were a man," says Nora Ephron, a *Newsweek* "mail
girl" in 1962. The women reported on the murder of a colleague, the State
Department, and the 1968 campaign. But when it came to writing, they were
forced to hand over their reporting to their male colleagues. "It was a very
hopeless time," remembers Brownmiller. "After a while you really did start to
lose your confidence. You started to think, 'Writing is what the men do.'"

Over dinner one night, a young researcher poured out her frustration to a 11
lawyer friend, who ordered her to call the Equal Employment Opportunity
Commission. She did, and slowly her colleagues signed on to a class-action
suit. They found a fiery young lawyer—now D.C. Congresswoman Eleanor
Holmes Norton—and they waited, nervously, until the time was right. "We
were very staid, ladylike, not guerrilla-theater types," says Pat Lynden, one of
the group's early organizers, who wrote cover stories for the *Atlantic Monthly*
and the *New York Times Magazine* even while she wasn't allowed to write for
Newsweek. "But eventually we just couldn't take it anymore."

A year later, as the national women's movement gathered steam, *News-* 12
week's all-male management decided to put feminism on their cover. Oblivi-
ous to the rebellion brewing at home, they looked past the legions of *Newsweek*
women and went outside the building for a writer—to the wife of one of their
top brass, whom they would ultimately describe, in an editor's note, as "a top-
flight journalist who is also a woman." It was the final straw. The night before
the issue hit newsstands, the *Newsweek* women sent a memo announcing a
press conference. They pooled their money to fly a colleague to Washington to
present a copy to Katharine Graham, the magazine's owner, who later asked,
"Which side am I supposed to be on?" Then on Monday, March 16, 1970, the
Newsweek women did what journalists do best: they took their story public.
Crowded into a makeshift conference room at the ACLU, *Newsweek*'s "news
hens" (as a local tabloid called them) held up a copy of their magazine, whose
bright yellow cover told their own story: "Women in Revolt." Two days later the
women of the *Ladies' Home Journal* would stage their own sit-in; others were
soon to follow.

It was a moment of hope, one that set the stage for a wave of progress that 13
continued rapidly through the 1990s. Twenty years after the *Newsweek* dollies
rose up, mothers were entering the workforce in unprecedented numbers,
women's organizations such as NOW saw surges in membership, and expanded
affirmative-action programs ensured that girls had equal access to education.
"Girl power" became the new female mantra, and young women's empower-
ment groups sprang up at YWCAs. By 2000, when the female employment rate
peaked, many women thought the job was done.

In the years since, there has been what Douglas describes as "a subtle, 14
insidious backlash." In the face of 9/11, two wars, and now the Great Recession,

gender equality—and stereotyping—became a secondary concern. Feminism was no longer a label to be worn with pride; Britney Spears and Paris Hilton now dominated airwaves. But the changes were more than cultural. The Global Gender Gap Index—a ranking of women's educational, health, political, and financial standing by the World Economic Forum—found that from 2006 to 2009 the United States had fallen from 23rd to 31st, behind Cuba and just above Namibia. Companies may have incorporated policies aimed at helping women, but they haven't helped as much as you'd think. "The U.S. always scores abysmally in terms of work-life balance," says the WEF's Kevin Steinberg. "But even here, [women] still rank 'masculine or patriarchal corporate culture' as the highest impediment to success." Exhibit A: the four most common female professions today are secretary, registered nurse, teacher, and cashier—low-paying, "pink collar" jobs that employ 43 percent of all women. Swap "domestic help" for nurse and you'd be looking at the top female jobs from 1960, back when want ads were segregated by gender.

The women of *Newsweek* thought, or hoped, they'd begun to solve these 15 problems four decades ago. Yet here we are. "It's sad," says Lynden, now 72. "Because we fought for all that." There's no denying that we're enjoying many of the spoils of those women's victories. We are no longer huddled in secret; we're reporting for a national magazine, and we're the ones doing the writing. We have a president whose first act in office was to sign a law that promises equal pay for equal work. Yet the fact that such a law is necessary makes the point: equality is still a myth. "We've got the entire weight of human history behind us, making us feel like we're kind of lucky to have jobs," says writer Ariel Levy. "And I think it takes a lot of fearlessness to think, 'F—k it, go ahead and yell at me, I'm going to fight for what I deserve.'" We've come a long way, baby. But there's still a long way to go.

⊙ READING ARGUMENTS

1. According to the writers, "Motherhood has long been the explanation for the persistent pay gap" between men and women (para. 4). What do they think is wrong with this explanation? According to the writers, why is the pay gap especially problematic now?

2. The writers spend much of the essay discussing female *Newsweek* employees in the late 1960s and early 1970s. Why do they include this historical background? Is it necessary?

3. What is the writers' position on the issue they discuss? Where do they refute opposing arguments? Do you find their refutations of these arguments effective? Why or why not?

4. In what sense is this essay an evaluation argument? Identify specific elements of this strategy.

THE REAL REASON SO FEW WOMEN ARE IN THE BOARDROOM

MARTY NEMKO

On average, women are rated as slightly better managers than men. Also, 1
women better understand the female consumer's mindset. That's important
because women make most purchases. So why are only 11% of Fortune 500
senior executives women?

The standard answer is "glass ceiling," a term that evokes the image of a 2
cabal of top male executives scheming to preserve an old boy's club.

While vestiges of old-boy hiring may remain, most top executives at 3
Fortune 500 companies are too worried about the bottom line to let any clubby
cravings affect who they hire as senior executives.

The primary reason for the 11% figure is that men, on average, are willing 4
to devote more time to their career. And time it takes. A study conducted by
The Business Roundtable, an association of CEOs, found that the average CEO
works 58 hours per week. Fortune 500 CEOs likely work even more.

Unlike in typical media portrayals, few male senior executives spend much 5
time hang-gliding. In the real world, here's how it more often plays out, as
reported to me by my many clients who are male senior executives. Their exercise is more likely to be on a treadmill while doing professional reading. If he's
married, when his wife urges him to do more of the domestic chores and parenting, he is likely to say something like, "I want to rise to the top and you want
me to, too. I like my work and you like our lifestyle. That requires lots of evenings and weekends. I spend as much time with the family as I can."

Most women make different choices. The October 10, 2004, lead story on 6
60 Minutes and the September 2003 *New York Times Magazine* story documented that a majority even of Ivy- and Stanford-educated female alumni did
not work full-time. Harvard Business School reports that only 38% of its
female MBA graduates, during their childbearing years, work full-time.

Dr. Warren Farrell, author of the 7
forthcoming book *Why Men Earn More*
(Amacom, 2005), found that a key reason
men earn more than women is number
of hours worked. In addition to providing abundant statistics, he interviewed a
number of successful senior executive
women. Each one stated that crucial to their success was their willingness to
work longer than most women are. For example, when I interviewed Lillian
Vernon (of Lillian Vernon Corporation), she said, "Many people who dream

> "A key reason men earn more than women is number of hours worked."

about their own businesses and don't have one, are not prepared to work that hard—to think about their job while they're getting dressed, showering, waiting for somebody—to think of every minute as an opportunity."

Theresa Metty, senior VP at Motorola, agreed, "Successful people don't see after-hour 'demands' as demands, but as opportunities. The opportunity to surprise, invent, create. . . ." 8

All this doesn't surprise me. Having been career coach to 2,000 professional clients, 2/3 female, I know that more women than men prioritize work/life balance, wanting more time for family, home, friends, and recreation. 9

In the privacy of my office, many capable, highly educated women who, in public, may mouth politically correct mantras decrying the dearth of women in the boardroom, admit that what they'd really like is to work part-time if at all, and only on a pleasant job, so they can have ample time for home, family, friends, etc. Far fewer women than men are willing to work 58+ hours a week and to take work home or do extensive after-work professional development activities during evenings and weekends. 10

Steven Rhoades, author of the new book *Taking Sex Differences Seriously*, cites study after study indicating that the main reason most women want ample family time is their biological drive to have children and be the primary family caregiver. Feminist activists argue that is social conditioning by "the male hegemony." But if that were true, then why do women take on most family caregiving in every society from Iceland to New Guinea, in every era from ancient times to today, and in all political contexts from communist to capitalist? Women's desire to prioritize family caregiving is mainly biological predisposition, not cultural brainwashing. 11

Some women argue that it's men's fault that women don't spend more time at work. For example, *Career Journal* senior correspondent Perri Capell wrote, "If more women had men at home doing for them what women traditionally do for men, they might be able to stay at the office longer." 12

Fact is, many women don't do it for men. They do it for themselves. On average, it is women, more than men, who want to have children. So it is unfair of them to insist that the men share heavily in the child rearing. 13

It is the woman, on average, who cares more about having lots of time with children. (And the data doesn't support the importance of that—after controlling for socioeconomic status, quantity of time matters little. Quality of time does.) Even many wealthy women, who could afford and have access to high-quality child care, choose to forego that so they can be with their children. If quantity of family time matters more to women, it is unfair for them to impose that value on their husbands. 14

And regarding domestic chores, most men aren't as concerned about a tastefully decorated and sparkling clean home. On average, women care more about this. 15

It is unfair for women to force men to spend time on what the woman wants. If a man were to insist that a woman devote equal time to the things he cares about—for example, financial and tax issues, that fix-it/build-it project, 16 or playing basketball, most people would think that unfair, selfish. Yet when women do it, we're expected to consider it reasonable.

I predict that if women—before they got married—informed their career-minded future husbands that they insist he fully share domestic and child-rearing responsibilities and that they don't expect to earn much money, many men would decide it isn't worth getting married. So, most women withhold those demands until afterwards. 17

A 2004 study by Catalyst, a women's advocacy organization, found that women aspire to senior executive positions at the same rate as men. But a woman (or a man) can't have it both ways. If she wants a moderate workweek, for the reasons I will outline below, she cannot fair-mindedly aspire to the boardroom. 18

Corporations, governments, and non-profits need plenty of good 20 to 40 hour-a-week workers, but not in the top spots. Here's why. 19

Imagine you were the CEO of a company and were considering two employees for a senior position. Candidate A had—over her or his 20-year career—worked 50 to 60 hours a week, and in spare time, made great efforts to keep upgrading skills. Meanwhile, Candidate B worked 40 hours a week, and in spare time, focused on family, home, friends, and recreation, and had taken years off to raise children—thereby losing professional contacts and currency with the latest information and technology. You'd almost certainly hire Candidate A. Fact is, more men than women are like Candidate A. That, and not a sexist glass ceiling, is the main reason why women represent only 11% of senior executives in Fortune 500 companies. 20

But let's say that you, the CEO, did what feminist activists advocate: install a family-friendly workplace that prioritizes work-life balance, and hired many women who had worked only 40 hours a week and taken years off to raise children. You might hire lots of people like Candidate B. If so, your company would likely go out of business. 21

Here's why. Your competitors would hire lots of Candidate A's. That would result not only in those senior executives—the company's more important people—being more productive, but their supervisees too. Dedicated, passionate leadership is infectious. 22

A company with such committed employees is an exciting, passion-filled place. The argument that working more than 40 hours a week is ineffective and leads to burnout is not true. What leads to burnout is meaningless or too difficult work in a passionless workplace, not additional hours of meaningful, doable work in a passionate environment. Some of the most alive people I know work long hours. The argument that working more than 40 hours a week leads to burnout is unsupported by sound research. Such rhetoric is a shoot-from-the-hip pitch that feminist advocates use to sell work-life balance to employers. We all know how being around dedicated people makes us more energized, not less. 23

A workplace with long, hard-working passionate people results in the company's products being better or more cost-effective, which makes thousands 24 of people—the customers—happier. Aren't you grateful when your home, TV, car, etc., is wonderful, reliable, and didn't cost too much? Creating excellent products, in turn, causes a company's profits to grow, which allows the company to invest in more innovation, provides money to the thousands of shareholders who entrusted their savings to the company, and increases the sense of pride and passion among the company's employees.

Meanwhile, your employees, mostly Candidate B's, zealots for work-life 25 balance, in the short run, will appreciate being able to leave work earlier than workers at your competitors' companies. When, in the middle of a brainstorming meeting, someone says, "Sorry, I have a parent-teacher conference. I have to leave," and you say, "Fine," everyone will smile at how family-friendly their workplace is. But inside, those with passion about their work will feel that passion just slightly diminished. Each such event—for example, every time an employee takes advantage of the Family Leave Act—diminishes your workplace's passion just a little more. A number of your employees, who had taken years off to raise a family, are less up-to-date and lack current professional contacts. In the intermediate term, your employees will be working for a company in decline because their competitors, filled with more passionate, dedicated, more knowledgeable, better connected employees, are producing a better product. And in the long term, such companies are far more likely to go out of business, leaving your boardroom with 0 percent women and 0 percent men.

The media's headline message is, "Hire more women and make the workplace 26 more family-friendly. Stop demanding that executives work 50 to 60 hours a week. Be more like France that mandates a 35-hour average workweek." The media is far less eager to trumpet the fact that despite France having a better-educated population and 35-hour workweek, its unemployment rate is more than twice the US rate and there's talk of changing the law. Advocating "family-friendly, work-life balance" workplaces will likely create different headlines a few years from now: "More jobs offshored to India." "More companies open new facilities in China." "Unemployment soars."

For the reasons stated at the outset, if I were a CEO, I would certainly want 27 to hire women in senior positions, but only those with a proven track record of having put in long hours at work and in professional development, and who could be counted on to continue doing so. Those are the same criteria I would use to evaluate male candidates.

Women, if you want to be considered for the boardroom, it doesn't cut it 28 to say you're working smart so you needn't work long hours. There are plenty of men competing for those slots who work both long and smart. You can't have it both ways: either plan on working long and smart or accept a lower-level job in exchange for work/life balance.

There would be plenty of room in my company for women and men who 29 want to work a moderate workweek, but not at the top. I don't care whether my executives have a y chromosome, but I want their priority not to be work-life balance, but rather, helping my company to ethically develop the best products in the world.

⊙ READING ARGUMENTS

1. In his opening paragraph, Nemko cites evidence that suggests that women should be better represented among business executives. Why do you think he includes this evidence? How does this opening support his argument?

2. What is Nemko's thesis? Restate it in your own words.

3. At several points in his argument, Nemko appeals to his own authority. How does he establish *ethos*? Do you find him credible? Why or why not?

4. In what respects is this a causal argument? Identify the specific elements of this strategy.

5. In paragraph 20, Nemko introduces a scenario with "Imagine. . . ." What does he hope to accomplish? Is he creating a **straw man**? Explain.

6. In paragraph 26, Nemko writes, "The media's headline message is, 'Hire more women and make the workplace more family-friendly. Stop demanding that executives work 50 to 60 hours a week. Be more like France that mandates a 35-hour workweek." What is Nemko's response to this message?

This essay is from Forbes.com, where it appeared on March 14, 2011.

DEBUNKING MYTHS OF GENDER EQUALITY

LISA QUAST

Countless numbers of women have worked for many years around the globe trying to achieve career parity to men; everything from equal pay for equal work to breaking through the proverbial "glass ceiling." 1

But a new report seeks to debunk the long-held myth that sex differences at work are "self-evident proof of widespread sex discrimination and sex-role stereotyping" and are instead, "the result of personal choices and preferences." The report is titled "Feminist Myths and Magic Medicine: The flawed thinking behind calls for further equality legislation." 2

In the report, written by Catherine Hakim, a senior research fellow in the London School of Economics and published by The Centre for Policy Studies, Dr. Hakim believes feminist demands for further equality legislation rest on faulty assumptions and outdated or partial evidence. Her research report attempts 3 to demonstrate that most of the theories and ideas built up around gender equality over the last few decades are actually wrong.

She notes that "despite feminist claims, the truth is that most men and 4 women have different career aspirations and priorities. Men and women often have different life-goals and policy makers should therefore not expect the same job outcomes." There are a dozen feminist myths Dr. Hakim believes have no solid basis in social science research, yet which are widely believed and reinforced in the media.

Here are just a few of the myths Dr. Hakim works to debunk in the report: 5

Myth: Higher female employment promotes gender equality. Dr. Hakim uses 6 a study by the International Labour Office (ILO) and several other academic studies that show raising female employment has actually led to a *reduction* in gender equality. How can this be? Because higher levels of female employment are associated with female-dominated service-type occupations, which are rarely high-status jobs. Also, more women with lower levels of education and less careerist attitudes are entering the workforce.

Myth: Women's access to higher education brings gender equality into the 7 workplace. Dr. Hakim cites studies that demonstrate how women with high-powered jobs tend to reduce or eliminate work-life balance issues by remaining childless or subcontracting childcare and domestic work to others. By contrast, "almost all their male colleagues are married, with several children, but also with wives who typically remain fulltime mothers and homemakers."

Myth: Men and women do not differ in careerist attitudes, values, or life 8 goals. Differences in attitudes and values are emerging from new studies as the "hidden hand shaping employment histories and career paths as well as private lives" of women and men. Dr. Hakim cites national interview surveys that show women divide into three very different groups in terms of life goals, values, and aspirations. A minority are career focused; a minority are centered on home and family life; and a majority seek a combination of paid work and family work. In contrast, the majority of men are more likely to be careerist in their attitudes and goals.

Myth: Women prefer to earn their own living and hate financial dependence on 9 men. Dr. Hakim believes one indicator of women's lifestyle preferences can be found in patterns of educational homogamy (whether women choose husbands with equal levels of education, or prefer a better-educated and higher-earning spouse). According to studies throughout Europe, women in most European countries still prefer to "marry up" to a man who is better educated and earns more money. Apparently, financial dependence on a man "has lost none of its attractions after the equal opportunities revolution." Dr. Hakim believes this is because "symmetrical family roles are not the ideal sought by most couples, even though they are popular among the minority of highly educated professionals."

Bottom Line . . . while equal opportunity policies have been successful over 10 the years in advancing women's workplace equality, it is also important to take into consideration career attitudes, values, and life goals when creating additional measures to promote equality—as these may differ between men and women and may even differ on a geographical basis.

What do you think? Will women ever be able to achieve career equality to men or will personal choices and preferences such as different career attitudes, values, and life goals keep us from achieving parity?

> "What do you think? Will women ever be able to achieve career equality to men?"

11

⊘ READING ARGUMENTS

1. This essay originally appeared in *Forbes*, a magazine that focuses on finance, industry, and investing. Who is the audience for this essay? How can you tell?

2. In paragraph 2, Quast says that there is a "long-held myth" that sex differences at work (such as a lack of women in high-level corporate jobs) are proof of discrimination and stereotyping. Do you agree this belief is indeed a myth? Explain.

3. What is the function of paragraphs 2–4? Are they necessary? Would the essay be more or less effective if these paragraphs were removed?

4. Quast relies heavily on a report by Catherine Hakim, a researcher at the London School of Economics. Does this source provide enough support for Quast's argument, or should she have included additional sources?

5. Much of Quast's essay refutes commonly held beliefs about gender discrimination. How convincingly does she refute these assumptions? Explain.

⊛ AT ISSUE: IS THE GLASS CEILING A MYTH OR A REALITY?

1. This essay originally appeared as a blog post, which Quast concluded by asking, "What do you think? Will women ever be able to achieve career equality to men or will personal choices and preferences such as different career attitudes, values, and life goals keep us from achieving parity?" How would you respond to these questions?

2. In paragraph 15, Kochanowski discusses "threat-rigidity theory," which predicts that "at an individual level, any perceived threat will increase both genders' reliance upon gender stereotypes." What evidence of this phenomenon do you see in "Are We There Yet?," "The Real Reason So Few Women Are in the Boardroom," or "Debunking Myths of Gender Equality"? Be specific.

3. According to the writers of "Are We There Yet?," we live in a "highly sexualized, post-PC world," where "navigating gender roles at work is more confusing than ever" (para. 9). What do you think they mean? Is this generalization consistent with your own experiences and observations? Why or why not?

⊛ WRITING ARGUMENTS: IS THE GLASS CEILING A MYTH OR A REALITY?

1. After reading these arguments about gender equality in the workplace, what are your views on the issue? Write an essay that presents your own position on whether the glass ceiling is a "myth" or a "reality."

2. The writers whose essays appear in this casebook make various claims about the real or perceived differences between men and women. For example, Kochanowski refers to studies showing "women's leadership styles to be more interactive and transformational whereas men's style has been identified as more directive" (para. 22). Similarly, Nemko contends that "women better understand the female consumer's mindset" (1). How significant are the differences between men and women in the context of education, business, and the workplace? Do men and women have different strengths and weaknesses? Do you think gender differences matter— that is, that they affect work habits and leadership styles? Answer these questions in an argumentative essay.

CHAPTER 26

Does the United States Need a Federal DREAM Act?

As a flashpoint in the immigration debate, the DREAM Act—the Development, Relief, and Education for Alien Minors Act—provokes strong opinions from both its supporters and its detractors. Given this debate, it may be surprising to learn that the legislation was originally suggested as a bipartisan compromise and as an alternative to more controversial policy proposals, such as amnesty or guest worker programs. Senator Orrin Hatch (R-Utah) drafted the first DREAM Act in 2001. Under its provisions, undocumented immigrants brought to the United States as children could earn legal resident status or citizenship. Although various versions of the bill have come up for a vote several times since then, the federal DREAM Act has never received enough congressional support to become law. Over the last decade, some of the bill's details have changed, but its broad outline and purpose remain the same.

The DREAM Act addresses a complex problem. Many children come to the United States with parents who either enter illegally or overstay their visas. The DREAM Act focuses on this demographic: it is applicable only to those brought to the United States before age sixteen. To apply for its provisions, undocumented immigrants must have lived in the country for at least five years and be between the ages of twelve and thirty-five. Applicants are also required to meet other criteria, such as having a high school diploma (or GED) and being of "good moral character" as determined by the Department of Homeland Security. (The DREAM Act specifically excludes some applicants, such as convicted felons and those who pose a public health risk.) Successful applicants would receive conditional resident status, thus qualifying for in-state tuition at public universities and colleges. Ultimately, they could achieve U.S. citizenship by earning a college degree (or by completing at least two years toward a degree) or serving in the military.

For comprehension quizzes,
see bedfordstmartins.com/practicalargument.

Supporters of the bill argue that current immigration policy blocks young immigrants from educational opportunities, professional advancement, and assimilation even though they were brought to the United States illegally through no fault of their own. Supporters also believe that the DREAM Act would have social and economic benefits, including reduced crime, lower social services costs, and greater economic productivity and tax revenue from higher-earning workers. Opponents of the bill are concerned that the DREAM Act rewards illegal behavior and creates incentives for "chain migration." Finally, some opponents ask why illegal immigrants should receive in-state discounts to attend colleges and universities that many U.S. citizens cannot afford.

As the essays that follow illustrate, this controversy is highly politicized. In "The Message the DREAM Act Sends," the *Economist* frames its support of the DREAM Act as a matter of decency and urges America to live up to its image as "a land of opportunity." Mark Krikorkian enumerates the DREAM Act's "four fatal flaws"; he also implies that the bill's proponents use emotionally manipulative stories of young immigrant children to "bootstrap a larger amnesty." In "Harry Reid's Illegal Alien Student Bailout," Michelle Malkin criticizes the DREAM Act as well as the activists and politicians of both parties who support it. Finally, Marshal Fitz's "Myth vs. Fact: The DREAM Act" offers a strong defense of the legislation, seeking to refute the "deceptive arguments" of the DREAM Act's opponents.

This unsigned essay was posted to the Web site of the *Economist* on November 21, 2010.

THE MESSAGE THE DREAM ACT SENDS

THE ECONOMIST

Last week Harry Reid said he would reintroduce a bill (thecaucus.blogs .nytimes.com/2010/11/17/reid-trying-again-on-immigration-bill) that would create a route to citizenship for certain undocumented young adults who were brought to America as children. According to the so-called DREAM Act, an undocumented immigrant will qualify for "conditional permanent residency" if he or she satisfies the following conditions (taken from the DREAM Act Portal, dreamact.info/students):

- Must have entered the United States before the age of 16 (i.e., 15 and younger)

- Must have been present in the United States for at least five consecutive years prior to enactment of the bill

- Must have graduated from a United States high school, or have obtained a GED, or have been accepted into an institution of higher education (i.e., college/university)

- Must be between the ages of 12 and 35 at the time of application

- Must have good moral character

Then, if the qualifying individual enlists in the armed forces or enrolls in 2 college, and completes two years of military service or two years of work toward a bachelor's (or higher) degree within six years of having gained conditional permanent residency, he or she will qualify for plain vanilla legal permanent residency, which entails the right to apply for citizenship.

Suppose your parents moved to America from Mexico without legal permis- 3 sion when you were five years old. You grow up in America. You graduate from high school in America. You're an American in every sense except the legal one. You want to go to college, but because your parents came into the country illicitly, you don't qualify for government financial aid, and you can't get legal work. If caught by immigration authorities, you face the pos- sibility of detention or deportation, even though this is, in every sense, your home. That doesn't seem fair. Every year, over 60,000 kids like you graduate high school in the United States. And unless some- thing like the DREAM Act becomes law, you and they will become part of a grow- ing class of marginalized and unprotected Americans without papers. Even then, the papers are no sure thing. You've got to serve in the military or get a couple years of college under your belt, and stay out of trouble. But at least you'll someday have the chance to enjoy the same rights and opportunities as your date to the prom.

> "You're an American in every sense except the legal one."

This strikes me as sensible and humane, if a little over-demanding. But 4 here's what the *National Review*'s Heather MacDonald has to say about it (nationalreview.com/corner/253569/trust-reason-not-emotion-dream-act -heather-mac-donald):

> The act signals to prospective illegal aliens the world over that if they can just get their child across the border illegally, they have put him on the path towards U.S. citizenship—and, as significant, the child will then be able to apply for legal status for his parents and siblings. . . .
>
> DREAM Act beneficiaries are certainly the most sympathetic cate- gory of amnesty candidates, and opponents of the act have been accused of hard-heartedness. Yet the act indisputably encourages and incentivizes more illegal behavior. It continues to send the message that the U.S. is not serious about its immigration laws, but will always eventually confer the same benefits on people who break the law entering the country as on those immigrants who respected American law.

I think it's useful in this debate to be as clear as we can be. We're mostly talk- 5 ing about Mexicans, so let's just talk about Mexicans. Lots and lots and lots of Mexicans come across the border to the United States not because they're a nation of heedless antinomians, but because this is (was?) where the work is. Many come because much of their family resides here, legally or illegally. It's worth noting that the southwestern portion of the United States *just was* Mexico, once upon a time.

There is an undeniable economic and cultural continuity between Mexico and the United States. The border distorts and disrupts it, but it cannot and will never put an end to it. The pattern of traffic between these two countries is not something to choke off, but something sensibly to regulate and rationalize.

"But we do regulate it sensibly!" you may insist. Well, suppose you're a hard- 6 working and ambitious Mexican with no family legally in the States and not much education, but you've got friends there, 50 miles away, and they tell you they're getting steady, relatively well-paying work. One of the things that's so attractive to you about America is its sound institutions, including its sturdy rule of law. You would very much like to migrate to the United States legally. So what are your options? Zip. Zilch. Zero. You have no options! There is no way to "get in line" and "wait your turn" (reason.org/files/a87d1550853898a9b306ef458f116079.pdf) because there is no line for you to stand in that leads to the legal right to live and work in the United States. So you pack up one day, take a hair-raising hike through the desert with your young daughter, meet up with your friends in Tucson, and get to work on the American dream. What were you supposed to do? Consign yourself and your daughter to a life on the edge of poverty out of respect for the American rule of law? Please.

The DREAM Act sends the message that although American immigration 7 law in effect tries to make water run uphill, we are not monsters. It says that we will not hobble the prospects of young people raised and schooled in America just because we were so perverse to demand that their parents wait in a line before a door that never opens. It signals that we were once a nation of immigrants, and even if we have become too fearful and small to properly honor that noble legacy, America in some small way remains a land of opportunity.

Yes, the DREAM Act also incentivizes illegal activity. But if the activity is 8 not one that ought to be illegal, perhaps we should consider changing the law? Something to consider, anyway. In the meantime, this small reform will make America a somewhat more decent place.

⊖ READING ARGUMENTS

1. How does the writer use causal argument? In what sense is this essay making an ethical argument?

2. In paragraph 3, the writer presents a hypothetical example: "Suppose your parents moved to America from Mexico without legal permission when you were five years old." What is the purpose of this strategy? Why do you think the writer uses the second person (*you*) here and elsewhere?

3. In paragraph 3 and in the essay's last paragraph, the writer addresses an opposing argument. What is this argument? How does he refute it? Do you find his refutation convincing? Why or why not?

4. According to the writer, what is the "message the DREAM Act sends"?

This essay was posted to *National Review Online* on December 1, 2010.

DREAM ON

MARK KRIKORIAN

Harry Reid and Nancy Pelosi have pledged a vote as early as this week on the DREAM Act (Development, Relief, and Education for Alien Minors), a bill that would legalize illegal aliens who arrived here before the age of 16 and who comply with certain educational or military-service requirements.

The core principle behind this amnesty proposal is that it is aimed at those who have grown up here and are, psychologically and emotionally, Americans. In the words of America's Voice, a hard-left open-borders group, the beneficiaries of the measure are "patriotic young Americans in all but paperwork."

There's no doubt that this is the most sympathetic group of illegal immigrants. That is precisely why DREAM has been dangled as bait for the more general amnesty proposals described as "comprehensive immigration reform," with amnesty advocates brandishing the situation of these young people as justification for a broader amnesty. (Though no one seems to have stopped to ask: If such a comprehensive bill would provide amnesty for all illegals, then why would we need DREAM?)

Nonetheless, now that the amnesty crowd has belatedly decided to move ahead on DREAM as a standalone measure, many in the public and Congress are open to the idea of addressing the situation of such young people. But the DREAM Act, in every one of its iterations over the years, has four fatal flaws.

1. The act is billed as legalizing those brought as infants or toddlers, and yet it covers people brought here up to age 16. The examples used by advocates are nearly always people who were brought here very young. The student-body president at Fresno State University, Pedro Ramirez—who was "coincidentally" revealed to be an illegal alien just as the DREAM Act lame-duck effort got under way—came here at age three. Harvard student Eric Balderas was brought here at age four. Yves Gomes was brought here at 14 months, Juan Gomez at two years, Marie Gonzalez at five, Daniel Padilla at four, and so on.

So why set the age cutoff at 16? If the point is to provide amnesty to those whose identity was formed here, then you'd need a much lower age cutoff. I have a 15-year-old, and if I took him to live illegally in Mexico (and living illegally is a lot harder to do there than here), he would always remain, psychologically, an American, because his identity is already formed. The Roman Catholic Church and English common law set the age of reason at seven. That, combined with a requirement of at least ten years' continuous residence here, seems like a much more defensible place to draw the line. Unless, of course, you're just using those who came as young children to bootstrap a larger amnesty.

2. Next, all amnesties have at least three harmful consequences, and the DREAM Act ignores all three. The first of these is massive fraud. Perhaps

one-fourth of those legalized under the 1986 Immigration Reform and Control Act received amnesty fraudulently, including Mahmud Abouhalima, a leader of the first World Trade Center attack. The fraud in

> "All amnesties have at least three harmful consequences."

that first big amnesty program was so pervasive as to be almost comical, with people claiming work histories here that included picking watermelons from trees and digging cherries out of the ground.

And yet what does the DREAM Act say about fraud? As Sen. Jeff Sessions 8 (R., Ala.) points out in "Ten Things You Need to Know about S-3827, the DREAM Act," the measure "prohibits using any of the information contained in the amnesty application (name, address, length of illegal presence that the alien admits to, etc.) to initiate a removal proceeding or investigate or prosecute fraud in the application process." This is like playing a slot machine without having to put any money in—any illegal alien can apply, and if he wins, great, but if he loses, he can't be prosecuted *even if he lied through his teeth about everything*. No amnesty proposal can be taken seriously unless applicants are made to understand, right up front, that any lies, no matter how trivial, will result in arrest and imprisonment.

3. Another problem with DREAM, which all amnesties share, is that it will 9 attract new illegal immigration. Prospective illegal immigrants, considering their options, are more likely to opt to come if they see that their predecessors eventually hit the jackpot. In 1986, we had an estimated 5 million illegals, 3 million of whom were legalized. We now have more than twice as many as before the last amnesty, and they've been promised repeatedly that if they hold out a little longer they'll be able to stay legally. Any new amnesty, even if only for those brought here as children, will attract further illegal immigration.

There's really no way to prevent this, but to minimize it, you need strin- 10 gent enforcement measures. This was the logic of the 1986 law and the recent "comprehensive immigration reform" proposals. The critique of such "grand bargains" has been that the illegals get their amnesty but the promised enforcement never materializes—and that critique remains valid. But if the sponsors of DREAM were serious about addressing the plight of people brought here as infants and toddlers, they would include muscular enforcement measures as proof of their bona fides. These would include mandatory use of E-Verify for all new hires, explicit authorization of state and local governments to enforce civil immigration law, and full implementation of an exit-tracking system for all foreign visitors, for starters. And the legal status of all the amnesty beneficiaries would remain provisional until the enforcement measures were up and running and passed judicial muster. Even these might not be sufficient to turn back a new wave of illegal immigration sparked by the amnesty, but the lack of such measures speaks volumes about the real intentions of the DREAM Act's sponsors.

4. Finally, all amnesties reward illegal immigrants—in this case, both those   11
brought here as children *and* the adults who subjected them to this limbo. Any
serious proposal to legalize young people brought here as infants or toddlers
would need to prevent the possibility that their parents and other adults
responsible for bringing them here illegally would ever receive any benefit
from the amnesty, namely, future sponsorship as legal immigrants. This could
be done in two ways: Either the amnesty recipients would not be put on a
"path to citizenship" at all, but instead be given a time-limited work visa,
indefinitely renewable so long as they stay out of trouble. This would mean
they could not petition for any relatives to immigrate in the future. Alternatively, the amnesty beneficiaries could receive green cards and eventual citizenship, but we would abolish all the legal-immigration categories for family
members other than spouses and minor children of U.S. citizens. Either way,
the adults who knew what they were doing would never be rewarded.

A DREAM Act 2.0 that addressed these problems—that prosecuted fraud,   12
implemented enforcement, prevented downstream legal immigration, and
focused much more narrowly on those who came very young—would possibly
be something that even I, were I a congressman, might be able to vote for. But
the lack of these elements is clear proof that the amnesty crowd isn't interested
in fixing the specific problem of a sympathetic but small group of people;
rather, these young people are simply poster children who have been used for
years to try to justify a general amnesty for all illegal aliens. And when the
DREAM Act fails, as it will, Pedro Ramirez and his fellows will need to ask
the pro-amnesty politicians and lobbying groups why they were sacrificed on
the altar of "comprehensive immigration reform."

⊘ READING ARGUMENTS

1. What is Krikorkian's thesis? Restate it in your own words.

2. Krikorkian acknowledges that the DREAM Act may benefit some
    young people who "have grown up here and are, psychologically
    and emotionally, Americans" (para. 2). He also concedes that they
    are "the most sympathetic group of illegal immigrants" (3). Do these
    concessions weaken his argument? Why or why not?

3. Krikorkian states that he could possibly support a revised version of
    the DREAM Act. What specific changes does he recommend? Does
    his willingness to compromise strengthen or weaken his argument?
    Explain.

This syndicated newspaper column was published on September 17, 2010.

HARRY REID'S ILLEGAL ALIEN STUDENT BAILOUT

MICHELLE MALKIN

The so-called DREAM Act would create an official path to Democrat voter registration for an estimated 2 million, college-age illegal aliens. Look past the public relations–savvy stories of "undocumented" valedictorians left out in the cold. This is not about protecting "children." It's about preserving electoral power through cap-and-gown amnesty.

Senate Majority Leader Harry Reid announced this week that he's attaching the DREAM Act to the defense authorization bill. With ethnic activists breathing down his neck and President Obama pushing to fulfill his campaign promise to Hispanics, Reid wants his queasy colleagues to vote on the legislation next week. Open-borders lawmakers have tried and failed to pass the DREAM Act through regular channels for the last decade. That's because informed voters know giving green cards to illegal alien students undermines the rule of law, creates more illegal immigration incentives, and grants preferential treatment to illegal alien students over law-abiding native and naturalized American students struggling to get an education in tough economic times. This bad idea is compounded by a companion proposal to recruit more illegal aliens into the military with the lure of citizenship (a fraud-ridden and reckless practice countenanced under the Bush administration).

DREAM Act lobbyists are spotlighting heart-wrenching stories of high-achieving teens brought to this country when they were toddlers. But instead of arguing for case-by-case dispensations, the protesters want blanket pardons. The broadly-drafted Senate bill would confer benefits on applicants up to age 35 and the House bill contains no age ceiling at all. The academic achievement requirements are minimal. Moreover, illegal aliens who didn't arrive in the country until they turned 15—after they laid down significant roots in their home country—would be eligible for DREAM Act benefits and eventual U.S. citizenship. And like past amnesty packages, the Democrat plan is devoid of any concrete eligibility and enforcement mechanisms to deter already-rampant immigration benefit fraud.

The DREAM Act sponsors have long fought to sabotage a clearly worded provision in the 1996 Illegal Immigration Reform and Immigrant Responsibility Act (IIRIRA) that states: "Notwithstanding any other provision of law, an alien who is not lawfully present in the United States shall not be eligible on the basis of residence within a State (or a political subdivision) for any postsecondary education benefit unless a citizen or national of the United States is eligible for such a benefit (in no less an amount, duration, and scope) without regard to whether the citizen or national is such a resident." Ten states defied that federal law and offered

DREAM Act–style tuition preference to illegal aliens: California, Illinois, Kansas, Nebraska, New Mexico, New York, Oklahoma, Texas, Utah, and Washington. The last time the DREAM Act champions tried to tack their scheme onto a larger immigration proposal, they snuck in language that would absolve those ten states of their law-breaking by repealing the 1996 law retroactively—and also offering the special path to green cards and citizenship for illegal alien students.

Despite the obvious electoral advantage this plan would give Democrats, several pro–illegal alien amnesty Republicans crossed the aisle to support the DREAM Act, including double-talking Sens. John McCain, Richard Lugar, Bob Bennett, Sam Brownback, Norm Coleman, Susan Collins, Larry Craig, Chuck Hagel, Kay Bailey Hutchison, Mel Martinez, Olympia Snowe, and presidential candidate Mike Huckabee (who champions even greater illegal alien student benefits than those proposed by Democrats). After paying lip service to securing the borders, McCain promised DREAM Act demonstrators this week that he supported the bill and would work to "resolve their issues." 5

Out-of-touch pols might want to pay attention to the world outside their bubble. A recent Quinnipiac University poll shows that Americans across the political spectrum favor tougher enforcement of existing immigration laws over rolling out the amnesty welcome wagon. When asked "Do you think immigration reform should primarily move in the direction of integrating illegal immigrants into American society or in the direction of stricter enforcement of laws against illegal immigration?," solid majorities of registered Republicans, Democrats, and independents chose stricter enforcement over greater integration of the illegal alien population. 6

> "Out-of-touch pols might want to pay attention to the world outside their bubble."

Democrats outside the Beltway have grown increasingly averse to signing on to illegal alien incentives—especially as the Obama jobs death toll mounts and economic confidence plummets. Here in Colorado, a handful of Democrats joined Republican lawyers to kill a state-level DREAM Act amid massive higher-ed budget cuts and a bipartisan voter backlash. Asked why she opposed the illegal alien student bailout, one Democrat lawmaker said quite simply: "I listened to my constituents." 7

An alien concept in Washington, to be sure. 8

⊙ READING ARGUMENTS

1. Can you identify any elements of a **Rogerian argument** in Malkin's essay? Explain.

2. Malkin believes that the DREAM Act is a "bad idea" (para. 2). Why? How does she use causal argument to support her position?

3. What is Malkin's attitude toward those who support the DREAM Act? What words and phrases does she use to characterize their goals and

their motives? Do you find her language effective and persuasive? Why or why not?

4. Although Malkin focuses on the DREAM Act and its supporters, she also criticizes national politicians. On what basis does she criticize them? How does she support these criticisms?

This essay was posted to the Web site of the Center for American Progress in December 2010.

MYTH VS. FACT: THE DREAM ACT

MARSHALL FITZ

The arguments mustered in opposition to the Development, Relief, and Education for Alien Minors Act, or DREAM Act, have never been particularly persuasive. It's hard to make a straight-faced argument against providing kids who lack immigration status through no fault of their own an opportunity to go to college or serve the country through military service. 1

That's why dozens of House members spoke in favor of the bill, which passed when it came to the floor on December 8. Only a few hardliners stood to oppose it. The extreme broadsides levied by those House conservatives have been echoed by senators seeking to block consideration of the bill. More than anything, these deceptive arguments clearly expose the moral callousness of the opponents. 2

It's important to expose the flaws and blatant misrepresentations in DREAM Act opponents' most common arguments against the bill. It should be clear that the Senate has no good reason not to pass it. 3

Myth: America can't afford the DREAM Act.

Fact: America can't afford not to pass the DREAM Act.

One of the most baseless excuses for opposing the bill is fiscal. Opponents of the bill have tried to throw a series of sensational and utterly unsupported cost figures into the debate, hoping something will stick. But the nonpartisan Congressional Budget Office, or CBO, did the analysis and concluded that the DREAM Act would reduce the deficit by $2.2 billion over the next 10 years. 4

DREAM-eligible youths would not be eligible for health care subsidies, including Medicaid, or other federal means-tested benefits like food stamps or Pell grants. More importantly, the alternative of removing the 700,000 eligible kids would cost taxpayers $16.2 billion over five years. 5

The far stronger argument is: "America can't afford not to pass the DREAM Act."

> "America can't afford not to pass the DREAM Act." 6

Myth: The DREAM Act would reward illegal behavior.

Fact: This isn't amnesty. Eligible youth who had no say in the decision to come to the United States would have to work hard to earn permanent residence, and the earliest they could gain citizenship would be 13 years.

Opponents grasp for the moral high ground with this feeble contention. The 7 dubious claim that providing a path to legal status somehow violates our commitment to the rule of law is standard fare for opponents of immigration reform. But this tired "anti-amnesty" argument lacks all resonance when applied to this population.

These kids were brought to the United States before they had a say in their 8 life circumstances. Denying them hope and opportunity is punishment for an act beyond their control. Enabling them to work hard and earn the privilege of citizenship is hardly "rewarding" illegal behavior.

Moreover, the hypocrisy of some of the elected officials who would con- 9 demn these kids to marginalization is shameful. Sen. David Vitter (R-LA), who has confessed to moral waywardness, complains with a straight face that these kids are subverting the rule of law.

Myth: Passing the DREAM Act would encourage more illegal immigration.

Fact: The bill has strict requirements that make only a discrete one-time universe of individuals eligible for relief.

When immigration reform of any sort is under consideration, the "magnet" 10 excuse returns to vogue like clockwork. To be sure, this bill is not a solution to the problem of illegal immigration. But neither is it a magnet for more undocumented migration. And according to the secretary of homeland security the DREAM Act will enable DHS to better focus its resources on criminals and security threats.

To be eligible for relief under the DREAM Act an individual must have 11 come to the United States before they were 16 years old, and they must have been in the United States for more than five years on the date of enactment. In addition, they must be under 30 years old on the date of enactment and they must prove that they have possessed good moral character from the time they arrived in the United States. Those types of strict requirements—particularly the mandatory number of years in the United States—ensure there will be no surge of undocumented immigrants at the border.

Myth: The DREAM Act would trigger large-scale "chain migration."

Fact: It would be at least 10 years before a DREAM Act beneficiary could sponsor their spouse or child for permanent residence and at least 13 years before they could sponsor their parents or siblings.

Another claim rolled out with monotonous regularity is the "chain migration" 12 excuse. Opponents falsely suggest that the nation's immigration system authorizes sponsorship of extended family, conjuring up hordes of great-aunts, step-uncles, and third cousins immigrating to the United States once the DREAM Act beneficiary gains legal status.

The reality is that our immigration laws only permit sponsorship of 13 immediate relatives. And the soonest these youths would be able to sponsor their spouses or minor children to come to the United States would be 10 years after enactment. They could not sponsor their parents or siblings until after they became U.S. citizens, which is a minimum of 13 years after gaining legal status. Moreover, if their parents or siblings were in the United States unlawfully they would be required to leave the United States for 10 years before becoming eligible for sponsorship.

A 23-year wait to bring your parents to the United States doesn't square 14 with the chain migration menace promoted by opponents.

Myth: We have to secure the border before doing anything else on immigration.

Fact: Our border is more secure than ever.

A prevalent tactic designed to delay taking a position on immigration issues is 15 the "sequence" excuse. "We have to secure our borders first" has become the most common and perhaps least defensible talking point to prevent consideration of immigration-related legislation.

In fact, the singular focus of our immigration policies for the last nine 16 years has been ramping up resources and implementing enforcement strategies. There are exponentially more boots and barriers on the ground at the southern border, and it is more secure than ever in our history. We spend more than $17 billion each year on our immigration enforcement agencies—a 70 percent increase over the last five years. And just six months ago we added another $600 million in emergency funding.

Myth: We can't bother with issues like the DREAM Act when we have more pressing priorities.

Fact: It is not an either/or proposition. Congress can address more than one important issue at a time.

During this lame duck period we've seen a new delay tactic deployed: the 17 "prioritization" excuse. Yes, there is an array of pressing priorities facing the country right now requiring congressional attention. Sadly, the one issue senators opposing the DREAM Act leveraged to try to block progress on the nation's agenda was way down that list: tax breaks for the wealthy. If they showed as much concern for the next generation as they do for millionaires, they would realize that this is an investment in future leaders, thinkers, and entrepreneurs.

Dealing with the expiring tax cuts was certainly an important topic for 18 congressional attention. But it should not have been to the exclusion of other critical issues. We elect our officials on the assumption, or at least the hope, that they can walk and chew gum at the same time. With the tax cut debate now in the rearview mirror, some senators are pivoting to argue that we are out of time and that impinging on the holidays is sacrilegious. What is truly immoral is that these senators would try to put their vacations before the lives of these youths.

Myth: We need more time to analyze the DREAM Act.

Fact: The basic elements of the bill are well understood and have been considered many times over the last nine years.

Last but not least is the process excuse, a standard ploy to justify delaying a 19 vote. Opponents complain that numerous versions of the bill have been introduced and they need more time to thoroughly analyze it.

But this is not a new or complicated bill. The basic elements of the 20 DREAM Act are straightforward, well understood, and have been considered numerous times over the last nine years. It has been introduced by every Congress since 2001. It passed the Senate Judiciary Committee by a 16–3 vote in October 2003. And it passed the Senate Judiciary Committee again in 2006 by voice vote as part of the McCain-Kennedy comprehensive bill, which passed the full Senate by a 62–36 margin.

Conclusion

We have three basic options for addressing the situation confronting these 21 young undocumented people: deport them to a country they barely know; preserve the status quo and consign these talented kids—who include valedictorians—to a hopeless future; or pass the DREAM Act and give them an opportunity to work hard and earn the privilege of citizenship.

The first and second options are morally bankrupt and fiscally irrespon- 22 sible. As mentioned earlier, deporting the 700,000 youths whom the Congressional Budget Office has concluded would qualify for benefits under the bill would cost taxpayers about $16.2 billion over five years. Preserving the status quo is to accept system failure and allow these youngsters to languish unproductively on the margins of society. Both options run counter to America's economic interests and to core American values.

The truth is, only the third alternative—passing the DREAM Act—makes 23 economic, practical, and moral sense. Indeed, most (but not all) of the bill's opponents fear the politics around the bill more than they object to the substance. That tension between fear of the far right's backlash and what's right as a matter of policy and justice has driven them to evade the obligations of governance. The evidence of evasion lies in the transparent dissembling used to justify preventing a vote.

It's time for Congress to quit machinating and start solving problems. 24 No more stale, flimsy excuses. The American public strongly supports the DREAM Act. The time has come for Congress to stand and deliver. This dream has waited long enough.

⊖ READING ARGUMENTS

1. Writing in support of the DREAM Act, Fitz seeks to debunk the "myths" about the legislation. What are these myths? How does Fitz use them to define the DREAM Act? Why is definition central to his purpose?

2. Fitz uses a series of opposing arguments to structure his essay. Choose one of these opposing arguments, and evaluate the evidence he uses to refute it. Do you find his refutation effective?

3. Fitz implies that critics of the DREAM Act rely on logical fallacies. What are these fallacies? Do you agree with Fitz's characterization of these critics' arguments? Why or why not?

4. In his concluding paragraphs, Fitz discusses the "three basic options" (para. 21) for addressing the problem of young undocumented immigrants in the United States. What are these options? What objections does Fitz have to the first two?

5. Fitz accuses some of the DREAM Act's opponents of "shameful" hypocrisy. For example, he points out that "Sen. David Vitter (R-LA), who has confessed to moral waywardness, complains with a straight face that these kids are subverting the rule of law" (9). Is this an **ad hominem** attack, or is Fitz's point about Vitter's past relevant to the issue?

⊖ AT ISSUE: DOES THE UNITED STATES NEED A FEDERAL DREAM ACT?

1. In "Myth vs. Fact: The DREAM Act," Marshall Fitz writes that opponents of the bill try to claim the "moral high ground" (para. 7), but supporters of the DREAM Act also make ethical arguments. How would you summarize the ethical claims on each side of this issue, as represented in these essays? How are the writers' standards of right and wrong different? Which side do you believe makes the more persuasive ethical case? Why?

2. According to Michelle Malkin, DREAM Act lobbyists spotlight "heart-wrenching stories of high-achieving teens brought to this country when they were toddlers" (3). Here and elsewhere, she suggests that supporters of the bill make manipulative and misleading emotional appeals. Do you agree? Does her criticism apply to the supporters of

the DREAM Act represented in this casebook? What role does *pathos* play in America's public discussion of immigration?

3. Fitz asserts that "most (but not all) of the bill's opponents fear the politics around the bill more than they object to the substance" (23). As a result, politicians "evade the obligations of governance." What distinction is Fitz making? How might Malkin respond to Fitz's claim? How do these two writers' contrasting views reflect different assumptions about the role of elected officials?

◑ WRITING ARGUMENTS: DOES THE UNITED STATES NEED A FEDERAL DREAM ACT?

1. Do you believe the United States should pass a federal DREAM Act? After reading the essays in this casebook and thinking about this issue, write an essay that presents your position on the question.

2. In "The Message the DREAM Act Sends," the writer ties immigration policy to the national identity of the United States: "The DREAM Act sends the message that . . . we were once a nation of immigrants, and even if we have become too fearful and small to properly honor that noble legacy, America in some small way remains a land of opportunity" (para. 7). Do you think that immigration generally makes America stronger, or do you believe that it harms the country in some fundamental way? Write an argumentative essay explaining your point of view. (You may use your own personal experiences and family history to support your position.)

Plato

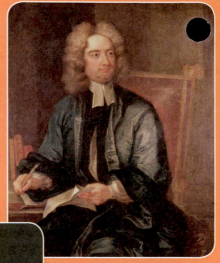

Jonathan Swift

Martin Luther King Jr.

Betty Friedan

Rachel Carson

James Baldwin

THE ALLEGORY OF THE CAVE

PLATO

Plato (428 BCE–347 BCE) was an important Greek philosopher. In The Republic, *from which "The Allegory of the Cave" is drawn, Plato examines the nature of reality, how we know what we know, and how we should act. An* **allegory** *is a dramatic representation of abstract ideas by characters and events in a story or image. "The Allegory of the Cave" is an imagined dialogue between Plato's teacher (Socrates) and brother (Glaucon).*

And now, I said, let me show in a figure how far our nature is enlightened or 1 unenlightened:—Behold! human beings living in an underground den, which has a mouth open towards the light and reaching all along the den; here they have been from their childhood, and have their legs and necks chained so that they cannot move, and can only see before them, being prevented by the chains from turning round their heads. Above and behind them a fire is blazing at a distance, and between the fire and the prisoners there is a raised way; and you will see, if you look, a low wall built along the way, like the screen which marionette players have in front of them, over which they show the puppets.

I see. 2

And do you see, I said, men passing along the wall carrying all sorts of 3 vessels, and statues and figures of animals made of wood and stone and various materials, which appear over the wall? Some of them are talking, others silent.

You have shown me a strange image, and they are strange prisoners. 4

Like ourselves, I replied; and they see only their own shadows, or the shad- 5 ows of one another, which the fire throws on the opposite wall of the cave?

True, he said; how could they see anything but the shadows if they were 6 never allowed to move their heads?

And of the objects which are being carried in like manner they would only 7 see the shadows?

Yes, he said. 8

And if they were able to converse with one another, would they not sup- 9 pose that they were naming what was actually before them?

Very true. 10

 For comprehension quizzes,
see bedfordstmartins.com/practicalargument.

And suppose further that the prison had an echo which came from the 11
other side, would they not be sure to fancy when one of the passers-by spoke
that the voice which they heard came from the passing shadow?

No question, he replied.   12

To them, I said, the truth would be literally nothing but the shadows of the 13
images.

That is certain.   14

And now look again, and see what will naturally follow if the prisoners are 15
released and disabused of their error. At first, when any of them is liberated
and compelled suddenly to stand up and turn his neck round and walk and
look towards the light, he will suffer sharp pains; the glare will distress him,
and he will be unable to see the realities of which in his former state he had
seen the shadows; and then conceive someone saying to him, that what he saw
before was an illusion, but that now, when he is approaching nearer to being
and his eye is turned towards more real existence, he has a clearer vision—
what will be his reply? And you may further imagine that his instructor is
pointing to the objects as they pass and requiring him to name them,—will he
not be perplexed? Will he not fancy that the shadows which he formerly saw
are truer than the objects which are now shown to him?

Far truer.   16

And if he is compelled to look straight at the light, will he not have a pain 17
in his eyes which will make him turn away to take refuge in the objects of
vision which he can see, and which he will conceive to be in reality clearer than
the things which are now being shown to him?

True, he said.   18

And suppose once more, that he is reluctantly dragged up a steep and rugged
ascent, and held fast until he is forced into the presence of the sun himself, is he not
likely to be pained and irritated? When he approaches the light his eyes will be dazzled, and he will not be able to see anything at all of what are now called realities.

Not all in a moment, he said.   20

He will require to grow accustomed to the sight of the upper world. And 21
first he will see the shadows best, next the reflections of men and other objects
in the water, and then the objects themselves; then he will gaze upon the light
of the moon and the stars and the spangled heaven; and he will see the sky and
the stars by night better than the sun or the light of the sun by day?

Certainly.   22

Earth's star, often associated
in Plato's work with reason,
absolute good, intellectual
illumination, and God

Last of all he will be able to see the sun,° and not mere reflections of him 23
in the water, but he will see him in his own proper place, and not in another;
and he will contemplate him as he is.

Certainly.   24

He will then proceed to argue that this is he who gives the season and the 25
years, and is the guardian of all that is in the visible world, and in a certain way
the cause of all things which he and his fellows have been accustomed to
behold?

Clearly, he said, he would first see the sun and then reason about him.   26

27 And when he remembered his old habitation, and the wisdom of the den and his fellow prisoners, do you not suppose that he would felicitate himself on the change, and pity them?

28 Certainly, he would.

29 And if they were in the habit of conferring honors among themselves on those who were quickest to observe the passing shadows and to remark which of them went before, and which followed after, and which were together; and who were therefore best able to draw conclusions as to the future, do you think that he would care for such honors and glories, or envy the possessors of them? Would he not say with Homer,°

    Better to be the poor servant of a poor master,

and to endure anything, rather than think as they do and live after their manner?

A blind Greek poet from the eighth century BCE, author of the epics The Iliad *and* The Odyssey

30 Yes, he said, I think that he would rather suffer anything than entertain these false notions and live in this miserable manner.

31 Imagine once more, I said, such an one coming suddenly out of the sun to be replaced in his old situation; would he not be certain to have his eyes full of darkness?

32 To be sure, he said.

33 And if there were a contest, and he had to compete in measuring the shadows with the prisoners who had never moved out of the den, while his sight was still weak, and before his eyes had become steady (and the time which would be needed to acquire this new habit of sight might be very considerable), would he not be ridiculous? Men would say of him that up he went and down he came without his eyes; and that it was better not even to think of ascending; and if any one tried to loose another and lead him up to the light, let them only catch the offender, and they would put him to death.

34 No question, he said.

35 This entire allegory, I said, you may now append, dear Glaucon,° to the previous argument; the prison house is the world of sight, the light of the fire is the sun, and you will not misapprehend me if you interpret the journey upwards to be the ascent of the soul into the intellectual world according to my poor belief, which, at your desire, I have expressed—whether rightly or wrongly God knows. But, whether true or false, my opinion is that in the world of knowledge the idea of good appears last of all, and is seen only with an effort; and, when seen, is also inferred to be the universal author of all things beautiful and right, parent of light and of the lord of light in this visible world, and the immediate source of reason and truth in the intellectual; and that this is the power upon which he who would act rationally either in public or private life must have his eye fixed.

Plato's brother, who responds to the questions, ideas, and arguments Socrates poses in The Republic

36 I agree, he said, as far as I am able to understand you.

37 Moreover, I said, you must not wonder that those who attain to this beatific vision are unwilling to descend to human affairs; for their souls are ever hastening into the upper world where they desire to dwell; which desire of theirs is very natural, if our allegory may be trusted.

38 Yes, very natural.

And is there anything surprising in one who passes from divine contem- 39
plations to the evil state of man, misbehaving himself in a ridiculous manner; if, while his eyes are blinking and before he has become accustomed to
the surrounding darkness, he is compelled to fight in courts of law, or in
other places, about the images or the shadows of images of justice, and is
endeavoring to meet the conceptions of those who have never yet seen absolute justice?

Anything but surprising, he replied.   40

Anyone who has common sense will remember that the bewilderments of 41
the eyes are of two kinds, and arise from two causes, either from coming out of
the light or from going into the light, which is true of the mind's eye, quite as
much as of the bodily eye; and he who remembers this when he sees anyone
whose vision is perplexed and weak, will not be too ready to laugh; he will first
ask whether that soul of man has come out of the brighter life, and is unable to
see because unaccustomed to the dark, or having turned from darkness to the
day is dazzled by excess of light. And he will count the one happy in his condition and state of being, and he will pity the other; or, if he have a mind to laugh
at the soul which comes from below into the light, there will be more reason in
this than in the laugh which greets him who returns from above out of the
light into the den.

That, he said, is a very just distinction.   42

But then, if I am right, certain professors of education must be wrong 43
when they say that they can put a knowledge into the soul which was not there
before, like sight into blind eyes.

They undoubtedly say this, he replied.   44

Whereas, our argument shows that the power and capacity of learning
exists in the soul already; and that just as the eye was unable to turn from darkness to light without the whole body, so too the instrument of knowledge can
only by the movement of the whole soul be turned from the world of becoming into that of being, and learn by degrees to endure the sight of being, and of
the brightest and best of being, or in other words, of the good.

Very true.   46

And must there not be some art which will effect conversion in the easiest 47
and quickest manner; not implanting the faculty of sight, for that exists already,
but has been turned in the wrong direction, and is looking away from the truth?

Yes, he said, such an art may be presumed.   48

And whereas the other so-called virtues of the soul seem to be akin to 49
bodily qualities, for even when they are not originally innate they can be
implanted later by habit and exercise, the virtue of wisdom more than anything else contains a divine element which always remains, and by this
conversion is rendered useful and profitable; or, on the other hand, hurtful and
useless. Did you never observe the narrow intelligence flashing from the keen
eye of a clever rogue—how eager he is, how clearly his paltry soul sees the way
to his end; he is the reverse of blind, but his keen eyesight is forced into the
service of evil, and he is mischievous in proportion to his cleverness?

Very true, he said. 50

But what if there had been a circumcision of such natures in the days of 51
their youth; and they had been severed from those sensual pleasures, such as
eating and drinking, which, like leaden weights, were attached to them at their
birth, and which drag them down and turn the vision of their souls upon the
things that are below—if, I say, they had been released from these impediments
and turned in the opposite direction, the very same faculty in them would have
seen the truth as keenly as they see what their eyes are turned to now.

Very likely. 52

Yes, I said; and there is another thing which is likely, or rather a necessary 53
inference from what has preceded, that neither the uneducated and uninformed of the truth, nor yet those who never make an end of their education,
will be able ministers of State; not the former, because they have no single aim
of duty which is the rule of all their actions, private as well as public; nor the
latter, because they will not act at all except upon compulsion, fancying that
they are already dwelling apart in the islands of the blessed.

Very true, he replied. 54

Then, I said, the business of us who are the founders of the State will be to 55
compel the best minds to attain that knowledge which we have already shown
to be the greatest of all—they must continue to ascend until they arrive at the
good; but when they have ascended and seen enough we must not allow them
to do as they do now.

What do you mean? 56

I mean that they remain in the upper world: but this must not be allowed; 57
they must be made to descend again among the prisoners in the den, and par-
take of their labors and honors, whether they are worth having or not.

But is not this unjust? he said; ought we to give them a worse life, when 58
they might have a better?

You have again forgotten, my friend, I said, the intention of the legislator, 59
who did not aim at making any one class in the State happy above the rest; the
happiness was to be in the whole State, and he held the citizens together by
persuasion and necessity, making them benefactors of the State, and therefore
benefactors of one another; to this end he created them, not to please themselves, but to be his instruments in binding up the State.

True, he said, I had forgotten. 60

Observe, Glaucon, that there will be no injustice in compelling our philos- 61
ophers to have a care and providence of others; we shall explain to them that in
other States, men of their class are not obliged to share in the toils of politics:
and this is reasonable, for they grow up at their own sweet will, and the government would rather not have them. Being self-taught, they cannot be expected to
show any gratitude for a culture which they have never received. But we have
brought you into the world to be rulers of the hive, kings of yourselves and of
the other citizens, and have educated you far better and more perfectly than
they have been educated, and you are better able to share in the double duty.
Wherefore each of you, when his turn comes, must go down to the general

underground abode, and get the habit of seeing in the dark. When you have acquired the habit, you will see ten thousand times better than the inhabitants of the den, and you will know what the several images are, and what they represent, because you have seen the beautiful and just and good in their truth. And thus our State, which is also yours, will be a reality, and not a dream only, and will be administered in a spirit unlike that of other States, in which men fight with one another about shadows only and are distracted in the struggle for power, which in their eyes is a great good. Whereas the truth is that the State in which the rulers are most reluctant to govern is always the best and most quietly governed, and the State in which they are most eager, the worst.

Quite true, he replied.   62

And will our pupils, when they hear this, refuse to take their turn at the toils of State, when they are allowed to spend the greater part of their time with one another in the heavenly light?   63

Impossible, he answered; for they are just men, and the commands which we impose upon them are just; there can be no doubt that every one of them will take office as a stern necessity, and not after the fashion of our present rulers of State.   64

Yes, my friend, I said; and there lies the point. You must contrive for your future rulers another and a better life than that of a ruler, and then you may have a well-ordered State; for only in the State which offers this, will they rule who are truly rich, not in silver and gold, but in virtue and wisdom, which are the true blessings of life. Whereas if they go to the administration of public affairs, poor and hungering after their own private advantage, thinking that hence they are to snatch the chief good, order there can never be; for they will be fighting about office, and the civil and domestic broils which thus arise will be the ruin of the rulers themselves and of the whole State.   65

Most true, he replied.   66

And the only life which looks down upon the life of political ambition is that of true philosophy. Do you know of any other?   67

Indeed, I do not, he said.   68

⊖ READING ARGUMENTS

1. Do you find Plato's allegory persuasive? What are its strengths and weaknesses?

2. According to Plato, what are the benefits of becoming educated about the true nature of reality? What are the drawbacks and costs of this process?

3. "The Allegory of the Cave" contains elements of a proposal argument. What does Plato propose? In what sense, if any, does his proposal apply to contemporary politics?

4. This argument is presented in the form of a dialogue, in which Glaucon responds to Socrates. How do Glaucon's responses move Plato's argument along?

⊕ WRITING ARGUMENTS

Both Plato and Thomas Jefferson (p. 770) discuss political leadership. How are their views similar? Where do their beliefs about the proper conduct and nature of political leaders differ? Which writer's argument seems more persuasive, and why? Develop your ideas in an argumentative essay.

TO HIS COY MISTRESS

ANDREW MARVELL

Andrew Marvell (1621–1678) was a member of the English Parliament for twenty years, starting in 1658. His poetry, which he wrote for his own enjoyment, was not published until after his death. "To His Coy Mistress" is his best-known poem.

Had we but world enough, and time,   1
This coyness, lady, were no crime.
We would sit down, and think which way
To walk, and pass our long love's day.
Thou by the Indian Ganges° side   5 *A river in India*
Should'st rubies find: I by the tide   *A river in England that flows*
Of Humber° would complain.° I would   *past the city of Hull*
Love you ten years before the Flood,   *To write poems or songs of*
And you should, if you please, refuse   *unrequited love*
Till the conversion of the Jews.°   10 *The belief that Jews would*
My vegetable love° should grow   *be converted to Christianity*
Vaster than empires, and more slow.   *during the Last Judgment;*
An hundred years should go to praise   *the end of time*
Thine eyes, and on thy forehead gaze: *A slow-growing love*
Two hundred to adore each breast:
But thirty thousand to the rest.   15
An age at least to every part,
And the last age should show your heart.
For, lady, you deserve this state,
Nor would I love at lower rate.   20
    But at my back I always hear
Time's winged chariot hurrying near;
And yonder all before us lie
Deserts of vast eternity.

25

Thy beauty shall no more be found,
Nor in thy marble vault shall sound
My echoing song; then worms shall try
That long preserved virginity,
And your quaint honor turn to dust,
And into ashes all my lust.
The grave's a fine and private place,
But none, I think, do there embrace.
          Now therefore, while the youthful hue
Sits on thy skin like morning dew,
And while thy willing soul transpires
At every pore with instant fires,
Now let us sport us while we may;
and now, like am'rous birds of prey,
Rather at once our time devour,

Slowly chewing jaws   Than languish in his slow-chapt° power,
Let us roll all our strength, and all
Our sweetness, up into one ball;
And tear our pleasures with rough strife

Through   Thorough° the iron gates of life.
Thus, though we cannot make our sun
Stand still, yet we will make him run.

30
35
40
45

❯READING ARGUMENTS

1. "To His Coy Mistress" is divided into three sections. Paraphrase each section's main idea in a single sentence.

2. What does the phrase "coy mistress" suggest about the occasion and audience for the poem? How do you think the "coy mistress" would respond to the speaker's arguments?

3. How does the speaker's attitude toward time—and toward his relationship with the lady he addresses—change in line 21? How does this shift support his argument? What does he say will happen to the lady if she is not persuaded by his poem?

4. The concluding stanza of the poem begins with the phrase, "Now therefore." How does the speaker develop a deductive argument in the lines that follow?

❯WRITING ARGUMENTS

1. Write a letter from the "coy mistress" to the poem's speaker refuting his arguments.

2. "To His Coy Mistress" is generally considered to be a poem on the theme of *carpe diem*, which means "seize the day." The full quotation comes from the Roman poet Horace: "Seize the day, and place no trust in tomorrow." Does this seem like a good philosophy of life? Write an argumentative essay that develops your position on this issue.

A MODEST PROPOSAL

JONATHAN SWIFT

Jonathan Swift (1667–1745) was a Protestant clergyman (dean of St. Patrick's Cathedral in Dublin) and a member of the Irish ruling class. His other works include A Tale of a Tub *(1704) and* Gulliver's Travels *(1726). "A Modest Proposal," written in 1729, addresses the wretched condition of the Irish people under English rule: drought had caused crop failures in Ireland, and English landowners ignored the widespread famine while thousands died of starvation.*

1   It is a melancholy object to those who walk through this great town or travel in the country, when they see the streets, the roads, and cabin doors, crowded with beggars of the female sex, followed by three, four, or six children, all in rags and importuning every passenger for an alms. These mothers instead of being able to work for their honest livelihood, are forced to employ all their time in strolling to beg sustenance for their helpless infants: who as they grow up either turn thieves for want of work, or leave their dear native country to fight for the pretender in Spain,° or sell themselves to the Barbadoes.°

2   I think it is agreed by all parties that this prodigious number of children in the arms, or on the backs, or at the heels of their mothers, and frequently of their fathers, is in the present deplorable state of the kingdom a very great additional grievance; and, therefore, whoever could find out a fair, cheap, and easy method of making these children sound, useful members of the commonwealth, would deserve so well of the public as to have his statue set up for a preserver of the nation.

3   But my intention is very far from being confined to provide only for the children of professed beggars; it is of a much greater extent, and shall take in the whole number of infants at a certain age who are born of parents in effect as little able to support them as those who demand our charity in the streets.

4   As to my own part, having turned my thoughts for many years upon this important subject, and maturely weighed the several schemes of our projectors, I have always found them grossly mistaken in their computation. It is true, a

James Francis Edward Stuart (1688–1766), descendant of the Stuart royal line. After the Stuarts were expelled from Protestant England in 1689, they took refuge in Catholic countries.

A New World colony in the Caribbean. The poor sometimes emigrated from Ireland to Barbados to find work.

Just born

child just dropped from its dam° may be supported by her milk for a solar year, with little other nourishment; at most not above the value of 2s., which the mother may certainly get, or the value in scraps, by her lawful occupation of begging; and it is exactly at one year old that I propose to provide for them in such a manner as instead of being a charge upon their parents or the parish, or wanting food and raiment for the rest of their lives, they shall on the contrary contribute to the feeding, and partly to the clothing, of many thousands.

There is likewise another great advantage in my scheme, that it will pre- 5 vent those voluntary abortions, and that horrid practice of women murdering their bastard children, alas! too frequent among us! sacrificing the poor inno- cent babes I doubt more to avoid the expense than the shame, which would move tears and pity in the most savage and inhuman breast.

The number of souls in this kingdom being usually reckoned one million 6 and a half, of these I calculate there may be about 200,000 couple whose wives are breeders; from which number I subtract 30,000 couple who are able to maintain their own children (although I apprehend there cannot be so many, under the present distress of the kingdom); but this being granted, there will remain 170,000 breeders. I again subtract 50,000 for those women who mis- carry, or whose children die by accident or disease within the year. There only remain 120,000 children of poor parents annually born. The question there- fore is, how this number shall be reared and provided for? which, as I have already said, under the present situation of affairs, is utterly impossible by all the methods hitherto proposed. For we can neither employ them in handicraft nor agriculture; we neither build houses (I mean in the country) nor cultivate land; they can very seldom pick up a livelihood by stealing, till they arrive at six years old, except where they are of towardly parts, although I confess they learn the rudiments much earlier, during which time they can, however, be properly looked upon only as probationers; as I have been informed by a principal gen- tleman in the county of Cavan, who protested to me that he never knew above one or two instances under the age of six, even in a part of the kingdom so renowned for the quickest proficiency in that art.

I am assured by our merchants, that a boy or a girl before twelve years old 7 is no salable commodity; and even when they come to this age they will not yield above 3£. or 3£. 2s. 6d. at most on the exchange; which cannot turn to account either to the parents or kingdom, the charge of nutriment and rags having been at least four times that value.

I shall now therefore humbly propose my own thoughts, which I hope will 8 not be liable to the least objection.

I have been assured by a very knowing American of my acquaintance in 9 London, that a young healthy child well nursed is at a year old a most deli- cious, nourishing, and wholesome food, whether stewed, roasted, baked, or broiled; and I make no doubt that it will equally serve in a fricassee or a ragout.

I do therefore humbly offer it to public consideration that of the 120,000 10 children already computed, 20,000 may be reserved for breed, whereof only one-fourth part to be males; which is more than we allow to sheep, black cattle, or swine; and my reason is, that these children are seldom the fruits of marriage, a circumstance not much regarded by our savages; therefore one male will be sufficient to serve four females. That the remaining 100,000 may, at a year old, be offered in sale to the persons of quality and fortune through the kingdom; always advising the mother to let them suck plentifully in the last month, so as to render them plump and fat for a good table. A child will make two dishes at an entertainment for friends; and when the family dines alone, the fore and hind quarter will make a reasonable dish, and seasoned with a little pepper or salt will be very good boiled on the fourth day, especially in winter.

11   I have reckoned upon a medium that a child just born will weigh 12 pounds, and in a solar year, if tolerably nursed, will increase to 28 pounds.

12   I grant this food will be somewhat dear, and therefore very proper for landlords, who, as they have already devoured most of the parents, seem to have the best title to the children.

13   Infants' flesh will be in season throughout the year, but more plentiful in March, and a little before and after: for we are told by a grave author, an eminent French physician, that fish being a prolific diet, there are more children born in Roman Catholic countries about nine months after Lent than at any other season; therefore, reckoning a year after Lent, the markets will be more glutted than usual, because the number of popish infants is at least three to one in this kingdom: and therefore it will have one other collateral advantage, by lessening the number of papists° among us.

Catholics. The term papists *suggests their allegiance to the Pope rather than to the Church of England.*

14   I have already computed the charge of nursing a beggar's child (in which list I reckon all cottagers, laborers, and four-fifths of the farmers) to be about 2s. per annum, rags included; and I believe no gentleman would repine to give 10s. for the carcass of a good fat child, which, as I have said, will make four dishes of excellent nutritive meat, when he has only some particular friend or his own family to dine with him. Thus the squire will learn to be a good landlord, and grow popular among the tenants; the mother will have 8s. net profit, and be fit for work till she produces another child.

15   Those who are more thrifty (as I must confess the times require) may flay the carcass; the skin of which artificially dressed will make admirable gloves for ladies, and summer boots for fine gentlemen.

16   As to our city of Dublin, shambles° may be appointed for this purpose in the most convenient parts of it, and butchers we may be assured will not be wanting: although I rather recommend buying the children alive, and dressing them hot from the knife as we do roasting pigs.

Butcher shops

17   A very worthy person, a true lover of his country, and whose virtues I highly esteem, was lately pleased in discoursing on this matter to offer a refinement upon my scheme. He said that many gentlemen of this kingdom, having of late destroyed their deer, he conceived that the want of venison might be well supplied by the bodies of young lads and maidens, not exceeding fourteen years of age nor under twelve; so great a number of both sexes in every country being now ready to starve for want of work and service; and these to be disposed of by their parents, if alive, or otherwise by their nearest relations. But

with due deference to so excellent a friend and so deserving a patriot, I cannot be altogether in his sentiments; for as to the males, my American acquaintance assured me from frequent experience that their flesh was generally tough and lean, like that of our schoolboys by continual exercise, and their taste disagreeable; and to fatten them would not answer the charge. Then as to the females, it would, I think, with humble submission be a loss to the public, because they soon would become breeders themselves: and besides, it is not improbable that some scrupulous people might be apt to censure such a practice (although indeed very unjustly), as a little bordering upon cruelty; which, I confess, has always been with me the strongest objection against any project, how well soever intended.

But in order to justify my friend, he confessed that this expedient was put into his head by the famous Psalmanazar,° a native of the island Formosa, who came from thence to London about twenty years ago: and in conversation told my friend, that in his country when any young person happened to be put to death, the executioner sold the carcass to persons of quality as a prime dainty; and that in his time the body of a plump girl of fifteen, who was crucified for an attempt to poison the emperor, was sold to his imperial majesty's prime minister of state, and other great mandarins° of the court, in joints from the gibbet,° at 400 crowns. Neither indeed can I deny, that if the same use were made of several plump young girls in this town, who without one single groat° to their fortunes cannot stir abroad without a chair, and appear at the playhouse and assemblies in foreign fineries which they never will pay for, the kingdom would not be the worse.   18

Some persons of a desponding spirit are in great concern about the vast number of poor people, who are aged, diseased, or maimed, and I have been desired to employ my thoughts what course may be taken to ease the nation of so grievous an encumbrance. But I am not in the least pain upon that matter, because it is very well known that they are every day dying and rotting by cold and famine, and filth and vermin, as fast as can be reasonably expected. And as to the young laborers, they are now in as hopeful condition: They cannot get work, and consequently pine away for want of nourishment, to a degree that if at any time they are accidentally hired to common labor, they have not strength to perform it; and thus the country and themselves are happily delivered from the evils to come.

I have too long digressed, and therefore shall return to my subject. I think the advantages by the proposal which I have made are obvious and many, as well as of the highest importance.   20

For first, as I have already observed, it would greatly lessen the number of papists, with whom we are yearly overrun, being the principal breeders of the nation as well as our most dangerous enemies; and who stay at home on purpose to deliver the kingdom to the Pretender, hoping to take their advantage by the absence of so many good Protestants, who have chosen rather to leave their country than stay at home and pay tithes against their conscience to an Episcopal curate.   21

George Psalmanazar (1679?–1763), who falsely claimed to be the first person from Formosa (modern-day Taiwan) to visit Europe. He described Formosan native customs that included cannibalism.

Chinese nobles, court officials, or magistrates

A post for hanging; a gallows

A small coin

Secondly, The poor tenants will have something valuable of their own, 22
which by law may be made liable to distress° and help to pay their landlord's
rent, their corn and cattle being already seized, and money a thing unknown.

Able to be seized to pay a debt

Thirdly, Whereas the maintenance of 100,000 children from two years old 23
and upward, cannot be computed at less that 10s. a-piece per annum, the
nation's stock will be thereby increased £50,000 per annum, beside the profit
of a new dish introduced to the tables of all gentlemen of fortune in the kingdom who have any refinement in taste. And the money will circulate among
ourselves, the goods being entirely of our own growth and manufacture.

Fourthly, The constant breeders beside the gain of 8s. sterling per annum 24
by the sale of their children, will be rid of the charge of maintaining them after
the first year.

Fifthly, This food would likewise bring great custom to taverns, where the 25
vintners will certainly be so prudent as to procure the best receipts for dressing
it to perfection, and consequently have their houses frequented by all the fine
gentlemen, who justly value themselves upon their knowledge in good eating;
and a skillful cook who understands how to oblige his guests, will contrive to
make it as expensive as they please.

Sixthly, This would be a great inducement to marriage, which all wise 26
nations have either encouraged by rewards or enforced by laws and penalties.
It would increase the care and tenderness of mothers toward their children,
when they were sure of a settlement for life to the poor babes, provided in
some sort by the public, to their annual profit instead of expense. We should
see an honest emulation among the married women, which of them would
bring the fattest child to the market. Men would become as fond of their wives
during the time of their pregnancy as they are now of their mares in foal, their
cows in calf, their sows when they are ready to farrow; nor offer to beat or kick
them (as is too frequent a practice) for fear of a miscarriage.

Many other advantages might be enumerated. For instance, the addition 27
of some thousand carcasses in our exportation of barreled beef, the propaga-
tion of swine's flesh, and improvement in the art of making good bacon, so
much wanted among us by the great destruction of pigs, too frequent at our
table; which are no way comparable in taste or magnificence to a well-grown,
fat, yearling child, which roasted whole will make a considerable figure at a
lord mayor's feast or any other public entertainment. But this and many others
I omit, being studious of brevity.

Supposing that 1,000 families in this city would be constant customers for 28
infants' flesh, besides others who might have it at merry-meetings, particularly
at weddings and christenings, I compute that Dublin would take off annually
about 20,000 carcasses; and the rest of the kingdom (where probably they will
be sold somewhat cheaper) the remaining 80,000.

I can think of no one objection that will possibly be raised against this 29
proposal unless it should be urged that the number of people will be thereby
much lessened in the kingdom. This I freely own, and it was indeed one principal design in offering it to the world. I desire the reader will observe, that I

*The indigenous Sami people
of northern European
countries, including Sweden,
Norway, and Finland. The
term is now considered
pejorative.*
Brazil

*Jerusalem, which was
conquered by the Roman
commander Titus in 70* AD

England

calculate my remedy for this one individual kingdom of Ireland and for no
other that ever was, is, or I think ever can be upon earth. Therefore let no man
talk to me of other expedients: of taxing our absentees at 5s. a pound: of using
neither clothes nor household furniture except what is of our own growth and
manufacture: of utterly rejecting the materials and instruments that promote
foreign luxury: of curing the expensiveness of pride, vanity, idleness, and gam-
ing in our women: of introducing a vein of parsimony, prudence, and temper-
ance: of learning to love our country, in the want of which we differ even from
Laplanders.° and the inhabitants of Topinamboo:° of quitting our animosities
and factions, nor acting any longer like the Jews, who were murdering one
another at the very moment their city° was taken: of being a little cautious not
to sell our country and conscience for nothing: of teaching landlords to have at
least one degree of mercy toward their tenants: lastly, of putting a spirit of
honesty, industry, and skill into our shopkeepers; who, if a resolution could
now be taken to buy only our native goods, would immediately unite to cheat
and exact upon us in the price, the measure, and the goodness, nor could ever
yet be brought to make one fair proposal of just dealing, though often and earnestly invited to it.

Therefore I repeat, let no man talk to me of these and the like expedients, 30
till he has at least some glimpse of hope that there will be ever some hearty and
sincere attempt to put them in practice.

But as to myself, having been wearied out for many years with offering 31
vain, idle, visionary thoughts, and at length utterly despairing of success, I fortunately fell upon this proposal; which, as it is wholly new, so it has something
solid and real, of no expense and little trouble, full in our own power, and
whereby we can incur no danger in disobliging England. For this kind of commodity will not bear exportation, the flesh being of too tender a consistence to
admit a long continuance in salt, although perhaps I could name a country°
which would be glad to eat up our whole nation without it.

After all, I am not so violently bent upon my own opinion as to reject any 32
offer proposed by wise men, which shall be found equally innocent, cheap,
easy, and effectual. But before something of that kind shall be advanced in contradiction to my scheme, and offering a better, I desire the author or authors
will be pleased maturely to consider two points. First, as things now stand, how
they will be able to find food and raiment for 100,000 useless mouths and
backs. And secondly, there being a round million of creatures in human figure
throughout this kingdom, whose subsistence put into a common stock would
leave them in debt 2,000,000£. sterling, adding those who are beggars by profession to the bulk of farmers, cottagers, and laborers, with the wives and
children who are beggars in effect; I desire those politicians who dislike my
overture, and may perhaps be so bold as to attempt an answer, that they
will first ask the parents of these mortals, whether they would not at this day
think it a great happiness to have been sold for food at a year old in the manner
I prescribe, and thereby have avoided such a perpetual scene of misfortunes as
they have since gone through by the oppression of landlords, the impossibility

of paying rent without money or trade, the want of common sustenance, with neither house nor clothes to cover them from the inclemencies of the weather, and the most inevitable prospect of entailing the like or greater miseries upon their breed for ever.

I profess, in the sincerity of my heart, that I have not the least personal   33 interest in endeavoring to promote this necessary work, having no other motive than the public good of my country, by advancing our trade, providing for infants, relieving the poor, and giving some pleasure to the rich. I have no children by which I can propose to get a single penny; the youngest being nine years old, and my wife past childbearing.

❯READING ARGUMENTS

1. Swift's "A Modest Proposal" is **satire**: it takes a position that is so extreme that readers must necessarily disagree with it. By taking such a position, Swift ridicules the English political system that he considers corrupt and insensitive and implies another, more reasonable argument that the reader must infer. What is the real argument that Swift is making in "A Modest Proposal"? What social reforms does he propose?

2. Where does "A Modest Proposal" use inductive reasoning?

3. In what sense is "A Modest Proposal" an ethical argument?

4. Swift's use of **irony**—saying one thing but meaning another—is a useful technique for making an argument, yet it also has limitations. What are some of these limitations?

5. What elements of a proposal argument appear in this essay? Which elements, if any, are missing?

❯WRITING ARGUMENTS

1. Write your own "modest proposal." Choose a contemporary issue or controversy (political, cultural, or social). Then, write an argumentative essay that uses **irony**, **satire**, and **hyperbole** (intentional exaggeration) to make your point.

2. "A Modest Proposal" includes population data, economic projections, and other kinds of support. What point do you think Swift is making about actual proposals to solve social or political problems? Do you think his point is relevant today? Why or why not?

THE DECLARATION OF INDEPENDENCE

THOMAS JEFFERSON

Thomas Jefferson, born in 1743, was one of the founding fathers of the United States. He served in the Virginia House of Burgesses and the Continental Congress, as governor of Virginia, minister to France, secretary of state in President George Washington's cabinet, vice president, and president of the United States for two terms. He also founded the University of Virginia. In 1776, he was chosen to draft the Declaration of Independence, the founding document of American liberties. Jefferson died on July 4, 1826.

In Congress, July 4, 1776
The Unanimous Declaration of the
Thirteen United States of America

When in the Course of human events it becomes necessary for one people to 1 dissolve the political bands which have connected them with another, and to assume among the powers of the earth, the separate and equal station to which the Laws of Nature and of Nature's God entitle them, a decent respect to the opinions of mankind requires that they should declare the causes which impel them to the separation.

We hold these truths to be self-evident, that all men are created equal, that 2 they are endowed by their Creator with certain unalienable Rights, that among these are Life, Liberty, and the pursuit of Happiness. That to secure these rights, Governments are instituted among Men, deriving their just powers from the consent of the governed. That whenever any Form of Government becomes destructive of these ends, it is the Right of the People to alter or to abolish it, and to institute new Government, laying its foundation on such principles and organizing its powers in such form, as to them shall seem most likely to effect their Safety and Happiness. Prudence, indeed, will dictate that Governments long established should not be changed for light and transient causes; and accordingly all experience hath shewn that mankind are more disposed to suffer, while evils are sufferable, than right themselves by abolishing the forms to which they are accustomed. But when a long train of abuses and usurpations, pursuing invariably the same Object evinces a design to reduce them under absolute Despotism, it is their right, it is their duty, to throw off such Government, and to provide new Guards for their future security. Such has been the patient sufferance of these Colonies; and such is now the necessity which constrains them to alter their former Systems of Government. The history of the present King of Great Britain is a history of repeated injuries and usurpations, all having in direct object the establishment of an absolute Tyranny over these States. To prove this, let Facts be submitted to a candid° world.

Impartial, without prejudice

He has refused his Assent to Laws, the most wholesome and necessary for the public good.

4   He has forbidden his Government to pass laws of immediate and pressing importance, unless suspended in their operation till his Assent should be obtained; and when so suspended, he has utterly neglected to attend to them.

5   He has refused to pass other Laws for the accommodation of large districts of people, unless those people would relinquish the right of Representation in the Legislature, a right inestimable to them and formidable to tyrants only.

6   He has called together legislative bodies at places unusual, uncomfortable, and distant from the depository of their Public Records, for the sole purpose of fatiguing them into compliance with his measures.

7   He has dissolved Representative Houses repeatedly, for opposing with manly firmness his invasions on the rights of the people.

8   He has refused for a long time, after such dissolutions, to cause others to be elected; whereby the Legislative Powers, incapable of Annihilation, have returned to the People at large for their exercise; the State remaining in the mean time exposed to all the dangers of invasion from without, and convulsions within.

9   He has endeavored to prevent the population of these States; for that purpose obstructing the Laws for Naturalization of Foreigners; refusing to pass others to encourage their migration hither, and raising the conditions of new Appropriations of Lands.

10   He has obstructed the Administration of Justice, by refusing his Assent to Laws for establishing Judiciary Powers.

11   He has made Judges dependent on his Will alone, for the tenure of their offices, and the amount and payment of their salaries.

12   He has erected a multitude of New Offices, and sent hither swarms of Officers to harass our people, and eat out their substance.

13   He has kept among us, in times of peace, Standing Armies without the Consent of our legislatures.

14   He has affected to render the Military independent of and superior to the Civil Power.

15   He has combined with others to subject us to a jurisdiction foreign to our constitution, and unacknowledged by our laws; giving his Assent to their Acts of pretended Legislation: For quartering large bodies of armed troops among us: For protecting them, by a mock Trial, from punishment for any Murders which they should commit on the Inhabitants of these States: For cutting off our Trade with all parts of the world: For imposing Taxes on us without our Consent: For depriving us in many cases, of the benefits of Trial by Jury: For transporting us beyond Seas to be tried for pretended offenses: For abolishing the free System of English Laws in a neighboring Province,° establishing therein an Arbitrary government, and enlarging its Boundaries so as to render it at once an example and fit instrument for introducing the same absolute

Quebec, whose residents were deprived of political representation by the British government in 1774

rule into these Colonies: For taking away our Charters, abolishing our most valuable Laws and altering fundamentally the Forms of our Governments: For suspending our own Legislatures, and declaring themselves invested with power to legislate for us in all cases whatsoever.

He has abdicated Government here, by declaring us out of his Protection and waging War against us. 16

He has plundered our seas, ravaged our Coasts, burnt our towns, and destroyed the lives of our people. 17

He is at this time transporting large Armies of foreign Mercenaries to complete the works of death, desolation and tyranny, already begun with circumstances of Cruelty & Perfidy scarcely paralleled in the most barbarous ages, and totally unworthy the Head of a civilized nation. 18

He has constrained our fellow Citizens taken Captive on the high Seas to bear Arms against their Country, to become the executioners of their friends and Brethren, or to fall themselves by their Hands. 19

He has excited domestic insurrections amongst us, and has endeavored to bring on the inhabitants of our frontiers, the merciless Indian Savages, whose known rule of warfare, is an undistinguished destruction of all ages, sexes, and conditions. 20

In every stage of these Oppressions We have Petitioned for Redress in the most humble terms: Our repeated Petitions have been answered only by repeated injury. A Prince, whose character is thus marked by every act which may define a Tyrant, is unfit to be the ruler of a free people. 21

Nor have We been wanting in attention to our British brethren. We have warned them from time to time of attempts by their legislature to extend an unwarrantable jurisdiction over us. We have reminded them of the circumstances of our emigration and settlement here. We have appealed to their native justice and magnanimity, and we have conjured them by the ties of our common kindred to disavow these usurpations, which would inevitably interrupt our connections and correspondence. They too have been deaf to the voice of justice and of consanguinity. We must, therefore, acquiesce in the necessity, which denounces our Separation, and hold them, as we hold the rest of mankind, Enemies in War, in Peace Friends. 22

We, THEREFORE the Representatives of the UNITED STATES OF AMERICA, in General Congress, Assembled, appealing to the Supreme Judge of the world for the rectitude of our intentions, do, in the Name, and by Authority of the good People of these Colonies, solemnly publish and declare, That these United Colonies are, and of Right ought to be FREE AND INDEPENDENT STATES; that they are Absolved from all Allegiance to the British Crown, and that all political connection between them and the State of Great Britain, is and ought to be totally dissolved; and that as Free and Independent States, they have full Power to levy War, conclude Peace, contract Alliances, establish Commerce, and to do all other Acts and Things which 23

Independent States may of right do. And for the support of this Declaration, with a firm reliance on the protection of Divine Providence, we mutually pledge to each other our Lives, our Fortunes, and our sacred Honor.

⊖READING ARGUMENTS

1. What are the purposes of the first and second paragraphs of the Declaration of Independence? Do these opening paragraphs present information deductively or inductively?

2. In paragraph 2, Jefferson writes, "Governments long established should not be changed for light and transient causes." Why is this qualification important to his argument? What objections does it anticipate?

3. According to the Declaration, what is the purpose of government? What makes a government legitimate?

4. In what sense is the Declaration of Independence a causal argument?

5. What specific evidence does Jefferson supply to support his case? How effective is this evidence? What do you consider his most convincing piece of evidence?

⊖WRITING ARGUMENTS

1. Write a one-page rhetorical analysis of the Declaration of Independence in terms of the Toulmin model. Begin by identifying the claim, the grounds, and the warrant. (See Chapter 6 for more on Toulmin argument; see Chapter 4 for information on writing a rhetorical analysis.)

2. Jefferson writes that revolutionary action should not be taken for "light and transient causes" (para. 2). After an armed uprising several years before the American Revolution, he also said, "God forbid we be 20 years without such a rebellion. . . . The tree of liberty must be refreshed from time to time with the blood of patriots and tyrants." In your view, what conditions or actions on the part of an established government justify its overthrow? Explain your answer in an argumentative essay.

THE GETTYSBURG ADDRESS

ABRAHAM LINCOLN

Abraham Lincoln (1809–1865) was the sixteenth president of the United States. Raised in frontier Kentucky and Indiana, he rose from rural poverty to become a lawyer, an Illinois state legislator, and a member of the U.S. House of Representatives. He also became one of America's mythic figures. Elected to the White House in 1861, Lincoln led the United States through the cataclysm of the Civil War and was assassinated in 1865. His 1863 Gettysburg Address, delivered at the dedication of the Soldier's National Cemetery in Gettysburg, Pennsylvania, is arguably the most famous speech in American history.

Four score and seven years ago our fathers brought forth on this continent, a 1 new nation, conceived in Liberty, and dedicated to the proposition that all men are created equal.

Now we are engaged in a great civil war, testing whether that nation, or 2 any nation so conceived and so dedicated, can long endure. We are met on a great battle-field of that war. We have come to dedicate a portion of that field, as a final resting place for those who here gave their lives that that nation might live. It is altogether fitting and proper that we should do this.

But, in a larger sense, we can not dedicate—we can not consecrate—we 3 can not hallow—this ground. The brave men, living and dead, who struggled here, have consecrated it, far above our poor power to add or detract. The world will little note, nor long remember what we say here, but it can never forget what they did here. It is for us the living, rather, to be dedicated here to the unfinished work which they who fought here have thus far so nobly advanced. It is rather for us to be here dedicated to the great task remaining before us—that from these honored dead we take increased devotion to that cause for which they gave the last full measure of devotion—that we here highly resolve that these dead shall not have died in vain—that this nation, under God, shall have a new birth of freedom—and that government of the people, by the people, for the people, shall not perish from the earth.

⊖READING ARGUMENTS

1. According to Lincoln, what is the obligation of "the living" (para. 3)? Explain this obligation in your own words.

2. Does the Gettysburg Address make an argument? If so, is it a deductive argument or an inductive argument? Explain.

3. Lincoln gave this speech at the dedication of a cemetery, yet he concedes that "in a larger sense, we can not dedicate—we can not consecrate—we can not hallow—this ground" (3). Is he undercutting his own implicit purpose here? How does this concession support his larger point?

4. What strategies does Lincoln use to support his position? Does he make an ethical argument? A causal argument? Is this speech in any sense a proposal argument?

❯ WRITING ARGUMENTS

1. Consider Lincoln's prose style—in particular, its rhythm and word choice. For example, is "Four score and seven years ago" (para. 1) the clearest, simplest phrasing he could have chosen? Rewrite this sentence—or any other sentence—in your own words. How does your version compare to his? What do you learn about Lincoln's language—and his argument—when you try to paraphrase his speech?

2. In a well-known 1920 essay, the American critic H. L. Mencken lauded the Gettysburg Address as "eloquence brought to a pellucid and almost gem-like perfection—the highest emotion reduced to a few poetical phrases." However, Mencken qualified his praise of Lincoln's speech by saying, "But let us not forget that it is poetry, not logic; beauty, not sense." He said of Lincoln's main point: "It is difficult to imagine anything more untrue." How do you respond to Mencken's assessment? Do you find Lincoln's argument "true" or "untrue"? Do you think the speech's "eloquence," "poetry," and "beauty" undercut its "logic," "sense," and "truth"? Why or why not?

DECLARATION OF SENTIMENTS AND RESOLUTIONS

ELIZABETH CADY STANTON

Elizabeth Cady Stanton (1815–1902) was a prominent leader in the struggle for the rights of women, advocating for the right of women to vote, divorce, and be equal to men under law. In 1848, when Stanton's Declaration of Sentiments and Resolutions was written for a women's rights convention in Seneca Falls, New York, married women were not allowed to own property. Stanton's declaration is modeled on Thomas Jefferson's Declaration of Independence.

When, in the course of human events, it becomes necessary for one portion of 1
the family of man to assume among the people of the earth a position different
from that which they have hitherto occupied, but one to which the laws of nature
and of nature's God entitle them, a decent respect to the opinions of mankind
requires that they should declare the causes that impel them to such a course.

We hold these truths to be self-evident: that all men and women are created 2
equal; that they are endowed by their Creator with certain inalienable rights; that
among these are life, liberty, and the pursuit of happiness; that to secure these
rights governments are instituted, deriving their just powers from the consent of
the governed. Whenever any form of government becomes destructive of these
ends, it is the right of those who suffer from it to refuse allegiance to it, and to
insist upon the institution of a new government, laying its foundation on such
principles, and organizing its powers in such form, as to them shall seem most
likely to effect their safety and happiness. Prudence indeed, will dictate that governments long established should not be changed for light and transient causes;
and accordingly all experience hath shown that mankind are more disposed to
suffer, while evils are sufferable, than to right themselves by abolishing the forms
to which they were accustomed. But when a long train of abuses and usurpations, pursuing invariably the same object evinces a design to reduce them under
absolute despotism, it is their duty to throw off such government, and to provide
new guards for their future security. Such has been the patient sufferance of the
women under this government, and such is now the necessity which constrains
them to demand the equal station to which they are entitled.

The history of mankind is a history of repeated injuries and usurpations on 3
the part of man toward woman, having in direct object the establishment of an
absolute tyranny over her. To prove this, let facts be submitted to a candid world.

He has never permitted her to exercise her inalienable right to the elective 4
franchise.

He has compelled her to submit to laws, in the formation of which she 5
had no voice.

He has withheld from her rights which are given to the most ignorant and 6
degraded men—both natives and foreigners.

Having deprived her of this first right of a citizen, the elective franchise, 7
thereby leaving her without representation in the halls of legislation, he has
oppressed her on all sides.

He has made her, if married, in the eye of the law, civilly dead. 8

He has taken from her all right in property, even to the wages she earns. 9

He has made her, morally, an irresponsible being, as she can commit many 10
crimes with impunity, provided they be done in the presence of her husband.
In the covenant of marriage, she is compelled to promise obedience to her husband, he becoming, to all intents and purposes, her master—the law giving
him power to deprive her of her liberty, and to administer chastisement.

He has so framed the laws of divorce, as to what shall be the proper causes, 11
and in case of separation, to whom the guardianship of the children shall be
given, as to be wholly regardless of the happiness of women—the law, in all
cases, going upon a false supposition of the supremacy of man, and giving all
power into his hands.

After depriving her of all rights as a married woman, if single, and the 12
owner of property, he has taxed her to support a government which recognizes
her only when her property can be made profitable to it.

He has monopolized nearly all the profitable employments, and from 13
those she is permitted to follow, she receives but a scanty remuneration. He
closes against her all the avenues to wealth and distinction which he considers
most honorable to himself. As a teacher of theology, medicine, or law, she is
not known.

He has denied her the facilities for obtaining a thorough education, all 14
colleges being closed against her.

He allows her in Church, as well as State, but a subordinate position, 15
claiming Apostolic authority for her exclusion from the ministry, and, with
some exceptions, from any public participation in the affairs of the Church.

He has created a false public sentiment by giving to the world a different 16
code of morals for men and women, by which moral delinquencies which
exclude women from society, are not only tolerated, but deemed of little
account in man.

He has usurped the prerogative of Jehovah himself, claiming it as his right 17
to assign for her a sphere of action, when that belongs to her conscience and to
her God.

He has endeavored, in every way that he could, to destroy her confidence 18
in her own powers, to lessen her self-respect, and to make her willing to lead a
dependent and abject life.

Now, in view of this entire disfranchisement of one-half the people of this 19
country, their social and religious degradation—in view of the unjust laws
above mentioned, and because women do feel themselves aggrieved, oppressed,
and fraudulently deprived of their most sacred rights, we insist that they have
immediate admission to all the rights and privileges which belong to them as
citizens of the United States.

In entering upon the great work before us, we anticipate no small amount 20
of misconception, misrepresentation, and ridicule; but we shall use every
instrumentality within our power to effect our object. We shall employ agents,
circulate tracts, petition the State and National legislatures, and endeavor to
enlist the pulpit and the press in our behalf. We hope this Convention will be
followed by a series of Conventions embracing every part of the country.

⊘READING ARGUMENTS

1. Why do you think Stanton chose to echo the style and structure of the
   Declaration of Independence? What point was she trying to make?

2. How do Stanton's general political aims contrast with Jefferson's goals in the Declaration of Independence (p. 770)?

3. According to Stanton, "The history of mankind is a history of repeated injuries and usurpations on the part of man toward woman, having in direct object the establishment of an absolute tyranny over her" (3). How does she support this generalization? Do you find her evidence convincing? Why or why not?

4. Stanton writes that man has "usurped the prerogative of Jehovah himself, claiming it as his right to assign for [women] a sphere of action" (para. 17). What do you think she means? Do you think her point is valid today?

5. In her conclusion, Stanton summarizes how women will fulfill the goals of her declaration. What specific steps does she expect women to take?

❯ WRITING ARGUMENTS

1. Stanton accuses male-dominated society not only of "monopoliz[ing] nearly all the profitable employments" (para. 13) but also of "giving to the world a different code of morals for men and women" (16). Do you think these gender restrictions and double standards still exist today? Write an argumentative essay that takes a stand on this issue.

2. In paragraph 2, Stanton quotes Thomas Jefferson's claim that "all experience hath shown that mankind are more disposed to suffer, while evils are sufferable, than to right themselves by abolishing the forms to which they were accustomed." What view of human nature is implied here? Do you agree with this view? Do you think it is still held by people today? Explain your views in an argumentative essay.

POLITICS AND THE ENGLISH LANGUAGE

GEORGE ORWELL

George Orwell was the pen name of journalist, critic, and novelist Eric Blair (1903–1950), best known for his allegorical satire Animal Farm *(1945) and his dystopian novel* 1984 *(1949). Orwell also wrote nonfiction about many different subjects, from his experiences in the Spanish Civil War to his affection for English cooking. He was especially preoccupied with language and political writing—for*

example, the ways in which political orthodoxy leads to a "lifeless, imitative style."
Orwell himself rejected orthodoxy: he was a democratic socialist who criticized
socialism, a lover of England who attacked British colonialism, and a literary
highbrow who enjoyed popular culture. Although it was written in 1946, "Politics
and the English Language" remains an excellent guide for avoiding the bad writ-
ing habits of "political conformity."

Most people who bother with the matter at all would admit that the English   1
language is in a bad way, but it is generally assumed that we cannot by conscious
action do anything about it. Our civilization is decadent and our language—so
the argument runs—must inevitably share in the general collapse. It follows
that any struggle against the abuse of language is a sentimental archaism, like
preferring candles to electric light or hansom cabs to aeroplanes. Underneath
this lies the half-conscious belief that language is a natural growth and not an
instrument which we shape for our own purposes.

    Now, it is clear that the decline of a language must ultimately have politi-   2
cal and economic causes: it is not due simply to the bad influence of this or
that individual writer. But an effect can become a cause, reinforcing the original cause and producing the same effect in an intensified form, and so on
indefinitely. A man may take to drink because he feels himself to be a failure,
and then fail all the more completely because he drinks. It is rather the same
thing that is happening to the English language. It becomes ugly and inaccurate because our thoughts are foolish, but the slovenliness of our language
makes it easier for us to have foolish thoughts. The point is that the process is
reversible. Modern English, especially written English, is full of bad habits
which spread by imitation and which can be avoided if one is willing to take
the necessary trouble. If one gets rid of these habits one can think more clearly,
and to think clearly is a necessary first step towards political regeneration: so
that the fight against bad English is not frivolous and is not the exclusive concern of professional writers. I will come back to this presently, and I hope that
by that time the meaning of what I have said here will have become clearer.
Meanwhile, here are five specimens of the English language as it is now habitually written.

    These five passages have not been picked out because they are especially   3
bad—I could have quoted far worse if I had chosen—but because they illustrate various of the mental vices from which we now suffer. They are a little
below the average, but are fairly representative samples. I number them so that
I can refer back to them when necessary:

> (1) I am not, indeed, sure whether it is not true to say that the Milton who
> once seemed not unlike a seventeenth-century Shelley had not become,
> out of an experience ever more bitter in each year, more alien [*sic*] to the
> founder of that Jesuit sect which nothing could induce him to tolerate.
>   Professor Harold Laski (Essay in *Freedom of Expression*)

(2) Above all, we cannot play ducks and drakes with a native battery of idioms which prescribes such egregious collocations of vocables as the basic *put up with* for *tolerate* or *put at a loss* for *bewilder*.

Professor Lancelot Hogben (*Interglossa*)

(3) On the one side we have the free personality: by definition it is not neurotic, for it has neither conflict nor dream. Its desires, such as they are, are transparent, for they are just what institutional approval keeps in the forefront of consciousness; another institutional pattern would alter their number and intensity; there is little in them that is natural, irreducible, or culturally dangerous. But *on the other* side, the social bond itself is nothing but the mutual reflection of these self-secure integrities. Recall the definition of love. Is not this the very picture of a small academic? Where is there a place in this hall of mirrors for either personality or fraternity?

Essay on psychology in *Politics* (New York)

(4) All the "best people" from the gentlemen's clubs, and all the frantic fascist captains, united in common hatred of Socialism and bestial horror of the rising tide of the mass revolutionary movement, have turned to acts of provocation, to foul incendiarism, to medieval legends of poisoned wells, to legalize their own destruction of proletarian organizations, and rouse the agitated petty-bourgeoisie to chauvinistic fervour on behalf of the fight against the revolutionary way out of the crisis.

Communist pamphlet

(5) If a new spirit *is* to be infused into this old country, there is one thorny and contentious reform which must be tackled, and that is the humanization and galvanization of the B.B.C. Timidity here will bespeak cancer and atrophy of the soul. The heart of Britain may be sound and of strong beat, for instance, but the British lion's roar at present is like that of Bottom in Shakespeare's *Midsummer Night's Dream*—as gentle as any sucking dove. A virile new Britain cannot continue indefinitely to be traduced in the eyes or rather ears, of the world by the effete languors of Langham Place, brazenly masquerading as "standard English." When the Voice of Britain is heard at nine o'clock, better far and infinitely less ludicrous to hear aitches honestly dropped than the present priggish, inflated, inhibited, school-ma'amish arch braying of blameless bashful mewing maidens!

Letter in *Tribune*

Each of these passages has faults of its own, but, quite apart from avoidable ugliness, two qualities are common to all of them. The first is staleness of imagery: the other is lack of precision. The writer either has a meaning and cannot express it, or he inadvertently says something else, or he is almost indifferent as to whether his words mean anything or not. This mixture of vagueness and sheer incompetence is the most marked characteristic of modern

English prose, and especially of any kind of political writing. As soon as certain topics are raised, the concrete melts into the abstract and no one seems able to think of turns of speech that are not hackneyed: prose consists less and less of *words* chosen for the sake of their meaning, and more and more of *phrases* tacked together like the sections of a prefabricated hen-house. I list below, with notes and examples, various of the tricks by means of which the work of prose-construction is habitually dodged:

Dying Metaphors

A newly invented metaphor assists thought by evoking a visual image, while on 5 the other hand a metaphor which is technically "dead" (e.g., *iron resolution*) has in effect reverted to being an ordinary word and can generally be used without loss of vividness. But in between these two classes there is a huge dump of worn-out metaphors which have lost all evocative power and are merely used because they save people the trouble of inventing phrases for themselves. Examples are: *Ring the changes on, take up the cudgels for, toe the line, ride roughshod over, stand shoulder to shoulder with, play into the hands of, no axe to grind, grist to the mill, fishing in troubled waters, on the order of the day, Achilles' heel, swan song, hotbed.* Many of these are used without knowledge of their meaning (what is a "rift," for instance?), and incompatible metaphors are frequently mixed, a sure sign that the writer is not interested in what he is saying. Some metaphors now current have been twisted out of their original meaning without those who use them even being aware of the fact. For example, *toe the line* is sometimes written *tow the line*. Another example is *the hammer and the anvil*, now always used with the implication that the anvil gets the worst of it. In real life it is always the anvil that breaks the hammer, never the other way about: a writer who stopped to think what he was saying would be aware of this, and would avoid perverting the original phrase.

Operators or Verbal False Limbs

These save the trouble of picking out appropriate verbs and nouns, and at the 6 same time pad each sentence with extra syllables which give it an appearance of symmetry. Characteristic phrases are: *render inoperative, militate against, make contact with, be subjected to, give rise to, give grounds for, have the effect of, play a leading part (role) in, make itself felt, take effect, exhibit a tendency to, serve the purpose of, etc., etc.* The keynote is the elimination of simple verbs. Instead of being a single word, such as *break, stop, spoil, mend, kill*, a verb becomes a *phrase*, made up of a noun or adjective tacked on to some general-purposes verb such as *prove, serve, form, play, render*. In addition, the passive voice is wherever possible used in preference to the active, and noun constructions are used instead of gerunds (*by examination of* instead of *by examining*). The range of verbs is further cut down by means of the *-ize* and *de-* formation, and the banal statements are given an appearance of profundity by means of the *not un-* formation. Simple conjunctions and prepositions are replaced by such phrases as *with respect to, having regard to, the fact that, by dint of, in view of, in the interests of, on the hypothesis that*; and the ends of sentences are saved from anticlimax by such resounding commonplaces as *greatly to be desired, cannot be left out of account, a development to be expected in the near future, deserving of serious consideration, brought to a satisfactory conclusion*, and so on and so forth.

Pretentious Diction

Words like *phenomenon, element, individual* (as noun), *objective, categorical, effective, virtual, basic, primary, promote, constitute, exhibit, exploit, utilize, eliminate, liquidate*, are used to dress up simple statements and give an air of scientific impartiality to biased judgments. Adjectives like *epoch-making, epic, historic, unforgettable, triumphant, age-old, inevitable, inexorable, veritable*, are used to dignify the sordid processes of international politics, while writing that aims at glorifying war usually takes on an archaic color, its characteristic words being: *realm, throne, chariot, mailed fist, trident, sword, shield, buckler, banner, jackboot, clarion*. Foreign words and expressions such as *cul de sac, ancien régime, deus ex machina, mutatis mutandis, status quo, gleichschaltung, weltanschauung*, are used to give an air of culture and elegance. Except for the useful abbreviations *i.e., e.g.*, and *etc.*, there is no real need for any of the hundreds of foreign phrases now current in English. Bad writers, and especially scientific, political, and sociological writers, are nearly always haunted by the notion that Latin or Greek words are grander than Saxon ones, and unnecessary words like *expedite, ameliorate, predict, extraneous, deracinated, clandestine, subaqueous*, and hundreds of others constantly gain ground from their Anglo-Saxon opposite numbers.[1] The jargon peculiar to Marxist writing (*hyena, hangman, cannibal, petty bourgeois, these gentry, lackey, flunky, mad dog, White Guard*, etc.) consists largely of words and phrases translated from Russian, German, or French; but the normal way of coining a new word is to use a Latin or Greek root with the appropriate affix and, where necessary, the *-ize* formation. It is often easier to make up words of this kind (*deregionalize, impermissible, extramarital, nonfragmentatory*, and so forth) than to think up the English words that will cover one's meaning. The result, in general, is an increase in slovenliness and vagueness.

Meaningless Words

In certain kinds of writing, particularly in art criticism and literary criticism, it is normal to come across long passages which are almost completely lacking in meaning.[2] Words like *romantic, plastic, values, human, dead, sentimental, natural, vitality*, as used in art criticism, are strictly meaningless in the sense

7

8

---

[1]An interesting illustration of this is the way in which the English flower names which were in use till very recently are being ousted by Greek ones, *snapdragon* becoming *antirrhinum, forget-me-not* becoming *myosotis*, etc. It is hard to see any practical reason for this change of fashion: it is probably due to an instinctive turning-away from the more homely word and a vague feeling that the Greek word is scientific.

that they not only do not point to any discoverable object, but are hardly ever expected to do so by the reader. When one critic writes, "The outstanding feature of Mr. X's work is its living quality," while another writes, "The immediately striking thing about Mr. X's work is its peculiar deadness," the reader accepts this as a simple difference of opinion. If words like *black* and *white* were involved, instead of the jargon words *dead* and *living*, he would see at once that language was being used in an improper way. Many political words are similarly abused. The word *Fascism* has now no meaning except in so far as it signifies "something not desirable." The words *democracy, socialism, freedom, patriotic, realistic, justice*, have each of them several different meanings which cannot be reconciled with one another. In the case of a word like *democracy*, not only is there no agreed definition, but the attempt to make one is resisted from all sides. It is almost universally felt that when we call a country democratic we are praising it: consequently the defenders of every kind of régime claim that it is a democracy, and fear that they might have to stop using the word if it were tied down to any one meaning. Words of this kind are often used in a consciously dishonest way. That is, the person who uses them has his own private definition, but allows his hearer to think he means something quite different. Statements like *Marshal Pétain was a true patriot, The Soviet Press is the freest in the world, The Catholic Church is opposed to persecution*, are almost always made with intent to deceive. Other words used in variable meanings, in most cases more or less dishonestly, are: *class, totalitarian, science, progressive, reactionary, bourgeois, equality.*

Now that I have made this catalog of swindles and perversions, let me give 9 another example of the kind of writing that they lead to. This time it must of its nature be an imaginary one. I am going to translate a passage of good English into modern English of the worst sort. Here is a well-known verse from *Ecclesiastes*:

> I returned and saw under the sun, that the race is not to the swift, nor the battle to the strong, neither yet bread to the wise, nor yet riches to men of understanding, nor yet favor to men of skill; but time and chance happeneth to them all.

Here it is in modern English:

> Objective consideration of contemporary phenomena compels the conclusion that success or failure in competitive activities exhibits no tendency to be commensurate with innate capacity, but that a considerable element of the unpredictable must invariably be taken into account.

---

[2]Example: "Comfort's catholicity of perception and image, strangely Whitmanesque in range, almost the exact opposite in aesthetic compulsion, continues to evoke that trembling atmospheric accumulative hinting at a cruel, an inexorably serene timelessness . . . Wrey Gardiner scores by aiming at simple bull's-eyes with precision. Only they are not so simple, and through this contented sadness runs more than the surface bittersweet of resignation" (*Poetry Quarterly*).

This is a parody, but not a very gross one. Exhibit (3), above, for instance, contains several patches of the same kind of English. It will be seen that I have not made a full translation. The beginning and ending of the sentence follow the original meaning fairly closely, but in the middle the concrete illustrations—race, battle, bread—dissolve into the vague phrase "success or failure in competitive activities." This had to be so, because no modern writer of the kind I am discussing—no one capable of using phrases like "objective consideration of contemporary phenomena"—would ever tabulate his thoughts in that precise and detailed way. The whole tendency of modern prose is away from concreteness. Now analyze these two sentences a little more closely. The first contains forty-nine words but only sixty syllables, and all its words are those of everyday life. The second contains thirty-eight words of ninety syllables: eighteen of its words are from Latin roots, and one from Greek. The first sentence contains six vivid images, and only one phrase ("time and chance") that could be called vague. The second contains not a single fresh, arresting phrase, and in spite of its ninety syllables it gives only a shortened version of the meaning contained in the first. Yet without a doubt it is the second kind of sentence that is gaining ground in modern English. I do not want to exaggerate. This kind of writing is not yet universal, and outcrops of simplicity will occur here and there in the worst-written page. Still, if you or I were told to write a few lines on the uncertainty of human fortunes, we should probably come much nearer to my imaginary sentence than to the one from *Ecclesiastes.*

As I have tried to show, modern writing at its worst does not consist in   11
picking out words for the sake of their meaning and inventing images in order to make the meaning clearer. It consists in gumming together long strips of words which have already been set in order by someone else, and making the results presentable by sheer humbug. The attraction of this way of writing is that it is easy. It is easier—even quicker, once you have the habit—to say *In my opinion it is a not unjustifiable assumption that* than to say *I think.* If you use ready-made phrases, you not only don't have to hunt about for words; you also don't have to bother with the rhythms of your sentences, since these phrases are generally so arranged as to be more or less euphonious. When you are composing in a hurry—when you are dictating to a stenographer, for instance, or making a public speech—it is natural to fall into a pretentious, Latinized style. Tags like *a consideration which we should do well to bear in mind* or *a conclusion to which all of us would readily assent* will save many a sentence from coming down with a bump. By using stale metaphors, similes, and idioms, you save much mental effort, at the cost of leaving your meaning vague, not only for your reader but for yourself. This is the significance of mixed metaphors. The sole aim of a metaphor is to call up a visual image. When these images clash—as in *The Fascist octopus has sung its swan song, the jackboot is thrown into the melting pot*—it can be taken as certain that the writer is not seeing a mental image of the objects he is naming; in other words he is not really thinking. Look again at the examples I gave at the beginning of this essay. Professor Laski (1) uses five negatives in fifty-three words. One of these is superfluous,

making nonsense of the whole passage, and in addition there is the slip *alien* for akin, making further nonsense, and several avoidable pieces of clumsiness which increase the general vagueness. Professor Hogben (2) plays ducks and drakes with a battery which is able to write prescriptions, and, while disapproving of the everyday phrase *put up with*, is unwilling to look *egregious* up in the dictionary and see what it means. (3), if one takes an uncharitable attitude towards it, is simply meaningless: probably one could work out its intended meaning by reading the whole of the article in which it occurs. In (4), the writer knows more or less what he wants to say, but an accumulation of stale phrases chokes him like tea leaves blocking a sink. In (5), words and meaning have almost parted company. People who write in this manner usually have a general emotional meaning—they dislike one thing and want to express solidarity with another—but they are not interested in the detail of what they are saying. A scrupulous writer, in every sentence that he writes, will ask himself at least four questions, thus: What am I trying to say? What words will express it? What image or idiom will make it clearer? Is this image fresh enough to have an effect? And he will probably ask himself two more: Could I put it more shortly? Have I said anything that is avoidably ugly? But you are not obliged to go to all this trouble. You can shirk it by simply throwing your mind open and letting the ready-made phrases come crowding in. They will construct your sentences for you—even think your thoughts for you, to a certain extent—and at need they will perform the important service of partially concealing your meaning even from yourself. It is at this point that the special connection between politics and the debasement of language becomes clear.

In our time it is broadly true that political writing is bad writing. Where it 12 is not true, it will generally be found that the writer is some kind of rebel, expressing his private opinions and not a "party line." Orthodoxy, of whatever color, seems to demand a lifeless, imitative style. The political dialects to be found in pamphlets, leading articles, manifestos, White Papers, and the speeches of under-secretaries do, of course, vary from party to party, but they are all alike in that one almost never finds in them a fresh, vivid, home-made turn of speech. When one watches some tired hack on the platform mechanically repeating the familiar phrases—*bestial atrocities, iron heel, bloodstained tyranny, free peoples of the world, stand shoulder to shoulder*—one often has a curious feeling that one is not watching a live human being but some kind of dummy: a feeling which suddenly becomes stronger at moments when the light catches the speaker's spectacles and turns them into blank discs which seem to have no eyes behind them. And this is not altogether fanciful. A speaker who uses that kind of phraseology has gone some distance towards turning himself into a machine. The appropriate noises are coming out of his larynx, but his brain is not involved as it would be if he were choosing his words for himself. If the speech he is making is one that he is accustomed to make over and over again, he may be almost unconscious of what he is saying, as one is when one utters the responses in church. And this reduced state of consciousness, if not indispensable, is at any rate favorable to political conformity.

In our time, political speech and writing are largely the defense of the 13 indefensible. Things like the continuance of British rule in India, the Russian purges and deportations, the dropping of the atom bombs on Japan, can indeed be defended, but only by arguments which are too brutal for most people to face, and which do not square with the professed aims of political parties. Thus political language has to consist largely of euphemism, question-begging, and sheer cloudy vagueness. Defenseless villages are bombarded from the air, the inhabitants driven out into the countryside, the cattle machine-gunned, the huts set on fire with incendiary bullets: this is called *pacification.* Millions of peasants are robbed of their farms and sent trudging along the roads with no more than they can carry: this is called *transfer of population* or *rectification of frontiers.* People are imprisoned for years without trial, or shot in the back of the neck, or sent to die of scurvy in Arctic lumber camps: this is called *elimination of unreliable elements.* Such phraseology is needed if one wants to name things without calling up mental pictures of them. Consider for instance some comfortable English professor defending Russian totalitarianism. He cannot say outright, "I believe in killing off your opponents when you can get good results by doing so." Probably, therefore, he will say something like this:

"While freely conceding that the Soviet régime exhibits certain features 14 which the humanitarian may be inclined to deplore, we must, I think, agree that a certain curtailment of the right to political opposition is an unavoidable concomitant of transitional periods, and that the rigors which the Russian people have been called upon to undergo have been amply justified in the sphere of concrete achievement."

The inflated style is itself a kind of euphemism. A mass of Latin words falls upon the facts like soft snow, blurring the outlines and covering up all the details. The great enemy of clear language is insincerity. When there is a gap between one's real and one's declared aims, one turns as it were instinctively to long words and exhausted idioms, like a cuttlefish squirting out ink. In our age there is no such thing as "keeping out of politics." All issues are political issues, and politics itself is a mass of lies, evasions, folly, hatred, and schizophrenia. When the general atmosphere is bad, language must suffer. I should expect to find—this is a guess which I have not sufficient knowledge to verify—that the German, Russian, and Italian languages have all deteriorated in the last ten or fifteen years, as a result of dictatorship.

But if thought corrupts language, language can also corrupt thought. A bad 16 usage can spread by tradition and imitation, even among people who should and do know better. The debased language that I have been discussing is in some ways very convenient. Phrases like *a not unjustifiable assumption, leaves much to be desired, would serve no good purpose, a consideration which we should do well to bear in mind*, are a continuous temptation, a packet of aspirins always at one's elbow. Look back through this essay, and for certain you will find that I have again and again committed the very faults I am protesting against. By this morning's post I have received a pamphlet dealing with conditions in Germany. The author tells me that he "felt impelled" to write it. I open it at random, and here is almost the first sentence that I see: "(The Allies) have an opportunity not only of achieving a radical transformation of Germany's social and political structure in such a way as to avoid a nationalistic reaction in Germany itself, but at the same time of laying the foundations of a cooperative and unified Europe." You see, he "feels impelled" to write—feels, presumably, that he has something new to say—and yet his words, like cavalry horses answering the bugle, group themselves automatically into the familiar dreary pattern. This invasion of one's mind by ready-made phrases (*lay the foundations*, *achieve a radical transformation*) can only be prevented if one is constantly on guard against them, and every such phrase anaesthetizes a portion of one's brain.

I said earlier that the decadence of our language is probably curable. 17 Those who deny this would argue, if they produced an argument at all, that language merely reflects existing social conditions, and that we cannot influence its development by any direct tinkering with words and constructions. So far as the general tone or spirit of a language goes, this may be true, but it is not true in detail. Silly words and expressions have often disappeared, not through any evolutionary process but owing to the conscious action of a minority. Two recent examples were *explore every avenue* and *leave no stone unturned*, which were killed by the jeers of a few journalists. There is a long list of flyblown metaphors which could similarly be got rid of if enough people would interest themselves in the job; and it should also be possible to laugh the *not un-* formation out of existence,[3] to reduce the amount of Latin and Greek in the average sentence, to drive out foreign phrases and strayed scientific words, and, in general, to make pretentiousness unfashionable. But all these are minor points. The defense of the English language implies more than this, and perhaps it is best to start by saying what it does not imply.

To begin with it has nothing to do with archaism, with the salvaging of 18 obsolete words and turns of speech, or with the setting up of a "standard English" which must never be departed from. On the contrary, it is especially concerned with the scrapping of every word or idiom which has outworn its usefulness. It has nothing to do with correct grammar and syntax, which are of no importance so long as one makes one's meaning clear, or with the avoidance of Americanisms, or with having what is called a "good prose style." On the other hand it is not concerned with fake simplicity and the attempt to make written English colloquial. Nor does it even imply in every case preferring the Saxon word to the Latin one, though it does imply using the fewest and shortest words that will cover one's meaning. What is above all needed is to let the meaning choose the word, and not the other way about. In prose, the worst thing one can do with words is to surrender to them. When you think of a concrete object, you think wordlessly, and then, if you want to describe the thing you have been visualizing you probably hunt about till you find the exact words that seem to fit.

---

[3]One can cure oneself of the *not un-* formation by memorizing this sentence: *A not unblack dog was chasing a not unsmall rabbit across a not ungreen field.*

When you think of something abstract you are more inclined to use words from the start, and unless you make a conscious effort to prevent it, the existing dialect will come rushing in and do the job for you, at the expense of blurring or even changing your meaning. Probably it is better to put off using words as long as possible and get one's meaning as clear as one can through pictures or sensations. Afterwards one can choose—not simply *accept*—the phrases that will best cover the meaning, and then switch round and decide what impression one's words are likely to make on another person. This last effort of the mind cuts out all stale or mixed images, all prefabricated phrases, needless repetitions, and humbug and vagueness generally. But one can often be in doubt about the effect of a word or a phrase, and one needs rules that one can rely on when instinct fails. I think the following rules will cover most cases:

1. Never use a metaphor, simile, or other figure of speech which you are used to seeing in print.

2. Never use a long word where a short one will do.

3. If it is possible to cut a word out, always cut it out.

4. Never use the passive where you can use the active.

5. Never use a foreign phrase, a scientific word, or a jargon word if you can think of an everyday English equivalent.

6. Break any of these rules sooner than say anything outright barbarous.

These rules sound elementary, and so they are, but they demand a deep 19 change of attitude in anyone who has grown used to writing in the style now fashionable. One could keep all of them and still write bad English, but one could not write the kind of stuff that I quoted in those five specimens at the beginning of this article.

I have not here been considering the literary use of language, but merely 20 language as an instrument for expressing and not for concealing or preventing thought. Stuart Chase and others have come near to claiming that all abstract words are meaningless, and have used this as a pretext for advocating a kind of political quietism. Since you don't know what Fascism is, how can you struggle against Fascism? One need not swallow such absurdities as this, but one ought to recognize that the present political chaos is connected with the decay of language, and that one can probably bring about some improvement by starting at the verbal end. If you simplify your English, you are freed from the worst follies of orthodoxy. You cannot speak any of the necessary dialects, and when you make a stupid remark its stupidity will be obvious, even to yourself. Political language—and with variations this is true of all political parties, from Conservatives to Anarchists—is designed to make lies sound truthful and murder respectable, and to give an appearance of solidity to pure wind. One cannot change this all in a moment, but one can at least change one's own habits, and from time to time one can even, if one jeers loudly enough, send some worn-out and useless phrase—some *jackboot*, *Achilles' heel*, *hotbed*, *melting pot*, *acid test*, *veritable inferno*, or other lump of verbal refuse—into the dustbin where it belongs.

⊘READING ARGUMENTS

1. What two qualities do Orwell's "five specimens" (para. 2) share? According to Orwell, what is the "most marked characteristic of modern English prose, and especially of any kind of political writing" (4)?

2. Where in this essay does Orwell use deductive reasoning?

3. How does Orwell use causal argument in his essay? For instance, how does he use it to explain why political speech and writing are bad? What other examples of causal argument can you identify?

4. Orwell argues that "political language" consists "largely of euphemism, question-begging, and sheer cloudy vagueness" (13). What is a euphemism? What does "question-begging" mean?

5. Where does Orwell make a proposal argument? What does he propose?

⊘WRITING ARGUMENTS

1. In paragraph 16, Orwell concedes, "Look back through this essay, and for certain you will find that I have again and again committed the very faults I am protesting against." Find three examples of these "faults" in Orwell's prose. Then, write a paragraph for each "fault," explaining why it meets his standard for "bad" writing.

2. Surveying the state of the English language in 1946, Orwell asserts that "it is broadly true that political writing is bad writing" (12). Is this still "broadly true"? Reread paragraphs 12 through 15 of Orwell's essay. Then, develop your own argument about the language of contemporary politics, updating Orwell's examples with contemporary examples.

THE OBLIGATION TO ENDURE

RACHEL CARSON

Rachel Carson (1907–1964) received a master's degree in zoology and worked as editor-in-chief of publications for the U.S. Bureau of Fisheries. Her books include Under the Sea-Wind *(1941);* The Sea around Us *(1951), a best-seller and winner of the National Book Award;* The Edge of the Sea *(1955); and* The Sense of Wonder *(published in 1965 after her death). Her most famous work is* Silent Spring *(1962), from which "The Obligation to Endure" is drawn. In this book,*

Carson argues that agricultural pesticides are destructive to wildlife and to the environment, an idea that predates the modern environmental movement and to this day remains controversial. Silent Spring, *an extremely influential work, led to bans of DDT as well as other chemicals.*

The history of life on earth has been a history of interaction between living things and their surroundings. To a large extent, the physical form and the habits of the earth's vegetation and its animal life have been molded by the environment. Considering the whole span of earthly time, the opposite effect, in which life actually modifies its surroundings, has been relatively slight. Only within the moment of time represented by the present century has one species—man—acquired significant power to alter the nature of his world.

During the past quarter century this power has not only increased to one of disturbing magnitude but it has changed in character. The most alarming of all man's assaults upon the environment is the contamination of air, earth, rivers, and sea with dangerous and even lethal materials. This pollution is for the most part irrecoverable; the chain of evil it initiates not only in the world that must support life but in living tissues is for the most part irreversible. In this now universal contamination of the environment, chemicals are the sinister and little-recognized partners of radiation in changing the very nature of the world—the very nature of its life. Strontium 90, released through nuclear explosions into the air, comes to earth in rain or drifts down as fallout, lodges in soil, enters into the grass or corn or wheat grown there, and in time takes up its abode in the bones of a human being, there to remain until his death. Similarly, chemicals sprayed on croplands or forests or gardens lie long in soil, entering into living organisms, passing from one to another in a chain of poisoning and death. Or they pass mysteriously by underground streams until they emerge and, through the alchemy of air and sunlight, combine into new forms that kill vegetation, sicken cattle, and work unknown harm on those who drink from once pure wells. As Albert Schweitzer has said, "Man can hardly even recognize the devils of his own creation."

It took hundreds of millions of years to produce the life that now inhabits the earth—eons of time in which that developing and evolving and diversifying life reached a state of adjustment and balance with its surroundings. The environment, rigorously shaping and directing the life it supported, contained elements that were hostile as well as supporting. Certain rocks gave out dangerous radiation; even within the light of the sun, from which all life draws its energy, there were short-wave radiations with power to injure. Given time—time not in years but in millennia—life adjusts, and a balance has been reached. For time is the essential ingredient; but in the modern world there is no time.

The rapidity of change and the speed with which new situations are created follow the impetuous and heedless pace of man rather than the deliberate pace of nature. Radiation is no longer merely the background radiation of rocks, the bombardment of cosmic rays, the ultraviolet of the sun that have existed before there was any life on earth; radiation is now the unnatural creation of man's tampering with the atom. The chemicals to which life is asked to make its adjustment are no longer merely the calcium and silica and copper and all the rest of the minerals washed out of the rocks and carried in rivers to the sea; they are the synthetic creations of man's inventive mind, brewed in his laboratories, and having no counterparts in nature.

To adjust to these chemicals would require time on the scale that is 5 nature's; it would require not merely the years of a man's life but the life of generations. And even this, were it by some miracle possible, would be futile, for the new chemicals come from our laboratories in an endless stream; almost five hundred annually find their way into actual use in the United States alone. The figure is staggering and its implications are not easily grasped—500 new chemicals to which the bodies of men and animals are required somehow to adapt each year, chemicals totally outside the limits of biologic experience.

Among them are many that are used in man's war against nature. Since the 6 mid-1940's over 200 basic chemicals have been created for use in killing insects, weeds, rodents, and other organisms described in the modern vernacular as "pests"; and they are sold under several thousand different brand names.

These sprays, dusts, and aerosols are now applied almost universally to 7 farms, gardens, forests, and homes—nonselective chemicals that have the power to kill every insect, the "good" and the "bad," to still the song of birds and the leaping of fish in the streams, to coat the leaves with a deadly film, and to linger on in soil—all this though the intended target may be only a few weeds or insects. Can anyone believe it is possible to lay down such a barrage of poisons on the surface of the earth without making it unfit for all life? They should not be called "insecticides," but "biocides."

The whole process of spraying seems caught up in an endless spiral. Since 8 DDT° was released for civilian use, a process of escalation has been going on in which ever more toxic materials must be found. This has happened because insects, in a triumphant vindication of Darwin's principle of the survival of the fittest, have evolved super races immune to the particular insecticide used, hence a deadlier one has always to be developed—and then a deadlier one than that. It has happened also because, for reasons to be described later, destructive insects often undergo a "flareback," or resurgence, after spraying, in numbers greater than before. Thus the chemical war is never won, and all life is caught in its violent crossfire.

*Dichlorodiphenyltrichloroeth-
ane, a synthetic pesticide that
was used to control disease-
spreading insect populations*

Along with the possibility of the extinction of mankind by nuclear war, 9 the central problem of our age has therefore become the contamination of man's total environment with such substances of incredible potential for harm—substances that accumulate in the tissues of plants and animals and even penetrate the germ cells to shatter or alter the very material of heredity upon which the shape of the future depends.

Some would-be architects of our future look toward a time when it will be 10 possible to alter the human germ plasm by design. But we may easily be doing so now by inadvertence, for many chemicals, like radiation, bring about gene mutations. It is ironic to think that man might determine his own future by something so seemingly trivial as the choice of an insect spray.

All this has been risked—for what? Future historians may well be amazed 11 by our distorted sense of proportion. How could intelligent beings seek to control a few unwanted species by a method that contaminated the entire environment and brought the threat of disease and death even to their own kind? Yet this is precisely what we have done. We have done it, moreover, for reasons that collapse the moment we examine them. We are told that the enormous and expanding use of pesticides is necessary to maintain farm production. Yet is our real problem not one of *overproduction*? Our farms, despite measures to remove acreages from production and to pay farmers *not* to produce, have yielded such a staggering excess of crops that the American taxpayer in 1962 is paying out more than one billion dollars a year as the total carrying cost of the surplus-food storage program. And is the situation helped when one branch of the Agriculture Department tries to reduce production while another states, as it did in 1958, "It is believed generally that reduction of crop acreages under provisions of the Soil Bank will stimulate interest in use of chemicals to obtain maximum production on the land retained in crops."

All this is not to say there is no insect problem and no need of control. I 12 am saying, rather, that control must be geared to realities, not to mythical situations, and that the methods employed must be such that they do not destroy us along with the insects.

The problem whose attempted solution has brought such a train of disaster in 13 its wake is an accompaniment of our modern way of life. Long before the age of man, insects inhabited the earth—a group of extraordinarily varied and adaptable beings. Over the course of time since man's advent, a small percentage of the more than half a million species of insects have come into conflict with human welfare in two principal ways: as competitors for the food supply and as carriers of human disease.

Disease-carrying insects become important where human beings are 14 crowded together, especially under conditions where sanitation is poor, as in time of natural disaster or war or in situations of extreme poverty and deprivation. Then control of some sort becomes necessary. It is a sobering fact, however, as we shall presently see, that the method of massive chemical control has had only limited success, and also threatens to worsen the very conditions it is intended to curb.

Under primitive agricultural conditions the farmer had few insect prob- 15 lems. These arose with the intensification of agriculture—the devotion of immense acreages to a single crop. Such a system set the stage for explosive increases in specific insect populations. Single-crop farming does not take advantage of the principles by which nature works; it is agriculture as an engineer might conceive it to be. Nature has introduced great variety into the landscape, but man has displayed a passion for simplifying it. Thus he undoes the built-in checks and balances by which nature holds the species within bounds. One important natural check is a limit on the amount of suitable habitat for each species. Obviously then, an insect that lives on wheat can build up its population to much higher levels on a farm devoted to wheat than on one in which wheat is intermingled with other crops to which the insect is not adapted.

The same thing happens in other situations. A generation or more ago, the 16 towns of large areas of the United States lined their streets with the noble elm tree. Now the beauty they hopefully created is threatened with complete destruction as disease sweeps through the elms, carried by a beetle that would have only limited chance to build up large populations and to spread from tree to tree if the elms were only occasional trees in a richly diversified planting.

Another factor in the modern insect problem is one that must be viewed 17 against a background of geologic and human history: the spreading of thousands of different kinds of organisms from their native homes to invade new territories. This worldwide migration has been studied and graphically described by the British ecologist Charles Elton in his recent book *The Ecology of Invasions*. During the Cretaceous Period, some hundred million years ago, flooding seas cut many land bridges between continents and living things found themselves confined in what Elton calls "colossal separate nature reserves." There, isolated from others of their kind, they developed many new species. When some of the land masses were joined again, about 15 million years ago, these species began to move out into new territories—a movement that is not only still in progress but is now receiving considerable assistance from man.

The importation of plants is the primary agent in the modern spread of 18 species, for animals have almost invariably gone along with the plants, quarantine being a comparatively recent and not completely effective innovation. The United States Office of Plant Introduction alone has introduced almost 200,000 species and varieties of plants from all over the world. Nearly half of the 180 or so major insect enemies of plants in the United States are accidental imports from abroad, and most of them have come as hitchhikers on plants.

In new territory, out of reach of the restraining hand of the natural ene- 19 mies that kept down its numbers in its native land, an invading plant or animal is able to become enormously abundant. Thus it is no accident that our most troublesome insects are introduced species.

These invasions, both the naturally occurring and those dependent on 20 human assistance, are likely to continue indefinitely. Quarantine and massive chemical campaigns are only extremely expensive ways of buying time. We are faced, according to Dr. Elton, "with a life-and-death need not just to find new technological means of suppressing this plant or that animal"; instead we need the basic knowledge of animal populations and their relations to their surroundings that will "promote an even balance and damp down the explosive power of outbreaks and new invasions."

Much of the necessary knowledge is now available but we do not use it. 21 We train ecologists in our universities and even employ them in our governmental agencies but we seldom take their advice. We allow the chemical death rain to fall as though there were no alternative, whereas in fact there are many, and our ingenuity could soon discover many more if given opportunity.

Have we fallen into a mesmerized state that makes us accept as inevitable ²² that which is inferior or detrimental, as though having lost the will or the vision to demand that which is good? Such thinking, in the words of the ecologist Paul Shepard, "idealizes life with only its head out of water, inches above the limits of toleration of the corruption of its own environment. . . . Why should we tolerate a diet of weak poisons, a home in insipid surroundings, a circle of acquaintances who are not quite our enemies, the noise of motors with just enough relief to prevent insanity? Who would want to live in a world which is just not quite fatal?"

Yet such a world is pressed upon us. The crusade to create a chemically ²³ sterile, insect-free world seems to have engendered a fanatic zeal on the part of many specialists and most of the so-called control agencies. On every hand there is evidence that those engaged in spraying operations exercise a ruthless power. "The regulatory entomologists . . . function as prosecutor, judge and jury, tax assessor and collector and sheriff to enforce their own orders," said Connecticut entomologist Neely Turner. The most flagrant abuses go unchecked in both state and federal agencies.

It is not my contention that chemical insecticides must never be used. I do ²⁴ contend that we have put poisonous and biologically potent chemicals indiscriminately into the hands of persons largely or wholly ignorant of their potentials for harm. We have subjected enormous numbers of people to contact with these poisons, without their consent and often without their knowledge. If the Bill of Rights contains no guarantee that a citizen shall be secure against lethal poisons distributed either by private individuals or by public officials, it is surely only because our forefathers, despite their considerable wisdom and foresight, could conceive of no such problem.

I contend, furthermore, that we have allowed these chemicals to be used ²⁵ with little or no advance investigation of their effect on soil, water, wildlife, and man himself. Future generations are unlikely to condone our lack of prudent concern for the integrity of the natural world that supports all life.

There is still very limited awareness of the nature of the threat. This is an era ²⁶ of specialists, each of whom sees his own problem and is unaware of or intolerant of the larger frame into which it fits. It is also an era dominated by industry, in which the right to make a dollar at whatever cost is seldom challenged. When the public protests, confronted with some obvious evidence of damaging results of pesticide applications, it is fed little tranquilizing pills of half truth. We urgently need an end to these false assurances, to the sugar coating of unpalatable facts. It is the public that is being asked to assume the risks that the insect controllers calculate. The public must decide whether it wishes to continue on the present road, and it can do so only when in full possession of the facts. In the words of Jean Rostand, "The obligation to endure gives us the right to know."

⬤ READING ARGUMENTS

1. In her opening paragraphs, Carson makes broad and provocative claims about human beings and their place in the natural world.

What evidence does she use to support these assertions? Do you find this evidence convincing?

2. According to Carson, what problem (in addition to the threat of nuclear war) was the greatest threat to human beings in the middle of the twentieth century?

3. In what sense is "The Obligation to Endure" an evaluation argument?

4. In paragraph 2, Carson refers to "man's assaults upon the environment." How does she characterize human beings throughout her essay? For example, how does she describe their interaction with the environment? How does her characterization of human beings support her essay's main point?

5. Where in her essay does Carson address opposing arguments? Do you think she refutes them effectively? Why or why not?

❯ WRITING ARGUMENTS

1. Carson contrasts the "heedless pace of man" with the "deliberate pace of nature" (para. 4). Is this distinction valid? Do you think her view of people and their relationship with the environment is accurate? For example, do you think human beings are engaged in a "war against nature" (6)? Do you generally share Carson's view of scientific progress and industrial society? Write an argumentative essay that takes a stand for or against her views.

2. As a result of Carson's book, DDT was banned worldwide. Since then, some scientists have challenged this ban, blaming it for the rise of malaria, among other diseases. Write an essay arguing that the United States should reconsider its response to Carson's book.

THE IMPORTANCE OF WORK
BETTY FRIEDAN

An activist, an author, and the first president of the National Organization for Women, Betty Friedan (1921–2006) sparked the second wave of American feminism with her manifesto The Feminine Mystique. *This 1963 book examined the "problem that has no name"—the deep dissatisfaction of American women, who were trapped by domestic roles and feminine ideals that limited their individuality, freedom, and growth. In the following excerpt from this book, Friedan argues that women need "to break out of their comfortable concentration camps"—a metaphor that, like the book, remains shocking and controversial more than fifty years later.*

The question of how a person can most fully realize his own capacities and thus achieve identity has become an important concern of the philosophers and the social and psychological thinkers of our time—and for good reason. Thinkers of other times put forth the idea that people were, to a great extent, defined by the work they did. The work that a man had to do to eat, to stay alive, to meet the physical necessities of his environment, dictated his identity. And in this sense, when work was seen merely as a means of survival, human identity was dictated by biology.

But today the problem of human identity has changed. For the work that defined man's place in society and his sense of himself has also changed man's world. Work, and the advance of knowledge, has lessened man's dependence on his environment; his biology and the work he must do for biological survival are no longer sufficient to define his identity. This can be most clearly seen in our own abundant society; men no longer need to work all day to eat. They have an unprecedented freedom to choose the kind of work they will do; they also have an unprecedented amount of time apart from the hours and days that must actually be spent in making a living. And suddenly one realizes the significance of today's identity crisis—for women, and increasingly, for men. One sees the human significance of work—not merely as the means of biological survival, but as the giver of self and the transcender of self, as the creator of human identity and human evolution.

For "self-realization" or "self-fulfillment" or "identity" does not come from looking into a mirror in rapt contemplation of one's own image. Those who have most fully realized themselves, in a sense that can be recognized by the human mind even though it cannot be clearly defined, have done so in the service of a human purpose larger than themselves. Men from varying disciplines have used different words for this mysterious process from which comes the sense of self. The religious mystics, the philosophers, Marx, Freud—all had different names for it: man finds himself by losing himself; man is defined by his relation to the means of production; the ego, the self, grows through understanding and mastering reality—through work and love.

Erik Erikson (1902–1994): A German-born American psychologist who coined the phrase "identity crisis"

The identity crisis, which has been noted by Erik Erikson° and others in recent years in the American man, seems to occur for lack of, and be cured by finding, the work, or cause, or purpose that evokes his own creativity. Some never find it, for it does not come from busy-work or punching a time clock. It does not come from just making a living, working by formula, finding a secure spot as an organization man. The very argument, by Riesman and others, that man no longer finds identity in the work defined as a paycheck job, assumes that identity for man comes through creative work of his own that contributes to the human community: the core of the self becomes aware, becomes real, and grows through work that carries forward human society.

Work, the shopworn staple of the economists, has become the new fron- 5
tier of psychology. Psychiatrists have long used "occupational therapy" with
patients in mental hospitals; they have recently discovered that to be of real
psychological value, it must be not just "therapy," but real work, serving a real
purpose in the community. And work can now be seen as the key to the problem that has no name. The identity crisis of American women began a century
ago, as more and more of the work important to the world, more and more of
the work that used their human abilities and through which they were able to
find self-realization, was taken from them.

Until, and even into, the last century, strong, capable women were needed 6
to pioneer our new land; with their husbands, they ran the farms and planta-
tions and Western homesteads. These women were respected and self-respecting
members of a society whose pioneering purpose centered in the home.
Strength and independence, responsibility and self-confidence, self-discipline
and courage, freedom and equality were part of the American character for
both men and women, in all the first generations. The women who came by
steerage from Ireland, Italy, Russia, and Poland worked beside their husbands
in the sweatshops and the laundries, learned the new language, and saved to
send their sons and daughters to college. Women were never quite as "feminine," or held in as much contempt, in America as they were in Europe. American women seemed to European travelers, long before our time, less passive,
childlike, and feminine than their own wives in France or Germany or England. By an accident of history, American women shared in the work of society longer, and grew with the men. Grade- and high-school education for boys
and girls alike was almost always the rule; and in the West, where women
shared the pioneering work the longest, even the universities were coeduca-
tional from the beginning.

The identity crisis for women did not begin in America until the fire and 7
strength and ability of the pioneer women were no longer needed, no longer
used, in the middle-class homes of the Eastern and Midwestern cities, when
the pioneering was done and men began to build the new society in industries
and professions outside the home. But the daughters of the pioneer women
had grown too used to freedom and work to be content with leisure and passive femininity.

It was not an American, but a South African woman, Mrs. Olive Schreiner, 8
who warned at the turn of the century that the quality and quantity of women's
functions in the social universe was decreasing as fast as civilization was
advancing; that if women did not win back their right to a full share of honored and useful work, woman's mind and muscle would weaken in a parasitic
state; her offspring, male and female, would weaken progressively, and civilization itself would deteriorate.

The feminists saw clearly that education and the right to participate in the 9
more advanced work of society were women's greatest needs. They fought for
and won the rights to new, fully human identity for women. But how very few
of their daughters and granddaughters have chosen to use their education and

their abilities for any large creative purpose, for responsible work in society? How many of them have been deceived, or have deceived themselves, into clinging to the outgrown, childlike femininity of "Occupation: housewife"?

It was not a minor matter, their mistaken choice. We now know that the 10 same range of potential ability exists for women as for men. Women, as well as men, can only find their identity in work that uses their full capacities. A woman cannot find her identity through others—her husband, her children. She cannot find it in the dull routine of housework. As thinkers of every age have said, it is only when a human being faces squarely the fact that he can forfeit his own life, that he becomes truly aware of himself, and begins to take his existence seriously. Sometimes this awareness comes only at the moment of death. Sometimes it comes from a more subtle facing of death: the death of self in passive conformity, in meaningless work. The feminine mystique prescribes just such a living death for women. Faced with the slow death of self, the American woman must begin to take her life seriously.

"We measure ourselves by many standards," said the great American psy- 11 chologist William James, nearly a century ago. "Our strength and our intelligence, our wealth and even our good luck, are things which warm our heart and make us feel ourselves a match for life. But deeper than all such things, and able to suffice unto itself without them, is the sense of the amount of effort which we can put forth."

If women do not put forth, finally, that effort to become all that they have 12 it in them to become, they will forfeit their own humanity. A woman today who has no goal, no purpose, no ambition patterning her days into the future, making her stretch and grow beyond that small score of years in which her body can fill its biological function, is committing a kind of suicide. For that future half a century after the child-bearing years are over is a fact that an American woman cannot deny. Nor can she deny that as a housewife, the world is indeed rushing past her door while she just sits and watches. The terror she feels is real, if she has no place in that world.

The feminine mystique has succeeded in burying millions of American 13 women alive. There is no way for these women to break out of their comfortable concentration camps except by finally putting forth an effort—that human effort which reaches beyond biology, beyond the narrow walls of home, to help shape the future. Only by such a personal commitment to the future can American women break out of the housewife trap and truly find fulfillment as wives and mothers—by fulfilling their own unique possibilities as separate human beings.

⊙ READING ARGUMENTS

1. In what respects is this essay a definition argument? What key term is being defined? Why is the meaning of this term essential to Friedan's argument?

2. According to Friedan, how do modern people establish their identities? What gives these identities meaning?

3. In paragraph 6, Friedan writes about eighteenth- and nineteenth-century women who helped "to pioneer" the United States. How does she characterize these women? Why is their history important to her overall point?

4. In her next-to-last paragraph, Friedan refers to "a kind of suicide." What does she mean?

⟿ WRITING ARGUMENTS

1. According to Friedan, men and women need work that satisfies their creativity and contributes to human society. Do you agree with her implication that doing paid work is the only way to create a meaningful life? Is it possible to find fulfillment by focusing on domestic tasks such as child-rearing? How do you view such questions in the context of your own life and career ambitions? Write an essay that responds to Friedan's argument about the importance of work—that is, of meaningful paid employment.

2. This essay is from Friedan's 1963 book *The Feminine Mystique*. Does the "identity crisis" that Friedan describes still exist? Many aspects of society have changed over the last five decades. Do her arguments seem relevant to men and women today? Why or why not? Write an essay that presents your point of view.

LETTER FROM BIRMINGHAM JAIL
MARTIN LUTHER KING JR.

Martin Luther King Jr. (1929–1968), the foremost civil rights leader in America in the 1950s and 1960s, was an ordained minister and held a doctorate in theology. As head of the Southern Christian Leadership Conference, King fought against segregation through nonviolent means. At that time in the South, African Americans were forced to sit in the back of buses and were prohibited from drinking from water fountains used by whites. They also often attended segregated schools. After a protest in Birmingham, Alabama, in 1963, King was arrested. His "Letter from Birmingham Jail" is a response to a statement made by eight local clergymen who questioned his methods. In this letter, he makes the point that "injustice anywhere is a threat to justice everywhere" (para. 4). King's efforts toward ending segregation eventually bore fruit when Congress passed the Civil Rights Act of 1965. In 1964, he was awarded the Nobel Peace Prize.

My Dear Fellow Clergymen:

While confined here in the Birmingham city jail, I came across your recent   1
statement calling my present activities "unwise and untimely." Seldom do I pause to answer criticism of my work and ideas. If I sought to answer all the criticisms that cross my desk, my secretaries would have little time for anything other than such correspondence in the course of the day, and I would have no time for constructive work. But since I feel that you are men of genuine good will and that your criticisms are sincerely set forth, I want to try to answer your statement in what I hope will be patient and reasonable terms.

I think I should indicate why I am here in Birmingham, since you have   2
been influenced by the view which argues against "outsiders coming in." I have the honor of serving as president of the Southern Christian Leadership Conference, an organization operating in every southern state, with headquarters in Atlanta, Georgia. We have some eighty-five affiliated organizations across the South, and one of them is the Alabama Christian Movement for Human Rights. Frequently we share staff, educational, and financial resources with our affiliates. Several months ago the affiliate here in Birmingham asked us to be on call to engage in a nonviolent direct-action program if such were deemed necessary. We readily consented, and when the hour came we lived up to our promise. So I, along with several members of my staff, am here because I was invited here. I am here because I have organizational ties here.

But more basically, I am in Birmingham because injustice is here. Just as   3
the prophets of the eighth century B.C. left their villages and carried their "thus saith the Lord" far beyond the boundaries of their home towns, and just as the Apostle Paul left his village of Tarsus and carried the gospel of Jesus Christ to the far corners of the Greco-Roman world, so am I compelled to carry the gospel of freedom beyond my own home town. Like Paul, I must constantly respond to the Macedonian call for aid.

Moreover, I am cognizant of the interrelatedness of all communities and   4
states. I cannot sit idly by in Atlanta and not be concerned about what happens in Birmingham. Injustice anywhere is a threat to justice everywhere. We are caught in an inescapable network of mutuality, tied in a single garment of destiny. Whatever affects one directly, affects all indirectly. Never again can we afford to live with the narrow, provincial "outside agitator" idea. Anyone who lives inside the United States can never be considered an outsider anywhere within its bounds.

You deplore the demonstrations taking place in Birmingham. But your 5 statement, I am sorry to say, fails to express a similar concern for the conditions that brought about the demonstrations. I am sure that none of you would want to rest content with the superficial kind of social analysis that deals merely with effects and does not grapple with underlying causes. It is unfortunate that demonstrations are taking place in Birmingham, but it is even more unfortunate that the city's white power structure left the Negro community with no alternative.

In any nonviolent campaign there are four basic steps: collection of the 6 facts to determine whether injustices exist; negotiation; self-purification; and direct action. We have gone through all these steps in Birmingham. There can be no gainsaying the fact that racial injustice engulfs this community. Birmingham is probably the most thoroughly segregated city in the United States. Its ugly record of brutality is widely known. Negroes have experienced grossly unjust treatment in the courts. There have been more unsolved bombings of Negro homes and churches in Birmingham than in any other city in the nation. These are the hard, brutal facts of the case. On the basis of these conditions, Negro leaders sought to negotiate with the city fathers. But the latter consistently refused to engage in good-faith negotiation.

Then, last September, came the opportunity to talk with leaders of 7 Birmingham's economic community. In the course of the negotiations, certain promises were made by the merchants—for example, to remove the stores' humiliating racial signs. On the basis of these promises, the Reverend Fred Shuttlesworth and the leaders of the Alabama Christian Movement for Human Rights agreed to a moratorium on all demonstrations. As the weeks and months went by, we realized that we were the victims of a broken promise. A few signs, briefly removed, returned; the others remained.

As in so many past experiences, our hopes had been blasted, and the 8 shadow of deep disappointment settled upon us. We had no alternative except to prepare for direct action, whereby we would present our very bodies as a means of laying our case before the conscience of the local and the national community. Mindful of the difficulties involved, we decided to undertake a process of self-purification. We began a series of workshops on nonviolence, and we repeatedly asked ourselves: "Are you able to accept blows without retaliating?" "Are you able to endure the ordeal of jail?" We decided to schedule our direct-action program for the Easter season, realizing that except for Christmas, this is the main shopping period of the year. Knowing that a strong economic withdrawal program would be the by-product of direct action, we felt that this would be the best time to bring pressure to bear on the merchants for the needed change.

Then it occurred to us that Birmingham's mayoral election was coming up 9 in March, and we speedily decided to postpone action until after election day. When we discovered that the Commissioner of Public Safety, Eugene "Bull" Connor,° had piled up enough votes to be in the runoff, we decided again to postpone action until the day after the runoff so that the demonstrations could

Eugene "Bull" Connor (1897–1974), the public safety commissioner for the city of Birmingham, Alabama, in the 1960s. He was known for his segregationist views and violent response to civil rights marchers.

not be used to cloud the issues. Like many others, we wanted to see Mr. Connor defeated, and to this end we endured postponement after postponement. Having aided in this community need, we felt that our direct-action program could be delayed no longer.

You may well ask, "Why direct action? Why sit-ins, marches, and so forth? Isn't negotiation a better path?" You are quite right in calling for negotiation. Indeed, this is the very purpose of direct action. Nonviolent direct action seeks to create such a crisis and foster such a tension that a community which has constantly refused to negotiate is forced to confront the issue. It seeks so to dramatize the issue that it can no longer be ignored. My citing the creation of tension as part of the work of the nonviolent-resister may sound rather shocking. But I must confess that I am not afraid of the word "tension." I have earnestly opposed violent tension, but there is a type of constructive, nonviolent tension which is necessary for growth. Just as Socrates felt that it was necessary to create a tension in the mind so that individuals could rise from the bondage of myths and half-truths to the unfettered realm of creative analysis and objective appraisal, so must we see the need for nonviolent gadflies to create the kind of tension in society that will help men rise from the dark depths of prejudice and racism to the majestic heights of understanding and brotherhood.

The purpose of our direct-action program is to create a situation so crisis- 11 packed that it will inevitably open the door to negotiation. I therefore concur with you in your call for negotiation. Too long has our beloved Southland been bogged down in a tragic effort to live in monologue rather than dialogue.

One of the basic points in your statement is that the action that I and my associates have taken in Birmingham is untimely. Some have asked: "Why didn't you give the new city administration time to act?" The only answer that I can give to this query is that the new Birmingham administration must be prodded about as much as the outgoing one, before it will act. We are sadly mistaken if we feel that the election of Albert Boutwell° as mayor will bring the millennium to Birmingham. While Mr. Boutwell is a much more gentle person than Mr. Connor, they are both segregationists, dedicated to maintenance of the status quo. I have hoped that Mr. Boutwell will be reasonable enough to see the futility of massive resistance to desegregation. But he will not see this without pressure from devotees of civil rights. My friends, I must say to you that we have not made a single gain in civil rights without determined legal and nonviolent pressure. Lamentably, it is an historical fact that privileged groups seldom give up their privileges voluntarily. Individuals may see the moral light and voluntarily give up their unjust posture, but, as Reinhold Niebuhr° has reminded us, groups tend to be more immoral than individuals.

We know through painful experience that freedom is never voluntarily 13 given by the oppressor; it must be demanded by the oppressed. Frankly, I have yet to engage in a direct-action campaign that was "well timed" in the view of

Albert Boutwell (1904–1978), the mayor of Birmingham, Alabama, from 1963 to 1967

Reinhold Niebuhr (1892–1971), an American Protestant theologian who focused on the relationship between Christian faith and modern politics

those who have not suffered unduly from the disease of segregation. For years now I have heard the word "Wait!" It rings in the ear of every Negro with piercing familiarity. This "Wait" has almost always meant "Never." We must come to see, with one of our distinguished jurists, that "justice too long delayed is justice denied."

We have waited for more than 340 years for our constitutional and God-given rights. The nations of Asia and Africa are moving with jet-like speed toward gaining political independence, but we still creep at horse-and-buggy pace toward gaining a cup of coffee at a lunch counter. Perhaps it is easy for those who have never felt the stinging darts of segregation to say, "Wait." But when you have seen vicious mobs lynch your mothers and fathers at will and drown your sisters and brothers at whim; when you have seen hate-filled policemen curse, kick, and even kill your black brothers and sisters; when you see the vast majority of your twenty million Negro brothers smothering in an airtight cage of poverty in the midst of an affluent society; when you suddenly find your tongue twisted and your speech stammering as you seek to explain to your six-year-old daughter why she can't go to the public amusement park that has just been advertised on television, and see tears welling up in her eyes when she is told that Funtown is closed to colored children, and see ominous clouds of inferiority beginning to form in her little mental sky, and see her beginning to distort her personality by developing an unconscious bitterness toward white people; when you have to concoct an answer for a five-year-old son who is asking, "Daddy, why do white people treat colored people so mean?"; when you take a cross-country drive and find it necessary to sleep night after night in the uncomfortable corners of your automobile because no motel will accept you; when you are humiliated day in and day out by nagging signs reading "white" and "colored"; when your first name becomes "nigger," your middle name becomes "boy" (however old you are), and your last name becomes "John," and your wife and mother are never given the respected title "Mrs."; when you are harried by day and haunted by night by the fact that you are a Negro, living constantly at tiptoe stance, never quite knowing what to expect next, and are plagued with inner fears and outer resentments; when you are forever fighting a degenerating sense of "nobodiness"—then you will understand why we find it difficult to wait. There comes a time when the cup of endurance runs over, and men are no longer willing to be plunged into the abyss of despair. I hope, sirs, you can understand our legitimate and unavoidable impatience.

You express a great deal of anxiety over our willingness to break laws. This is certainly a legitimate concern. Since we so diligently urge people to obey the Supreme Court's decision of 1954 outlawing segregation in the public schools, at first glance it may seem rather paradoxical for us consciously to break laws. One may well ask: "How can you advocate breaking some laws and obeying others?" The answer lies in the fact that there are two types of laws: just and unjust. I would be the first to advocate obeying just laws. One has not only a legal but a moral responsibility to obey just laws. Conversely, one has a moral

St. Augustine (354–430), a Catholic Church father, philosopher, theologian, and important figure in the development of European Christianity

St. Thomas Aquinas (1225–1274), a Roman Catholic priest, theologian, and philosopher

Martin Buber (1878–1965), an Austrian-born Jewish philosopher

Paul Tillich (1886–1965), a German American theologian and philosopher

Brown v. Board of Education of Topeka, *which declared that laws establishing separate schools for black and white students were unconstitutional*

responsibility to disobey unjust laws. I would agree with St. Augustine° that "an unjust law is no law at all."

Now, what is the difference between the two? How does one determine whether a law is just or unjust? A just law is a man-made code that squares with the moral law or the law of God. An unjust law is a code that is out of harmony with the moral law. To put it in the terms of St. Thomas Aquinas:° An unjust law is a human law that is not rooted in eternal law and natural law. Any law that uplifts human personality is just. Any law that degrades human personality is unjust. All segregation statutes are unjust because segregation distorts the soul and damages the personality. It gives the segregator a false sense of superiority and the segregated a false sense of inferiority. Segregation, to use the terminology of the Jewish philosopher Martin Buber,° substitutes an "I-it" relationship for an "I-thou" relationship and ends up relegating persons to the status of things. Hence segregation is not only politically, economically, and sociologically unsound, it is morally wrong and sinful. Paul Tillich° has said that sin is separation. Is not segregation an existential expression of man's tragic separation, his awful estrangement, his terrible sinfulness? Thus it is that I can urge men to obey the 1954 decision of the Supreme Court° for it is morally right; and I can urge them to disobey segregation ordinances, for they are morally wrong. 16

Let us consider a more concrete example of just and unjust laws. An unjust law is a code that a numerical or power majority group compels a minority group to obey but does not make binding on itself. This is *difference* made legal. By the same token, a just law is a code that a majority compels a minority to follow and that it is willing to follow itself. This is *sameness* made legal. 17

Let me give another explanation. A law is unjust if it is inflicted on a minority that, as a result of being denied the right to vote, had no part in enacting or devising the law. Who can say that the legislature of Alabama which set up that state's segregation laws was democratically elected? Throughout Alabama all sorts of devious methods are used to prevent Negroes from becoming registered voters, and there are some counties in which, even though Negroes constitute a majority of the population, not a single Negro is registered. Can any law enacted under such circumstances be considered democratically structured? 18

Sometimes a law is just on its face and unjust in its application. For instance, I have been arrested on a charge of parading without a permit. Now, there is nothing wrong in having an ordinance which requires a permit for a parade. But such an ordinance becomes unjust when it is used to maintain segregation and to deny citizens the First-Amendment privilege of peaceful assembly and protest. 19

I hope you are able to see the distinction I am trying to point out. In no sense do I advocate evading or defying the law, as would the rabid segregationist. That would lead to anarchy. One who breaks an unjust law must do so openly, lovingly, and with a willingness to accept the penalty. I submit that an 20 individual who breaks a law that conscience tells him is unjust, and who willingly accepts the penalty of imprisonment in order to arouse the conscience of the community over its injustice, is in reality expressing the highest respect for law.

Of course, there is nothing new about this kind of civil disobedience. It was evidenced sublimely in the refusal of Shadrach, Meshach, and Abednego° to obey the laws of Nebuchadnezzar, on the ground that a higher moral law was at stake. It was practiced superbly by the early Christians, who were willing to face hungry lions and the excruciating pain of chopping blocks rather than submit to certain unjust laws of the Roman Empire. To a degree, academic freedom is a reality today because Socrates practiced civil disobedience. In our own nation, the Boston Tea Party represented a massive act of civil disobedience. 21

Biblical figures who chose to be burned alive in a furnace rather than worship the Babylonian king, Nebuchadnezzar II, and survived through divine intervention

We should never forget that everything Adolf Hitler did in Germany was "legal" and everything the Hungarian freedom fighters did in Hungary was "illegal." It was "illegal" to aid and comfort a Jew in Hitler's Germany. Even so, I am sure that, had I lived in Germany at the time, I would have aided and comforted my Jewish brothers. If today I lived in a Communist country where certain principles dear to the Christian faith are suppressed, I would openly advocate disobeying that country's antireligious laws. 22

I must make two honest confessions to you, my Christian and Jewish brothers. First, I must confess that over the past few years I have been gravely disappointed with the white moderate. I have almost reached the regrettable conclusion that the Negro's great stumbling block in his stride toward freedom is not the White Citizen's Counciler or the Ku Klux Klanner, but the white moderate, who is more devoted to "order" than to justice; who prefers a negative peace which is the absence of tension to a positive peace which is the presence of justice; who constantly says, "I agree with you in the goal you seek, but I cannot agree with your methods of direct action"; who paternalistically believes he can set the timetable for another man's freedom; who lives by a mythical concept of time and who constantly advises the Negro to wait for a "more convenient season." Shallow understanding from people of good will is more frustrating than absolute misunderstanding from people of ill will. Lukewarm acceptance is much more bewildering than outright rejection. 23

I had hoped that the white moderate would understand that law and order exist for the purpose of establishing justice and that when they fail in this purpose they become the dangerously structured dams that block the flow of social progress. I had hoped that the white moderate would understand that the present tension in the South is a necessary phase of the transition from an obnoxious negative peace, in which the Negro passively accepted his unjust plight, to a substantive and positive peace, in which all men will respect the dignity and worth of human personality. Actually, we who engage in nonviolent direct action are not the creators of tension. We merely bring to the surface the hidden tension that is already alive. We bring it out in the open, where 24 it can be seen and dealt with. Like a boil that can never be cured so long as it is covered up but must be opened with all its ugliness to the natural medicines of air and light, injustice must be exposed, with all the tension its exposure creates, to the light of human conscience and the air of national opinion, before it can be cured.

In your statement you assert that our actions, even though peaceful, must 25 be condemned because they precipitate violence. But is this a logical assertion? Isn't this like condemning a robbed man because his possession of money precipitated the evil act of robbery? Isn't this like condemning Socrates because his unswerving commitment to truth and his philosophical inquiries precipitated the act by the misguided populace in which they made him drink hemlock? Isn't this like condemning Jesus because his unique God-consciousness and never-ceasing devotion to God's will precipitated the evil act of crucifixion? We must come to see that, as the federal courts have consistently affirmed, it is wrong to urge an individual to cease his efforts to gain his basic constitutional rights because the quest may precipitate violence. Society must protect the robbed and punish the robber.

I had also hoped that the white moderate would reject the myth concern- 26 ing time in relation to the struggle for freedom. I have just received a letter from a white brother in Texas. He writes: "All Christians know that the colored people will receive equal rights eventually, but it is possible that you are in too great a religious hurry. It has taken Christianity almost two thousand years to accomplish what it has. The teachings of Christ take time to come to earth." Such an attitude stems from a tragic misconception of time, from the strangely irrational notion that there is something in the very flow of time that will inevitably cure all ills. Actually, time itself is neutral; it can be used either destructively or constructively. More and more I feel that the people of ill will have used time much more effectively than have the people of good will. We will have to repent in this generation not merely for the hateful words and actions of the bad people, but for the appalling silence of the good people. Human progress never rolls in on wheels of inevitability; it comes through the tireless efforts of men willing to be co-workers with God, and without this hard work, time itself becomes an ally of the forces of social stagnation. We must use time creatively, in the knowledge that the time is always ripe to do right. Now is the time to make real the promise of democracy and transform our pending national elegy into a creative psalm of brotherhood. Now is the time to lift our national policy from the quicksand of racial injustice to the solid rock of human dignity.

You speak of our activity in Birmingham as extreme. At first I was rather 27 disappointed that fellow clergymen would see my nonviolent efforts as those of an extremist. I began thinking about the fact that I stand in the middle of two opposing forces in the Negro community. One is a force of complacency, made up in part of Negroes who, as a result of long years of oppression, are so drained of self-respect and a sense of "somebodiness" that they have adjusted to segregation; and in part of a few middle-class Negroes who, because of a degree of academic and economic security and because in some ways they profit by segregation, have become insensitive to the problems of the masses. The other force is one of bitterness and hatred, and it comes perilously close to advocating violence. It is expressed in the various black nationalist groups that are springing up across the nation, the largest and best-known being Elijah Muhammad's Muslim movement. Nourished by the Negro's frustration over the continued existence of racial discrimination, this movement is made up of people who have lost faith in America, who have absolutely repudiated Christianity, and who have concluded that the white man is an incorrigible "devil."

I have tried to stand between these two forces, saying that we need emulate neither the "do-nothingism" of the complacent nor the hatred and despair of the black nationalist. For there is the more excellent way of love and nonviolent protest. I am grateful to God that, through the influence of the Negro church, the way of nonviolence became an integral part of our struggle. 28

If this philosophy had not emerged, by now many streets of the South would, I am convinced, be flowing with blood. And I am further convinced that if our white brothers dismiss as "rabble-rousers" and "outside agitators" those of us who employ nonviolent direct action, and if they refuse to support our nonviolent efforts, millions of Negroes will, out of frustration and despair, seek solace and security in black-nationalist ideologies—a development that would inevitably lead to a frightening racial nightmare. 29

Oppressed people cannot remain oppressed forever. The yearning for freedom eventually manifests itself, and that is what has happened to the American Negro. Something within has reminded him of his birthright of freedom, and something without has reminded him that it can be gained. Consciously or unconsciously, he has been caught up by the *Zeitgeist*, and with his black brothers of Africa and his brown and yellow brothers of Asia, South America, and the Caribbean, the United States Negro is moving with a sense of great urgency toward the promised land of racial justice. If one recognizes this vital urge that has engulfed the Negro community, one should readily understand why public demonstrations are taking place. The Negro has many pent-up resentments and latent frustrations, and he must release them. So let him march; let him make prayer pilgrimages to the city hall; let him go on freedom rides—and try to understand why he must do so. If his repressed emotions are not released in nonviolent ways, they will seek expression through violence; this is not a threat but a fact of history. So I have not said to my people, "Get rid of your discontent." Rather, I have tried to say that this normal and healthy discontent can be channeled into the creative outlet of nonviolent direct action. And now this approach is being termed extremist. 30

But though I was initially disappointed at being categorized as an extremist, as I continued to think about the matter I gradually gained a measure of satisfaction from the label. Was not Jesus an extremist for love: "Love your enemies, bless them that curse you, do good to them that hate you, and 31

An Old Testament prophet

Martin Luther (1483–1546), a German priest, philosopher, and primary figure in the Protestant Reformation

John Bunyan (1628–1688), an English writer and Christian preacher best known for writing The Pilgrim's Progress

pray for them which despitefully use you, and persecute you." Was not Amos° an extremist for justice: "Let justice roll down like waters and righteousness like an ever-flowing stream." Was not Paul an extremist for the Christian gospel: "I bear in my body the marks of the Lord Jesus." Was not Martin Luther° an extremist: "Here I stand; I cannot do otherwise, so help me God." And John Bunyan:° "I will stay in jail to the end of my days before I make a butchery of my conscience." And Abraham Lincoln: "This nation cannot survive half slave and half free." And Thomas Jefferson: "We hold these truths to be self-evident, that all men are created equal. . . ." So the question is not whether we will be extremists, but what kind of extremists we will be. Will we be extremists for hate or for love? Will we be extremists for the preservation of injustice or for the extension of justice? In that dramatic scene on Calvary's hill three men were crucified. We must never forget that all three were crucified for the same crime—the crime of extremism. Two were extremists for immorality, and thus fell below their environment. The other, Jesus Christ, was an extremist for love, truth, and goodness, and thereby rose above his environment. Perhaps the South, the nation, and the world are in dire need of creative extremists.

I had hoped that the white moderate would see this need. Perhaps I was 32 too optimistic; perhaps I expected too much. I suppose I should have realized that few members of the oppressor race can understand the deep groans and passionate yearnings of the oppressed race, and still fewer have the vision to see that injustice must be rooted out by strong, persistent, and determined action. I am thankful, however, that some of our white brothers in the South have grasped the meaning of this social revolution and committed themselves to it. They are still all too few in quantity, but they are big in quality. Some—such as Ralph McGill, Lillian Smith, Harry Golden, James McBride Dabbs, Ann Braden, and Sarah Patton Boyle—have written about our struggle in eloquent and prophetic terms. Others have marched with us down nameless streets of the South. They have languished in filthy, roach-infested jails, suffering the abuse and brutality of policemen who view them as "dirty nigger-lovers." Unlike so many of their moderate brothers and sisters, they have recognized the urgency of the moment and sensed the need for powerful "action" antidotes to combat the disease of segregation.

Earl Stallings, one of the eight clergymen King was responding to and pastor of the First Baptist Church in Birmingham

Let me take note of my other major disappointment. I have been so greatly 33 disappointed with the white church and its leadership. Of course, there are some notable exceptions. I am not unmindful of the fact that each of you has taken some significant stands on this issue. I commend you, Reverend Stallings,° for your Christian stand on this past Sunday, in welcoming Negroes to your worship service on a nonsegregated basis. I commend the Catholic leaders of this state for integrating Spring Hill College several years ago.

But despite these notable exceptions, I must honestly reiterate that I have 34 been disappointed with the church. I do not say this as one of those negative critics who can always find something wrong with the church. I say this as a minister of the gospel, who loves the church; who was nurtured in its bosom;

who has been sustained by its spiritual blessings and who will remain true to it as long as the cord of life shall lengthen.

When I was suddenly catapulted into the leadership of the bus protest in 35 Montgomery, Alabama, a few years ago, I felt we would be supported by the white church. I felt that the white ministers, priests, and rabbis of the South would be among our strongest allies. Instead, some have been outright opponents, refusing to understand the freedom movement and misrepresenting its leaders; all too many others have been more cautious than courageous and have remained silent behind the anesthetizing security of stained-glass windows.

In spite of my shattered dreams, I came to Birmingham with the hope that 36 the white religious leadership of this community would see the justice of our cause and, with deep moral concern, would serve as the channel through which our just grievances could reach the power structure. I had hoped that each of you would understand. But again I have been disappointed.

I have heard numerous southern religious leaders admonish their wor- 37 shipers to comply with a desegregation decision because it is the law, but I have longed to hear white ministers declare: "Follow this decree because integration is morally right and because the Negro is your brother." In the midst of blatant injustices inflicted upon the Negro, I have watched white churchmen stand on the sideline and mouth pious irrelevancies and sanctimonious trivialities. In the midst of a mighty struggle to rid our nation of racial and economic injustice, I have heard many ministers say: "Those are social issues, with which the gospel has no real concern." And I have watched many churches commit themselves to a completely otherworldly religion which makes a strange, un-Biblical distinction between body and soul, between the sacred and the secular.

I have traveled the length and breadth of Alabama, Mississippi, and all the 38 other southern states. On sweltering summer days and crisp autumn mornings I have looked at the South's beautiful churches with their lofty spires pointing heavenward. I have beheld the impressive outlines of her massive religious-education buildings. Over and over I have found myself asking: "What kind of people worship here? Who is their God? Where were their voices when the lips of Governor Barnett° dripped with words of interposition and nullification? Where were they when Governor Wallace° gave a clarion call for defiance and hatred? Where were their voices of support when bruised and weary Negro men and women decided to rise from the dark dungeons of complacency to the bright hills of creative protest?"

Yes, these questions are still in my mind. In deep disappointment I have 39 wept over the laxity of the church. But be assured that my tears have been tears of love. There can be no deep disappointment where there is not deep love. Yes, I love the church. How could I do otherwise? I am in the rather unique position of being the son, the grandson, and the great-grandson of preachers. Yes, I see the church as the body of Christ. But, oh! How we have blemished and scarred that body through social neglect and through fear of being nonconformists.

Ross Robert Barnett (1898–1987), segregationist governor of Mississippi from 1960 to 1964

George Wallace (1919–1998), a governor of Alabama (1963–1967, 1971–1979, 1983–1987). Although a segregationist early in his political career, he abandoned that conviction later in life.

There was a time when the church was very powerful—in the time when   40
the early Christians rejoiced at being deemed worthy to suffer for what they
believed. In those days the church was not merely a thermometer that
recorded the ideas and principles of popular opinion; it was a thermostat that
transformed the mores of society. Whenever the early Christians entered a
town, the people in power became disturbed and immediately sought to con-
vict the Christians for being "disturbers of the peace" and "outside agitators."
But the Christians pressed on, in the conviction that they were "a colony of
heaven," called to obey God rather than man. Small in number, they were big
in commitment. They were too God-intoxicated to be "astronomically intimidated." By their effort and example they brought an end to such ancient evils
as infanticide and gladiatorial contests.

Things are different now. So often the contemporary church is a weak,   41
ineffectual voice with an uncertain sound. So often it is an archdefender of the
status quo. Far from being disturbed by the presence of the church, the power
structure of the average community is consoled by the church's silent—and
often even vocal—sanction of things as they are.

But the judgment of God is upon the church as never before. If today's   42
church does not recapture the sacrificial spirit of the early church, it will lose
its authenticity, forfeit the loyalty of millions, and be dismissed as an irrelevant social club with no meaning for the twentieth century. Every day I meet
young people whose disappointment with the church has turned into outright disgust.

Perhaps I have once again been too optimistic. Is organized religion too   43
inextricably bound to the status quo to save our nation and the world? Perhaps I must turn my faith to the inner spiritual church, the church within the
church, as the true *ekklesia*° and the hope of the world. But again I am thankful to God that some noble souls from the ranks of organized religion have
broken loose from the paralyzing chains of conformity and joined us as active
partners in the struggle for freedom. They have left their secure congregations
and walked the streets of Albany, Georgia, with us. They have gone down the
highways of the South on tortuous rides for freedom. Yes, they have gone to
jail with us. Some have been dismissed from their churches, have lost the support of their bishops and fellow ministers. But they have acted in the faith
that right defeated is stronger than evil triumphant. Their witness has been
the spiritual salt that has preserved the true meaning of the gospel in these
troubled times. They have carved a tunnel of hope through the dark mountain of disappointment.

I hope the church as a whole will meet the challenge of this decisive hour. But   44
even if the church does not come to the aid of justice, I have no despair about the
future. I have no fear about the outcome of our struggle in Birmingham, even if
our motives are at present misunderstood. We will reach the goal of freedom in
Birmingham and all over the nation, because the goal of America is freedom.
Abused and scorned though we may be, our destiny is tied up with America's destiny. Before the pilgrims landed at Plymouth, we were here. Before the pen of

Greek for "church"

Jefferson etched the majestic words of the Declaration of Independence across the pages of history, we were here. For more than two centuries our forebears labored in this country without wages: they made cotton king; they built the homes of their masters while suffering gross injustice and shameful humiliation—and yet out of a bottomless vitality they continued to thrive and develop. If the inexpressible cruelties of slavery could not stop us, the opposition we now face will surely fail. We will win our freedom because the sacred heritage of our nation and the eternal will of God are embodied in our echoing demands.

Before closing I feel impelled to mention one other point in your state- 45 ment that has troubled me profoundly. You warmly commended the Birmingham police force for keeping "order" and "preventing violence." I doubt that you would have so warmly commended the police force if you had seen its dogs sinking their teeth into unarmed, nonviolent Negroes. I doubt that you would so quickly commend the policemen if you were to observe their ugly and inhumane treatment of Negroes here in the city jail; if you were to watch them push and curse old Negro women and young Negro girls; if you were to see them slap and kick old Negro men and young boys; if you were to observe them, as they did on two occasions, refuse to give us food because we wanted to sing our grace together. I cannot join you in your praise of the Birmingham police department.

It is true that the police have exercised a degree of discipline in handling 46 the demonstrators. In this sense they have conducted themselves rather "nonviolently" in public. But for what purpose? To preserve the evil system of segregation. Over the past few years I have consistently preached that nonviolence demands that the means we use must be as pure as the ends we seek. I have tried to make clear that it is wrong to use immoral means to attain moral ends. But now I must affirm that it is just as wrong, or perhaps even more so, to use moral means to preserve immoral ends. Perhaps Mr. Connor and his policemen have been rather nonviolent in public, as was Chief Pritchett° in Albany, Georgia, but they have used the moral means of nonviolence to maintain the immoral end of racial injustice. As T. S. Eliot° has said, "The last temptation is the greatest treason: To do the right deed for the wrong reason."

Laurie Pritchett (1926–2000), the police chief in Albany, Georgia, during the 1961 Albany Movement, a desegregation campaign

I wish you had commended the Negro sit-inners and demonstrators of 47 Birmingham for their sublime courage, their willingness to suffer, and their amazing discipline in the midst of great provocation. One day the South will recognize its real heroes. They will be the James Merediths,° with the noble sense of purpose that enables them to face jeering and hostile mobs, and with the agonizing loneliness that characterizes the life of the pioneer. They will be old, oppressed, battered Negro women, symbolized in a seventy-two-year-old woman in Montgomery, Alabama, who rose up with a sense of dignity and with her people decided not to ride segregated buses, and who responded with ungrammatical profundity to one who inquired about her weariness: "My feets is tired, but my soul is at rest." They will be the young high school and college students, the young ministers of the gospel and a host of their elders, courageously and nonviolently sitting in at lunch counters and

T. S. Eliot (1888–1965), an American-born poet, playwright, and critic

James Meredith (b. 1933), in 1961 the first African-American student to attend the University of Mississippi

willingly going to jail for conscience' sake. One day the South will know that when these disinherited children of God sat down at lunch counters, they were in reality standing up for what is best in the American dream and for the most sacred values in our Judaeo-Christian heritage, thereby bringing our nation back to those great wells of democracy which were dug deep by the founding fathers in their formulation of the Constitution and the Declaration of Independence.

Never before have I written so long a letter. I'm afraid it is much too long 48 to take your precious time. I can assure you that it would have been much shorter if I had been writing from a comfortable desk, but what else can one do when he is alone in a narrow jail cell, other than write long letters, think long thoughts, and pray long prayers?

If I have said anything in this letter that overstates the truth and indicates 49 an unreasonable impatience, I beg you to forgive me. If I have said anything that understates the truth and indicates my having a patience that allows me to settle for anything less than brotherhood, I beg God to forgive me.

I hope this letter finds you strong in the faith. I also hope that circum- 50 stances will soon make it possible for me to meet each of you, not as an integrationist or a civil-rights leader but as a fellow clergyman and a Christian brother. Let us all hope that the dark clouds of racial prejudice will soon pass away and the deep fog of misunderstanding will be lifted from our fear-drenched communities, and in some not too distant tomorrow the radiant stars of love and brotherhood will shine over our great nation with all their scintillating beauty.

Yours for the cause of Peace and Brotherhood,

Martin Luther King Jr.

⤷ READING ARGUMENTS

1. In what sense is "Letter from Birmingham Jail" a Rogerian argument? What specific elements of Rogerian argument does King use? Why is this form of argument suited to King's overall purpose?

2. Where does King use analogies—historical and otherwise—to strengthen his arguments? Why do you think he makes these particular comparisons? How are they related to his political goals?

3. According to King, what is "direct action" (para. 6), and what is its purpose?

4. In many parts of his letter, King writes in a detached, almost scholarly style, citing philosophers and theologians. Where does he use more emotional language? What do you think he is trying to achieve with

this language? Do you think this language effectively supports his argument? Do you think it appealed to his original audience?

5. King makes "two honest confessions" in his letter (23). What are they? Why do you think he characterizes these points as confessions?

⊙ WRITING ARGUMENTS

1. According to King, people have a moral obligation to obey just laws and to disobey unjust laws. What is his standard for determining which laws are just and unjust? Is there a current law you would consider breaking for the reasons King describes? Write an argumentative essay in which you defend such a choice.

2. King agrees with the theologian Reinhold Niebuhr that "groups tend to be more immoral than individuals" (12). Do you think this statement is generally true? Take a position on the issue, and argue your case.

IF BLACK ENGLISH ISN'T A LANGUAGE, THEN TELL ME, WHAT IS?

JAMES BALDWIN

Although the Harlem-born novelist, playwright, poet, and critic James Baldwin spent much of his life abroad, he remained an American writer. That is evident in well-known works like Go Tell It on the Mountain *(1953),* Notes of a Native Son *(1955), and* The Fire Next Time *(1963), which explore the problem of race in the United States. He also wrote powerfully about class, culture, and sexual identity in both his fiction and his essays. Baldwin was especially perceptive about the complex relationship between "self" and "society," as is clear in the following essay. For Baldwin, language "reveals the private identity, and connects one with, or divorces one from, the larger, public, or communal identity."*

The argument concerning the use, or the status, or the reality, of black English   1 is rooted in American history and has absolutely nothing to do with the question the argument supposes itself to be posing. The argument has nothing to do with language itself but with the role of language. Language, incontestably, reveals the speaker. Language, also, far more dubiously, is meant to define the other—and, in this case, the other is refusing to be defined by a language that has never been able to recognize him.

People evolve a language in order to describe and thus control their circumstances or in order not to be submerged by a situation that they cannot articulate. (And if they cannot articulate it, they are submerged.) A Frenchman living in Paris speaks a subtly and crucially different language from that of the man living in Marseilles; neither sounds very much like a man living in Quebec; and they would all have great difficulty in apprehending what the man from Guadeloupe, or Martinique, is saying, to say nothing of the man from Senegal—although the "common" language of all these areas is French. But each has paid, and is paying, a different price for this "common" language, in which, as it turns out, they are not saying, and cannot be saying, the same things: They each have very different realities to articulate, or control.

What joins all languages, and all men, is the necessity to confront life, in order, not inconceivably, to outwit death: The price for this is the acceptance, and achievement, of one's temporal identity. So that, for example, though it is not taught in the schools (and this has the potential of becoming a political issue) the south of France still clings to its ancient and musical Provençal, which resists being described as a "dialect." And much of the tension in the Basque countries, and in Wales, is due to the Basque and Welsh determination not to allow their languages to be destroyed. This determination also feeds the flames in Ireland for among the many indignities the Irish have been forced to undergo at English hands is the English contempt for their language.

It goes without saying, then, that language is also a political instrument, means, and proof of power. It is the most vivid and crucial key to identity: It reveals the private identity, and connects one with, or divorces one from, the larger, public, or communal identity. There have been, and are, times and places, when to speak a certain language could be dangerous, even fatal. Or, one may speak the same language, but in such a way that one's antecedents are revealed, or (one hopes) hidden. This is true in France, and is absolutely true in England: The range (and reign) of accents on that damp little island make England coherent for the English and totally incomprehensible for everyone else. To open your mouth in England is (if I may use black English) to "put your business in the street." You have confessed your parents, your youth, your school, your salary, your self-esteem, and, alas, your future.

Now, I do not know what white Americans would sound like if there had never been any black people in the United States, but they would not sound the way they sound. *Jazz*, for example, is a very specific sexual term, as in *jazz me, baby*, but white people purified it into the Jazz Age. *Sock it to me*, which means, roughly, the same thing, has been adopted by Nathaniel Hawthorne's° descendants with no qualms or hesitations at all, along with *let it all hang out*

Nathaniel Hawthorne (1804–1864), an American novelist and short story writer whose work often focused on Puritan New England

and *right on! Beat to his socks*, which was once the black's most total and despairing image of poverty, was transformed into a thing called the Beat Generation,° which phenomenon was, largely, composed of *uptight*, middle-class white people, imitating poverty, trying to *get down*, to *get with it*, doing their *thing*, doing their despairing best to be *funky*, which we, the blacks, never dreamed of doing—we were funky, baby, like *funk* was going out of style.

A group of post–World War II American writers that valued freedom, authenticity, spontaneous expression, antimaterialism, and nonconformity

Now, no one can eat his cake, and have it, too, and it is late in the day to attempt to penalize black people for having created a language that permits the nation its only glimpse of reality, a language without which the nation would be even more *whipped* than it is. 6

I say that the present skirmish is rooted in American history, and it is. Black English is the creation of the black diaspora. Blacks came to the United States chained to each other, but from different tribes. Neither could speak the other's language. If two black people, at that bitter hour of the world's history, had been able to speak to each other, the institution of chattel slavery could never have lasted as long as it did. Subsequently, the slave was given, under the eye, and the gun, of his master, Congo Square, and the Bible—or, in other words, and under those conditions, the slave began the formation of the black church, and it is within this unprecedented tabernacle that black English began to be formed. This was not, merely, as in the European example, the adoption of a foreign tongue, but an alchemy that transformed ancient elements into a new language: *A language comes into existence by means of brutal necessity, and the rules of the language are dictated by what the language must convey.* 7

There was a moment, in time, and in this place, when my brother, or my mother, or my father, or my sister, had to convey to me, for example, the danger in which I was standing from the white man standing just behind me, and to convey this with a speed and in a language, that the white man could not possibly understand, and that, indeed, he cannot understand, until today. He cannot afford to understand it. This understanding would reveal to him too much about himself and smash that mirror before which he has been frozen for so long. 8

Now, if this passion, this skill, this (to quote Toni Morrison)° "sheer intelligence," this incredible music, the mighty achievement of having brought a people utterly unknown to, or despised by "history"—to have brought this people to their present, troubled, troubling, and unassailable and unanswerable place—if this absolutely unprecedented journey does not indicate that black English is a language, I am curious to know what definition of languages is to be trusted. 9

Toni Morrison (1931–) an African-American writer who won the 1993 Nobel Prize in Literature

A people at the center of the western world, and in the midst of so hostile a population, has not endured and transcended by means of what is patronizingly called a "dialect." We, the blacks, are in trouble, certainly, but we are not inarticulate because we are not compelled to defend a morality that we know to be a lie. 10

The brutal truth is that the bulk of the white people in America never had [11] any interest in educating black people, except as this could serve white purposes. It is not the black child's language that is despised. It is his experience. A child cannot be taught by anyone who despises him, and a child cannot afford to be fooled. A child cannot be taught by anyone whose demand, essentially, is that the child repudiate his experience, and all that gives him sustenance, and enter a limbo in which he will no longer be black, and in which he knows that he can never become white. Black people have lost too many black children that way.

And, after all, finally, in a country with standards so untrustworthy, a [12] country that makes heroes of so many criminal mediocrities, a country unable to face why so many of the nonwhite are in prison, or on the needle, or standing, futureless, in the streets—it may very well be that both the child, and his elder, have concluded that they have nothing whatever to learn from the people of a country that has managed to learn so little.

➲ READING ARGUMENTS

1. How does Baldwin use deductive reasoning in the first three paragraphs of this essay? Construct a syllogism for this argument. Do you find the syllogism's conclusion persuasive? Why or why not?

2. Baldwin writes, "It goes without saying, then, that language is a political instrument, means, and proof of power" (4). What does he mean? Does this really "go without saying"? In other words, is this point self-evident? How does he support his claim?

3. According to Baldwin, black people "created a language that permits the nation its only glimpse of reality" (6). What does he mean? Do you agree? Why or why not?

➲ WRITING ARGUMENTS

1. For Baldwin, language is the "most vivid and crucial key to identity" (para. 4). When you speak, you reveal "your parents, your youth, your school, your salary, your self-esteem, and, alas, your future" (4). In your experience, have you found this to be true? Are these aspects of your life evident in the sounds of your own speech? Write an essay that presents your point of view on these questions.

2. Baldwin discusses black contributions to American English. He also points out how white Americans "purified" (5) certain black terms from

jazz culture and transformed black poverty into the "Beat Generation." Why would people imitate the language of poverty? Is this process still at work today? If so, where do you see it? Address these questions in an argumentative essay, using examples to support your points.

Writing Literary Arguments

When you write an essay about literature, you have a number of options. For example, you can write a **response paper** (expressing your reactions to a poem, play, or story), or you can write an **explication** (focusing on a work's individual elements, such as a poem's imagery, meter, figurative language, and diction). You can also write an **analysis** of a work's theme, a character in a play or a story, or a work's historical or cultural context. Another option, which is discussed in the pages that follow, is to write a literary argument.

What Is Literary Argument?

When you write a literary argument, you do more than just react to, explicate, or analyze a work of literature. When you develop a **literary argument**, you take a position about a literary work (or works), support that position with evidence, and refute possible opposing arguments. You might, for example, take the position that a familiar interpretation of a well-known work is limited in some way, that a work's impact today is different from its impact when it was written, or that two apparently very different works have some significant similarities.

It is important to understand that not every essay about literature is a literary argument. For example, you might use a discussion of Tillie Olsen's short story "I Stand Here Ironing," with its sympathetic portrait of a young mother during the Great Depression, to support an argument in favor of President Franklin D. Roosevelt's expansion of social welfare programs. Alternatively, you might use Martin Espada's poem "Why I Went to College" to support your own decision to continue your education. But writing a literary argument involves much more than using a literary work as support for an argument or referring to a literary character to shed light on your own intellectual development or to explain a choice you made. A literary argument *takes a stand* about a work (or works) of literature.

Stating an Argumentative Thesis

When you develop an argumentative thesis about literature, your goal is to state a thesis that has an edge—one that takes a stand on your topic. Like

any effective thesis, the thesis of a literary argument should be clearly worded and specific; it should also be more than a statement of fact.

INEFFECTIVE THESIS (TOO GENERAL)	In "A&P," Sammy faces a difficult decision.
EFFECTIVE THESIS (MORE SPECIFIC)	Sammy's decision to quit his job reveals more about the conformist society in which "A&P" is set than about Sammy himself.
INEFFECTIVE THESIS (STATES A FACT)	The theme of *Hamlet* is often seen as an Oedipal conflict.
EFFECTIVE THESIS (TAKES A STAND)	Although many critics have identified an Oedipal conflict in *Hamlet*, Shakespeare's play is also a story of a young man who is struggling with familiar problems—love, family, and his future.

Here are some possible thesis statements that you could support in a literary argument:

- Charlotte Perkins Gilman's short story "The Yellow Wallpaper," usually seen as a feminist story, is actually a ghost story.

- The two characters in August Strindberg's play *The Stronger* seem to be rivals for the affection of a man, but they are really engaged in a professional rivalry to see who gives the better performance.

- Although many readers might see Wilfred Owen's "Dulce et Decorum Est" as the more powerful poem because of its graphic imagery of war, Carl Sandburg's understated "Grass" is likely to have a greater impact on modern readers, who have been overexposed to violent images.

(For more on developing a thesis statement, see Chapter 7.)

Choosing Evidence

Like any argument, a literary argument relies on evidence. Some of this evidence can be found in the literary work itself. For example, to make a point about a character's antisocial behavior, you would cite specific examples of such behavior from the work. To make a point about a poet's use of biblical allusions, you would present examples of such allusions from the poem.

> **NOTE**
>
> Be careful not to substitute plot summary for evidence. For example, summarizing everything that happens to a character will not convince your readers that the character is motivated by envy. Choose only *relevant* examples—in this case, specific instances of a character's jealous behavior, including relevant quotations from the literary work.

Evidence can also come from **literary criticism**—scholarly articles by experts in the field that analyze and evaluate works of literature. For example, to argue that a particular critical position is inaccurate, outdated, or oversimplified, you would quote critics who take that position before you explain why you disagree with their interpretation. (For more on evaluating potential sources for your essay, see Chapter 8.)

Writing a Literary Argument

The structure of a literary argument is similar to the structure of any other argument: it includes a **thesis statement** in the introduction, supporting **evidence**, **refutation** of opposing arguments, and a strong **concluding statement**. However, unlike other arguments, literary arguments follow specific conventions for writing about literature:

- In your essay's first paragraph, include the author's full name and the title of each work you are discussing.

- Use **present tense** when discussing events in works of literature. For example, if you are discussing "I Stand Here Ironing," you would say, "The mother *worries* [not *worried*] about her ability to provide for her child." There are two exceptions to this rule. Use past tense when referring to historical events: "The Great Depression *made* things difficult for mothers like the narrator." Also use past tense to refer to events that came before the action described in the work: "The mother is particularly vulnerable because her husband *left* her alone to support her children."

- Italicize titles of plays and novels. Put titles of poems and short stories in quotation marks.

- If you quote more than four lines of prose (or more than three lines of poetry), indent the entire quotation one inch from the left-hand margin. Do not include quotation marks, and add the parenthetical documentation after the end punctuation. Introduce the quotation with a colon, and double-space above and below it.

- When mentioning writers and literary critics in the body of your essay, use their full names ("Emily Dickinson") the first time you mention them and their last names only ("Dickinson," not "Miss Dickinson" or "Emily") after that.

- Use **MLA documentation style** in your paper, and include a works-cited list. (See Chapter 10 for information on MLA documentation.)

- In your in-text citations, cite page numbers for stories, act and scene numbers for plays, and line numbers for poems. Use the word *line* or *lines* for the first in-text citation of lines from each poem. After the first in-text citation, you may omit the word *line* or *lines*.

The following literary argument, "Confessions of a Misunderstood Poem: An Analysis of 'The Road Not Taken,'" takes a stand in favor of a particular way of interpreting poetry.

CONFESSIONS OF A MISUNDERSTOOD POEM: AN ANALYSIS OF "THE ROAD NOT TAKEN"

MEGAN McGOVERN

Introduction (identifies titles and authors of works to be discussed)

The word *lines* is omitted from the in-text citation after the first reference to lines of a poem.

Thesis statement

In his poem "Introduction to Poetry," Billy Collins suggests that rather than dissecting a poem to find its meaning, students should use their imaginations to experience poetry. According to Collins, they should "drop a mouse into a poem / and watch him probe his way out" (lines 5–6). However, Collins overstates his case when he implies that analyzing a poem to find out what it might mean is a brutal or deadly process, comparable to tying the poem to a chair and "beating it with a hose" (15). Rather than killing a poem's spirit, a careful and methodical dissection can often help the reader better appreciate its subtler meanings. In fact, with patient coaxing, a poem often has much to "confess." One such poem is Robert Frost's familiar but frequently misunderstood "The Road Not Taken." An examination of Frost's "The Road Not Taken" reveals a complex and somewhat troubling message

1

about the arbitrariness of our life choices and our need to idealize those choices.

2   On the surface, Frost's poem seems to have a fairly simple meaning. The poem's speaker talks about coming to a fork in the road and choosing the "less-traveled" path. Most readers see the fork in the road as a metaphor: the road represents life, and the fork represents an individual's choices in life. By following the less-traveled road, the speaker is choosing the less conventional—and supposedly more emotionally rewarding—route. At the end of the poem, the speaker indicates his satisfaction when he says his choice "made all the difference" (line 20). However, Frost himself, referring to "The Road Not Taken," advised readers "'to be careful of that one; it's a tricky poem—very tricky,'" encouraging readers not to accept the most appealing or obvious interpretation (qtd. in Savoie 7–8). Literary critic Bojana Vujin urges readers to look for "poetic booby traps such as irony or deceit" in this poem and to enjoy the pleasures and rewards of discovering instances of "deliberate deceit on the poet's part" (195). Indeed, after the speaker's tone and word choice are carefully examined, the poem's message seems darker and more complicated than it did initially.

Refutation of opposing argument

3   The speaker's tone in the first three stanzas suggests indecision, regret, and, ultimately, lack of power. Rather than bravely facing the choice between one common path and one uncommon path, the speaker spends most of the poem considering two seemingly equal roads, "sorry" not to be able to "travel both" (2). Even after choosing "the other" road in line 6, the speaker continues for two more stanzas to weigh his options. The problem is that the two roads are, in fact, indistinguishable. As several critics have observed, "the difference between the two roads, at least when it comes to the amount of treading they have been exposed to, is but an illusion: they 'both that morning equally lay' and neither is particularly travelled by" (Vujin 197). The roads are worn "really about the same" (10). If there is virtually no difference between the two, then why does Frost draw our attention to this fork in the road—this seemingly critical moment of choice? If Frost had wanted to dramatize a meaningful decision, the roads would be different in some significant way.

Evidence: Analysis and explication of Frost poem

Evidence: Literary criticism

Evidence: Literary criticism

One critic, Frank Lentricchia, argues that Frost is demonstrating "'that our life-shaping choices are irrational, that we are fundamentally out of control'" (qtd. in Savoie 13). Similarly, another critic, Sterling Eisiminger, connects "The Road Not Taken" to an essay Frost wrote years later to show that Frost was interested in "the impulsiveness and arbitrariness with which most important decisions are made" (114). These critical views help to explain the speaker's indecision in the first three stanzas. The speaker impulsively chooses "the other" road but

Evidence: Analysis and explication of Frost poem

cannot accept the arbitrariness of his choice; therefore, he cannot stop considering the first road. He exclaims in the third stanza, "Oh, I kept the first for another day!" (13). In the next two lines, when he finally gives up the possibility of following that first road, he predicts, "Yet knowing how way leads on to way, / I doubted if I should ever come back" (14–15). Here, the speaker further demonstrates a lack of control over his own decisions. He describes a future guided not by his own active, meaningful choices but rather by some arbitrary force. In a world where "way leads on to way," he is a passive traveler, not a decisive individualist.

Evidence: Analysis and explication of Frost poem

Given the indecision that characterizes the previous stanzas, the poem's last two lines are surprisingly decisive: "I took the one less traveled by / And that has made all the difference" (19–20). Is the speaker contradicting himself? How has he suddenly become clear about the rightness of his decision? In fact, the last stanza does not make sense unless the reader perceives the irony in the speaker's tone. The speaker is imagining himself in the future, "ages and ages hence," telling the story of his moment at the crossroads (17). He imagines how he will, in hindsight, give his choice meaning and clarity that it did not have at the time. As Vujin argues, the poem's

Evidence: Literary criticism

speaker is already "mythologizing his self and his life" (198). The narrator, rather than anticipating the satisfaction that will come from having made the right and braver choice, is anticipating rewriting his own life story to make sense of an ultimately arbitrary chain of events. Vujin explains, "This is not a poem about individuality; this is a poem about self-deceit and the rewriting of one's own history" (198). Reading the last stanza ironically allows the reader to make sense of the poem as a whole.

6   There are many possible interpretations of "The Road Not   Conclusion
Taken," most of which can be supported with evidence from the poem
itself. However, to understand these interpretations, readers need to
take the poem apart, look at how its parts fit together, and reach a
thoughtful and logical conclusion. To do so, readers must go against
some of Billy Collins's well-meaning advice and be willing to tie the
poem—and themselves—to a chair: to read it carefully, ask questions,
and stay with it until it confesses.

Works Cited

Collins, Billy. "Introduction to Poetry." *Sailing Alone around the Room*.
    New York: Random, 1998. 16. Print.

Eisiminger, Sterling. "Robert Frost's Essay 'The Constant Symbol' and
    Its Relationship to 'The Road Not Taken.'" *American Notes and
    Queries* 19.7–8 (1981): 114–15. *Academic Search Premier*. Web.
    14 Mar. 2012.

Frost, Robert. "The Road Not Taken." *Mountain Interval*. New York:
    Holt, 1920. N. pag. *Bartleby.com: Great Books Online*. Web.
    14 Mar. 2012.

Savoie, John. "A Poet's Quarrel: Jamesian Pragmatism and Frost's 'The
    Road Not Taken.'" *New England Quarterly* 77.1 (2004): 5–24.
    Academic Search Premier. Web. 14 Mar. 2012.

Vujin, Bojana. "'I Took the Road Less Traveled By': Self-Deception in
    Frost's and Eliot's Early Poetry." *Annual Review of the Faculty of
    Philosophy* 36.1 (2011): 195–203. *Academic Search Complete*. Web.
    30 Apr. 2012.

The following literary argument, "Not Just a 'Girl,'" argues against the
commonly held position that a key character in the 1925 Ernest Hemingway short story "Hills Like White Elephants" is a stereotype.

NOT JUST A "GIRL"

LOREN MARTINEZ

Introduction

In Ernest Hemingway's famous story "Hills Like White Elephants," a couple, "the American and the girl with him," talk and drink while waiting for a train to Madrid (Hemingway 69). Most readers agree that the subject of their discussion is whether "the girl," called Jig, should have an abortion. Most of the story is told through dialogue, and although the word *abortion* is never mentioned, most readers agree that the pregnancy is the source of the tension between them. However, there are other aspects of the story about which readers do not agree. For example, some critics believe that Hemingway's portrayal of "the girl" is unfair or sexist. More specifically, some see in her the qualities of "the typically submissive Hemingway woman" (Nolan 19). However, **Thesis statement** a close reading of the story reveals the opposite to be true: "the girl" is not a one-dimensional stereotype but a complex, sympathetically drawn character.

Refutation of opposing arguments

Most critics who see Hemingway's portrayal of Jig as sexist base their interpretation on Hemingway's reputation and not on the story itself. For example, feminist critic Katherine M. Rogers points out that because Hemingway himself "openly expressed fear of and hostility to women" (263), it "seems fair" to see his male characters "as representative of Hemingway himself" (248). However, although "the American" in this story may see Jig as just "a pleasant pastime," it would be an oversimplification to confuse the character's opinion of her with the writer's as Rogers would encourage us to do (251). For example, one could argue (as many critics have done) that because the name "Jig" has sexual connotations, it reveals the author's sexism (Renner 38). However, as critic Howard Hannum points out, she is referred to by this name only twice in the story, both times by the male character himself, not by the narrator (qtd. in Renner 38). Critic Stanley Renner agrees with Hannum, rejecting the idea that Hemingway's choice to refer to the character as "the girl" is equally "belittling" (38). Renner argues that this use of the word *girl* is

1

necessary to show how the character changes and matures in this story. In fact, he sees "her achievement of mature self-knowledge and assertion [as] the main line of development in the story" (39). All in all, the evidence suggests that "the girl," not "the American," is actually the story's protagonist. Given this central focus on "the girl" and the complexity of her character, the accusations that Hemingway's sexism has led him to create a stereotype do not seem justified.

3   When students who are not familiar with Hemingway's reputation as a misogynist read "Hills Like White Elephants," they tend to sympathize more often with "the girl" than with "the American" (Bauer 126) and to see the female character's thoughtfulness and depth. Although "the American" refers to the abortion as "'really an awfully simple operation'" (Hemingway 72), downplaying its seriousness, "the girl" has a "more mature understanding" of what her decision might mean (Bauer 130). She recognizes that it is not so "simple," and she is not naive enough to think that having the baby will save the relationship. In fact, she responds to his own naive comments with sarcasm. He claims that they will be "'all right and happy'" if she goes through with the operation; he says he's "'known lots of people who have done it.' 'So have I,' said the girl. 'And afterward they were all so happy'" (Hemingway 73). Despite her sarcasm and her resistance to his suggestions, the man continues to insist that this problem will be easy to fix. Finally, the girl becomes irritated with him and, as readers can see by the dashes that end his lines midsentence, cuts him off, finishing his lines for him as he tries to tell her again how "perfectly simple" the operation is (Hemingway 76). Readers understand her pain and frustration when she finally says, "'Would you please please please please please please please stop talking?'" (Hemingway 76).

Evidence: First point in support of thesis

4   The argument that "the girl" is a flat, stereotypical character portrayed in sexist terms is hard to support. In fact, a stronger argument could be made that it is the man, "the American," who is the stereotype. As critic Charles J. Nolan Jr. points out, "Hemingway highlights Jig's maturity and superiority as he excoriates the selfishness and insensitivity of her companion" (19). Moreover, "the girl" is certainly the central character in this story—the one in conflict, the one who must

Evidence: Second point in support of thesis

make the final decision, and the one who grows over the course of the story. At times, she seems willing to listen to the man, even going so far as to say, "'Then I'll do it. Because I don't care about me'" (Hemingway 74). However, soon after, she responds defiantly to his comment, "'You mustn't feel that way'" with "'I don't feel any way'" (Hemingway 75). Thus, as Renner notes, Hemingway's dialogue reveals "the self-centered motives of his male character" while at the same time dramatizing the female character's complex inner struggle (38). By the end of the story, the shallow "American" still expects things to be all right between them. But when the man asks, "'Do you feel better?'" Hemingway shows the girl's quiet power—and her transformation—by giving her the final understated words of the story: "'I feel fine. . . . There's nothing wrong with me. I feel fine'" (Hemingway 77). Although we do not learn what her decision is, we can see that she is now in control: she has decided to shut down the conversation, and what the man has to say no longer matters.

Conclusion

In "Hills Like White Elephants," "the girl" proves herself to be neither "'weak *in* character'" nor "'weak *as* character'" as some have described Hemingway's female characters (Bauer 126). Far from being weak *in* character, she constantly questions and pushes against the male character's suggestions. And far from being weak *as* a character, she acts as the protagonist in this story, winning the reader's sympathies. A stereotypically drawn female character would not be able to carry off

Concluding statement

either of these feats. Although Hemingway may demonstrate sexism in his other stories—and demonstrate it in his own life—readers who evaluate *this* story will discover a complex, conflicted, sympathetic female character.

Works Cited

Bauer, Margaret D. "Forget the Legend and Read the Work: Teaching Two Stories by Ernest Hemingway." *College Literature* 30.3 (2003): 124–37. *Academic Search Premier*. Web. 22 Oct. 2012.

Hemingway, Ernest. "Hills Like White Elephants." *Men without Women*. New York: Scribner's, 1927. 69–77. Print.

Nolan, Charles J., Jr. "Hemingway's Women's Movement." *Hemingway Review* 4.1 (1984): 14–22. *Academic Search Premier.* Web. 22 Oct. 2012.

Renner, Stanley. "Moving to the Girl's Side of 'Hills Like White Elephants.'" *Hemingway Review* 15.1 (1995): 27–41. *Academic Search Premier.* Web. 22 Oct. 2012.

Rogers, Katherine M. *The Troublesome Helpmate: A History of Misogyny in Literature.* Seattle: U of Washington P, 1996. Print.

Documenting Sources: APA

APA documentation style was developed by the American Psychological Association and is commonly used in the social sciences. It helps readers understand new ideas in the context of previous research and shows them how current the sources are.* Citing sources in argumentative essays is important because readers expect arguments to be well supported by evidence and want to be able to locate those sources if they decide to delve deeper. Citing sources is also important to give credit to writers and to avoid plagiarism.

Using Parenthetical References

In APA style, parenthetical references refer readers to sources in the list of references at the end of the paper. In general, parenthetical references should include the author and year of publication. Here are some more specific guidelines:

- Refer to the author's name in the text, or cite it, along with the year of publication, in parentheses at the end of the sentence: Vang (2004) asserted . . . or (Vang, 2004). When quoting words from a source, also include the page number, if available: (Vang, 2004, p. 33). Once you have cited a source, you can refer to the author a second time without the publication date so long as it is clear you are referring to the same source: Vang also found . . .

- If no author is identified, use a shortened version of the title: ("Mind," 2007).

- If you are citing multiple works by the same author or authors published in the same year, include a lowercase letter with the year: (Peters, 2004a), (Peters, 2004b), and so on.

---

* American Psychological Association, *Publication Manual of the American Psychological Association*, Sixth Edition (2010).

e For comprehension quizzes,
see bedfordstmartins.com/practicalargument.

- When a work has two authors, cite both names, separated by an ampersand, and the year: (Tabor & Garza, 2006). For three to five authors, in the first reference, cite all authors, along with the year; for subsequent references, cite just the first author, followed by et al. When a work has six or more authors, cite just the first author, followed by et al. and the year: (McCarthy et al., 2010).

- Omit page numbers or dates if the source does not include them. (Try to find a .pdf version of an online source; it will usually include page numbers.)

- If you quote a source found in another source, cite the original author and the source in which you found it: Psychologist Gary Wells asserted . . . (as cited in Doyle, 2005, p. 122).

- Include in-text references to personal communications and interviews by providing the person's name, the phrase "personal communication," and the date: (J. Smith, personal communication, February 12, 2006). Do not include these sources in your reference list.

Parenthetical citations must be provided for all sources that are not common knowledge, whether you are summarizing, paraphrasing, or quoting. If a direct quotation is forty words or less, include it within quotation marks without separating it from the rest of the text. When quoting a passage of more than forty words, indent the entire block of quoted text one-half inch from the left margin, and do not enclose it in quotation marks. It should be double-spaced, like the rest of the paper.

Preparing a Reference List

Start your list of references on a separate page at the end of your paper. Center the title References at the top of the page, and follow these guidelines:

- Begin each reference flush with the left margin, and indent subsequent lines one-half inch.

- List your references alphabetically by the author's last name (or by the first major word of the title if no author is identified).

- If the list includes references for two sources by the same author, alphabetize them by title.

- Italicize titles of books and periodicals. Do not italicize article titles or enclose them in quotation marks.

- For titles of books and articles, capitalize the first word of the title and subtitle as well as any proper nouns. Capitalize words in a periodical title as they appear in the original.

When you have completed your reference list, go through your paper and make sure that every reference cited is included in the list in the correct order.

Examples of APA Citations

The following are examples of APA citations.

Periodicals
Article in a journal paginated by volume

Shah, N. A. (2006). Women's human rights in the Koran: An
   interpretive approach. *Human Rights Quarterly, 28,* 868–902.

Article in a journal paginated by issue

Lamb, B., & Keller, H. (2007). Understanding cultural models of
   parenting: The role of intracultural variation and response
   style. *Journal of Cross-Cultural Psychology, 38*(1), 50–57.

Magazine article

Collins, L. (2009, April 20). The vertical tourist. *The New Yorker,
   85*(10), 68–79.

Newspaper article

DeParle, J. (2009, April 19). Struggling to rise in suburbs where
   failing means fitting in. *The New York Times,* pp. A1, A20–A21.

Books
Books by one author

Venkatesh, S. A. (2006). *Off the books: The underground economy
   of the urban poor.* Cambridge, MA: Harvard University Press.

Books by two to seven authors

Guerrero, L. K., & Floyd, K. (2006). *Nonverbal communication in
   close relationships.* Mahwah, NJ: Erlbaum.

Books by eight or more authors

Barrett, J. M., Smith, V., Wilson, R. T., Haley, V. A., Clarke, P.,
   Palmer, N. B., . . . Fraser, D. (2012). *How to cite references in
   APA style.* New York: Cambridge University Press.

Edited book

Brummett, B. (Ed.). (2008). *Uncovering hidden rhetorics: Social issues in disguise*. Los Angeles, CA: Sage.

Essay in an edited book

Alberts, H. C. (2006). The multiple transformations of Miami. In H. Smith & O. J. Furuseth (Eds.), *Latinos in the new south: Transformations of place* (pp. 135–151). Burlington, VT: Ashgate.

Translation

Courville, S. (2008). *Quebec: A historical geography* (R. Howard, Trans.). Vancouver, British Columbia, Canada: UBC.

Revised edition

Johnson, B., & Christensen, L. B. (2008). *Educational research: Quantitative, qualitative, and mixed approaches* (3rd ed.). Los Angeles, CA: Sage.

Internet Sources
Entire Web site

Secretariat of the Convention on Biodiversity, United Nations Biodiversity Programmes. (2005). *Convention on biological diversity.* Retrieved from http://www.biodiv.org/

Web page within a Web site

The great divide: How Westerners and Muslims view each other. (2006, July 6). In *Pew global attitudes project*. Retrieved from http://pewglobal.org/reports/display.php?ReportID=253

University program Web site

National security archive. (2009). Retrieved from George Washington University website: http://www.gwu.edu/~nsarchiv/

Journal article found on the Web with a DOI

Because Web sites change and disappear without warning, many publishers have started adding a Digital Object Identifier (DOI) to their articles. A DOI is a unique number that can be retrieved no matter where the article ends up on the Web.

To locate an article with a known DOI, go to the DOI system Web site at http://dx.doi.org/ and type in the DOI number. When citing an article that has a DOI (usually found on the first page of the article), you do not need to include a URL in your reference or the name of the database in which you may have found the article.

> Geers, A. L., Wellman, J. A., & Lassiter, G. D. (2009). Dispositional optimism and engagement: The moderating influence of goal prioritization. *Journal of Personality and Social Psychology 94*, 913–932. doi:10.1037/a0014746

Journal article found on the Web without a DOI

> Bendetto, M. M. (2008). Crisis on the immigration bench: An ethical perspective. *Brooklyn Law Review*, 73, 467–523. Retrieved from http://brooklaw.edu/students/journals/blr.php/

Journal article from an electronic database

The name and URL of the database are not required for citations if a DOI is available. If no DOI is available, provide the home page URL of the journal or of the book or report publisher.

> Staub, E., & Pearlman, L. A. (2009). Reducing intergroup prejudice and conflict: A commentary. *Journal of Personality and Social Psychology*, *11*, 3–23. Retrieved from http://www.apa.org /journals/psp/

Electronic book

> Katz, R. N. (Ed.). (2008). *The tower and the cloud: Higher education in an era of cloud computing.* Retrieved from http://net .educause.edu/ir/library/pdf/PUB7202.pdf

Video blog post

> Baggs, A. (2007, January 14). In my language [Video file]. Retrieved from http://www.youtube.com/watch?v=JnylM1hl2jc

Presentation slides

> Hall, M. E. (2009) *Who moved my job!? A psychology of job-loss "trauma"* [Presentation slides]. Retrieved from http://www.cew .wisc.edu/docs/WMMJ%20PwrPt-Summry2.ppt

Student Essay

The following research paper, "The High Cost of Cheap Counterfeit Goods," follows APA format as outlined in the preceding pages.

APA PAPER GUIDELINES

- An APA paper should have a one-inch margin all around and be double-spaced throughout.

- The first line of every paragraph should be indented, and all pages of the paper, including the first, should be numbered consecutively.

- An APA paper has four sections: the *title page*, the *abstract*, the *body of the paper*, and the *reference list*:

  1. The **title page** (page 1) should include a running head at the top:

     Running Head: THE HIGH COST OF COUNTERFEIT GOODS

  2. The title page should also include the title of the paper (upper- and lower-case letters), your name (first name, middle initial, last name), and your school.

  3. The **abstract** (page 2) should be a 150- to 250-word summary of the paper. Type the word **Abstract** (centered); skip one line; and do not indent. After the abstract, skip one line and type *Keywords* (italicized and indented), followed by keywords that will help researchers find your essay in a database.

  4. The **body of the paper** should begin on page 3. After the title page, each page of the paper should include the title (in all capital letters), typed flush left, one-half inch from the top of the page:

     THE HIGH COST OF COUNTERFEIT GOODS

  5. The **reference list** should begin on a new page, after the body of the paper. (See pages 832–833 for a discussion of how to format the reference list.)

- Citations should follow APA documentation style.

The High Cost of Cheap Counterfeit Goods

Deniz Bilgutay

Humanities 101, Section 1

Professor Fitzgerald

March 4, 2012

Abstract

The global trade in counterfeit products costs manufacturers of luxury goods millions of dollars each year. Although this illegal trade threatens the free market, employs underage labor, and may even fund terrorism, many people consider it a victimless crime. Studies show that some consumers even take pride in buying knock-off products. But a closer look at this illicit trade in counterfeit goods shows that consumers in the United States—and around the world—do not understand the ethical implications of the choices they make. Consumers should stop supporting this illegal business, and law enforcement officials should prosecute it more vigorously than they currently do. In the final analysis, this illegal practice hurts legitimate businesses and in some cases endangers the health and safety of consumers.

Keywords: counterfeiting, terrorism, ethics, crime

THE HIGH COST OF CHEAP COUNTERFEIT GOODS   3

The High Cost of Cheap Counterfeit Goods

For those who do not want to pay for genuine designer
products, a fake Louis Vuitton bag or knock-off Rolex watch might
seem too good to pass up. Such purchases may even be a source
of pride. According to one study, two-thirds of British consumers
said they would be "proud to tell family and friends" that they
bought inexpensive knock-offs (Thomas, 2007). The trade in
counterfeit goods, however, is a crime—and not a victimless crime.
A growing body of evidence suggests that the makers and
distributers of counterfeit goods have ties to child labor, organized
crime, and even terrorism. In addition, the global economic cost
of counterfeiting is estimated at $600 billion a year, according to
recent data from the International Chamber of Commerce (Melik,
2011). For these reasons, consumers should stop buying these
products and funding the illegal activities that this activity supports.

Much of the responsibility for the trade in counterfeit
goods can be placed on the manufacturers and the countries
that permit the production and export of such goods. For
example, China, which dominates the world counterfeit
trade, is doing very little to stop this activity. According to
a recent article in *USA Today* by Calum MacLeod (2011), "a
major obstacle is China's *shanzhai* culture, whereby some
Chinese delight in making cheap imitations, sometimes
in parody, of expensive, famous brands." Chinese
counterfeiters have gone so far as to create entire fake
stores: fake Starbucks stores, fake Abercrombie & Fitch
stores, and even fake Apple stores. Although some of
these copycats have been prosecuted, there is a high level
of tolerance, even admiration, for counterfeiting in China.
This attitude towards *shanzhai* is reflected in the country's
lax intellectual property protection laws. As one Chinese
intellectual property lawyer observed, "The penalties don't

Introduction

Thesis
statement

outweigh the benefits" (as cited in MacLeod, 2011). Given this situation, the production of counterfeit goods in China is not likely to slow down any time soon.

Despite such cultural justifications for counterfeiting, there is still an ethical problem associated with the purchase of knock-offs. As Dana Thomas (2007) has written in *The New York Times*, many of these counterfeit products are made by children who are "sold or sent off by their families to work in clandestine factories." To American consumers, the problem of children laboring in Chinese factories may be remote, but it is serious. If it is reasonable to place blame for this flourishing market on the countries that allow it, it is also reasonable to blame the people who buy most of the counterfeit goods—namely, consumers in the United States and Europe. According to a report by U.S. Customs and Border Patrol, 62% of fake goods seized in the United States in 2011 were produced in China (as cited in Coleman, 2012). In Europe, the numbers are even higher. According to *The Wall Street Journal*, 85% of goods seized in the European Union come from China (Nairn, 2011). Consequently, the simple act of buying a counterfeit Coach handbag implicates the consumer in the practice of forced child labor.

Immoral labor practices are not the only reason why the counterfeit market needs to be stopped. Organized crime is behind much of the counterfeit trade, so "every dollar spent on a knockoff Gap polo shirt or a fake Kate Spade handbag may be supporting drug trafficking, . . . and worse" ("Editorial: The True Cost," 2007). Consumer dollars may also be supporting narcotics, weapons, and child prostitution (Thomas, 2007).

This illicit international system also helps to finance groups even more sinister than crime syndicates. American consumers of counterfeit goods should understand that profits from

Evidence: Point 1

Evidence: Point 2

THE HIGH COST OF CHEAP COUNTERFEIT GOODS   5

counterfeit goods support terrorist and extremist groups, including
Hezbollah, paramilitary organizations in Northern Ireland, and
FARC, a revolutionary armed faction in Colombia (Thomas, 2007).
According to the International Anti-Counterfeiting Coalition, the
sale of knock-off T-shirts may even have funded the 1993 attack on
the World Trade Center. Some observers speculate that terrorists
annually receive about 2% of the roughly $500 billion trade in
counterfeit goods ("Editorial: The True Cost," 2007). According
to Ronald K. Noble, secretary-general of the international
law enforcement agency Interpol, crime involving counterfeit
merchandise "is becoming the preferred method of funding for a
number of terrorist groups" (as cited in Langan, 2003).

    Beyond the moral and ethical implications of its links to
child labor, crime, and terrorism, counterfeit merchandise also
undermines the mainstay of Western business—respect for
intellectual property. In the context of a vast international market
of counterfeit luxury goods, the issue of intellectual property can
seem insignificant. But the creation of new products requires
time, energy, and money, and "unrestrained copying robs
creators of the means to profit from their works" (Sprigman,
2006). Copyright law exists to make sure that inventors and
producers will be motivated to create original work and be fairly
compensated for it. This principle applies to the designers of
luxury goods and fashion items as well. Christopher Sprigman
(2006) disagrees, however, noting that although intellectual
property law does little to protect fashion designs, this is as it
should be. "Trend-driven consumption," says Sprigman, is good
for the fashion industry because the industry's ability to create
trends "is based on designers' relative freedom to copy." But
even this argument—which addresses the influences of legitimate
fashion designers and manufacturers—cannot be used to justify
allowing counterfeiters to copy Prada handbags or Hugo

Evidence:
Point 3

Evidence:
Point 4

Opposing
argument

Refutation

Boss suits and pass them off as genuine branded articles. Such illicit activity creates no trends—other than perhaps increasing the market for counterfeit products, which siphons off more profits from original designers.

Evidence: Point 5

The knock-off market is not limited to fashion and luxury goods. For example, fake products such as shoddy brake pads have directly injured many consumers. In addition, each year millions of people in the United States and abroad buy counterfeit drugs that do not work and in many cases are dangerous. Some sources estimate that the majority of drugs used to treat life-threatening diseases in Africa are counterfeit. Not coincidentally, many of the same people who are making and distributing counterfeit luxury goods are also manufacturing these drugs ("Editorial: The True Cost," 2007).

Conclusion

It is time for people to realize the harm that is done by counterfeit merchandise and stop buying it. One way to combat this problem is to educate consumers about the effects of their purchases. As James Melik (2011) of the BBC explains, "People try to save money without realising that the purchase of counterfeit goods can actually harm themselves, the economy and ultimately, their own pockets." Melik urges consumers to "think twice" before buying "products which promote and fund crime." Another way to confront the problem is for law enforcement to address this issue aggressively. Not only should local authorities do more to stop this illegal trade, but national governments should also impose sanctions on countries that refuse to honor international treaties concerning intellectual property. Only by taking this issue seriously can we ensure that this "victimless" crime does not continue to spread and claim more victims.

THE HIGH COST OF CHEAP COUNTERFEIT GOODS   7

References

Coleman, S. (2012, January 20). China still accounts for majority
of US counterfeit goods. *Canadian Manufacturers and
Exporters*. Retrieved from http://www.cme-mec.ca/?lid
=JCKNC-E742G-1W6JA&comaction=show&cid=DVU6K
-CVBRZ-C6TZQ

Editorial: The true cost: Illegal knockoffs of name-brand products
do widespread harm. [Editorial]. (2007, December 2). *The
Columbus* [OH] *Dispatch*, p. 4G.

Langan, M. (2003, July 24). Counterfeit goods make real
terrorism. *Pittsburgh Post-Gazette*, p. A17.

MacLeod, C. (2011, August 2). China takes knock-offs to a
new level, copying entire stores. *USA Today*. Retrieved
from http://www.usatoday.com/money/industries
/technology/2011-07-31-China-counterfeiting-fake-Western
-goods-stores_n.htm

Melik, J. (2011, December 18). Fake goods save money but at
what cost? *BBC News*. Retrieved from http://www.bbc
.co.uk/news/business-16087793

Nairn, G. (2011, October 18). Countering the counterfeiters. *The
Wall Street Journal*. Retrieved from http://online.wsj.com
/article/SB10001424052970204226204576600462442044764
.html

Sprigman, C. (2006, August 22). The fashion industry's piracy
paradox [Online forum comment]. Retrieved from http://
www.publicknowledge.org/node/597

Thomas, D. (2007, August 30). Terror's purse strings. *The New
York Times*, p. A23.

Accurate evidence: Evidence from reliable sources that is quoted carefully and in context.

Ad hominem fallacy: The logical fallacy of undermining an argument by attacking the person who is making the argument instead of addressing the argument itself.

Allusion: A reference within a work to a person, literary or biblical text, or historical event. This shorthand device reminds the reader of something that enlarges the context of the situation being written about.

Analogy: An extended comparison that explains an unfamiliar item, concept, or situation by comparing it to a more familiar one.

Antithesis: An opposing statement that tests whether an argumentative **thesis** is debatable.

Appeal to doubtful authority: The use of nonexperts to support an argument.

Applied ethics: The field of philosophy that applies **ethical principles** to real-life issues (such as abortion, the death penalty, animal rights, or doctor-assisted suicide).

Argument: A logical and persuasive presentation of **evidence** that attempts to convince people to accept (or at least to consider) the writer's position.

Argument by analogy: An argument that claims that its position is valid because it is similar in some ways to a position on another issue that readers are likely to accept.

Backing: In a **Toulmin argument**, the evidence that supports the warrant.

Bandwagon appeal: An attempt to convince people that something is true because it is widely held to be true.

Begging-the-question fallacy: An illogical assumption that a statement is self-evident (or true) when it actually requires proof.

Bias: Preconceived ideas or prejudices, which are often used in an argument instead of factual **evidence**.

Brainstorming: Making quick notes on a topic to generate ideas.

Causal argument: An argument that explains an event or a situation by considering its likely causes or outcomes.

Causal chain: A sequence of events in which one event causes the next, which in turn causes the next, and so on.

Circular reasoning: An attempt to support a statement by simply repeating the statement in different terms.

Claim: In a **Toulmin argument**, the main point, usually stated as a **thesis**.

Common ground: Points of agreement that are shared by those on opposing sides of an argument.

Common knowledge: Factual information (such as a writer's date of birth, a scientific fact, or the location of a famous battle) that can be found in several credible sources. Common knowledge does not require documentation.

Conclusion: The last part of a **syllogism**.

Confirmation bias: The tendency that people have to accept information that supports their own beliefs and to ignore information that does not.

Confrontational argument: A kind of argument that is characterized by conflict and opposition.

Contributory causes: The less important causes in a **causal argument**.

Credibility: Trustworthiness. A credible source is believable.

Criteria for evaluation: Standards by which a subject (or source) is evaluated.

Critical response: A passage in which a writer examines the ideas that are presented in an argument and evaluates them.

Current source: A source containing up-to-date information. Current sources are especially important in discussions of scientific subjects and may be less important in other subjects.

Debatable thesis: A thesis statement that presents a position with which people might disagree.

Deductive reasoning: A form of reasoning that moves from general statements (or **premises**) to specific conclusions. See **inductive reasoning**.

Definition argument: An argument that is based on the idea that something fits or does not fit a particular definition of a key term.

Dictionary definition: A structure for definition that consists of the term to be defined, the general class to which the term belongs, and the qualities that differentiate the term from other items in the same class.

Dilemma: A choice between two or more unfavorable alternatives.

Distortion: An unfair tactic of argument in which the writer misrepresents evidence—for example, by presenting an opponent's view inaccurately or by exaggerating his or her position.

Documentation: Information that identifies the sources used in an argument.

Editing and proofreading: The final steps in the writing process, which check that an essay is well organized, convincing, and clearly written and has no distracting grammatical, spelling, and mechanical errors.

Either/or fallacy: Faulty reasoning that presents only two choices when there are actually three or more choices.

Equivocation: The use of two different meanings for the same key term in an argument.

Ethical argument: An argument that focuses on whether something should be done because it is good or right.

Ethical dilemma: A conflict between two or more possible actions, each of which will potentially have negative outcomes.

Ethical principles: A set of ideas or standards that guides someone to an ethically correct conclusion.

Ethics: The field of philosophy that studies the standards by which an act can be judged right or wrong or good or bad.

Ethos: An appeal to the trustworthiness or credibility of a speaker or writer.

Evaluate: To express an opinion about the quality of something.

Evaluation argument: An argument that presents a positive or negative judgment, asserts that someone else's positive or negative judgment is not accurate or justified, or demonstrates that one thing is or is not superior to another.

Evidence: The facts, observations, expert opinion, examples, and statistics that support a thesis statement. In a **Toulmin argument**, the evidence is called the **grounds**.

Fact: A statement that can be verified (proven to be true).

Fallacy: An error in reasoning that undermines the logic of an argument.

False dilemma: See **either/or fallacy**.

Formal argument: An argument developed according to set rhetorical principles in academic discussion and writing. See **informal argument**.

Formal outline: A presentation of an essay's main and subordinate points that uses a number/letter system to designate the order in which the points will be discussed.

Freewriting: Writing continuously for a set time to generate ideas without worrying about spelling or grammar.

Grounds: In a **Toulmin argument**, the evidence that is used to support the claim.

Hasty generalization: An error in reasoning that occurs when a conclusion is based on too little evidence or when the gap between the evidence and conclusion is too wide.

Identifying tag: A phrase that identifies the source of a **quotation**, **paraphrase**, or **summary**.

Immediate cause: In a **causal argument**, the cause that occurs right before an event.

Inductive leap: In **inductive reasoning**, a stretch of the imagination that enables a writer to draw a reasonable conclusion from the existing information.

Inductive reasoning: A form of reasoning that begins with specific observations (or evidence) and moves to a general conclusion. See **deductive reasoning**.

Inference: A statement that uses what is known to draw a conclusion about what is unknown.

Informal argument: An **argument** that occurs in daily life about politics, sports, social issues, and personal relationships. See **formal argument**.

Informal outline: A list of the ideas that will be discussed in an essay. See **formal outline**.

Jumping to a conclusion: See **hasty generalization**.

Logic: The principles of correct reasoning that enable someone to tell whether a conclusion correctly follows from a set of statements or assumptions.

Logical fallacy: A flawed argument.

Logos: An appeal to logic.

Main cause: In a **causal argument**, the most important cause.

Major premise: See **syllogism**.

Means of persuasion: The appeals—*logos, pathos,* and *ethos*—that writers use to persuade their audience.

Metaphor: A comparison in which two dissimilar things are compared without the word *like* or *as*.

Middle term: The term in a **syllogism** that appears in both the major and minor premises but not in the conclusion.

Minor premise: See **syllogism**.

Non sequitur **fallacy**: Illogical reasoning that occurs when a conclusion does not follow from the premises or is supported by weak or irrelevant evidence or by no evidence at all.

Objective source: A source that is not unduly influenced by personal opinions or feelings.

Operational definition: A definition of how something acts or works that transforms an abstract concept into something concrete, observable, and possibly measurable.

Opinion: A personal judgment; therefore, an idea that is open to debate.

Parallelism: The use of the same or a similar structure in the repetition of words, phrases, or clauses.

Paraphrase: A passage that presents a source's ideas in detail, including its main idea and key supporting points and perhaps key examples.

Parenthetical references: In MLA and APA **documentation**, citations that identify the source of a paraphrase, quotation, or summary.

Pathos: An appeal to the emotions.

Peer review: The process of having colleagues examine and critique written work. Informally, school work is read by friends or classmates; formally, scholarly work is read by experts in the field to confirm its accuracy.

Persuasion: The act of influencing an audience to adopt a particular belief or to follow a specific course of action.

Plagiarism: The use of the words or ideas of another person without attributing them to their rightful author.

Popular magazine: A periodical that is aimed at general readers. It generally is not an acceptable source for research.

Post hoc **fallacy**: Faulty reasoning that asserts that because two events occur closely in time, one event must have caused the other.

Premises: Statements or assumptions on which an **argument** is based or from which a conclusion is drawn.

Previewing: During active reading, forming a general impression of a writer's position on an issue, the argument's key supporting points, and the context for the writer's remarks.

Propaganda: Biased or misleading information that is spread about a particular viewpoint, person, or cause.

Proposal argument: An argument that attempts to convince people that a problem exists and that a particular solution is both practical and desirable.

Qualifiers: In a **Toulmin argument**, statements that limit the **claim**.

Quotation: Words or sentences taken directly from a source.

Quoting out of context: Removing a quotation from its original setting for the purpose of distorting its meaning.

Reading critically: Questioning or challenging material instead of simply accepting it as true. This often involves assessing the accuracy of facts in sources and considering the evidence that supports them.

Reason: In a **Toulmin argument**, a statement that supports the **claim**.

Rebuttals: In a **Toulmin argument**, refutations of opposing arguments.

Red herring fallacy: An irrelevant side issue that diverts attention from the real issue.

Refutation: The section of an argumentative essay that identifies opposing arguments and presents arguments against them.

Refute: To disprove or call into question.

Relevant evidence: Evidence that applies specifically (not just tangentially) to the topic under discussion.

Remote causes: In a **causal argument**, incidents that occurred in the past but may have had a greater impact than more recent events.

Representative evidence: Evidence that is drawn from a fair range of sources, not just from sources that support a particular position.

Revision: The careful and critical review of a draft.

Rhetoric: The effect of various elements working together to form a convincing and persuasive **argument**.

Rhetorical analysis: A systematic examination of the strategies that a writer employs to achieve his or her purpose.

Rhetorical question: A question that encourages readers to reflect on an issue but does not call for a reply.

Rhetorical situation: The combination of the writer, the writer's purpose, the writer's audience, the topic, and the context.

Rhetorical strategies: The ways in which argument writers present ideas and opinions, including but not limited to thesis, organization, evidence, and stylistic techniques (**simile**, **metaphor**, **allusion**, **parallelism**, repetition, and **rhetorical questions**).

Rhetorical triangle: A graphic representation of the three kinds of appeals in an argument—*logos* (reason), *ethos* (credibility), and *pathos* (values and beliefs).

Rogerian argument: A model of argument that assumes that people of good will can avoid conflict by identifying **common ground** and points of agreement. It is based on the work of Carl Rogers, a twentieth-century psychologist who felt that traditional confrontational arguments could be counterproductive.

Scholarly journal: A periodical that is usually written by experts, documented, and peer reviewed.

Scientific method: A way of using induction to find answers to questions. It involves proposing a hypothesis, making a series of observations to test the hypothesis, and arriving at a conclusion that confirms, modifies, or disproves the hypothesis.

Self-evident: A proposition that requires no proof or explanation.

Simile: A figure of speech that compares two unlike things by using *like* or *as*.

Skeptical: Having an open mind but still needing to be convinced.

Slanting: An unfair tactic that makes an argument appear stronger by presenting only evidence that supports a particular position and ignoring evidence that challenges it.

Slippery-slope fallacy: An illogical argument that holds that one thing will cause a series of events that ends in an inevitable, unpleasant conclusion, usually with no evidence that such a sequence will actually occur.

Sound syllogism: A syllogism that is both true and valid. See **true syllogism** and **valid syllogism**.

Straw man fallacy: An intentional oversimplification of an opposing argument to make it easier to refute.

Sufficient evidence: Evidence that includes enough facts, statistics, and expert opinion to support the essay's thesis.

Summary: A concise restatement of the main idea of a passage (or article or book) without the examples, explanations, and stylistic devices of the source.

Sweeping generalization: See **hasty generalization**.

Syllogism: A model for **deductive reasoning** that includes a **major premise**, a **minor premise**, and a **conclusion**.

Synthesis: A combination of **summary**, **paraphrase**, **quotation**, and a writer's own ideas that supports an original conclusion.

Taking a stand: Expressing a position in the form of a **thesis statement**.

Thesis: The position that an argument supports.

Thesis statement: A single sentence in an argumentative essay that states a position on an issue.

Thinking critically: Questioning rather than accepting ideas at face value.

Toulmin argument: An argument that includes the **claim** (the main point), the grounds (the **evidence** a writer uses to support the claim), and the **warrant** (the inference—either stated or implied—that connects the claims to their grounds).

Unfair appeal: An appeal to an audience's fears or prejudices.

Valid syllogism: A syllogism in which a conclusion follows logically from its premises.

Visual: An image—such as a chart, graph, table, photo, drawing, or diagram.

Visual argument: An advertisement, chart, graph, table, diagram, Web page, photograph, painting, or other representation that communicates a position through images.

Warrant: In a **Toulmin argument**, the inference or assumption, either stated or implied, that connects a claim to its grounds.

Works-cited list: An alphabetical list of sources that appears at the end of an essay that follows MLA style.

Writing process: The process of planning, drafting, revising, and editing an argument.

You-also fallacy (*tu quoque*): An illogical assertion that a statement is false because the speaker has said or done the opposite. It attacks a person for doing the thing that he or she is arguing against.

Art Credits

519 Image courtesy of People for the Ethical Treatment of Animals, www.PETA.org. 521 Copyright © 2009 Sunshine Week/American Society of News Editors (asne.org). All rights reserved. Reproduced with permission. 523 © Dale Sparks/AP Photo. 524 © Katvan Studios Inc. 558, 570 © Pool/Getty. 586, 608 © Thinkstock/Getty. 588 © Peter Dazeley/Getty. 591 (t) Bettmann/Corbis. 591 (b) Courtesy of the Library of Congress. 592 Bettmann/Corbis. 593 (t) © Rick Friedman/Redux. 593 (b) The Everett Collection. 594 © Cat's Collection/Corbis. 595 (l) © Tread Lightly!, Inc. (www.treadlightly.org). 595 (r) © Paul J. Richards/Getty. 619 Courtesy of Isothermal Community College, reproduced with permission. 623 Reproduced with permission by Amy Dion-Art Director S/U. 634 © ImageSource/Getty. 542 Mark Duncan/AP Photo. 650 David Pellerin/AP Photo. 658 © Aleksander Jaksic/istockphoto.com. 668 © Peter Cade/Getty. 684 © John Wilkes Studio/Corbis. 700 © Bloomberg/Getty. 714 © Norma Zuniga/Getty. 738 Reed Saxon/AP Images. 754 (t-l) © DEA/G. Dagli Orti/Getty. 754 (t-r) *Portrait of Jonathan Swift* (1667–1745) c. 1718 (oil on canvas), Jervas, Charles (1675–1739). National Portrait Gallery, London, UK/The Bridgeman Art Library. 754 (m) © SuperStock/Getty. 754 (b-l) © Rob Lewine/Getty. 754 (b-m) © Ulf Andersen/Getty. 754 (b-r) © Stock Montage/Getty. 818 © Peter Marlow/Magnum. 830 *Journal and Courier*, Tom Leininger/AP Photo.

Text Credits

Rachel Adams. "Bringing Down the Barriers—Seen and Unseen." From the *Chronicle of Higher Education*, November 6, 2011. Copyright © 2011 by Rachel Adams. Reproduced with the permission of the author. All rights reserved.

David Albert. "Change Honor Codes to Include Abuse of Non-Prescription Drugs." From *USA Today*, January 20, 2012. Copyright © 2012 Gannett. All rights reserved. Used by permission and protected by the Copyright Laws of the United States. The printing, copying, redistribution, or retransmission of this content without expressed, written permission is prohibited. http://www.usatoday.com.

Joyce Alcantara. "Keep Drinking Age At 21: Teens Aren't Mature Enough to Handle Consequence." From *Contra Costa Times*, July 7, 2011. Copyright © 2011 by Contra Costa Times. Reproduced with permission of TMS Reprints. All rights reserved.

Charlotte Allen. "College for the Intellectually Disabled." From *Minding the Campus*, September 23, 2010. Copyright © 2010 by Charlotte Allen. Reproduced with permission of the author. All rights reserved.

Amethyst Initiative. "Statement." From http://amethystinitiative.org/statement. Reproduced with permission of Choose Responsibility, Inc. www.chooseresponsibility.com.

Omar Ashmawy. "Ten Years After 9/11, We're Still in the Dark." From the *Washington Post*, September 9, 2010. Copyright © 2010 by Omar Ashmawy. Reproduced with permission of the author. All rights reserved.

Maria Aspan. "How Sticky Is Membership on Facebook? Just Try Breaking Free." From the *New York Times*, February 11, 2008. Copyright © 2008 by the New York Times. All rights reserved. Used by permission and protected by the Copyright Laws of the United States. The printing, copying, redistribution, or retransmission of this content without expressed, written permission is prohibited. http://www.nytimes.com.

Austin American-Statesman. "Cheaters Never Win." From the *Austin American-Statesman*, August 11, 2006. Copyright © 2006 by Austin American-Statesman. Reproduced with permission. All rights reserved.

Peter B. Bach and Robert Kocher. "Why Medical School Should Be Free." From the *New York Times*, May 28, 2011. Copyright © 2011 by the New York Times. All rights reserved. Used by permission and protected by the copyright laws of the United States. The printing, copying, redistribution, or retransmission of this content without expressed, written permission is prohibited. http://www.nytimes.com.

James Baldwin. "If Black English Isn't a Language, Then Tell Me, What Is?" From the *New York Times*, July 29, 1979. Collected in *The Price of the Ticket*, published by St. Martin's Press. Copyright © 1979 by James Baldwin. Reproduced by arrangement with the James Baldwin Estate.

Radley Balko. "Amethyst Initiative's Debate on Drinking a Welcome Alternative to Fanaticism." From FoxNews.com, August 25, 2008. Copyright © 2008 by Radley Balko. Reproduced with permission of the author. All rights reserved.

Billy Beane, New Gingrich, and John Kerry. "How to Take American Health Care from Worst to First." From the *New York Times*, October 24, 2008. Copyright © 2008 by the New York Times. All rights reserved. Used by permission and protected by the copyright laws of the United States. The printing, copying, redistribution, or retransmission of this content without expressed, written permission is prohibited. http://www.nytimes.com.

Jessica Bennett, Jesse Ellison, and Sarah Ball. "Are We There Yet?" From *Newsweek*, March 18, 2010. Copyright © 2010 by the Newsweek/Daily Beast Company LLC. All rights reserved. Used by permission and protected by the copyright laws of the United States. The printing, copying, redistribution, or retransmission of this content without expressed, written permission is prohibited. http://www.thedailybeast.com/newsweek.html.

David Brooks. "The Amateur Ideal." From the *New York Times*, September 23, 2011. Copyright © 2011 by the New York Times. All rights reserved. Used by permission and protected by the copyright laws of the United States. The printing, copying, redistribution, or retransmission of this content without expressed, written permission is prohibited. http://www.nytimes.com.

Tony Brummel. "Practical Experience Trumps Fancy Degrees." From *Bloomberg Business Week*, March 2011. Copyright © 2012 by Bloomberg L.P. Reproduced with permission. All rights reserved.

Patrick Buchanan. "Immigration Time-Out." From http://buchanan.org/blog/immigration-time-out-163, October 31, 1994. Copyright © 1994 by Patrick Buchanan. Reproduced with permission of Friedman, Inc. All rights reserved.

Missing something? To access the e-Pages that accompany this text, visit **bedfordstmartins.com/practicalargument**. Students who do not buy a new book can purchase access to e-Pages at this site.

Inside the e-Pages for *Practical Argument*

Quizzes in e-Pages provide helpful feedback. More than 200 quizzes on all the readings and instructional content allow instructors to quickly get a sense of what students understand and what they need help with.